Understanding Canadian
Public Administration

Understanding Canadian Public Administration

AN INTRODUCTION TO THEORY AND PRACTICE

THIRD EDITION   GREGORY J. INWOOD

RYERSON UNIVERSITY

PEARSON

Prentice
Hall

Toronto

Library and Archives Canada Cataloguing in Publication

Inwood, Gregory J.
    Understanding Canadian public administration: an introduction to theory and practice /
Gregory J. Inwood. — 3rd ed.

Includes index.
ISBN 978-0-13-206838-3

    1. Public administration—Canada—Textbooks.   2. Canada—Politics and government—
Textbooks.   I. Title.

JL108.I58 2009   351.71   C2008-900229-6

ISBN-13: 978-0-13-206838-3
ISBN-10: 0-13-206838-9

Vice President, Editorial Director: Gary Bennett
Senior Acquisitions Editor: Laura Forbes
Executive Marketing Manager: Judith Allen
Developmental Editor: Alexandra Dyer
Production Editor: Kevin Leung
Copy Editor: Colleen Ste. Marie
Proofreaders: Anne Borden, Kelli Howey
Production Coordinator: Andrea Falkenberg
Permissions Research: Cheryl Freedman
Composition: Integra
Art Director: Julia Hall
Cover and Interior Design: Jennifer Stimson
Cover Image: Eric Audras/Getty Images

2 3 4 5   12 11 10 09

Printed and bound in the United States of America.

PEARSON
Prentice
Hall

For Tish, Alison, and Matthew

Brief Contents

Chapter 1   Introduction: The Nature of Public Administration   1

Chapter 2   Public Administration and Democracy   26

Chapter 3   Theories of Organization   62

Chapter 4   Organization Theory and Canadian Public Administration   101

Chapter 5   Public Administration and Institutions: The Real World of Organizations and the Machinery of Government   121

Chapter 6   Public Administration, the Constitution, and Law   168

Chapter 7   Public Administration and Public Policy   205

Chapter 8   Public Administration and Evaluation   240

Chapter 9   Public Administration and the Management of Human Resources   262

Chapter 10   Public Administration, Management Reform, and Financial Management   306

Chapter 11   Public Administration and Ethics   341

Chapter 12   Public Administration and Accountability   368

Chapter 13   A Canadian Public Administration   401

Contents

Preface xv

Chapter 1   Introduction: The Nature of Public Administration 1

What You Will Learn   1

What Is Public Administration?   2

Public Administration and Democratic Government   6

Bureaucracy   7
  Personnel   8
  Formal Rules   8
  Policy Instruments   8
  Conventions of Behaviour   8
  Institutions   9

Comparing Public and Private Sectors   9
  Mandate and Goals   12
  Efficiency and Service   14
  Professionalism and Ethics   15

Restructuring the Public Sector and the Role of the State   17
  The Minimalist State   17
  The Keynesian Welfare State   18
  The Neoconservative State   18

What You Have Learned   20

Chapter 2   Public Administration and Democracy 26

What You Will Learn   26

Power, Politics, and Public Administration   28

What Is Democracy?   31
  Direct Democracy   32

Representative Democracy   33
Political Democracy   33
Economic Democracy   34

State and Government   36

Political Culture   39
Geography   41
Demography   42
Three Founding Cultures   42
Continentalism   42
Interpretations of Canadian Political Culture   43

The Interplay of Democracy, Political Culture, and the Institutions
of Public Administration   48
The Canadian Constitution   48
The North American Free Trade Agreement   49
Federalism   50
The Parliamentary Actors   51
The Extra-Parliamentary Actors   54

What You Have Learned   56

Chapter 3   **Theories of Organization**   62

What You Will Learn   62

Perspectives on Bureaucratic Organization   63

The Classic Theorists   64
Karl Marx   64
The Neo-Marxists   67
Criticisms of Marxist Theory   68
Max Weber   68
Criticisms of the Weberian Model   70

Structuralist Theories   77
Scientific Management   77
Criticisms of Scientific Management   82

Humanist Theories   83
The Human Relations Approach   83
Criticisms of the Human Relations School   90

Other Theoretical Approaches   92

What You Have Learned   96

Chapter 4   Organization Theory and Canadian Public
             Administration   101

What You Will Learn   101
The Impact of Organization Theory   102
Contemporary Developments   104
       Participatory Management   105
       New Public Management   112
What You Have Learned   117

Chapter 5   Public Administration and Institutions: The Real World
             of Organizations and the Machinery of Government   121

What You Will Learn   121
Factors Influencing Organizational Structure   122
       Capitalist Democracy   122
       Federalism   123
       Cabinet-Parliamentary Government   125
Political-Administrative Relationships   131
Departmental Organizations   132
       Central Agencies   138
       Alternative Service Delivery   142
       Ministerial Responsibility   144
       The Deputy Minister   145
Regulatory Agencies   150
Crown Corporations   154
What You Have Learned   160

Chapter 6   Public Administration, the Constitution, and Law   168

What You Will Learn   168
The Law, the Courts, and the Administration of Justice   169
What Is a Constitution?   174
       A History of Canada's Constitution   177
       Federalism and the Constitution   181
Constitutional Law   184
       Peace, Order, and Good Government   184
       Federal–Provincial Bargaining   186

Administrative Law   189
What You Have Learned   197

Chapter 7   **Public Administration and Public Policy**   205

What You Will Learn   205
Defining Public Policy   206
    Scope   207
    Means   208
    Resources   209
Formulating Public Policy   211
    Environmental Factors   212
    Distribution of Power   213
    Social Attitudes and Ideas   213
    Institutional Structures   214
    Procedural Factors   214
    Frameworks, Models, and Theories   214
Implementing Public Policy: How Does Anything Get Done?   224
    Choice of Governing Instrument   227
    Recent Developments in Policy Implementation   231
Evaluating Public Policy   232
What You Have Learned   234

Chapter 8   **Public Administration and Evaluation**   240

What You Will Learn   240
The Development of Evaluation   241
Problems of Evaluation   247
Evaluation in Action   250
Contemporary Evaluation Practices   251
What You Have Learned   257

Chapter 9   **Public Administration and the Management of Human Resources**   262

What You Will Learn   262
A Brief History of the Public Service: Who Works There, Anyway?   263

The Public Service Today: An Overview   276
    The Theory of Representativeness   282
    Region   283
    Language   285
    Equity   286
    Unionization of the Public Service   293
    Public Servants and Politics   295
Human Resources Management   296
What You Have Learned   298

Chapter 10   **Public Administration, Management Reform,**
            and Financial Management   306

What You Will Learn   306
Restructuring the Public Service: The Management View   307
    PS2000   311
    Program Review   313
    La Relève and the Leadership Network   314
    The Policy Research Initiative (PRI)   317
    The Public Service Modernization Act   317
    The Gomery Commission   318
Financial Management   319
    The State and Economy   319
    Managing Government Fiscal Resources   324
    The Budgetary Cycle   331
What You Have Learned   335

Chapter 11   **Public Administration and Ethics**   341

What You Will Learn   341
Ethical Dilemmas in the Public Service   342
    Discretion   350
    Partisanship   351
    Public Comment   352
    Conflict of Interest   352
    Lying for the Public Good   353
    Public Sector versus Private Sector Ethics   354

Codes of Conduct   356
    Do Codes of Conduct Work?   357
    Training and Education   360
    Role Models   361
    An Attentive Public   363
What You Have Learned   364

Chapter 12   Public Administration and Accountability   368

What You Will Learn   368
Accountability and Democracy   369
Ministerial Responsibility   375
Accountability and Public Servants   381
Accountability in Action: The Role of the Office of the Auditor General   384
Contemporary Issues of Accountability and Control   388
What You Have Learned   394

Chapter 13   A Canadian Public Administration   401

What You Will Learn   401
Models of Canadian Public Administration   402
A *Canadian* Public Administration?   409
What You Have Learned   416

Glossary   420

Index   430

PREFACE

This third edition of *Understanding Canadian Public Administration: An Introduction to Theory and Practice* builds on the main purposes for which the original was conceived and executed. It addresses the need for an introductory text on the theory and practice of public administration in Canada. As with the first two editions, this edition provides an overview of the essential theoretical issues in the field and then uses that theoretical grounding to examine the actual practice of public administration. As an introduction, both in a historical context and in the contemporary context of rapid change, the goal of this work is to foster an understanding of the basic elements of public administration, leaving detailed analysis of specific sub-fields to more specialized sources. As such, this text is geared to undergraduate university and college students, as well as public servants, who require a clear and concise introduction to the topic. It is meant to be used as the primary text for courses in public administration.

One of the striking features of public administration is that it is constantly in a state of flux. As this edition goes to press, sweeping reforms of the federal public service are ongoing. Legislation has been introduced over the past few years intended to modernize the public service, alter the relationship between the government and its unions, change the definition of merit, reform the process of hiring, firing, and managing federal public servants, adapt a new code of conduct and rules for ethical behaviour, introduce a new accountability framework for senior public servants, and make numerous other changes. What, if anything, will come of these reforms remains to be seen – there have been approximately 37 inquiries into the state of the public service in the past 40 years, after all. However, the fact that many of these reforms are being mandated in law will make a difference which students of public administration will be able to observe.

Understanding Canadian Public Administration begins with an introduction to the basic elements of public administration and explains the field in the context of democratic government. It also focuses on the impact of recent developments such as restructuring. In particular, it compares the roles of the private and public sectors and examines the impact that the latter has had on the former. The text examines theories of public administration, grouping them broadly into three categories: classic, structuralist, and humanist. It critically analyses the impact of each category on public administration in Canada and concludes with an assessment of how recent theoretical innovations, such as the New Public Management and Participatory Management, have reshaped our thinking.

The real world of government organizations is examined, allowing students to see how theoretical ideas are translated into practice in the Canadian government. Here, the student learns about the executive, legislative, and judicial branches of government, as well as the nature of bureaucratic organizations.

The relationship between democracy and bureaucracy is a recurring theme, illustrated with real-life examples.

This introductory material sets the stage for an analysis of how public policy is actually set within the context of a federal state. Policy outcomes and processes are also considered in the context of the roles of key government players: the executive, legislative, and judicial branches of government, the bureaucracy, and the central agencies. Outside government, other actors are examined, such as political parties, interest groups and social movements, and the media. The text explains policy formulation, implementation, and evaluation and examines the issue of choosing governing instruments. Specific key issues such as financial and personnel management are also considered. Finally, the text concludes with a chapter on the question of the extent to which a distinctly *Canadian* public administration exists.

Understanding Canadian Public Administration addresses the outstanding need and demand for an easily accessible introductory text in the field that is neither encyclopedic nor esoteric. It is meant to be a simple (though not simplistic) explanation of the basics of Canadian public administration. The narrative is in an interrogative style that can be easily understood by undergraduate students. In addition, the text provides real-life examples that are relevant to students' experiences and incorporates these examples into the analysis of public administration. In this way, the topic is brought to life and made immediately relevant. The text invites students to examine the issues of public administration from their own viewpoints, through their own experiences, by posing questions about day-to-day issues that they may not have realized relate to the way public administration affects them.

A variety of pedagogical features in *Understanding Canadian Public Administration* enhances the student's learning experience. These include sections, found at the beginning and end of each chapter, entitled *What You Will Learn* and *What You Have Learned*, which clarify learning objectives through brief introductory and concluding passages. There are lists of *Key Words and Concepts* (boldfaced within the text) and suggested lists for *Further Reading* and useful *Weblinks*. Each chapter also contains summary questions with which the instructor can test the students' understanding of the material or generate essay questions; students can use these questions to self-test their comprehension of the material. Sidebars complement the main text; these short asides illuminate issues with supplementary information that might otherwise interrupt the flow of the narrative. Occasional editorial cartoons highlight points in a humorous, but effective, manner.

This third edition features many updates on topical issues and new developments in the field of public administration. While retaining the intention of providing a solid grounding in the basics, this edition addresses issues and themes which have emerged since the first edition was published. In particular, the chapters on public policy, human resources, and financial management have been substantially restructured. Throughout the text, updated data, statistical information, and policy issues have been introduced as well.

Understanding Canadian Public Administration is divided into 13 chapters. Chapter 1 provides an overview of some central issues of public administration. It defines the field, examines what bureaucracy means, and compares the public sector with the private sector. As well, it introduces the concept of the role of the state, a central notion that is re-examined in the final chapter.

Chapter 2 explores the link between public administration and democracy by illuminating the meaning of concepts such as responsible and representative government.

Chapter 3 deals with organization theory and is divided into three broad sections. The first critically examines classic theories and theorists; the second assesses structuralist theories and theorists; and the third assesses humanist theories and theorists. In this chapter, students are introduced to Weber, Marx, Taylor, and many other key actors in the development of public administration as both theory and practice.

Chapter 4 applies organization theory to the Canadian experience. It explores the impact of various approaches to public administration on Canadian thinking and practice, and examines the most recent trends and developments affecting the organization of the Canadian government, including emerging post-New Public Management issues.

Chapter 5 turns to the "real world" of public administration by examining the actual organizations and machinery of governing in Canada. It does so within a framework of factors that influence the organizational structure of government.

Chapter 6 discusses the relationship between public administration and law—both constitutional and administrative.

In Chapter 7, the wide-ranging issue of public policy is explored. The term is defined and placed within the context of the policy cycle, which involves the formulation, implementation, and evaluation of public policy. Various theoretical perspectives on public policy decision-making are also surveyed.

Chapter 8 builds on the insights provided in the previous chapter by focusing in more detail on the increasingly important concept of policy evaluation.

Public administration is nothing without the people who make up the public service, and so Chapter 9 has been reworked to focus more sharply on the key elements that shape the world of those who work in government administration. Merit and patronage, equity and collective bargaining, and recruitment and retention are all considered. So, too, are the many issues surrounding the recent restructuring of the public service.

This leads us to consider the role of management in public administration, which is the topic of Chapter 10. Specifically, management reform and management of financial resources are explored in the context of current reforms of the public service.

The ethical dilemmas confronting public administrators are many and are of a different nature than those facing private-sector administrators. Chapter 11 explains why this is so and explores various public administration issues related to ethics and morality.

Chapter 12 focuses on accountability, a fundamental issue of public administration given increasing prominence in the wake of scandals like the Sponsorship Program and Gomery Commission. Chapter 12 assesses the ways in which accountability is maintained in the public sector by looking at issues such as ministerial and Cabinet responsibility. It also explores the structures of accountability while revealing the inherent tensions among democracy, bureaucracy, efficiency, and other important values within public administration.

Finally, Chapter 13 ties together several of the main themes by analyzing the extent to which a distinctly Canadian public administration has emerged. The chapter considers the academic literature as well as governmental innovations. It also places the issue in a comparative context by considering what other countries have done in public administration.

No text on a topic as broad as public administration is going to cover every possible issue and development in the depth each deserves. No attempt has been made to do so in *Understanding Canadian Public Administration*; rather, an overview is provided, recognizing that the literature is both rich and deep, and that students with particular interests not covered explicitly here can pursue them through the Further Readings or Weblinks listed herein. As well, it should be admitted that the focus is unabashedly federal, which is not to suggest that provincial and municipal public administration are not worthy of attention. Certainly they are, but space and time are cruel masters for those writing about so complex a matter as the public administration of this country, necessitating a sharper focus than we might otherwise prefer.

It is extremely gratifying to be asked to produce a third edition of this book. Doing so simply reminds me that a text such as *Understanding Canadian Public Administration* is the product of the distillation of years of reading and thinking inspired by countless intellectual contributions from others too numerous to list. As such, my debts are many but must mainly go unnamed. Still, happily, there are those whose direct contribution to this text I can acknowledge. The reviews and comments supplied by Susan Blankenship (University of Ontario Institute of Technology), Geoffrey Booth (Georgian College), Nathalie Burlone (University of Ottawa),Ted Dionne (Durham College), John Fakouri (Algonquin College), Marc D. Froese (University of Guelph-Humber), Adrian (Andy) Knetsch (Conestoga College), Andrea Riccardo Migone (Simon Fraser University), Jason Morris (University of Northern British Columbia), Robert V. Segsworth (Laurentian University), Lynne Siemens (University of Victoria), Kimberly Speers (University of Manitoba), and Christopher Stoney (Carleton University) were helpful in the genesis of the text. My own public administration students at Ryerson University—many of them practising civil servants—have provided invaluable feedback as I field-tested my ideas on them. Many of my colleagues in the Department of Politics and Public Administration have provided unstinting support and encouragement for which I am very grateful. The team at Pearson Education Canada has been extraordinarily patient with me and understanding of the pressures on my time. I particularly want to thank Alexandra Dyer, Kevin Leung, Colleen Ste. Marie, Christine Cozens, and Laura Forbes.

All of the above made important contributions to the writing of this book. Of course, responsibility for whatever errors and defects which appear in the text is mine alone.

Gregory J. Inwood

Department of Politics and Public Administration,
Ryerson University

Chapter 1

Introduction: *The* Nature *of* Public Administration

WHAT YOU WILL LEARN

Your study of public administration will require you to canvass many issues from a variety of perspectives. You will discover that the field's theory and practice range across a surprisingly broad spectrum. This first chapter introduces the topic by addressing some basic issues related to the nature of public administration in Canada. By the end of the chapter, you will be able to answer the following questions:

- How has the field of public administration been defined?
- What is the relationship between public administration and democratic government?
- What are some of the common assumptions about bureaucratic organizations, and how do these assumptions influence how we view public sector organization and management in Canada?
- What are the major differences and similarities between public and private sector administration?
- How can the growth and ongoing restructuring of the bureaucratic state be explained, and what are the implications for democracy?

In order to answer these questions, this chapter highlights five central issues:

1. What Is Public Administration?

This introductory section addresses the following questions: How do we define public administration? What key terms and concepts are used in its study and practice? The intent is to familiarize you with the basic language used in this area in order to lay the basis for an understanding of later material.

2. — Public Administration and Democratic Government

The second section concerns the tensions between democratic representation and bureaucracy. You will consider the following question: If elected politicians, acting as representatives of the people, are responsible for government policy, how do nonelected public servants influence policy? Is the will of the people realized through the institutions of public administration?

3. — Bureaucracy

This section focuses on the nature of bureaucracy by briefly examining its component parts: personnel, formal rules, policy instruments, conventions of behaviour, and institutions. This section also asks you to consider what happens when values like democracy and efficiency clash within the organizational structure of bureaucracy.

4. — Comparing Public and Private Sectors

The fourth section compares the public and private sectors. You will note important differences between the two with regard to the following questions: What are the mandates and goals of the public sector compared to the private sector? How do the issues of efficiency and service differ in each? What roles do professionalism and ethics play in the one sector compared to the other?

5. — Restructuring the Public Sector and the Role of the State

The fifth section looks at the extent, significance, and consequences of government restructuring. This section asks the following: Why is organizational change taking place? What forms does it take? How has organizational change redefined the nature and scope of public administration?

These five sections are followed by a comparison of Canadian and international perspectives on the top 10 issues vital to the study and practice of public administration.

What Is Public Administration?

So, you have embarked on the study (and perhaps career) of **public administration**. When you excitedly told your family and friends the news, though, you were probably greeted with polite but quizzical looks. They may not have said it aloud, but many were probably thinking to themselves, "What the heck is that?" Perhaps you yourself are a little unsure of what direction your studies will take you. This is not unusual. As one author puts it,

To the practitioner seeking a bit of advice or the student trying to understand the operation of government, a journey into the literature of public administration can be a bewildering experience. The collective wisdom of public administration emerges from at least six separate fields and disciplines; bits of knowledge sought by one set of experts may be hidden behind another's disciplinary boundary; principles drawn from one field have a tendency to contradict lessons drawn from additional sources; no unifying theory exists to help guide the investigator. Experts frequently cannot agree on a definition of public administration. Some view the subject broadly so as to include the entire process of running a modern government, while others view it as narrowly confined to the administrative policies that governments formulate, such as laws regulating the hiring and firing of personnel. The field comes from so many places—and leads to so many subjects—that even people who make a profession out of studying the subject have trouble keeping up with it all.[1]

However, the depth and breadth of the field, though intimidating, are precisely the features that make it such an interesting study as well as a challenging career.

While the systematic and organized academic study of public administration is relatively young (dating from around the start of the 1900s), the practice of public administration is ancient. One account of public administration that discusses the administrative practices of every civilization in recorded history shows that in ancient China and Egypt, there were incredible feats of organization (the construction of the pyramids, for example) as well as massive public bureaucracies, red tape, and corruption of the sort we often associate with contemporary bureaucracy.[2] Many characteristics of present-day public bureaucracy also existed during the period of the Roman Empire. The Roman Catholic Church kept many of the Roman administrative practices alive during the Dark Ages, and the rise of the Enlightenment in seventeenth-century Western Europe, as well as the emergence of the modern nation-state, beginning in Germany shortly thereafter, contained the seeds of modern public administration. By the 1800s the characteristics of contemporary systems of bureaucracy were emerging in Europe, Great Britain, the United States, and Canada. But what exactly is public administration?

Rather than get bogged down in a definitional quagmire, we will dispense with the traditional list of definitions.[3] For our purposes, public administration will be viewed from two perspectives. It is a field of academic study derived from several disciplines, including political science, business administration, sociology, psychology, law, and economics. But public administration is also a set of administrative practices and institutional arrangements geared toward providing public services and regulations through the public bureaucracy. The knowledge derived from the academic side of public administration supports the practices of the field, while, at the same time, the practices continuously feed academic study, requiring a constant reviewing and updating of findings in light of the increasingly professionalized real world of government.

The relationship between study and practice, then, is mutually reinforcing. Education for public administration careers can be eclectic, based as it is on several different disciplines. Professor of public administration Dwight Waldo draws an analogy between the study of public administration and that of medicine: aspiring doctors must draw on a variety of sciences to prepare for their careers;[4] similarly, practitioners of public administration educate themselves by drawing on a range of academic literatures.

Writings on public administration, in fact, go back thousands of years. But the first modern statement referring to public administration as a distinct professional field came in an essay written in 1887 by Woodrow Wilson, later a president of the United States (see Box 1.1). Wilson argued that political scientists had ignored the fundamental question of how governments are administered. He advocated focusing on personnel, organization, and management of the public sector in the interest of greater efficiency and economy. These are concerns that animate the field to this day. But overlying these concerns are ones about the democratic nature of governing.

BOX 1.1 | Woodrow Wilson on "The Study of Administration"

Woodrow Wilson (1856–1924) made an important contribution to the understanding of public administration in an essay he wrote in 1887 for the journal *Political Science Quarterly*. Wilson later became president of the United States, but at the time he was an instructor at a college for women. He wrote, "It is the object of administrative study to discover, first, what government can properly and successfully do, and secondly, how it can do these proper things with the utmost possible efficiency and at the least possible cost either of money or of energy." Wilson also said that an important distinction needed to be made between "politics" and "administration." This observation served as the underpinning for the important theory of the politics-administration dichotomy, discussed in Box 1.2 (p. 6).

Source: Woodrow Wilson, "The Study of Administration," in Jay M. Shafritz and Albert C. Hyde, eds. *Classics of Public Administration, Third Edition*, (Pacific Grove, California: Brooks Cole Publishing, 1992): 11–24.

The American influence on Canadian public administration is indisputable.[5] Indeed, while a 1914 study entitled *Canada and Its Provinces* addressed some aspects of public administration and bureaucracy in Canada, the first study looking at a particular problem in Canadian public administration was actually written in 1918 by two Americans![6] American writers were originally concerned with corruption and the party "bosses" who ruled local politics with iron fists. Thus, administrative reform became an early concern, as did the management of personnel and budgets, and finding the "one best way" of administratively organizing the workplace through the systematic adoption and application of scientific theory and rationalism.[7] As we will see later, assumptions made in these approaches came under attack by the middle part of the century, fuelling debates about the theory and practice of public administration that continue today.

These issues spilled over the border into Canada (as well as elsewhere in the world).[8] But public administration was long regarded as the poor cousin to political science, with its teachers and students buried somewhere in the recesses of political science departments. For several generations, R. MacGregor Dawson's book *The Government of Canada* (1947) served as the main (and indeed only) text for students studying Canadian political science. But Dawson also published the first two Canadian books on public administration, *The Principle of Official Independence* in 1922, and *The Civil Service of Canada* in 1929.[9] A number of universities began to offer degrees in public administration, starting with Dalhousie University in 1936 and Carleton College (now Carleton University) in 1946.[10] In 1957 the Institute of Public Administration of Canada (IPAC) was formed, and a year later the journal *Canadian Public Administration* was launched to disseminate the views and experiences of both practitioners and scholars. Then, in 1987, the Canadian Association of Programs in Public Administration (CAPPA) was launched. Debates about the purpose of the association, the institute, the journal, and indeed the field of Canadian public administration revealed a belief that educational training in public administration should not simply be restricted to learning the administrative techniques necessary to run a government department. Rather, the study of public administration should be tied to the broader social sciences to produce a well-rounded approach rooted in a wider conception of the management of the state.[11]

From about the 1960s onward, efforts increased to position public administration as a more distinct field of study. A rapid growth in the size of the public service contributed to this trend by fuelling the need for highly trained professionals versed in the art of public administration. Today, there are several colleges and over 20 universities in Canada with programs in public administration. As you work your way through your undergraduate degree, you might keep in mind that an increasing number of universities—now over 20—also offer master's degrees in public administration.[12] Generally, these programs offer opportunities through political science or administrative studies faculties or through specialized schools of public administration. In addition, Carleton University and l'École Nationale d'Administration Publique offer doctorate programs in public administration.

There is no single model for the location of public administration programs within universities. About an equal number of programs are located in faculties of social science or in faculties of administrative and business studies (44 percent each). Only about 8 percent are located in separate schools of public administration and management, with the remainder scattered in a variety of other places.[13] This orphan-like characteristic of the discipline reflects its hybrid nature as the product of a variety of academic influences. A report on graduate studies in Canadian public administration concluded there is a "considerable degree of variety in our master's programs because of differing objectives, institutional emphasis and opportunities for specialization or combined degrees."[14]

While in the 1990s, government downsizing and layoffs led to doubts about the viability of public administration as both a career and a course of study,[15] recent trends indicate quite the opposite. Governments are again hiring as aging baby boomers retire from the public service and because most governments are back in surplus fiscal positions after decades of deficit financing. As well, schools of public administration are experiencing increased interest. For example, the Universities of Toronto, Ottawa, Ryerson, and York have all launched new degree programs in public administration and policy in the past few years in anticipation of a hiring boom in the public service.[16] Another sign of the discipline's health is the rapidly growing and vibrant literature on Canadian public administration. This all bodes well for you, the student of public administration.

Public Administration and Democratic Government

Since public administration is about the public provision of services and regulations, it is necessary to talk about politics. Politics is about who gets what, when, and how; or how the state responds to the demands and wants of the public. This response will be different from how the private-sector marketplace answers this question through the law of supply and demand. State action involves myriad complex decisions and actions by various actors and institutions in what we call the public sector.

We will explore these issues in more detail in Chapter 2, "Public Administration and Democracy." For now, we will briefly consider that a handy but somewhat artificial division of labour exists in the practice of public administration between those who make the decisions and those who carry out the decision-makers' wishes. In a **democratic society** such as Canada, these roles fall into the hands of **elected representatives** (the decision-makers) and public servants or bureaucrats (who carry out the decision-makers' wishes). This neat little division of labour is referred to as the **politics-administration dichotomy** (see Box 1.2). In this sense, then, public administration is the process of public servants carrying out politicians' public decisions. There is a division or dichotomy between politics and administration.

BOX 1.2 | The Politics-Administration Dichotomy

The politics-administration dichotomy reflects the notion that "politics" is about deciding what government should do, while "administration" is about how to do it; thus, there should be clearly defined responsibilities that differentiate the roles of politicians and public servants. The concept manifests itself in the desire to find the "one best way" of administering public affairs and reflects the desire to achieve the ultimate in efficiency in the provision of public services and in the business of government by putting public administration on the most rational basis possible. This means, for example, hiring and promoting the best possible candidate for a job (the **merit principle**) rather than a minister's political supporter (patronage). Public servants' political neutrality is vital to the realization of the politics-administration dichotomy. Public servants should serve the *government* of the day, not the political party that happens to hold power.

In reality, of course, the politics-administration dichotomy is less straightforward than the theory implies. Not only do public servants respond to orders from politicians, but they also sometimes initiate action on their own. In other words, the traditional role of public servants, which is to implement policy on the instructions of their political bosses, is accompanied by the role they play in policy formulation. This is because public servants enjoy a fair amount of discretionary power. After all, no elected official who is given the job of heading up a large and complex government department or ministry can know absolutely everything that goes on within it. So in aiding the elected representatives, public servants engage in policy formulation as well as implementation.

During the 1960s and 1970s, it became fashionable to assert that public servants were highly trained technocratic experts who knew and understood the "ins and outs" of government and who ought to have a more responsible role in areas traditionally left up to politicians. Some theorists and practitioners went so far as to suggest that since front-line public servants (i.e., those dealing directly with members of the public) had first-hand and intimate experience with the needs of citizens, they ought to have a more hands-on role in formulating and implementing policy. In the 1980s and 1990s, however, the view emerged that the bureaucracy had usurped too much power from the politicians, and many governments enacted reforms to restore the proper relationship between the two sets of actors. These views represent some of the many attempts to sort out the proper balance between the power of public servants and elected representatives in a democratic society.

Bureaucracy

The public provision of services and regulations, and how the state answers the political question of who gets what, when, and how take place within a structure known generically as a **bureaucracy**. We have all encountered bureaucracy. When you go to renew your driver's licence, file your income tax, register in a program at a community centre, go to court, apply for a passport or a parking permit, etc., you are involved in a relationship with a bureaucracy whose job it is to satisfy your needs and wants as a *citizen*. Of course, bureaucracy is also the organizational form for the private sector. Think of dealing with a bank, cable company, or department store, for instance, as a *customer*.

The term *bureaucracy* comes from a combination of the French word *bureau,* which means "desk," and a Greek word, meaning "rule." Given the remarkable accomplishments of human societies that have emerged from bureaucratic organizations in both the public and private sector through the ages, it is striking that the term carries such pejorative connotations. It is often negatively associated with red tape, inefficiency, rigid lines of control, corruption, petty officiousness, delay, and so on. But this is nothing new. Honoré de Balzac (1799–1850) said that "bureaucracy is a giant mechanism operated by pygmies." Czar Nicholas I (1796–1855) claimed that "I do not rule Russia: Ten thousand clerks do." And Winston Churchill (1874–1965) once complained that "some civil servants are neither servants nor civil."

Bureaucracies are made up of a mixture of elements: personnel, formal rules, policy instruments, conventions of behaviour, and institutions, all of which importantly affect the provision of services for citizens in any political system. But in a democracy there are particular issues in terms of these components and how citizens hold governments accountable. In the following paragraphs each of these components of bureaucracy is considered in relation to democracy.

Personnel

When you seek a government service you may meet a public servant face-to-face, but behind that person stands a veritable army of people, usually arranged in a hierarchical relationship characterized by a division of labour. The public service in Canada employs hundreds of thousands of people at all three levels of government (federal, provincial, and municipal) in an array of professions. From firefighters to diplomats, from judges to environmental scientists, from presidents of Crown corporations to street sweepers—all serve in bureaucracies dedicated to providing services, enforcing regulations, and formulating, implementing, and evaluating policies for citizens. None of these people are elected, yet together they wield a tremendous amount of influence. This raises the issue of whom they are accountable to and how that accountability is realized. This is discussed next and in chapter 12.

Formal Rules

Bureaucracy is notorious for its "red tape," but there must be clearly laid-out rules to ensure that all services are provided equally to all citizens, and that all regulations are fairly enforced. This is due to the special requirement of **accountability** in public bureaucracies. After all, the money spent to support the services and regulations being provided is *your* money—i.e., taxpayers' money—and so must be accounted for. However, this buildup of formal rules sometimes comes at the expense of efficiency, which may conflict with the values of democracy (through accountability). This is an important ongoing public administration conundrum.

Policy Instruments

Policy instruments are the means by which services are provided and regulations enforced. The government has at its disposal a vast array of tools to ensure that citizen needs and wants are satisfied.[17] These range from instruments that rely on voluntary compliance on the part of citizens all the way to tools that use coercion or even violence. Laws, regulations, Crown corporations, expenditures, and taxes are but a few examples of different types of policy or governing instruments (see chapter 7).

Conventions of Behaviour

Bureaucracies often develop their own internal logic and way of doing things, emphasizing formal rules, hierarchies of power, and divisions of labour. In a perfect world, there would always be "one right way" of doing something. Bureaucracies often behave as though they live in such a world, when they develop conventions of behaviour about how to fulfill their mandates based on the "one right way" of doing things. Bureaucracies must not appear to be arbitrary and unfair but must treat each citizen equally. This is why elaborate conventions of behaviour exist, even though they sometimes make institutions appear hidebound and inflexible.

Institutions

This term refers to the complex of government ministries and departments, regulatory bodies, Crown corporations, special operating agencies, and other institutions responsible for translating the will of the people into action (see chapter 5). The democratization of modern society has resulted in ever more elaborate structures to ensure that all interests in society are accommodated within the institutions of the state. But, ironically, as bureaucracy has increased in size, the level of responsiveness has sometimes declined due to the growth of red tape and bureaucratic procedure within those institutions.

All five of these components of bureaucracy profoundly affect the type and quality of public administration we get. In a democratic society, there is the expectation that each component contributes to administration that is fair and equitable in its treatment of citizens. But in fulfilling this mandate, bureaucracies often appear to lack efficiency. Thus, there often is a real tension between the value of democracy and efficient provision of service.

To illustrate how this tension can play out, imagine a government focused solely on efficiency. Such a government might, for instance, cut back on the number of politicians, the number of personnel within the public service, reduce and eliminate regulations and red tape, streamline the delivery of services, or, in some cases, turn them over entirely to the private sector and re-engineer the institutions of government to make them leaner. But democratic accountability could be trampled in the rush to create a more efficient public administration. Reducing the number of politicians may indeed save money, but citizens will get less representation. Fewer elected officials also means centralizing power in the hands of the leader and cabinet, which may reduce the democratic quality of debate and discussion within government. Reduction of personnel, privatization, and deregulation are all recipes for diminishing the quality of democratic life—a process that leaves ordinary citizens with fewer avenues through which to force the government to explain itself.

But this debate about efficiency versus democracy is neither new nor particular to Canada. It is part of the larger ongoing debate in democracies about the values appropriate to the administration of the public will. An important part of that debate is the issue of what the role of government (that is, the **public sector**) ought to be. Are there some things the marketplace (that is, the **private sector**) can better attend to? These questions are considered in the next section.

Comparing Public and Private Sectors

The question of the differences between public and private administration goes back a long way in both the study and practice of the field.

Since Woodrow Wilson wrote his classic essay exhorting reformers to help make the busi-
ness of government "less unbusinesslike," the field of public administration has been seeking
to differentiate itself from business administration. But comparisons between business and
government are inevitable. In fact, they are important to understanding how management
ideas from the private sector have been imposed on public administration and how this
process affects what is actually done in public organizations. A key question is, how appro-
priate are these ideas, and how well has the transfer worked? [18]

Especially since the 1980s, the line between public and private administration has become increasingly blurred. Public administration has been placed on a
more businesslike footing and uses more business techniques, theories, and
methods to run government. Furthermore, contracting out to the private sector
has increased, and more and more services are being privatized outright. Public
sector and private sector managers interact more frequently, and their career
paths often cross over between the two sectors.

Today's students are sometimes surprised to learn that in Canada, the
career of public servant was once held in high esteem as a noble calling in
which individuals dedicated themselves to the service of their country.[19] But
then, this attitude changed. Private sector managers were often seen as inherently superior, more intelligent, industrious, and efficient than their public sector counterparts, who were disdained as incompetent, lazy, and wasteful. This
view is simplistic, patently unfair, and inaccurate. In any event, attitudes do
seem to be changing again (see Box 1.3). Still, you may have heard the following popular refrain: "If only they would run the government like a business,
then things would get done!" And in fact, at least superficially, business and
public administration are alike in that they perform many of the same basic
functions. Both engage in the management of complex organizations of people
through planning, organizing, staffing, and budgeting.

Box 1.3 | **Bureaucrat is not a dirty word; Bureaucratic ethics**
may slowly erode in the face of unrelenting contempt.

By Matt Young
The Globe and Mail, Tuesday, May 3, 2005, Page A20

"I want to be a bureaucrat."

When was the last time you heard someone say those words? Not too recently, I bet.
Do you wonder why not? Let me tell you, because somehow, the proper name of this
profession has been transformed into a dirty word, a barb to be slung about, a euphemism
for waste, inefficiency, sloth, rote action, obstructionism and, perhaps worst of all, the
complete absence of any sartorial acumen. Now do you see why so few people proclaim
their bureaucratic aspirations?

On the cusp of graduating with a professional degree specializing in the bureaucratic arts and sciences, I have yet to enroll in Obfuscation 101, study Introduction to Time Mismanagement, or attend lectures on Advanced Fiscal Ineptitude. No, my classmates and I are eager, experienced, highly skilled, and committed to making a difference. Daily, we debate issues of public importance. We promptly complete our projects and assignments, and I'm quite certain I've even witnessed a number of innovative thoughts and approaches during my schooling.

When we talk of bureaucracy, we use a different vocabulary altogether. We discuss ideals such as the rule of law, justice, fairness, effectiveness and service to the public interest above all else. We identify collective problems and strive to craft solutions for them. We assess models of public accountability. We measure the use of common resources to evaluate efficiency. We confront the reconciling of competing social demands. And we do all of this with gusto. . . .

We are the bureaucrats of tomorrow. We aspire not to profit nor to be recognized, but to make our communities, however large or small, better than before our arrival. And we're committed to doing that while upholding the rule of law, stewarding public resources, and treating everyone equally and with fairness. That's the credo of the bureaucrats I know.

So, what does it matter if we poke a little fun at government officials, if we disparage them for a laugh? It matters because it undermines the sense of public duty, the ethic of public service that drives each of us into this profession. It belittles our commitment to an ideal and mocks our faith in our professional values. If this banter corrodes the bureaucratic ethos to the point that civil servants only half-heartedly engage in their responsibilities, we all suffer. The true cost will be measured by the degradation of our international development, law enforcement, environmental protection, health and social service programs.

Nonetheless, I'm pleased to report that government institutions will be shortly infused with another eager cohort, a cohort that sees beyond the derision to the highest aspirations of our profession: integrity, commitment to the public interest, public service, and some of the best public programs in the world. This is our pledge, and your assurance, of the kind of Canada we want into the next generation.

Source: Matt Young, "Bureaucrat is not a dirty word: Bureaucratic ethics may slowly erode in the face of unrelenting contempt." *The Globe and Mail,* (Tuesday, May 3, 2005): A20.

But this ignores the underlying differences between business and government. As public administration theorist Wallace Sayre once noted, "Business and public administration are alike only in all unimportant respects."[20] After all, we refer to the "business of business" but to the "art of government." We can distinguish between private and public administration by examining the mandate and goals, efficiency and service, and professionalism and ethics of both.

Mandate and Goals

It may be easiest to grasp these differences by referring to what public administration is not. It is not the same as administration dedicated to the pursuit of private profit. Public administration is geared toward the provision of public services, not the "bottom line." This has important implications for the way bureaucracies function in the private and public sectors.

According to political scientist Graham Allison, the first difference between the public and private sectors is temporal.[21] Government managers tend to work with relatively short time frames dictated by the political calendar. A related difference is duration of service. Top-level public sector managers usually serve for a relatively short time before moving to another position, while, on average, private sector managers hold tenure for longer periods of time.

Third, goal measurement distinguishes the public from the private sector. The public sector manager often faces multiple or contradictory ends sought by governments. For example, the Ministry of Finance may want to reduce government spending. Simultaneously, another department may want to reduce child poverty, a goal that requires the expenditure of more money. Moreover, certain intangible goals unique to government are impossible to measure—for instance, whether an increased "quality of life" has been achieved through the implementation of family service policies. This contrasts with the relatively straightforward measurement of goals in the private sector: profits, market share, financial performance, and so on. Indeed, some would argue that public sector managers actually have to be more creative and imaginative than their private sector counterparts.

A fourth difference between the public and private sectors relates to human resource management. It is a much more complicated process to hire or fire someone in the public service. Consider the merit principle, that all Canadian citizens should have a reasonable opportunity for employment and promotion in the public sector based exclusively on fitness to do the job.[22] The strict application of this principle means that a detailed, time-consuming, and thorough process must be initiated to ensure that every hiring in the public service is done fairly and equitably. Firings, too, must be carefully justified by extensive documentation of failure to perform or malfeasance in duty. In addition, provisions such as bilingualism and employment equity may mean that extra effort must be put into recruiting and training employees. These steps guide (some would say constrain) the public sector manager through a maze of regulations intended to ensure that human resource management is scrupulously fair and equitable. Overlying the process is the requirement that the public sector be representative of the population it serves (that is, all of Canada). The private sector manager has few such requirements.

Fifth, equity and efficiency concerns are different in the public and private sectors. Public sector managers emphasize providing equity among various constituents. The private sector, on the other hand, is more oriented toward efficiency and competitiveness.

Sixth, the public sector continues to be open to scrutiny by the attentive public and the media in a way that private business is not. Looking over the shoulder of every senior public sector manager is a reporter. Watching the actions of every government member are the opposition parties. The public scrutinizes the actions of every front-line clerk. Service to the public is the raison d'être of the public service, but along with this mandate comes a level of attention that simply is not present in the private sector. While recent corporate scandals, like those involving Hollinger, Enron, WorldCom, and Bre-X, have drawn increased attention to private sector malfeasance, most corporate executives operate in relative obscurity, but the limelight frequently shines on public sector managers and, especially, on political leaders. Success seems to be downplayed, while errors are often magnified by a media looking for that juicy lead story for the news—a point made more than 50 years ago by Paul Appleby, journalist turned administrator turned academic, who said administrators live in a goldfish bowl, where "each employee hired, each one demoted, transferred, or discharged, every efficiency rating, every assignment of responsibility, each change in administrative structure, each conversation, each letter, has to be thought about in terms of possible public agitation, investigation, or judgement."[23]

A seventh difference between public and private administration with regard to mandate and goals is the provision of what are called *public goods*. These are goods provided for the benefit of all members of society, such as national defence or roads and bridges. Sometimes these services are inherently unprofitable, but they must be provided nonetheless. So the state assumes responsibility for doing so. In any event, the value of the provision of some goods is often intangible. How, for instance, does one measure the efficient production of national defence?

An eighth factor is accountability. According to the Office of the Auditor General, the watchdog agency that conducts audits and examinations of government programs and departments,

Parliament, the government and the public service are the guardians of public funds entrusted to them for delivering programs and services to benefit Canadians. An important part of the confidence that people have in our democratic institutions is their belief that public funds are spent wisely and effectively. There must be, and there must be seen to be, value from money spent, compliance with authority and environmental stewardship. In a significant way, then, confidence in our national government depends upon clear and timely accountability by the government for its performance.[24]

The public sector faces standards of accountability that are simply absent in the private sector. The public sector's actions must be available to public scrutiny, there must be a "paper trail" documenting every step, and its services must be transparent and above board. Lines of authority and responsibility are complex. Public sector managers are scrutinized as well by legislatures and the courts. Parliament keeps an eye on the public service through a variety of watchdog agencies, such as the Office of the Auditor General and the Canadian Human Rights Commission. Moreover, a whole body of administrative law has built up that is overseen by the courts, adjudicating disputes between the public service and the public (see chapter 6). Such scrutiny, both legislative and judicial, tends to constrain public sector managers, whereas their private sector equivalents enjoy more freedom from this kind of unrelenting attention. The private sector simply does not labour under these types of standards.

Finally, in the private sector, efficient operation leads to enhanced profitability. There is a clear and sobering focus on the "bottom line," which is often absent in the public sector. Thus, private businesses will shy away from operations that are inefficient and from which a profit cannot be derived. The private sector, in effect, receives its mandate from the marketplace through the law of supply and demand. But where do public sector managers get their mandate? From their political bosses, who, theoretically, are seeking to express the broadly understood will of the people. And that popular will must be turned into action through legislative or regulatory means—that is, by the passing of laws and regulations—which may or may not result in profitable activities by government.

Efficiency and Service

Notwithstanding the differences noted above, efficiency has become a dominant value of our time and there has been an increasing trend to impose it on the public sector.[25] Indeed, the "three Es" of *efficiency, economy,* and *effectiveness* are now prominent in the minds of many public sector managers; a major aspect of holding public servants accountable has been to measure whether they have provided efficient, economical, and effective service. In response, a series of old and new government institutions have evolved. The Treasury Board, one of the government's central agencies (see chapter 5), helps ensure that the public service as a whole is run efficiently and effectively; it has introduced numerous innovations over the years to ensure that "the managers are being managed properly." Other government institutions, such as the Office of the Comptroller General and the Office of the Auditor General, assist public sector managers and cajole them into performing their jobs more efficiently, economically, and effectively.

But how does one "measure" success in the three Es? How, for instance, does a public sector manager—given the job of implementing programs to enhance the "quality of life" of citizens—determine success? How can increased national security be measured? Or how can anyone determine that preventive policies have been effective? Even defining the service provided can be a challenge. If the Ministry of Health has a mandate of securing the mental health of citizens, what is "mental health"? Without this basic information, how can you determine whether it has been efficiently, economically, and effectively increased? Along with the three Es, government has the responsibility of providing services to citizens equitably and fairly. For instance, subsidizing air or rail links to remote communities may not be economical but may be undertaken in the interests of fairness. Thus, the three Es alone cannot be the guiding principle of public administration, as they are in the private sector. In any event, the public sector lacks the same motivation for efficiency as in the private sector: compete efficiently or perish. Indeed, many times governments make decisions that are patently inefficient in a strict economic sense. For instance, it may not be efficient to decentralize a program by setting up regional offices across the country. But it may make good political sense to do so, as the government appears responsive to regional needs. Indeed, many government services are monopolistic; that is, they have no competition. For example, there is only one police force, and it does not need to be conscious of the efficient provision of services in the same way that a private corporation does. This does not mean that it should not be as efficient as possible. But the standard of efficiency is different from that of the private sector because there is no competition. And in cases in which government activities *do* generate a profit against which efficiency can be measured, some people argue that those activities should be turned over to the private sector.

There are, however, different incentives for governments to provide services efficiently. While they do not compete in the free market to make a profit, government departments do compete with one another for public funds. This can be especially tough during periods of reduced government revenues and expenditures, which cause government institutions to impose more efficiency on their internal operations, including reducing staff, introducing performance measurement, rationalizing program delivery, contracting out, and operating programs on a cost-recovery basis.

Another incentive in the public realm is that politicians must seek re-election. To achieve this, they must run an efficient government so that voters do not withdraw their support. But in reality, the public pays little attention to the nuts-and-bolts of effective public sector management unless a scandal is uncovered. Thus, this incentive for efficient management by politicians is a relatively weak one.

Professionalism and Ethics

When Sir John A. Macdonald and the Fathers of Confederation founded Canada in 1867, there was little need for a large, sophisticated professional public service.[26] The activities of government were extremely limited, and governing could be accomplished with a ratio of about 100 public servants per politician. Today there are several thousand public servants per politician, since government has become involved in so many more aspects of life than was common in Macdonald's day.

But there is more to the differences than simply numbers of public servants. Back then, many bureaucrats owed their positions to **patronage**—the practice of rewarding loyal supporters, friends, and relatives with government positions. Today, however, most jobs in the public service are based on merit.

A patronage-based public service is by definition amateurish and unprofessional. The office-holders are not hired for *what* they know, but rather *who* they know. The result is a lack of skills and ability compounded by a high turnover rate, since every time a new government is elected, the old government's supporters get fired and are replaced by the new government's supporters. Thus, the capability of developing a professional, well-trained, and dedicated public service is undermined. As well, service to the public is compromised, since the best person for a job is not always hired.

Calls for reform of the patronage-based system of appointments started almost as soon as the new Dominion was created. In 1911, a group of Ontario businessmen made a proposal to the leader of the opposition, Robert Borden. The group promised support for Borden's Conservative Party in the next election if he promised to initiate a merit system of appointment to the public service. "Since they also wanted a stronger role for the federal government in promoting Canadian trade around the world," according to political scientist Reginald Whitaker, "they obviously saw a merit-based administration as the prerequisite to a more effective government that could act in their interests."[27]

Borden did win the subsequent election, and reforms were implemented after the First World War when the Civil Service Act, 1918 was passed. The Act called for the Civil Service Commission (later the Public Service Commission) to oversee all appointments to the public service, rather than leave them in the hands of the politicians. As well, competitive exams were initiated as the basis of appointments, political activity by public servants was prohibited, the public service was reorganized, and a new job classification system was introduced. Many of these steps, you may have noticed, reflect the principles of the politics-administration dichotomy. In addition, special provisions were included in the reforms to favour returning war veterans, setting a precedent as an early form of affirmative action.

The long-term result of these changes was to foster professionalism within the public service. Further reforms followed that reinforced its competency and ability, particularly with regard to ongoing training and education, and issues like affirmative action programs related to language, gender, ethnicity, and disability (discussed in chapter 9). As new technological, economic, and social developments shaped modern Canada, the government responded by continuously reforming the operation and organization of the public service. From the 1918 reforms to the Royal Commission on Government Organization (the Glassco Commission) in the 1960s to the Public Service Employment Act of 1967 to the Public Service Modernization Act in 2003 and beyond to the present day, successive governments have engaged in a never-ending process of maintaining and building the professionalism of the public service.

Related to professionalism is the issue of ethics, which raises particular concerns in the context of government bureaucracies. Governments are entrusted with a special responsibility to act in the best interests of society as a whole. Thus, government personnel are held up to the highest standards of ethical behaviour. But governments are composed of individuals, and individuals are susceptible to temptation. As two theorists of Canadian public administration put it, "Nothing is more dangerous than a public servant who is technically fit but ethically flabby."[28] To prevent individuals from succumbing to temptation, elaborate systems of checks and balances are built into government bureaucracy.

Ethics involves the study, implementation, and enforcement of activities designed to promote "proper" behaviour and to punish "improper" behaviour. Various formal methods of promoting ethics within government have emerged that can be applied both to politicians and public servants. In general, the stipulation is that public office is not to be used for private gain. Of course, the concern not to overstep the bounds of ethical behaviour sometimes means that high-ranking public servants must take extraordinary steps. "It's no wonder that to be a senior public servant these days is to live constantly on your guard," according to a former deputy minister in the Ontario government.

"If someone sends you flowers for any reason, you immediately give them away. You politely decline an offer of free baseball tickets, no matter who is giving them to you and regardless of the fact that the person offering them has nothing to do with your job."[29]

To enforce ethical behaviour of government personnel, a complex set of cumbersome rules has been built up over the years[30] that often results in delays in developing or implementing a policy. However, these rules also ensure that taxpayers know that decisions are being made on the merits of a particular issue and not because of the material self-interest of particular government officials. Because public servants are guardians of the public interest, ethical codes and rules ensure that there is some way of guarding the guardians. A series of scandals in Ottawa in the 1990s and early 2000s intensified interest in the issue of ethics and values in government, resulting in numerous reforms and initiatives (see chapter 11).

Comparing the issues of mandate and goals, efficiency and service, and professionalism and ethics between the private and public sectors reveals some important distinctions. The issues are complex, yet we frequently hear the rather simplistic and dogmatic call for government to somehow achieve businesslike standards in what it does. What this ignores are the profound differences between public and private administration.

Restructuring the Public Sector and the Role of the State

Many recent reforms to the public service reflect the conflict between the values of efficiency and democracy. But to place these developments in context requires understanding the evolution of the public sector in the longer term. This evolution can, for convenience's sake, be divided into three eras: the **minimalist state**, from roughly 1867 to the 1930s; the **Keynesian welfare state**, from the 1930s to the late 1970s; and the **neoconservative state**, from the late 1970s to the present.

The Minimalist State

Confederation in 1867 was accomplished by a state with minimal responsibilities. The prevailing ideology was a laissez-faire attitude that suggested the role of the state be limited to national defence and the provision of infrastructure (roads, canals, railways) to help facilitate the expansion of business. There was little or no role for government in the provision of welfare and social services, which were regarded as private matters to be attended to by family or by religious or charitable organizations. Even the state's role in education was relatively limited by today's standards. Consequently, the public service was small.

This is not to suggest that it was nonexistent, of course. The early Canadian state played an important role in building the national economy, for instance, through the three planks of Sir John A. Macdonald's 1878 National Policy: a system of tariffs to protect infant Canadian industries from foreign (i.e., American) competition; an aggressive immigration policy to settle the great Western prairies, which supplied raw materials and markets for central Canadian industry; and a transcontinental railway to further assist in the creation of a national economy. Thus, from early on the Canadian state established a presence in the nation's economic life. But apart from the economy, the provision of law and order, national defence, the post office, and a handful of other areas, the role of the state was minimal.

The Keynesian Welfare State

The middle part of the twentieth century witnessed the emergence of a much more activist, interventionist state in areas beyond economic matters. The horrors of the Great Depression of the 1930s starkly revealed that laissez-faire capitalism could not function unregulated, as hundreds of thousands of Canadians were thrown out of work without means of support. The strain this placed on private charities, religious agencies, and families proved unbearable. Thus, gradually and reluctantly, the Canadian state began providing welfare and other social services previously regarded as the domain of the private sector.

But how could a society that had preached self-reliance now justify allowing government to accept responsibility for private concerns? The theoretical underpinning for this new view was provided by the British economist John Maynard Keynes, who argued that in bad economic times the government could prime the pump of economic growth by investing and spending. Spending on infrastructure as well as on social programs was thus justified.

The result was the Keynesian welfare state. In Canada, it included a commitment to full employment as well as the construction of the social safety net (welfare, unemployment insurance, pensions, family allowance, Medicare, etc.), which began in the 1940s. The acceptance of Keynesianism implied that the government would be providing more and more services, which in turn spurred growth in the public sector. A large, sophisticated well-trained public service emerged first at the federal level, and later at the provincial and municipal levels. Indeed, because the provinces in Canada have constitutional responsibility for most social policy issues, overall provincial government growth eventually outstripped that of the federal government.

The Neoconservative State

More recently, we have entered a new era that in many ways reflects the attitudes and ideologies that rationalized the original minimalist state. Globalization has prompted questions about the apparent inability of the Keynesian welfare state to perform as theory predicted.[31] Growing deficits, both real and exaggerated, informed the ideological framework within which the expanded interventionist role of the state was brought under question. A concerted attack on the state, by business and right-wing think tanks and the corporate-controlled media, successfully conveyed the image of Canada on the edge of a precipice, and convinced many citizens that we could only pull back from sure disaster if we curtailed the state. From the 1970s onward, provincial governments in Manitoba (under Conservative Sterling Lyon), in British Columbia (under Social Credit's Bill Bennett and Bill Vander Zalm and the Liberal party's

Gordon Campbell), in Alberta (under Conservative Ralph Klein), and in Ontario (under Conservative Mike Harris), as well as federal governments (under Conservatives Brian Mulroney and Stephen Harper and Liberals Jean Chrétien and Paul Martin) all preached fiscal responsibility above all else. This emphasis on efficiency, economy, and effectiveness usually translated into massive cutbacks in the public sector, coupled with drastically reduced government spending on social policies.

A period of retrenchment of the public sector resulted. Privatization, contracting out of services, deregulation, firing of public servants, re-engineering, restructuring, and devolution became commonplace. Transferring services to the private sector and to the newly emergent "third sector"—i.e., non-profit and voluntary organizations—became significant. Moreover, the role of the family, religious agencies, and private charities re-emerged, as in earlier times, to fill the void left by the retreating state.

We can measure and compare the three eras by looking at how the expenditures and revenues of Canadian governments have changed over time. One common method for doing so is note the percentage of Canada's gross domestic product (GDP) accounted for by government. GDP represents the total value of all goods and services produced in the country (see Figure 1.1).

You will likely notice that the greatest increase in revenues and expenditures over time occurred at the provincial level. Why is this? During the expansion of

FIGURE 1.1 **Public Finance in Canada: Revenue and Expenditure as Percentages of GDP for Each Level of Government, 1950 and 2001.**

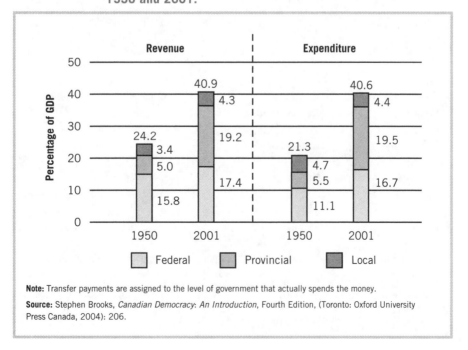

Note: Transfer payments are assigned to the level of government that actually spends the money.

Source: Stephen Brooks, *Canadian Democracy: An Introduction*, Fourth Edition, (Toronto: Oxford University Press Canada, 2004): 206.

the social welfare state, a variety of social security programs was enacted by governments in Canada. Since the constitution stipulates that the provinces are primarily responsible for social policy fields, such as health, education, and welfare, we should not be surprised that most government growth occurred at this level.

As we proceed from here, ask yourself why the state was originally small in scope and what factors contributed to its growth. Today, can you think of an area of your own life in which the state does *not* have a role? These kinds of questions are central to public administration because they touch on the issue of what size, shape, and form the government ought to take. We will examine these questions in more detail in chapter 5, when we look at factors affecting the organization of government.

WHAT YOU HAVE LEARNED

There are several more issues surrounding public administration addressed in the next chapters in this book. For now, to summarize what we have studied so far as well as to signal what is to come, consider the differing perspectives on what constitutes the "top 10" concerns of public administration (see Box 1.4).

BOX 1.4 — Top 10 Concerns of Canadian and International Public Administration

Johnson's Top 10 List	International Scholar's Top 10 List	Canadian Public Servants' Top 10 List
Political power	Regulation	Leadership development
Public policy	Health policy	Alignment between the needs of the organization and employee skills
Institutions	Organizational culture	Collaboration within the public sector
The public service	Environmental policy	Management accountability
Democracy	Democratic dialogue	Information sharing
Law	Public administration of quasi-public organizations	Ethics
Management	Governance	Work/life balance
Evaluation	Technology change and policy	Democracy/public engagement
Ethics	Municipal and urban public administration	Results-based management
Accountability	Performance and evaluation	Inter-jurisdictional relations

Sources: David Johnson, "Public Administration's Top Ten List," in John James Guy, ed. *Expanding Our Political Horizons: Readings in Canadian Politics and Government,* (Toronto: Harcourt Brace, 1997): 124–132; Michael McConkey with Patrice Dutil, *The Top Ten Topics in Public Administration Scholarship: An International Perspective,* (Toronto: Institute of Public Administration of Canada, 2006).

Political scientist David Johnson's list and two other top-10 lists highlight some of the most important but very broad issues surrounding the practice and theory of public administration.

It is interesting to compare this list to a recent survey of the top 10 topics in international public administration scholarship. Forty-eight scholarly journals from around the world were surveyed, analyzing their contents from 2004 to 2006. In addition, practitioners of Canadian public administration were also surveyed. As you can see, the study and practice of public administration are many and varied. The discrepancies in these lists reflect two things we noted earlier in this chapter— that public administration draws on a number of academic disciplines for its theoretical underpinnings (hence the variety of scholarly concerns), and that it covers a remarkably wide range of human activity and behaviour in the public realm.

Key Words and Concepts

public administration (2)

democratic society (6)

elected representatives (6)

politics-administration dichotomy (6)

merit principle (6)

bureaucracy (7)

accountability (8)

private sector/public sector (9)

patronage (15)

minimalist state (17)

Keynesian welfare state (17)

neoconservative state (17)

Review Questions

This chapter was divided into five substantive sections, each reflecting a key issue for public administration. You should be familiar with these issues, and be able to address the questions associated with each.

1. What Is Public Administration?

At this stage, you should ask yourself, Can I adequately define public administration as both an academic field and a practice, and can I explain the concept of bureaucracy?

2. Public Administration and Democratic Government

In considering the tensions between democracy and bureaucracy, ask yourself, What is the nature of the relationship between elected and non-elected officials, and why is this important in public administration? How do public servants influence governance? Is this problematic for democracy, or supportive of it? What is meant by the "politics-administration dichotomy"? Is it realistic or is its value simply theoretical?

3. Bureaucracy

Ask yourself, Can I explain the significance of personnel, formal rules, policy instruments, conventions of behaviour, and institutions for public administration? How can I describe the tension between the values of democracy and efficiency within government organizations? Which value should prevail?

4. Comparing Public and Private Sectors

In thinking about the public and private sectors, ask yourself, How do the mandates and goals of each differ? What set of characteristics set the two apart and how? Are the differences between public administration and private administration clear to me?

5. Restructuring the Public Sector and the Role of the State

Ask yourself, What major factors have influenced reforms to public administration over the years? List as many public services as you can. Select one and argue why it should, or should not, be turned over to the private sector. Do you know enough about the role of the state to be able to explain how and why the public sector has been undergoing a period of restructuring?

Weblinks

Institute of Public Administration of Canada (IPAC)
www.ipaciapc.ca

Canadian Association of Programs in Public Administration (CAPPA)
www.cappa.ca

Public Service Commission of Canada
www.psc-cfp.gc.ca

Canadian Political Science Association
www.cpsa-acsp.ca

Canada School of Public Service
www.myschool-monecole.gc.ca

Canada Public Service Agency
www.psagency-agencefp.gc.ca

United Nations Public Administration Country Profiles
www.unpan.org/dpepa/country%20profiles/countries.asp

Further Reading

1. What Is Public Administration?

White, Leonard D. "Introduction to the Study of Public Administration," in Jay M. Shafritz and Albert C. Hyde, eds. *Classics of Public Administration. Third Edition.* Pacific Grove, California: Brooks Cole Publishing, 1992: 57–65.

Wilson, Woodrow. "The Study of Administration," in Jay M. Shafritz and Albert C. Hyde, eds. *Classics of Public Administration. Third Edition.* Pacific Grove, California: Brooks Cole Publishing, 1992: 11–24.

2. Public Administration and Democratic Government

MacDonald, Flora. "Who Is on Top? The Minister or the Mandarins?" and Mitchell Sharp, "A Reply From a Former Minister and Mandarin," in Paul W. Fox and Graham White, eds. *Politics Canada. Eighth Edition.* Toronto: McGraw-Hill, 1995: 448–56.

Whitaker, Reginald. "Politics Versus Administration: Politicians and Bureaucrats," in Michael S. Whittington and Glen Williams, eds. *Canadian Politics in the 21st Century. Sixth Edition.* Toronto: Thomson Nelson, 2004: 57–84.

3. Bureaucracy

Breton, Albert and Ronald Wintrobe. "Bureaucracy and State Intervention: Parkinson's Law?" in Barbara Wake Carroll, David Siegel and Mark Sproule-Jones, eds. *Classic Readings in Canadian Public Administration*. Toronto: Oxford University Press, 2005: 427–42.

Brooks, Stephen. "Bureaucracy," in James P. Bickerton and Alain-G. Gagnon, eds. *Canadian Politics. Second Edition*. Peterborough: Broadview Press, 1994: 307–27.

Kernaghan, Kenneth, Brian Marson and Sandford Borins. *The New Public Organization*. Toronto: Institute of Public Administration of Canada, 2000.

4. Comparing Public and Private Sectors

Allison, Graham T. "Public and Private Management: Are They Fundamentally Alike in All Unimportant Respects?" in Jay M. Shafritz and Albert C. Hyde, eds. *Classics of Public Administration. Third Edition*. Pacific Grove, California: Brooks Cole Publishing, 1992: 457–75.

Candler, Gaylord George. "The Comparative Evolution of Public Administration in Australia, Brazil and Canada," *Canadian Public Administration* 49, 3 (Autumn 2006): 334–49.

5. Restructuring the Public Sector and the Role of the State

Pal, Leslie A. "New Public Management in Canada: New Whine in Old Bottles?" in James P. Bickerton and Alain-G. Gagnon, eds. *Canadian Politics. Fourth Edition*. Peterborough: Broadview Press, 2004: 185–202.

Roberts, Alasdair. "A Fragile State: Federal Public Administration in the Twentieth Century," in Christopher Dunn, ed. *The Handbook of Canadian Public Administration*. Toronto: Oxford University Press, 2002: 18–36.

Endnotes

1. Howard E. McCurdy, *Public Administration: A Bibliographic Guide to the Literature*, (New York: Marcel Dekker Inc., 1986): iii.

2. See E.N. Gladden, *A History of Public Administration*, (London: Frank Cass and Company, 1972).

3. On various definitions of public administration, see David H. Rosenbloom, *Public Administration: Understanding Management, Politics and Law in the Public Sector, Fourth Edition*, (New York: McGraw-Hill, 1998): 4–5. For one of the earliest definitions of the field, see Leonard D. White, *Introduction to the Study of Public Administration*, (New York: Macmillan, 1926). See also Grover Starling, *Managing the Public Sector*, (Homewood, Illinois: The Dorsey Press, 1977): 1; and Frederick C. Mosher, "Public Administration," in Frederick S. Lane, ed. *Current Issues in Public Administration*, (New York: St. Martin's Press, 1978): 4.

4. See Dwight Waldo, "Education for Public Administration in the Seventies," in Frederick C. Mosher, ed. *American Public Administration*, (University, Alabama: University of Alabama Press, 1975).

5. See O.P. Dwivedi and James Iain Gow, *From Bureaucracy to Public Management: The Administrative Culture of the Government of Canada*, (Peterborough: Broadview Press, 1999): 55–6.

6. H.S. Villard and W.W. Willoughby, *The Canadian Budgetary System*, (New York: Harper and Row, 1918).

7. See Alasdair Roberts, *So-Called Experts: How American Consultants Remade the Canadian Civil Service 1918–21*, (Toronto: Institute of Public Administration of Canada, 1996).

8. A. Paul Pross and V. Seymour Wilson, "Graduate Education in Canadian Public Administration: Antecedents, Present Trends and Portents," *Canadian Public Administration*, 19, (Winter, 1976): 515–41.

9. Robert MacGregor Dawson, *The Principle of Official Independence With Particular Reference to the Political History of Canada*, (London: P.S. King, 1922); *The Civil Service of Canada*, (London: Humphrey Milford, 1929); *The Government of Canada*, (Toronto: University of Toronto Press, 1947).

10. By comparison, the first American university to offer a program in public administration was Syracuse University in 1924, followed by Princeton and the University of Southern California in 1929 and 1930. See Gaylord George Candler, "The Comparative Evolution of Public Administration in Australia, Brazil and Canada," *Canadian Public Administration* 49, 3 (Autumn 2006): 335.

11. See J.E. Hodgetts, "The Intellectual Odyssey of Public Administration in English Canada," *Canadian Public Administration*, 40, 2 (Summer, 1997): 171–85.

12. For a current list of graduate and undergraduate programs, see the CAPPA website, www.cappa.ca. See also Donald J. Savoie, "Studying Public Administration," *Canadian Public Administration*, 33, 3 (Fall, 1990): 389–413; and Sanford F. Borins, "The Role of Universities in Public Administration Education," *Canadian Public Administration*, 33, 3 (Fall, 1990): 348–65.

13. David A. Good, "2002 CAPPA/CCMD Survey of Schools and Programs of Public Administration and Public Policy: Report of the Findings," Presentation to the University Seminar of the Canadian Centre for Management Development, (Ottawa: April, 2002).

14. See James Iain Gow and Sharon L. Sutherland, "Comparison of Canadian Master's Programs in Public Administration, Public Management and Public Policy," *Canadian Public Administration*, 47, 3, (Fall, 2004): 404. See also Fazley Siddiq and Lindsay Hardy, "A Survey on the Recruitment of Graduates of Master's Programs in Public Administration and Public Policy," report prepared for the 20th Annual University Seminar, Canada School of Public Service, (Ottawa, May, 2006).

15. See Jonathan Malloy, "The Next Generation? Recruitment and Renewal in the Federal Public Service," in G. Bruce Doern, ed. *How Ottawa Spends 2004–2005: Mandate Change in the Paul Martin Era*, (Montreal: McGill-Queen's University Press, 2004): 277–95.

16. See Kathryn May, "Specialized Programs to Help Fill Thousands of Vacancies," *Ottawa Citizen*, (November 6, 2006).

17. See Leslie A. Pal, *Beyond Policy Analysis: Public Issue Management in Turbulent Times. Third Edition*, (Toronto: Thomson Nelson, 2006): chapter 4; and Pearl Eliadis, Margaret M. Hill and Michael Howlett, eds. *Designing Government: From Instruments to Governance*, (Montreal: McGill-Queen's University Press, 2005).

18. James L. Perry and Kenneth L. Kraemer, *Public Management: Public and Private Perspectives*, (Palo Alto, California: Mayfield, 1983): x. Cited in Shafritz and Hyde, eds. *Classics of Public Administration*, (1992): 443.

19. See, for example, J.L. Granatstein, *The Ottawa Men: The Civil Service Mandarins 1935–1957*, (Toronto: Oxford University Press, 1982).

20. See Graham T. Allison, "Public and Private Management: Are They Fundamentally Alike in All Unimportant Respects?" in Jay M. Shafritz and Albert C. Hyde, eds. *Classics of Public Administration: Third Edition*, (Pacific Grove, California: Brooks Cole Publishing, 1992): 457–75.

21. See Graham T. Allison, "Public and Private Management: Are They Fundamentally Alike in All Unimportant Respects?" cited in Shafritz and Hyde, *Classics of Public Administration*, (1992): 462.

22. For a discussion of the merit principle, see Fred Ruemper, "Beyond Merit: The Representative Principle," in Randy Hoffman *et al.*, *Public Administration: Canadian Materials, Third Edition*, (Toronto: Captus Press, 1998): 252–71.

23. Paul Appleby, *Big Democracy*, (New York: Alfred A. Knopff, 1945): 7, cited in Howard E. McCurdy, *Public Administration: A Synthesis*, (Menlo Park, California: Cummings Publishing Company, 1977): 107.

24. See Canada, Office of the Auditor General of Canada, *Auditing for Parliament*, (Ottawa: Minister of Public Works and Government Services Canada, 1997): 1.

25. See Janice Gross Stein, *The Cult of Efficiency*, (Toronto: Anansi, 2001). For an early consideration of the issue, see A.W. Johnson, "Efficiency in Government and Business," in Barbara Wake Carroll, David Siegel and Mark Sproule-Jones, eds. *Classic Readings in Canadian Public Administration*, (Toronto: Oxford University Press, 2005), 299–312.

26. See Ralph Heintzman, "Introduction: Canada and Public Administration," in Jacques Bourgault, Maurice Demers and Cynthia Williams, eds. *Public Administration and Public Management: Experiences in Canada*, (Quebec: Les Publications du Quebec, 1997): 1–12.

27. Reginald Whitaker, "Politics Versus Administration: Politicians and Bureaucrats," in Michael Whittington and Glen Williams, eds. *Canadian Politics in the 21st Century, Sixth Edition*, (Toronto: Thomson Nelson, 2004): 59.

28. Kenneth Kernaghan and John W. Langford, *The Responsible Public Servant*, (Halifax: The Institute for Research on Public Policy: 1990): 3.

29. Elaine Todres, "The Ethical Dimension in Public Service," *Canadian Public Administration,* 34, 1 (Spring, 1991): 14.

30. See Kenneth Kernaghan, "East Block and Westminster: Conventions, Values and Public Service," in Christopher Dunn, ed., *Handbook of Canadian Public Administration*, (Toronto: Oxford University Press, 2002): 104–19.

31. See Timothy Lewis, *In the Long Run We're All Dead: The Canadian Turn to Fiscal Restraint*, (Vancouver: UBC Press, 2003).

Chapter 2

Public Administration *and* Democracy

WHAT YOU WILL LEARN

This chapter considers how democracy and power relate to the theory and practice of public administration in Canada. In order to examine Canadian public administration in any serious way, we must address the basics:

■ What do we understand by the terms *democracy* and *power*?

■ What is politics? What is the state? What is government? Are they the same thing? If not, how are they different, and how are they related? Why might we draw a distinction among them?

■ How is power exercised in Canada? Who has it and who lacks it?

■ What is the basis of power relations within society? Is it notions of equity? Equality? Freedom? Or is it simply that the person with the most toys gets to determine the rules of the game? In other words, what role do economic factors play in Canadian public administration?

Accountability is a prominent issue in any consideration of democracy and public administration. But since accountability is given fuller treatment in chapter 12, it is raised here only in passing, as a subset of the broader philosophical approach to democracy. This chapter is divided into five sections, each dealing with a particular but related aspect of democracy, political power, and public administration. It is prefaced with a brief section defining power and politics, followed by a consideration of the concept of democracy. This is followed by a brief analysis of the concepts of state and government. Some observations on political culture are made, and its interplay with the democratic context of public administration is then assessed by examining the issues of the constitution and the key parliamentary and extra-parliamentary actors who play a role in public administration in Canada. We want to demystify Canadian public administration and its democratic context, to show that it has a very real and practical impact on our everyday lives. So we will draw connections among what happens, how it happens, to whom it happens, and why it happens. By the end you will hopefully find yourself empowered toward the political system and prepared as a citizen to participate in and engage yourself proactively with public administration, beyond simply casting a ballot once every few years or passively submitting to the bureaucratic machine as it steamrolls along. The chapter is divided in the following way:

1. Power, Politics, and Public Administration

This brief section sets the table for our discussions of democracy by asking simply, What is power? What is influence? Who has power and influence in Canadian society, and why? What is politics? What is the relationship between power and politics? This section also presents the debate about the public sector versus the private sector in a slightly different manner than in chapter 1, in light of democratic theory. We ask, How is it determined what is rightly in the public domain? What kind of struggle must be engaged to move issues from the private world to the public, or vice versa?

2. What Is Democracy?

This section asks, What is democratic theory? What does democracy mean to the theory and practice of public administration? What is the relationship of democracy to political power? This section assesses the concepts of direct democracy and representative democracy. How do these affect the way government is structured and run in Canada?

3. State and Government

These two terms are often used interchangeably. But they actually refer to two different things. We ask, What is the difference between state and government? Why is it important to have a conceptual difference between the two?

4. Political Culture

This section looks at several definitions and theories of this concept and poses the following questions: What are the major theoretical explanations for the quality and type of democratic life in Canada? Is there a single theory that explains how democratic Canada is (or is not)? What impact does this have on public administration in Canada?

5. The Interplay of Democracy, Political Culture, and the Institutions of Public Administration

Finally, this section resurrects the theme of democratic theory to introduce both parliamentary and extra-parliamentary actors who influence and exercise power in the state and government in Canada. We ask, What is a constitution, and what impact does it have on the relations of power within Canadian public administration? We further ask, What are those relations? Who are the actors? What are the key institutions, both parliamentary and extra-parliamentary, that affect public administration?

Power, Politics, and Public Administration

Politics is fundamentally about **power**. The element of power always lurks beneath the surface of public administration, and in many cases is overt and plain to see (see Box 2.1). If you could imagine the origins of society, you might see where power comes from. You might see the interactions of individuals devolving into conflict or evolving into co-operation over the division of goods among them. There will virtually always be conflict or co-operation simply because there will never be enough goods for all those who want them, all the time. Therefore, some means must be devised to co-operatively divide those goods and to prevent conflict from degenerating into violence. This is where the exercise of power comes into play. Someone must be designated (or designate themselves) the arbiter over the division of the goods and have **authority** to exercise power and make decisions on behalf of the members of the society. This is the core of politics. Public administration, in turn, is the mechanism by which political decision making takes place.

Power is typically defined in public administration and politics as the ability to authorize, influence, or coerce behaviour. In other words, someone has power over you because they can direct or instruct you to do something (or refrain from doing something) by virtue of 1) their legal position of authority; 2) their status or position; or 3) their use of force.

Why people consent to alter their behaviour is a fascinating sociological question. The famous German sociologist Max Weber (see chapter 3) suggested that those in positions of power derived their authority from one of three sources of legitimacy. The first is **traditional legitimacy**, wherein rule is justified on the basis of long-established custom or habit. Because things have always been ordered in a certain way means that the exercise of power is justified. The second is **charismatic legitimacy**. Under these circumstances, a leader is believed to be vested with exceptional personal qualities that make him or her uniquely suited to lead. In many cases, such leaders will claim to have been divinely chosen. Third, Weber refers to **legal-rational legitimacy**, in which a set of rationally created rules and legal statutes serve as the basis of power and sanctioned authority.[1]

Box 2.1 | **Power in the Nation's Capital**

This description of power in the nation's capital was written by Christina McCall-Newman more than 25 years ago.

Ottawa is a city that talks incessantly about power: who has it, who wants it, who's misusing it, who's losing it. The talk starts first thing in the morning as soon as the busses begin to lumber around Confederation Square and the sun glances off the windows of the West Block. As the day wears on, the buzz becomes nearly visible, blowing in the wind like the sulphur fumes that used to waft over the area from the paper company on the Ottawa River's farther shore. . . .

> *. . . Everybody talks, talks, talks about power all day long, spreading rumours, flying kites, seeking leaks, formulating strategies, and telling lies.*
>
> **Source:** Christina McCall-Newman, *Grits: An Intimate Portrait of the Liberal Party,* (Toronto: Macmillan, 1982): 177–78.

Increasingly, modern states have moved to systems of legal-rational legitimacy, although there are many examples of the other two systems as well.[2] Still, tradition-based and charisma-based systems tended to predominate in non-democratic societies in the past. The reasons for the rise of the legal-rational model are many. For one, modern societies have a degree of literacy and education with which citizens can question the basis of power. At one time it served the purposes of a king to suggest that some holy book decreed that he should rule. As long as people lacked the skills to read and interpret such a source of authority, the king could maintain his power. But the rise of mass literacy was accompanied by the rise of "public opinion," which increasingly could intelligently ask (and answer) the question, "Who ought to rule?" This example also illustrates the diminishing role in many societies of religion, which often served as the rationale for charismatic and some traditional systems of legitimacy.

Moreover, a rational-legal system makes clear, "How will they rule?" For instance, leaders could justify their actions in traditional and charismatic systems simply by stating that this was what they had ordained. Under a legal-rational system, however, this arbitrariness is reduced by features such as rules of accountability and the **rule of law**, which is the principle that no one—not even a lawmaker—is above the law. In a democratic society, decisions about who holds power—and can therefore legitimately authorize, influence, or coerce you into behaving in a certain way—are made through elected and nonelected institutions of public administration. These range from the prime minister, Cabinet, public service, and Parliament to the judiciary, police, and army—all of whom are given clearly prescribed roles.

Where do politics come into play? As political scientist Larry Johnston suggests, "The world we inhabit is political. We may choose to study politics or not, or having studied politics, decide that we will do so no more, but we *cannot choose to opt out of the political world*."[3] [Emphasis in original.] But it is not always perfectly obvious what we mean by *politics*, although we may intuitively know what the term means. For some, it is simply the goings-on on Parliament Hill, far removed from real life, which intrude on us only when a scandal or particularly flashy issue emerges. Relatively few Canadians are passionately involved in this sphere. The majority remain at a distance from political life. If you are typical of most Canadians, you probably are not a member of a political party and you follow politics only casually, if at all. Indeed, fewer and fewer Canadians are even bothering with the most fundamental democratic political act—voting.

Still, politics is all around us, and failure to come to grips with this too often makes us citizen-victims, as other interests in society play the political game to their advantage. For the most basic fact about politics is that it arises out of scarcity: there are not enough resources available in the world for all people to satisfy all of their basic wants and needs all of the time. Limits on what is available, especially on what is desirable, such as wealth, mean that conflicting claims will be made as to who gets what. So, competition over scarce resources is at the heart of politics. But if politics was just perpetual conflict, then presumably we would be in a state of perpetual war with each other. Politics, then, is about more than just conflict; but also about how rival claims are settled through the resolution of conflict.

Moreover, it is obvious that conflict and competition are not the only forces driving humans. Co-operation is also important, indeed inevitable, to settle disputes over scarce resources. Organization theory reveals (see chapter 3) that co-operation, as much as conflict, has led us to create many complex systems and organizations. Since humans are naturally sociable animals, it did not take us long to deduce that co-operation could further the interests of all. Hence we developed organizations, with divisions of labour and hierarchy, to realize societal goals through co-operation. Thus, in our understanding of power and politics, we might just as easily speak of co-operation as well as conflict and competition.

At the core of every definition of politics is notions about the exercise of power. One commonly cited definition is by American David Easton, who developed the "systems" approach to the study of politics. His definition is somewhat general and abstract: *politics* is the authoritative allocation of values.[4] What this mouthful of terms means is really quite simple when you break it down. *Authoritative* refers to the idea that there must be a legitimate authority who can make decisions on behalf of society. Decisions about what? About what values will prevail. For instance, you may value freedom, but someone else may value security. So how do we decide whether society should invest in, say, human rights commissions to safeguard our freedoms or the armed forces to safeguard our security? We give the job to authorities, who then allocate values.

Another perhaps more straightforward definition by Harold Laswell is that politics is about "who gets what, when and how."[5] This is essentially another way of expressing what Easton said. But this definition's virtue—besides brevity—is its clarity and simplicity. Vladimir Lenin, the founder of the Soviet Union, said politics was "who does what to whom."[6] China's Communist leader, Mao Zedong, called politics "bloodless war."[7] Otto von Bismarck, the chancellor of Germany, called politics "the doctrine of the possible: the attainable."[8] Karl Marx argued that "political power, properly so called, is merely the organized power of one class for oppressing another."[9] Virtually all definitions of politics have this common underlying theme of power.

Today, we engage in conflict resolution and co-operative activities in all aspects of our lives: in familial settings, in the workplace, over grades in school, etc. But there are two things about politics that distinguish it from other forms of conflict resolution and co-operation: first, the nature of the issues are public, not private; second, we use public authority to settle them.

The issue of establishing which relations within society count as political, i.e. public, and which are private is often contentious. It was not until the twentieth century, for example, that relations between men and women were deemed political. But the women's movement has raised our consciousness about the political factors underlying the subjugation of women. For instance, where public administration is concerned,[10] the very structures of bureaucracy have contributed to the oppression of women by men, according to feminist scholar Camilla Stivers.[11] Similarly, at one time relations between bosses and workers were considered to be a private affair in which public authorities had no business. That changed with the advent of a strong labour movement that politicized workplace relations and appealed to public authorities—the government—to do something about wage levels, unsafe working conditions, child labour, and so on.[12] In these views about women's roles and the conflict between capitalists and the working class, understanding manifestations of oppression are the key to the concept of power.

The boundary between political (or public) and private may not be distinct, but it is crucial for understanding politics. For much of political conflict occurs over where exactly this line should be drawn: what should be considered a matter for public life and decisions by the state, and what should remain private.

This is fundamentally important, for it is only by clarifying the line between public and private that our democratic rights and responsibilities can be discerned. Only those power relations in the public realm can legitimately be associated with the use of coercion or force. Only public authorities—the state—have the legitimate right to back up decisions with the full power of society, because the state is the only entity that can claim to speak and act on behalf of the entire community. It alone is responsible for some measure of social order, which is a necessary condition for all other societal activities. Without the state, there is no peaceful basis for reconciling conflicts in society.

What Is Democracy?

The term *democracy* is one of those words that everyone uses, but no one defines. We all have an intuitive sense of what democracy is. If you were asked what democracy is, how would you reply? Elections? Parliamentary government? Freedom? The reality is that democracy is what political scientists call a "contested concept," meaning there is not always agreement on what the term means. If you sat down with a group of people—say, the other students in this course—and canvassed their views, you might find broad agreement on the outlines of democracy but differences on the details. It may be quite hard, in fact, for your group to reach a consensus.

We are interested here in noting where democracy intersects with public administration, and so will not digress too far into the definitional quagmire. But it is important to keep in mind that the values an individual or a society holds help determine what that individual or society means by *democracy*. In turn, these values are translated into political institutions and structures, roles, and actors that assume responsibility for enacting the public will; in other words, for governing.

Given the variety of nations with different governmental forms, politics, and policies, all of which call themselves "democratic," how can we be sure what the concept really entails? The word *democracy* comes from two Greek roots: *demos,* meaning "the people," and *kratos,* meaning "authority." In ancient Greek culture, *democracy* meant "government by the many." In some Greek city-states, all citizens participated in making laws (all, that is, except women and slaves, who were not considered citizens). Save for a few rare examples, such as some Swiss Cantons and the New England "town halls" of the seventeenth and eighteenth centuries, such systems, known as **direct democracy**, do not exist. In direct democracy, citizens exercise authority and power personally. Instead, most democracies, including Canada, now consist of a body of elected representatives that makes laws. This is **representative democracy**, in which citizens delegate others to exercise authority on their behalf. Let us briefly consider each model.

Direct Democracy

The model of democracy that approaches most people's conception of "pure" democracy is one in which popular assemblies are constituted by the people to directly govern themselves. Strictly speaking, this ideal did not even prevail in the Athenian example, since elections were often carried out by lotteries rather than voting. The Athenians believed that elections could be manipulated by wealthy individuals who could afford to run as candidates, while ordinary citizens couldn't (much like the impression that prevails today). Currently, few people expect democracy to be rule by the people as a whole, since societies have become so large and complex. Ironically, though, for the first time, we may have the technological capability to effect direct democracy with the internet and interactive telecommunications, although few concrete steps have yet been taken in this direction.[13]

There are, however, some mechanisms in Canada that approximate the direct democracy model. These include, for instance, *referenda,* in which citizens directly express their approval of or objection to a particular issue via a simple vote. Two referenda, in 1980 and 1995, asked Quebecers whether they would authorize their provincial government to negotiate sovereignty with the rest of Canada. Referenda were also held in British Columbia and Prince Edward Island in 2005 and in Ontario in 2007, asking citizens if they wanted to reform their electoral systems. Referenda results are generally binding on a government. Another form of direct vote is a *plebiscite,* which is a vote, the results of which are *not* binding on the government. Shades of direct democracy can also be seen in extending the election of governmental officials to include not just politicians, but also judges and other administrative officials.

Other direct democracy mechanisms include recall, wherein voters can effectively "fire" their representative before an election by getting a certain number of voters to sign a petition to that effect. However, it is noteworthy that in jurisdictions that use these techniques of direct democracy, there is often a low participation rate by citizens. And wealthy and powerful interests are often the only ones who can afford to spend money on campaigns that will influence citizens' choices.

Representative Democracy

Democracy in Canada is not equivalent to rule by the people as a whole. The Canadian form of government is, properly speaking, a representative democracy in which those elected to public office derive legitimacy to act authoritatively for others and are thus vested with power to make decisions having the force of law. This system allows a method of choosing representatives and monitoring their activities on an ongoing basis. It also permits regular opportunities for changing those responsible for governing through the institution of elections.

In a representative democracy, then, citizens are one step removed from the actual exercise of decision making. Almost all modern democracies are representative democracies, where government is carried out by an elected legislature. Citizens delegate law-making authority to their representatives, holding them responsible for their actions through various institutions of government (Parliament, for instance) and through periodic elections. Representative democracy can be summed up as a system in which "public policies are made, on a majority basis, by representatives subject to effective popular control at periodic elections which are conducted on the principle of political equality and under conditions of political freedom."[14]

Political Democracy

We can usefully subdivide these conceptions about representative democracy into "political democracy" and "economic democracy." Both direct and representative democracy have at their core some notion of equality. This implies, for example, that all citizens have equal rights. But in the real world, equality is an elusive quantity. Certain features of the Canadian system are associated with the idea of political democracy: majority rule; one person, one vote; competitive elections; and cabinet-parliamentary government. Theoretically, we might expect that, with all these principles and mechanisms, some measure of equality could be realized. And in fact, a formal political type of equality does apply in that we all have rights to and access to these political mechanisms. Thus, oppressive government, in which equality is undermined or denied, should be virtually impossible.

But consider the following possibility: what if the majority of Canadians voted for a party that supported the suppression of French-language rights? Would that be democratic? The point is that the appearance of equality as vested in the mechanisms of democracy can be deceiving. What this hypothetical example points to is the imperfection of a democracy in which the simple principles, such as majority rule, can actually be used to achieve ends that seem antidemocratic, since there is nothing "democratic" about depriving citizens of their rights.

To avoid these consequences, we build protection against what may be called the "tyranny of the majority" into our institutions and processes. These might take the form of constitutional limits on the power of the state. For example, while a majority might vote to suppress French-language rights, no such law would stand up against the rights and freedoms protected in the Constitution.

As well, particular protection for groups and individuals in society may be entrenched in the formal and informal rules and procedures of politics. For example, the Canadian electoral system reinforces the power of the country's French Canadian minority, most of whom live in Quebec and can therefore vote as a block to protect their own interests. Moreover, federalism and the division of powers in the constitution mean that citizens aggrieved by one level of government can seek redress from the other.

But beyond formal and informal constitutional rules and procedures, the social and cultural values of a society also come into play. This is a point made by political scientists Gabriel Almond and Sidney Verba in their book, *The Civic Culture*.[15] A political culture that acknowledges and recognizes a multiplicity of group identities is likely to give rise to values such as tolerance. These group identities become important in protecting minority rights when individuals perceive, and society recognizes, that some members of society belong to discrete groups, whether religious, ethnic, linguistic, regional, occupational, etc., in addition to sharing a common citizenship with everyone else. Under these circumstances, the likelihood of a democratic state being turned to oppressive ends is reduced, since everyone ultimately has a stake in the tolerance of society.

Can we say that political democracy ensures freedom and equality—two values of primary importance in contemporary Canadian society? If all the rules and procedures are followed, and if there are guarantees for minority rights against the tyranny of the majority derived from political culture, have we achieved some near-ideal form of representative democracy? To answer this question, we must look at democracy from yet another angle, and consider what may be called *economic democracy*.

Economic Democracy

In Canada, we claim to have a democratic system because there is a fairly equal chance that all citizens can participate in the political system and because we as citizens can "throw the rascals out" if we disagree with the government of the day. But in the absence of economic and social equality, can we really claim to have a democratic society?

Look at it this way. Political democracy guarantees that there are institutions in place through which the will of the people can be realized. These include Parliament, and theoretically everyone has a chance to run for election, become a member of Parliament, and exercise authority on behalf of the people. However, it is prohibitively expensive to run for Parliament. Increasingly, it seems this key symbol of Canadian democracy is becoming the preserve of the wealthy. Certainly, lower-income Canadians, welfare recipients, and those on social assistance, among other less well-off Canadians, are grossly under-represented in the halls of power. The same holds true for the upper reaches of the public service. The senior public servants tend to be well educated and from middle- and upper-income families. They can afford the university education that prepares them for a position in the public service. The question that arises is whether they, along with their parliamentary masters, can adequately and fairly represent and understand the views and needs of those who are systematically excluded from positions of power. There is no easy answer to this question. Though we explore it in more detail in chapter 9, it is flagged here as a disputed element in any discussion of the quality of democracy in a society.

Socialists critique democracy by suggesting that it is unrealistic to expect ordinary citizens, who are overburdened with the concerns of making ends meet, to have the time, energy, and resources to engage the political system in a meaningful way. They argue that political equality without economic equality is a sham. Politics becomes the preserve of the idle rich, while the majority toil endlessly with little time or opportunity to substantively affect the political system. Marxists go a step further and argue that any system, democratic or not, that exists within the framework of capitalism is by its nature unequal. This is because capitalism divides society into classes, with the upper (capitalist) class exploiting the lower (working) class through their disproportionate ownership of property and the means of production. The minority, then, exploits the majority, and this makes a mockery of notions of political democracy. In this view, only when some form of economic democracy is realized through the overthrow of capitalism can there be true equality.

In short, political democracy lacks a commitment to economic or social equality. There are societies that devote a considerable amount of effort to ensuring the economic and social equality of their citizens but that lack many of the institutional features that we assume characterize democracy, such as free, fair open elections. So, does attaching greater importance to the social and economic equality of individuals than to rules and procedures make those societies any less democratic than our own?[16]

There is one more aspect to democracy that needs to be considered—one still related to the question of equality. That is, respect for rights and freedoms. But which rights and freedoms warrant protection in a democratic society, and which may be legitimately limited by government? These questions form the basis of a debate about democracy that has been ongoing since ancient Greek times. For example, some would argue that any level of taxation is a restriction on the personal freedom of individuals to dispose of their income as they see fit. Others argue that taxation promotes freedom by paying for policies that provide opportunities that the disadvantaged would not otherwise enjoy. Even a value such as freedom of speech becomes controversial. Are limits on spending to advertise a political point of view during an election a legitimate limit on freedom of speech, since only the wealthy and powerful in society can afford to try to influence public opinion in this way?

Rights and freedoms are important, but almost everyone recognizes that no right is absolute and that certain kinds of limits on rights actually promote democracy. The struggle between expanding and limiting rights is sometimes seen as the struggle between the competing pulls of individual rights and group rights, or between the private and public realms. Society must constantly find the balance between these conflicting impulses if it is to be considered democratic. And it expresses its findings through the mechanisms of public administration.

State and Government

Most of us are familiar with the debate over how much the state should be involved in the economy: e.g., in public broadcasting through the CBC; in the airline business, as with Air Canada; or in the selling of alcohol through provincial liquor boards. As we saw in chapter 1, there is a long history of state involvement in the economy in Canada, stretching back to the pre-Confederation era. Canadian society has evolved from one in which there was little need or desire for state involvement in the lives of its citizens, to one in which the state is intimately and intricately involved in our lives in countless ways.

The great, clamorous debate about the appropriate role of the state in society is largely organized around ideological world views. We are naive if we think that the level and extent of state involvement in society is somehow "natural"—that it is the result of forces beyond our control. For what the state's role in society clearly reflects is the nature of power relations in society. It reflects in whose interests the power of the state has been exercised. Why did the welfare state develop? Was it simply because politicians in power felt generous? Why has that same welfare state been under a savage attack for the past 20 years? Who benefits and who loses in a strong state, as opposed to a laissez-faire system in which the state disengages itself from the economy and from social life? How do these interests affect public administration?

To sort out these issues we must ask the following: what exactly do we mean when we use the term *the state*? Some use it interchangeably with *government*, but, in fact, it means something somewhat different. For example, to argue that a government is corrupt or wasteful and that it should be turfed out is not the same as arguing for the overthrow of the state. It simply challenges the authority of the people who at a particular moment in time have their hands on the state's levers of power. Most political activity is aimed at influencing and changing the government, rather than at reforming the state.

Weber suggested that it is most useful to view the state not in terms of its ends but of its means. He quoted the Communist revolutionary Leon Trotsky, who said that "every state is founded on force," and went on to suggest that the elemental characteristic of any state is this feature of the legitimate use of violence and coercion. Weber wrote,

A state is a human community that (successfully) claims the monopoly of the legitimate use of physical force within a given territory. Note that "territory" is one of the characteristics of the state. Specifically, at the present time, the right to use physical force is ascribed to other institutions or to individuals only to the extent to which the state permits it. The state is considered the sole source of the "right" to use violence. Hence, "politics" for us means striving to share power or striving to influence the distribution of power, whether among states or among groups within a state.[17]

Marx claimed that society as a whole was splitting into two classes directly facing each other: bourgeoisie (the capitalist class) and proletariat (the working class). In a famous and often-quoted line from the *Communist Manifesto*, he claimed that "the executive of the modern State is but a committee for managing the common affairs of the whole bourgeoisie."[18] But if class differences were obliterated by a revolution in which private property was abolished, there would be no need for the state to continue since the bourgeoisie in whose interests it acted would no longer exist. Hence, Marx argued, the state would "wither away."

Political economist Ralph Miliband explained the importance of the state in this way:

More than ever before men [sic] now live in the shadow of the state. What they want to achieve, individually or in groups, now mainly depends on the state's sanction and support. But since that sanction and support are not bestowed indiscriminately, they must, ever more directly, seek to influence and shape the state's power and purpose, or try and appropriate it altogether. It is for the state's attention, or for its control, that men compete; and it is against the state that beat the waves of social conflict. It is to an ever greater degree the state which men encounter as they confront other men. This is why, as social beings, they are also political beings, whether they know it or not. It is possible not to be interested in what the state does; but it is not possible to be unaffected by it.[19]

According to Brooks, the state has three main characteristics:[20]

1. territorial boundaries, beyond which the state has no legitimate authority;
2. a complex set of institutions that wield public authority;
3. power.

Asserting, as Weber has, that the state has a legitimate monopoly on the use of force to maintain order says nothing about in whose interests this power is exercised. Some have tried to incorporate this question into their understanding of the state. Marxists, for example, see the state as an instrument used by the ruling class to oppress and exploit the working class. Feminists view the state as a patriarchal institution designed and maintained to ensure the dominance of men over women in society.

Later on, we will consider whose interests the state serves. But for now, we want to make sure that we understand the difference, and the relationship, between the state and government. The latter is a term usually reserved for those who have been elected to power. This is a more personal conception, usually associated with a particular group of people, often through the instrument of a political party. We speak, for example, of the "Harper government," but not of the "Harper state," even though the prime minister and the political party and the elections that he may contest are all part of the larger state structure. Governments come and go; but the rules, procedures, and institutions of the state are more enduring than is the government and its policies. You might think of the state as the forum within which government exists.

A state is also characterized by the feelings its citizens have about it. In developed democracies, such as Canada, the state elicits widespread public identification with its institutions and values. Normally, the people strongly identify with their state. When citizens accept that a government ought, or has the right, to make decisions for them, political scientists refer to the system as having *legitimacy.*

Legitimacy in this sense is closely linked to the concept of authority: the legitimate right to exercise power. Underlying the distinction between state and government is an important practical difference in the basis on which each compels the obedience of citizens within its jurisdiction. The willingness of citizens to obey the decisions of the government, even though they may strongly disagree with them (for example, the Goods and Services Tax), is fundamentally based on the view that the state's authority is legitimate; that is, the rules and institutions of the state that determine how governments are chosen are accepted by most people as reasonable. The legitimacy of the state is therefore based on the *consent* of those who are governed.

Government may be upheld by consent of the governed. Or it may be upheld by the use of force. Usually both come into play to a varying extent. The state's authority may be questioned from time to time, as when citizens stage a tax revolt or protest in the streets over some issue. Thus, the state's authority is sometimes questioned, and it may resort to the use of force, crushing civil disobedience to maintain its ability to govern. Of course, governments that rely on threats or violence to stay in power are usually unstable and actually serve to undermine the legitimacy of the state, because one of the cornerstones—consent by the governed—is missing. How consent is manufactured is the topic of some debate. In some societies, such as Canada, it arises out of the combined ideological forces of the education system, the media, family, government, the workplace, and various other political, social, and economic institutions that influence the ideological outlook of citizens. In other societies, more overt and sometimes quite crude attempts are made to manufacture the consent of the people through propaganda, or the stifling of opposition parties or media censorship, and so on. This is frequently resorted to in totalitarian systems.

The ability of a state and its political institutions to govern a given population and territory rests on its legitimacy to exercise power. In the resolution of conflict, a government requires the consent necessary to authoritatively allocate values and resources. All states attempt to maintain political order and viability, to resolve societal conflicts without tearing the country apart, to defend the territory against external enemies, and to maintain essential services for its citizens. The manner in which these and other policy-making activities are performed, while a balance is maintained between power on the one hand and legitimacy on the other, is at the core of the study of politics and government as realized through public administration.

More specifically, the issue may also be cast in terms of the tensions between the institutional arms of the state—the bureaucracy—and the value of democracy.[21] How we reconcile the challenges of modern government—with its requirement of large, complex bureaucracies—with the imperatives of democracy is a difficult, ongoing issue. Bureaucracies are hierarchical institutions designed to execute complex tasks, but are often criticized for being "undemocratic" or even "anti-democratic." But the requirements of efficiency, professionalism, and skills found in bureaucracies are necessary to the functioning of societies, including democratic ones. And serving democratic ends sometimes means taking actions that are inimical to the bureaucratic values of efficiency, effectiveness, and economy. These considerations are flagged here but are taken up in more detail in subsequent chapters.

Political Culture

To fully understand the nature of political power and democracy, we must also look at the question of **political culture**, which, though an important concept for public administration, is not without some controversy as to its precise meaning and application.[22] For example, understanding political culture can help us understand why Western Canada feels alienated from the rest of Canada, and what this means for public administration. Understanding political culture can also assist in understanding the impact of language; the relationship between Quebec and the rest of the country; the growing participation of women in politics, in the workplace, and in public life; how multiculturalism has affected the governance of the country; and a legion of other issues.

There is a vast literature dealing with political culture, and definitions of it abound. Most refer to the values, attitudes, and beliefs citizens possess in relation to political life in the society. Political culture was first introduced as a concept by Gabriel Almond in his 1956 essay "Comparative Political Systems," where he claimed it was "the particular distribution of patterns of orientation toward political objects among the members of the nation."[23]

There are four broad areas we look at in the study of political culture. First, we can look at attitudes toward political symbols and institutions and ask, How strongly do you, as a citizen, feel about political symbols, such as the flag? Do you feel sheepish about singing the national anthem at sporting events, or do you belt it out with gusto? Are there historical heroes from Canada's past that you look back on with pride? Or villains? Do you believe political institutions, such as Parliament, the courts, and the public service, are effective? Can government be trusted? What kinds of duties and obligations are implied by the idea of "citizenship"? How do citizens view the constitution?

Second, we can look at attitudes toward others in the political system. Do citizens have strong loyalties to particular groups or regions of the country? Are you a "Canadian" first and foremost, or are you an "Albertan" or a "Newfoundlander"? How tolerant should majorities be toward minorities? Should you be tolerant of those expressing alternative political viewpoints or of those who are critical of the status quo? What types of protest are acceptable behaviour? How important is freedom of speech?

Third, we can look at political knowledge, values, and evaluations. How much do you, as a citizen, know about politics, about the workings of institutions, policy making, and political leaders? What kinds of beliefs, values, and sentiments do citizens have? How widely are they shared? How should resources be distributed? How much support should be given to the poor or disadvantaged groups in society?

Finally, we can look at the acquisition and transmission of political beliefs. Where do your beliefs and expectations about political life come from? How are they learned? How effectively are they transmitted from one generation to the next? Are citizens' beliefs becoming more coherent, more ideological?

This long list of questions suggests that political culture, as a concept, covers an awful lot of ground. This is partly because political cultures are so dynamic: that is, they are constantly changing and evolving. Indeed, the broad configuration of political culture today may well be the result of events from the distant past. Conditions change over time, populations grow or shrink, and remote historical episodes that were at one time terribly important fade from our collective memories. But just because we don't consciously remember the events of our collective past does not mean that they don't continue to influence the way we view political life today and continue to affect public administration.

Much of political culture is oriented toward our *subjective* perspectives on political life (that is, how we *feel* things are, as opposed to how they actually are) and relates directly to our political behaviour (that is, how we vote, the way parties work, the effectiveness of political institutions, the formation of policy, interest group behaviour, the workings of the constitution, and so on). Public administration must respond to these subjective perspectives, which give rise to actions that can ripple through the entire socio-political and economic system, affecting it in large and small ways (see Box 2.2).

Isolating and analyzing the precise way that Canadians feel about political life is a difficult task. Canada shares with many other industrialized democracies certain political values rooted in the Western tradition and containing essentially liberal elements modified by conservative and socialist democratic practices that

> **Box 2.2 | Charlie Brown and Seniors' Pensions**
>
> In the late 1980s, the government of Brian Mulroney attempted to save money by de-indexing seniors' old age pensions. There was an outcry from "grey power" groups across the country. Many seniors developed the subjective perception that their income was under threat. Whether this was the case was a matter of some dispute, but ultimately incidental. Once they felt threatened, they mobilized. A demonstration on Parliament Hill encapsulated the feelings and power behind this threat. Prime Minister Mulroney waded into the crowd, affecting his most statesmanlike demeanour for the cameras, no doubt sensing a photo opportunity in the making. But he was confronted by a tiny octogenarian named Solange Denis, who loudly berated him for his government's stand. The sight of this ordinary Canadian standing up to the power of the prime minister created a striking image. She admonished him for messing around with seniors' pensions, loudly proclaiming, "You lied to us, Charlie Brown." The prime minister's blustering reply was lost in the face of this forthright challenge, which was repeated on the airwaves for days afterward. The government backed down from its plan to de-index pensions. Apparently attacking seniors' entitlements is outside the bounds of acceptable behaviour in Canadian political culture.

have evolved since the eighteenth century. Thus, Canadian political culture embraces such values as equality before the law, the right to hold private property, the right of free speech and assembly, the right to vote and run for office, and so on. But these values do not set us apart from numerous other political communities that also share the same general political culture. In any event, these values have increasingly been overlain with new values brought by a range of immigrants contributing to the multicultural reality that is now Canada. To understand the uniqueness of the Canadian political culture, we need to consider how geography, economics, culture, and politics historically combined to shape this country.

Geography

First, the sheer geographic size of Canada has had an immense impact on its political development and the structure of political life. Canada is the second-largest country in the world, after Russia; it occupies some 9.2-million square kilometres; it spans six time zones; and it sprawls across half of an entire continent. Distance, climate, and natural geographic barriers, such as the Canadian Shield, the St. Lawrence Seaway, the Prairies, the Rockies, and the tundra, have all had an impact on attempts to carve a political community out of this land mass.

Demography

Relative to its land size, Canada's population is small. As well, the population is unevenly distributed. About 80 percent of all Canadians live within three hours of the U.S. border, and 60 percent reside in one of two provinces: Ontario or Quebec. The cultural distribution of the population is also uneven. Eighty percent of all francophones live in Quebec, and Canada's Native peoples form majorities in the sparsely inhabited Nunavut and Northwest Territories. The major urban centres, meanwhile, are by far the most multicultural parts of the country.

So the physical size and expanse of the country and the size, makeup, and distribution of the population posed unique problems of communication, transportation, and governance in Canada. The decision to adopt a federal political framework—that is, a division of powers among regional and central governments—is an institutional response to those kinds of problems; federalism aims to make government less remote to a far-flung and diverse population, as well as representative of distinctive regions.

Three Founding Cultures

The presence of a significant linguistic minority—francophones—concentrated in one part of the country is a significant factor in Canadian political culture. The debate in 2006 about Parliament designating Quebec as "a nation within Canada" revealed the extent to which this is still true. The French–English relationship is sometimes summed up by the term *dualism,* and was captured in Lord Durham's famous 1839 pronouncement that Canada was "two nations warring in the bosom of a single state." Add to this the presence of a civilization that predates European settlement by several thousand years—Native Canadians—and that has always played a significant but largely ignored role in political, economic, and cultural affairs, and you have a unique mixture that defines Canadian political culture.

Continentalism

The relationship between Canada and the United States as co-tenants on one continent, who share what was once referred to as "the longest undefended border in the world," is basic to the essence of both countries. But it is perhaps more significant to Canada because of the immense imbalance in power between the two countries, which has resulted in an ongoing challenge to Canadians to find and define their "national identity." Canadians may not be good at articulating what they *are,* but at least most can agree that what they are *not* is American. But Canada's ongoing struggle to maintain itself as a distinct political culture has been seriously compromised by the penetration of U.S. economic and cultural influences. The continuous fight against absorption into the U.S. empire is a particularly important theme in the study of Canadian political culture, as was the struggle to emerge from the shadows of Great

Britain in an earlier age. Indeed, this process has been called "the evolution of Canada from colony to nation to colony."

Interpretations of Canadian Political Culture

There is widespread agreement that factors such as geography, demography, the presence of three founding cultures and proximity to the U.S. all contributed to Canadian political culture. But how? These different elements must have created immense barriers to the creation of a single, united, and focused political culture, which has given rise to several different interpretations of how Canadian political culture got its unique colouration. We will look briefly at the contributions of four important theorists: Louis Hartz, Seymour Martin Lipset, John Porter, and Harold Adams Innis.[24]

One very influential interpretation has been that offered by the U.S. sociologist Louis Hartz in his book, *The Founding of New Societies*.[25] There are three main points in Hartz's thesis: the nature of the founding "fragment"; the point of departure of the emigrants; and the point of congealment in the new society. Hartz argued that "new" societies, such as Canada, Australia, and the United States, were profoundly shaped by the values carried to those societies by early settlers and immigrants (he tended to ignore the presence of Natives in his study). He argued that one had to look at the specific segment of the culture that the settlers came from in order to understand the political culture they established in the new land.

A second, complementary explanation of Canadian political culture is offered by the American sociologist Seymour Martin Lipset in his book, *Continental Divide*.[26] He emphasizes the importance of "formative events," historical episodes such as the British conquest of Quebec, which has forever since shaped Quebecers' views about their position in Canadian society. Other formative events include the American Revolution, which resulted in the displacement of tens of thousands of Americans loyal to Britain. These United Empire Loyalists fled to Canada, carrying with them conservative, elitist, loyalist world views. In addition, the rebellions of 1837 and 1838 in Upper and Lower Canada, and the Riel rebellions of 1870 and 1885, are all examples of the kind of nation-shaping events to which Lipset is referring.

A third interpretation focuses on the central role that elites play in Canadian society. John Porter's important book, *The Vertical Mosaic*, is a study of how power is organized and exercised in Canadian society.[27] It provides a provocative analysis of the ways in which Canadian elites exercise far more influence over the state and Canadian society than is typical in other advanced industrial states. These elites, he contends, are crucial "gatekeepers," who exercise control over the economy, the public service, elected officials, the media, and intellectual and religious life. All societies have elites, but Porter argues that Canadian elites are particularly powerful because they are a small, closed group with overlapping membership in different sectors of Canadian society. Moreover, because such small groups exercise influence over all these domains, they have been able to deflect attention away from class division in Canadian society, and toward ethnic, religious, and regional divisions.

Harold Adams Innis has been one of the most influential interpreters of Canadian society, spawning a whole subdiscipline called the *staples approach* within the academic discipline of Canadian political economy.[28] He contended that an understanding of the broad economic forces, and particularly the importance of such primary resources as fish, fur, lumber, minerals, and wheat, is germane to understanding Canadian political culture. These primary resources, or "staples," formed the core of the Canadian export economy from the outset, and that economy in turn has shaped the political and cultural outlines of Canadian society. A country such as Canada, which is overly dependent on the whims of the international marketplace into which it seeks to export its goods, has little control over its economy. Demand is dictated by economic forces beyond its boundaries. Thus, Innis maintained, Canadians have developed conservative, cautious, and even pessimistic or fatalistic attitudes, largely because they are not able to control their own economic destinies. This cautiousness is not just limited to economic matters, though; it filters through to the way Canadians think about their society and about political life, and helps to explain why Canadians hold such cautious views about social and political change.

These four interpretations of Canadian political culture do not necessarily contradict one another. In fact, in many ways they are complementary, though each scholar emphasizes different areas. However you want to explain the making of Canadian political culture, a long-range, historical perspective on Canadian society is useful—indeed necessary. When we turn to more recent developments, however, we seem as far as ever from a single, harmonious, unified national culture. We are bedevilled by ongoing debates about Native rights, what constitutes a "nation," the limits of multiculturalism, same-sex marriage, and so on. This suggests that, in fact, there are deep fractures or divisions in Canadian society. And one way to look at these fractures is in terms of different political cultures within society, in conflict with one another.

Why is Canada so politically fragmented? At least part of the answer can be found when we look more closely at three key dynamics of Canadian society: Quebec nationalism, and relations between the English and French in this country; the ongoing vitality of regionalism; and the pull of continentalism.

When the Englishman, General Wolfe, defeated his French counterpart, Marquis de Montcalm, on the Plains of Abraham at Quebec City on September 13, 1759, the immediate problem facing the French was how to sustain a viable francophone culture under British rule. The solution presented itself in the form of the Quebec Act of 1774, whereby the French were permitted to retain their religion and legal traditions—their culture—in return for not supporting the Americans in their revolution against the English.[29] These rights remain intact, are at the root of Canada's linguistic duality, and are the chief instruments of the survival of Canada's francophone community. Those rights, along with the expanding shield of the provincial government, have formed the historical basis of Quebec's political self-definition as a "nation" and, by extension, the moral claim to national self-determination (see Box 2.3).

Describing Canada as "two nations within a single state" focuses attention on the historic role that anglophone-francophone relations and conflicts has

> **Box 2.3** | **The Government Recognizes Quebec as a Nation**
>
> On November 27, 2006, the House of Commons passed the following motion, introduced by Prime Minister Stephen Harper: "That this House recognizes that the Québécois form a nation within a united Canada." The motion passed by a vote of 266 to 16 with all Conservatives, most Liberals, the NDP, and the Bloc voting in favour.

played in the evolution of Canadian political culture. Language, however, is but one aspect of political culture, and it is clear that other relevant regional divisions also shape the collective lives of Canadians in significant ways. In fact, some observers have gone so far as to suggest that Canadian politics is the politics of regions.

Evidence of the political importance of regions is all around us. Imagine, for instance, that you are the prime minister and you want to form a Cabinet composed of the best and the brightest of your Members of Parliament. But there is a long-standing tradition of taking regional representatives into the federal Cabinet: for example, by making sure the minister of fisheries is from the Atlantic region or British Columbia, that the minister of agriculture is from the Prairies, that the minister of finance is from Toronto or Montreal, and so on. Think about the spectacle of the First Ministers' Conference, at which the premiers get to unload their regional concerns into the lap of the prime minister. Think about the way debates about the distribution of economic resources take place: why does Ontario want lower oil prices while the Western provinces want higher ones? Think of the regional orientation of the party system. We have had up to five political parties represented in the House of Commons at any one time. There were four parties in the 2004 and 2006 elections, but none had enough support country-wide to form a majority. Indeed, one of those parties, the Bloc Québécois, does not even try to run candidates in all parts of the country. In these and a thousand other ways, regionalism intrudes on Canadian political life and must be accommodated within the workings of public administration.

Regionalism is partly a function of patterns of immigration and settlement. Different groups of people have settled in different parts of the country at various times in our history, reinforcing the regional nature of the political culture. But immigration and settlement are also a function of economics. Regional differences in economic activity have contributed to the development of regional political cultures. Innis was among the earliest proponents of this view. In the industrialized heartland of Quebec and Ontario, the occupational mix of working populations is quite different from that found in the Prairies, the Atlantic provinces, or British Columbia, all of which rely heavily on resource-based economic activities or staples. Economies that over-rely on staples are subject to the fluctuations of world demand for their products, a factor over which they have no control. So the regional economies fluctuate in terms of prosperity at different rates and times depending on the particular economic base of the region. Thus, while some regions enjoy prosperity, others falter, and the uneven performance of different segments of the Canadian economy aggravates regional political differences.

What is the importance of the regional dynamic of political culture for the political community as a whole? Well, one thing it does is frustrate the development of a strong national political community. First, there is the bare fact of electoral arithmetic; that is, about 60 percent of Canada's population live in only two of the provinces, which means that the votes in that region carry enormous electoral weight; they can make or break nationally elected governments. This can only contribute to a feeling of alienation and powerlessness among Canadians in regions other than Quebec and Ontario, who have few reasons to believe that their influence will be felt nationally.

Second, it has been argued that Canada's particular style of a federal parliamentary institution tends to aggravate rather than moderate regional divisions. The fact that Canada's Senate is an appointed body, in the first place, decreases the legitimacy of the institution. And the fact that the appointment process is highly politicized—that is, often based on political patronage rather than on merit—is another blow to the Senate's legitimacy. The Senate's seeming ineffectuality in the main task for which it was created, representing regional interests, also decreases respect for the institution and creates the feeling among regional populations that they are without an effective champion in Ottawa's halls of power.

Party discipline is a third institutional practice that frustrates balanced regional representation; hence, the development of a national political community. In the British parliamentary tradition that Canada follows, party discipline is central to the workings of **responsible government**, which is government in which the prime minister and Cabinet are accountable to, and can be removed by a majority of, the legislature. While MPs from various regions may be able to try to influence their colleagues on the merits of a certain course of action for their region, they have few real opportunities to place the interests of their region over those of the party, due to party discipline.

However, there is another contextual dynamic at work: namely, Canada's continental location, which also obscures the evolution of a strong and easily identifiable political culture. There is a multiplicity of ways in which the United States dominates the North American continent: its population size, the power of its economy, the vitality of its cultural institutions, and so on. Most recently, questions related to the security of the continent in the wake of September 11, 2001, have brought to the fore issues of identity and sovereignty.

The extent of Canada's economic ties to the United States is astonishing. Canada and the United States have the largest single trading relationship in the entire world. Since the Second World War, U.S. direct and indirect investment in Canada has grown to account for more than 75 percent of all foreign investment in the country. Furthermore, U.S. control over a variety of key industrial sectors, such as fuels, rubber, chemicals, transportation, and others, is remarkably high. U.S. enterprises account for more than 60 percent of the Canadian manufacturing sector, for example. Virtually no other free and sovereign country in the world has permitted this kind of foreign economic domination of its domestic economy. But our ambivalence as a nation about these issues is apparent through the lens of public administration. Free trade with the United States was a central issue in the 1911 election, in the late 1940s, and in the 1980s and 1990s. In the past 25 years, we have seen the Canadian government create an agency to *monitor and limit* foreign direct investment in Canada (the Foreign Investment Review Agency), then replace it with an agency that *facilitates and welcomes* it (Investment Canada).[30]

This U.S. penetration of Canada is, of course, a mixed blessing. Undoubtedly, Canada enjoys a high standard of living partly because of high levels of American investment. But at the same time, the levels and types of U.S. investment in Canada have limited the abilities of the Canadian government to exercise complete control over domestic economic policy making. Indeed, it has been suggested that with the progressive integration of Canada into the U.S. economy, Canada has become little more than a branch plant of the United States.[31] The **Free Trade Agreement (FTA)** and its successor, the **North American Free Trade Agreement (NAFTA)**, according to this view, simply provide the institutional mechanism to continue this process. Some also argue that the continentalization of the economy both undermines Canadian political sovereignty and erodes the distinctiveness of Canada's social and cultural fabric. Consequently, some have called NAFTA Canada's "real constitution."[32]

Economics have had a major effect on the continentalization of Canada, but it is difficult to precisely measure the extent to which they have consequences for political and cultural life in Canada. Supporters of the FTA and NAFTA argue that these are merely economic agreements with no impact on politics or culture. They are simply tools to enhance the nation's economic well-being and strength. Nor is it possible to measure the extent to which Canadians have absorbed American values. But certainly economic ties, proximity, population distribution, and the fact that a majority of Canadians share a language with Americans means that U.S. cultural values are easily transmitted to Canadians.

What else shows the distinctiveness of Canadian political culture?[33] Researchers have noted the apparent absence of a strong or consistent relationship between class and vote in Canada. In other words, Canadians do not tend to support political parties that appeal to them on the basis of which class they belong to. A second significant finding that sets Canadian political belief systems apart from those in other countries is the apparent weakness of left–right orientations within the population. In other words, Canadians do not generally think of themselves in class or ideological terms in relation to the political system—although this may be changing.

Until recently, a common observation was that one thing Canada shares with other nations is a citizenry that demonstrates a great deal of political trust, which is reflected in a fairly high regard for those who govern. But this, too, seems to be changing. It has been noted that Canadians were more likely to defer to authority figures than were citizens of the U.S. and publics in other industrial countries, but that recently there has been a "decline in deference" among Canadians.[34] Canadians and Americans are also quite different in their attitude toward the role of government in society and the economy: Canadians have a much more positive view of the state.

However, despite the linguistic and regional differences that raise substantial obstacles to developing an easily identifiable national political identity, and despite the powerful pull of continental forces, there are distinctive, discernible political values that together delineate Canadian political culture. But what is the relationship of political culture to the other topics raised in this chapter, such as democracy and power? This is the concern of the next section.

The Interplay of Democracy, Political Culture, and the Institutions of Public Administration

While chapter 5 looks at some of the key actors and institutions of public administration, a brief introduction is included here in the context of our discussion of democracy. Specifically, we are interested in how the interplay of democracy and political culture produces certain types of institutions, and in turn how those institutions contribute to democracy and political culture. Rather than viewing the relationship as one-way and linear, then, we will look at the interplay between these things as circular and mutually reinforcing.

The Canadian Constitution

The Constitution, both the written document and the unwritten set of conventions that accompany it, is the guidepost of society. It is the supreme law of the land, embodying the fundamental beliefs and values of a society, such as democracy and freedom. Any constitution typically does three things: it orders the relationship between the state and its citizens; it orders the relationships among citizens; and, in a federal system such as Canada, it orders the relationships among the different levels of government. It is within the parameters set by the Constitution that public administration takes place.

The Canadian Constitution has evolved to reflect changing conditions in Canadian society. For example, the British North America Act, 1867, set out a division of powers between the federal government and the provinces that reflected the roles of the state in the latter half of the nineteenth century. And it sketched out the responsibilities of some of the government's major institutions. It is perhaps a testament to the flexibility of the original constitutional agreement that it has been formally amended only 18 times. Strikingly, most constitutional change has occurred outside the written Constitution, through alterations to the informal traditions and customs known as *constitutional conventions,* as well as to the common law. For example, the prime minister is clearly the most powerful figure in government, yet nowhere are the duties and responsibilities of this post spelled out in the BNA Act. They have evolved largely through habit and tradition, rather than in formal written constitutional rules.

The most significant amendment to the Constitution came in 1982, when it was patriated (that is, brought home from Great Britain, where it had resided as an ordinary statute of the British Parliament), and a **Charter of Rights and Freedoms** was added to it. The addition of the Charter most obviously signalled changing attitudes in the Canadian political culture about democracy, the role of the state, and the relationship of citizens to government.[35] The Charter has spawned a whole new set of issues for public administration, including, for example, whether the judges who interpret the legality of legislation through the Charter are, in fact, usurping Parliament's traditional role.[36] This alleged "politicization" of the judges resurfaced as a controversial topic in 2007 when Prime Minister Harper changed the process of judicial appointments, apparently to ensure that individuals with more socially conservative views could be appointed to the judiciary.[37] Citizens have embraced the Charter to protect their basic freedoms (of conscience and religion, association, and peaceful assembly), as well as basic legal rights (such as the right to be secure against unreasonable search and seizure, and the right to life, liberty, and the security of the person). In addition, the Charter guarantees equal protection and equal benefit of the law without discrimination based on race, national or ethnic origin, colour, religion, sex, age, or mental or physical disability. All these and other rights specified in the Charter are only subject to such reasonable limits by law as can be demonstrably justified in a free and democratic society. The catalogue of rights and freedoms strongly reflects the prevailing political culture, and their protection has had a profound effect on the practice of public administration, in that government institutions and public servants have had to conform in policy and behaviour to the Charter.

The North American Free Trade Agreement

The great debate that raged in Canada around the 1988 election concerning free trade is deeply resonant of the political culture of the country, and touches on all aspects of public administration. Essentially, the nationalists who opposed the signing of a free trade agreement with the United States argued that Canada's national identity was at risk if it submitted to the lure of the U.S. empire. They argued that as Canada integrated itself economically with the United States, it would only be a matter of time before Canada was culturally and politically integrated as well. The continentalists scoffed at these charges, arguing that the Free Trade Agreement was nothing more than an economic arrangement that would bring enhanced economic wealth and opportunity to Canada. It had nothing to do with sovereignty, or political or national identity.[38] The continentalists prevailed, and the FTA was signed into law in 1989. It was extended to Mexico in 1990 and rechristened NAFTA. Its provisions created a tariff-free border among Canada, the United States, and Mexico, and improved market access in areas such as services, agriculture, and resources. But NAFTA does much more than this. It entrenches a supranational dispute resolution process that requires the Canadian government to sacrifice decision-making powers over the economy to a commission. In addition, Canada cannot act unilaterally in certain policy initiatives. Instead, it must give advance notice of its intentions to its partners. Moreover, it cannot apply traditional trade remedies in the event of a dispute with the United States or Mexico. Thus, some have argued that NAFTA is a new pillar in the constitution of the country that constrains the state from taking certain policy actions. Moreover, in political culture terms, the free trade debate has become a flash point for those who argue for the supremacy of the free market versus those who argue for a positive, interventionist state—all of which has a direct impact on public administration.[39]

Federalism

The Canadian Constitution divides jurisdiction between a federal government and provincial governments (municipal governments fall under the jurisdiction of the provinces). Why don't we have a unitary system with just one government? The Fathers of Confederation struck a bargain in 1867, in which the rights of linguistic and religious minorities would be protected. The only practical way they could do that was to create two levels of government and divide jurisdiction between the two. The federal government was given the majority of powers to construct and maintain the national economy, while the provinces were given powers to safeguard social and cultural issues.

Clearly, the decision to divide powers in this way reflects the political culture of the country at the time, and has also had a lasting effect on public administration. One inescapable issue that continuously resurfaces is the French presence in Canada. At the same time, though, we must consider the other regions of Canada that are acknowledged through the Constitution and federal system. Ultimately, federalism is based on the desire to balance regional interests with a sense of national unity. Concretely, it tries to do this through sections 91, 92, and 95 of the Constitution Act, 1867. Section 91 lists powers that are the exclusive preserve of the federal government. Section 92 lists provincial powers. And section 95 indicates that agriculture and immigration are areas of shared jurisdiction, but that in the event of a dispute, federal law prevails.

Conflict between the two levels over this division of powers is endemic in Canadian federalism. The resolution of disputes can occur in one of two main ways. The two levels of government can sit down at the bargaining table and talk through their problems, a process that necessarily gives a prominent role to provincial premiers as the spokespersons for regional interests. A whole machinery of intergovernmental relations has arisen around this development, including ministries in each government responsible for relations with the other level of government, and permanent intergovernmental secretariats to coordinate relations between Ottawa and the provinces.[40] This process has come to be known as *executive federalism,* since it is the executive of each level of government (the prime minister, premiers and Cabinet ministers and their senior advisors) who take the lead role.[41] The second major form of dispute resolution is the courts. The role of the judiciary in federalism has been vital. In a long series of judgments since Confederation, the judges have interpreted the division of powers between the two levels of government whenever governments could not settle their differences at the bargaining table (see chapter 6). In some instances, the judges have tended to rule in favour of the provinces, shifting the pendulum of power toward a decentralized form of federalism. In other instances, they have upheld Ottawa's position, contributing toward a centralized federal system. In any event, the role of the judiciary has been key to shaping the federal system.[42]

The Parliamentary Actors

One of the elemental questions of public administration is, Who decides? Who decides, for example, that tuition is going to be increased? Did you? Who decides that we should purchase sophisticated helicopters for the Canadian navy at a cost of some $5 billion? Did you? Who decided that we should forgo a national, universally accessible day-care system? Did you? Who decided that we should enter into a free trade agreement with the U.S. and extend it to Mexico? Did you? Who decided that the community-based policing model is the preferable approach to dealing with modern crime problems? Did you?

Perhaps the facile answer is that our elected politicians decide these things. But a sophisticated analysis reveals that the waters of public administration run much deeper than this. There is a whole legion of players, some known to us, but most not, that makes these decisions. Who are these people? How public is the process of public administration? Do we as ordinary citizens have access to the decision-making process in any meaningful way? Do we even understand the stages of the decision-making process? Hopefully we can cast a little light on this aspect of Canadian public administration, if only to bring some understanding to the sometimes seemingly incomprehensible decisions our political representatives take. As well, it may help us to understand where, within the complex process, effective input is possible, and help to reveal who the main players are in the system of decision making.

We will begin with the *parliamentary actors* within government that influence public administration. They include the executive (which includes the public service), legislative, and judicial branches of government. We will then look at the *extra-parliamentary actors*: that is, the individuals, groups, and organizations that influence public administration from outside government. These include political parties, interest groups, social movements, and the media.

The Executive What is the **executive** branch of government? It is first the Crown, represented in Canada by the Governor General, whose role has evolved into a purely symbolic one. The prime minister and the Cabinet compose the politically significant parts of the executive branch. Together, they direct and control the public service, which is also part of the executive. (These relationships are presented in more detail in chapter 5). The prime minister and the Cabinet are the key decision-makers. Together they initiate policy and legislation and have their hands on the purse strings of government. Cabinet is organized into committees, and its overall work is coordinated by powerful bodies called central agencies.

Of course, the prime minister and Cabinet do not act alone or in isolation. Instead, they are supported and assisted by a veritable army of public servants, whose job it is to proffer advice and carry out the decisions of their political masters. This largely faceless, nameless cast of thousands is headed by senior officials who not only administer on behalf of their political masters, but also influence the policy process with their advice and actions. Among the important issues this raises is this: to whom are they accountable? We need to understand how an appointed authority, such as the public service, can be held accountable and is reconcilable to a system of responsible government. This raises all sorts of thorny questions. For example, if there is a major screw-up or scandal in the government, as with the infamous Sponsorship Program scandal, who would you hold responsible? Is it the minister who heads the department? Or is it the public servant who gave bad advice? Furthermore, how responsive is this massive bureaucratic machine to individual citizens and interest groups? Is it just the wealthy and powerful who have the wherewithal to gain access to the corridors of power? What about ordinary citizens who may lack the financial resources, organizational skills, or sophisticated knowledge and understanding of how government works? These questions have important implications for public administration and democracy.

The Legislature We also must consider the role of the **legislature** in the Canadian political system. After all, is this not what democracy is all about? We elect representatives to take our concerns to Parliament, where free and open debate about the merits of different positions takes place, and decisions are taken and passed into law on the basis of what is good for Canadians. This is typical of what many Canadians think the legislature is and what it does.

The Canadian Parliament is based on the British model. It consists of two parts: the elected House of Commons, and the appointed Senate. Given that the Senate is appointed, it generally lacks legitimacy in the eyes of most Canadians. Its members are appointed by the prime minister, usually as a reward for faithful service; it is thus a major vestige of patronage. The Senate was originally meant to fulfill two roles: as a forum for regional interests, and as a voice to protect minority rights. As to the second function, the property requirements for membership in the Senate ensured that it became a preserve of the well-off, but as Sir John A. Macdonald noted, the Senate should protect minorities—and the rich are always a minority. Macdonald also saw the Senate as a forum for "sober second thought." This attitude reflects the elitist political culture that is cautious and conservative and wary of the democratizing influences of the House of Commons. As for defending regional interests, the Senate has failed miserably in this regard. Since, proportionately, Ontario and Quebec have the most seats in the Senate, central Canadian interests have tended to prevail there—hence the calls emanating particularly from Western Canada to reform the Senate on the lines of a triple-*E* model: elected, equal, and effective. In addition, recent attempts at reform have included limiting Senators' terms of office.

The House of Commons is really where most of the action is. Democratically elected in one of 308 geographically defined constituencies, each Member of Parliament (MP) is charged with holding the government to account. He or she does this by supporting or opposing the party that has the majority of seats. This is the essence of responsible government. The party with the most seats, whose leader is the prime minister, is primarily responsible for initiating policy, especially through the powers of taxing and spending. But it only retains power so long as it retains the support of the majority in the House. This would appear to give ordinary MPs a tremendous amount of leverage and power. But the practice of party discipline constrains them. This is the convention whereby MPs vote in the House according to the wishes of their leaders. In this way, some stability is achieved in government, and the business of passing laws is facilitated. But this also means that in many circumstances ordinary MPs are caught between a rock and a hard place: that is, they are forced to support their leader even when their constituents demand they act otherwise. Failure to subscribe to the rules of party discipline can mean a short and inglorious parliamentary career: rogue MPs are denied promotion to Cabinet minister or any of the other perks and privileges that the prime minister dishes out to ensure the loyalty of the troops. The dominance of the executive branch over the legislative branch is firmly entrenched.[43]

This is not to suggest that Parliament is completely toothless and ineffectual. Legislators do play an important role in holding the executive accountable through mechanisms such as question period in the House of Commons, through various legislative committees that investigate government policies, and through the actions of the opposition parties in mobilizing public opinion. In addition, the power of the legislature is elevated under conditions of minority government when prime ministers have to pay more attention to the desires of MPs in order to ensure the government is not defeated prematurely. But, overall, it is best to regard Parliament as a *law-passing* body rather than as a *law-making* body, whose role is secondary to that of the executive.

Can Parliament control the prime minister and Cabinet, or keep the public service accountable for its actions? Should the Senate be reformed, or should we just abolish it and put it out of our misery? Does Parliament respond to the needs of ordinary citizens? Where party discipline is concerned, should MPs be allowed to vote according to their conscience—assuming they have one? Should they be allowed more free votes in the House of Commons? Or does this pose a threat to the underpinnings of responsible government? All these questions animate public administration where these parliamentary actors are concerned.

The Judiciary The courts and the judges constitute the third branch of government in Canada: the **judiciary**. Judges are appointed rather than elected. The top court is the Supreme Court of Canada, which became so only in 1949. Prior to this, the **judicial committee of the Privy Council**, a British body of law lords, was the final court of appeal for Canadian judicial cases.

The judicial branch of government is important to public administration in two ways. First, it is responsible for interpreting constitutional law.[44] The judges are asked to make judgments on two broad types of issues. The first involves the division of powers in the Constitution. They are asked to determine whether a law passed by one level of government is within its jurisdiction as spelled out in the Constitution. If it infringes on the jurisdiction of the other level of government, the courts rule that it is ultra vires and, therefore, illegal. If it does not infringe on the other level of government, the courts rule that it is intra vires, or legal. As well, since the introduction of the Charter of Rights and Freedoms in 1982, the courts have been asked to rule on the constitutionality of laws related to human rights.

The second way that the judicial branch is important to public administration is through its responsibility for the area of administrative law.[45] This essentially means that the judges are required to ensure that public servants do not overstep the law in fulfilling their duties and obligations, that regulations are followed according to the rules and procedures set out in legislation, that citizen rights are not abridged or denied in the process of carrying out the instructions of government, and that penalties are levied for violations of administrative procedure and process.

The Extra-Parliamentary Actors

Political Parties The traditional view of political parties in Canada is that they play an important role in recruiting political leaders, and that they aggregate and articulate disparate interests, which are then mobilized for electoral purposes.[46] In Canada, the political party system has evolved from two dominant parties (the Liberals and the Conservatives) to three (with the addition of the New Democratic Party) to a multiparty system with as many as five parties holding seats in Parliament at any one time. Parties are a particularly important reflection of the political culture. For example, the Liberals and Conservatives—the only two parties to form the government at the federal level—have usually been viewed as "brokerage parties" engaged in the task of downplaying divisions within Canadian society and forging the broadest possible coalition of voters to win power. This typically means pitching their appeal to the region with the most votes: central Canada. They are often regarded as subsuming principles to the pursuit of power, which has resulted in a range of "protest parties" emerging. These include the NDP and its predecessor, the Co-operative Commonwealth Federation (CCF), as well as the Social Credit Party, the Progressives, and several others. Regionalism is mirrored in the party system, as we can see from the rise of the Western-based Reform Party (which became the Canadian Alliance, which then merged with the Progressive Conservative Party to become the Conservative Party), and the Bloc Québécois, exclusively rooted in Quebec.

Elections and political parties are, of course, central to our general under-standing of democracy in Canada. But think about parties in political culture terms. They reflect a political culture in which class issues are subordinated to issues of language and region (and earlier in our history, religion). Moreover, low participation by Canadians in the party system reflects our tendency to defer to elites. We lack the kind of mass populism that characterizes party systems in some other countries. Parties generate policy ideas, but these are rarely acted on unless they have the support of the leadership of the parties. In other words, they do not tend to reflect "grassroots" democracy. Still, parties are the key organiza-tional variable in the House of Commons, as we saw earlier in the section on party discipline.

Interest Groups Interest groups are organizations of like-minded individuals that attempt to further their common interests by affecting public policy. Increasingly, they seem to dominate the policy-making process in Canada.[47] They arise as a result of citizens banding together to promote their own inter-ests, but they often end up in conflict with other groups doing the same thing. All these competing groups try to get the attention of bureaucratic and political decision-makers. Almost every imaginable interest in Canadian society is represented by organized groups; you yourself are probably a member of several such groups at any one time. Besides the major business and labour groups, there are hundreds of organizations representing women, students, environmentalists, seniors, Aboriginals, farmers, musicians and artists, religions, and so on. The term *social movement* is generally applied to those groups with a social policy orientation, an increasing number of which have appeared in the political system in the past 30 years.

Clearly, though, not all interest groups are equal in their influence. As a result, it is perhaps overstating the case to say that the system of interest groups represents the pinnacle of democracy in large, complex modern societies, since everyone can be represented. Some groups are well-funded, institutionalized, and have the resources to pursue their interests effectively. Others, though, are just the opposite. They lack financial resources, knowledge of who the key decision-makers are, and how to get to them. This is not to say that they are totally ineffective, but clearly the odds of success are improved if you have the wherewithal to play the game well. Typically, business groups have the resources at their disposal to target decision-makers and public opinion at the same time; thus the ideological dominance of business values is reinforced through the interest group system. While business interests do not "win" on every issue they try to influence, clearly their position is predominant in the constellation of interest groups trying to influence public administration.

It is perhaps axiomatic that a society that values free association should feature interest-group politics. Interest groups provide important services to their members, but are also oriented toward influencing policy-making by advocating change or mobilizing to prevent change unfavourable to their interests. Interest groups also provide expert knowledge and information to policy-makers and often support governments sympathetic to their aims. They target Cabinet ministers and senior public servants as well as ordinary MPs. They use techniques such as personal lobbying, public information campaigns, the media, protests, and other tactics to get their messages across. Recent concern over undue influence has prompted legislative reform to control the activities of interest groups, such as requiring lobbyists to register themselves with the government, and prohibiting public servants who quit their jobs from immediately turning around and lobbying their old departments.

The Media Finally, we need to consider the role of the media and its influence on public administration.[48] Again, political culture reveals that Canada is a society that values freedom of speech and a free press as a cornerstone of democracy. Hence the media plays an important role as a purveyor of information as well as of political attitudes and values. The media is constantly engaged in a process of defining what is political and of setting political discourse—that is, the way we talk about politics.

The media plays an extremely important role in matters such as selecting and evaluating political leaders. As well, the media plays a key role in the communication functions of government. But in so doing, it should be noted that the media carries its own set of biases, contrary to the widely held view that the media is objective. This means that what the media chooses *not* to report can be every bit as important as what it chooses *to* report. In this way the media helps set the agenda for public discussion and debate, legitimizing certain actors and institutions and conferring or withholding status.

In the context of a nation that sits next door to the most powerful media empire on earth, a whole other set of issues becomes important, such as the Americanization of Canada and the national identity question. The decision to have a public broadcasting network, the CBC, was in part a reaction to this reality. Moreover, the regulatory regime that has been developed in Canada concerning the media is complex and contains many contentious issues. Should the CBC be privatized? Do we need Canadian content regulations as stipulated by the Canadian Radio-television and Telecommunications Commission (CRTC)? Should Canadian magazines be protected from U.S. competition? Should the reporting of poll results be restricted during elections? All these questions, and many others, imply that the role, function, and place of the media are issues of ongoing concern for public administration.

WHAT YOU HAVE LEARNED

We began this chapter with some basic concepts: *power, politics, democracy, state,* and *government.* Each term, while susceptible to a variety of interpretations, plays an important part in the world of Canadian public administration. We then examined some related questions to demystify Canadian public administration and its democratic context. It is important to draw connections between *what* happens, *how* it happens, *to whom* it happens, and *why* it happens. This helps us understand how power is exercised in Canada, who has it, and who lacks it. Furthermore, by introducing the topic of political culture and its interplay with democracy and public administration, we can begin to see the basis of power relations within society and the importance of values such as equality and freedom.

This chapter considered how the concept of democracy relates to the theory and practice of public administration in Canada. Finally, the context of public administration was assessed by examining the issues of the constitution, NAFTA, federalism, and the key parliamentary and extra-parliamentary actors who play a role in public administration in Canada.

Key Words and Concepts

power (28)	responsible government (46)
authority (28)	FTA (47)
traditional legitimacy (28)	NAFTA (47)
charismatic legitimacy (28)	Charter of Rights and Freedoms (49)
legal-rational legitimacy (28)	executive (51)
rule of law (30)	legislature (52)
direct democracy (32)	judiciary (53)
representative democracy (32)	judicial committee of the Privy
political culture (39)	Council (53)
party discipline (46)	interest groups (54)

Review Questions

The chapter was divided into five sections. You should now be able to address the following set of questions:

1. *Power, Politics, and Public Administration*
You should now know something about democracy, power, and politics. Ask yourself, What is the relationship between power and politics? How are issues moved from the private to the public realm?

2. *What Is Democracy?*
After reading this section, ask yourself, What is the importance of democratic theory in public administration? What kinds of democracy are there, and which pertain most to Canadian public administration?

3. *State and Government*
Ask yourself, What is the difference between state and government, and how is each important to public administration?

4. *Political Culture*
In explaining the nature of democracy and governance, ask yourself, What is political culture? What theories help us understand it? And how does it influence public administration? What is the relationship of political culture to democracy and to the institutions of governing in Canada?

5. *The Interplay of Democracy, Political Culture, and the Institutions of Public Administration*
Ask yourself, how do both parliamentary and extra-parliamentary actors influence and exercise power in the state and government in Canada? What impact does the Canadian constitution have on the relations of power within Canadian public administration?

 ## Weblinks

Canadian Political Science Association
www.cpsa-acsp.ca

Mapleleafweb
www.mapleleafweb.com

Democracy Watch
www.dwatch.ca

Elections Canada
www.elections.ca

Parliament of Canada
www.parl.gc.ca

Supreme Court of Canada
www.scc-csc.gc.ca

United Nations Public Administration Country Profiles
www.unpan.org/dpepa/country%20profiles/countries.asp

Further Reading

1. Power, Politics, and Public Administration

Almond, Gabriel. *Comparative Politics: A Theoretical Framework*. New York: HarperCollins, 1993.

Brodie, Janine. "Power and Politics," in Janine Brodie and Sandra Rein, eds. *Critical Concepts: An Introduction to Politics. Third Edition*. Toronto: Pearson Prentice Hall, 2005: 2–20.

Easton, David. *A Framework for Political Analysis*. Englewood Cliffs, New Jersey: Prentice Hall, Inc., 1965.

2. What Is Democracy?

Dahl, Robert. *Democracy and Its Critics*. New Haven: Yale University Press, 1989.

Schmitter, Philippe C. and Terry Lynn Karl. "What Democracy Is . . . And Is Not," in George A. MacLean and Brenda O'Neill, eds. *Ideas, Interests and Issues: Readings in Introductory Politics*. Toronto: Pearson Prentice Hall, 2006: 166–76.

3. State and Government

Clement, Wallace, ed. *Understanding Canada: Building on the New Canadian Political Economy*. Kingston: McGill–Queen's University Press, 1997.

Miliband, Ralph. *The State in Capitalist Society: The Analysis of the Western System of Power*. London: Quartet Books, 1973.

Panitch, Leo, ed. *The Canadian State: Political Economy and Political Power*. Toronto: University of Toronto Press, 1977.

4. Political Culture

Ball, Terence, Richard Dagger, William Christian and Colin Campbell. *Political Ideologies and the Democratic Ideal. Canadian Edition*. Toronto: Pearson, 2006.

Bell, David V.J. "Political Culture in Canada," in Michael S. Whittington and Glen Williams, eds. *Canadian Politics in the 21st Century. Sixth Edition*. Toronto: Thomson Nelson, 2004: 317–45.

Pye, Lucian W. and Sidney Verba, eds. *Political Culture and Political Development*. Princeton: Princeton University Press, 1965.

5. The Interplay of Democracy, Political Culture, and the Institutions of Public Administration

Bradford, Neil. *Commissioning Ideas: Canadian National Policy Innovation in Comparative Perspective*. Toronto: Oxford University Press, 1998.

Nevitte, Neil and Mebs Kanji. "'New' Cleavages, Value Diversity, and Democratic Governance," in James Bickerton and Alain-G. Gagnon, eds. *Canadian Politics. Fourth Edition*. Peterborough: Broadview Press, 2004: 79–97.

Simeon, Richard and David Elkins. "Regional Political Cultures in Canada," *Canadian Journal of Political Science*, 7, 3 (September, 1974).

Endnotes

1. Max Weber, "Politics as a Vocation," in H.W. Gerth and C. Wright Mills, eds. From *Max Weber: Essays in Sociology*, (New York: Oxford University Press, 1958): 79.

2. For profiles of different systems of public administration in the world today, see United Nations, Public Administration Programme *Public Administration Country Profiles* **www.unpan.org/ dpepa/country%20profiles/countries.asp**.

3. Larry Johnston, *Politics: An Introduction to the Modern Democratic State*, (Peterborough: Broadview, 1997): 15.

4. David Easton, *Systems Analysis of Political Life*, (New York: John Wiley and Sons, 1965): 21.

5. Harold D. Laswell, *Politics: Who Gets What, When and How*, (New York: McGraw-Hill, 1936).

6. V.I. Lenin, "Left Wing Communism: An Infantile Disorder," in *Selected Works*, (New York: International Publishers, 1943).

7. See Stuart Schram, ed. *The Political Thought of Mao Tse Tung*, (New York: Frederick A. Praeger, 1969): 287.

8. Cited in James John Guy, *People, Politics and Government: A Canadian Perspective, Fourth Edition*, (Scarborough: Prentice Hall, 1998): 2.

9. Karl Marx and Frederick Engels, "The Communist Manifesto," in Arthur P. Mendel, ed. *The Essential Works of Marxism*, (New York: Bantam Books, 1961).

10. For an overview of the role of women in the public service, see Caroline Andrew, "Women and the Public Sector," in Christopher Dunn, ed. *The Handbook of Canadian Public Administration*, (Toronto: Oxford University Press, 2002): 159–68.

11. Camilla Stivers, *Gender Images in Public Administration*, (Newbury Park, California: Sage Publications, 1993): 4. See also Susan D. Phillips, "Discourse, Identity and Voice: Feminist Contributions to Policy Studies," in Laurent Dobuzinskis, Michael Howlett and David Laycock, eds. *Policy Studies in Canada: The State of the Art*, (Toronto: University of Toronto Press, 1996): 242–65.

12. See Leo Panitch and Donald Swartz, *From Consent to Coercion: The Assault on Trade Union Freedoms. Third Edition*, (Toronto: Garamond, 2003).

13. See Darin Barney, *Communication Technology*, (Vancouver: UBC Press, 2005); Ronald J. Diebert, "Civil Society Activism on the World Wide Web: The Case of the Anti-MAI Lobby," in David R. Cameron and Janice Gross Stein, eds. *Street Protests and Fantasy Parks: Globalization, Culture and the State*, (Vancouver: UBC Press, 2002): 88–108; and Cynthia Alexander and Leslie Pal, eds. *Digital Democracy: Policy and Politics in the Wired World*, (Toronto: Oxford University Press, 1998).

14. Henry B. Mayo, *An Introduction to Democratic Theory*, (New York: Oxford University Press, 1960): 70.

15. Gabriel A. Almond and Sidney Verba, *The Civic Culture*, (Princeton, New Jersey: Princeton University Press, 1963).

16. See C.B. Macpherson, *The Real World of Democracy*, (Toronto: CBC Enterprises, 1965).

17. H.H. Gerth and C. Wright Mills, *From Max Weber: Essays in Sociology*, (New York: Oxford University Press, 1946): 78.

18. Karl Marx and Frederick Engels, "The Communist Manifesto," in Arthur P. Mendel, ed. *Essential Works of Marxism*, (New York: Bantam Books, 1961): 15.

19. Ralph Miliband, *The State in Capitalist Society: The Analysis of the Western System of Power*, (London: Quartet Books, 1969): 3.

20. Stephen Brooks, *Canadian Democracy: An Introduction, Fourth Edition*, (Toronto: Oxford University Press, 2004): 8.

21. See Kenneth J. Meier and Laurence J. O'Toole, *Bureaucracy in a Democratic State*, (Baltimore: The Johns Hopkins Press, 2006).

22. See Stephen Brooks, "Political Culture in Canada: Issues and Directions," in James B. Bickerton and Alain-G.Gagnon, eds. *Canadian Politics: Fourth Edition*, (Peterborough: Broadview Press, 2004): 55–78.

23. Gabriel Almond, "Comparative Political Systems," *World Politics*, 18 (1956): 396.

24. For an overview, see David J. Bell, *The Roots of Disunity: A Study of Canadian Political Culture*, (Toronto: Oxford University Press, 1992). See also Heather MacIvor, *Parameters of Power: Canada's Political Institutions*, (Toronto: Thomson Nelson, 2006).

25. Louis Hartz, *The Founding of New Societies: Studies in the History of the United States, Latin America, South Africa, Canada and Australia*, (New York: Harcourt, Brace and World, 1964). See also Gad Horowitz, "Conservatism, Liberalism and Socialism in Canada: An Interpretation," *Canadian Journal of Economics and Political Science*, 32, 2 (May, 1966): 143–77; and H.D. Forbes, "Hartz-Horowitz at Twenty: Nationalism, Toryism and Socialism in Canada and the United States," *Canadian Journal of Political Science*, 20, 2 (June, 1987): 287–316.

26. Seymour Martin Lipset, *Continental Divide*, (New York: Routledge, 1990).

27. John Porter, *The Vertical Mosaic: An Analysis of Social Class and Power in Canada*, (Toronto: University of Toronto Press, 1965). See also Wallace Clement, *The Canadian Corporate Elite: An Analysis of Economic Power*, (Toronto: McClelland and Stewart, 1975).

28. Harold Adams Innis, *The Fur Trade in Canada: An Introduction to Canadian Economic History*, (Toronto: University of Toronto Press, 1956).

29. See Bayard Reesor, *The Canadian Constitution in Historical Perspective*, (Scarborough: Prentice Hall, 1992): 9.

30. See John McDougall, *Drifting Together: The Political Economy of Canada-US Integration*, (Peterborough: Broadview Press, 2006); and David M.Thomas and Barbara Boyle Torrey, eds. *Canada and the United States: Differences That Count*. Third Edition, (Peterborough: Broadview, 2008).

31. Among the first statements of this position was Kari Levitt, *Silent Surrender: The Multinational Corporation in Canada*, (Toronto: Macmillan, 1970).

32. See Stephen Clarkson, *Uncle Sam and US: Globalization, Neoconservatism and the Canadian State*, (Toronto: University of Toronto Press, 2002).

33. See Michael Adams, *Sex in the Snow: Canadian Social Values at the End of the Millennium*, (Toronto: Penguin Books, 1998). For an earlier look at this question, see Richard Simeon and David Elkins, *Small Worlds: Provinces and Parties in Canadian Political Life*, (Toronto: Methuen, 1980).

34. See Neil Nevitte, *The Decline of Deference*, (Peterborough: Broadview Press, 1996).

35. See Alan Cairns and Cynthia Williams, eds. *Constitutionalism, Citizenship and Society in Canada*, (Toronto: University of Toronto Press, 1985).

36. See Raymond Bazowski, "The Judicialization of Canadian Politics," in James B. Bickerton and Alain-G.Gagnon, eds. *Canadian Politics: Fourth Edition*, (Peterborough: Broadview Press, 2004): 203–22; and Michael Mandel, *The Charter of Rights and the Legalization of Politics in Canada*, (Toronto: Thompson Educational Publishing, 1994).

37. Campbell Clark, "Harper Brushes Off Judicial Critics on Appointments," *Globe and Mail* (February 22, 2007): A5.

38. See Gregory J. Inwood, *Continentalizing Canada: The Politics and Legacy of the Macdonald Royal Commission*, (Toronto: University of Toronto Press, 2005). See also Jeffrey M. Ayres, *Defying Conventional Wisdom: Political Movements and Popular Contention Against North American Free Trade*, (Toronto: University of Toronto Press, 1998). For arguments against free trade, see Duncan Cameron, ed. *The Free Trade Deal*, (Toronto: Lorimer, 1988). For arguments in favour of free trade, see John Crispo, ed. *Free Trade: The Real Story*, (Toronto: Gage, 1988). A collection of papers on both sides of the debate can be found in Marc Gold and David Leyton-Brown, eds. *Trade-Offs on Free Trade*, (Toronto: Carswell, 1988).

39. See Bruce Campbell and Ed Finn, eds. *Living With Uncle: Canada-US Relations in an Age of Empire*, (Toronto: Lorimer, 2006).

40. See Gregory J. Inwood, Carolyn M. Johns and Patricia L. O'Reilly, "Intergovernmental Officials in Canada," in J. Peter Meekison, Hamish Telford and Harvey Lazar, eds. *Canada: The State of the Federation 2002: Reconsidering the Institutions of Canadian Federalism*, (Montreal: McGill-Queen's University Press, 2004): 249–84; and Carolyn M. Johns, Patricia L. O'Reilly and Gregory J. Inwood, "Intergovernmental Innovation and the Administrative State in Canada," *Governance*, 19, 4 (October 2006): 627–49.

41. See D.V. Smiley, *The Federal Condition in Canada*, (Toronto: McGraw-Hill Ryerson, 1987); and Richard Simeon, *Federal-Provincial Diplomacy: The Making of Recent Policy in Canada. With a New Preface and Postscript*, (Toronto: University of Toronto Press, 2006).

42. See Peter H. Russell. *Constitutional Odyssey: Can Canadians Become a Sovereign People? Third Edition*, (Toronto: University of Toronto Press, 2004).

43. See Donald J. Savoie, *Governing From the Centre: The Concentration of Power in Canadian Politics*, (Toronto: University of Toronto Press, 1999); Donald J. Savoie, "Power at the Apex: Executive Dominance," in James B. Bickerton and Alain-G.Gagnon, eds. *Canadian Politics: Fourth Edition*, (Peterborough: Broadview Press, 2004): 145–61; and Graham White, *Cabinets and First Ministers*, (Vancouver: UBC Press, 2005).

44. See Peter H. Russell, *Leading Constitutional Decisions, Fourth Edition*, (Ottawa: Carleton University Press, 1987).

45. See Sara Blake, "An Introduction to Administrative Law in Canada," in Christopher Dunn, ed. *The Handbook of Canadian Public Administration*, (Toronto: Oxford University Press, 2002): 466–79; and David Phillip Jones and Anne S. de Villars, *Principles of Administrative Law, Second Edition*, (Scarborough: Carswell, 1994).

46. See William Cross, ed. *Political Parties, Representation, and Electoral Democracy in Canada*, (Toronto: Oxford University Press, 2002); and Hugh G. Thorburn and Alan Whitehorn, eds. *Party Politics in Canada, Eighth Edition*, (Toronto: Prentice Hall, 2001).

47. See Lisa Young and Joanna Everitt, *Advocacy Groups*, (Vancouver: UBC Press, 2004).

48. See Paul Nesbitt-Larking, *Politics, Society and the Media: Canadian Perspectives*, (Peterborough: Broadview Press, 2001); and Rand Dyck, *Canadian Politics: Critical Approaches, Fourth Edition*, (Toronto: Thomson Nelson, 2003).

Chapter ③

Theories *of* Organization

WHAT YOU WILL LEARN

In this chapter, we will focus on theoretical approaches to public administration by examining several schools of thought on bureaucratic organization. This chapter asks the following questions:

- What are the main concerns of organization theory?

- What are the origins of organization theory?

- What contesting values underlie the development of theories of public administration?

- What are the major classical theories of organization, and who were the major theorists?

- What types of debates have ensued over the nature and form of organization in both the private and the public sectors?

- What exactly are theoretical innovations meant to accomplish when translated into practice?

The discussion is organized around five central issues.

1. — *Perspectives on Bureaucratic Organization*

This section provides a brief overview of how we can approach organizations from a theoretical perspective, and why we should do so to enhance our understanding of the development of bureaucracy and public administration over time. It notes the contribution of business management thinking and its uneasy marriage with public sector values and concerns.

2. The Classic Theorists

This section focuses mainly on the vital contributions of Karl Marx and Max Weber to our understanding of bureaucratic organizations. It outlines the contributions of these two great thinkers, as well as the influence they have had on subsequent theorizing.

3. Structuralist Theories

This section looks at one of the two main schools of thought that have, historically, dominated the theories of organization literature—that is, the scientific management approach pioneered by F.W. Taylor.

4. Humanist Theories

Structuralist theories spawned a backlash in the form of *organizational humanism*. A variety of theorists are canvassed in this section, many associated with the famous Hawthorne experiments.

5. Other Theoretical Approaches

There is large constellation of theories in addition to the main ones outlined above. This section reveals a small sampling of some of the other significant approaches. After reading this chapter, you should have a firm grasp of the major contending theories of public administration, and be familiar with the thinkers associated with each.

Perspectives on Bureaucratic Organization

The literature on bureaucratic organization is rich and well developed. Indeed, there are a multiplicity of approaches to understanding the role and impacts of bureaucracies (both private and public sector).[1] You will recall from the first chapter that public bureaucracy is the organizing principle of government. Despite its pejorative reputation, it is nonetheless central to the study and practice of public administration. As American public administration scholar Robert Denhardt reminds us, "although we often think of the public bureaucracy as an impersonal mechanism, in fact, behind each of our encounters with public organizations lies a lengthy and complex chain of human events, understandings, and behaviours developed in the everyday lives of people just like us."[2]

Bureaucratic organizations are ubiquitous—that is, they exist everywhere, in all parts of our lives. When you registered in your program at university and signed up for your courses, you dealt with a bureaucratic organization. If you ran into difficulties, you might have cursed the "red tape" and bureaucratic mindset that held up the smooth processing of your registration. But chances are, you have spent little time thinking through the reasons for that red tape or the complexities of processing your application. What factors lay behind that red tape? Why is registration done the way it is done? How can the process be made more efficient? More fair? Cheaper? Quicker? More convenient? If you have ever pondered any of these questions (and who hasn't, while standing in a line or waiting on hold on the phone?), then you have confronted questions about the role of bureaucracy in our lives.

While bureaucratic organizations are ubiquitous, opinion over their role and function is quite divided. Most organization theory originated from studies about how to improve the management of private sector organizations, particularly large corporations. Hence, academically, organization theory is often associated with schools of business management. But issues that affect how businesses organize themselves are also of great concern to both practitioners and scholars in other disciplines, including public administration. In some cases, theories derived from business practices have been adapted to the public sector in an attempt to understand how government organizes itself. In other cases, the social sciences, and especially sociology, have developed their own unique explanations and analyses of government organization. In either case, when we talk about "organization theory," we are talking about our need to understand what people do, how things get done, and why we have organizations.

In the nineteenth and twentieth centuries, organizations became increasingly administered according to values of rationality, impersonality, and efficiency. If you designed an organization based on these values, what might it look like? In the public sector, other values come into play, such as democracy and fairness. Compare the design of an organization premised on rationality, impersonality, and efficiency to one based on democracy and fairness. Chances are, you would come up with two quite different animals. The problem has been how to marry these sets of values in organizations whose primary task is to serve the public interest through the formulation, implementation, and evaluation of government policies. So, in a sense, the development of the theory and practice of public administration has been the story of struggling to adapt and extend aspects of private sector management into the public sector, and blend those with theory and practice unique to the problems and opportunities of governing.

The Classic Theorists

We begin with an overview of what might be called the "classic theorists" of bureaucracy and organizations—Karl Marx and Max Weber—as well as some other important contributors to the foundations of our thinking about organizations. The classic theorists pondered the effect on the power structure of society of the development of large-scale organizations. How does "big" government or "big" business influence a society's political life? Is bureaucracy simply an administrative apparatus designed to meet societal goals? Or does it actually come to shape those goals? Again, we find ourselves confronting the nature of the relationship between bureaucracy and democracy, first raised in chapter 1.

Karl Marx

The first major figure in the classic school of thought is **Karl Marx** (1818–1883), for whom the concepts of **class conflict** and **alienation** were central to understanding bureaucracy. Marx was influenced in his ideas about bureaucracy by the German philosopher G.W.F. Hegel. For Hegel, the bureaucracy represented a bridge between the state and civil society (the various interests in society outside the government itself). The state, on the other hand, represented the overall general or common interest. The state bureaucracy, in Hegel's view, was the medium through which the transformation of the particular interest into the general interest could take place. For Hegel, the bureaucracy was in fact the "universal class" par excellence because it represented the generalized communal interest of all.

Marx rejected Hegel's characterization of the state bureaucracy. For Marx, bureaucracy was not some kind of ideal representation of the general will of society. It was more concrete than that: it was real people involved in a particular set of social relationships involving the exercise of power. Marx particularly disagreed with Hegel's conception of the bureaucracy as the "universal" element in society.

Such a notion was illusory, according to Marx, since the bureaucracy's interests were anything but universal. The bureaucracy was nothing more than a special interest in itself. It might hide behind the more dignified picture of a faithful servant of the general will and, therefore, appear somehow to be above personal interests, but reality was quite different. Whereas in society various interests struggled for possession of private property (the basis of wealth in capitalist societies), he said, within the bureaucracy the struggle was over positions. In Marx's view, the desire to claw one's way up the bureaucratic career ladder in the quest for increased power, status, and prestige is what motivates bureaucrats.

Hegel had raised the question of how the people were to be safeguarded against abuse from bureaucratic authority. He answered by referring to **hierarchy**. The hierarchical structure of government meant that abuse by lower officials could be redressed by their superiors. Marx refuted this contention. He argued that hierarchy only leads to the punishment of officials who commit offences against the hierarchy itself. However, it protects the official whenever the hierarchy commits an offence against the people. Hierarchy, then, was far more likely to abuse citizens than were the petty actions of lower officials.

Marx's theory is distinctive because bureaucracy is not seen as merely an unfortunate tumour on the otherwise healthy body of the state but, rather, as inherent and inseparable from that body itself. In a capitalist society, Marx said, the role of the bureaucracy was to maintain the class distinctions and domination that sustained the rule of the business class. But at the same time, the bureaucracy must mask this domination by presenting itself as representing the general interest. To maintain this facade, it must retain a certain degree of **autonomy** (freedom of action) from the ruling business class. Because of this autonomy, the bureaucracy occasionally acts in a way that may appear to counter the interests of the business class. But, overall, the bureaucracy will always act in the long-term interests of the capitalist class, since its main purpose is to sustain the power of the dominant class. Moreover, the bureaucracy is an organization that serves as an instrument of rule from above, institutionally detached from the mass of the people it is ostensibly designed to serve.

The concept of alienation is a major aspect of Marx's views about bureaucracy, and he saw bureaucracy as one of the primary institutions responsible for it.

Bureaucracy is felt by most citizens as a distant, impersonal, and oppressive force—a perception promoted by bureaucrats themselves through the invention of special myths and symbols that make the bureaucracy a bewildering institution that compels compliance. Moreover, alienation occurs not just between citizens and the bureaucracy, but also within the bureaucracy itself. The true nature of the bureaucracy is hidden from itself so that those occupying its posts view their jobs as essential rather than as oppressive or parasitic, as Marx would contend. This image is sustained within the bureaucracy by hierarchy, discipline, and authority, all of which promote alienation among bureaucrats themselves. For Marx, bureaucracy stifled its workers' initiative and imagination while reinforcing the fear of taking any responsibility and risk. (See Box 3.1.)

Marx did not initially consider that bureaucracy might, in fact, be a class unto itself. He was only concerned with disabusing Hegel's notion of the "universal class." But as he began to examine the historical role of bureaucracies, he concluded that during the transition from feudalism to capitalism (the transition from rule by the aristocracy to rule by the bourgeoisie), there was a contest for political power in which the state took a "relatively autonomous" position. He felt that the bureaucracy was able to stay above the fray, more or less, and gain an "abnormal" level of independence and political influence. The bureaucracy helped pave the way for capitalism, according to Marx, but once capitalism was established, the bureaucracy reverted to its previous role of supporting the ruling interests of society. As a result, Marx saw bureaucracy as a "parasitic" body that did not contribute to the productive forces of society but, rather, fed off the rest of society, its real task being to maintain the status quo.

BOX 3.1 Karl Marx on Bureaucracy

In his *Critique of Hegel's Philosophy of Right* (1843–44), Marx outlines the true character of bureaucracy and presents some ideas that would be expanded upon later by the other great classic theorist, Max Weber. Marx wrote,

Authority is . . . the principle of its knowledge . . . authority is its mentality. But inside the bureaucracy itself spiritualism becomes a crass materialism, faith in authority, mechanization of a fixed and formal behaviour, fixed principles, views, and traditions. As far as the individual bureaucrat is concerned, the state's ends become his private ends, namely, chasing after higher posts and carving out a career. . . . The state continues to exist only as various bureau mentalities connected by relations of subordination and passive obedience.

The universal spirit of bureaucracy is secrecy, the mystery, which it secures internally by hierarchy, and against external groups by its character as a closed corporation.

Source: Karl Marx, "Contribution to the Critique of Hegel's *Philosophy of Right*," in Robert C. Tucker, ed. *The Marx-Engels Reader, Second Edition*, (New York: Norton, 1978): 25.

Marx's hope for society was for the triumph of communism over capitalism. Under communism, exploitation of one class by another would end, and, therefore, there would no longer be any need for institutions that sustained that exploitation. As a result, the state would wither away along with the bureaucracy, and we would have a classless society. Beyond this, Marx said little about this new world.

To summarize briefly, Marx argued the following:

- Capitalist society is marked by class conflict in which the capitalist (business) class oppresses and exploits the working class in the pursuit of profitability.

- The state (of which the bureaucracy is a key part) is "relatively autonomous" from the capitalist class but ultimately serves its long-term interests.

- The bureaucracy also has interests of its own, focused on its own survival and the career-building activities of its employees.

- Both the society at large and bureaucrats suffer from alienation derived from the hierarchical nature of bureaucracy.

- Class struggle will result in revolution, leading to a classless society in which the state (and bureaucracy) will gradually wither away.

The Neo-Marxists

Marx inspired a number of subsequent thinkers who have modified his original ideas, such that we can talk about a school of thought known as *neo-Marxism*. In general, these theorists consider the modern capitalist state to have two primary functions. One is to foster capital **accumulation**, meaning that the state passes policies that make it possible for capitalist enterprises to make profits. These might include low corporate tax rates, subsidies, grants, or other similar measures. The second is to ensure that the working class does not rise up and revolt against the dominant class. Thus, the state passes policies of **legitimation** to appease the working class without interfering with the accumulation of profits by capitalists. These may include social welfare policies, for instance. But if they do not keep the workers more or less quiescent, the state may also use coercion or even force to ensure that the working class complies with the needs of the capitalist class.

Neo-Marxists are divided, though, over the precise nature of the state and its role in supporting capitalism. Some point to the close personal and professional relationships and networks between senior state officials and the corporate elite as evidence of the commonality of interests between the state and the bureaucracy. In a groundbreaking study, sociologist John Porter (although not a Marxist himself) documented the common social origins and ties between these groups in Canada as evidence that public policy naturally tends to favour the dominant classes in society.[3] Other neo-Marxists contend that bureaucracy serves the capitalist class not because of common social origins but because the state operates in a capitalist system and is thereby constrained by the structures of that system. Because of these "structural constraints," the interests of the state and the capitalist class coincide.

Neo-Marxists do agree, however, on the notion that the modern bureaucratic state is a threat to democracy. They contend that it has grown so powerful that it is no longer as responsible to elected legislatures as it should be, and that in any case the bureaucracy is politicized in many countries, which enables the ruling party to appoint its own supporters to influential positions within the bureaucracy.

Criticisms of Marxist Theory

One of the basic problems with Marx's analysis is that he himself did not elaborate on his ideas in this area, so they have been subject to a variety of interpretations (and misinterpretations). More concretely, the neo-Marxists have been criticized for trying to have their cake and eat it, too. Neo-Marxists claim that any state policy that assists capital is evidence of the state serving the capitalist class. But any policy that assists the working class is also interpreted as ultimately serving the interests of capital by legitimating the capitalist system. Neo-Marxists are also criticized for arguing that the bureaucracy is merely a tool of the capitalist class, while at the same time arguing that the bureaucracy has become too powerful in its own right. In any event, there is no doubt that Marx and his followers have exerted a tremendous influence over the way we think about the role and nature of bureaucracy.

Max Weber

Perhaps the greatest influence on our thinking about organizations is derived from the literature on the sociology of organization, and the dominant writer in this area remains **Max Weber**.

Contemporary thinking . . . [about bureaucracy] begins with the work of the brilliant German sociologist Max Weber (1864–1920). His analysis of bureaucracy, first published in 1922 after his death, is still the most influential statement—the point of departure for all further analyses—on the subject. Drawing on studies of ancient bureaucracies in Egypt, Rome, China and the Byzantine Empire, as well as on the more modern ones emerging in Europe during the 18th and 19th centuries, Weber used an "ideal-type" approach to extrapolate from the real world the central core of features characteristic of the most fully developed bureaucratic form of organization. [4]

Weber argued that bureaucracy was essentially a system of administration carried out on a continuous basis by trained professionals, according to prescribed rules. He identified four main features common to modern systems of organization:

1. *hierarchy*, in which everyone has a clearly defined role within a division of labour and answers to a superior;
2. *continuity*, in the sense of full-time salaried occupations and career structures;
3. *impersonality*, in which work is based on prescribed rules and a written record; and

4. *expertise*, whereby personnel, selected on the basis of what they know rather than who they know (that is, on the basis of merit), are trained, and control access to knowledge stored in files.[5]

Weber felt that the closer an organization could be to this model, the more efficient it would be and the larger it would grow (see Box 3.2). Weber identified bureaucracy with efficiency since its central feature is rationality. Rationality is reflected in bureaucracy's complex division of labour, coupled with its impersonality and uniformity in the treatment of all citizens—all of which enhanced its potential for efficiency. Weber felt that bureaucratic organization was becoming more prevalent in all political systems and in all organizations where complex and large-scale administrative tasks were undertaken, including businesses, trade unions, political parties, etc. Weber saw bureaucracy as central to modernization. Its source of power was the monopolization of knowledge and organization, and the concentration of this power was within the political domain.

Weber regarded the growth of the modern organization and the bureaucratic form it took as the single most important phenomenon of the modern world.

BOX 3.2 | **Weber's Views on Organization**

Weber's views on organization are summarized by Adie and Thomas in the following way:

In bureaucracy there is a clearly defined layering of authority, a hierarchy, with each person under the control and supervision of a superior. Each person in the organization fills an office, or position, on the basis of free, contractual agreement, and following from a division of labour based on specialization of function, each person is appointed to a position on the basis of competence demonstrated to superiors. Each office has a specified sphere of competence, in that duties are specifically attached to it along with the necessary authority to carry them out. Each person obeys authority because that authority is attached to the position above his or her own. Each person obeys another only because the other has the "legal" right to give orders. At the same time, no person is entitled to give orders to others unless his or her office clearly allows it, and the orders must pertain to the functions of that office. At all times, however, the individual is subject to strict and systematic supervision and discipline based on the principle of hierarchy. To avoid arbitrary, personalistic use of authority, it is clearly stated that the individual is always free to resign but that the employing authority can end a subordinate's appointment only under certain circumstances, e.g. dereliction of duty.

Source: Robert F. Adie and Paul G. Thomas, *Canadian Public Administration: Problematical Perspectives, Second Edition,* (Scarborough: Prentice-Hall, 1987): 17–18. Reprinted with permission by Pearson Education Canada Inc.

That growth was the result of the superiority of bureaucratic forms of organization based on rationality and efficiency. Because individuals working within such an organization develop skills through training and experience, they develop into a body of professionals and experts. Because their positions are determined by their skills, and not by inheritance or purchase, as was common in earlier times, there is an ineluctable logic in the expansion, development, and evolution of bureaucracy as the dominant organizational form in modern society.

Weber saw bureaucratization as a rational, systematic, logical, and scientific approach to organization. Weber argued that, historically, people and societies were guided in their actions and behaviours by tradition, habit, instincts, and passions. But in the sixteenth and seventeenth centuries, the ideas of the Enlightenment elevated reason and rationality and largely replaced those earlier guides to action. Consider the concept of *authority*, for instance, and the decisions in society about who has the right to wield it. Weber argued that in the past, authority could be attributed to tradition (e.g., you are the king because your father was the king, as was his father, etc.) or to the charisma of an individual leader (e.g., you are able to secure compliance to your authority by the force of your personality). But the increasing rationalization of modern life undermined the grounds upon which these justifications stood. An ideally rational organization in the Weberian sense was an organization performing its tasks with maximum efficiency. But bestowing authority on an individual for reasons of tradition or charisma was not logical in that it did not guarantee that the best person for the job would exercise authority. As a result, efficiency could actually be impeded. An ideal type of organization would be perfectly rational, since rationality enhanced efficiency, whereas tradition and charisma did not, according to Weber.

But Weber also noted that the nature of bureaucratic organizations had a profound effect on people as individuals. The tendency toward impersonality of bureaucracy, which is realized through the application of impersonal rules (i.e., rules that apply to all, regardless of station in life), means that bureaucracy depersonalizes individuals. Also, the idea that bureaucrats advance through the strict application of rules contributes to that spirit of impersonality, since it promotes the pursuit of personal career goals through rigid application of formulistic rules. In some cases, following these rules supersedes other considerations due to the bureaucrat's desire for advancement and security within the organization. We will examine these kinds of pathologies in more detail later on.

Criticisms of the Weberian Model

We know that organizations do not always work the way Weber prescribed. There is a disconnect between his model and the real world, and therein lies a problem with organization theory in general. It seeks to describe and explain *what is,* but often falls short. For example, we know that many organizations that display Weber's characteristics of an ideal bureaucracy (i.e., they are hierarchical, have continuity, are impersonal, and are staffed by experts) are, in fact, inefficient! Moreover, some are downright dysfunctional. For instance, hierarchy can generate a lack of initiative and individual responsibility; continuity can lead to ennui and apathy in the delivery of services; impersonality can foster indifference and insensitivity; expertise can result in inflexibility, hidebound tradition, and arrogance.

Moreover, while the impersonality of bureaucratic rules and authority is consistent with the democratic ideal of the equality of everyone before the law, in some cases it actually impedes values such as democracy and equality. For instance, the education level required for one to hold a position of authority in a government bureaucracy prevents many individuals from disadvantaged circumstances from becoming rule-makers themselves. Or, while impersonal rules may protect individuals from arbitrary treatment at the hands of officials, they may also be used to frustrate popular demands for social justice. For instance, in the past, the hiring criteria of your local fire department might have required potential employees be a certain height and weight. Ostensibly, these are objective criteria that are deemed necessary due to the physical requirements of fighting fires. But what if they inadvertently discriminate against a whole group of people who do not meet those qualifications? For instance, women and some visible minorities tend to be shorter and of slighter stature than the white male average against which the standards were set. As a result, demands for equality of opportunity in employment run up against allegedly impersonal and objective rules and regulations. The result, systemic discrimination, is neither foreseen nor desired by the rule-makers but is, nonetheless, a reality in this situation.

Some argue that bureaucracy has significantly contributed to the destruction of privileges based on heredity (due to the merit principle) and made the organization of large-scale industry and commerce possible. But right-wing critics of the Weberian view argue that increasing government bureaucracy, marked by greater regulation and intervention in the economy, has hindered capitalist development and the risk-taking initiative and entrepreneurial spirit of capitalism.

Critics on the left focus on a different problem with the Weberian model. They suggest that Weber's model assumes a view about human nature that is contestable, to say the least. Weber sees humans as constantly striving for power and self-gain and in need of discipline and control. Workers in the bureaucratic machine are subsumed under the organization, rather than possessing some sense of individuality. Thus, "the impact of bureaucracy on the individual is the extreme limitation of our personal freedom and spontaneity, and an increasing incapacity to understand our own activities in relation to the whole organization. We become cogs in a machine."[6]

From this perspective, bureaucracy has profoundly negative implications for democracy. Democracy requires participation by citizens who have a strong sense of self and belonging and who feel able to participate in decision making, but bureaucratic forms of organization stress obedience to authority, and the sublimation of the self to the greater interests of the organization. These points are important to keep in mind when we look at some later theorists who argue that managers in bureaucracies would be more successful in attaining their goals if they permitted more democratic forms of decision making and participation to take place within organizations.

Weber's work on bureaucracy was premised on the notion of an *ideal-type;* that is, a model of the perfect bureaucratic machine. In his view, the closer you come to approximating the ideal-type, the closer you come to creating the most perfectly efficient type of organization. But the work of subsequent social scientists, who observed how bureaucratic organizations actually functioned in the real world, gave rise to some trenchant critiques of Weber's views. Some concluded that there was more to bureaucracy than the rules and structures of Weber's ideal model. There were informal patterns of behaviour co-existing with the formal rules, which, when they functioned in harmony, could produce greater efficiency and effectiveness. But when they were in conflict, efficiency and effectiveness were impeded.

The work of several theorists who followed Weber modified his views about bureaucracy. For instance, they took Weber's notion that politicians were at the top of the hierarchical ladder, giving orders to faithful public servants, and examined real-life cases where it appeared that the bureaucrats were actually following their own agendas. These new theorists noted that the politician was often at a distinct disadvantage in that he was a generalist with a lack of specific technical knowledge of how government departments functioned or how policy was made and implemented. The public servants, on the other hand, were often technical experts with many long years of experience. Picture yourself in the following situation:

You are the newly elected Member of Parliament for your riding, and the prime minister calls to tell you that she wants you to be the minister of the environment in her Cabinet. Chances are, you may not be an expert in environmental issues. But even if you are, the first day you walk into your office, you are met by the deputy minister and other senior bureaucratic officials, who have spent years developing policy in this area. Moreover, they have all developed an intimate knowledge of how government works. You, as the rookie, will have to be an awfully quick study to get up to speed, but in the meantime you may find yourself at the mercy of the "experts" who are supposedly also your "servants."

While Weber acknowledged that tensions could develop between politicians and their bureaucrats, it took the work of other theorists to document how this could affect the running of governmental bureaucracies. For instance, S.M. Lipset, in his book *Agrarian Socialism,* used a case study that showed that the political values and ideologies of public servants could directly influence and even override the express wishes of their political masters.[7] Lipset studied the 1944 government formed by the Co-operative Commonwealth Federation (CCF), the forerunner of the New Democratic Party (NDP), in Saskatchewan and the difficulties it had in initiating its socialist platform. Many of the top public servants in the province were opposed to socialism and were successful in having the CCF's reforms modified or even thwarted altogether, often by arguing that the reforms were "administratively unfeasible," although this was not necessarily the case. Although they did not have it all their own way, some senior public servants boasted of "running my department completely" and of "stopping the harebrained radical schemes" of the CCF.

Lipset's study clearly outlined how the values and ideological predispositions of top public servants could have an important impact on the formal orders passed down from their political superiors. His study also revealed that the bureaucracy was not simply a passive tool but could itself develop informal values and even policy goals.

Another feature not accounted for by Weber is bureaucracy's pathological or distorted character. An example from popular culture is presented in the novel *One Flew Over the Cuckoo's Nest* by Ken Kesey, which was made into a movie starring Jack Nicholson.[8] In the story, a nurse in a mental hospital runs a ward in an authoritarian manner, following the organization's rules and regulations with no flexibility or allowance for individual circumstance or personality. The inmates passively accept the nurse's orders but are never "cured." When a new patient arrives (played by Nicholson in the movie), he challenges the nurse's authority and her insistence that "therapy" consists of routine schedules and rigid rules of behaviour. He organizes poker and basketball games, and tries to have the nurse rearrange the patients' schedule so they can watch the World Series. The nurse refuses, but with every refusal to indulge the patients in new activities outside the rigidly defined rules of the institution, the new patient introduces ever more radical and risky activities, culminating in a daylong fishing trip outside the institution, and a wild party with alcohol and prostitutes. This is too much for the nurse to bear, even though the patients display a marked improvement in their conditions. She orders the disruptive new patient to the surgical wing of the hospital, where he is lobotomized—the thinking part of his brain removed.

This is a highly dramatic and fictional account of how a bureaucracy with the best of intentions can display pathological behaviour that actually impedes the goals it sets for itself. The rules of the organization came to take precedence over the very objectives the rules were intended to realize. When the new patient defied the established routine and rules, the nurse used those same rules to beat him down, even though his unorthodox solutions to the patients' mental disorders were having positive effects.

The sociologist Robert K. Merton studied such dysfunctions in bureaucracies. In an important article, entitled "Bureaucratic Structure and Personality," he argued that certain aspects of bureaucratic procedure may, in fact, be dysfunctional to the organization and actually discourage behaviour that might otherwise be beneficial to the organization's goals.[9] He suggested that when an official is trained to comply with a set of rules and regulations, any situation that arises that is not covered by those rules may lead to inflexibility and timidity. The bureaucrat is not taught to be innovative or creative. He may actually be afraid to deviate from the rules, even in the face of absurd outcomes, because of fear of jeopardizing chances for promotion. This is sometimes referred to as *trained incapacity,* referring to the state of affairs in which one's learned abilities function as inadequacies or blind spots. The analogy is sometimes used of chickens trained to interpret the sound of a bell as a signal for food. That same bell may also be used to summon the trained chickens to the slaughterhouse!

Merton also notes that the devotion to rules often becomes an end in itself for officials. The bureaucrat loses sight of the goals of the organization and, instead, becomes bound up in red tape, trying to ensure that the rules are followed without deviation. Merton characterizes this kind of behaviour as *goal displacement,* an example of which is clearly present in *One Flew Over the Cuckoo's Nest.* But it is worth remembering that Weber's model of bureaucracy stressed the importance of impersonally applying prescribed rules and regulations to maximize efficiency. In many cases, bureaucrats are trained to be skeptical of complaints, since they are led to believe that universal impersonal application of rules is for the good of the organization. In time, bureaucrats come to identify the disciplined application of rules with their own self-interest and desire for promotion and status.

This notion of the substitution of self-interest for organizational interest is crucial. It means that bureaucrats will come to interpret any challenge to the existing rules as a threat to their own security. To protect themselves, they will apply the rules even more rigidly, since this is the only procedure they know that will bring the praise of their superiors. In time, they will cease to question whether the rules are relevant to the organization's objectives. For example, in 1803, the British government created a post that required a civil servant to stand on the cliffs of Dover with a spyglass and ring a bell if he saw Napoleon coming. The position was not abolished until 1945!

Merton also focused on the impersonality of bureaucratic procedures and the problems this raised. He noted, in particular, the cold impersonal treatment jobless individuals met when applying for benefits from employment offices. The bureaucrats interpreted their own behaviour as "businesslike." They had little time for pleasantries since they were so rushed and overworked, so they went about applying the rigid rules of the application process with little regard to the feelings of their clients, who were often emotionally distressed due to their unemployment. But the clients interpreted the clerks' behaviour as arrogance, and felt that they were being looked down upon. Many complaints from the public resulted, but no action was taken in response by the bureaucrats, who had been trained to impersonally apply a set of predetermined rules in a prescribed manner.[10] Two other post-Weberians, Victor Thompson (*Modern Organizations*) and Alvin Gouldner (*Patterns of Industrial Behaviour*), approached these issues from another angle.[11] They focused on the behaviour of clients on the receiving end of the bureaucracy. They argued that clients are notoriously insensitive to the needs of bureaucrats, and that clients tend to act like children when they encounter big organizations. Clients seem to want instant gratification and fulfillment of their needs, irrespective of how difficult or complicated it is for the bureaucrat to fulfill those needs. They argued that clients tended to view bureaucratic organizations in personal terms, as either a friend or an enemy. All attempts by bureaucrats to evaluate clients are perceived as intrusions upon their personal lives. While the clients are willing to accept the services provided by bureaucracies, they resent having to give anything in return. Moreover, while clients realize that they depend on large institutions for a variety of services, they feel powerless in their presence, which fosters feelings of alienation and anger.

Such responses, Thompson insisted, were nothing more than the dysfunctional persistence of childish patterns of behaviour.

Thompson and Gouldner had come across the role of *passion* in human affairs as it related to large organizations. Bureaucracies require that people be patient, accept impersonal treatment, submit to evaluation, and place obligation above rights—in short, that they substitute self-discipline for passion. In the era of large bureaucracies, passion is a human attribute that is out of place, since bureaucracy draws its morality from the old Protestant work ethic, with its commitment to self-discipline and rationalism.

Weber's ideas were reassessed from another perspective, as well. His work was the basis of what other theorists called the *politics-administration dichotomy*. You will recall from chapter 1 that this was a view first articulated by Woodrow Wilson, who developed the notion that politics and administration are separate things. Frank J. Goodnow took up this theme in his book, *Politics and Administration,* published in 1900.[12] Goodnow took the view that public administration, as practised under the party "boss system" in the United States, was in many ways corrupt and thereby inefficient since leaders typically apportioned jobs to their supporters, family, and friends rather than to the best-qualified candidates for a position. An ardent reformer, Goodnow argued for the separation of politics and administration. But while this "principle" of public administration prevailed for many years, it also increasingly came under attack. Indeed, few would admit the theory has much utility today. It is factually inaccurate in that politics and administration are inextricably linked in countless large and small ways, even if we do not want them to be. Nonetheless, as a "principle" it remains desirable in guiding public administration in areas such as appointments to the public service (where merit has replaced patronage).

But Herbert Simon, the only non-economist ever to win the Nobel Prize in economics, postulated that the "principles of public administration" were really nothing more than "proverbs of administration."[13] As a result, these principles were often contradictory, inconsistent, inapplicable, and confusing. In short, public administration was anything but scientific, notwithstanding the claims of a couple of generations of theorists. For example, Simon noted that proverbs often come in mutually contradictory pairs ("look before you leap" is countered by "he who hesitates is lost"). Similarly, in administration, apparently contradictory principles seem to be at work. The Peter Principle states that every individual reaches her level of competence in an organization; yet the Great Shelf Principle suggests that individuals are generally shelved somewhere in the organization long before they have realized their potential. More directly, Simon cited the example of the span of control in organizations. **Span of control** refers to the structure of the hierarchy within an organization. Around 1750 BC, the Egyptians assigned 10 workers to each supervisor while building the pyramids in what may be the first recorded application of the concept of span of control. Traditional literature had argued that efficiency was maximized with a narrow span of control; that is, each manager "controls" only a limited number of subordinates. The theory was that too many subordinates resulted in poor

FIGURE 3.1   Span of Control

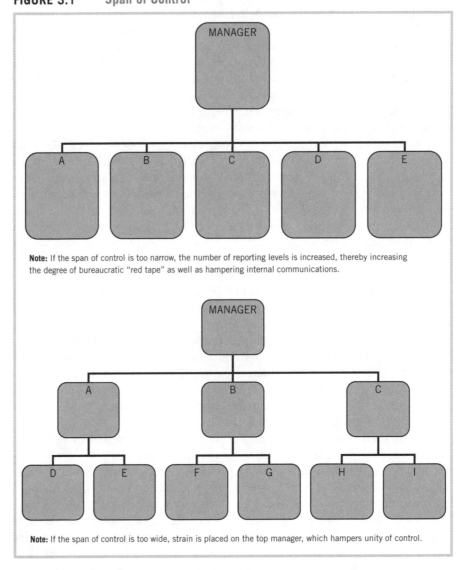

Note: If the span of control is too narrow, the number of reporting levels is increased, thereby increasing the degree of bureaucratic "red tape" as well as hampering internal communications.

Note: If the span of control is too wide, strain is placed on the top manager, which hampers unity of control.

communications within the organization and progressively looser and less effective control. But Simon pointed out that the literature also argued that, for an organization to maximize effective communications, there should be as few hierarchical levels as possible. These are two mutually contradictory principles, making it impossible for managers to "do the right thing" as far as the structure of their organization is concerned. The two span of control systems are represented in Figure 3.1.

As you have seen, Weber's basic model contained vitally important insights, but it has not gone unchallenged. The fact that he really only considered the formal structure of bureaucracy, with its official rules and procedures and authorized structure of hierarchy, meant that he ignored the unofficial practices that also contribute to the functioning of organizations. But various bureaucratic pathologies also exist that impede the achievement of maximum efficiency and rationality as espoused in the Weberian model. Many of these new insights found expression through the theorists we will now turn to in the structuralist and humanist schools of thought.

Structuralist Theories

Generally speaking, **structuralist theories** view workers in administrative organizations as little more than interchangeable parts—cogs in a machine lubricated by money. In this view, the goal of organization theory is to devise structures within which the work of individuals can be rationalized so as to maximize the organization's efficiency. Little regard is paid to the needs or desires of the individual workers, who are expected to subsume their interests to the administrative machine. These theories rely on a particular view of human nature that suggests individuals are motivated by material gain (wages, career advancement, etc.) and that workers require a strict regime of rules and regulations, determined and clearly spelled out by management, in order to function at maximum efficiency.

Scientific Management

A profoundly important evolution in thinking about public administration came about as a result of new demands from business managers arising at the turn of the twentieth century, as a consequence of industrial capitalism. The term **scientific management** characterized this school of thought. Increasing industrialization and technological change in the workplace in the late 1800s created a great deal of disorganization in industry. Major adjustment problems were encountered in the transition from small-scale, craft-based production to large-scale, industrial factory-based production, where the work of employees was increasingly deskilled (for example, on the newly invented assembly line). The growing classes of capitalist owners and workers had to adapt to new forms of workplace organization to remain competitive, if large-scale efficiency was going to be achieved.

The growth of business operations increasingly separated owners from the daily routine of workers. Thus, a more rationalized form of organization and control was needed to maximize productivity and profit. The pioneers in this reorganizational challenge were those in industry who were strategically located in the production process—namely, the mechanical engineers— because of their central position in organizing factory production on a daily basis. The cost accountants also became key players, due to their role of measuring and controlling costs. These people and the theorists who supported their work tackled the question of organizations and administration from the point of view of what can be called the *managerial* tradition. Thus, scientific management's origins and ideas were clearly directed at and for management in contrast, as we will see, to the humanist theories of bureaucracy.

The father of scientific management was Frederick Winslow Taylor (1856–1915) (see Box 3.3). He was not so much interested in the organizational problems of society's power structure as he was in the practical problem of efficiency. In other words, Taylor's main unit of analysis was not society as a whole or bureaucracy as such, but the individual worker in the bureaucratic/organizational setting (i.e., the workplace). Taylor began to develop his system in the 1880s while employed as a pattern maker and machinist at the Midvale Steel Company in Philadelphia. At the time, work in factories was still not particularly "routinized" or "rationalized." The skilled craft worker still predominated, and workers were largely left on their own to perform their duties; the pace of the work was not yet set by the machines; and the individual worker placed his own "stamp" on the product—i.e., work was individualized. Foremen were also generally left to set their own standards and to regulate work breaks, etc. The tyranny of the clock had not yet been imposed.

BOX 3.3 | **Frederick Winslow Taylor: The Father of Scientific Management**

Although Taylor is regarded as the father of scientific management, the term actually originated elsewhere.

Strangely enough, while Taylor's 1911 book Principles of Scientific Management is the work for which he is best known, the credit for coining the term scientific management belongs not to Taylor but to an associate of his, Louis D. Brandeis (1856–1941). Brandeis, who would later become a Supreme Court justice, needed a catchy phrase to describe the new style management techniques of Taylor and his disciples when he was to present arguments before the Interstate Commerce Commission that railroad rate increases should be denied. Brandeis dramatically argued that the railroads could save "a million dollars a day" by applying scientific management methods. The highly publicized hearings beginning in 1910 caused a considerable sensation and vastly expanded Taylor's reputation. Ironically, Taylor was initially opposed to the phrase, thinking that it sounded too academic. But he quickly learned to embrace it. So did the rest of the country. In the first half of the century, scientific management was gospel and Frederick W. Taylor was its prophet.

Source: Jay M. Shafritz and Albert C. Hyde, *Classics of Public Administration, Third Edition,* © 1992 Wadsworth, a part of Cengage Learning, Inc. Reproduced by permission. www.cengage.com/permissions

---

Taylor came to regard such practices as haphazard and inefficient. The Midvale plant was run on a piecework basis: machines ran around the clock, and labourers were paid on the basis of how many pieces they produced. Taylor observed this process and determined that workers could triple their productivity (and their wages) simply by reorganizing the flow of work. So Taylor attempted to regulate the work routine and speed up its pace. Rather than allow individual workers to set the pace and to carry out their own tasks, Taylor set a time for how long any particular job should take, and outlined in a strict way the manner in which the job should be done. The workers reacted unfavourably to Taylor's attempted reorganization. They called him a "piecework hog" for working so hard; he was the kind of guy you love to hate in the workplace— the keener who volunteered to work on Sundays, and who rose every day at 5:00 a.m. to walk the two miles to work, never leaving before 5:00 p.m., etc. He was born into an upper-class Philadelphia family and studied law at Harvard for a while but quit, complaining that he was going blind from all the reading. After this he signed up with the Midvale plant and engaged his fascination with time management and scientific solutions to workplace problems. (Incidentally, he applied this thinking to his personal life, too. Plagued by nightmares, he noticed that he always woke up on his back. He therefore concluded that if he did not sleep on his back, he would not have nightmares. So he rigged up an elaborate harness of leather straps and wooden prods that he wore while sleeping. If he rolled onto his back, he would be prodded awake. Thus he applied a scientific-type solution to his problem.)

In the workplace, Taylor sought to scientifically discover the shortest time possible for performing any particular task, and his tool was the stopwatch. Standing behind each worker, Taylor would record the time it took to perform even the most elementary motions: finding a steel rod, setting it on a lathe, picking up a tool, and so on. By studying a large number of workers, he felt he could identify the shortest possible time for performing each individual motion. By combining the best times, discarding useless motions, and adding gaps for unavoidable delays or rest breaks, Taylor could establish a pattern of work that was invariably shorter than the workers' informal pace. These experiments became known as the infamous **time and motion studies**.

When Taylor asked for help from management to implement his system, the workers responded by running their machines so fast and hard that pieces fell off! Taylor responded by fining them. Ultimately, he convinced management to use the ultimate weapon against the workers: cut the piecework rate in half so that the workers would have to speed up their production to financially survive. Taylor's battles with the Midvale workers were to last three years (see Box 3.4). Before leaving Midvale, Taylor astonished the plant engineers by revealing that he had conducted upward of 50 000 experiments on these problems, which he published in the book *On the Art of Cutting Metal*.

He then began to look beyond time and motion studies to determine that workers were also using improper tools and defective equipment. He contended that there was "one best way" of performing any task, and his work resulted in a complete reorganization of the firm—planning, engineering, purchasing, and inventory control were all centralized, as was maintenance and cost accounting; assembly line techniques were introduced as well. Management's job, Taylor argued, was to "discover" this "one best way" by applying scientific principles to work procedures. The workers should not be left to solve the problems of production themselves; this was management's role. The worker should simply

---

BOX 3.4 | **Taylor's View of Workers**

Taylor based part of his view of the division of labour in the workplace on a view of workers that can only be considered repulsive by today's standards. Consider the following quote from his book, *The Principles of Scientific Management*:

Now one of the very first requirements for a man who is fit to handle pig iron as a regular occupation is that he shall be so stupid and so phlegmatic that he more nearly resembles in his mental make-up the ox than any other type. . . . Therefore the workman who is best suited to handling pig iron is unable to understand the real science of doing this class of work. He is so stupid that the word "percentage" has no meaning to him, and he must consequently be trained by a man more intelligent than himself into the habit of working in accordance with the laws of this science before he can be successful.

Source: F.W. Taylor, *The Principles of Scientific Management*, (New York: Harper and Brothers, 1911): 59.

---

be told how to carry out the "one best way." What this implied was a radical separation of planning and performing, of thinking and doing.

While Taylor's theories were initially developed for the private sector, Taylor also attempted to introduce his system into public administration, beginning in 1906 in government-run arsenals and navy yards. The most famous incident took place at Watertown Arsenal near Boston. The arsenal was run by rule of thumb: the workers would receive an order for a set number of gun carriages and fill it by milling assorted parts found in the yard according to designs someone sketched in chalk on the factory floor. Taylor contended this was not the "one best way" of doing the job. Furthermore, he argued that the selection of workers must be based on scientific criteria, too—i.e., some workers were better suited for some jobs than others, and the best person for each job must be determined and chosen. When the workers at Watertown heard that Taylor was coming, they went on strike, and the army was sent in to guard the arsenal with fixed bayonets. Later, a special congressional committee was formed that summoned Taylor to explain his system. So contentious was Taylor's time and motion system that the U.S. Congress passed a law banning stopwatches in government-run factories—a law that remained in place for 40 years—because of the unpopularity of Taylor and his ideas among working class voters.

Two more theorists in the scientific management tradition argued that there are universal principles of administration that should govern arrangements for human organizations. Luther Gulick and Lyndall Urwick produced an important collection of papers on the state of the art of organization theory, entitled "Papers on the Science of Administration."[14] The French theorist Henri Fayol had documented the five functions common to all managers in all organizations as planning, organizing, commanding, coordinating, and controlling;[15] Gulick expanded on this approach in a famous acronym, **POSDCORB**, which stands for Planning, Organizing, Staffing, Directing, Coordinating, Reporting, and Budgeting. By subdividing all the tasks of an organization along these lines, efficiency could be maximized. This was Gulick's attempt to define the "one best way" for organization management by focusing on the top of the hierarchical pyramid in organizations. He was concerned with developing scientific principles and practices that management should systematically employ.

But it is the underlying philosophy behind Taylorism and scientific management, the assumption of worker–management co-operation, that was problematic. In the absence of this, all other principles of his approach were useless. Taylor saw scientific management as a solution both to productivity problems and to class conflicts, which he viewed as wasteful. He wrote, "Once the natural laws governing work and production are discovered, the determination of the proper time for doing a job and the proper amount of pay can be determined in an objective, scientific way." Once these things were scientifically established, there would be no need for bargaining or conflict between labour and management, because one could not bargain with scientific fact. Thus, Taylor was hostile to trade unions, feeling that they served to generate conflict and were against the real best interests of the workers. He preferred to deal with workers as individuals rather than in groups (unions) because he felt that workers in groups exerted social pressure on individuals to conform to unscientific, more comfortable production norms (i.e., to "slack off"). Taylor wished to prevent such groups from developing, by making it in the workers' economic interest to co-operate with scientific management techniques.

Interestingly, the underlying premise of scientific management in terms of the relationship of workers to the industrial environment was explained by Taylor in analogies between people and machines. First, in terms of production, people were considered to be like machines (the mechanomorphic world image) whose specifications and performance could be scientifically measured and rated, and whose efficiency could be improved through mechanical adjustments, such as reducing superfluous motions. Second, he argued that the factory structure should be considered as a complex productive mechanism—a combination of machines and workers involved in the process of transforming raw material in the cheapest possible manner. Rationalization was the key, defined as producing a product in the most efficient manner. Goals were to be set and achieved by using workers and machines as standardized, interchangeable parts to be manipulated with the aim of maximizing productivity at minimum cost.

Mechanization of industry in the late 1800s and early 1900s had resulted in unprecedented productivity growth, particularly in America, it is true. But it also resulted in human organizational problems, the solution to which, according to scientific management, was to treat humans as machines. In terms of efficiency, this was a solution that resulted in amazing gains in productivity. Thus, scientific management represents not just a theory of organization, but one of motivation and human behaviour. It characterizes the individual as driven by fear of hunger and deprivation, and by a desire for profit. These characteristics were manipulable, according to scientific management, in a manner compatible with efficiency, so long as it was possible to view humans as mere machines.

Taylor saw the **division of labour** as a basic principle controlled by a hierarchical pyramid of authority driven by efficiency. The emphasis on managerial control attracted American capitalists engaged in a bitter struggle with labour over control of the modern industrial workplace. But even once Taylorist measures were implemented in workplaces, they did not have all the desired effects of transferring decision-making authority to management and producing the most efficient and profitable form of operation. Henry Ford's adoption of scientific management in his assembly line, for instance, did not result in the workers quietly acquiescing to the highly regulated and automated routine of the production line. Instead, they unionized and adapted their own defensive techniques to counter management's attempts to gain total control over the labour process. Their responses culminated in the sit-down strikes of the 1930s, the wildcat strikes of the 1940s, as well as labour militancy in the 1960s and 1970s. These struggles showed the alienating power for workers of Taylor's approach, and demonstrated that scientific management rationality did not necessarily result in the most efficient, effective production process. Instead, it often resulted in worker resistance or even sabotage of the production process. The often inhumane working conditions fostered by Taylor's techniques impeded efficiency, ironically destroying the very "rationality" of the system. Thus, the observation is appropriate that the quickest way of doing a job may not be the most efficient way.

Nonetheless, Taylorism attracted a diverse range of supporters. Besides American capitalists and industrialists, Italian Fascists in the 1930s made scientific management an important plank in their ideology; but it was also picked up by the left, too. Lenin, the father of the Communist revolution in Russia, was an enthusiastic admirer of Taylor, as were several socialist parties in the U.S., strangely enough. The attraction can be explained by remembering that there was widespread admiration in societies of the day for "scientific" advancement, which often overcame more ideologically based concerns about the welfare of workers.

Criticisms of Scientific Management

Scientific management techniques caught on across the United States and the industrialized world. But critiques of scientific management also emerged and sometimes found expression in popular culture. Charlie Chaplin's *Modern Times* and Fritz Lang's *Metropolis,* for instance, were trenchant and biting commentaries on the dehumanizing tendencies of this approach to workplace organization. By now, some of the weaknesses of the scientific management school should be apparent to you. For instance, by focusing on the individual worker as the main unit of analysis, it fails to see the worker as a member of a broader social group. There is no recognition that the worker is socially influenced in his or her behaviour and attitudes by colleagues and by the social structure and culture of the group.

Moreover, Taylorism represents a theory of organization based on a particular model of human behaviour: a machine model. This was an engineer's perspective, which saw human relations in mechanistic terms. The organization member was seen as an instrument of production like any other tool, to be manipulated and used. Taylor assumed that the individual feelings of workers were more or less irrelevant to the problems of productivity. In this sense, Taylor's conception of the worker is very similar to Weber's view of the ideal bureaucrat: both are devoid of personal feelings, ambitions, and independent actions that might jeopardize the systems Taylor and Weber constructed. Thus, there is no consideration of the individual's feelings, attitudes, and private goals. In short, Taylor (like Weber) neglected the psychological and sociological variables of organizational behaviour.

Thus, the same types of criticisms levelled against Weber by the post-Weberians apply in some instances to Taylor. Taylor, for instance, looked at the problem of morale and productivity exclusively in terms of economic reward and punishment; the primary motivation of workers is assumed to be economic. But this is obviously an oversimplified view of human nature; clearly other, non-economic motivations also guide worker behaviour (e.g., alienation). Furthermore, Taylor's pro-management perspective led him to mistakenly believe that the interests of management and labour were reconcilable and could exist in harmony through scientific management. But this is naive; as long as there are bosses and workers and a prevailing capitalist economy wherein a dollar that goes to profit cannot also go to wages, tensions and hostilities will persist.

Over the years, a growing chorus of criticisms of Taylorism led to a contrary school of thought, which we can classify as the humanist or human relations approach to organization theory.

Humanist Theories

Popular culture can often be seen as a barometer of society's attitudes; hence the alienating hyper-rationalism of industrial capitalism became the subject matter for numerous critical films and novels, from Charlie Chaplin's *Modern Times*, to Arthur Miller's *Death of a Salesman*, to George Orwell's *1984*. Similarly, in the realm of management and public administration, the **humanist** school arose as a critique of the dehumanizing structuralist approach. Humanist theorists argued that to maximize efficiency required paying attention to the workers as individuals with identifiable needs beyond mere material rewards. It was the job of managers, according to this school of thought, to be sensitive to those needs in order to maximize efficiency, since a happy and contented worker who feels a part of the decision-making process is more likely to produce efficiently than one who is disgruntled and must be coerced by restrictive institutional structures and rules.

The Human Relations Approach

As we saw above, a main concern of Taylorism was with scientifically selecting workers on the basis of their aptitude for a position. Given such an orientation, it was only a matter of time before the industrial psychologist would join the engineer and accountant to discover the most efficient conditions for work. The turn toward the industrial psychologist was largely prompted by workers' hostile reactions to scientific management's attempts to implement its mechanistic principles in the working environment. Industrial psychologists went beyond scientific management, taking into account more than the mere physical elements of the human in relation to work suitability. They attempted to modify scientific management's "machine model" of organizational behaviour, and were concerned with the following: how to devise tests to select the best person for a job; how to discover whether that person was working at full efficiency or not; how work conditions, such as lighting, humidity, and temperature affect productivity; how the effects of boredom, brought on by doing repetitive tasks, impeded productivity, etc. This approach, then, began to emphasize the human element in the work enterprise—hence the name *human relations approach.*

But rather than simply an altruistic response to structuralism, it is important to keep in mind another rather more prosaic reason for this approach's evolution. Serious labour disruption brought about by the introduction of scientific management erupted in every advanced industrial nation by the early 1900s. The mobilization of organized labour into unions and the sometimes violent strikes around this process prompted some theorists to wonder how workers themselves felt about the organization of work, if only to keep the wheels of industry turning.

One important theorist who anticipated the shift in attitudes and approaches was Mary Parker Follett, who wrote a groundbreaking reflection in 1926, called "The Giving of Orders," several years before the humanist tradition really took hold.[16] She argued for an approach that today we would identify as "participatory management" (discussed in chapter 4), in which leadership and decision making was not a linear process from the top down but, rather, a kind of continuous feedback loop. When a manager made a decision, his or her subordinates responded to and reacted to that decision, and their response fed back up to management, according to Parker Follett. Thus, she was questioning the command-and-control structure so lionized by scientific management and suggesting that both the *formal* power of management and the *informal* power of employees affected the organization's functions and success.

To gain insight into workers' feelings and opinions, theorists began to use techniques such as questionnaires, surveys, and workplace observations. They wished to tap into the influence of the "human factor." This new approach was reflected in a slogan adopted by much of the American business community in the 1930s: "The human element is the most important element in business." This gave recognition to problems inherent in scientific management.

The receptiveness of some business people to such studies provided industrial psychologists with a real working environment in which to apply academic theories. The worksite became their "laboratory" for studying human behaviour in an organizational (primarily industrial) setting. Among the most famous of these experiments were the **Hawthorne experiments**. In 1924, the American National Academy of Sciences sent a team of researchers to the Western Electric Company's Hawthorne Works near Chicago to study the effects of illumination on worker efficiency. Taylor had pointed to the need for well-placed work breaks that would give workers relief from the strains of their job and thereby improve efficiency. The researchers in the Hawthorne study were keenly aware of the studies of fatigue and monotony that had attempted to reduce these phenomena and consequently cut down on the problems of absenteeism and turnover and increased overall worker productivity. Researchers believed that an improved physical work environment would result in increased worker productivity.

The Hawthorne Works employed about 29 000 men and women. It was a massive industrial complex, producing telephone equipment. The researchers initially conducted their lighting tests on various broad groups of workers throughout the plant, but the results were inconclusive, so they decided to focus on a narrower, more controlled group of workers who wound small induction coils onto wooden spools. The researchers improved the lighting in the room and found that worker productivity went up. But some researchers were not convinced of the certainty of the results; they argued that if productivity was tied to illumination, then a *decrease* in lighting would result in a *decrease* in productivity. So the scientists then tested this proposition; they replaced the higher intensity light bulbs with lower ones, and what happened surprised them: productivity slowly but steadily increased! The scientists kept lowering the light level, and productivity continued to slowly rise. Finally the experimenters replaced the electric lights with three-foot candles; at this point the workers complained—noting that they were hardly able to see what they were doing—and the production rate decreased.

The researchers attempted to check their unusual findings by establishing a control group in another area of the plant. Here the level of lighting was never altered in the work room, yet the productivity of the workers in this control group continued to increase! This baffled the scientists. So they began a second series of experiments in 1927, in which they recruited five women who built telephone relays and segregated them from the other employees in a special room where the scientists could control temperature and humidity and their hours of work. The objective was to test the role of fatigue and monotony on productivity. The scientists experimented with longer rests and shorter workdays. In their conversations with the women, they discovered that the women frequently had no time to have breakfast, so the scientists provided them with sandwiches, coffee, and soup. Productivity went up. Moreover, productivity steadily went up until the rumour spread through the plant that the Hawthorne executives were about to dismiss the research team because of the effects of the experiments on other workers in the plant. At this point the workers in the experiment began producing an extraordinarily large number of telephone relays. At about the same time, scientists decided to observe the effects of increasing the women's fatigue by restoring the old 48-hour workweek. Productivity continued to climb! They eliminated the lunch break. Absenteeism went down! They cut down the rest breaks. There were still no signs of fatigue! No matter how the researchers tinkered with the rest periods or the workweek, they could not get the women to slow down.

What they finally figured out after about five years of study was that the workers were actually responding to the *researchers*, not to the conditions imposed on them or to the manipulation of their work environment. In the beginning, the women had responded to the novelty of having the researchers there; they felt it meant that management was worried about productivity. Then the women began to respond to the style of supervision. Given greater freedom, said the researchers, less strict supervision, and the opportunity to vary from a fixed pace without reprimand by a gang boss, worker morale increased, as did productivity.

The researchers felt they needed to know more about the effects of supervision, so they interviewed 20 000 workers but got so many different responses that they decided to conduct another experiment. This time the researchers would not supervise the workers directly but would watch them from a distance. The most important of these experiments began in 1931 in the bank wiring room where workers produced telephone switchboards. At the time, management was trying to improve worker productivity through a combination of wage incentives and low-key supervision. By industrial standards of the time, Hawthorne was a good place to work (given the Great Depression of the 1930s, just having *anywhere* to work was a good thing). But the employees were naturally concerned about losing their jobs. As a result, they artificially depressed their own productivity so that each worker wired no more than two banks a day. Any worker, of his or her own initiative, could have made more money by working harder. But the employees attacked those who did and berated those who worked too slowly. Thus, two banks a day was considered by all to be a fair day's work.

This phenomenon finally revealed the source of the researchers' confusion over their findings: the **informal group**. The researchers concluded that the dominant factor in employee productivity was the informal group and its attitudes. The most powerful motivators on the job were the social norms and values of the group and the ability of supervisors to act as leaders in modifying those norms and values. Workers might acquire their sentiments on the basis of individual experience, but on the job they acted as members of groups.

Elton Mayo, who was one of the key researchers from the Harvard Business School at Hawthorne, is considered to be the father of the human relations approach in the same way that Taylor was the father of scientific management.[17] Mayo made the following observation: human collaboration in work has always depended upon the evolution of a nonlogical social code that regulates the relations between persons and their attitudes to one another. Insisting on a merely economic logic of production interferes with the development of such a code and, consequently, gives rise in the group to a sense of human defeat. The human relations school came to the conclusion that economic incentives, rest breaks, free breakfasts, improved physical working conditions, etc., could never be as powerful as the "social controls" exercised by the group in the workplace. In other words, the key finding of the decade-long study was one that we might assume is rather obvious today: workers are more responsive to peer pressure than to management controls.

Despite the findings of the human relations school, however, the approach did not really begin to catch on until the late 1930s, with the publication of a book in 1938 called *The Functions of the Executive* by Chester Barnard, a career executive and president of the New Jersey Telephone Company.[18] Barnard was closely associated with the experimenters from the

Harvard Business School who conducted the Hawthorne experiments. Barnard argued that organizations by their very nature were co-operative, rather than mechanical. They were held together by good communications and the continuing desire of individuals within an organization to see it thrive. Members of an organization make contributions to it but only when they receive adequate inducements to do so. There must, therefore, be a balance between the two, and it was the task of the executive to maintain the dynamic equilibrium between the needs of the organization and the needs of the employees. Inducements include not only money but loyalty, good working conditions, and pride. Barnard gave credence to such ideas as upward communications and authority from below, rather than just hierarchical structuring. He recognized the existence of natural informal groupings in the work setting—giving support to the growing human relations school by pointing out that one cannot understand how an organization works simply by studying its organization chart, its charter, or its rules and regulations. You cannot really understand how the government of Canada works, for instance, by simply reading the Constitution. "'Learning the organization ropes' in most organizations," he claimed, "is chiefly learning who's who, what's what, why's why, of its informal society."[19]

Two other Hawthorne experimenters from 1927–1932, F.J. Roethlisberger and William Dickson, published *Management and the Worker*—the first empirical study to test for the relationship between productivity and social relations.[20] This book, containing the definitive account of the Hawthorne studies, investigated the importance of informal groups, and looked into the effects of psychological manipulation of workers and resulting productivity. They tended to confirm empirically some of Barnard's earlier intuitive assertions concerning the efficient functioning of organization and the existence of informal groups.

This work, and Elton Mayo's contributions, are key to understanding the significant findings of this school of thought. Mayo developed a general philosophy concerning problems brought about by industrial civilization. He said these problems stemmed largely from the social disorganization generated by industrialization (i.e., the weakening of the family and other traditional groups that the individual had been associated with, such as the church and community). He said this resulted in the atomization (isolation) of the individual, leading to loneliness and anxiety and a sense of defeat called *anomie* (a term coined by the French sociologist Emile Durkheim), not unlike the phenomenon of alienation described by Marx. This created a social vacuum whereby a person might be in a crowd (in the workplace or community) but still feel alone, and feel no real sense of identity with her social surroundings. Mayo contrasted this with the past social cohesion rooted in the neighbourhood, centred around small towns and villages. He hoped, through the human relations approach, to recreate the communal village of rural times within the work group of a modern factory. For Mayo, this required a new society within the workplace to replace the decaying family and social institutions of the past. It would be in this workplace that individuals would find emotional security and social satisfaction as a result of the harmony of both the formal and informal organizations. Such individual worker satisfaction, Mayo argued, rested on open communications between the ranks, participation in decision making by workers, job security, and a spirit of democracy wherein the administrator became concerned not just with the work, but with the workers.

Its most optimistic adherents felt that the application of human relations to the work setting would bring an end to industrial strife and establish a new industrial order based on co-operation and harmony. This was the philosophy that guided Mayo's work and the early stages of the human relations approach. The key question in this approach became, How do you marry harmony and efficiency?

Mayo's philosophy, plus the research findings from Hawthorne, outlined the basic principles of human relations, which can be summarized in the following five points:

1. *Social Norms.* The level of organizational effectiveness is determined by social norms. The early experiments on illumination and fatigue demonstrated that the physiological capability of the worker was not the crucial factor in productivity; neither were the principles of administration, such as the division of work. Neither factor was as important as the social norms. To put it another way, the amount of work carried out by a worker is not determined by his or her physical capacity but, rather, by the worker's social capacity.

2. *The Group.* Group standards strongly influence the behaviour of individuals in organizations. The bank wiring room experiment showed how the group could enforce a standard level of productivity on all members. The group also provided a shield against executive reprisals. In both ways the group acted as a restraint on management power.

3. *Rewards and Sanctions.* Social rewards and sanctions are the strongest motivators on the job. The Hawthorne workers responded to the respect, affection, and appeals to group loyalty provided by their fellow workers. Management's system of economic incentives was, by contrast, less powerful.

4. *Supervision.* The most effective system of supervision is created when the managers consult the group and its informal leaders in order to win acceptance of organizational objectives. Human relations specialists would advise managers to: a) be human; b) be good listeners; c) not be "bosses"; and d) give the impression that the workers are making the decisions. They believe that effective communication, supplemented by a willingness to allow workers to participate in decision making, is the key to effective supervision.

5. *Democratic Administration.* Workers will achieve their highest level of effectiveness when they are allowed to manage their own affairs with no gang boss looking over their shoulder. Re-analysis of the Hawthorne experiments revealed that improvements in productivity in the relay assembly room followed the decision of the researchers to allow the women to become a collegial, self-managing group. This point also relates to the issue of specialization: democratic administration also implies that specialization is by no means the most efficient form of division of labour.

Another theorist, psychologist Abraham Maslow, took the Hawthorne findings a step further. The experiments had challenged the scientific management view that workers were essentially economic animals motivated simply by financial incentives. Maslow argued that the notion of monetary incentives for workers was too simplistic. He argued that people were motivated by a **hierarchy of human needs**, of which there were five categories, ranging from physiological to self-actualization. People are motivated to satisfy the first categories, the most basic physiological ones, and only once those have been satisfied do they move up to the next level (see Box 3.5). Moreover, once they have satisfied the lower needs, these cease to be motivators of human behaviour. But higher needs cannot be satisfied until lower ones are met.[21] Contrary to the scientific management literature, Maslow contended that there was no "one best way" to motivate employees. Instead, management had to be sensitive to the idea that workers have a variety of needs and motivations.

Thus, the human relations school no longer saw the worker as an isolated physical being but considered her as a group member whose behaviour was greatly

---

BOX 3.5 | Maslow's Hierarchy of Human Needs

1. *Physiological*: Food, shelter, clothing, sex, sleep
2. *Safety*: Security, stability, freedom from fear
3. *Belongingness and Love*: Friendship, love, membership in some community
4. *Esteem*: Achievement, competence, independence, prestige, status
5. *Self-Actualization*: Self-fulfillment, attaining ultimate goals in life

Source: Maslow, A.H. *Motivation and Personality, Second Edition*, (New York: Harper and Row, 1970).

Maslow's hierarchy can be further subdivided into higher and lower level needs, as depicted here:

Source: www.fotosearch.com/LIF140/nu220002/.

controlled by group norms and values, and motivated by a complex hierarchy of needs and desires. The lesson, then, was that management must *not* try to destroy the informal organization on the worksite but, rather, take it into consideration and use supervisors trained in human relations to harmonize the informal norms and values with the goals of the formal organization. Ultimately, then, the human relations skills of the organization's leadership by and large set the tone of human relations. The good leader was one who was considerate of the workers' positions and problems.

Criticisms of the Human Relations School

From a historical perspective, the Hawthorne study went in a new direction—it recognized that human beings are a complex and influential factor in organizational performance. Humans are not machines, and scientific management's "one best way" had to be tempered to recognize the effect of group behaviour. Many have taken the human relations movement as a counterbalance to Taylor and scientific management, and it is true that human relations certainly filled a blind spot in the earlier school of thought. However, in reality, the distinction between the two is more academic than practical. What managers in the real world tended to do was graft the principles of human relations onto the more formal principles of scientific management, seeking to maximize production as efficiently as possible behind the facade of a humane face. After all, the Hawthorne experiments were no less interested in improving efficiency than was Taylor; they shared the common desire to find principles that would aid managers in running a more efficient shop. The "iron fist" had been replaced by the "velvet glove," but the hand still belonged, ultimately, to management.

Criticisms of human relations theory are often centred on its neglect of organizational conflict in favour of a one-sided emphasis on harmony and on the fact that, notwithstanding their apparent concern with workers' needs and motivations, human relations theorists ultimately display pro-management values. For instance, one of the Hawthorne experiments involved 300 workers who were given the job of wandering around the factory floor, listening to the complaints of other employees. But management never intended to do anything about the complaints; it simply wanted to create the impression that it actually cared about the workers. In any event, these theorists' preaching about the virtues of internal democracy and worker participation in decision making were, when viewed against reality, certainly utopian. Advising that workers be given active participation in the workings of the firm immediately gives rise to a dilemma—either they construct a pseudo-democracy where employees are given the opportunity to participate only in decisions that do not hurt management, or they propose real, meaningful participation, which in the end means that management must voluntarily cede part of its power and prerogatives over their employees. Given this situation, it becomes clear that managers would be unwilling to sacrifice their own power for such an altruistic purpose. Real participation on a large scale would imply sacrificing the predominant position of management—an unlikely development in a capitalist enterprise.

To put it another way, human relations theorists wanted to revolutionize the organization without a revolution, without touching its societal foundations.

This sort of critique found another form of expression in the work of Swiss sociologist Robert Michels, who documented the fundamentally antidemocratic tendencies of modern bureaucracies.[22] He posited the "iron law of oligarchy," in which he claimed all large organizations—political parties, corporations, religious bodies, government bureaucracies, etc.—ultimately fall under the sway of oligarchies—that is, small groups of ruling elites. Thus, a concentration of power at the top is inevitable, in Michels' view.

Other critics, such as the sociologists Clark Kerr and Abraham Siegel, challenged the notion that industrial co-operation rested primarily on the skills and understanding of industrial leaders.[23] They pointed to areas of work activity where industrial conflict was persistent and other areas where conflict was rare. Kerr and Siegel asked if differences in workplace harmony could really be accounted for in terms of the leadership skills (the human relations skills) of management. Was it that some industries adopted a human relations approach and others did not? Or were the roots of these differences in workplace conflict to be found elsewhere? Kerr and Siegel pointed to the powerful influence that job structure had on human relations on the job. For instance, the resource industries are notoriously strike-ridden because of structural factors—the jobs are dangerous, such industries are boom-and-bust, employment is often centred in small, highly class-polarized towns, etc. All of these factors contribute to the conflict-prone nature of the industry, notwithstanding the best efforts and theories of the human relations model. In some industries, the issue of technological change is vital. For the textile industry, the lack of conflict can be explained by the large numbers of unorganized marginal workers—mainly women and immigrants—who are less likely to strike. The reason for differing job structures in various working environments also has much to do with the nature of the work, and in most cases little to do with the orientation of management, whether trained in human relations or not.

Furthermore, human relations theorists have given little consideration to the effect that the worker's experience has on work behaviour, beyond the confines of the organization. It makes little sense, in this view, to talk about basic needs of all workers. If such needs exist, they are conditioned by the individual's place in the social structure or class structure outside work (e.g., white-collar versus blue-collar individuals). Thus, the human relations school is limited by its failure to look beyond the factory gates for explanations of the behaviour of humans in organizations.

Another criticism is that human relations is management-centred. Human relations theorists were as preoccupied with efficiency as were scientific management theorists. The human relations specialists simply emphasized different principles; they were concerned with informal groups and improved communications, and thought that executives should be benevolent toward employees because this would raise productivity and make workers happy. But critics found this view superficial and irrelevant to workers' real needs.

For instance, the position of Mayo and other human relations theorists was that unions and collective bargaining emphasized the divisions between workers and management, preventing effective communication and increasing the kind of conflict that bred anomie. That there was a natural community of interests between worker and management was not substantiated by the human relations specialists, according to the critics. In addition, the point that financial incentives were not all that important in motivating workers was challenged; after all, wages and benefits are usually at the heart of collective bargaining disputes. These criticisms undermined the human relations approach to a certain extent, although this approach continues to have an influential legacy in both private and public organizations.

Other Theoretical Approaches

Our survey of organization theory, while covering a lot of ground, cannot of course be comprehensive. To round out this overview, though, we will finish with a brief sample of other modern theoretical approaches.

One important attempt to develop a more sophisticated understanding of management styles utilizing both the structuralist and humanist frameworks is found in the work of Douglas McGregor, an American management scholar, who crafted what he called the **"Theory X and Theory Y"** explanations of organizational behaviour. In an article entitled "The Human Side of Enterprise" McGregor constructed a two-part typology, contrasting structuralist and humanist approaches (see Box 3.6).

Among the post–Second World War developments in organization theory, **systems theory** established itself as important. We might credit the origins of systems theory to the great English poet John Donne (1572–1631), who famously wrote that "No man is an Island, entire of itself;/ every man is a piece of the Continent,/ a part of the main." In this eloquent statement of our interconnectedness, Donne was laying the groundwork for modern social science. He also wrote "Any man's death diminishes me because/ I am involved in mankind; And therefore/ never send to know for whom the bell tolls;/ it tolls for thee," suggesting the extent to which we are collectively invested in a human social system.[24]

Systems theory explains organizations as *open systems* and methodologically studies those systems through the application of computers, statistical analysis, information systems, and quantitative measurement. These techniques attracted the attention of theorists who expressed a confidence in the same kind of rationality espoused generations earlier by structuralist theorists. The central work in this area was by Daniel Katz and Robert Khan, who wrote *The Social Psychology of Organizations* in 1966.[25] This was followed in 1967 by the publication of *Organizations in Action* by James D. Thompson.[26]

Systems theory sees organizations as made up of complex and dynamic interconnected elements: e.g., inputs, processes, outputs, and a feedback loop, whereby outputs re-enter the system as new inputs. This approach relied on the

Box 3.6	Theory X and Theory Y

Theory X	Theory Y
Management is responsible for organizing the elements of productive enterprise—money, materials, equipment, people—in the interest of economic ends.	Management is responsible for organizing the elements of productive enterprise—money, materials, equipment, people—in the interest of economic ends.
With respect to people, this is a process of directing their efforts, motivating them, controlling their actions, modifying their behaviour to fit the needs of the organization.	People are *not* by nature passive or resistant to organizational needs. They have become so as a result of experience in organizations.
Without the active intervention by management, people would be passive—even resistant—to organizational needs. They must, therefore, be persuaded, rewarded, punished, controlled—their activities must be directed. This is management's task. We often sum it up by saying that management consists of getting things done through other people.	The motivation, the potential for development, the capacity for assuming responsibility, the readiness to direct behaviour toward organizational goals are all present in people. Management does not put them there. It is a responsibility of management to make it possible for people to recognize and develop these human characteristics for themselves.
The average man is by nature indolent—he works as little as possible.	The essential task of management is to arrange organizational conditions and methods of operation so that people can achieve their own goals *best* by directing *their* own efforts toward organizational objectives.
He lacks ambition, dislikes responsibility, prefers to be led.	
He is inherently self-centred, indifferent to organizational needs.	
He is by nature resistant to change.	
He is gullible, not very bright, the ready dupe of the charlatan and the demagogue.	

Source: Douglas Murray McGregor, "The Human Side of Enterprise," in J. Steven Ott, Sandra J. Parkes, and Richard B. Simpson, eds. *Classic Readings in Organizational Behavior. Third Edition*, (Toronto: Nelson Thomson, 2003): 163–68.

metaphor of the organization as an organism. To survive, any organism must seek inputs from its environment (food, for instance, or material for shelter), which it then converts into outputs (energy or housing). Those outputs in turn feed back to the organism, helping it in its ongoing quest for more inputs. In organizational terms—say, in a corporation—a business needs labour, capital, knowledge, and technology (inputs), which are converted into finished products for sale (outputs), which generates cash to purchase more inputs (feedback). There are elements in this process that are knowable and understandable, but there are also others whose presence and impact is hard to discern. Thus, when a manager makes a decision, she sets in motion unanticipated consequences due to the dynamic, multidimensional, and interconnected nature of the organization as a whole. Systems theorists sought to study this by focusing on decision-making processes, the flow of information through the system, and the measure and degree of controls present in it. They noted the ability of an organization to adapt in order to keep functioning, mainly by storing more inputs than it immediately needs to survive so that it can draw on them in hard times or crises.

The adaptability of an organization gained attention through theorists' work in the field of *cybernetics*, a term derived from the Greek word for "steersman"; as applied to organizations it means "the multidisciplinary study of the structures and functions of control and information processing systems in animals and machines. The basic concept behind cybernetics is self-regulation—through biological, social, or technological systems that can identify problems, do something about them, and then receive feedback to adjust themselves automatically."[27]

But another stream of thought within systems theory, known as **contingency theory**, suggests that there are no absolutes or universal rules that apply to all organizations in all circumstances. It argues ". . . the effectiveness of an organizational action (for example, a decision) is viewed as dependent upon the relationship between the element in question and all other aspects of the system— at the particular moment."[28] Those elements most importantly include the environment of the organization, its technology, and its size. Thus, all the actors with which the organization may interact—clients, customers, competitors, suppliers, regulators, etc.—as well as its technological systems and capabilities, and its size (i.e., small, and relatively intimate contact between the top, middle, and bottom layers; or large and dispersed), are all contingent factors affecting success and failure. Everything depends on (is contingent upon) the situation at hand. This view places a large emphasis on an organization's ability to develop rapid and accurate information systems to successfully adapt.

Systems theory ran into criticisms by the 1970s, however. In particular, human relations theorists argued that the systems theory model paid inadequate attention to issues such as the negative role of computers and information technology in dominating human organizations; the impact of centralized decision making; and the freedom of individuals within organizations to escape the tyranny of technological imperatives. Methodological problems arose as well. Faith in computer analysis, econometric modelling, and statistical analysis often proved misplaced when analyses of organizations revealed outcomes different from those predicted by the model. In Canada, cybernetics and systems theory received the imprimatur of Prime Minister Trudeau and his government, which attempted to initiate reforms built on the inherent rationalism of the approach.[29] But repeated frustrations led to its virtual abandonment by the 1980s. The standard diagrammatic depiction of systems theory as applied to the Canadian government is captured in Figure 3.2, which shows a model of the political system that contains the essential elements of inputs, process, and outputs feeding back into the inputs.

One of the offspring of systems and contingency theory is *population ecology theory*. Theorists working in this area view organizations as organisms with a life cycle of birth, growth, and death. They also note the diversity of

FIGURE 3.2   A Model of the Political System

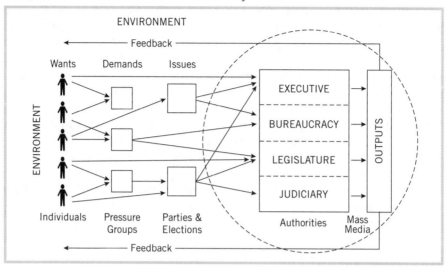

organizational types that exist. In these regards they owe an intellectual debt of gratitude to Darwinism, since much of their approach can be likened to evolution theory. Competition for scarce resources among populations, the need to reproduce, and survival of the fittest are all concepts borrowed from the natural sciences and applied to organizations. Population ecology theory also pays attention to the different environments within which organizations exist and attempts to understand the impact of environment on organizational form and durability. The theory also argues that a process of natural selection is at work among organizations. Those that adapt, thrive; those that remain static, die. At a more subtle level, this theory suggests that decision making by managers does not in itself lead to adaptation. Instead, the environment itself selects organizational forms (consistent with the process of natural selection in the animal world).[30]

As with the other theoretical models outlined above, population ecology has had its share of critics, who began with questioning the applicability of models from the natural sciences to organization theory. Critics also pointed out the methodological difficulties inherent in tracing causal factors for the success and failure of organizations, which do not lend themselves to easy identification or measurement. Still, the population ecology approach added to the diversity of organization theory and offers yet another way of thinking about how organizations function.

Given the diversity of approaches outlined (and again, this is not a comprehensive overview), students of public administration may be forgiven for feeling a little overwhelmed. One way of sorting through the morass of approaches is provided by management professor Gareth Morgan. He developed a typology of different "images" of organizations—a classification system of several different metaphors that can be used to describe the attributes of organizations. He suggests we can classify organizations as, among other things, machines, organisms, brains, cultures, and instruments of domination.[31] If you give some consideration to the theories and theorists studied here, you should be able to make some sense of them in terms of this template. For instance, it is clear that some theorists, like Weber and Taylor, undertake their study of organizations while regarding them as machines, as we noted. The work of the human relations school can be seen to privilege the view of organizations as organisms, as can systems, contingency, and population ecology theories. Proponents of cybernetics and similar models see organizations as brains. Marx and, to some extent, Weber view organizations as instruments of domination. In short, a rich and varied set of perspectives has been brought to bear on our understanding of organizations.

But what about Canadian public administration more specifically? How have these varied approaches affected the organization of the public sector in Canada? This is the concern of the next chapter.

WHAT YOU HAVE LEARNED

This chapter has focused on the theory of public administration. As such, it has sought to elucidate the ideas behind that ubiquitous presence of contemporary life—the modern organization. It is important, in studying public administration, to understand the theoretical premises upon which organizations are constructed. It is also important to appreciate that organization theory crosses from the private to the public sector and back again. This makes for some difficulty in drawing conclusions and in constructing organizations, since, as you saw in chapter 1, the public and private sectors are two quite different beasts. Nonetheless, theoreticians tell us that the study of one aids us in the understanding of the other. Hence, this examination of the theoretical literature reveals the interrelationship between the dominant ideas that animate our understanding of both sectors.

But another point about organization theory needs to be emphasized. It should be obvious to you by now that no one theory explains all there is to know about organizations. You should, therefore, be considering the utility of particular theories by subjecting them to a series of questions:

■ What aspects of organizational reality does a given theory purport to explain? Is it concerned with the methods managers use to maximize efficiency, or with the well-being of workers and their role in decision making?

■ What level of analysis is the theory aimed at? Individuals within organizations? Parts of organizations? The whole organization? The society within which the organization is located? Or some combination of all of these?

■ What conception of human nature underlies the theory? We saw that Taylor assumed people were lazy and indolent unless motivated by personal monetary gain. But Maslow felt that humans were motivated by a much more complex set of factors. What does this tell us about the way each theorist viewed human nature?

■ Does the theory appear to make sense of what actually goes on in the real world of organizations? Does it explain only the workings of private sector organizations, or is it applicable to the public sector as well?

■ Does the theory make sense in light of your own knowledge and experience?

This is not a comprehensive list of questions but it should, nonetheless, give you some idea of the nature and utility of the theoretical aspects of public administration as it has been affected by organization theory.

Key Words and Concepts

Karl Marx (64)	time and motion studies (79)
class conflict (64)	POSDCORB (81)
alienation (64)	division of labour (82)
hierarchy (65)	humanist theory (83)
autonomy (65)	Hawthorne experiments (84)
accumulation (67)	informal group (86)
legitimation (67)	hierarchy of human needs (89)
Max Weber (68)	theory X and theory Y (92)
span of control (75)	systems theory (92)
structuralist theories (77)	contingency theory (94)
scientific management (77)	

Review Questions

This chapter was divided into five sections, each of which addressed key issues regarding theoretical approaches to understanding organizations within public administration. You should now be able to answer the questions associated with each.

1. Perspectives on Bureaucratic Organization

The development of bureaucratic organizations is central to public administration. This section noted the contribution of business management thinking and its uneasy marriage with public sector values and concerns, asking the following questions: What are the main concerns of organization theory? What are the origins of organization theory? What contesting values underlie the development of theories of public administration?

2. The Classic Theorists

Karl Marx and Max Weber are two thinkers whose contributions to understanding organizations and bureaucracy, though widely divergent, are the basis for much subsequent theorizing. The section examined the strengths and weaknesses of their ideas and asked, What impact have the classic theories and theorists had on public administration? What are the strengths and weaknesses of their respective theories?

3. Structuralist Theories

The scientific management approach, pioneered by F.W. Taylor, arose in response to the need to improve the efficiency of large-scale modern organizations, as well as the conditions of those who worked in these structures. This led us to ask the following: What types of debates have ensued over the nature and form of organization in both the private and the public sectors? What exactly were these theoretical innovations meant to accomplish when translated into practice?

4. Humanist Theories

This school of thought arose in response to the dehumanizing and alienating aspects of structuralist approaches to organizational management. But it also was ultimately concerned with improving the efficiency of organizations, though with a "human" face. This section asked, How did the human relations approach originate? How did it differ from structuralism, and what impact did it have? Finally, we also briefly canvassed other theories, asking, What are some of the offshoots of the classic, structuralist, and humanist theoretical schools?

5. Other Theoretical Approaches

This section canvasses a handful of other theoretical approaches arising out of the work of earlier schools of thought. It asks, What other theoretical approaches have emerged? How have they drawn upon theories that went before and/or innovated new approaches to understanding public administration?

Weblinks

Marx/Engels Archive
www.marxists.org

Max Weber
www.faculty.rsu.edu/~felwell/Theorists/Weber/Whome.htm

Dead Sociologists Index
http://media.pfeiffer.edu/lridener/DSS

F.W. Taylor
http://attila.stevens-tech.edu/~rdowns

Further Reading

1. Perspectives on Bureaucratic Organization

Denhardt, Robert B. *Theories of Public Organization: Fourth Edition.* Toronto: Nelson Thomson, 2004.

2. The Classic Theorists

Marx, Karl. "Contribution to the Critique of Hegel's *Philosophy of Right,*" in Robert C. Tucker, ed. *The Marx-Engels Reader. Second Edition.* New York: Norton, 1978.

Merton, Robert K. "Bureaucratic Structure and Personality," in Jay M. Shafritz and J. Steven Ott, eds. *Classics of Organization Theory. Fifth Edition*. Belmont, California: Wadsworth Publishing, 1999: 103–11.

Weber, Max. "Bureaucracy," in Jay M. Shafritz and J. Steven Ott, eds. *Classics of Organization Theory. Fifth Edition*. Belmont, California: Wadsworth Publishing, 1999: 73–78.

3. Structuralist Theories

Barnard, Chester. "Informal Organizations and Their Relation to Formal Organization," in Jay M. Shafritz and Albert C. Hyde, eds. *Classics of Public Administration. Third Edition*. Pacific Grove, California: Brooks/Cole Publishing, 1992: 96–100.

Gulick, Luther. "Notes on the Theory of Organization," in Jay M. Shafritz and J. Steven Ott, eds. *Classics of Organization Theory. Fifth Edition*. Belmont, California: Wadsworth Publishing, 1999: 79–87.

Simon, Herbert. "The Proverbs of Administration," in Jay M. Shafritz and Albert C. Hyde, eds. *Classics of Public Administration. Third Edition*. Pacific Grove, California: Brooks/Cole Publishing, 1992: 150–65.

Taylor, Frederick W. "Scientific Management," in Jay M. Shafritz and J. Steven Ott, eds. *Classics of Organization Theory. Fifth Edition*. Belmont, California: Wadsworth Publishing, 1999: 61–72.

4. Humanist Theories

Follett, Mary Parker. "The Giving of Orders," in J. Steven Ott, Sandra J. Parkes and Richard B. Simpson, eds. *Classic Readings in Organizational Behavior. Third Edition*. Toronto: Nelson Thomson, 2003: 42–47.

Maslow, A.H. "A Theory of Human Motivation," in Jay M. Shafritz and J. Steven Ott, eds. *Classics of Organization Theory. Fifth Edition*. Belmont, California: Wadsworth Publishing, 1999: 167–78.

Mayo, Elton. *The Human Problems of an Industrial Civilization*. New York: The Viking Press, 1960.

5. Other Theoretical Perspectives

Mills, Albert J., Tony Simmons and Jean Helms Mills. *Reading Organization Theory: A Critical Approach to the Study of Organizational Behaviour and Structure*. Third Edition. Toronto: Garamond, 2005.

Endnotes

1. See Jay M. Shafritz and J. Steven Ott, eds. *Classics of Organization Theory: Fifth Edition*, (Belmont: Wadsworth, 2001).

2. Robert B. Denhardt, *Theories of Public Organization*, (Toronto: Nelson Thomson, 2004): 1.

3. John Porter, *The Vertical Mosaic: An Analysis of Social Class and Power in Canada*, (Toronto: University of Toronto Press, 1965).

4. Jay M. Shafritz and Albert C. Hyde, eds. *Classics of Public Administration, Third Edition*, (Pacific Grove, California: Brooks/Cole Publishing, 1992): 40.

5. See H.H. Gerth and C. Wright Mills, eds. *From Max Weber: Essays in Sociology*, (New York: Oxford University Press, 1946): 196–244.

6. Robert F. Adie and Paul G. Thomas, *Canadian Public Administration: Problematical Perspectives, Second Edition*, (Scarborough: Prentice-Hall, 1987): 18.

7. S.M. Lipset, *Agrarian Socialism*, (Berkeley: University of California Press, 1950). For an insider's views on the CCF experience in government, see A.W. Johnson, *Dream No Little Dreams: A Biography of the Douglas Government, 1944–1961*, (Toronto: University of Toronto Press, 2004).

8. This example is cited in Howard E. McCurdy, *Public Administration: A Synthesis*, (Menlo Park, California: Cummings Publishers, 1977).

9. See Robert K. Merton, *Social Theory and Social Structure*, (New York: The Free Press, 1957).

10. Merton's observations on the cold, impersonal characteristic of welfare officers were first made in 1940. The persistence of these attitudes over time is striking, though. See "The Dark Side," *St. John's Evening Telegram,* 1973. Cited in Albert J. Mills and Tony Simmons, *Reading Organization Theory: A Critical Approach,* (Toronto: Garamond, 1999): 41–42.

11. See Alvin Gouldner, *Patterns of Industrial Bureaucracy,* (New York: The Free Press, 1954), and Victor A. Thompson, *Modern Organization,* (New York: Alfred A. Knopf, 1961).

12. Frank J. Goodnow, *Politics and Administration: A Study in Government,* (New York: Russell and Russell, 1900).

13. See Herbert A. Simon, "The Proverbs of Administration," in Shafritz and Hyde, eds. *Classics of Public Administration,* (1992): 150–65; and Herbert A. Simon, *Administrative Behaviour,* (New York: The Free Press, 1954).

14. See Luther Gulick and L. Urwick, eds. *Papers on the Science of Administration,* (New York: Augustus M. Kelly Publishers, 1937).

15. Henri Fayol, *General and Industrial Management*, (London: Pitman, 1971). Translated by Constance Storrs.

16. Mary Parker Follett, "The Giving of Orders," in J. Steven Ott, Sandra J. Parkes and Richard B. Simpson, eds. *Classic Readings in Organizational Behavior. Third Edition*, (Toronto: Nelson Thomson, 2003): 42–7.

17. See Elton Mayo, *The Human Problems of an Industrial Civilization,* (New York: The Viking Press, 1960). The first five chapters of this book provide short summaries of some of the Hawthorne experiments.

18. Chester Barnard, *The Functions of the Executive,* (Cambridge, Massachusetts: Harvard University Press, 1938).

19. Chester Barnard, "Informal Organizations and Their Relation to Formal Organization," cited in Shafritz and Hyde, eds. *Classics of Public Administration,* (1992): 99.

20. F.J. Roethlisberger and William J. Dickson, *Management and the Worker,* (Cambridge, Massachusetts: Harvard University Press, 1939).

21. A.H. Maslow, "A Theory of Human Motivation," in Shafritz and Hyde, eds. *Classics of Public Administration,* (1992): 129–37.

22. Robert Michels, *Political Parties: a Sociological Study of the Oligarchical Tendencies of Modern Democracy*, (New York: Collier, 1962).Translated by Edan and Cedar Paul.

23. See Clark Kerr et al. *Industrialism and Industrial Man: The Problems of Labour and Management in Economic Growth, Second Edition,* (Harmondsworth, England: Penguin Books, 1973); and Albert J. Mills, Tony Simmons and Jean Helms Mills, *Reading Organization Theory: A Critical Approach to the Study of Organizational Behaviour and Structure. Third Edition,* (Toronto: Garamond, 2005).

24. See Jay M. Shafritz, Karen S. Layne and Christopher P. Borick, eds. *Classics of Public Policy,* (New York: Pearson Longman, 2005): 3.

25. Daniel Katz and Robert Khan, *The Social Psychology of Organizations*, (New York: Wiley, 1966).

26. James D. Thompson, *Organization in Action,* (New York: McGraw-Hill, 1967).

27. Jay M. Shafritz and J. Steven Ott, eds. *Classics of Organization Theory: Fourth Edition*, (Fort Worth: Harcourt Brace College Publishers, 1996): 255.

28. Shafritz and Ott, eds. *Classics of Organization Theory*, (1996): 258.

29. See Peter Aucoin, "Organizational Change in the Machinery of Canadian Government: From Rational Management to Brokerage Politics," *Canadian Journal of Political Science*, 29, 1 (March, 1986): 3–27.

30. See Michael Hannan and John Freeman, "The Population Ecology of Organizations," *American Journal of Sociology*, 82 (1977): 929–64.

31. Gareth Morgan, *Images of Organization: Second Edition*, (Thousand Oaks, California: Sage Publications, 1997). Morgan also uses the metaphors of organizations as political systems, psychic prisons, and unfolding logics of change.

Chapter 4

Organization Theory *and* Canadian Public Administration

WHAT YOU WILL LEARN

One notable characteristic of the theorists surveyed thus far is that few are Canadian. Indeed, the United States and Europe (especially Britain and Germany) have proven most influential in the spread of ideas about public administration. We will now assess in turn the impact of each of the major schools of thought on Canadian public administration. By the end of the chapter, you will be able to answer the following questions:

■ How influential have Marx, Weber, and the other theorists been in the Canadian context?

■ In what ways have Canadian thinkers adopted their ideas or developed their own counterpoints to those ideas?

■ Are there concrete instances of the impact of their thinking on the form and structure of the public sector?

■ How effective have applications of participatory management and other contemporary theories been in Canada?

■ What is the New Public Management, and how has it influenced thinking about recent reforms in Canadian public administration?

This chapter looks at these issues in two sections.

1. The Impact of Organization Theory

The practice of public administration in Canada is informed by the large international body of theoretical literature, going right back to the origins of the field. But exactly how inspirational have the classic, structuralist, and humanist thinkers been? The answer is not easy, for their influence has sometimes been subtle. But there are also ways in which the work of particular individuals and schools of thought has shaped both the practice and theory of Canadian public administration, which we elucidate in this section.

2. Contemporary Developments

This section considers the most recent developments in the theory and practice of public administration in Canada in light of the perspectives sketched out in chapter 3. The dynamism of the field should be evident to you as the ongoing evolution of theoretical approaches is canvassed.

The Impact of Organization Theory

Among the classic thinkers, Marx's critique of bureaucracy has shed light on how the power structures in society affect democracy and governing. For instance, his assertion that class is the most important division in society has important implications for who occupies decision-making posts in the political and bureaucratic realm. Some research in Canada points to a dominant **elite** representing, directly or indirectly, the capitalist class, whose dominance is reinforced through a network of social, economic, and political ties. They hang out at the same exclusive clubs; send their children to the same private schools; sit on the same boards of directors of major corporations; are wealthy and well educated; and are generally an ethnically and religiously homogeneous group historically, tending to be white, Anglo-Saxon male Protestants (if they are English) or Catholics (if they are French).[1]

This elite dominates the top positions in government, namely senior public servants and politicians, who generally act in the best interests of their own class. For instance, many prime ministers and Cabinet ministers were first corporate lawyers, business persons, and directors of important corporations.[2] Many members of the Canadian Senate sit on the boards of major corporations or have close connections to the corporate elite.[3] Moreover, there is a good deal of mobility among corporate, political, and bureaucratic careers.

Marxist theory suggests that the organizations of the state are designed to perpetuate this class's power and influence. On one level, the bureaucracy is a cold, uninviting and alienating place that is difficult to penetrate and understand. This tends to thwart ordinary citizens, most of the time, in questioning the government's actions and also permits those in control of the bureaucracy's complicated mechanisms to use them for their own ends. But the state is not solely organized for the purpose of the elite. This is too simplistic an assertion. Rather, the state is set up so that most of the time it acts in the long-term interests of the capitalist class. There are many debates among Marxist scholars about exactly how this process works, as well as criticisms of the theory by non-Marxists.

As for Weber, there is no doubt that his theories have been profoundly influential in Canadian public administration. For instance, the 1918 reforms to the public service (see chapter 1) very strongly reflect a Weberian sensibility. Those reforms introduced the concept of merit into the public service and entrenched hierarchy, a job classification system, professionalism, competitive exams, etc.

The intent—true to Weber's ideas—was to put the Canadian public service on a more rational basis and operate according to prescribed rules and regulations.

Taylor's scientific management approach has also been influential. Taylor's major contribution was, first, the principle that work ought to be divided up so as to take maximum advantage of employees' skills. The assembly line is the most obvious application of this principle in the private sector. In the public sector, elaborate job classification schemes have existed at least since the 1918 Civil Service Act. The second principle is that of **homogeneity**, also called **unity of direction**, which asserts that similar activities ought to be grouped together in the same unit under a single supervisor and a single plan. In public administration, then, those things related to health were organized under one department, to education under another, etc. Moreover, within departments, there is a further division of labour, with scientists grouped in one unit, policy analysts in another, clerical staff in yet another, and so on, for purposes of job function, promotion, and wages.

Furthermore, scientific management attempted to replace imprecise job criteria based on workers' personal characteristics (i.e., patronage) with the specification of job duties and requirements (i.e., merit). Public service recruits were expected to display only those "scientific qualities" that made them fit for the job. This was reflected in the Civil Service Reform Act of 1918, which was bent on eliminating all irrelevant considerations in the hiring of government workers. Thus, in Canadian public administration the impact of scientific management was felt fairly early, and was reflected in the concerns about efficiency and economy within the public service, giving rise to the reforms of 1918.

The reforms created a Civil Service Commission responsible, in part, for choosing government personnel based on scientific principles, and an elaborate classification scheme for government workers. What resulted, in short, was a system of scientific management that could satisfy the rising demand for the elimination of patronage and more efficient administration in government. Analysis of the component elements of jobs was inspired by the example of scientific management; once these were analyzed, examinations could be devised to determine which candidates were best qualified to fill specific positions. At the same time, development of new methods of uniform cost accounting necessitated a uniform job terminology, which would allow the legislature to more efficiently control the finances of the public service.

Having said all this, note that the many units of organization within the complex machinery of government are structured in a variety of ways. Some are close to the models set out by Weber or Taylor. The Canadian army, for example, or the fire and police services come closest to Weber's model. Still others reflect scientific management. For instance, in the Canada Revenue Agency, large numbers of employees work in data processing centres that are much like large factories, and there is strong pressure on employees to conform to the organization's rules and regulations to maximize the efficient processing of tax returns and other financial information. This type of organization is rigidly structured, with rules emanating from the top downward, and little attempt is made to seek employee input into management decisions. But not all government departments are best run in this way. For example, in some departments the workplaces are scattered throughout the country in small, regional offices, with a good deal of local control and initiative. Control is decentralized, and reporting systems are less hierarchical. Input from below is encouraged because front-line employees often have a better idea of what works than their seniors in distant Ottawa do.[4] So these organizations reflect some aspects of the human relations approach.

The point here is to ask yourself, Does any one model explain all there is to know and understand, given the complexity of modern government in Canada? Is there homogeneity in organizational types across government departments? Within departments? Are there some government organizations that display two or more of the models under consideration simultaneously?

Overall, the human relations school has been less successful in seeing its perspective adopted in Canadian public administration. You will recall that human relations theorists argued that organizations would produce the best work environments when they implemented non-routinized tasks, recognized the goals of their employees, decentralized decision making, and worked against a hierarchical decision-making structure. But in Canada, there seems to be little overt evidence that public administration was profoundly influenced by human relations; government in this country has persistently been characterized by rigid hierarchies, inflexible job classification structures, and other elements more reminiscent of Weber and of scientific management.

One exception in Canada is that decentralization became a major theme in government. In 1965, the Royal Commission on Government Organization (the Glassco Commission) pushed decentralization with the catchphrase "let the managers manage." Decentralization was aimed at securing employees' participation and commitment and was seen as a tool for reducing delays and red tape in decision making. Of course, politicians saw decentralization as aiding certain political objectives, and this was probably a greater motivation to its implementation than was human relations theory *per se*. But the human relations school did sensitize the government and public to its uses in curbing excess bureaucracy. Decentralization also aided in introducing freedom of information legislation and creating specialized government offices motivated to improve democracy within bureaucracies. Yet, 30 years after Glassco, another review of public administration practices entitled part of its report "Let the Managers Manage." Have we really gotten anywhere?

Contemporary Developments

Most recently, organization theory evolved further into a set of concepts that can loosely be referred to as **participatory management**. The general goal was to go beyond the platitudes of human relations theorists and implement genuine worker participation in decision making in the workplace. Participatory management was premised on the view that there is an innate tension in the work organization and that this is natural and unavoidable; however, such tension can be controlled and directed. Many different approaches exist under the broad heading of participatory management, including **Management by Objectives (MBO)**, **Organization Development (OD)**, and **Total Quality Management (TQM)**. But alongside participatory management, another set of developments has emerged. This is the New Public Management (NPM) approach, which incorporates private sector principles and techniques in a much more deliberate and systematic manner than has been the case in the past. We will look briefly at some trends in participatory management before turning our attention finally to the NPM.

Participatory Management

Management by Objectives (MBO) is derived from a theory by Peter Drucker, founder of MBO, that stood Weber's basic argument on its head.[5] MBO is centred on the notion that specialization and hierarchy can be overemphasized at the expense of the organization's overall efficiency. If you subdivide an organization into numerous specialized agencies, each with its own functions, the actions of one agency may conflict with the goals of another. For instance, the human resources department may require savings to be realized by eliminating employees to reduce payroll costs. But other departments may already be stretched to the limit in terms of personnel. Thus, if human resources does its job well, other parts of the organization may suffer. The problem, then, according to Drucker, is the inability of the organization's specialized parts to focus on the overall goals of the whole. The solution is MBO. While there is little agreement over the precise means of implementing MBO, several steps can be identified:

1. Consultation between top managers and their immediate subordinates to determine the organization's broad goals.
2. Preparation of a statement by top management of the overall results expected in the upcoming year.
3. Meeting between top managers and their subordinates to parcel out the responsibility for these results to individual organizational units. This task is subdivided by focusing on a) routine objectives; b) problem-solving objectives; and c) innovative objectives.
4. Repetition of the process of parceling out the responsibilities (outlined in step 3) throughout the organization.
5. Management review of this plan for consistency and to ensure that the desired goals are met.
6. Year-end comprehensive review.[6]

Some critics claim that MBO is a system that only pretends to offer greater participation in decision making, but that ultimately leaves control in the hands of senior management. Any participation in decision making that does take place is not really meaningful. Another problem is that establishing clear and measurable objectives is often difficult to do, especially in public administration (as was suggested earlier in chapter 1). Still, MBO was used in many organizations with varying degrees of success.

Organization Development (OD) is an approach traceable ultimately to the Hawthorne studies but more directly to a movement that started in the 1940s known as sensitivity training. American Kurt Lewin and his associates began conducting training workshops to improve racial relations and community leadership in a Connecticut town.[7] Originally aimed at individual development and growth, the workshops gradually expanded their focus to group organizational dynamics. The groups became a place where organization members learned to communicate their feelings and develop strategies around increasing organizational effectiveness through interpersonal communications. Gradually, the methodology expanded to include various research techniques, such as employee surveys and other feedback techniques in order to develop an action research model of organizational change (see Box 4.1).

BOX 4.1 **Organization Development Action Research**

According to Shafritz et al.:

The action research model is a process for identifying needs for organizational improvement through the use of external consultation but also through fostering psychological ownership of problems and solutions by organizational members. Briefly, action research involves the following:

1. *Collecting organizational diagnostic data (ascertaining the problem), usually either through written questionnaires or interviews.*

2. *Systematically feeding back information to the organization members who provided input.*

3. *Discussing what the information means to members and its implications for the organization in order to be certain if the "diagnosis" is accurate and to generate psychological ownership of the need for actions to improve the situation.*

4. *Jointly developing an improvement plan, using both the consultant's knowledge and skills and members' insider perspective.*

5. *Repeating all of the preceding as needed.*

Source: See Jay M. Shafritz, E.W. Russell and Christopher P. Borick, *Introducing Public Administration. Fifth Edition*, (New York: Pearson Longman, 2007): 271.

OD begins with the premise that organizations become rigid and inflexible over time, thus responding to changed conditions becomes difficult, if not impossible. The purpose of OD is to identify rigidities and prepare the organization to be flexible enough to adjust to changes in the broader environment before crisis or collapse occurs. Lewin's prescription saw development as a process of unfreezing, change, and refreezing. OD requires recognizing a culture or history within every organization that is often an impediment to positive reform, and then developing strategies to overcome that culture or history. Dysfunctional organizational behaviour is identified, and the organization is encouraged to "unlearn" that behaviour. For instance, objections to new innovations are often framed this way: "We tried something like that before, and it didn't work." This reflects the organization's historical memory but ignores that circumstances may have changed, making the suggested reforms more applicable. Then the reforms needed are identified and implemented. Finally, new behaviours are instituted to prevent the organization from slipping back into its old dysfunctional ways.

Total Quality Management (TQM) is an approach to participatory management that began to emerge in the 1980s, partly as an outgrowth of OD and partly as a response to Japanese management techniques. It is associated with the work of W. Edwards Deming, who taught his techniques to Japanese business leaders, especially in the automobile industry, after the Second World War.[8] In particular, the auto industry in Japan embraced TQM. In the American model, production focused on maximizing output and then employing a separate quality control group to detect and repair problems after the fact. The Japanese approach was to make each employee responsible for the quality of his segment of the work. Thus, while it might take longer to build a car, the overall quality was better, resulting in cost savings for the organization in the longer term, since repair and recalls were fewer. The guiding principle of TQM is "Get it right the first time." Therefore, quality control is no longer considered a discrete function of part of the organization but, rather, an integral part of what the entire organization does.

In Canadian public administration, these ideas were instituted by some governments starting in the mid-1970s with varying degrees of success. For instance, the federal department of Energy, Mines, and Resources; the Office of the Auditor General; and the department of Industry, Science, and Technology all adopted TQM. Committee structures were put in place, composed of both management and elected worker representatives. But most of these experiments failed, due primarily to the imbalance of power between management and workers, which was reinforced by the public service's rigid job classification system, which simply could not be overcome.

Attempts to institute participatory management in the Canadian public service have run into some serious roadblocks. The entrenched hierarchical system reflective of Weberian and Taylorist models has proven remarkably resistant to change. Even with the best of intentions, efforts to increase the participation of workers in decision-making structures have frequently floundered on the rocks of rigid job classification systems, rules and regulations, and hierarchy.

Moreover, approaches like OD encounter a set of problems unique to public administration—namely, that top management is fragmented.[9] It consists of both political and administrative executives, not to mention legislative oversight bodies, and outside actors like the media and the public, who may all influence key decision-makers directly and indirectly. Entrenched interests may resist the type of dynamic change required of OD, while internal competition, turf wars, and petty jealousies may intrude across levels of leadership rooted in political and administrative differences.

Another school of thought emerging in the 1960s and 1970s in American public administration asserted the "end of bureaucracy," whereby the Weberian model would be gradually supplanted by "more democratic, more flexible, though more complex, forms of large-scale organizations" which American administrative historian Dwight Waldo termed "postbureaucratic."[10] In place of assessing employees according to rank and status, they would be evaluated more flexibly according to competence; organizational charts would give way to project groups. Hierarchical lines of authority would give way to more democratic and participatory models. Moreover, presaging New Public Management (NPM), a call emerged for the "reinvention of government." A more strategic orientation geared to the deployment of increasingly scarce resources caused officials and theorists alike to look to changing expectations and values as well as to new structures and processes within government. Adaptivity was welcomed, even at the cost of morale and actual positions. Flattening of hierarchies, teamwork, processes of continuous learning, and a leadership style that excelled at articulating a vision rather than just giving orders was called for. The clearest expression of these new approaches in the federal government was found in a wide-scale review of the federal public service called *Public Service 2000* (discussed further in chapter 10), whose recommendations included "improved 'service to the public' . . . and an environment where 'public servants will be empowered and encouraged to decide themselves how best to use the resources made available to them in order to get the job done in the most efficient manner.'"[11] Some of the purported changes to Canadian public administration in recent years are shown in Table 4.1. Shields and Evans contrast traditional bureaucratic structures with the main features of newer models.[12] Following from trends in private sector management toward "virtual" forms of corporate organization, the view emerged that large, hierarchically and vertically integrated corporations and organizations were too slow and cumbersome in responding to customer demands under conditions of enhanced competitiveness brought on by globalization. As a consequence, attempts were made to flatten the organizational pyramid, create relatively autonomous operating units, and maximize the use of modern technologies to complete projects through teams that would come together for a project, disband upon its completion, and reform with other personnel for subsequent tasks.

TABLE 4.1   Traditional Bureaucratic Organizations

Traditional Bureaucratic Organizations	The New Public Sector Organization
A. Hierarchy and Central Command	**Flattened and Decentralized Organization and Decision-Making**
B. Rule-Governed and Upward Accountability	**Results-Centred** • achievement of goals rather than process is what counts
C. Static/Status Quo • all change is initiated and driven from above • emphasis given to continuity over continuous change	**Change-Driven High Performance Organizations** • risk-taking, continuous improvement and innovation are encouraged from all levels of the organization
D. Standardized Citizen's Right to Public Services • emphasis on universal legal rights to services	**Client-Focused** • emphasis upon individual customer satisfaction and service to selective client groups • clients as taxpayers
E. Tayloristic-Style Operating Structure	**Empowering Employees** • use of new human resource strategies such as Total Quality Management
F. Process-Driven Organization • static tasks, hierarchical institution, rigidly specified job categories	**The Learning Organization** • workforce is multiskilled • a learning and adapting environment
G. Fordist Production System • workforce based upon economies of scale, i.e., large workforce involved in all aspects of production and service delivery	**The Flexible Workplace** • "just-in-time" lean production • extensive use of part-time and contract workers • contracting out of tasks • alternative service delivery

Source: John Shields and B. Mitchell Evans, *Shrinking the State: Globalization and Public Administration "Reform,"* (Halifax: Fernwood, 1998): 44.

In the public sector, this model was emulated under the rubric of "flexible government." Presuming that traditional bureaucracies were rigid and unresponsive, advocates of flexible government called for an end to the permanence inherent in lifelong employment and careers in the public sector and for breaking down permanent structures and replacing them with more fluid virtual organizations. Concretely, this meant public sector downsizing, contingent public sector employment, contracting out, privatization, alternative service delivery, and deregulation. The reality, of course, was that these types of change were very problematic and controversial, and encountered considerable resistance.[13] Nonetheless, they presaged another major development in administrative theorizing and reform: NPM.

You may have noticed that in all the various theoretical models, there is a strange silence on certain issues, particularly gender and race/ethnicity. Until the past 30 years in Canada and abroad, scholars of public administration and organization theory seemed to assume away any ascriptive or socio-economic characteristics or differences among the individuals who populated organizations. The mainstream textbooks were largely silent on these issues. Mills, Simmons, and Mills report that a study of 107 textbooks widely used in Canada and the United States in courses on management, organization theory, and organizational behaviour between 1959 and 1995 showed that, prior to the mid-1980s, 21 texts (81 percent) said nothing about race and ethnicity while the remaining five (19 percent) made only passing references to it. Since 1985, they go on to report, 27 texts (45 percent) had nothing to say about race, 30 (50 percent) mentioned it in passing, and only three (5 percent) addressed it in depth. Where gender was concerned, 30 texts (34 percent), including nine that were published in the 1990s, had nothing to say. All but a handful of the rest of the texts barely scratched the surface of the topic. Another study of texts published between 1960 and 2000 found very little acknowledgement in management textbooks of the growing influence of feminist scholarship.[14]

If you think back to the major theorists we canvassed, you probably noticed that all of them are men, except for Mary Parker Follett. You may also have noticed that many of them, like Weber, Taylor, and the structuralists, privileged the idea of rationality—a masculine trait—and did not even consider the possibility of other ways of acting and knowing, such as intuition, emotionality, or non-rationality. You might have noticed as well that in the Hawthorne experiments, one group of subjects was exclusively male, while the other was female, yet no comment was made in the studies about the effect of gender on the experiments. Nor was it acknowledged that the experimenters were all male and that this may have prejudiced the findings in certain ways. Similarly, no account was taken of workers' and experimenters' differing class positions and how that might have conditioned the subjects' responses or the experiment design. In these and countless other examples, organizational theory has been myopic.

Feminist scholarship, in particular, has revealed the poverty of marginalizing differentiated groups. While feminist theory gave rise to a large body of literature critiquing the liberal state for its emphasis on individualism and a strict demarcation between the private and public sectors, very little of this theorizing was applied to public administration. "Feminist theories offered new theories of power, of virtue, of the nature of organizations, and of leadership and professionalism and brought to light fundamental ways in which women have shaped society and politics. Yet few if any of these ideas have made their way into conversations in public administration."[15]

One argument is that the genders operate in different ways in organizations. Women's growing participation in the workplace made this fact increasingly plain and caused feminist scholars to rethink organizational dynamics. This is particularly germane to public administration since the majority of public sector workers in Canada and many other countries are now women (although they are underrepresented in the executive and the technical categories, and over-represented in the administrative support category, a fact we explore in more detail in chapter 9). In addition, women have entered schools of public administration and related disciplines in increasing numbers in recent years. It is estimated that in the United States, three out of four public administration graduate students are women[16] (see Box 4.2). Yet relatively little reflection about these trends has made its way into the scholarship until fairly recently.

BOX 4.2 | **A Woman's Place in Public Administration**

The experience described here, while of an American woman, is not unique and likely reflects many Canadian women's experiences as well:

In 1981 I enrolled at Virginia Tech's Center for Public Administration and Policy. Launched on my doctoral studies, I occasionally grumbled to myself about the absence of discussion about women's issues, the all-male faculty, the fact that we never seemed to read anything by a woman (except for good old Mary Parker Follett), the articles that used he and his for the whole human race. I kept these complaints to myself, however; I wanted to be seen as a good student. I guess I hoped that my professors wouldn't notice—or at least attach any significance to the fact—that I was a woman.

Then came lengthy conversations with . . . other women students. I began to see both the absence of women from the course material and my own distance from women's concerns as moral issues. My intellectual curiosity was also aroused; I began to do some reading in feminist theory and decided I would do a paper on "something to do with women and public administration"—something that would explore the ways in which a feminist perspective might change thinking in the field. To prepare myself, I went back through Public Administration Review, intending to build on what had already been written. I was shocked (a sign of my naïveté) to find that in the past decade, there had been almost nothing written from a feminist viewpoint. . . . It seemed impossible (at the time), but despite what I knew was an outpouring of feminist work in political theory, organizational sociology, and even economics, public administration theory appeared to be innocent of a feminist theoretical perspective.

Source: Camilla Stivers, *Gender Images in Public Administration: Legitimacy and the Administrative State*, (Newbury Park, California: Sage, 1993): vii.

Early feminists in Canada focused on the structures of inequality in public bureaucracies, pointing out, for instance, the "ghettoization" of women in so-called "pink collar" positions and women's relative absence from the upper echelons of power.[17] Others focused on women's lack of representation in political positions of power.[18] Later feminists began to argue that the predominance of male scholarship in organization theory has meant that organizations have mainly been seen from male perspectives. Gendered processes reinforce and perpetuate the maleness of organizations, including gendered divisions that produce gender patterning of jobs; masculine-rooted organizational symbols and images; and male-based values, such as dominance and subordination, characterizing interactions in the workplace.[19] A considerable body of research has also emerged that shows that women have different management styles than men: for instance, they act more co-operatively and share leadership more, and are less likely to fall back on the "command-and-control" Weberian models preferred by men. Women privilege different values than men, such as trust, openness, and acceptance, and they are less aggressive than men. Another approach argues that the state, rather than being inherently patriarchal, should be viewed as being constituted by individual institutions that vary in their makeup, some of which are "culturally marked as masculine," since the state is not some kind of monolith that always acts to oppress or exclude women.[20]

These various theoretical approaches are of increasing importance given women's growing participation in organizations that are traditionally the purview of men and in broadening the landscape of organizational theory as well. As American feminist scholar Camilla Stivers asserts, as long as administration is seen as genderless, women will continue to face the unpalatable choice of either adopting a masculine administrative identity or accepting marginalization in the bureaucratic hierarchy.[21] To assess for yourself the significance of feminist arguments about the role of women in organizations, you might ask yourself, What difference would it make if women were in charge of all major government organizations and if all the leading scholars in the field were women? (See Figure 4.1.)

New Public Management

Much contemporary organization theory centres on the **New Public Management (NPM)**. NPM found its origin in the approach to governing pioneered by Britain's former prime minister Margaret Thatcher and later followed by former American president Ronald Reagan and former Canadian prime minister Brian Mulroney. NPM has been motivated by three things:

- the debt and deficit problems of governments that resulted in a search for more economical ways of governing;

- a growing alienation from politics and politicians among ordinary citizens, a rise in apathy, distrust of governments, and a decline in public confidence in public policies and services provided by governments; and

- globalization and the emergence of a new economic order in which the traditional nation-state has declined in significance in comparison to transnational corporations and other global actors.

FIGURE 4.1   Power in the Institutions of the Canadian State

♀ = Majority Female
♂ = Majority Male

Judicial Branch:
Courts ♂

Executive Branch:
Cabinet ♂
Prime Minister ♂

Legislative Branch:
Senate ♂
House of Commons ♂

Public Service:
Executive ♂
Clerical ♀
Military ♂
Police ♂

Crown Corporations:
The Bank of Canada ♂
CBC ♂

Source: Adapted from Jill Vickers, *Reinventing Political Science*, (Halifax: Fernwood Publishing, 1997): 10.

The NPM theory's basic response to these developments was to argue for a rolling back of the state and its withdrawal from a number of areas. Changes in public administration thus focused on **privatization, deregulation, contracting out** of public services, decentralization, **downsizing** and expenditure reduction initiatives (including layoffs of public servants, wage freezes, and rollbacks), the introduction of **user fees**, commercialization of public enterprises, and other similar measures.

According to political scientist Peter Aucoin, the NPM requires state administrators to accommodate themselves to certain assumptions: public servants have gained too much power over politicians in recent years; the organizational mechanisms of government have become too complex and now actually impede political leadership in exercising authority and managing government; management in government has become too concerned with rigid adherence to rules and procedures and too prone to bureaucratic pathologies.[22] Thus, criticisms of government bureaucracy emerged that focused on *re-engineering* the whole apparatus and role of government. More precisely, such criticisms prompted a search for management techniques that put the operation of government on a more businesslike footing.

The intellectual roots of NPM can be found in theorists' attempts to go beyond structuralist and humanist approaches, particularly to private sector management. An early source was Thomas Peters and Robert Waterman's *In Search of Excellence*, published in 1982.[23] The authors studied a number of well-run American corporations, looking for a formula in large organizations that suggested the necessary qualities for success. They argued for de-emphasizing Weberian rationality and focusing more closely on the messy human side of organizational life, as well as paying sharper attention to customers' needs. While their book was not without its critics, it was nonetheless widely read in business circles and, eventually, in the public sector, too.

Among the most influential proponents of NPM were David Osborne and Ted Gaebler, who argued that "governments must steer, not row." Their 1992 book, *Reinventing Government,* outlined 10 principles on the assumption that while government is necessary, it does not necessarily have to act like government but could be much more businesslike in its operations. They argued the following:

Most entrepreneurial governments promote competition between service providers. They empower citizens by pushing control out of the bureaucracy, into the community. They measure the performance of their agencies, focusing not on inputs but on outcomes. They are driven by their goals—their missions—not by their rules and regulations. They redefine their clients as customers and offer them choices—between schools, between training programs, between housing options. They prevent problems before they emerge, rather than simply offering services afterward. They put their energies into earning money, not simply spending it. They decentralize authority, embracing participatory management. They prefer market mechanisms to bureaucratic mechanisms. And they focus not simply on providing public services, but on catalyzing all sectors—public, private, and voluntary—into action to solve their community's problems.[24]

One theorist suggests that NPM arose in part as critique of bureaucracy. British public management professor Christopher Pollitt puts it this way:

Bureaucracy is pictured as ruling the pre-NPM earth like a dinosaur. Like a dinosaur, it was too big, too slow-moving, too insensitive, insufficiently adaptable, and seriously underpowered as far as brains were concerned. Messages took too long to get all the way down the hierarchy from the tiny little head to the cumbersome feet and claws, and, by the same token, information travelled up from the ground level to the brain at an agonizingly slow pace. The large size demanded a huge and continuous supply of resources. . . . So bureaucracy was cast as the enemy of freedom, creativity and efficiency.[25]

Of course, this characterization is problematic for a number of reasons. For instance, it assumes that "bureaucracy" is one big, undifferentiated whole. It is not. It is made up of countless components, some of which may fit the description above under certain circumstances but most of which are highly effective and efficient in the execution of their duties. Put another way, the critique ignores entirely the positive features of public service by painting a simplistic picture of some kind of singular "creature" when, in fact, we are talking about a diverse array of animals with a rich variety of organizational forms and structures.

The NPM is largely driven by the same values that underlie those of the private sector: the **three Es** of *efficiency, effectiveness,* and *economy.* These are placed within the framework of "quality service" to citizens, who are referred to as "customers" or "clients." A much greater level of attention is paid to the relationship between expenditures and revenues, even at the cost of sacrificing long-established and cherished government policies and programs as administrators are confronted with "clients" demanding improved services at less cost. As Aucoin notes, "Concerns for economy and efficiency have thus been given a new priority in public management. Enhancing cost-consciousness, doing more with less and achieving value for money became the objectives of this finance-centred perspective on public management reform."[26] This entails effectively "debureaucratizing" organizations. Donald Savoie suggests that "the philosophy [of NPM] is rooted in the conviction that private sector management is superior to public administration. The solution, therefore, is to transfer government activities to the private sector through privatization and contracting out." But, as he goes on to suggest, it is hardly practical to transfer *all* government activities to the private sector, so "the next best solution is to transfer business management practices to government operations."[27]

But political scientist Alan Tupper cites a trenchant critique of the NPM idea of treating citizens as clients or customers. He argues that "new public management debases Canadian democracy in deep but subtle ways. It denigrates democratic citizenship by portraying citizens as customers of government." He goes on to suggest "new public management's stress on private sector management theories, market tests, and partnerships transforms government from a unique institution into a commonplace fixture that can be managed by the same principles as a grocery store."[28]

In any event, a literature on public administration has emerged that suggests NPM was never very thoroughly applied in the Canadian context or, more precisely, that the Canadian variant of NPM that evolved was softer than the model imposed on Britain, New Zealand, and other places. Some theorists argue that we are already moving beyond NPM.[29] For now, it is suffice to note that the impact of NPM is apparent in a series of reforms instituted by the federal government in the 1990s, like Program Review and PS2000 (see chapter 10), which called for improved service to the public, support for innovation, better human resource management practices, and new forms of accountability focused on results and performance.

But a variety of impediments frustrated the wholesale application of NPM, not the least of which was lack of political will, with the result that Canadian reforms paled in comparison to those in other countries.[30] Nonetheless, the introduction of reforms to improve client satisfaction with government services proliferated (e.g., the 1995 Quality Service Initiative), as did new innovations deemed "alternative service delivery" mechanisms. What emerged was "an increasing number of instruments, ranging from traditional ones such as departments, Crown corporations and mixed enterprises to newer ones such as special operating agencies, privatized public organizations, single-window service-delivery units, and partnerships," which, according to some theorists of public administration, are derived from NPM but move beyond it to the post-bureaucratic model.[31]

Critics of NPM point out that wholesale reform has been taking place without public consultation or popular approval. Others suggest that NPM represents yet another fad in a long line of changing tastes. Moreover, the critics contend, proponents of NPM have forgotten Wallace Sayre's law that public and private administration are fundamentally alike in all unimportant respects. Aucoin argues that,

> it is increasingly acknowledged that public service reform cannot be based on a paradigm that assumes that public administration is essentially the same as private administration. The public policy dimension is unique to public management as governance. Citizen-centred service requires attention to critical issues of law, rights, and due process not present in the marketplace of private service delivery. And managing the public service entails managing in a context of constraints and motivations that are distinct to the public sector. To the degree that privatization and contracting out cannot be extended to all functions of government, public administration, even in a highly devolved management regime, remains subject to political and administrative dynamics that require their own distinctive modes of reform and renewal.[32]

Responding to the shortcomings of NPM, American public administration theorists Janet and Robert Denhardt argue for a new framework for the reaffirmation of democratic values, citizenship, and service in the public interest organized around a core of seven principles:

1. Serve citizens, not customers;
2. Seek the public interest;
3. Value citizenship and public service above entrepreneurialism;
4. Think strategically, act democratically;
5. Recognize that accountability isn't simple;
6. Serve, rather than steer;
7. Value people, not just productivity.[33]

They also argue that "government should not be run like a business; it should be run like a democracy."[34]

As you can see, the development of organization theory has proceeded through several different stages, each having an impact on the public administration of Canada. You may be forgiven if the array of theories seems a little daunting. Imagine for a moment you are a public sector manager having to implement some version of one of them! The complexities of doing so show that there is sometimes a gap between theory and practice, a point illustrated by two former public servants in an article that argued that there is often a distinction between the "surreal" world of theory and the "real" world of practice.[35] To put these developments into more focus, we turn in the next chapter to that "real" world of organizations, looking at the actual machinery of government to see more concretely the impact of theory on practice.

WHAT YOU HAVE LEARNED

This chapter has illuminated some of the ways in which various theoretical approaches to the concept of organization have influenced Canadian public administration. It observed that Canadian ideas have been heavily influenced by foreign ones in this area, particularly American, British, and German. The classic thinkers have been influential, though sometimes in subtle ways. The basic Weberian-type model has largely prevailed in the structure and organization of Canadian public administration, while structuralist and humanist theories have waxed and waned over time. And various alternative theoretical approaches arising out of these schools have also left their mark on Canadian public administration.

Key Words and Concepts

elite (102)
homogeneity (103)
unity of direction (103)
participatory management (104)
Management by Objectives (MBO) (105)
Organization Development
  (OD) (105)
Total Quality Management
  (TQM) (105)

New Public Management
  (NPM) (112)
privatization (113)
deregulation (113)
contracting out (113)
downsizing (113)
user fees (113)
three Es (efficiency, effectiveness,
  and economy) (115)

Review Questions

This chapter was divided into two sections, addressing the impact of organization theory on Canadian public administration. You should now be able to answer the questions associated with each.

1. The Impact of Organization Theory

Sometimes it is hard to see the relevance of theoretical arguments to the real world. To discern which approaches have been most influential in shaping the organization of the Canadian government, this section explored the ways in which theory has been concretely applied in the Canadian experience. We asked the following questions: What theories have had the most influence on the development of Canadian public administration? How have contending schools of thought affected the actual organization and functioning of the Canadian public sector?

2. Contemporary Developments

Finally, the most recent developments in the theory of organizations were briefly examined. Again, in trying to wed the theoretical with the concrete, we asked,

How have recent theoretical developments affected organizations in the public sector in practice? After reading this chapter and the previous one, you should have a firm grasp of the major contending theories of public administration, the thinkers associated with each, and the impact of organizational life on the Canadian government and on us as individuals.

Weblinks

Canada Site
www.canada.gc.ca

Canada Gazette
www.canadagazette.gc.ca

Canada Public Service Agency
www.psagency-agencefp.gc.ca

Further Reading

1. The Impact of Organization Theory

Johnson, David. *Thinking Government: Public Sector Management in Canada. Second Edition.* Peterborough: Broadview Press, 2006: Chapters 5 and 10.

Mills, Albert J., Tony Simmons and Jean Helms Mills. *Reading Organization Theory: A Critical Approach to the Study of Organizational Behaviour and Structure. Third Edition.* Aurora, Ontario: Garamond Press, 2005.

Mintzberg, Henry and Jacques Bourgault. *Managing Publicly.* Toronto: Institute of Public Administration of Canada, 2000.

2. Contemporary Developments

Borins, Sandford. "The New Public Management Is Here to Stay," *Canadian Public Administration*, 38, 1 (1995).

Hood, Christopher. "A Public Management for All Seasons," *Public Administration*, 69, (Spring, 1991): 3–19.

Savoie, Donald. "What Is Wrong With the New Public Management?" *Canadian Public Administration*, 38, 1, (1995): 113.

Shields, John and B. Mitchell Evans. *Shrinking the State: Globalization and Public Administration "Reform."* Halifax: Fernwood, 1998.

Tupper, Allan. "New Public Management and Canadian Politics," in Janine Brodie and Linda Trimble, eds. *Reinventing Canada: Politics of the 21st Century.* Toronto: Prentice Hall, 2003: 231–42.

Endnotes

1. The groundbreaking study in this regard was John Porter's *The Vertical Mosaic: An Analysis of Social Class and Power in Canada*, (Toronto: University of Toronto Press, 1965). See also Dennis Olsen, *The State Elite*, (Toronto: McClelland and Stewart, 1980); Wallace Clement, *The Canadian Corporate Elite: An Analysis of Economic Power*, (Toronto: McClelland and Stewart, 1975); and Wallace Clement, *Class, Power and Property: Essays on Canadian Society*, (Toronto: Methuen, 1983).

2. See, for example, Gregory J. Inwood, *Continentalizing Canada: The Politics and Legacy of the Macdonald Royal Commission*, (Toronto: University of Toronto Press, 2006): chapter 10.

3. An early analysis of the class ties between the Senate and the business community in Canada is Colin Campbell's *The Canadian Senate: A Lobby Within*, (Toronto: Macmillan, 1978).

4. For an analysis of different styles of organization within Canadian departments and agencies, see Henry Mintzberg and Jacques Bourgault, eds. *Managing Publicly*, (Toronto: Institute of Public Administration of Canada, 2000).

5. Peter F. Drucker, *The Practice of Management*, (New York: Harper and Row, 1954).

6. See Drucker, *The Practice of Management*, (1954). Adapted from *Public Administration in Canada*, by Kenneth Kernaghan and David Siegel (Scarborough: ITP Nelson, 1995): 71. Reprinted by permission of ITP Nelson.

7. See Jay M. Shafritz, E.W. Russell and Christopher P. Borick, *Introducing Public Administration. Fifth Edition*, (New York: Pearson Longman, 2007): 270–71.

8. See W. Edwards Deming, *Quality, Productivity and Competitive Position*, (Cambridge, Massachusetts: M.I.T. Centre for Advanced Engineering Study, 1982).

9. See Shafritz, Russell and Borick, *Introducing Public Administration,* (2007): 270; and Christopher Pollitt, "New Forms of Public Service: Issues in Contemporary Organizational Design," in Thomas J. Courchene and Donald J. Savoie, eds. *The Art of the State: Governance in a World Without Frontiers,* (Montreal: Institute for Research on Public Policy, 2003): 209–35.

10. Cited in Shafritz, Russell and Borick, *Introducing Public Administration,* (2007): 289.

11. Canada, *Public Service 2000: The Renewal of the Public Service of Canada,* (Ottawa: Supply and Services, 1990): 46. Cited in Laurent Dobuzinskis, "Public Administration," in Michael Howlett and David Laycock, eds. *Puzzles of Power: An Introduction to Political Science, Second Edition,* (Toronto: Oxford University Press, 1998): 159. For an analysis from the perspective of the culture and values of public administration, see O.P. Dwivedi and James Iain Gow, *From Bureaucracy to Public Management: The Administrative Culture of the Government of Canada,* (Peterborough: Broadview Press, 1999).

12. John Shields and B. Mitchell Evans, *Shrinking the State: Globalization and Public Administration "Reform,"* (Halifax: Fernwood, 1998): 44.

13. See Donald J. Savoie, "Fifteen Years of Reform: What Have We Learned?" in B. Guy Peters and Donald J. Savoie, eds. *Taking Stock: Assessing Public Sector Reforms,* (Montreal: McGill-Queen's University Press, 1998): 394–414.

14. See Albert J. Mills, Tony Simmons and Jean Helms Mills, *Reading Organization Theory: A Critical Approach to the Study of Organizational Behaviour and Structure. Third Edition,* (Aurora, Ontario: Garamond Press, 2005), 39, fn 1.

15. Camilla Stivers, *Gender Images in Public Administration: Legitimacy and the Administrative State,* (Newbury Park, California: Sage, 1993): 3.

16. Stivers, *Gender Images in Public Administration,* (1993).

17. On the history of women in the Canadian public service, see Nicole Morgan, *The Equality Game: Women in the Federal Public Service 1908–1987,* (Ottawa: Canadian Advisory Council on the Status of Women, 1988).

18. See Jane Arscott and Linda Trimble, eds. *In the Presence of Women: Representation in Canadian Governments,* (Toronto: Harcourt Brace, 1997).

19. Shafritz, Russell and Borick, *Introducing Public Administration,* (2007): 295.

20. Louise A. Chappell, *Gendering Government: Feminist Engagement with the State in Australia and Canada,* (Vancouver: UBC Press, 2003): 11. See also Susan B. Boyd, ed. *Challenging the Public/ Private Divide: Feminism, Law and Public Policy,* (Toronto: University of Toronto Press, 1997).

21. Stivers, *Gender Images in Public Administration,* (1993).

22. Peter Aucoin, *The New Public Management: Canada in Comparative Perspective,* (Montreal: The Institute for Research on Public Policy, 1995): 3–4.

23. Thomas Peters and Robert Waterman, *In Search of Excellence: Lessons From America's Best-Run Companies,* (New York: Harper and Row, 1982).

24. David Osborne and Ted Gaebler, *Reinventing Government: How the Entrepreneurial Spirit Is Transforming the Public Sector,* (New York: Penguin, 1993): 19–20. Cited in Leslie A. Pal, *Beyond Policy Analysis: Public Issue Management in Turbulent Times,* (Scarborough: Nelson, 1997): 56–57.

25. Christopher Pollitt, *The Essential Public Manager*, (Philadelphia: Open University Press, 2003): 32–33.

26. Aucoin, *The New Public Management*, (1995): 9.

27. Donald Savoie, "What Is Wrong With the New Public Management?" *Canadian Public Administration*, 38, 1 (1995): 113.

28. Alan Tupper, "New Public Management and Canadian Politics," in Janine Brodie and Linda Trimble, eds. *Reinventing Canada: Politics of the 21st Century*, (Toronto: Prentice Hall, 2003): 239–40.

29. Peter Aucoin, "Beyond the 'New' in Public Management Reform in Canada: Catching the Next Wave?" in Christopher Dunn, ed. *The Handbook of Canadian Public Administration*, (Toronto: Oxford University Press, 2002): 50.

30. See Aucoin, "Beyond the 'New' in Public Management Reform in Canada," (2002): 36–52; and Kenneth Kernaghan, Brian Marson and Sandford Borins, *The New Public Organization*, (Toronto: The Institute of Public Administration of Canada, 2000).

31. See Donald J. Savoie, *Thatcher, Reagan and Mulroney: In Search of a New Bureaucracy*, (Toronto: University of Toronto Press, 1994); and Aucoin, *The New Public Management*, (1995).

32. Aucoin, "Beyond the 'New' in Public Management Reform in Canada," (2002): 50.

33. Janet V. Denhardt and Robert B. Denhardt, *The New Public Service: Serving, Not Steering*, (Armonk, New York: M.E. Sharpe, 2003): 42–43.

34. Denhardt and Denhardt, *The New Public Service*, (2003): 3.

35. Ian D. Clark and Harry Swain, "Distinguishing the Real From the Surreal in Management Reform: Suggestions for Beleaguered Administrators in the Government of Canada," *Canadian Public Administration* 48, 4 (Winter, 2005): 453–76.

Chapter 5

Public Administration *and* Institutions: *The* Real World *of* Organizations *and the* Machinery *of* Government

WHAT YOU WILL LEARN

In this chapter we will consider the place at which public administration theory and public administration practice in Canada intersect. To this end, we will look closely at the following questions:

- What contextual factors shape the structure and organization of public administration in Canada?
- What are the key relationships within those structures?
- What are the key institutions within which those relationships play themselves out, and why does structure matter in the provision of programs and services for Canadians?

Chapter 5 is divided into the following sections:

1. *Factors Influencing Organizational Structure*

Here we look at the basic framework of the Canadian political system and ask, How have capitalist democracy, federalism, and cabinet-parliamentary government influenced the organization of the Canadian government? How have the very outlines of the state influenced public administration?

2. *Political-Administrative Relationships*

Chapter 1 introduced you to the relationship between public administration and democratic government. This section elaborates on this relationship by focusing on the roles of politicians and public servants in more detail, and asks, Who is in control of the machinery and actions of the state?

3.— *Departmental Organizations*

Why do governments grow and shrink over time? Why do some prime ministers prefer large Cabinets with many departments, while others opt for more stripped-down models? This section introduces you to the actual organizational units of the Canadian government, including new mechanisms of alternative service delivery (ASD). In so doing, we will explain why, organizationally speaking, the government looks the way it does.

4.— *Regulatory Agencies*

What role do regulatory bodies play in public administration? In an era of deregulation and downsizing government, we have been rethinking the areas that government should be regulating. Why is this?

5.— *Crown Corporations*

The role of Crown corporations in Canada has been important. But recently, the wisdom of public ownership (i.e., the use of Crown corporations) to achieve policy goals has been questioned. What explains their use over time in Canada, and why are Crown corporations as policy instruments being re-evaluated?

After reading this chapter, you should be able to explain the relationship between politicians and public servants, and the main factors influencing the organization of the public sector, including departments, regulatory agencies, Crown corporations, and alternative service delivery mechanisms, while keeping in mind the organizational theories studied earlier.

Factors Influencing Organizational Structure

Before we dive into the nature of political and administrative relationships, we must be clear about some fundamentals. The first point is that public administration in Canada takes place within a capitalist democracy. Second, Canada has a federal system. And third, within that federal system, we have a cabinet-parliamentary government. What exactly do these terms mean? It is worth spending a moment clarifying them, since these systems are the framework for Canadian public administration. Then, we will look more closely at the organization of government within this framework.

Capitalist Democracy

The first point about factors shaping the organization of government is that governing in Canada takes place within the context of capitalist democracy.[1] This is a political-economic system whose broad rules impose themselves on the scope of action of governments in obvious and subtle ways. At the most basic level, it combines capitalist relations of production with democratic electoral institutions that shape public administration; ultimately, organizational life must conform to this system.

You might look at it this way. At the root of capitalist economic systems is the right to private property. To defend that right, state structures are created that act in the interests of those who hold property. If we define *property* here to mean the "means of production" (i.e., capital, machines, factories, natural resources, information systems, etc.), then in a capitalist system, state structures act in the interests of the capitalists. In other words, business interests (capital) must be defended through the structures of the state. But at the same time, in a democratic society, the will of the majority must prevail. And since the majority of Canadians are not capitalists (ownership of the means of production in Canada is concentrated in few hands), the state must also respond to the democratically expressed will of ordinary citizens. Geoffrey Hale, an expert on business–government relations, says, "the frequent dependence of politicians and governments on businesses, large and small, for economic development, job creation, and political support has made the mobilization of this support a major element of democratic political life since the late-eighteenth and early-nineteenth centuries."[2] Political scientist Neil Bradford asserts,

This combination of capitalism and democracy must reasonably be seen to set broad and general parameters on policy-making. Elected officials clearly rely heavily on private investors to sustain growth, employment, revenue, and so forth. Given the value voters placed on these outputs, this dependence on "business confidence" reduces the political incentive for certain kinds of policy innovation, for example, those that directly challenge the existing property system.[3]

So the organization of government must meet the needs of the property-holding capitalists by creating the conditions for profitability, to ensure that business confidence is maintained. But this must be balanced against the interests of others in the system, whose interests may be in direct contrast to the capitalists.

For instance, it may enhance profitability for a corporation to simply dump its waste in a nearby river. But that action certainly is not in the interests of the communities situated along the river. The citizens may mobilize and demand that the government do something about industrial pollution, and, hence, a ministry of the environment is created. But the corporation may resist attempts by the new ministry to impose restrictions on polluting by threatening to move its plant to some other jurisdiction that has less severe environmental laws. Less drastically, it may look to other parts of the state structure for assistance. There may be, for instance, a ministry of industry that provides subsidies for the purchase of pollution-control equipment for corporations. Or the ministry of finance may provide tax breaks to corporations that promise to meet certain environmental goals. Whatever the case, the organization of the state flows in a very direct way from the interaction and tension between capitalism and democracy.

Federalism

A federal system of government is one in which the constitutional authority to make laws is divided between a national government and regional governments. Neither the national government acting alone nor the regional governments acting together have the authority to alter the power of the other level of government. They are coordinate and equal in their own constitutional spheres. Where there is a dispute, the governments negotiate or resort to the courts to adjudicate between them. According to K.C. Wheare, a British authority on federalism,

federal government exists . . . when the powers of government for a community are divided substantially according to the principle that there is a single independent authority for the whole area in respect of some matters and that there are independent regional authorities for other matters, each set of authorities being co-ordinate with and not subordinate to the others within its own prescribed sphere.[4]

What does this mean in the Canadian context? It means simply that we have a national government and 10 provincial governments (as well as three territories, but these are under federal jurisdiction and are not constitutionally a third level of government). Beyond this obvious point, though, lies a range of complex issues that affect public administration in myriad ways.

In the Canadian federal system, power is divided through the Constitution. Section 91 lists most of the federal government's powers, and section 92 lists most of the provincial governments' powers. Therefore, the organization of both levels of government is shaped by each level's respective constitutional responsibilities and the resulting relationship between the two levels of government. For example, section 91.7 confers the power to enact laws in the area of "Militia, Military and Naval Service, and Defence" exclusively to the federal government. Therefore, it would make little sense, and indeed would be in violation of the Constitution, for the provinces to have a department to create programs in this area.

Complicating this, though, is the ambiguous language of much of the Constitution combined with the overlapping nature of many issues confronting modern governments. Thus, both levels of government set up administrative organizations (e.g., departments, regulatory bodies, Crown corporations, etc.) in the same area of jurisdiction. For instance, even though the Constitution stipulates that health care is a provincial responsibility, there are both federal and provincial ministries of health. While this may appear to contradict the constitutional division of powers, it in fact reflects the flexibility of the federal system. In this case, while the federal government lacks jurisdictional authority over the delivery of health care, it both administers the Canada Health Act and provides fiscal resources to support this expensive policy area. And in federalism, it is said that the golden rule always prevails: i.e., he who has the gold makes the rules. In constitutional terms, this is because the national government has what is called the "**spending power**." Although not listed anywhere in the formal written Constitution, the spending power is the convention that if the federal government has money to spend, it has the authority to do so even in an area of provincial jurisdiction.

An important irony shapes the Canadian federal system. In 1867, the Fathers of Confederation gave most powers over issues such as education, health, and social policy to the provinces. In the context of the times, these were relatively unimportant areas in which governments were only minimally involved, as we noted in chapter 1 when we discussed the minimalist state. Furthermore, the Fathers of Confederation gave most of the powers to raise and spend money to the federal level of government, in the interests of creating a national economic and social union. The result is that today, the provinces are constitutionally responsible for the most expensive policy areas but lack the fiscal capacity to pay for them. The federal government, on the other hand, has tremendous fiscal resources but lacks constitutional jurisdiction in the most expensive policy areas. This has recently led to the charge that a "fiscal imbalance" exists in Canadian federalism, fuelling considerable controversy over management of the federation's fiscal affairs.[5]

The ongoing search for ways around this basic dilemma is at the root of organizational reform for both levels of government. An elaborate network of intergovernmental institutions has emerged,[6] where senior public servants and ministers from both levels of government regularly meet to discuss the federation's administration. So entrenched is this network that political scientist Richard Simeon refers to it as a system of "federal-provincial diplomacy."[7] In fact, by the 1960s, meetings of federal and provincial ministers and their expert advisers became so numerous that they were supplanting legislatures as the primary arena of Canadian policy making.[8] Then, over the succeeding 50 years, intergovernmental relations intensified as the provinces in particular built up their capacity to engage the already well-endowed federal government. This gave rise to an increasing number and type of administrative institutions—central agencies, line departments, secretariats, conferences, partnerships, accords and agreements, and so on, as well as a large informal network of intergovernmental specialist officials.[9] So, ultimately, Canadian public administration is profoundly affected by our federal system of government.

Cabinet-Parliamentary Government

The third major part of the framework of Canadian public administration is cabinet-parliamentary government. To place this in context, look at Figure 5.1, which outlines the three major *branches* of the Canadian government.

The **executive branch** consists of the monarch, the Governor General, and the Cabinet (which includes the prime minister). The public service is considered a part of the executive as well, in that it administers the programs devised by the executive and tenders advice on the formulation of those programs. The **legislative branch** consists of Parliament, which in turn is divided into a lower elected chamber called the House of Commons and an appointed upper chamber called the Senate. Finally, the **judicial branch** consists of the Supreme Court and all the courts and judges below it in the federal and provincial court systems.

There are two main features of cabinet-parliamentary government. The first is the relationship between the branches of government. The second, related feature is that the Constitution tells us that certain offices are conferred with tremendous

FIGURE 5.1 **Basic Institutions of Canadian Government**

Source: James John Guy, *People Politics and Government: A Canadian Perspective*, Sixth Edition, (Toronto: Pearson Prentice Hall, 2006): 134. Reprinted with permission by Pearson Education Canada Inc.

powers, but practice reveals that they do not actually exercise those powers. In effect, to understand the relationship between the branches of government, you need to understand the "myth and reality" of cabinet-parliamentary government. Another way to conceive of this is to compare the "formal" and "political" powers of each branch of government.

To begin with, the "myth" asserts that tremendous powers are accorded by the Constitution to the monarch as the formal head of state. In Canada, the monarch is represented by the Governor General (and Lieutenant-Governor at the provincial level), who has the power on behalf of the monarch to decide which political party will form the government, when Parliament will be dissolved, and when a new election will be called, and the right to confer royal assent upon all legislation. In reality, these powers are almost completely symbolic. Because of the historical evolution of democratic government, the role and position of the nonelected monarch and Governor General have become essentially ceremonial.

So, in reality, who gets to exercise the formidable powers cited in the Constitution as the prerogative of the monarch? The answer: another part of the executive branch of government, the **Privy Council**, which is an advisory body. This is a term with which you might not be familiar, since it is hardly ever used anymore. Strictly speaking, it consists of all current and former ministers of the Crown; more commonly it is known nowadays as the **Cabinet**. Only current members of the Cabinet exercise the powers spelled out in the Constitution. They are chosen by the prime minister, who heads the Cabinet, and are usually government members of the House of Commons. Indeed, so much power has come to be vested in the prime minister and the Cabinet that it is common to refer to the Canadian system as executive-dominated.[10]

Why does the Constitution tell us that power is held in one place, while in reality it is exercised somewhere else? Partly because of **constitutional convention**. This is the idea of habit or tradition: that is, when things have been done a certain way for a long period of time, it becomes a convention. And conventions can be every bit as important as the actual written Constitution. The other reason is the doctrine of **responsible government**. This is the principle that the government (as represented by the Cabinet) must explain itself and be accountable to the elected representative of the people (as represented by the House of Commons). For this to take place, there must be some mechanism by which power can be removed from the government by the people's representatives. In order to govern, the prime minister and Cabinet must have the *confidence* of the elected House of Commons. If a government loses that confidence (i.e., loses the support of the majority of members of the House), it loses the right to govern and can, therefore, be removed from power. The doctrine of responsible government has evolved to ensure that those who actually hold and exercise power (in the Cabinet) can be held accountable (by Parliament).

The other important issue is where the Cabinet comes from. Since its members are also members of the Parliament, we talk about a *fusion of powers* in the Canadian system. This differs from the American system, for instance, where there is a *separation of powers*. In the United States, the president (the executive branch) is not a member of Congress (the legislative branch), nor does he require the support of a majority of its members to retain power. This is a crucial difference. The fusion of powers in the Canadian system facilitates accountability, in that the prime minister and Cabinet must participate every day in question period and other activities of the House of Commons, explaining their policies and actions (or inaction) on a daily basis to their opponents and to the country as a whole. This is the heart of responsible cabinet-parliamentary government.

You should be able to infer that the second branch of government—the legislative branch—plays a significant role in the theory of responsible government, holding the executive to account. Some people mistake this power for the power to make laws. The truth about the legislative branch is that it is a law-*passing*, rather than a law-*making*, body. The main decisions about what laws the government seeks to introduce are made in Cabinet, and indeed in almost all cases it is Cabinet ministers who introduce legislation into Parliament for debate and approval. Ordinary members of Parliament in the governing party who are not in the Cabinet (called *backbenchers*) and opposition party members of Parliament have a circumscribed role in law-making. This is because of the doctrine of *party discipline*, which suggests party members always vote according to the instructions of their leaders. This is necessary to ensure that Cabinet can have its legislative desires realized, since the government, to pass laws, must have the support of the majority in the House of Commons. In times of minority government, of course, the power of the legislature vis-à-vis the executive is enhanced, since the executive must be more responsive as it cannot command a majority in the House without attracting the support of at least some of the opposition party members.

The third branch of Canadian government is the judicial branch, which, unlike in some other countries, is composed of appointed rather than elected officials. The judges and courts are called upon to act as arbiters in the event of disputes between the other branches of government, between the two levels of government, and between citizens and government. Where constitutional law is concerned, the judicial branch mediates two types of disputes. The first are disputes related to the division of powers in the Constitution. If one or the other level of government passes a law that infringes on the jurisdiction of the other, a court action can be initiated to see if the law is intra vires (constitutional) or ultra vires (unconstitutional). The other type of constitutional law the judicial branch deals with relates to the relationship of government and citizens. When citizens feel their rights have been infringed or denied, they may appeal to the courts to rule whether a government's actions or law has violated the Canadian Charter of Rights and Freedoms. The Charter, added to the Constitution in 1982, provides a list of rights that governments may not infringe when they pass laws, "subject only to such reasonable limits prescribed by law as can be demonstrably justified in a free and democratic society."

The judicial branch is also concerned with administrative law, making sure that the administrative processes, rules, and regulations of policy are followed. The courts ensure that the administrators do not transgress the law in carrying out their duties and that there are penalties assigned if they do. The courts are the principal agency through which controls over the administrative process are exercised.[11] The courts may examine three aspects of the administrative process. First, they may consider the validity of the way in which power was delegated to an administrative unit by the legislature. Here, the courts are looking to make sure that the delegation of power does not violate the principles of law, including the Constitution, and that there has not been an inappropriate or excessive delegation of power. Second, the courts may look into the rule-making process to ensure that the administrative body has not exceeded the powers granted to it in the making of rules and procedures. Finally, the courts may investigate whether the administrative body has applied the rules with which it is empowered in a fair and consistent manner to individual citizens.

The hallmark of the relationship between the judicial branch and the two other branches is that the judicial branch is regarded as independent of the control of the two other branches, far removed from the taint of political interference or partisanship. The principle of noninterference in judicial affairs is reflected in the fact that individual judges have complete liberty to hear and decide any cases that come before them. How do we know how important this principle is? On a number of occasions Cabinet ministers have been forced to resign their positions because of the reality, or even the perception, that they have interfered with a member of the judiciary.

In summary, you should now have a basic understanding of the importance of capitalist democracy, federalism, and cabinet-parliamentary government to public administration in Canada. To illustrate their importance, try to conceive of a Canada in which business interests and property rights are not pre-eminent in influencing public policy. For instance, what would the organization of public administration look like if the state, rather than private interests, owned everything? Or consider what Canada would look like with a unitary system of government. What would be different if there were no provincial governments? What if there were no division of powers between two levels of government in the constitution to worry about? Now think about a government without a cabinet-parliamentary form. Imagine, for instance, that power had not devolved through historical practice and convention into the hands of the Cabinet, held accountable by the elected representatives of the people, but had instead been retained in the hands of the monarch. How different would the provision of services and the formulation, implementation, and evaluation of public policy be?

Now imagine that it is July 1, 1867. Prime Minister Sir John A. Macdonald invites you into his office to tell you that you are to organize the government of the new Dominion of Canada. What would that government look like, organizationally? How many and which ministries and departments would be needed to serve the needs of Canadians in the mid- to late-1800s? What would the composition of Macdonald's new government be?

Flash ahead to the year 2015. The new prime minister has invited you into her office with the same assignment Macdonald gave you. Would the government you now design look the same as the earlier one? What would be different? Why? What factors did you take into account as you thought about how government would be designed in each of the two eras?

Let's suppose that the first principle you settled on was that the organization of government should allow for the most efficient provision of services possible. Presumably, you would opt for a streamlined model of government, with as few departments as possible. This requires you to think very precisely about what exactly government should do—i.e., what activities it should engage in and what services it should provide. You might start, for instance, by noting the obvious ones: you need structures that serve the interests of the main actors in a capitalist democracy, that respond to the opportunities and constraints of a federal system, and that respond to the rules and processes of cabinet-parliamentary government.

You must ask what government is to be responsible for. The safety and defence of the nation might be a starting point. Therefore, you would want to create an army and a department of defence to run it. Governments are also responsible for dealing with foreign countries, so you would need a department of foreign affairs. Beyond these two duties, what else does government need to do? Communications and transportation are important services, and therefore you might consider creating a post office and a department of transportation. There ought to be a department responsible for coordinating the government's spending and revenues, so a finance ministry seems like a logical choice.

We could continue adding to this list in a number of other areas, too. But keep in mind that each time you add a department, agency, board commission, or other government body, you increase the complexity of governing, thereby potentially decreasing its efficiency.

But where do you draw the line? What interests in society need to be served? When considering a country like Canada, there are certain obvious features that need to be taken into consideration: regionalism; class; language; gender; ethnicity; economic factors (business, labour, popular sector); geography; climate; and so on. At some point, you will also need to think about how to coordinate the various organizations within the government to ensure that there is no overlap of duties and that money is being raised and spent in the most propitious manner. So you need to construct some "watchdog" organizations, adding another layer of complexity to your design.

While speculating in this manner is an interesting intellectual exercise, the fact is that capitalist democracy, federalism, and cabinet-parliamentary government prevail in the real world of Canadian public administration. In some ways, the basic conundrum of making a society run smoothly can be expressed this way: the pursuit of common goals requires organization. Within the bounds of capitalist democracy, federalism, and cabinet-parliamentary government, we have a variety of structures and organizations designed to facilitate the public's business.

To illustrate, let us now focus on the actual organizational features of the federal government. Over 3 million Canadians currently work in the public sector (federal, provincial, territorial, and municipal). This should give you some sense of the complexity and size of the public sector. For now, we will focus only on the organization of the federal government. The structure of the federal government is divided into three broad components: departments, regulatory agencies, and Crown corporations. These are the main organizing structures, but they exist alongside a large number of other bodies as well. Before considering each component specifically, we will provide a brief overview of the political-administrative relationships that oversee this impressive machinery.

Political-Administrative Relationships

Let us return here to a concept we introduced in chapter 1: the politics-administration dichotomy. This is the principle that in the organization of government, there is a division between the elected officials and the appointed ones. The elected officials (the politicians) are the key decision-makers because, as the theory of representative government tells us, they represent the people. The appointed officials—the public servants—are there to take orders, administer programs, and assist the politicians in formulating, implementing, and evaluating the government's policies.

But, as we also noted in chapter 1, this relationship does not always work the way the theory suggests. Politicians run for public office as members of political parties. But ask yourself this: does it really matter which party wins office in an election? Doesn't the ongoing, professional public service march to the beat of its own drummer, regardless of which party wins elections? Sometimes it seems like this is the case. For instance, the Chrétien Liberals campaigned in the 1993 federal election against the dreaded Goods and Services Tax and the North American Free Trade Agreement, promising to repeal both pieces of legislation passed by the earlier Conservative government. Yet once in power, the Liberals kept both. Is it possible that the public servants within government convinced the new ruling party to keep both policies? If so, what does this suggest about the politics-administration dichotomy?

At various times in history, the alarm has been raised that the public interest has been sacrificed to the self-interest of public servants and their organizations. The fear of "rule by officials" is often cited in connection with bureaucracies that appear to be too powerful, which raises questions about the goals and values that public servants may have. After all, the traditional view is that public servants are concerned with the means by which government accomplishes its goals—not the ends that society aims for. In recent years, though, there has been a growing recognition that the values public servants have as individuals should be expressly acknowledged, and that those values should guide them in their actions. But then this brings us back to the age-old problem: how can public servants, who are not elected, be held accountable? What if public servants, guided by their own personal value systems, take actions that contradict official rules or procedures?

Imagine yourself in this position: you are a front-line worker in a government employment office. The rules say that each applicant for a job must be treated in exactly the same manner. Over time, you have gotten to know the case of one hard-luck individual who has just about used up his employment insurance benefits, hasn't yet qualified for provincial social assistance, has a young family, and is about to lose his apartment. His search for a job has been futile. One day, you are contacted by an employer who needs someone immediately. Your hard-luck case meets all the qualifications. But the rules say that you must post the job so that everyone has a fair chance to apply, and that you can send the employer a maximum of only three applicants. Your hard-luck case had just been in to see you before you learned of this new job. What do you do if your value system says that this person should be given first crack at the job, but the rules say that the job must be processed in the usual manner, even if it means the individual concerned will have virtually no opportunity to apply?

If you follow your own value system, you contribute to the concern that powerful bureaucracies acting in their own interests can actually undermine democracy, since you are accountable to no one, in this example, but your own conscience. You will recall that some of the theorists of public administration, such as Marx (and others), raised just this issue. But if you follow the prescribed rules, an individual may suffer dire consequences.

Think about it this way: governments are involved in making countless choices about what policies to enact. This necessarily involves making compromises between competing groups and individuals in societies, since not everyone is going to get all of what they want all of the time. It is the people's representatives who theoretically make the choices about whose interests are to be satisfied, since they have the legitimacy to exert authority in democratic societies. And if the people do not like their decisions, they can replace those representatives in the next election. Elections, therefore, are the mechanisms by which citizens hold governments accountable for their actions (or inactions). But what if the function of compromising is tainted by the fact that those responsible for enacting the compromises bring their own narrow self-interest to the process? What if, instead of faithfully serving the government of the day, the public service really serves only its own interests? Clearly, the democratic process would be undermined.

This underlying tension between bureaucracy and democracy is a recurrent theme in public administration, which is wrestled with by theorists and practitioners alike. Clearly, there are no easy answers to the dilemmas raised by these tensions.

Departmental Organizations

About half the employees who work in the federal public service work directly or indirectly in **departments** (also referred to as **ministries**). These are statutory bodies: that is, they are created by law passed by Parliament. The head of each department is the **minister**, who is appointed by the prime minister. The prime minister and the other ministers together constitute the Cabinet and are responsible individually for their departments and collectively for the actions of the government as a whole.

The convention exists that the prime minister will always select Cabinet ministers from individuals who sit in Parliament. This means that both senators and Members of the House of Commons are eligible to become ministers; in reality, the prime minister virtually always limits his or her selection of ministers to those who are elected to the House of Commons because senators are appointed (by the prime minister) and, therefore, have less legitimacy as representatives of the people. Prime Minister Harper ran into a storm of protest in 2006 when he violated these conventions. Harper selected his friend and supporter

Michael Fortier, who had neither run in the election nor held a Senate seat, to sit in Cabinet. Fortier had been a Conservative Party candidate in previous elections, had run for the leadership of the party, was co-chair of Harper's successful leadership campaign in 2004, and co-chair of the Conservatives' election campaigns in 2004 and 2006. Harper got Fortier into the Cabinet by instantly appointing him to the Senate, arguing that he needed some representation from the Montreal area (which the Canadian people, in exercising their political wisdom, had declined to give him in the election).

The talent the prime minister can draw on ultimately depends on the composition of the House of Commons. There is usually a strong correlation between the distribution of Cabinet seats and provincial population. Moreover, certain regional, linguistic, and other constraints limit the prime minister's choices. For instance, a French-Canadian prime minister will usually select an English Canadian to be deputy prime minister. A Western Canadian is usually made minister of agriculture, while a Maritimer or British Columbian is usually made minister of fisheries.

There has been a gradual growth in the number of departments (and hence of Cabinet ministers) over time until recently in Canada (see Table 5.1). Sir John A. Macdonald got by in 1867 with 13 ministers, but since the 1970s the wholesale growth in government responsibilities has necessitated ever larger Cabinets. Brian Mulroney felt compelled to appoint 40 in 1984! Pierre Trudeau's largest Cabinet had 37 members, nine more than his predecessor, Lester Pearson. Joe Clark, who followed Trudeau, reduced the Cabinet to 29 members, the same number used by John Turner. Kim Campbell continued the trend toward a reduced Cabinet with just 24 ministers, which was followed by Jean Chrétien, who had 23 ministers (although he also maintained a large number of "Secretaries of State," which are like junior ministers). Paul Martin had a large ministry, with close to 40 ministers, while Stephen Harper appointed 27 ministers in 2006.[12] The number and types of departments (and hence Cabinet ministers) is entirely at the discretion of the prime minister. This considerable power is exercised through the Public Service Rearrangement and Transfer of Duties Act, which reads, in part, "The Governor in Council may (a) transfer any powers, duties or functions or the control or supervision of any portion of the federal public administration from one minister to another, or from one department in, or portion of, the federal public administration to another; or (b) amalgamate and combine any two or more departments under one minister and under one deputy minister."[13]

The federal government, under the Financial Administration Act and the Public Service Employment Act, defines departments and the other parts of government in terms of statutory lines of control and accountability, according to financial and personnel criteria. More broadly, political scientist J.E. Hodgetts defines a *department* as an administrative unit consisting of one or more organizational components under the direct management and control of a minister of the Crown.[14] Departments provide services and administer programs either for the public or for other parts of the government. Personnel are mainly drawn from the Public Service Commission, which establishes merit-based hiring criteria and administers the hiring and firing process. Funding for each department comes from an annual appropriation act passed by Parliament as part of the government's overall budget.

TABLE 5.1   Government Departments, 1867 and 2007

Government Departments in 1867	Government Departments in 2007
Agriculture	**Government Departments**
Customs	Department of Agriculture and Agri-Food
Finance	Department of Canadian Heritage and Status of Women
Inland Revenue	Department of Citizenship and Immigration
Justice	Department of Environment Canada
Marine and Fisheries	Department of Fisheries and Oceans
Militia and Defence	Department of Foreign Affairs and International Trade
Post Office	Department of Health
Privy Council Office	Department of Human Resources and Social Development
Receiver General	Department of Indian Affairs and Northern Development
Secretary of State	Department of Industry Canada
Secretary of State for Provinces	Department of Justice Canada
	Department of Labour
	Department of National Defence
	Department of National Revenue
	Department of Natural Resources
	Department of Public Safety
	Department of Public Works and Government Services Canada
	Department of Transport, Infrastructure and Communities
	Department of Veterans Affairs
	Central Agencies
	Department of Finance
	Prime Minister's Office
	Privy Council Office
	Treasury Board Secretariat
	Special Agencies and Other Bodies
	Atlantic Canada Opportunities Agency
	Canada Revenue Agency
	Canadian International Development Agency
	Economic Development Agency of Canada for the Regions of Quebec
	Western Economic Diversification

Source: Updated for 2007 from Government of Canada's Privy Council Office Information Resources section online at **www.pco-bcp.gc.ca/default.asp?Language=E&Page=home**

BOX 5.1 What's in a Name?

As political scientists Jackson and Jackson point out, the names of departments reflect the predominant values and biases of the government of the day. Consider the evolution of the department responsible for immigration:

1867–1892:	Canadian Immigration and Quarantine Services
1892–1917:	Immigration Branch, Department of the Interior
1917–1936:	Department of Immigration and Colonization
1936–1950:	Immigration Branch, Department of Mines and Resources
1950–1966:	Department of Citizenship and Immigration
1966–1977:	Department of Manpower and Immigration
1977–1993:	Canada Employment and Immigration Commission
1993–	Immigration divided between Department of Public Security and the Department of Human Resources
1993–2007:	Department of Citizenship and Immigration

Source: Adapted from Robert J. Jackson and Doreen Jackson, *Politics in Canada: Culture, Institutions, Behaviour and Public Policy*, (Toronto: Pearson Prentice Hall, 2006): 353.

How do you distinguish the different types of departments? One common typology of departments divides them into three broad types of organizations (see Table 5.2).[15] First, and most commonly, there are the *vertical constituency* departments. Their primary function is to provide services directly to the public (e.g., Health or Industry), or some particular segment or group thereof (e.g., Indian Affairs and Northern Development). They are described as *vertical* departments because they represent direct links between citizens and the government.

The second type of department is the *horizontal administrative coordinative* type, whose main role is to provide services to other departments. For instance, the Department of Public Works and Government Services provides and coordinates a range of services, such as printing and purchasing, and real estate and office space, for other departments.

The third type of department is the *horizontal policy coordinative,* whose responsibilities include developing the broad policy framework within which other government functions are carried out, and coordinating policies and programs across government. The Department of Finance is among the most important in this regard, along with other "central agencies" (described in a following paragraph), including the Department of Foreign Affairs as well as Justice. Each provides coordination and policy advice to other departments regarding external relations and legal issues, respectively. Although usually small in size and budget, these are generally the key actors in the overall coordination of government policy. They can intervene in the affairs of the other departments, for instance, for this purpose.

Not all departments are alike in organization or function. But we can generalize about the structure of departments to some extent. They are hierarchical bodies, with

TABLE 5.2   A Typology of Departments

Horizontal Policy Coordinative	Horizontal Administrative Coordinative	Vertical Constituency
Finance	Public Works and Government Services	Agriculture and Agri-Food
Foreign Affairs and International Trade		
		Canadian Heritage and Status of Women
Justice		Citizenship and Immigration
Privy Council Office Treasury Board Secretariat		Environment
		Fisheries and Oceans
		Health
		Human Resources and Social Development
		Indian Affairs and Northern Development
		Industry
		Labour
		National Defence
		Natural Resources
		Transport, Infrastructure and Communities
		Veterans Affairs

the minister, as the political head, at the apex. Below the minister is the administrative head of the department, the deputy minister (who is discussed in more detail in a following paragraph). Below that are a number of assistant deputy ministers, directors, managers, and so on. The problem with this type of structuring is in knowing how many subdivisions or units optimize both efficiency in decision making and democracy in terms of accountability. While increased bureaucratization of government functions has been the response to the increased complexity of governing modern society, at some point bureaucracy becomes dysfunctional, as we saw in chapter 3.

Just as too many departments can make Cabinet decision making too unwieldy, too many internal subdivisions within departments can hamper their effective operation. This is part of the span of control problem, which, as we noted in chapter 3, refers to the number of subordinates that report to one supervisor. Ideally, a balance must be reached between too narrow and too broad a span of control. In a narrow span of control, there are too many supervisors and the number of reporting levels is increased, thereby increasing the degree of red tape and impeding internal communications. In a broad span of control, on the other hand, there are too few supervisors, placing strain on top management. Luther Gulick was among the first to think systematically about this problem. "Just as the hand of man can span only a limited number of notes on the piano," he wrote, "so the mind and will of man can span but a limited number of immediate managerial contacts. . . . The limit of control is partly a matter of the limits of time and of energy. As a result the executive of any enterprise can personally direct only a few persons. He must depend upon these to direct others, and upon them in turn to direct still others, until the last man in the organization is reached."[16] (See Figure 5.2.)

There is no sure way of knowing what constitutes an acceptable span of control, since any of a number of factors can come into play in the functioning of an organization. For instance, the number and type of tasks to be performed, the competence of individuals, the quality and amount of assistance available to the manager, and the geographical and physical setting (whether, for example, a department must have a

FIGURE 5.2   **Department of Foreign Affairs and International Trade**

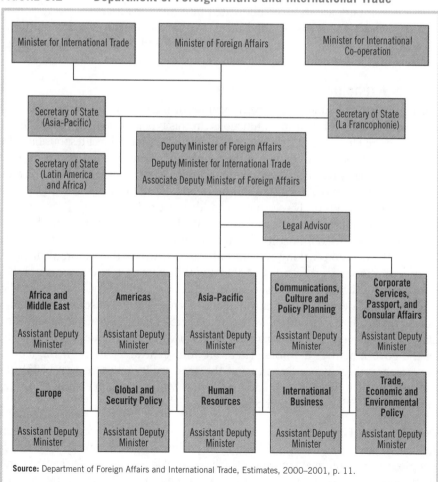

Source: Department of Foreign Affairs and International Trade, Estimates, 2000–2001, p. 11.

number of regional offices, or can be centralized in Ottawa) can all be factors influencing the organizational design of departments.

These points can be illustrated by looking at the organizational chart of a typical federal government department. Figure 5.2 shows the organizational structure of the Department of Foreign Affairs and International Trade. Notice the hierarchical arrangement of offices, beginning with the ministers for each of International Trade, Foreign Affairs, and International Co-operation, where ultimate authority rests. Below the ministers are the deputy ministers and other top management, including an associate deputy minister. There are six functional branches, and four geographic branches. As you study this organization chart, ask yourself: what type of span of control is evident here?

A generic model of the general categories of offices in federal government departments would look like this: the deputy minister (DM) sits at the administrative apex of a pyramidal hierarchy, with two or more assistant deputy ministers (ADMs) heading branches or bureaus of the department and reporting directly to the DM. Below the ADMs are directorates or branches, each headed by a director-general or director. These directorates are in turn subdivided into divisions headed by directors or divisional chiefs, which are also subdivided into sections, regions, districts, and areas. In general, this structure is used at both the federal and provincial levels, although different titles are sometimes used for roughly the same position in the hierarchy.

Central Agencies

Another way of thinking about government departments is to divide them into two categories in terms of their main functions. In this typology, some departments are simply referred to as *line departments,* which means they have direct responsibility for the delivery of goods and services to the people of Canada. These departments tend to consist of a large number of subunits and employ a large staff to deal with the public. The Department of Agriculture and Agri-Food, for instance, is a line department employing thousands of civil servants in a wide range of jobs.

Other departments are referred to as **central agencies**, which means that they are responsible for coordinating the line departments. Their main purpose is to support the decision-making activities of Cabinet, which they do in a variety of ways.[17] For instance, they supply Cabinet with information and advice, and they communicate Cabinet decisions to other parts of the public service, to the public, and to other governments. Central agencies ensure there is some consistency across departments—in other words, that there is *horizontal coordination*—and that the departments' overall spending habits fit with the revenue-raising capacity of the government as a whole. There are four central agencies in the federal government: the Finance Department; the Treasury Board Secretariat (TBS); the Privy Council Office (PCO); and the Prime Minister's Office (PMO). Let us consider briefly the role of each central agency.

Department of Finance In many respects, this is the most powerful actor in the federal government. It plays a leading role in making economic policy, which contributes to its informal reputation as the centre of key economic decision making. Preparation and delivery of the government's revenue and expenditure budgets rest with this department, as does jurisdiction over taxation and trade and tariff policy.

Moreover, the Finance Department manages federal borrowing on financial markets, and administers major federal transfers to provinces and territories. It also develops regulatory policy for the financial sector, and represents Canada within international financial institutions. It provides the government with analysis and advice on the broad economic and financial affairs of the country.

To fulfill its mandate, the Finance Department monitors and researches the performance of the Canadian economy in all important aspects, from output and growth to employment and income to price stability and monetary policy to the impact of globalization, and so on. In addition, the Finance Department is in constant communication with the other departments of government to coordinate initiatives that have an impact on the economy. Created in 1867 to replace the old office of Inspector General, Finance officials numbered 38. The department grew as large as 6000, but currently it employs just under 1000. It is generally conceded that the best and the brightest in the public service aspire to work in this powerful central agency. Concerns expressed by the Finance Department about the economic health of the country usually become the concerns of other departments as well. In other words, Finance often sets the tone for the rest of government in terms of whether new policies and programs can be launched, or whether there will be cutbacks and restraint. Initiatives from other departments in government generally require the support of Finance if they are to go ahead, since Finance controls the purse strings.

Treasury Board Secretariat The Treasury Board Secretariat (TBS) is the administrative arm of the Treasury Board, which is the only Cabinet committee that has a statutory basis. TBS supports the Treasury Board by providing advice on policies, directives, regulations, and program expenditure proposals regarding the management of the government's financial, human, and material resources (e.g., lands and buildings). TBS also supports the Treasury Board in its role as the general manager and employer of the public service. It is "management" where employee relations are concerned within government. In other words, it is the agency that assumes the interest of the employer in collective bargaining and personnel issues within government. In 2003, the Canada Public Service Agency was created to assume some aspects of the TBS's human resources management functions (see chapter 10). TBS is also the key actor in administrative policy within the government, overseeing departmental audits and ensuring that accounting practices and standards are uniformly adhered to across the government.

TBS is also responsible for evaluating policy and particular programs. TBS assists the Cabinet by providing information about expenditures and the financial and personnel resources required by each department. And TBS also prepares the main estimates for the government, which are the detailed spending plans that the government introduces each year in the House of Commons.

The Privy Council Office As an organizational body, the Cabinet requires support to function on an ongoing, day-to-day basis. This support primarily comes from the Privy Council Office (PCO), which acts essentially as the Cabinet's secretariat (see Figure 5.3).

The PCO reports directly to the prime minister and is headed by the Clerk of the Privy Council and Secretary to the Cabinet, which is the highest position in the

FIGURE 5.3   Basic Privy Council Office Structure Under Stephen Harper

Source: Office of the Assistant Deputy Minister, Corporate Services.

public service (see Box 5.2). The Clerk and the PCO are intimately involved in the sensitive process of Cabinet decision making, and particularly in strategic planning and policy formulation. The PCO is both the Cabinet secretariat and the prime minister's source of public service advice across the entire spectrum of policy questions and operational issues that confront the government. This includes matters relating to the management of federal-provincial relations and constitutional issues.

BOX 5.2 Clerk of the Privy Council and Secretary to the Cabinet

This is the most senior public servant in the government. In his or her role supporting the prime minister, the clerk has three primary responsibilities:

- As the prime minister's deputy minister, provides advice and support to the prime minister on a full range of responsibilities as head of government, including management of the federation.

- As the secretary to the Cabinet, provides support and advice to the ministry as a whole, and oversees the provision of policy and secretariat support to Cabinet and Cabinet committees.

- As the head of the Public Service, is responsible for the quality of expert, professional, and nonpartisan advice provided by the Public Service to the prime minister, the ministry, and to all Canadians.

The PCO also provides support to the deputy prime minister, government leaders in the House of Commons and the Senate, the president of the Privy Council and minister of Intergovernmental Affairs, as well as the minister designated as the federal interlocutor for Metis and nonstatus Indians. Box 5.3 shows the responsibilities of the divisional units within PCO, the secretariats.

The Prime Minister's Office The Prime Minister's Office (PMO) stands apart from the other central agencies in that it is staffed by partisan supporters of the government in power rather than by nonpartisan public servants. This is the prime minister's personal staff (see Figure 5.4). As such, the PMO deals with the prime minister's voluminous correspondence; speech writing; scheduling the prime minister's time and appearances; dealing with media relations; liaising with other ministers, the government caucus, and party; and providing advice on appointments and policy. The PMO is headed by a chief of staff, who has ongoing daily contact with the prime minister. The PMO drafts the annual Speech from the Throne, which is the statement of the government's legislative and policy intentions for the coming year.

To a large extent, the success or failure of any given prime minister rides on the quality of advice he or she gets from the PMO. Not surprisingly, the style of the prime minister is reflected in the role and functioning of the PMO. Pierre Trudeau was the first prime minister to really expand the PMO, which previously had been a relatively small organization. Today it is an extremely influential body. Some academic

---

BOX 5.3 | **About PCO Secretariats**

Secretariats are the basic building blocks of the Privy Council Office (PCO). Although each secretariat plays a distinct role within PCO, many share common functions.

Some secretariats support the Cabinet and committees of Cabinet and keep track of developments within specific policy sectors. Others provide advice on appointments, mandates, and government organization, legislation and counsel issues, security and intelligence, communications issues, and other direct concerns of the prime minister.

Key roles include the following:

Supporting Cabinet Committees

■ Assisting the Cabinet and its committees in preparing for and conducting meetings

■ Transmitting decisions and documents to departments

Managing the Flow of Cabinet Business

■ Helping ensure the Cabinet decision-making process functions smoothly according to the standards, design, and instructions of the prime minister

■ Managing changes in committee structure and the use of ad hoc committees (to focus on special policy areas and problems)

Facilitating Policy Development

■ Working with departments to prepare ministerial proposals for Cabinet

■ Ensuring complementarity between new proposals, existing policies, and government objectives

■ Arranging for follow-up measures for implementation

Source: Canada. Privy Council Office, *PCO Secretariats.* **www.pco-bcp.gc.ca/default.asp? Language=E&page= PCOsSecretariats**

---

observers have maintained that there is an unhealthy concentration of power in the PMO. Not surprisingly, at least one occupant of an influential position therein claims this is not true, arguing government is too complex to be dominated by one agency.[18]

Taken together, these four central agencies play a vital series of coordinating and supportive roles for the government; they are powerful and important actors in the overall structure. An understanding of their place in the organization of the Canadian government is vital to understanding public administration.

Alternative Service Delivery

Apart from the traditional structures reviewed above, governments have been resorting to a variety of new innovations to provide services to Canadians.[19]

FIGURE 5.4 **The Prime Minister's Office (Basic Form)**

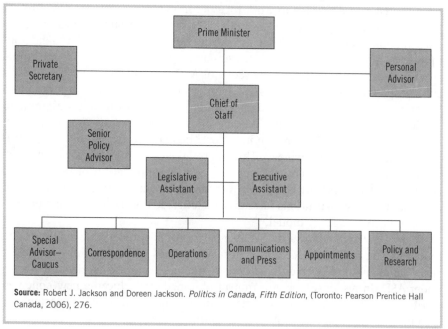

Source: Robert J. Jackson and Doreen Jackson. *Politics in Canada, Fifth Edition*, (Toronto: Pearson Prentice Hall Canada, 2006), 276.

These so-called **"alternative service delivery"** (ASD) arrangements come in a number of packages: bodies created by restructuring existing institutions within government; bodies partnering with actors in other departments within government, with other governments, or outside government altogether; and structures outside government entirely. According to the Treasury Board Secretariat, "While departments continue to play an important role in service delivery, a growing need for flexibility, interdependence and innovation has produced an increasing diversity of organizational forms and service delivery arrangements to provide more responsive service to Canadians."[20]

The motivations behind ASD are varied. They include the desire to offer a more "citizen-centred" approach to service provision, in response to the growing disillusionment with government evident in the broader society. They also are a result of the drive toward "less government," which has been predominant in recent years. In addition, they are seen as potential cost-saving innovations. Moreover, rigidities in existing institutions have increasingly been seen as impediments to service delivery, and more flexible alternatives to departments might address this problem. There is also the desire to break down the "silo mentality," in which government departments exist in isolation from each other, resulting in duplication of activities and frustration for citizens trying to find information across departments that never speak to or interact with one another. This is directly related to the trend toward "horizontality" in management, wherein attempts are made to cut across traditional boundaries (be they departmental, programmatic, issue-based, etc.) to more fully integrate and rationalize service delivery. ASD promotes horizontality by requiring different institutional actors to learn to work together in new ways. Finally, ASD mechanisms are often designed to accommodate the growing desire for greater citizen participation in governance. They provide interested actors with the "hands-on" opportunity to shape, create, and implement programs in ways traditional structures cannot or will not. The scope of ASD is impressive.[21] It can include special operating agencies (SOAs), service agencies, and Crown corporations, a variety of partnership arrangements, and the devolution of programs and services to other governments. It sometimes involves the commercialization of services, such that they are run in a more "businesslike" fashion than government is thought able to achieve. This might take the form of innovations such as employee takeovers, contracting out, and the application of user fees. In addition, outright privatization of government services is an option. In short, a plethora of new institutions have arisen alongside the traditional line department and central agency model.[22]

However, the trend toward ASD has not been problem-free. One important and difficult issue is that of accountability. While lines of responsibility are clear and unambiguous with traditional bodies, such as departments, they are less so under ASD. In response, the government of Canada introduced a new policy on April 1, 2007, setting out in greater detail and with more precision the accountability relationships of ASD mechanisms.[23]

Ministerial Responsibility

Whether we are talking about line department, central agency, or ASD, the ultimate responsibility for what government does or does not do rests with the political head of the institution, namely the minister. As a member of Cabinet, the minister is responsible for all the official acts of the public servants under his or her supervision. This is known as the doctrine of **ministerial responsibility**, an extremely important concept in understanding how government is held accountable to the people. This is particularly significant when you remember that a department can employ thousands of people and spend millions of dollars of taxpayers' money. Reinforcing this principle is another: **collective ministerial responsibility**.[24] This is the convention whereby ministers must always show solidarity with their colleagues in Cabinet. Once a decision has been taken in a Cabinet meeting, the whole Cabinet supports it publicly. These concepts are discussed in detail in chapter 12.

But how can an individual minister heading up a department employing thousands of people and spending millions of dollars really be held responsible for everything that goes on in that department? Realistically and logistically, it is impossible for a given minister to know the intimate details of the thousands of decisions taken every year within his or her department, let alone those taken by the government as a whole. Still, there is the expectation that the principle of ministerial responsibility will be observed. In this way, a link is established that sees the public service connected to the political realm through the minister. Political scientists Jackson and Jackson put it this way:

The Prime Minister appoints members of the Cabinet to assume responsibility for particular ministries or portfolios, and their associated departments, commissions, boards and corporations. Ministers are constitutionally responsible for all of the operations of their departments. Thus, legally, it is ministers who are assigned the powers and duties to be exercised by their departments. Departmental officials, on the other hand, are given scant attention in the law and are responsible exclusively to their ministers, not to Parliament. They are supposed to be non-partisan, objective and anonymous—shielded from the glare of public attention and from the partisan political arena of Parliament by their minister—in order to safeguard their neutrality and ensure their ability to serve faithfully whichever government is in power. In the event of a serious error in the formulation or administration of policy within a department, convention dictates that the minister, rather than officials, be held responsible to Parliament; and if the minister cannot account for the failures to the satisfaction of Parliament, then convention dictates that the minister should resign.[25]

There are, however, limits to the application of this doctrine. As a consequence of these limits as well as the outbreak of the "sponsorship scandal," the federal government sought to institute a vastly reformed accountability regime in 2006. Accountability became one of the Conservative government's five policy priorities, and the Federal Accountability Act was passed. We assess these developments more fully in chapter 12.

The Deputy Minister

While the minister is the *political* head of a department, the *administrative* head is the **deputy minister (DM)**. This is the senior-most public servant, an extremely powerful and influential post in the workings of government. DMs receive their positions "at the pleasure of the prime minister," which is to say that it is the prime minister who hires and fires them. (Most other personnel in departments are recruited through the Public Service Commission, which is like a giant human relations department for the government.)

What exactly is the relationship between a minister and his or her top bureaucratic advisor—the deputy minister? This is an important question. The popular British sitcom *Yes, Prime Minister* portrays a series of often hilarious episodes in which the senior advisor to the prime minister is engaged in a constant game of trying to control and shape the prime minister's decisions. The series portrays the clash between the "political will and the administrative won't." Interestingly, the writers for the series were former public servants and claim their inspiration came from real-life examples within the British government.

In the real world of governing, there are several factors that may make it difficult for a minister to resist the influence of his or her DM or other senior advisors. The experience of Flora MacDonald, former secretary of state for External Affairs in the Joe Clark government, points to this. A minister is typically pulled in several different directions at once. There are Cabinet responsibilities, party duties, attendance in the House of Commons, press conferences, constituency work, foreign travel, political brushfires, and countless other distractions. Invariably, most ministers have little time to effectively concentrate on their departments' day-to-day administrative needs. This must be left to the deputy minister and other senior staff. But MacDonald claimed that her senior staff went beyond simply tendering advice on the administration of the department she headed. MacDonald claimed that her senior advisors engaged in a concerted effort to impose their own agendas on both the running of the department and the development of policy. She felt that as a rookie Cabinet minister, she was at the mercy of the more experienced public servants.[26]

Another view is provided by Mitchell Sharp, who was a public servant early in his career and later became a Cabinet minister. He argued that top civil servants are powerful individuals in the machinery of government. After all, they hold their positions because they have demonstrated a high level of skill and ability in administrative matters. Weak ministers may be susceptible to manipulation by crafty civil servants, but Sharp also argues that most of the time this is not the case. A government, he argues, cannot be run by amateurs, and so a trained and professional civil service is vital. But ministers must be able to determine what constitutes good advice from their advisors. Moreover, Sharp felt that a first-class nonpartisan civil service dedicated to the public interest was a hallmark of parliamentary government that enabled elected "amateurs" to make the political decisions needed to govern effectively.[27]

There is also the issue of the longevity of ministers. Most serve for relatively short periods of time before being shuffled to another position in the Cabinet (or removed from Cabinet altogether). To ensure continuity in departments, DMs are not appointed by the ministers they serve. Rather, the prime minister appoints them, according to an 1896 order-in-council.[28] DMs thereby have some measure of security, knowing that they will not lose their jobs if ministers change. This is reinforced by the nonpartisanship of DMs. They are not members or supporters of any political party but, rather, serve the government of the day no matter who is in power. Thus, when the government changes hands, the senior public servants retain their jobs, allowing for a measure of stability and continuity in the administration of government. Admittedly, though, this places the DM in a somewhat awkward position, sandwiched between the nonpolitical public service and the political minister.

Apart from the appointment question, there are other questions surrounding the DM. What, exactly, are the DM's role and duties? And what is the relationship of the DM to other actors in the political-administrative structure?[29] It is the primary duty of the DM to create the conditions under which the minister and prime minister can provide the best possible government. To this end, the DM plays a vital role in both formulating and implementing policy. There are several important conventions that guide the DM in his or her role: neutrality, anonymity, the politics-administration dichotomy, and loyalty. Let us consider each in turn.

The convention of *neutrality* suggests that the DM is nonpartisan, as we noted above. The DM should be politically neutral in serving the minister, but this convention is often difficult to maintain. Political pressures swirl around the

BOX 5.4 | **Deputy Ministers in International Perspective**

Canada has a long-standing tradition of apolitical senior public servants. How does this compare to the practices in other countries? According to political scientist Jacques Bourgault,

In the last few years, it seems that Canada has become quite a unique case, some would say anachronistic, due to the apolitical character of its senior officials. The United States have a spoils system for Deputy Secretaries positions (and the six levels immediately below. . . .) France uses a system of internal lists of public servants for the positions of chiefs of staff, Secretaries General and several Director General positions. . . . Socialist States insist on the necessary politicization of the administration provided by the Marxist-Leninist doctrine, because of the role of the State in the class struggle.

Only countries that use the Whitehall model (Westminster political system) practice a certain separation between administration and politics. New public management, imple-mented in Australia, New Zealand and Great Britain, recommends a greater dependency of the administration on political leaders, in the name of greater democracy and efficiency. This manifests itself by a more political selection of incumbents, the contracturalization of hiring, and performance contracts with large financial bonuses. None of this seems to have really disrupted the Canadian practice.

Source: Jacques Bourgault, *Profile of Deputy Ministers in the Government of Canada*, (Ottawa: Canada School of Public Service, 2005): 16.

DM constantly. Political interaction occurs in almost all facets of the DM's job, from dealing with Parliament and Cabinet to meeting with interest groups and citizens, all of whom have some vested stake in policy matters. Moreover, while remaining officially nonpartisan, the DM must be sensitive to political develop-ments, trends, and issues. This is an extraordinarily difficult balancing act.

The second convention is that of *anonymity*. Can you name a Cabinet minister? Most people can. Can you name a deputy minister? Most of us would be hard-pressed to identify a single one at either level of government. Since it is the minister who is formally responsible for the actions of the government, it is the minister who must accept praise or blame for those policies. The DM toils anonymously in the shadows for two reasons. First, the DM is not elected by anyone and, therefore, is not directly accountable to anyone other than the minister and the prime minister. Second, the DM must be free to provide frank and impartial advice in a private and confidential manner. In return, the DM is shielded from public attack by the minister, who rightly accepts public responsibility for the department's actions.

This is part of the doctrine of ministerial responsibility. Having said this, it should be noted that this doctrine of anonymity has been eroding in recent years. Senior public servants have been singled out and asked to appear in public before Parliamentary committees in a number of high-profile scandals.[30] But overall, to retain anonymity the DM must renounce any desire for public recognition of his or her efforts or personal identification with the government's policies.

The third convention relates to the *politics-administration dichotomy*. It is the minister's duty to direct the public service and the DM's to see to it that directions are executed faithfully. In reality, as we discussed in chapter 1, this is an artificial division of duties. The senior civil service is very much involved in both administration and policy formulation. Interestingly enough, though, the same cannot be said of the minister, who is so consumed by other duties that he or she is rarely concerned with the department's administration.

Ironically, while the precepts of the politics-administration dichotomy are supposed to be followed, it is also expected that the DM will regularly provide policy advice to the minister. What does this policy advisory role cover? It entails initiating policy suggestions without seeking to usurp the minister's decision-making role. In other words, the DM should be able to say, "The government ought to adopt policy X for all these reasons." But the minister ultimately says "yes" or "no" to this suggestion. Some have criticized this as providing the DM with "power without responsibility." Others have said that it is quite the opposite: "responsibility without power." Whichever view is correct, there is a fine line that DMs ought not to cross between simply providing advice and making decisions.

Finally, there is the convention of *loyalty*. The DM must in all circumstances remain loyal to the minister in providing the best possible government. But the DM's loyalties conflict, making this a complicated problem. DMs have a loyalty to Parliament as well as to the policies their departments implement. And the DM has a loyalty to the profession of public servant. These various pressures may compel the DM to speak out against certain policies as a matter of conscience. But the DM's position compels the DM to remain silent.

The relationship of the DM to his or her staff is also an important consideration. As the head of the administration, the DM must set the example for the other public servants, instill a sense of public service, an understanding of the power of bureaucracy, and a respect for what is most important in every department, program, and policy: the rights of the citizen. The DM also has a responsibility to keep abreast of public reaction to government policies, and to have a staff that can evaluate when policies are working properly or not. Thus, the DM must keep in close touch with his or her subordinates and be sensitive to their views.

The DM must also develop a good working relationship with the interest groups and citizens most directly affected by the policies of the government in a given area. The DM actively seeks out public opinion on these issues to represent the most current views of the public to the minister in the development of policy. At the same time, the DM must be careful not to become captive to any one group or interest. To avoid this pitfall, good DMs constantly seek countervailing sources of information and advice: they talk not only to the proponents of a particular policy, but also to opponents, and they seek independent advice on various issues, often from disinterested parties, such as academics. To effectively do their jobs, DMs canvass a range of views to get the best possible advice to tender to the minister.

A major job of the DM is to implant in the ministry an understanding of broader social and economic trends, and to effectively evaluate those trends in relation to the department's responsibilities and programs. This means that besides administering the day-to-day minutiae, the DM must also be able to see the big picture of governing. The DM is responsible for understanding the long-term impacts of social and economic change, and anticipating when and where those changes will affect his or her department. This contrasts with the short-term view typical of the minister, whose main concern is the next election just over the horizon. The juxtaposition of these two views often creates tensions between the DM and minister that a skilful and sensitive DM must nonetheless work around.

The DM has some particular administrative responsibilities in the area of personnel and finance. He or she must deal with matters of personnel, such as changes in the collective agreement, employment equity, bilingualism in the public service, and so on. As well, the DM is responsible for the overall preparation of departmental expenditure budgets. In all these duties, the DM must be responsible to other actors in government besides the minister, such as the Public Service Commission, and especially to central agencies like the Treasury Board Secretariat, the Ministry of Finance, and the Privy Council Office.

In 2007, the responsibilities of deputy ministers were further modified. In a controversial move (discussed in chapter 12), new accounting officer provisions of the Financial Administration Act (FAA) designated deputy ministers and deputy heads of designated government entities as the accounting officers for their organizations. This means that they now have a legal obligation to appear before committees of the Senate and House of Commons and answer questions on the management responsibilities set out in the FAA. While the framework of ministerial responsibility and accountability to Parliament still prevails, this new designation creates new legal obligations for deputy ministers, the consequences of which are not yet fully known. Ministers, and ministers alone, remain accountable to Parliament for all actions of the executive, including management, but the accounting officer is legally obliged to appear before the Senate and House of Commons. While he or she is to do so in support of the minister's accountability, it is not hard to imagine situations in which the deputy minister is made to accept responsibility that rightly belongs to the minister.[31]

Clearly, the role of the DM is a demanding and complex one that requires an incredible amount of administrative management ability combined with a remarkable degree of political sophistication. The DM must constantly satisfy, at the same time, the demands of both the bureaucratic constituency and his or her political master. It is a remarkably sensitive balancing act but one that must be maintained for a department to be successful in fulfilling its mandate.

Regulatory Agencies

Besides *making* policy, government is also in the business of *enforcing* policy. Enforcement can take many forms, the most common of which is regulation. According to the Economic Council of Canada, regulation is "the imposition of constraints, backed by government authority, that are intended to modify economic behaviour of individuals in the private sector significantly."[32] Regulation is intended to ensure that the behaviour of private sector actors conforms with the desires of government by modifying the behaviour of those private sector actors through a number of possible mechanisms. For instance, the government may decide that promoting Canadian culture is a worthwhile goal and may, as a result, craft regulations to ensure that broadcasters include a certain percentage of Canadian content on the airwaves. The Canadian Radio-television and Telecommunications Commission (CRTC) does exactly this.

Among their varied functions, **regulatory agencies** can influence private sector behaviour with respect to prices, conditions, and quality of service, contents of goods for sale, methods of production, and so on. Many regulatory agencies also have investigative powers and can undertake research and can launch inquiries. Some regulatory bodies are imbued with quasijudicial power. This means they can "judge specific cases involving the granting, denial, or removal of licences, the approval of rates or fares and the censuring of failure to comply with terms of licences."[33] The senior levels of regulatory bodies are staffed by government appointees, usually for five- or ten-year terms. These are often patronage appointments, used by the prime minister to reward loyal supporters. In general, these appointees enjoy an arm's-length relationship with the department that oversees their activities, thus creating a climate of independence from direct political interference. With some exceptions, their members are not appointed by the Public Service Commission, nor are they employees of the Treasury Board. But accountability is maintained in that regulatory bodies must submit their budgets to the Treasury Board for review, and present annual reports through the responsible minister to the House of Commons.

Regulation takes place in a range of areas. Besides radio, television, and telecommunications, cited above, the government also regulates matters as varied as atomic energy (Atomic Energy Control Board), labour relations (Canadian Labour Relations Board), old age pensions (Canadian Pension Commission), and many others. Regulatory agencies receive their powers—which are often considerable—and their mandates through legislation. While some regulations are actually laws that require enforcement by the police and judicial system, most are simply administrative directives managed on an ongoing basis by a specialized government body.

Political scientists Howlett and Ramesh point out that the nature of regulations varies, depending on whether they are economic or social:

Economic regulations control aspects of the production processes specific to particular goods and services, such as the prices and the volumes of production, or return on investment, or the entry into or exit of firms from an industry. A good example of this type of regulation is that carried out by the various kinds of marketing boards, regulatory bodies that are particularly prominent in the agricultural sector. The intent of such boards is to keep farm commodity prices high by restricting supply. Their objective is to correct perceived imbalances or inequities that may emerge as a result of the operation of market forces. Economic regulations have been the traditional form of regulation; their social counterparts are of more recent origin.

Social regulations refer to controls in matters of health, safety and social practices such as civil rights and discrimination of various sorts. They have more to do with our physical and moral well-being than with our pocketbooks. Examples of social regulation include rules regarding liquor consumption and sales, gambling, consumer product safety, occupational hazards, water-related hazards, air pollution, noise pollution, discrimination on the basis of religion, race, gender or ethnicity, and pornography. Many areas of regulation, such as environmental protection, liquor consumption and gambling, exist as hybrids between pure economic and pure social regulation, because the problems may have economic origins but their adverse effects are mostly social. While there is a great deal of overlap between the two, social regulations tend to be more general than economic ones and do not focus on particular industries (for example banks or telecommunications), as do economic regulations, but on broader problems or functions such as pollution, safety or morality. This has important implications for their administration and enforcement because social regulation tends to cut across several sectors and come under the jurisdiction of several government agencies.[34]

In some cases, regulations place directed constraints on behaviour, leaving little or no discretion to the body concerned in implementing the regulations. In other cases, the government steps back and allows the private actors to self-regulate, sometimes through the adoption of voluntary codes of conduct.[35] This is the case, for instance, with the medical and legal professions, which are given substantial power to regulate their members and their activities. These powers are limited only where they contradict the broad guidelines provided in the government regulations. The government will often choose this option because it may be the least expensive form of regulation, reducing administration costs by passing them on to the profession concerned. In addition, it allows those with the most intimate knowledge of the activity being regulated to administer the rules. Governments have neither the time nor the inclination to enter the labyrinthine worlds of doctors and lawyers, and so are content to allow these (and other) groups to regulate themselves.

Why do governments use regulation rather than other administrative or organizational forms? First, regulation is justified on the grounds of "public interest." This means that government intervention in the market is sometimes needed to correct market failures: that is, situations in which private sector actors cannot or will not act as effective regulatory instruments themselves. The most obvious case of market failure is monopoly, where firms may earn excessive profits by exploiting consumers by charging excessive rates for their services, or by engaging in discriminatory behaviour toward certain customers. This argument has been under fire, though, on the basis that the public interest is not always served by regulation in these circumstances. Instead, the regulator becomes "captured" by the interests that it was supposed to be regulating. As a result, the very public purposes of the regulatory agency are undermined and the private corporate interest is promoted at public expense.

Another motivation for regulation is to protect individual firms from competition. Such was the case, for instance, when Air Canada was created. Another reason is to create a policy tool that can engage in some planning for a specific sector of the economy. This may be most obvious in the telecommunications sector, where ongoing planning under the auspices of the CRTC has been used to moderate the impact of new television technologies, from antennae to cable to satellites to digital, for instance.

The most important recent development concerning regulation, however, is the trend toward deregulation.[36] According to political economists Shields and Evans, "deregulation may entail the complete or partial withdrawal of the state from a specific activity, such as enforcement of labour standards or occupational health and safety, through privatizing the enforcement function, shifting towards a compliance framework based on workplace or sectoral self-regulation, or both."[37] Deregulation is an important component of the New Public Management, discussed in chapter 4.

As early as 1978, Prime Minister Trudeau and the premiers embraced deregulation, though in only a lukewarm manner. Since then, the Mulroney, Chrétien, Martin, and Harper governments have made it central to administrative reform for their governments, as have several provincial governments. Federally, the government has deregulated the oil and gas industry, foreign investment, financial services, transportation, and other areas. Indeed, various governments proceeded with deregulation in a pronounced manner by reorganizing government structures, sometimes even designating a specific minister responsible for deregulation.[38]

Sociologist Gary Teeple argues that there are several reasons for the accelerating pace of deregulation.[39] He suggests that there is usually a strong relationship between the development and application of new technology and the use of regulation. When new technology comes on line, a number of consequences are discernable: increased competition between producers with the same technology; competition between producers with different technology; monopolies in which only one or a small number of firms have access to the new technology for a period of time; damage to humans or the natural environment. In all of these situations, regulation can be justified, according to Teeple. Thus, he argues, the growth of government regulation corresponds more or less to the rate of technological growth in society. Since the Second World War, technological growth has proceeded at a pace unprecedented in human history and, not surprisingly, so, too, has the growth in regulatory bodies and agencies. But "with the present stage of permanent technological revolution beginning in the 1970s, the imposition of government regulations can no longer keep up with industrial innovation and its implications for society and nature."[40] Thus, regulation has come under attack as a hindrance to innovation and development.

Teeple further argues that the original rationale for much regulation was to prevent or control monopolies and other market failures. But, increasingly, the economy is made up of global monopolies, oligopolies, and cartels. So the rationale for seeking to control competition among national corporations is being swept aside. In any event, global corporations can move their operations to countries with minimal regulations as a means of lowering the costs of doing business. The mere threat of this action by a major employer in Canada is often enough to send government officials scurrying to find ways to repeal or tone down the regulatory framework. Moreover, the construction of global trade regimes and international free trade areas often means that one country has to modify its regulations to match those of its partners. In Canada's case, there is pressure to lessen regulations to the lowest common denominator of its NAFTA partners. Since both the United States and (especially) Mexico have much less government intervention than Canada does, this implies reducing the regulatory role of the Canadian state to match that of the other two parties.

Teeple goes on to argue, though, that the impact of deregulation is frequently negative. For instance, deregulation actually reduces competition in some cases. It sometimes even opens the doors to illicit financial activities, since the watch-dog role of regulatory bodies is relaxed. Nonetheless, deregulation has recently been embraced by governments of many different ideological stripes.

Recently, governments have moved toward a program of regulatory reform, according to economist John Strick, in which they

"regulate smarter" through greater efficiency, greater accountability, and increased sensitivity to those affected by regulation. Regulatory procedures were streamlined to reduce bureaucratic red tape and delays. Regulations were relaxed and modified in areas where it was deemed they impeded efficiency in the marketplace. A form of regulating the regulators was introduced through the application of cost-benefit analysis to new regulatory proposals in recognition of the potential high costs to the economy of regulation.[41]

On March 24, 2005, the president of the Treasury Board announced Smart Regulation and launched a new website (**www.regulation.gc.ca**) dedicated to regulatory renewal. The government said,

Smart Regulation is aimed at improving the Government of Canada's regulatory system so that it can keep pace with today's realities and our evolving needs. This means building a regulatory system that is more effective in safeguarding the health and safety of all Canadians, ensuring a clean and sustainable environment, and creating the conditions for an innovative and competitive economy. In meeting these goals, Smart Regulation recognizes the interdependence of social, environmental, and economic objectives. It strives for a better coordinated system that remains forward-thinking, progressive and accountable to the citizens it serves.

Smart Regulation is based on public desire for high standards and transparency in regulation, combined with the advice provided by the Organisation for Economic Co-operation and Development (OECD), and the recommendations of both the

Auditor General and the External Advisory Committee on Smart Regulation (EACSR), which released its report, Smart Regulation: A Regulatory Strategy for Canada, on September 23, 2004.[42]

On April 1, 2007, the *Cabinet Directive on Streamlining Regulation* came into effect, further refining the regulatory regime of the federal government.[43]

A moment's reflection about your own personal daily routine will reveal that government is intimately involved in almost every aspect of your life. And regulations are a prominent part of that involvement. Bleary-eyed, you wake up to the sound of your alarm clock-radio, the electronic parts of which are regulated by safety standards set by the government. The DJ screams at you to rise and shine, as he plays the latest Canadian hit song, as required by government regulations covering Canadian content on the airwaves. You stumble into the bathroom, flip on the light and turn on the water, both of which are supplied by public utilities heavily regulated with regard to delivery, service, and maintenance. You fumble for the toothpaste, whose ingredients are carefully regulated to ensure that they do not include anything harmful. As you head out for your morning walk with the dog, you put its leash on, mindful of municipal regulations (which also require that you suffer the indignity of having to "stoop and scoop"). If you drive to school, you are travelling in an invention that is among the most regulated technologies ever developed, from the additives in the fuel that propels it, to its safety systems, to the speed at which it can travel, and so on. If you take public transit, another legion of regulations governs everything from smoking to number of passengers to hours of operation. And the list goes on and on. In short, the world of regulation has truly penetrated every aspect of our lives. Former prime minister Pierre Trudeau once said that the state had no place in the bedrooms of the nation. He might have reconsidered that observation in light of the pervasive growth of the state's regulatory powers.

Crown Corporations

Another important organizational unit of government is the **Crown corporation**, which includes a variety of nondepartmental organizations involved in regulating the private sector through public ownership. There are about 400 such federal corporations in Canada, usually headed by boards of directors, whose members are usually appointed by the prime minister. These are typically patronage appointments. The legal definition of Crown corporations revolves around the issue of government ownership. Government doesn't have to own 100 percent of an enterprise for that enterprise to be publicly owned; a minority holding of less than 50 percent of the shares of a corporation qualifies as public ownership. But the legislation covering Crown corporations refers only to enterprises that are 100-percent government owned.

A general definition supplied by Adie and Thomas suggests that "a Crown corporation could be described as an institution with a corporate form brought into existence by government action to serve a public function."[44] Crown corporations are a sort of blend between the private and public sectors. They function in most cases as private corporations but under conditions of greater accountability to government than private corporations. They enjoy a higher level of autonomy from Parliament than do departments, although they are ultimately responsible to Parliament through a designated minister. For instance, one of the most prominent Crown corporations is the Canadian Broadcasting Corporation (CBC), which reports to Parliament through the Canadian Heritage Minister. But Crown corporations are not subject to direct ministerial control. As a result, they have more autonomy with regard to personnel, finance, and service provision than do regular departments.

Crown corporations are also called government business enterprises (GBEs), Crown agencies, or public enterprises. According to Hale, their role

has changed significantly in recent years with the maturing of the Canadian economy and changes in the political and management philosophies of many Canadian governments. These changes variously described as "the new governance" or "new public management," have blurred many traditional distinctions between government and business. In so doing, the range of policy tools or instruments available to governments for the delivery of public services and the delivery of public policy goals has been greatly expanded.[45]

Crown corporations can act as *alternatives* to private sector businesses that fail or refuse to provide certain services; act in *competition* with them; act in *co-operation* or *partnership* with them; or *complement* or *supplement* them in the marketplace. They generally have the following characteristics:

- They are legal entities engaged in the sale of goods and/or services to citizens, businesses, or other governments (domestic or foreign).
- They are hybrid creatures with varying degrees of operational autonomy from governments.
- They typically serve some public policy goal or, more generally, the "public interest."
- They usually have a commercial orientation requiring more attention to customer service and operational efficiency than most traditional government departments.
- They may have legal or regulatory privileges unavailable to private sector actors.[46]

Why would governments create Crown corporations in the first place? Why not simply rely on the traditional structures of government—that is, on departments? These questions are central to any explanation of the role of government ownership in Canada. We will consider several related explanations: nation building, resistance to the pull of continentalism, regional economic development, other economic rationales, ideology, and efficiency.

Crown corporations have historically been used in Canada as nation-building tools in the promotion of transportation, communication, and resource development, and to make Canada competitive with its neighbour to the south. For instance, pre-Confederation governments were heavily involved in developing infrastructure, such as canals and roads—a practice that continued after 1867 in other areas, such as airports. The Canadian National Railway, created in 1917, and Air Canada (Trans-Canada Air Lines), created in 1936, were needed to unite the country through transportation links from sea to sea. Petro-Canada was created in 1976 to give the Canadian government a "window" into the oil and gas industry, which was mainly foreign (i.e., U.S.) owned and controlled. The CBC was created in 1936 to protect and promote Canadian culture and cultural industries. At the provincial level, countless Crown corporations have been created over the years to pursue the goals of economic development and diversification. Ontario Hydro, for example, was created in 1906 by taking over the many private utility companies in the province so as to provide cheap and reliable sources of electric power to the province's manufacturers. By the 1970s and 1980s, every province in the country had established some sort of provincial development corporation to attract investment and jobs. So nation- and province-building have been important factors in explaining the proliferation of Crown corporations at both levels of government in Canada.

Sir John A. Macdonald once said in defence of government involvement in the economy that without it Canada would become "a bundle of sticks . . . without binding cord, [which would] fall, helpless, powerless, and aimless, into the hands of the neighbouring republic."[47] Later in the 1930s, an early advocate for a national public broadcasting system, Graham Spry, argued that the choice for Canadians was either "the state or the United States." These arguments reflect what economist Hugh G.J. Aitken termed the practice of "defensive expansionism." This is the notion that Canadian governments adopt an active role in the economy in order to resist or prevent continentalism—the economic, cultural, and, ultimately, political domination of Canada by the United States. In this view, Crown corporations are viewed as policy tools that permit Canadian governments to resist the overwhelming influence of the world's most powerful nation.

The third common explanation for the use of Crown corporations also has economic roots. This is the view that these policy tools promote regional economic development. Canada is regionally divided in a number of ways. Uneven economic development means that some regions are poorer and less economically diversified than other regions. At various times in Canadian history, governments have attempted to overcome this problem by targeting economic development at particular areas to stimulate the economies of these regions. For example, the Cape Breton Development Corporation was established by the federal government in 1967 to take over some failing coal mines that the private sector was about to abandon. The Maritime provinces have been particular targets of federal intervention in the form of Crown corporations, but such corporations have also been used in other depressed regions from time to time. In many of these situations, the government steps into an area where the private sector has failed or refuses to go. The bottom line of the private sector is profits, but governments must also take into consideration the health and welfare of communities, the costs of unemployment insurance and welfare, the possibility of mass migrations of people out of depressed regions into other parts of Canada, and so on. These are considerations that corporate officials do not need to worry about.

Regional economic development is also fostered when governments create Crown corporations in industries that tend to have wide fluctuations in prices and incomes from year to year. For instance, the Canadian Wheat Board was established to add some stability to the price of wheat by regulating supply and demand, and ensuring that farmers would get a fair price year in and year out, notwithstanding fluctuations in the world price for their products. Finally, some Crown corporations are used in order to provide low-interest loans and risk capital to private sector corporations to promote economic activity in particular regions. All these measures are intended to ensure that some healthy level of economic activity exists in all the regions of Canada.

Another economic argument for Crown corporations says that, in some circumstances, particular industries may lend themselves to a natural monopoly. For instance, until recent technological change altered the landscape, it was often argued that the provision of services such as transit, sewage, telephone, hydro, or natural gas were most efficiently and effectively provided by one big company in each field. Whether the one company was to be public or private was a matter of some debate, but in many instances there was a proper and defensible role for the state, as the monopoly provider of a given service, to ensure that customers were not gouged by high prices, poor service, or discriminatory practices.

Besides the economic arguments, there are also ideological ones. Some commentators have focused on the differences between Canadian political culture and U.S. political culture, arguing that Canada has a stronger sense of the collective or community, and is more willing to use the state to defend that sense of community than are the Americans, where a more "rugged individualism" prevails. This manifests itself in a more pluralistic set of political ideologies than is found in the United States. There is a specific content to the ideologies of socialism, liberalism, and conservatism in Canada. Each has important consequences for the choice and implementation of economic development strategies by the Canadian state,[48] and will be considered in turn:

- Socialism is associated with the idea that society should be organized on the basis of co-operation rather than competition and that the collective is of paramount importance in securing the liberty of the individual, whose self-worth is recognized in the idea that all in society are equal. In this view, the state is seen as an active agent of intervention in the marketplace, up to and including nationalization of industry.

- Liberalism asserts that the individual is the single most important element in a society, a notion derived from political philosophers, such as Thomas Hobbes and John Locke, who essentially saw the community as an atomistic collection of individuals who best further societal living by pursuing their self-interests in healthy competition with others. The liberal, like the socialist, believes in equality. But unlike the socialist, the liberal asserts that equality of opportunity is sufficient for the pursuit of personal fulfillment, while the socialist asserts that equality of condition is necessary. Freedom of the individual from state interference is of primary importance for liberals, and shapes their view of economic development, which is that the market should operate unencumbered by state intervention.

■ In conservatism, the organic community is most important, and notions of social equality give way to deference to authority and tradition that guide societal relations. This view asserts that society is naturally hierarchically organized, and is evidenced in the Canadian tradition by such well-known features of Canadian history and development as the absence of a lawless, egalitarian, American-style frontier, by a preference for Britain rather than the United States as a social model, and generally by a weaker emphasis on social equality than is found in either socialism or liberalism. A particular trait of Canadian conservatism is the willingness of the political and business elites to use the power of the state for developing and controlling the economy, especially where staples (i.e., natural resource) development is concerned. This partly explains why it was Conservative governments in Canada that created Crown corporations, such as the CBC, Air Canada, Ontario Hydro, and others.

The presence of conservatism and socialism alongside liberalism permits a greater diversity of views about the role of the state to exist in Canada than does the more monolithic ideology of liberalism that dominates in the United States. Hence the more common use of public ownership in Canada than in the United States.[49]

Indeed, almost all aspects of social and economic life in Canada are represented in the proliferation of Crown corporations at both the federal and provincial levels. Their use as policy tools has some advantages over the use of regular departments in providing services for citizens. For instance, as alluded to above, Crown corporations are one step removed from direct political control. This immunizes Crown corporations from compromising positions—for example, where the provision of a good or service may appear as a political favour from a minister to a supporter or friend (e.g., in the awarding of a contract).

In addition, there is often an advantage of efficiency in Crown corporations that is absent in departments. Departments can be weighed down with processes, procedures, rules, and regulations that impede the speedy and efficient achievement of a particular goal. Departments may also be less efficient due to contradictory, competing, or multiple goals. Budgeting and personnel policy may be more streamlined in Crown corporations than in government departments. For instance, labour relations in many Crown corporations come under the Labour Code instead of the more onerous legislation that governs personnel in departments. This allows for greater flexibility in a number of areas, such as setting wages and salaries. Finally, Crown corporations may be preferable to departments under certain circumstances for the simple reason that departments have enough on their plates already, making it preferable to "farm out" tasks and work to another government body.

Recently, Crown corporations have been under sustained attack by the right wing in Canada as costly, bloated, unresponsive, and unaccountable creatures that compete unfairly in the marketplace against private sector corporations. What began in the 1970s and 1980s as a call for increased accountability and control over Crown corporations has evolved into a call for their dismantling. Thus, neoconservatives in Canada have argued fairly successfully that many such corporations have outlived their usefulness and, more important, that they are inappropriate as a policy instrument, draining away taxpayer money and doing a job poorly that could be better done by the private sector. Thus, there has been a trend lately toward privatization of Crown corporations—that is, selling them to the private sector.

Advocates of privatization argue that the original public policy purposes of Crown corporations no longer apply, or that the public policy goals involved could be pursued more efficiently through private sector ownership. This has been the fate of Air Canada and Petro-Canada at the federal level (see Box 5.5).

BOX 5.5 | **Federal Crown Corporations and Privatizations**

Crown Corporations 2006	Privatizations—1980s–1990s
Canada Post Corporation	Canada Communications Group
Canadian Broadcasting Corporation	Canadian Arsenals
Atomic Energy of Canada	Canadian National Railway
VIA Rail Canada Inc	CN Subsidiaries: CN Hotels; CNCP
National Film Board of Canada	Telecommunications (CN half);
National Gallery of Canada	Northwestel Inc.; Terra Nova
National Arts Centre Corporation	Communications
National Capital Commission	Air Canada
Canada Mortgage and Housing Corporation	Eldorado Nuclear Limited
	Fishery Products International
Marine Atlantic Inc	Teleglobe Canada Inc
Bank of Canada	Telesat Canada
Royal Canadian Mint	Northern Canada Power Commission
Business Development Bank of Canada	Northern Transportation Company Ltd
	de Havilland Aircraft of Canada Inc.
Export Development Corporation	Canadair
St. Lawrence Seaway Authority	Petro-Canada
Canadian Wheat Board	Canada Development Corporation
Farm Credit Canada	Nanisivik Mines Ltd
Atlantic Canada Opportunities Agency	Pêcheries Canada
Western Canada Development Agency	Route Canada
	Terra Nova Telecommunications
	Co-Enerco Resources Ltd.
	Nordion International
	NAV Canada
	National Sea Products
	Theatronics International

Sources: Adapted from Alasdair Roberts, "A Fragile State: Federal Public Administration in the Twentieth Century," in Christopher Dunn, ed. *The Handbook of Public Administration*, (Toronto: Oxford University Press, 2002): 29; and David Johnson, *Thinking Government: Public Sector Management in Canada. Second Edition*, (Peterborough: Broadview Press, 2006): 172.

At the provincial level, the Liquor Control Board in Alberta and parts of Ontario Hydro in Ontario have been privatized. Many governments in Canada have established units within departments to look at which Crown corporations can be turned over to the private sector.

Those who oppose privatization argue that it is premised on shaky economic and ideological grounds. There is a good deal of skepticism that the free market can perform as well as its proponents claim. Certainly, there are underlying questions about whether nation building or resistance to continentalism can be realized without public ownership. And there is the lingering issue of whether the public interest is best served under conditions of free markets or under some mix of private and public ownership. Moreover, if privatization proceeds, who exactly is able to afford to buy the assets that the government puts up for sale? Generally, it is those corporate actors who are already powerful to begin with. Therefore, it is argued that privatization simply contributes to an undesirable concentration of wealth and power in fewer and fewer hands. In any event, the ongoing discussion in Canadian society about the usefulness of these policy instruments is part of the larger ideological debate about the proper role of government in general.

WHAT YOU HAVE LEARNED

The three categories of departments, regulatory bodies, and Crown corporations do not encompass all organizational units within the federal public service. As we noted, several new mechanisms for alternative service delivery have emerged. And certain other offices and institutions exist—for example, the Office of the Auditor General and the Commissioner of Official Languages. These are independent of Cabinet and report directly to Parliament. But the majority of organizational units do fall within the ambit of departments, regulatory bodies, and Crown corporations. Let us summarize this part by returning to some general observations about public service and how these units fit in the overall bureaucratic scheme of things.

You will recall that the term *bureaucracy* refers to a kind of organization with particular structural characteristics. As Weber pointed out, bureaucracies are characterized by a well-developed division of labour, within which officials perform certain clearly defined roles by following prescribed rules and regulations. Moreover, those roles are defined by the office held, not by the individual occupying the role. This ensures that there is some continuity in the functions and structures of government. Detailed written records of all the actions taken by public servants are also a feature of this system, which allows for a body of precedents to build up to guide future actions. The fact that office holding is a full-time occupation also contributes to continuity. Finally, the organizational structure is characterized by hierarchy. Decision making flows downward from above in a rigidly defined structure in which each level of the bureaucracy is responsible to the level above.

Adopting this type of bureaucratic organization has its benefits. It allows for a kind of equality of treatment of all citizens by "routinizing" the decision-making

Source: Josh Beutel, Saint John, N.B.

process, which in turn allows for maximum impartiality in dealing with citizens. It also allows for predictability, and thus fairness, in that the application of the law by bureaucratic officials must be the same for everyone. But clearly, these strengths are also weaknesses. Citizens with special circumstances may not fit into the routinized bureaucratic process. For example, certain university students applying for financial assistance may find they are unfairly disadvantaged by a bureaucratic interpretation of what constitutes an asset, which is appropriate in most cases, but not in their own. You have no doubt encountered a situation in which you pleaded for treatment appropriate to your own circumstances, only to be told by some bureaucratic official, "If we change the rules for you, we'll have to change them for everyone."

Notwithstanding these limitations, bureaucracy is the worst system we have—except for all the others (to paraphrase Winston Churchill on democracy). The organization of the Canadian bureaucratic system into departments, regulatory bodies, and Crown corporations both reflects the major characteristics of bureaucracy and represents our best attempts to construct a complex organizational structure that responds to the needs of citizens and can balance the tensions between democracy and efficiency within the framework of bureaucracy. The fact that alternative service delivery mechanisms have evolved, but not supplanted traditional mechanisms, speaks to both the strengths and weaknesses of the latter.

Key Words and Concepts

spending power (124)
executive branch (125)
legislative branch (125)
judicial branch (125)
Privy Council (127)
Cabinet (127)
constitutional convention (127)
responsible government (127)
departments (132)

ministries (132)
minister (132)
central agencies (138)
alternative service delivery (143)
ministerial responsibility (144)
collective ministerial responsibility (144)
deputy minister (145)
regulatory agencies (150)
Crown corporation (154)

Review Questions

This chapter was divided into five sections, each reflecting a key issue for public administration. You should now be familiar with these issues and be able to answer questions associated with each.

1. Factors Influencing Organizational Structure

Among the many factors influencing Canadian public administration, we isolated three for particular attention. How in your view would the structure of government differ if one or more of capitalist democracy, federalism, and/or cabinet-parliamentary government was absent from the Canadian setting? Can you explain the significance of each in terms of how they influence the very outlines of the state itself and have influenced public administration?

2. Political-Administrative Relationships

We returned here to some issues surrounding the relationship between public administration and democratic government. You may have some assumptions about who controls government, and how. Did this section confirm those assumptions, or challenge them? How? Can you explain the relationship between politicians and public servants, and explain who is actually in control of the machinery and actions of the state?

3. Departmental Organizations

The main organizational units of the Canadian government are dynamic, growing and shrinking over time, rising and falling in influence and importance. Why do some prime ministers prefer large Cabinets with many departments, while others opt for more stripped-down models? How does the traditional departmental model stack up against alternative service delivery agencies? Why have these newer bodies emerged?

4. Regulatory Agencies

The presence of government in our lives is evident in examining the nature of regulatory bodies. Can you think of an area of life that government does not regulate? These most common of organizational forms of government, although increasingly under attack, sometimes seem ubiquitous. What role do regulatory bodies play in public administration? In an era of deregulation, why have we been rethinking the areas of life that government should be regulating?

5. Crown Corporations

Can you claim to have an understanding of the historical place of public ownership in Canadian public administration? Why has the role of Crown corporations as a policy tool recently been questioned?

Weblinks

The Prime Minister of Canada
www.pm.gc.ca

The Privy Council
www.pco-bcp.gc.ca

Treasury Board
www.tbs-sct.gc.ca

Department of Finance
www.fin.gc.ca

Cabinet Ministers and Their Portfolios
canada.gc.ca/howgoc/glance_e.html

Parliament of Canada
www.parl.gc.ca

Federal Government Departments Canada
http://canada.gc.ca/depts/major/depind_e.html

Canadian Public Service Commission
www.psc-cfp.gc.ca

Supreme Court of Canada
www.scc-csc.gc.ca

Intergovernmental Online Information Kiosk
www.intergov.gc.ca

Government of Canada Intergovernmental Affairs
www.pco-bcp.gc.ca/aia

Institute of Intergovernmental Relations (IIGR)
www.iigr.ca/iigr.php

Centre for Constitutional Studies
www.law.ualberta.ca/centres/ccs

Forum of Federations
http://forumfed.org

Further Reading

1. Factors Influencing Organizational Structure

Johnson, David. *Thinking Government: Public Sector Management in Canada, Second Edition*. Peterborough: Broadview Press, 2006.

Peters, B. Guy and Donald J. Savoie, eds. *Governance in the Twenty-First Century: Revitalizing the Public Service*. Montreal: McGill-Queen's University Press, 2000.

2. Political-Administrative Relationships

Bourgault, Jacques. "The Role of Deputy Ministers in Canadian Government," in Christopher Dunn, ed. *The Handbook of Canadian Public Administration*. Toronto: Oxford University Press, 2002: Chapter 23.

Dwivedi, O.P. and James Iain Gow. *From Bureaucracy to Public Management: The Administrative Culture of the Government of Canada*. Peterborough: Broadview Press, 1999.

Franks, C.E.S. "The Respective Accountability and Responsibilities of Ministers and Public Servants: A Study of the British Accounting Officer System and Its Relevance for Canada," in Donald Savoie, ed. *Restoring Accountability: Research Studies, Volume 3, Commission of Inquiry into the Sponsorship Program and Advertising Activities*. Ottawa: Public Works and Government Services Canada, 2006: 157–230.

MacDonald, Flora. "Who Is on Top? The Minister or the Mandarins?" in Paul Fox and Graham White, eds. *Politics: Canada. Eighth Edition*. Toronto: McGraw-Hill, 1995: 488–552.

Savoie, Donald J. "The Public Service Has a Personality," *Canadian Public Administration*, 49, 3 (Fall 2006): 261–81.

Sharp, Mitchell. "A Reply From a Former Minister and Mandarin," in Paul Fox and Graham White, eds. *Politics: Canada. Eighth Edition*. Toronto: McGraw-Hill, 1995: 453–56.

3. Departmental Organizations

Aucoin, Peter. "The Staffing and Evaluation of Canadian Deputy Ministers in Comparative Westminster Perspective: A Proposal for Reform," in Donald Savoie, ed. *Restoring Accountability: Research Studies, Volume 3, Commission of Inquiry into the Sponsorship Program and Advertising Activities*. Ottawa: Public Works and Government Services Canada, 2006: 297–336.

Campbell, Colin and George J. Szablowski. "What Central Agencies May and Ought to Do: Structure of Authority," in Barbara Wake Carroll, David Siegel, and Mark Sproule-Jones, eds. *Classic Readings in Canadian Public Administration*. Toronto: Oxford University Press, 2005: 53–79.

Hodgetts, J.E. "Structural Heretics: The Non-Departmental Forms," in Barbara Wake Carroll, David Siegel, and Mark Sproule-Jones, eds. *Classic Readings in Canadian Public Administration*. Toronto: Oxford University Press, 2005: 87–102.

Hurley, James Ross. "Responsibility, Accountability and the Role of Deputy Ministers in the Government of Canada," in Donald Savoie, ed. *Restoring Accountability: Research Studies, Volume 3, Commission of Inquiry into the Sponsorship Program and Advertising Activities*. Ottawa: Public Works and Government Services Canada, 2006: 115–56.

Savoie, Donald J. "Power at the Apex: Executive Dominance," in James Bickerton and Alain-G. Gagnon, eds. *Canadian Politics. Fourth Edition*. Peterborough: Broadview Press, 2004: 145–62.

Sutherland, S.L. "The Role of the Clerk of the Privy Council," in Donald Savoie, ed. *Restoring Accountability: Research Studies, Volume 3, Commission of Inquiry into the Sponsorship Program and Advertising Activities*. Ottawa: Public Works and Government Services Canada, 2006: 21–114.

Tardi, Gregory. "Departments and Other Institutions of Government," in Christopher Dunn, ed. *The Handbook of Canadian Public Administration*. Toronto: Oxford University Press, 2002: Chapter 16.

Winfield, Mark. Alternative Service Delivery in the Natural Resources Sector: An Examination of Ontario's Forestry Compliance Self-Inspection System," *Canadian Public Administration*, 48, 4 (Winter 2005): 552–74.

4. Regulatory Agencies

Bird, Malcom and Christopher Stoney. "Government Approaches to the Regulation of 'Sin'." In G. Bruce Doern, ed. *How Ottawa Spends 2006–2007: In From the Cold: The Tory Rise and the Liberal Demise*. Montreal: McGill-Queen's University Press, 2006: 247–65.

Doern, G. Bruce. "Regulatory Processes and Regulatory Agencies," in Barbara Wake Carroll, David Siegel, and Mark Sproule-Jones, eds. *Classic Readings in Canadian Public Administration*. Toronto: Oxford University Press, 2005: 103–23.

Schultz, Richard. "Regulatory Agencies," in M.S. Whittington and G. Williams, eds. *Canadian Politics in the 1990s. Third Edition*. Scarborough: Nelson, 1990: 468–480.

5. Crown Corporations

Ashley, C.A. and G.H. Smails. "From Canadian Crown Corporations," in Barbara Wake Carroll, David Siegel, and Mark Sproule-Jones, eds. *Classic Readings in Canadian Public Administration*. Toronto: Oxford University Press, 2005: 124–43.

Canada. Treasury Board Secretariat. *Canada's Crown Corporations: Meeting the Expectations of Citizens*. Ottawa: Treasury Board Secretariat, 2005.

Endnotes

1. Neil Bradford, *Commissioning Ideas: Canadian National Policy Innovation in Comparative Perspective*, (Toronto: Oxford University Press, 1998): 15.

2. Geoffrey Hale. *Uneasy Partnership: The Politics of Business and Government in Canada*, (Peterborough: Broadview Press, 2006): 3

3. Bradford, *Commissioning Ideas*, (1998): 15–16.

4. For a discussion of Wheare's views and other definitions of federalism, see Garth Stevenson, *Unfulfilled Union: Canadian Federalism and National Unity, Fourth Edition*, (Montreal: McGill-Queen's University Press, 2004): chapter 1. For an overview of the evolution of federalism, see Gregory J. Inwood, "Federalism, Democracy and the (Anti-) Social Union," in Mike Burke, Colin Mooers and John Shields, eds. *Restructuring and Resistance: Canadian Public Policy in an Age of Global Capitalism*, (Halifax: Fernwood Press, 2000): 124–44.

5. The federal and provincial governments launched major investigations into the question of the fiscal imbalance in 2006. For the provincial view, see The Council of the Federation, Advisory Panel on Fiscal Imbalance. Reconciling the Irreconcilable: Addressing Canada's Fiscal Imbalance. (Ottawa: Council of the Federation, March 2006). **www.councilofthefederation.ca/pdfs/ Report_Fiscalim_Mar3106.pdf.** For the federal view see The Expert Panel on Equalization and Territorial Formula Financing, Achieving a National Purpose: Putting Equalization Back on Track, (Ottawa: Department of Finance, May 2006). **www.eqtff-pfft.ca/english/index.asp**

6. See Gregory J. Inwood, Carolyn M. Johns and Patricia L. O'Reilly, "Intergovernmental Officials in Canada," in J. Peter Meekison, Hamish Telford and Harvey Lazar, eds. *Canada: The State of the Federation 2002: Reconsidering the Institutions of Canadian Federalism*, (Montreal: McGill-Queen's University Press, 2004): 249–84.

7. See Richard Simeon, *Federal-Provincial Diplomacy: The Making of Recent Policy in Canada. With a New Preface and Postscript*, (Toronto: University of Toronto Press, 2006).

8. Peter H. Russell, *Constitutional Odyssey: Can Canadians Become a Sovereign People? Third Edition*, (Toronto: University of Toronto Press, 2004): 81. See also Herman Bakvis and Grace Skogstad, "Canadian Federalism: Performance, Effectiveness, and Legitimacy," in Herman Bakvis and Grace Skogstad, eds. *Canadian Federalism: Performance, Effectiveness, and Legitimacy. Second Edition*, (Toronto: Oxford University Press, 2008): 3–22.

9. See Carolyn M. Johns, Patricia L. O'Reilly and Gregory J. Inwood, "Formal and Informal Dimensions of Intergovernmental Administrative Relations in Canada," *Canadian Public Administration*, 50, 1 (Spring, 2007); and Carolyn Johns, Patricia L. O'Reilly and Gregory J. Inwood, "Intergovernmental Innovation and the Administrative State in Canada," *Governance*, 19, 4 (October, 2006): 627–49.

10. See Donald Savoie, *Governing From the Centre: The Concentration of Power in Canadian Politics*, (Toronto: University of Toronto Press, 1999); and Graham White, *Cabinets and First Ministers*, (Vancouver: UBC Press, 2005).

11. Victor S. MacKinon, "Introduction to the Legal Environment: Theories and Principles," in Randy Hoffman et al., *Public Administration: Canadian Materials, Third Edition*, (Toronto: Captus Press, 1998): 199.

12. For an analysis of recent changes to cabinet structures, see Evert Lindquist, Ian Clark and James Mitchell, "Reshaping Ottawa's Centre of Government: Martin's Reforms in Historical Perspective," in G. Bruce Doern, ed. *How Ottawa Spends 2004–2005: Mandate Change in the Paul Martin Era*, (Montreal: McGill-Queen's University Press, 2004): 317–47.

13. Canada, Department of Justice. The Public Service Rearrangement and Transfer of Duties Act. **http://laws.justice.gc.ca/en/showdoc/cs/P-34/**

14. J.E. Hodgetts, *The Canadian Public Service: A Physiology of Government 1867–70*, (Toronto: University of Toronto Press, 1973): 89.

15. Robert J. Jackson and Doreen Jackson, *Politics in Canada: Culture, Institutions, Behaviour and Public Policy, Third Edition*, (Scarborough: Prentice Hall, 1994): 376–77.

16. Luther Gulick, "Notes on the Theory of Organization," in Jay M. Shafritz and Albert C. Hyde, eds. *Classics of Public Administration, Third Edition*, (Pacific Grove, California: Brooks/Cole Publishing, 1992): 83–84.

17. See Canada, Privy Council Office, "Decision-Making Processes and Central Agencies in Canada: Federal, Provincial and Territorial Practices," (Ottawa: Privy Council Office, 1998).

18. See Savoie, *Governing from the Centre*, (1999); and Eddie Goldenberg, *The Way it Works: Inside Ottawa*, (Toronto: McClelland and Stewart, 2006).

19. See Canada, Treasury Board of Canada Secretariat, "Policy on Alternative Service Delivery," (April 1, 2002): 1–2.

20. Canada, Treasury Board Secretariat, "Policy on Alternative Service Delivery," (April 1, 2002): 2.

21. See David Zussman, "Alternative Service Delivery," in Christopher Dunn, ed. *The Handbook of Canadian Public Administration*, (Toronto: Oxford University Press, 2002): 55.

22. See John C. Strick, *The Public Sector in Canada: Programs, Finance and Policy*, (Toronto: Thompson, 1999): Chapter 6.

23. See Canada, Treasury Board of Canada Secretariat, Policy on Reporting of Federal Institutions and Corporate Interests to Treasury Board Secretariat. **www.tbs-sct.gc.ca/pubs_pol/opepubs/ prfici-pmppif/prfici-pmppif01_e.asp#Toc149964094**

24. See David E. Smith, "Clarifying the Doctrine of Ministerial Responsibility as It Applies to the Government and Parliament of Canada," in Donald Savoie, ed. *Restoring Accountability: Research Studies, Volume 3, Commission of Inquiry into the Sponsorship Program and Advertising Activities*, (Ottawa: Public Works and Government Services Canada, 2006): 101–43.

25. See Jackson and Jackson, *Politics in Canada, Sixth Edition*, (Toronto: Pearson Prentice Hall Canada, 2004): 354.

26. Flora MacDonald, "Who Is on Top? The Minister or the Mandarins?" in Paul Fox and Graham White, eds. *Politics: Canada, Eighth Edition*, (Toronto: McGraw-Hill, 1995): 488–552.

27. Mitchell Sharp, "A Reply from a Former Minister and Mandarin," in Paul Fox and Graham White, eds. *Politics: Canada, Eighth Edition*, (Toronto: McGraw-Hill, 1995): 453–56.

28. Jacques Bourgault, *Profile of Deputy Ministers in the Government of Canada*, (Ottawa: Canada School of Public Service, 2005): 15.

29. See Gordon F. Osbaldeston, *Keeping Deputy Ministers Accountable*, (Toronto: McGraw-Hill Ryerson, 1989).

30. See, for example, Sharon L. Sutherland, "The Al-Mashat Affair: Administrative Accountability in Parliamentary Institutions," *Canadian Public Administration*, 34, 4 (Winter, 1991): 573–603.

31. Canada, Privy Council Office, Accounting Officers: Guidance on Roles, Responsibilities and Appearances before Parliamentary Committees 2007. **www.pco-bcp.gc.ca/default. asp?Language=E&Page=informationresources&Sub=publications&Doc=guidemin/account- guideonrole2007_e.htm**. For a critique of the accounting officer model, see Peter Aucoin and Mark D. Jarvis, *Modernizing Government Accountability: A Framework for Reform*, (Ottawa: Canada School of Public Service, 2005): 78–81.

32. Economic Council of Canada, Interim Report: Responsible Regulations. Cited in Jackson and Jackson, *Politics in Canada, Fifth Edition*, (2001): 341.

33. Richard Schultz, "Regulatory Agencies," in M.S. Whittington and G. Williams, eds. *Canadian Politics in the 1980s, Second Edition*, (Toronto: Methuen, 1984): 438.

34. Michael Howlett and M. Ramesh, *Studying Public Policy: Policy Cycles and Policy Subsystems. Second Edition*, (Toronto: Oxford University Press, 2003): 104.

35. See Strick, "Regulation and Deregulation," (2002): 262–78.

36. See Strick, "Regulation and Deregulation," (2002): 276.

37. John Shields and B. Mitchell Evans, *Shrinking the State: Globalization and Public Administration "Reform,"* (Halifax: Fernwood Press, 1998): 69–70.

38. Richard J. Schultz, "Regulating Conservatively: The Mulroney Record, 1984–1988," in Andrew B. Gollner and Daniel Salèe, eds. *Canada under Mulroney: An End of Term Report*, (Montreal: Véhicule Press, 1988): 198.

39. Gary Teeple, *Globalization and the Decline of Social Reform: Into the Twenty-First Century*, (Toronto: Garamond Press, 2000): 92–94.

40. Teeple, *Globalization and the Decline of Social Reform*, (2000): 93.

41. Strick, "Regulation and Deregulation," (2002): 277.

42. Canada. Treasury Board Secretariat of Canada. Government of Canada Reports Progress on Regulatory Review. **www.tbs-sct.gc.ca/media/nr-cp/2005/1028_e.asp#BG** Accessed July 4, 2007.

43. See Canada. Government of Canada. **www.regulation.gc.ca**. Accessed July 4, 2007.

44. Robert F. Adie and Paul G. Thomas, *Canadian Public Administration: Problematical Perspectives, Second Edition*, (Scarborough: Prentice Hall, 1987): 377. On the role of Crown corporations in particular sectors, see Matthew J. Bellamy. *Profiting the Crown: Canada's Polymer Corporation 1942–1990*, (Montreal: McGill-Queen's University Press, 2005); and Vanda Rideout, *Continentalizing Canadian Telecommunications: The Politics of Regulatory Reform*. (Montreal: McGill-Queen's University Press, 2003).

45. Geoffrey Hale, *Uneasy Partnership: The Politics of Business and Government in Canada* (Peterborough: Broadview Press, 2006): 271.

46. Hale, *Uneasy Partnership* (2006): 271.

47. Cited in Adie and Thomas, *Canadian Public Administration*, (1987): 387.

48. See Nelson Wiseman and David Whorley, "Lessons on the Centrality of Politics from Canadian Crown Enterprise," in Christopher Dunn, ed. *The Handbook of Canadian Public Administration*, (Toronto: Oxford University Press, 2002): 383–84.

49. See W. Christian and C. Campbell, *Political Parties and Ideologies in Canada, Second Edition*, (Toronto: McGraw-Hill Ryerson, 1983): 25–26; and Terrence Bell, Richard Dagger, William Christian and Colin Campbell, *Political Ideologies and the Democratic Ideal, Canadian Edition*, (Toronto: Pearson Longman, 2006).

Chapter 6

Public Administration, *the* Constitution, *and* Law

WHAT YOU WILL LEARN

Clearly, public administration is intimately connected to the law, particularly constitutional law and administrative law. In this chapter, we will frame our discussion of public administration and the law by first looking at the following issues:

- What is a constitution, and what does it do?

- What is the relationship between the constitution and the institutions of the state?

- How do elements of political culture relate to the law, and how does the British North America Act, 1867 (BNA Act) reflect the nature of Canadian society at Confederation, compared to how the Constitution Act of 1982 reflects the changed nature of Canadian society?

- How does the constitution deal with the question of rights and freedoms in the Canadian Charter of Rights and Freedoms?

- How has the Canadian Constitution evolved and changed, or, alternatively, why it has changed so little in over 140 years?

- What is the definition, nature, and scope of administrative law?

This chapter is divided into the following sections:

1. The Law, the Courts, and the Administration of Justice

This section asks you to consider political culture and the rule of law in Canada. It asks, What is the rule of law? What are common law and civil law? What is the structure of the court system in Canada? How is justice administered in Canada?

2. — *What Is a Constitution?*

While constitutions are fundamental to every society, they vary widely in their utility and application. This section asks, What is a constitution? What three main functions do constitutions serve? What are the component parts of the Canadian Constitution? What is constitutional law? How did the Canadian constitutional order come about?

3. — *Constitutional Law*

This section addresses constitutional law in terms of conflict over the division of powers in the Constitution. It asks, How are disputes resolved before the courts when federal and provincial governments cannot agree on the jurisdiction of a law? What powers in the Constitution have proven the most contentious, and how have disputes over them been resolved? What role have the courts played in the resolution of conflict? What has been the legacy of judicial review of constitutional law?

4. — *Administrative Law*

The last section in this chapter examines administrative law. It asks, What is administrative law? What is the power of discretion held by public servants? What happens when a dispute arises over the exercise of legal powers by an administrative agency? What is the relationship between constitutional and administrative law? What is the role of judicial review in administrative law?

The Law, the Courts, and the Administration of Justice

Institutions for the administration of justice are a feature common to virtually all societies. The Egyptian kings were perhaps the first to delegate the administration of justice to judges, starting around 2900 BC; the Code of Babylonia and Code of Hammurabi emerged a little later in ancient Mesopotamia; and courts were common to Hebrew, Hindu, Arab, Chinese, Greek, Roman, Aztec, and other societies.[1] The direct historical trajectory of Canada's legal traditions can be found in the legal systems developed first by Aboriginal societies, then imported from Europe by settlers mainly from Great Britain and France.

Canadians have a reputation as a peace-loving, orderly, cautious people. Our Constitution, it is said, reflects this in that its most memorable phrase is "peace, order, and good government." Compare this to the U.S. Constitution's declaration of "life, liberty, and the pursuit of happiness," or the French constitution's affirmation to "liberty, equality, fraternity." These phrases speak volumes about the political cultures of the three countries. Canada is said to be a nation that sent its police force into the wilderness to precede settlement and establish loyalty to the Crown, and hence the patterns of deference to authority were sown early on.

The early establishment of this firm belief in the law was fundamental to the evolution of the Canadian society. Moreover, we embraced the **rule of law**, which is the principle that both the rulers and ruled are answerable to the law, and both are prohibited from interfering with the independence of the courts, which uphold the rule of law through their positions as independent arbiters of societal disputes. This cornerstone of the Canadian constitutional order is evidenced daily by our obvious respect as a society for duly constituted authority.

The function of law is essentially to regulate human behaviour.[2] But to be effective, the law must be knowable—that is, people must be made aware of the standards of behaviour they are expected to uphold. And it must be predictable— that is, it cannot be arbitrary in its application. The law in Canada is based largely on statutes passed by the legislatures of the federal and provincial governments, and on the English **common law** tradition. This is a system of law wherein judges dispense justice on the basis of past custom and on the precedents built up over the years in prior legal findings. The cumulative body of law dating from the thirteenth century in England serves as the basis of common law.

Canada also has a system of **civil law**, most particularly in Quebec. This is based on Roman law, when the Emperor Justinian ordered the consolidation of all laws. Napoleon ordered the codification of French law on this model of Roman law, and the Napoleonic Code represented an authoritative written record of all laws. Judges in a civil law system are more constrained in making judgments than in common law. The civil code in Quebec, a legacy of the early relationship between French and English after the Conquest in 1759, is a key aspect of the distinctive political culture of the province. The Quebec Act of 1774 made Canada a "bijural" country. This awkward phrase simply means we have two types of law: common law, which is applied outside Quebec in matters of private law; and the Civil Code, which is applied to private law matters inside Quebec. Common law is used, though, for public law both inside and outside Quebec.[3]

Even though we continue to speak of a bijural system of law, we cannot forget the contribution of Aboriginal law. According to the federal Department of Justice,

Aboriginal peoples in Canada have also contributed to our legal system. Aboriginal rights and treaty rights are recognized and protected under the Constitution. Aboriginal rights are those related to the historical occupancy and use of the land by Aboriginal peoples; treaty rights are those set out in treaties entered into by the Crown and a particular group of Aboriginal people. Reserves, for example, are the responsibility of the federal government.

Aboriginal customs and traditions have also contributed to new ways of dealing with people, such as healing and sentencing circles, community justice and restorative justice.[4]

Interest in Aboriginal law has grown lately, particularly since the inclusion of Aboriginal rights in the Charter of Rights and Freedoms in 1982, the Royal Commission on Aboriginal Peoples (RCAP), the British Columbia treaty process, and numerous land claim settlement processes. But Aboriginal law is still a rapidly evolving legal area, and although the Supreme Court of Canada has passed a number of decisions regarding Aboriginal legal issues, it has not yet authoritatively determined the content of Aboriginal law.[5]

Because Canada adopted a federal system in 1867, the courts are federal (see Figure 6.1). There are separate federal and provincial courts in Canada, although in some circumstances cases from provincial courts can be appealed to the Supreme Court of Canada, illustrating that a degree of horizontal integration exists. Several parts of the Constitution relate to the courts. For instance, Section 92 authorizes the creation of courts by the provinces, which also appoint the judges. Section 96 authorizes the creation of courts by the

FIGURE 6.1   Section 92, 96, and 101 Courts

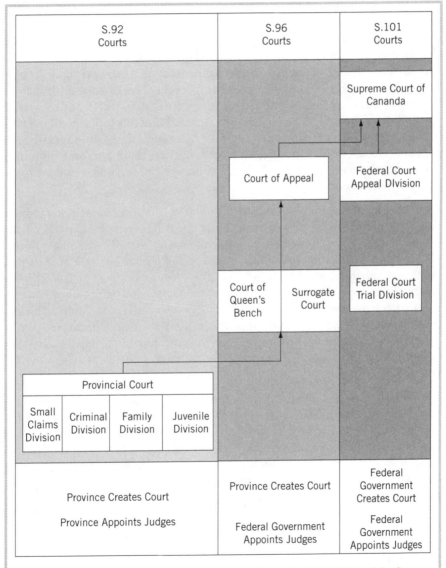

Source: F.L. Morton, ed. *Law, Politics and the Judicial Process in Canada. Third Edition.* Toronto: University of Calgary Press, 2002: 111.

provinces, but whose judges are appointed by the federal government. And Section 101 authorizes the creation of courts by the federal government whose judges are also appointed by the federal government. Together these bodies constitute a rather elaborate federal judicial system, at the apex of which stands the Supreme Court.[6] It was established in 1875 but did not become the final court of appeal until 1949. All types of law cases (common, civil, criminal, statutory, administrative, constitutional, federal, provincial) can be appealed to and be heard in the Supreme Court. It consists of nine learned and senior justices appointed by the prime minister. Three judges from Quebec hear civil law cases. The federal nature of our court system has resulted in a sometimes bewildering array of interrelated courts. The basic structure is derived from the English system, but of course England was a unitary country, not a federal one. So we adapted. But we did not do what the United States (a federal country) did. That court system has two parallel, independent sets of courts: state supreme courts and courts of appeal for matters falling within state jurisdiction; and federal district courts and courts of appeal for matters of federal jurisdiction. Instead, Canada replicated England's basic structure of inferior and superior trial courts and two appeal courts appended to a federal structure. As a consequence, there are three important and distinctive features of the Canadian court system, according to law professors Fitzgerald and Wright:

First, most matters arising under federal or provincial law are dealt with by courts that are administered by the provinces. These courts have remained largely as they had been when the province entered Confederation. Unlike the United States, there is no distinction between the courts that try matters of federal law and those that try matters of provincial law. Second, the judges of these courts may be federally—or provincially—appointed. The seriousness of the matter determines whether a case goes to a superior court for trial before a federally-appointed judge. Third, all appeals from provincially appointed courts, including matters of provincial law, are heard by federally-appointed judges. However, superior and provincial appeal courts are administered by each province while the supreme court of Canada is administered by the federal government.[7]

This brief sketch needs to include another important court that relates particularly to administrative law. In 1970 the Federal Court of Canada was created to replace the Exchequer Court, which had been responsible for hearing cases concerning federal taxes, patents, and copyrights. The Federal Court of Canada consists of a Trial Division and an Appeals Division, and its tasks were expanded to include federal administrative law cases concerning agencies, boards, commissions, and tribunals.

The labyrinth of courts and the very administration of justice itself, of course, require supportive bodies and agencies to facilitate the formulation and implementation of law. Hence, on May 22, 1869, Prime Minister John A. Macdonald established a federal Department of Justice headed by an Attorney General to do just that.[8] The mission of the current Department of Justice is shown in Box 6.1.

BOX 6.1 | **The Mission of the Department of Justice.**

The mission of the Department of Justice is to:

■ support the Minister of Justice in working to ensure that Canada is a just and law-abiding society with an accessible, efficient, and fair system of justice;

■ provide high-quality legal services and counsel to the government and to client departments and agencies; and

■ promote respect for rights and freedoms, the law, and the Constitution.

Source: Canada. Department of Justice Canada. *Canada's Department of Justice.* **www.justice.gc.ca/en/dept/pub/ about/** Accessed April 12, 2007.

The Department of Justice is headed by a politician chosen by the prime minister to play a dual role as both Minister of Justice and, by law, the Attorney General.[9] The minister is concerned with the administration of justice in areas like criminal law, family law, human rights, and Aboriginal justice. But as Attorney General, he or she must also act as the chief law officer of the Crown with responsibility for conducting all litigation for the federal government. This is a position that has its roots in an ancient practice of the sovereign appointing lawyers to represent the Crown in various courts. The department itself not only develops policy and drafts and reforms laws but also acts as the government's legal adviser. As such, it prosecutes cases under federal law and represents the Government of Canada in court. A related but separate ministerial position is that of Solicitor General, which came into being in fifteenth-century England as a deputy of the Attorney General. Today, reflecting the times we live in, the federal Solicitor General is called the Minister of Public Safety, and is responsible for overseeing the Royal Canadian Mounted Police, the Canadian Security Intelligence Service, Border Services, Emergency Management, Correctional Service of Canada, and the National Parole Board. Some provinces, though not all, also have Solicitors General.[10]

Supporting the minister of justice is a deputy minister, who also performs dual roles. The deputy minister manages the administration of the Department of Justice and advises the minister regularly on matters affecting the department. But the Deputy Minister of Justice is the Deputy Attorney General, too. As with most other departments, a pyramidal hierarchy describes the organization of the department, with a team of assistant deputy ministers, directors, and so on below the deputy minister. Not surprisingly, over half of the department personnel are lawyers.

Although it is not a large department, Justice is a very important actor. Some typologies of departments put it in the category of central agency since its influence is so widely felt. Legal advisers from the department can be found in over 40 other government agencies' legal units, and Justice Department personnel play a key role in drafting, reforming, and interpreting legislation, including that from other departments. For instance, one of the key responsibilities of the department since 1982 is ensuring that new legislation is consistent with the Charter of Rights and Freedoms. In addition, there are some 17 regional offices across Canada that provide legal advice to federal departments and agencies outside Ottawa. Thus Justice officials have their legal fingers in virtually everyone's pies.

According to the Justice Department, its administrative responsibilities for law making involve these steps:

Once Cabinet has decided what new laws should be introduced during a session of Parliament, work begins on preparing bills (drafts of proposed laws). When the subject in question is the responsibility of a department other than Justice, specialists in that department work with Justice lawyers, who provide the legal expertise to draft the bill. Justice is consulted in the early stages of the work and continues to be involved through each step, from obtaining Cabinet approval to drafting—and redrafting—the bill until it is enacted by Parliament. At that point, it becomes part of the law of the land, and is referred to as an "act" (also known as a "statute").[11]

Of course, we have focused on the federal Department of Justice here. But there are similar bodies in all the provinces that perform roughly the same set of tasks and have the same sets of administrative roles and responsibilities as their federal counterpart. One further element of confusion for the layperson, though, is the bewildering array of names of the courts in the provinces and territories (see Table 6.1). Some use American terminology, while others use British. This fact is derived from the constitutional provision in Section 92(14), which gives the provinces power over the administration of justice. Thus, each province is responsible for designing its own court system. In practice, however, the administration of justice is roughly similar across the country.

The law, the courts, and the administration of justice only exist within the framework of the Constitution. The Constitution encapsulates the rule of law, even though it is nowhere explicitly mentioned in the written documents of the Constitution. And it orders the positions and the roles of the courts and the supporting administrative institutions and actors—not always explicitly but certainly implicitly. We now turn to the Constitution before returning in more detail to constitutional and administrative law.

What Is a Constitution?

Constitutions are fundamental to the existence of virtually every organized society on earth.[12] They come in every size, description, length, and style. Some contain rules of behaviour and guidelines that are religiously adhered to even though they are nowhere written down. Others are not worth the paper they are written on. The simple fact that a nation has a constitution is no guarantee that it is necessarily a "democratic" society, that its constitution is observed, or even that the rights of citizens enshrined in the constitution will be protected. In fact, in several countries a form of state terrorism is conducted against their citizens, often depriving them of liberty and life, even while the constitutions of those countries contain ringing declarations of the rights of their citizens. A constitution, then, is no guarantee in and of itself that rights will be protected or that states will stay within the rules of the game.

TABLE 6.1   Canadian Provincial and Territorial Trial Courts

Province	Superior Court	Other Section 96 Courts	Provincial Court
BC	Supreme Court	NA	Provincial Court
AB	Court of Queen's Bench	Surrogate Court	Provincial Court
SK	Court of Queen's Bench Unified Family Court	Surrogate Court	Provincial Court
MB	Court of Queen's Bench *Trial Division *Family Division	NA	Provincial Court
ON	Superior Court	Unified Family Court	Ontario Court of Justice
QC	La Cour supérieure	NA	Cour du Québec *chambre civile *chambre criminelle et pénale *chambre de la jeunesse *chambre administrative *Cours municipales
NB	Court of Queen's Bench *Trial Division *Family Division	NA	Provincial Court
NS	Supreme Court	Supreme Court (Family Division)	Provincial Court
PEI	Supreme Court (Trial Division)	NA	Provincial Court
NF	Supreme Court (Trial Division)	Unified Family Court	Provincial Court
YT	Supreme Court	NA	Territorial Court
NWT	Supreme Court	NA	Territorial Court
NU	Nunavut Court of Justice	NA	NA

NA= Not applicable.
Source: Carl Baar, "Court Systems in the Provinces," in Christopher Dunn, ed. *Provinces: Canadian Provincial Politics. Second Edition.* Peterborough: Broadview, 2006: 287.

But without a constitution, the concept of rights, as well as the appropriate limits on the actions of the state, would not even exist. A constitution is the fundamental law of a political system. All other laws are supposed to follow from, and be subordinate to, the laws of the constitution. As well, a constitution provides a set of rules for the peaceful and civilized resolution of conflicts over scarce resources in society. Without it, there is no way of predicting either the powers of government or the rights of citizens. As political scientist J.R. Mallory put it, "the essence of a constitutional order is that it provides effective means of preventing abuses of power, and ensures that those in authority cannot take away the ultimate right of the governed to remove them or reject their policies."[13] Imagine a hockey game without a rule book. You can still play, but the game becomes largely meaningless unless there is some order imposed on the conduct of the participants. Otherwise, the law of the jungle may prevail, and the strongest, biggest, meanest players would impose their version of the game on the rest of us. Now imagine a society in which there is no constitution—a society in a "state of nature," in which chaos and anarchy prevail; a society in which no individual could feel secure in the possession of her property or life; a society in which life was, as seventeenth-century political philosopher Thomas Hobbes put it, "solitary, poor, nasty, brutish, and short." This insecurity can be remedied only when people agree to binding and authoritative rules: hence, the development and evolution of constitutions.

All constitutions are meant to do three things. First, constitutions define the relationship between citizens and the state. They empower the state to regulate citizens' behaviour by passing laws on behalf of the community, and generally they delineate the boundaries of the state's powers by identifying both individual and collective rights that the state is not allowed to violate. For example, the constitution prohibits the state from censoring the free expression of ideas and, therefore, protects the individual right to freedom of speech. However, it also allows the state to place limits on those individual rights in the interests of the greater community through anti-hate laws, libel and slander laws, and so on.

Second, constitutions define the responsibilities and relationships of the different parts of the state. As you now know, there are three main parts of the state: a) the executive, which makes and implements the law; b) the legislature, which passes the law; and c) the judiciary, which interprets the law. Since each of these elements is complex, we need to understand the roles of each and how they relate to one another. A constitution provides us with this information. Two political scientists put it this way:

In modern times, political power is understood to consist of three distinct types: Legislative power is the power to make law or policy. For instance, a political community might use its legislative power to pass a law stipulating that no one may drive an automobile when their blood has an alcohol content above .08%. Executive power is the power to "execute" or administer that law or policy. This would include the power to establish and maintain a police force to catch drunk drivers. Judicial power is the power to settle questions about specific violations of law (is there appropriate evidence to prove the driver's blood-alcohol level exceeded .08%?) and to choose a suitable punishment, from among those permitted in the relevant legislation, for those found guilty.[14]

Third, constitutions in federal systems (like Canada) also lay out the rules governing the relations between the levels of government. This aspect of the Canadian Constitution has captured the attention of politicians and constitutional experts throughout our history, during which federal–provincial relations have played a prominent role.

If you were asked what the Canadian Constitution was composed of, what would you say? In essence, there are three basic elements:

1. written documents, such as the BNA Act, 1867, the Constitution Act, 1982, and the Charter of Rights and Freedoms;
2. the common law; and
3. constitutional conventions—that is, practices that emerge over time and that are generally accepted as binding rules of the political system.

Note that constitutional conventions are not written anywhere into the constitutional documents; they are simply traditional habits and practices. But they can be just as significant as the other parts of the Constitution. Conventions are rules of the Constitution that are not enforced by the law courts. They can be regarded as nonlegal rules. An example would be the convention that the leader of the party that captures the most seats in the House of Commons is called on to form the government. Another convention stipulates that the Governor General will use his or her considerable powers only in accordance with the advice of the Cabinet or prime minister. For instance, the Queen, through the Governor General, enjoys the power of withholding royal assent from a bill that has been enacted by Parliament, but convention stipulates that royal assent is never withheld.

In Canada, the first two components of the Constitution—written documents and the common law—together make up the *constitutional law*. Conventions do not have the status of constitutional law. But this does not mean that constitutional law is more important. The major difference is that constitutional law is enforceable through the courts, whereas constitutional conventions are not.

In most countries, the bulk of the constitutional law is contained in a single constitutional document that came into being after independence, revolution, or war, and that was intended to symbolize and legitimize a new regime of law.[15] As we will see, the Canadian case is somewhat different. Before we turn our attention to the actual constitutional documents, let us look briefly at the reasons for and effects of Confederation, which resulted in the constitutional order we now have.

A History of Canada's Constitution

You are probably familiar with the less-than-stirring history of Canada's march from "colony to nation"[16] (and back to colony again, some would add). The outlines of the picture are clear: conservative, loyal Canada, rejecting the U.S. revolutionary experience, decides to take the slow, evolutionary path to nationhood. If nothing else, this picture seems to accurately reflect Canadian political culture, rooted in the formative experiences of accommodation with French Canada rather than assimilation, and the loyalist influence on English Canada.

Confederation reflected Canada's cautiousness and moderation, its preference for evolution over revolution, and its reluctance to break the imperial/colonial ties that bound it to Britain.

Thus, it is in British constitutional practices we discover the essential foundations of Canada's constitutional order. Long before Confederation the colonists had adopted many of the practices of British constitutionalism: the Crown, Parliament, Cabinet, responsible government, an independent judiciary, and the rudiments of party politics. Much of this heritage took the form of constitutional conventions that had evolved over a much earlier period of political experimentation in Britain. And, as well, it is to Britain we must turn to find the legislation that created and expanded upon Canada's constitutional life, both pre- and post-Confederation.

The BNA Act, 1867, gave effect to Confederation following conferences in Charlottetown in 1864, Quebec City in 1864, and London, England, in 1867. It united the provinces of Canada, Nova Scotia, and New Brunswick into a single "Dominion" under the name of Canada. As well, the BNA Act established a bicameral national Parliament with representation by population in the elected, lower House of Commons, and representation by region in the appointed, upper house, the Senate. It established a common market and allocated important economic powers to the new federal Parliament for maintaining peace, order, and good government, and authority over trade and commerce, transportation and communication, banking, currency, customs and excise, and other forms of taxation. Criminal law also became a federal responsibility, as did marriage and divorce. The provincial legislatures were given other powers, notably over property and civil rights, municipal institutions, education and the administration of justice, the power of direct taxation, and matters of a purely local or private nature within the province. Nova Scotia and New Brunswick retained their existing legislatures and other institutions of government. The province of Canada was divided into two new provinces: Ontario (the old Canada West, formerly Upper Canada); and Quebec (the old Canada East, formerly Lower Canada). The Act also established a legislature and other institutions of government for each of Ontario and Quebec. Thus, the BNA Act established the rules of federalism, allocating governmental power between the central and provincial institutions of government.

The BNA Act did not follow the U.S. model of codifying all the new nation's constitutional rules, since, as the preamble to the Act stated, the new nation was to have "a constitution similar in principle to that of the United Kingdom," which was not a written constitution. Apart from the changes needed to establish the new federation, the British North Americans wanted the old rules to continue in both form and substance. After 1867, therefore, much of Canada's constitutional law continued to be found in sources outside the BNA Act, such as in conventions and in the common law.

The result is that the BNA Act is silent on a number of issues you might suppose would be basic to the constitutional order. For instance, there is no general amending clause since the framers of the Constitution were content to let the amending power rest in the hands of the British Parliament. Consequently, the British Parliament enacted amendments to it right up until 1982, when the Constitution Act, 1982, finally supplied amending procedures that could be operated entirely within Canada.

The field of foreign relations is another notable gap in the BNA Act. It contains no express provision, for example, for a treaty-making power for the Canadian Parliament, except as it may relate to responsibilities as part of the British empire. Yet another gap in the BNA Act concerns the office of the Governor General. The Act vests executive authority for Canada in the Queen and confers several specific powers on a Governor General. But the office of Governor General is nowhere created by the BNA Act, and no rules are provided for the appointment or tenure of that officer. The reason for this gap was the assumption that the office would be created and filled in the same way colonial governorships had always been created and filled: by the Queen, acting on the advice of the British colonial secretary. And the office of the Governor General has never been formalized in an amendment to the BNA Act. The office is still constituted by royal prerogative, and appointments are still made by the Queen, although, needless to say, she now acts on the advice of her Canadian ministers.

It also never occurred to anyone to write the rules of responsible government into the BNA Act, and so there is no mention of the prime minister, or of the Cabinet, or of the dependence of the Cabinet on the support of a majority in the House of Commons. All these rather significant details were left in the form of unwritten conventions, as in the United Kingdom. Nor did the Canadians write into their BNA Act a new Supreme Court. Section 101 of the Act gave authority for such a court to be established, but it did not actually establish it, since we were accustomed to appealing our legal cases to the British Judicial Committee of the Privy Council (JCPC). The Supreme Court of Canada was finally established in 1875, but through an ordinary federal law or statute, and the right of appeal to the JCPC was retained until 1949, when our Supreme Court at last became "supreme."[17] Meanwhile, the existence, composition, and jurisdiction of the Supreme Court of Canada still depend upon that 1875 statute.

Finally, the BNA Act did not even include a bill of rights. The civil liberties of Canadians were instead left in the hands of our legislative bodies and in the rules of common law, as in Great Britain. Therefore, in 1960, the Canadian government of John Diefenbaker enacted a Bill of Rights—not as an amendment to the Constitution but as a simple statute that applied only to the federal government. The Constitution Act, 1982 finally added to the Constitution the Canadian Charter of Rights and Freedoms, which is now entrenched (that is, alterable only by the process of constitutional amendment) and applies to provincial as well as federal laws. We will expand on the importance of the Charter later.

The BNA Act served as Canada's central written constitutional document for 115 years. Changes were made to it occasionally prior to 1982, but most were relatively minor. With the passage of time, however, the original document became deficient for modern Canada. Repeated efforts were made, dating from the 1930s, to correct the anomaly of British control over the amending of the Canadian Constitution. But in every case, Canadian provincial premiers and prime ministers failed to agree on any domestic **amending formula** until, in

1980, Prime Minister Pierre Trudeau forced the issue by deciding to attempt to do it unilaterally. That decision, after a long battle with the provinces for public support and in the courts, eventually led to renewed federal–provincial negotiations in the fall of 1981. A settlement was finally reached on November 5, 1981, despite the vigorous opposition of René Lévesque, then premier of Quebec.[18] In the past, when Quebec had alone dissented from proposed amendment procedures—as with the 1964 Fulton-Favreau formula and the 1971 Victoria Charter—the deals fell apart, implying that Quebec enjoyed a veto over constitutional change.[19] This time, in 1981, a Supreme Court judgment ruled that Trudeau simply needed the "substantial agreement" of the provinces—and not their unanimous consent—for his patriation plan. After obtaining the consent of all provinces but Quebec, a constitutional resolution was passed by the Canadian Parliament on December 8, 1981, and transmitted to Westminster for its approval on March 29, 1982. Proclamation of the Canada Act, 1982, and the Constitution Act, 1982, by Queen Elizabeth followed in Ottawa on April 17, 1982.[20]

The constitutional deal of 1982 essentially did three things:

1. It added a domestic amending formula requiring the consent of 7 of 10 provinces representing 50 percent of the population for most constitutional amendments.
2. It terminated the authority of the United Kingdom parliament over Canada.
3. It created and adopted the Charter of Rights and Freedoms.

But the struggle was a long and arduous one, and it left some Québécois with a sense of betrayal. Indeed, November 5, 1982, the date the deal was struck between the federal government and the nine English-speaking provinces, is still referred to by some in Quebec as "the night of the long knives." The legitimacy of the 1982 deal, then, is diminished: Quebec still has not signed the Constitution Act, 1982.

Subsequent attempts by Prime Minister Brian Mulroney to bring Quebec back into the constitutional fold were stunning failures, and fed the momentum of separatist forces in the province.[21] The Meech Lake and Charlottetown Accords fanned the flames of Quebec nationalism and led to the second referendum in Quebec on sovereignty association in 1995. The result—the narrowest of victories by the federal government—prompted Prime Minister Jean Chrétien to introduce the "Clarity Bill" to test the constitutional validity of Quebec independence. In August 1998, Chrétien asked the Supreme Court of Canada to clarify whether Quebec enjoyed the legal right to unilaterally secede from Canada. The courts ruled that Quebec could not unilaterally secede but that the rest of Canada would be obliged to negotiate terms of secession if a *clear* majority of Quebecers voted to do so on the basis of a *clear* referendum question.[22] Subsequent to the "near-death" experience of the 1995 referendum and the failures of the Meech and Charlottetown Accords, political leaders in Canada lost their taste for constitutional politics. They backed down from the high-stakes negotiations and bargaining and began to focus on non-constitutional approaches to running the federation.[23] Canadians everywhere breathed a huge sigh of relief!

An integral part of the 1982 Constitution Act was the inclusion of the **Charter of Rights and Freedoms**, which makes formal distinctions among different kinds of rights: 1) fundamental political freedoms; 2) democratic rights; 3) mobility rights; 4) legal rights; 5) equality rights; and 6) language rights. Most of these rights were part of Canada's Constitution before 1982; some can be found in the BNA Act, 1867; some are considered part of the common law. But by specifically delineating these rights and including them in the Constitution, an important shift has occurred in the distribution of power in the Canadian constitutional system. Now, Canadian citizens are far more conscious of their common rights and the ways in which they can defend them. This has given rise to an increase in individual citizens becoming more "judicially conscious"—i.e., more willing to use the courts to defend their rights. It has also meant that interest groups have become more aware of this avenue of challenging governmental power. Court challenges to established authority have been on the rise, as Canadians got used to employing this new tool in the constitutional arsenal. Indeed, the Court Challenges Program of Canada is an innovative national non-profit organization that was set up in 1994 to provide financial assistance for important court cases that advance language and equality rights guaranteed under Canada's Constitution. Thus, even the disadvantaged could take advantage of the Charter to press their views if they felt discriminated against. But the program was cancelled in September 2006 by the government of Prime Minister Stephen Harper as a cost-saving measure.

The Charter also means that the judges and the judicial branch of government play an enhanced role in the Canadian political system and that old notions of parliamentary supremacy have had to be reassessed in light of a more activist judiciary.[24] Finally, it has meant that public servants have had to be more conscious in both the formulation of policy and the implementation of programs to ensure that citizens' Charter rights are not abridged or violated.

Federalism and the Constitution

At this stage, it is useful for us to return to the issue of federalism and focus on how the Constitution defines the nature of the relationship between the different levels of government and on the judicial interpretation of the division of powers. Federalism depends on its articulation within the Constitution: that is to say, it is a legal term, based in the Constitution, which vests power in at least two levels of government by virtue of a country's basic constitutional law. In this theoretical model of perfect federalism, or classical federalism, there are "watertight compartments" of power.[25] Jurisdictional authority is clearly laid out, and neither level of government ever crosses the line. In Canada, we have never really had "classical federalism." The Fathers of Confederation consciously developed a system whereby the federal level of government has certain powers allowing it to intrude in provincial jurisdiction; thus, we have never had the "watertight compartments" of classical federalism. The federal government was clearly intended to be the more powerful of the two levels of government. Indeed, Sir John A. Macdonald prophesied a role of little significance for provincial governments: he saw them as glorified municipal councils.[26] Macdonald turned out to be a better prime minister than he was a prophet.

The key sections of the Canadian Constitution that deal with federalism are those laying out the division of powers: primarily, sections 91 and 92, but also sections 93, 94, 95, 101, 117, and 132. Sections 91 and 92 are the most significant. Each section lists powers held exclusively by the national and provincial governments. But only a few subsections within sections 91 and 92 provide the basis for most of the power of the two levels of government, and most of the legal and political debate over jurisdiction.

Not surprisingly, the various players in the Confederation struggle had differing conceptions of the new system. We noted that Macdonald wanted to create a strong central government and weak, insignificant provincial governments. Others, though, felt differently. Oliver Mowat, for example, who would go on to become the longest serving premier in Ontario history (1872–1896) and was a champion of provincial rights, resisted the establishment of too strong a central government.[27] In any event, the agreement gave the central government what were then considered to be the most important legislative powers and sources of public revenue. Ottawa was thus given authority over trade and commerce, shipping, fisheries, interprovincial transportation, currency and banking, the postal service, and several other subjects largely related to managing the economy. Responsibility for immigration and agriculture was divided between the federal and provincial governments, but in the event of a conflict, Ottawa's legislation would prevail. The federal government was also assigned the job of building an intercolonial railway from Halifax to Montreal. When we consider that the two main functions of the state in the nineteenth century were military defence and economic growth, Ottawa certainly was assigned the major legislative powers of that era.

Customs and excise taxes were the most important sources of government revenue prior to Confederation, and these became the exclusive preserve of the federal government, which could raise money "by any Mode or System of Taxation," according to section 91(3) of the BNA Act. The provinces were limited to the less lucrative field of "direct taxation" through section 92(2), as well as royalties on provincially owned natural resources through section 109. So the provincial revenue sources were meagre compared to those available to the federal government. Recognizing this, the Confederation agreement also established the practice of transferring federal funds to the provinces. Thus, the economic dependence of the weaker provinces on federal funding began in 1867, and continues to this day.

In fact, there are sections of the BNA Act that appear to establish an almost colonial relationship between Ottawa and the provinces, by permitting the federal government to disallow laws passed by the provincial legislatures. In addition, the BNA Act gives provincial Lieutenant-Governors—appointees of Ottawa—the power to reserve approval of any act passed by a provincial legislature for up to one year after its passage. These powers of **reservation** (section 57) and **disallowance** (section 56) were widely used in the early years of Confederation, and periodically in the first 40 years of the twentieth century, and clearly established the primacy of the federal government over the provincial governments. In most cases, the federal government used these powers when a province challenged Ottawa's supremacy over economic matters. And section 92(10c) gives the federal government the authority to intervene in a provincial economy by declaring that the construction of a "public work" (which could mean a road or bridge, or similar type of structure) was in the national interest. This power has been used more than 470 times since Confederation, although not since 1961. Finally, sections 93(3) and (4) give Ottawa the power to pass laws respecting education, an area of provincial jurisdiction. It may do so when education rights, held by denominational minorities when a province entered Confederation, are abrogated by provincial law. This power, however, has never been used.

Whichever theory best explains the federal–provincial relationship, both levels of government exercise a range of powers assigned to each by the Constitution. So if you want to know which level of government is responsible for your particular misery, look at sections 91 and 92 of the Constitution Act, 1982. However, any reading of these sections must be undertaken cautiously, since conditions have changed considerably since they were first drafted. Moreover, new issues have arisen that could not even have been imagined by the Fathers of Confederation. In 1867, the framers of Confederation did not have to wrestle with problems such as old age pensions, air transportation, broadcasting and telecommunications technology, nuclear energy, climate change, and so on. As a result, none of these are explicitly assigned to either Ottawa or the provinces. In addition, issues that were of minor significance in 1867 took on tremendous importance in the twentieth century, as the role of the state has evolved over the past 150 years in ways unfathomable to the generation of the 1860s.

In addition, it is important to note that some powers are nowhere listed in the Constitution. The most important of these is the federal **spending power**, which is an implied power rather than a stated one. Ottawa spends billions of dollars every year on policies and programs that fall, strictly speaking, under provincial authority. As political scientist Keith Banting explains, "[A]ccording to the federal view, the spending power allows the federal government to make payments to individuals, institutions, or governments for purposes on which Parliament does not necessarily have the power to regulate. That is, it claims the power to give money away, and attach conditions if it wishes, even if the purposes involved clearly fall within provincial jurisdiction, as specified by the BNA Act."[28] Ottawa's "right" to spend money in any way it sees fit has never been definitely established by the courts, and provokes a good deal of controversy.[29] Nonetheless, that spending power has provided the constitutional basis for many major federal expenditures, which can cause friction between the two levels of government as Ottawa wades into a field and, consequently, distorts or usurps related provincial initiatives. In 1999, in the Social Union Framework Agreement (SUFA) that Ottawa signed with the territories and provinces (except Quebec), Ottawa agreed, for the first time, to certain limitations on the use of the spending power.[30] But the limitations seem muted since, as we noted in chapter 5, a major dispute emerged between Ottawa and the provinces over the question of whether a "fiscal imbalance" exists in the federation.[31] Contention over the federal use of spending power is but one area of federal–provincial conflict, though. How are disputes resolved over the division of powers within federalism? In several ways, including going to court—an issue we will now look at.

Constitutional Law

Constitutional law deals with the rules, practices, and institutions that constitute the state. Constitutional law issues occur when the courts are asked by an individual, group, corporation, or other government to declare a particular law unconstitutional. If they succeed, the law becomes null and void. One of the advantages of listing the **division of powers** in the Constitution is that it theoretically delineates what jurisdictional authority each level of government enjoys—or so we might think. In fact, the list of powers in sections 91 and 92 has often fuelled serious conflict between the two levels of government because items on the list are subject to a variety of interpretations. Powers such as "trade and commerce," "property and civil rights," and "direct taxation" may seem straightforward enough. But when important material interests are at stake for the constitutional experts, lawyers, judges, and citizens who launch constitutional challenges against federal or provincial law, words and phrases take on whole new meanings unintended by the Fathers of Confederation. Thus, the supposedly clear-cut list of powers becomes a source of endless haggling and interpretation, and, in fact, court interpretations over the division of powers have produced some unexpected results, effectively recasting Canadian federalism, for better or worse.

Let us begin by looking at the court's interpretation of perhaps the most sweeping power handed to the federal government. The preamble to section 91 authorizes the Parliament of Canada "to make Laws for the Peace, Order and Good Government of Canada, in relation to all Matters not coming within the Classes of Subjects by this Act assigned exclusively to the Legislatures of the Provinces . . ." while section 91(2) authorizes the federal government to make laws for "The Regulation of Trade and Commerce."

Peace, Order, and Good Government

At first blush, "Peace, Order, and Good Government" (P.O.G.G.) may appear to be a wide power, under which a variety of laws could be justified. But over time, this power has been reduced to one available to the federal government only in times of emergency. The restrictions on the use of P.O.G.G. began in 1896 with a ruling by the British Judicial Committee of the Privy Council (JCPC) in a case called *Local Prohibition*, concerning regulation of the lucrative sale of liquor. In an earlier case, *Russell v. The Queen* (1882), the JCPC held that the Canada Temperance Act, a federal law that established a local-option temperance scheme, was constitutional, since temperance did not fall under provincial jurisdiction. But later, in the *Local Prohibition* case, the provinces introduced their own local-option temperance schemes, and the JCPC ruled in their favour. However, to do so, it had to argue that the *Local Prohibition* case was upheld on the basis of the P.O.G.G. power, even though this had not been articulated at the time of the case. In rationalizing this decision, the judges argued that the federal government could only use P.O.G.G. if the issue at hand was one of "national dimensions": that is, if it was important nationally. Since, in the view of the judges, temperance was not an issue of national concern, the federal government was not justified in using P.O.G.G. to launch its own temperance scheme. But meanwhile, the judges in these cases left open the question of how to determine what constitutes "national dimensions."[32] Nonetheless, these cases represent the beginning of the winnowing away of the federal power of P.O.G.G.

The question of what, exactly, qualifies as "national dimensions" became moot in a sense, since three later cases determined that a new standard had to be met for the federal government to justify a law under P.O.G.G.: i.e., national emergency. In the Board of Commerce Act and Combines and Fair Prices Act, 1919, which was a case heard in 1922, the JCPC struck down two federal laws intended to prevent the development of monopolies and the hoarding of essential goods (food, clothing, and fuel), and which required fair prices for those goods after the First World War.[33] The courts struck down the laws but said that they might have been justifiable laws under the conditions of a national emergency. In so saying, the courts specified that P.O.G.G. should only be applied during times of war, or famine, or some similar condition. So, with the *Board of Commerce* case, the courts actually made it harder for the federal government to employ this power than if they had simply argued that an issue had acquired "national dimensions," as in the earlier *Local Prohibition* case. The fact that an issue had acquired "national dimensions" would no longer be sufficient to justify such exceptional legislation.

Subsequent rulings on P.O.G.G. also suggested it was a power to be used only in wartime or in similar, exceptional circumstances. In *Fort Frances Pulp and Power Company v. The Manitoba Free Press,* 1923, for instance, the JCPC declared that war-related circumstances were sufficient to warrant legislating under P.O.G.G., and indicated that the courts would be out of line in questioning Parliament's authority to do so under the conditions of a war or war-related emergency.[34] In this case, the courts argued that controlling the price and supply of newsprint would normally be a matter of provincial jurisdiction under section 92(13), "Property and Civil Rights in the Province." But it was willing to concede that under wartime conditions, P.O.G.G. could be used to "trump" provincial jurisdiction. Subsequent court rulings backed up this view.

In fact, in cases where the courts rejected the federal government's use of P.O.G.G. as a valid basis for federal legislation, the legislation dealt with peacetime circumstances. The first of these was the decision in *Toronto Electric Commissioners v. Snider,* 1925, in which the JCPC struck down Canada's major industrial relations legislation. It argued that relations between employers and employees were a matter of civil rights in the province and, therefore, within provincial jurisdiction. The JCPC also struck down the peacetime use of P.O.G.G. in three decisions in 1937 concerning the federal government's right to make laws regarding unemployment and social insurance, agricultural marketing boards, and labour relations.[35] The government of R.B. Bennett passed the laws as part of its New Deal legislation to mitigate the ravages of the Great Depression. But Bennett lost the 1935 election, and his successor, William Lyon Mackenzie King, referred the legislation to the courts to test the laws' constitutionality. The Bennett government had attempted to justify the laws on the basis that the Depression of the 1930s was a national concern, and that it threatened the well-being of the country. In all three cases, the JCPC considered this argument inadequate.

In the 1970s, the federal government again tried to use P.O.G.G. to justify legislation intended to deal with economic problems outside wartime. In a ruling on the constitutionality of Ottawa's Anti-Inflation Act, 1975, the federal government argued that growing inflation constituted an emergency, thereby justifying legislation that infringed on provincial jurisdiction. The judges agreed. This ruling made it easier for the federal government to use the P.O.G.G. power by detaching it from the emergency doctrine. The court also declared that it was really up to Parliament, and not the courts, to determine when an emergency existed.[36]

The "Regulation of Trade and Commerce" power in section 91(2) also appears to be a broad source of authority for Ottawa, but it, too, has been interpreted narrowly by the courts, limited largely to interprovincial and international trade. In contrast, the provincial power over "Property and Civil Rights in the Province" in section 92(13) has been interpreted more the way you might expect the trade and commerce power to have been interpreted. *Citizen's Insurance v. Parsons*, 1881, was the first major case to limit the trade and commerce power.[37] The JCPC ruled that a broad, literal interpretation of "trade and commerce" would unnecessarily restrict provincial rights under property and civil rights, and would bring all aspects of economic life under the authority of Ottawa. Never mind that this was the intention of the framers of Confederation! The JCPC nonetheless limited Ottawa's powers over trade and commerce in this case by suggesting that what the phrase "trade and commerce" meant was the regulation of trade in matters of interprovincial concern, and the general regulation of trade affecting the whole country.

The legacy of the *Parsons* case has been problematic. For example, it is possible that some federal laws that regulate trade between provinces may also affect trade that occurs strictly within a province. Is such a law constitutional? Until the 1950s, the courts said "no." But over the years, a series of court decisions gradually loosened the restrictions placed on the trade and commerce power in the *Parsons* case.[38] Nonetheless, the overall effect of the *Parsons* case, and others like it, was to severely restrict the powers of the federal government.

Federal–Provincial Bargaining

This brief overview of select examples of constitutional law judgments shows the impact of judicial review on federalism and, ultimately, on public administration in Canada. But the courts are only one avenue for addressing conflicts between Ottawa and the provinces, and their decisions do not always put an end to that conflict. Besides determining the constitutionality of law, the courts can also force the two levels of government back to the bargaining table.[39] For example, in *Employment and Social Service Act Reference*, 1937, the JCPC decision to strike down a federal law establishing a program to deal with national unemployment precipitated federal–provincial negotiations that led to a constitutional amendment giving the federal government power over unemployment insurance in 1940. In *Public Service Board v. Dionne*, 1978, the Supreme Court confirmed Ottawa's exclusive jurisdiction to regulate television broadcasting. But right after the decision, Ottawa indicated its willingness to negotiate with the provinces to share authority over this area. In *CIGOL v. Government of Saskatchewan*, 1978, a provincial tax on natural gas was found to be a direct tax and, therefore, outside provincial jurisdiction. Later, during the constitutional negotiations of 1981–1982, negotiations broadened the powers of the provinces in this area and permitted some form of resource taxation in section 92A of the Constitution Act, 1982, which had been ruled ultra vires in an earlier decision. In the *Patriation Reference*, 1981, the Supreme Court ruled that Ottawa's proposal to patriate the BNA Act and to change it in ways that affected provincial power was legal but that it was not constitutional in the conventional sense. This gave the federal government a legal victory but also suggested that the political consequences for proceeding were too high. The provinces and the federal government were forced back to the negotiating table.

More recently, the 1998 decision of the Supreme Court on the right of a province to unilaterally secede from Confederation is illustrative of the role of the courts in encouraging discussion and negotiations between the two levels of government. In this decision, the federal government asked the Supreme Court of Canada to rule on three questions:

1. Under the Constitution of Canada, can the National Assembly, legislature, or government of Quebec effect the secession of Quebec from Canada unilaterally?
2. Does international law give the National Assembly, legislature, or government of Quebec the right to effect the secession of Quebec from Canada unilaterally? In this regard, is there a right to self-determination under international law that would give the National Assembly, legislature, or government of Quebec the right to effect the secession of Quebec from Canada unilaterally?
3. In the event of a conflict between domestic and international law on the right of the National Assembly, legislature, or government of Quebec to effect the secession of Quebec from Canada unilaterally, which would take precedence in Canada?[40]

The court response to this potentially explosive set of questions gave a little bit to both sides (the federal government and the separatist government of Quebec). It suggested that unilateral secession was illegal and unconstitutional but that if the citizens of Quebec voted to separate, the federal government would be bound to negotiate the terms of the secession. As with the 1981 *Patriation Reference*, the ball was thrown squarely back into the laps of the politicians. The federal Parliament, in 2000, then passed the Clarity Act, under which the right to determine whether a question on separation was clear as well as what constitutes a majority were reserved to Parliament itself. Not surprisingly, there were howls of outrage from Quebec separatists, who declaimed that this was an unacceptable intrusion on the province's right to determine its own future. However, the election in 2003 of a federalist Liberal government in Quebec and its re-election in 2007 (albeit with a minority government) coupled with the relegation of the Parti Québécois to third place in the Quebec National Assembly seemed to mute the sovereignty debate in the province.

Constitutional law, though, is not the only or always the best way to resolve conflicts between governments. Over the years, a system of intergovernmental bargaining and negotiation has developed, whereby governments discuss their differences in much the same way that countries carry out international negotiation: that is to say, at the highest political and bureaucratic levels.[41] At these meetings, each province puts its own particular regional concerns on the table, while the federal government brings national concerns to the discussion. Since each province comprises many different economic, social, and cultural interests, intergovernmental conflict is, to some extent, the clash of conflicting regional demands in Canada.[42] As well, the state—federal or provincial—has its own set of interests, whether it is to constantly expand in size and influence and power, or to seek jurisdictional control of a particular area.[43] Thus, intergovernmental relations are driven by both the demands of regional societies within Canada and by the demands of the states that represent those regions.

Intergovernmental negotiations frequently focus on issues of jurisdiction, such as who has the authority to tax and spend in which areas. The arcane discussions and disputes that arise from these negotiations between the federal and provincial governments often seem remote and detached from the lives and concerns of ordinary Canadians. But from the state's point of view, how revenue sources and legislative jurisdiction are divided affects the ability of politicians to pursue their interest in re-election, career advancement, and personal prestige. The same is true of public servants.

The provincial governments in Canada have a long history of trying to wrestle power and jurisdiction away from the federal government. And frequently, provincial governments are backed up, from within, by powerful economic interests. We refer to this process as **province building**, when the political needs of governments are reinforced by the demands of provincially oriented economic interests. This is, in effect, the provincial counterpart to the nation building initiated by Sir John A. Macdonald. The term *province building* was originally applied to the efforts of then Ontario premier Oliver Mowat and then Quebec premier Honoré Mercier, who aggressively tried to expand the powers and rights of their provincial governments vis-à-vis the federal government in the late nineteenth century.

Divided jurisdiction has given rise to a sprawling and complicated network of relations linking the two levels of government. There are two basic elements to this network of relations: the part we see, and the part we don't. The part we see involves meetings between the prime minister and the provincial and territorial premiers (First Ministers' Conferences). These meetings always generate a great deal of media interest, and at least part of the proceedings usually takes place before the cameras. Less publicized, but far more frequent, are the hundreds of meetings between federal and provincial Cabinet ministers and their bureaucratic advisors.[44] Some of these are established as regular annual (or more often than annual) meetings; others are called as a new issue or demand arises. In any event, a complex web of intergovernmental meetings and conferences is now a regular feature of Canadian federalism, which, as we noted earlier, in some ways reflects the way sovereign countries carry on international negotiations.[45]

The meetings and relations between the prime minister and premiers and between Cabinet ministers and public servants from both levels of government have evolved into a formalized and regularized feature of Canadian federalism.[46] This feature is referred to as executive federalism because it involves meetings between the executives of both levels of government.[47] Executive federalism, by its nature, excludes the public, and it also excludes the elected members of the federal and provincial legislatures. Instead, negotiations and agreements are usually undertaken with little input from anyone but the federal and provincial executives. This, plus the fact that these negotiations are secret and private, often raises the charge that executive federalism is undemocratic because it undermines the elected legislatures, whose role, if any, is simply to approve what the executives have come up with.[48] As well, there is usually no opportunity for public input or debate. Thus, decisions about important public issues, such as health care, education, taxation, and other matters of real concern to ordinary citizens, are removed from the public realm and discussed behind closed doors. Citizens, political parties, interest groups, and others are generally excluded from a process of decision making dominated by the prime minister, premiers, and Cabinet ministers and their advisors.[49]

In addition to these criticisms, executive federalism has been blamed for distorting the political agenda by reinforcing regional differences and obscuring the national interest. At the same time, executive federalism undervalues the importance of nonregional interests. As well, it fuels government expansion because competitive relations between the two levels of government produce duplication of services. And it perpetuates intergovernmental conflict by, in effect, giving provincial premiers a stage from which to publicize and air their grievances. Still, in the absence of an alternative, executive federalism appears as an enduring institution of contemporary Canadian politics.

As this overview suggests, constitutional law is multifaceted and complex. It ranges across a number of issues having to do with the relations between the branches of government (executive, legislative, and judicial), the state and citizens (the Charter of Rights and Freedoms, for instance), and the relations between the levels of government (the division of powers in the Constitution). Administrative law is related to constitutional law but is focused more exclusively on the relations between citizens and the administrative arm of government. We now turn our attention to administrative law.

Administrative Law

Administrative law is closely related to constitutional law. It regulates the relationships between the individual and the state. If constitutional law looks at the *macro-legal* picture, administrative law looks at the *micro-legal* level. It is more concerned with the day-to-day legalities of how administration takes place.

The most visible government institution of which most citizens are conscious is the department or ministry, but below this is a huge array of other bodies with lesser powers and narrower functions. These bodies are termed *agency*, *board*, *commission*, *tribunal*, *bureau*, or any of a number of other names. Indeed, the variety of names for administrative bodies and the fact that the same name may imply different functions in two bodies is one thing that makes administrative law complicated and confusing to the outsider. For instance, the National Energy Board makes licensing decisions; sets rates and conditions regarding energy matters; revokes, suspends, or imposes conditions on licence holders; conducts research; and advises government on energy matters. By comparison, the Pension Review Board has a much more constrained and limited role, primarily involving the review of decisions by the Canadian Pension Commission (see Box 6.2).[50] This lack of uniformity in terms coupled with the legalistic language typical of administrative law makes it a challenging field. Moreover, procedures are not uniform across different agencies and are a source of many problems in the administrative process. Personnel selection is uneven and often complicated by patronage appointments. And the process by which citizens launch grievances against administrative bodies is not coordinated. As administrative law expert Alan Leadbeater has noted,

Independent administrative agencies at the federal level in Canada are not easily described or understood. They have a variety of powers and duties; their procedures differ and are not always formalized; their members are appointed in a closed and informal selection process; there is no uniform right of appeal from their decisions and no single appeal body to deal with those appeals; finally, their success in performing delegated functions efficiently and effectively is not regularly or adequately evaluated.[51]

BOX 6.2 Administrative Tribunals

At the federal level, there are roughly 18 administrative tribunals that exercise some form of quasi-judicial decision making.

The mandates and responsibilities of these tribunals vary widely but include human rights and freedoms, economic regulatory matters, socio-economic matters, and appeals. They vary in size as well. The Immigration and Refugee Board has more than 170 members and an annual budget of over $75 million, while the Copyright Board has four members and a budget of less than $1 million.

Some boards, such as the Canadian Transportation Agency, regulate a specific industry while others have jurisdiction over all sectors. As well, some boards may have a defined policy advisory role while others do not.

Source: Canada. Department of Justice Canada. *Justice and the Law in Canada.* Ottawa: Department of Justice Canada. **www.canada.justice.gc.ca/en/jl/index.html#court** Accessed April 13, 2007.

It is to both departments and to these less visible forums that much of administrative law relates.

Lawyer Sara Blake draws our attention to the ubiquity of officials whose decision-making powers affect our lives: immigration officers, securities commissioners, building inspectors, parole boards, labour relations boards, professional colleges (for example, of physicians and surgeons), and so on. She reminds us,

Much of our lives is governed by decisions made by administrative tribunals and government officials. Parliament and the provincial legislatures enact statutes that set out the framework of rules for a field of activity and then delegate the day-to-day decision-making power to tribunals and officials. These tribunals and officials then decide whether to admit an immigrant, whether to permit a person to trade in the stock market, whether to order an industry to clean up pollution, whether a person is eligible for Employment Insurance, whether to issue a building permit, whether to release a person from prison before the end of the sentence, the rights of employees, the licensing conditions imposed on a television broadcaster, professional discipline, and so on. . . . In Canada there are thousands of tribunals and officials who have statutory power to make decisions affecting our lives.[52]

An enormous amount of what government does takes place in administrative bodies at the discretion of public servants. This is because virtually no piece of legislation can be drafted so as to foresee every circumstance that might arise in the day-to-day application of its provisions. As a result, a great deal of power is left in the hands of public servants to determine how legislation is actually operationalized. But what happens when these officials stray from the spirit, intent, or letter of the law that they are implementing? What recourse do citizens have when they feel wronged by the actions or inactions of officials? This is where administrative law comes into play.

The growth of public administration has been accompanied by a concern that arbitrariness and inconsistency might arise in the treatment of citizens by the growing legions of administrators. Personal liberty and control over one's own destiny seem increasingly under siege as a result of administrative mechanisms and measures that, while effective in achieving internal goals, may fail to take into consideration the rights and freedoms of individuals. Moreover, the growth in administrative bodies has not always been well coordinated, either within the federal government, or across federal–provincial boundaries. Finally, a key problem for the administrative machine has been developing norms and standards of behaviour that will guarantee effectiveness while simultaneously retaining a measure of discretion and flexibility in the role performed by civil servants.[53] This is a circle not easily squared.

Administrative law is concerned with the manner in which government departments and regulatory agencies actually exercise the legal powers that they have been granted. When a dispute arises (for instance, if a citizen feels that a board is failing in its duties as prescribed by legislation), departments and regulatory agencies are obligated to abide by certain fundamental rules of administrative law enforced by the courts. Two theorists of administrative law explain,

Administrative Law deals with the legal limitations on the actions of governmental officials, and on the remedies which are available to anyone affected by a transgression of these limits. The subject invariably involves the question of the lawful authority of an official to do a particular act which, in the absence of such authority, might well be illegal. . . . In our legal system, the mere fact that the government is the government does not give it any particular rights or powers. On the contrary, all governmental actions must be specially authorized by either legislation or the Royal Prerogative. This need for governmental officials to be able to point to the lawful authority permitting their actions makes Administrative Law a close cousin to Constitutional Law.[54]

The modern state is characterized by a substantial delegation of authority and responsibility to various administrative bodies. One observer puts it this way:

The fact of the matter is that while the legislators may give legal effect and governmental force to certain directions in policy or priorities in terms of programmes and activities, it is in the process of implementation, by way of delegated powers and authority, that policies become meaningful and make their impact on particular groups or the society as a whole. It is no secret that much of the legislation which is enacted by Parliament or the legislative authority (as much as 80–90%) originates within the Civil Service, and certainly the regulations made to give practical effect to enabling legislation are almost always subject to the decisive influence of civil servants.[55]

Administrative law is intimately related to constitutional law, although it is a very young branch of the law overall. But constitutional law may be distinguished from administrative law "mainly by the fact that the former provides a skeleton of broad principles which the latter fleshes out."[56] Frank Scott, the great Canadian constitutional lawyer, once described constitutional law as "a law for the making of laws." Administrative law is concerned with the administrative actions of officials whose powers are derived from laws enacted under the Constitution. A law found to be unconstitutional, therefore, deprives the administrator of any right to exercise those powers and, further, may give rise to citizens who are adversely affected by the administrator's actions, seeking remedies in the event that the administrator's (illegal) actions caused damages. Administrative law has been defined as the branch of law that "is concerned with the legal limits on the actions of government or its agencies and with the remedies that are available to persons who feel aggrieved by an improper, illegal, or unauthorized act by the government or one of its agencies."[57] Typically, a statute passed by the government contains only the bare bones of a law. It must then be fleshed out during the implementation stage by the public servants who actually operationalize the law. But in so doing, many of their actions are left to discretion, and therein lies the need for administrative law. In effect, there must be a check against the arbitrary and discretionary interpretation of the law by unelected officials whose job it is to implement the wishes of the elected politicians, and through them, the people. These checks are provided in administrative law by administrative tribunals and, ultimately, the courts. The courts are the principal means by which controls over the administrative process are exercised through the power of judicial review.[58]

The courts play a role at several points in the review of administrative practice. Initially they might examine the validity of power delegated to an administrative body. They may look at the granting of power to the agency to ensure that it is authorized by the principles of law, including the Constitution, or that there has not been an excessive or inappropriate delegation of power. As well, the courts may look into the rule-making process: that is, they may check to see if the regulatory body that has been given power is exercising that power in its own rule making, or whether it has exceeded the grant of power in constructing its own rules. Finally, the courts may investigate the propriety of the way in which the administrative body has exercised its adjudicative power, which is the power to make decisions involving individual citizens.[59]

A whole series of legal principles, some of them centuries old, has infused the development of administrative law. For instance, there is the principle of *audi alteram partem,* which means that the individual must be given an opportunity to represent her side of an issue in a formal hearing or by some other process. Moreover, citizens generally have the following rights: representation by legal counsel, advance notice of any proceedings and disclosure of evidence that the state may bring, as well as the opportunity to cross-examine witnesses and to be heard by an impartial adjudicator. Not every one of these principles is necessarily in effect in every single case of administrative law. But over the years the courts have reinforced the importance of these principles of natural justice to an ever-widening range of administrative individuals and organizations. This ensures that public servants who are challenged by citizens cannot run roughshod over the rights of those citizens in their zeal in interpreting Parliament's will. Many of these legal principles are reflected in and reinforced by various Charter rights, especially concerning due process.[60] Legal rights in Sections 7–14 of the Charter are particularly relevant. For instance, Section 14 guarantees the right of a party or witness to an interpreter. The general right of protection from being deprived of "life, liberty and security of the person . . . except in accordance with principles of fundamental justice" is also obviously highly pertinent to administrative law.

These principles contribute to the elaborate decision-making process judges engage in, in deciding to overturn or support a particular administrative action. Judges must decide within the context of these principles whether an administrative action is based on an error of law, an error of fact, or inadequate evidence or information. They must also determine when not to intervene in an issue, allowing administrators to exercise their **discretion** in acting. But in the event that the judges do decide a wrong is committed, they must next determine what the remedy is for the aggrieved citizen. The courts have a number of options where remedies are concerned, ranging from simply quashing the administrative action or decision of the agency concerned, to ordering the agency to take some action that it had failed to take, to ordering the agency to compensate the citizen.

There are four main actors involved in administrative law. These are citizens, politicians, public servants, and judges. Each has a unique perspective on whether a law is working or has been administered properly. Somehow, at the intersection of these four groups of disparate perspectives, public policy must be made to work. It can be an imposing challenge.

Assuming that a given law is constitutionally valid, the next task is to determine the exact nature and scope of the powers delegated to officials. It is striking that most of the business of government is actually contained in delegated powers instead of in the actual laws passed by Parliament. Power can be delegated to a number of places (see Box 6.3). The legislation can say, for instance, that power is delegated to Cabinet, to a particular Cabinet minister, a particular public servant, a judge, or even to a private citizen. In theory, there is no limit to the powers that Parliament can delegate to others because of the doctrine of parliamentary supremacy, which means that Parliament has the right to make or unmake any law whatsoever, and no other body has the right to "override or set aside the legislation of Parliament."[61] Therefore, an important aspect of administrative law involves how Parliament devises ways to supervise and control the delegation of powers to administrators.

What happens when the delegated authority oversteps the bounds of the instructions imparted to it by Parliament? The judges step in and ask the delegate to reveal what statutory authority permitted her to take action. If the delegate cannot demonstrate that his or her actions are justified under the relevant statute, then the delegate's actions are declared **ultra vires** by the court, and thereby beyond the delegate's jurisdiction to act. This can be a daunting process, since legislation is often vague and unclear. Therefore, the judges are asked, essentially, to determine precisely what the legislation was intended to do or allow. Upon a court finding an administrator's actions ultra vires, the next step is to find a legal remedy. This process of **judicial review** is generally limited to determining whether an administrator has acted strictly within the statutorily delegated powers. In other words, judicial review looks at whether the administrator has legal jurisdiction to act.

BOX 6.3 | Delegating Power

According to Jones and de Villars, there are several reasons why Parliament delegates authority, including the following:

a) The sheer magnitude of the business of government means that not everything can be dealt with by Parliament or a legislature.

b) Much governmental activity is technical in nature, and only broad principles should be contained in legislation.

c) Delegating power to an administrator allows greater flexibility in applying broad statutory provisions to changing circumstances.

d) It may not be possible to devise a general rule to deal with all cases, which may be more conveniently determined in the discretion of a delegate.

e) The need for rapid governmental action may require faster administrative response than can be accommodated by the necessity of legislative amendment.

f) Innovation and experimentation in solving social problems may not be possible if legislation is required.

g) Someone actually has to apply legislation, and that person has to have authority to do so.

h) Emergencies may require broad delegation of powers with respect to a wide range of matters that would normally be dealt with by legislation.

Source: David P. Jones and Anne S. de Villars, *Principles of Administrative Law. Fourth Edition*, (Toronto: Carswell, 2004): 4–5.

One important court case that illustrates the working of judicial review in relation to the question of jurisdiction involved the premier of Quebec in the 1950s. Then premier Maurice Duplessis had ordered the revocation of a liquor licence belonging to a bar owner who had posted bail for some Jehovah's Witnesses[62] who had been arrested for distributing religious literature that attacked the Catholic Church. In predominantly Catholic Quebec, the actions of the Jehovah's Witnesses were seen by the premier as a provocation. However, in a court case entitled *Roncarelli v. Duplessis,* the courts ruled that there were jurisdictional errors in the administrative action of revoking Roncarelli's liquor licence. First, the legislature had not delegated power to the premier to revoke liquor licences but, rather, to a liquor licensing board. As well, revoking a licence because of posting bond for a group being prosecuted for their religious activity was an irrelevant and improper motive for the exercise of the power granted to the board. As a result, the board's actions (acting at the behest of the premier) were declared ultra vires; Roncarelli got to keep his licence and he was awarded damages.

Judicial review can occur for a number of reasons. If an action appears to be ultra vires, as the case above illustrates, it can be reviewed. Moreover, exercising discretion for an improper purpose, with malice, in bad faith, by reference to irrelevant considerations, or by not considering relevant matters, through procedural errors or through making an error in law, can all lead to judicial review. There are three central features of administrative law: the rule of law, which is the requirement that all government action must be expressly permitted by validly enacted laws; the denial of any special status to the government merely because it is the government; and the right of ordinary courts to determine such questions of legality.[63] If judicial review concludes that a delegated authority has overstepped the bounds of his or her authority, administrative law allows for the application of one of several types of remedies (see Box 6.4). But there are also nonjudicial remedies that can be sought. Parliamentarians are often alert to perceived abuses by administrative officials and, especially if they are from the opposition, are eager to point them out. The resulting embarrassment for the government may cause a review of administrative practices. In addition, the office of the ombuds is an increasingly common institution. It is responsible for reviewing the propriety and fairness of government actions. Reporting directly to Parliament, the ombuds draws attention to administrative action in such a way that few public servants want to be highlighted in its reports. Finally, administrative practice is itself sometimes self-correcting: that

BOX 6.4 | Remedies

When a citizen feels aggrieved by the actions of an administrative official, he or she can apply for a *prerogative remedy:* a declaration, an injunction, damages, or a statutory appeal to a court or another administrative body. Each is explained briefly below:

Certiorari an order from the superior court compelling an inferior tribunal or other statutory delegate to render up all records of its proceedings to permit the superior court to determine its lawfulness.

Prohibition similar to *certiorari,* except that this order occurs before the conclusion of the proceedings by the inferior body, and prohibits it from proceeding in a manner that would take it outside its jurisdiction.

Mandamus a command by the superior court compelling an inferior body to fulfill a delegated statutory duty.

Habeas corpus a command that compels the respondent to bring the person of the application before the superior court in order to determine the lawfulness of the respondent's detention of the applicant.

Quo warranto an order that requires the respondent to demonstrate by what authority he or she exercises the powers of a particular statutory office.

A declaration can be used to determine the lawfulness of an administrator's actions or the validity of the parent legislation. Claims for damages may be successful if the court finds that an illegal administrative action causes harm. Statutory appeal is sometimes expressly granted by the legislation setting up the administrative machinery in question.

Source: David P. Jones and Anne S. de Villars, *Principles of Administrative Law, Fourth Edition,* (Toronto: Carswell, 2004): 10–11.

is, administrators learn through trial and error or public criticism which practices are permissible, and then alter their behaviour and actions accordingly. In any event, judicial review can be entirely avoided if the legislation contains what are called *privative clauses.* These deprive the courts of any jurisdiction to review the actions of delegates. Thus, the legislation can expressly state that the administrator's actions shall not be reviewed in any court. The courts, naturally, do not appreciate being frozen out in this manner, and have devised a number of imaginative rulings to allow them to review administrators' actions even when privative clauses have been in effect.

What of the individuals who occupy the offices of administrative tribunals, agencies, boards, and so on? They are unique in the pantheon of public servants for several reasons. For instance, they perform adjudicative duties in many cases but lack the job security and independence that judges enjoy. Appointments to administrative bodies "are usually for a relatively short fixed term, until a specific purpose is achieved, or 'at the pleasure' of the government that made the appointment."[64] In other words, a position could be terminated at any moment—say, when a government changes and the new regime wants to have people in place that reflect its ideological or policy predispositions. One of the notable features about administrative appointments of this sort is that they can be much more political in nature than strictly merit-based.[65] Balancing the tension between the administrative and the political is thus one of the key ongoing issues related to administrative bodies and law.

In summary, administrative law, closely related to constitutional law, deals with the legal remedies available to citizens aggrieved by administrative actions. Determining what Parliament means when it delegates powers and authority is a large measure of what administrative law is all about. Thus, administrative law deals with three broad areas of public administration: the ways in which power is transferred from Parliament to administrative agencies; how those agencies use that power; and how the actions taken by administrative agencies are reviewed by the courts.[66] Administrative power has grown tremendously in Canada in terms of powers delegated to the approximately 1500 federal, provincial, and territorial administrative bodies that currently exist, raising questions about power, control, and accountability in democratic society. As arcane as it may seem to the uninitiated, administrative law is, thus, fundamentally important. Those concerned with administrative law must wrestle with many important questions: How much power should be delegated to administrative agencies? How much administrative discretion is too much? What constitutes a fair hearing for those aggrieved by administrative behaviour? Is it reasonable to allow administrative agencies to make law, implement law, and determine the fairness of that same law? How can administrative abuses be effectively checked? What internal and external safeguards are needed to prevent abuse by administrators? When should the courts become involved in the review of agency decisions? How can Parliament control the many and diverse administrative agencies for which it is ultimately responsible? Fundamentally, administrative law is about the making of fair procedures in administrative agencies, but this is a complex and daunting task.

WHAT YOU HAVE LEARNED

This chapter has shown that public administration is intimately connected to the law. While constitutional law deals with the rules, practices, and institutions that constitute the state and can be considered the macro-legal environment, administrative law is the micro-legal level, and deals with the discretionary actions of public servants in operationalizing the instructions of Parliament on a day-to-day basis.

Constitutional and administrative law issues are reflective of the broader political culture of the society. In Canada, our proclivity for constitutional wrangling is almost unprecedented anywhere else in the world. And the development of a complex web of administrative bodies and the judicial regime to ensure that administrators are observing the laws of the land is impressive, if somewhat arcane.

Key Words and Concepts

rule of law (169)
common law (170)
civil law (170)
amending formula (179)
Charter of Rights and
  Freedoms (181)
reservation (182)
disallowance (182)

spending power (183)
constitutional law (184)
division of powers (184)
province building (188)
administrative law (191)
discretion (193)
ultra vires (194)
judicial review (194)

Review Questions

The four sections of this chapter each dealt with a specific set of issues related to public administration, the constitution, and the law. You should now be able to address the following questions:

1. The Law, the Courts, and the Administration of Justice

The political culture of a society has an impact on the legal-constitutional regime, a point that should be evident from this section. How can you link the origins and application of the rule of law in Canada to its political culture? Why does Canada have both common law and civil law systems, and what do these terms mean? What is the structure of the court system, and what institutions are responsible for the administration of justice in Canada?

2. What Is a Constitution?

Can you define the term *constitution* and explain its three main functions? What exactly is the Canadian Constitution, and how did it evolve? What primary roles does the constitution play in public administration?

3. Constitutional Law

The division of powers in the Constitution is often a source of conflict. Why? What different means exist to resolve those conflicts? What is the significance of the courts when federal and provincial governments cannot agree on the jurisdiction of a law? What powers in the Constitution are most contentious, and why? What is the significance of the Charter of Rights and Freedoms? What is judicial review, and what has been its legacy?

4. Administrative Law

What is the difference between constitutional law and administrative law? How are the two related? What happens when a dispute arises over the exercise of legal powers by an administrative agency? What powers can the courts exercise in disputes concerning administrative bodies? What recourse do citizens have when wronged by an administrative body?

Weblinks

Canada in the Making: Primary and Secondary Sources in Government Documents
www.canadiana.org/citm/primary/primary_e.html

Canadian Bar Association
www.cba.org/CBA

Canada's Court System
www.justice.gc.ca/en/dept/pub/trib/page3.html

The Supreme Court of Canada
www.scc-csc.gc.ca

Supreme Court Decisions on the Charter of Rights and Freedoms
www.justice.gc.ca/en/dept/pub

Department of Justice Canada
www.justice.gc.ca

Provincial Courts:

British Columbia
www.provincialcourt.bc.ca

Alberta
www.albertacourts.ab.ca

Saskatchewan
www.sasklawcourts.ca

Manitoba
www.manitobacourts.mb.ca

Ontario
www.ontariocourts.on.ca

Quebec
www.justice.gouv.qc.ca

New Brunswick
www.gnb.ca/cour/06PCNB

Nova Scotia
www.courts.ns.ca

Prince Edward Island
www.gov.pe.ca/courts/provincial/index.php3

Newfoundland and Labrador
www.court.nl.ca/provincial

Further Reading

1. The Law, the Courts, and the Administration of Justice

Gall, Gerald. *The Canadian Legal System. Fifth Edition.* Toronto: Carswell, 2004.

Greene, Ian. *The Courts.* Vancouver: UBC Press, 2006.

Isaac, Thomas. *Aboriginal Law: Commentary, Cases and Materials.* Saskatoon: Purich Publishing, 2004.

McCormick, Peter. *Canada's Courts: A Social Scientist's Ground-Breaking Account of the Canadian Judicial System.* Toronto: James Lorimer, 1994.

McCormick, P. and I. Greene. *Judges and Judging: Inside the Canadian Judicial System.* Toronto: Lorimer, 1990.

Swainger, Jonathan. *The Canadian Department of Justice and the Completion of Confederation 1867–78.* Vancouver: UBC Press, 2000.

Tardi, Gregory. *The Legal Framework of Government: A Canadian Guide.* Aurora, Ontario: Canada Law Book, 1992.

2. What Is a Constitution?

Cheffins, R.I. and P.A. Johnson. *The Revised Canadian Constitution: Politics as Law.* Toronto: McGraw-Hill Ryerson, 1986.

Milne, David. *The New Canadian Constitution.* Toronto: Lorimer, 1982.

Morton, F.L. *Law, Politics and the Judicial Process in Canada. Third Edition.* Calgary: University of Calgary Press, 2002.

Rocher, François and Miriam Smith, "Four Dimensions of the Canadian Constitutional Debate," in François Rocher and Miriam Smith, eds. *New Trends in Canadian Federalism. Second Edition.* Peterborough: Broadview Press, 2003: 21–44

Russell, Peter. *Constitutional Odyssey: Can Canadians Become a Sovereign People? Third Edition.* Toronto: University of Toronto Press, 2004.

3. Constitutional Law

Finkelstein, Neil R. and Brian MacLeod Rogers, eds. *Administrative Tribunals and the Charter.* Toronto: Carswell, 1990.

Heard, Andrew D. "The Charter in the Supreme Court of Canada: The Importance of Which Judges Hear an Appeal," *Canadian Journal of Political Science,* 24 (June, 1991): 289–308.

Hogg, Peter W. *Constitutional Law of Canada: Student Edition 2002.* Toronto: Carswell, 2002.

Mellon, Hugh and Martin Westmacott, eds. *Political Dispute and Judicial Review: Assessing the Work of the Supreme Court of Canada.* Scarborough: Nelson, 2000.

4. Administrative Law

Blake, Sara. *Administrative Law in Canada. Second Edition.* Toronto: Butterworths, 1997.

Brown, Donald J.M. and John M. Evans. *Judicial Review of Administrative Action in Canada.* Toronto: Canvasback Publishing, 1998.

Elliott, David W. *Administrative Law and Process. Third Edition.* Toronto: Captus Press, 1999.

Macaulay, Robert W. and James L.H. Sprague. *Practice and Procedure before Administrative Tribunals.* Toronto: Carswell, 2001.

Mullan, David J. *Administrative Law: Essentials of Canadian Law.* Toronto: Irwin Law, 2001.

Salembier, Paul. *Regulatory Law and Practice in Canada.* Markham, Ontario: Butterworths, 2004.

Endnotes

1. John James Guy, *People, Politics and Government: A Canadian Perspective. Sixth Edition,* (Toronto: Pearson Prentice Hall, 2006): 245.
2. For a discussion of the legal system in Canada see F.L. Morton, ed. *Law, Politics and the Judicial Process in Canada. Third Edition,* (Calgary: University of Calgary Press, 2002).

3. Canada. Department of Justice Canada, Where Our Legal System Comes From, (Ottawa: Department of Justice Canada). **http://canada.justice.gc.ca/en/dept/pub/just/03.html** Accessed April 12, 2007.

4. Canada. Department of Justice Canada, Canada's System of Justice, (Ottawa: Department of Justice Canada). **http://canada.justice.gc.ca/en/dept/pub/just/03.html** Accessed April 12, 2007.

5. Thomas Isaac, *Aboriginal Law: Commentary, Cases and Materials*, (Saskatoon: Purich Publishing, 2004): 1.

6. See Peter McCormick, *Canada's Courts: A Social Scientist's Ground-Breaking Account of the Canadian Judicial System*, (Toronto: James Lorimer, 1994). For a history of the Supreme Court of Canada, see Peter H. Russell, *The Judiciary in Canada: The Third Branch of Government*, (Toronto: McGraw-Hill Ryerson, 1987).

7. Patrick Fitzgerald and Barry Wright, *Looking at Law: Canada's Legal System. Fifth Edition*, (Toronto: Butterworths, 2000): 96–97.

8. For a history of the founding and early development of the Department of Justice, see Jonathan Swainger, *The Canadian Department of Justice and the Completion of Confederation 1867–78*, (Vancouver: UBC Press, 2000).

9. The following description of the Department of Justice is adapted from Canada. Department of Justice Canada. Canada's Department of Justice. (Ottawa: Department of Justice Canada), **www.justice.gc.ca/en/dept/pub/about/** Accessed April 12, 2007.

10. See Fitzgerald and Wright, *Looking at Law*, (2000): 114–15.

11. Canada. Department of Justice Canada. Canada's Department of Justice. (Ottawa: Department of Justice Canada), **www.justice.gc.ca/en/dept/pub/about/** Accessed April 12, 2007.

12. The following discussion draws from Stephen Brooks, *Canadian Democracy: An Introduction, Fourth Edition*, (Toronto: Oxford University Press, 2004): chapter 5.

13. J.R. Mallory, *The Structure of Canadian Government*, (Toronto: Gage, 1971): 1.

14. Patrick Malcolmson and Richard Myers, *The Canadian Regime. Third Edition*, (Peterborough: Broadview Press, 2005): 25.

15. Peter Hogg, *Constitutional Law of Canada, Student Edition 2002*, (Toronto: Carswell, 2002): 2.

16. See A.R.M. Lower, *From Colony to Nation*, (Toronto: University of Toronto Press, 1946).

17. See Peter McCormick, *Supreme at Last: The Evolution of the Supreme Court of Canada*, (Toronto: James Lorimer, 2000).

18. See Robert Sheppard and Michael Valpy, *The National Deal: The Fight for a Canadian Constitution*, (Toronto: Fleet Books, 1982).

19. On the Fulton-Favreau formula, the Victoria Charter, and the ongoing search for an amending formula for the Canadian Constitution, see Garth Stevenson, *Unfulfilled Union: Canadian Federalism and National Unity, Fourth Edition*, (Montreal: McGill-Queen's University Press, 2004): chapter 10.

20. See Keith Banting and Richard Simeon, *And No One Cheered: Federalism, Democracy and the Constitution Act*, (Toronto: Methuen, 1983).

21. See Andrew Cohen, *A Deal Undone: The Making and Breaking of the Meech Lake Accord*, (Vancouver: Douglas and McIntyre, 1990); Patrick Monahan, *Meech Lake: The Inside Story*, (Toronto: University of Toronto Press, 1991); Martin Westmacott, "The Charlottetown Accord: A Retrospective Overview," in Martin Westmacott and Hugh Mellon, eds. *Challenges to Canadian Federalism*, (Scarborough: Prentice Hall, 1998): 100–11; and Robert M. Campbell and Leslie A. Pal, *The Real Worlds of Canadian Politics: Cases in Process and Policy, Third Edition*, (Peterborough: Broadview Press, 1994): chapter 3.

22. See Jose Woehrling, "The Supreme Court's Ruling on Quebec's Secession: Legality and Legitimacy Reconciled by a Return to Constitutional First Principles," in Hugh Mellon and Martin Westmacott, eds. *Political Dispute and Judical Review: Assessing the Work of the Supreme Court of Canada*, (Scarborough: Nelson, 2000): 83–101; and "Reference re the Secession of Quebec," in Morton, *Law, Politics and the Judicial Process in Canada*, (2002): 56–85.

23. See Harvey Lazar, ed. *Canada: The State of the Federation 1997. Non-Constitutional Renewal*, (Kingston: Institute of Intergovernmental Relations, 1998).

24. See Gerald Baier, "The Law of Federalism: Judicial Review and the Division of Powers," in François Rocher and Miriam Smith, eds. *New Trends in Canadian Federalism. Second Edition*, (Peterborough: Broadview Press, 2003): 111–33; Michael Mandel, *The Charter of Rights and the Legalization of Politics in Canada*, (Toronto: Thomson Educational Publishing, 1994); and Paul Howe and Peter H. Russell, eds. *Judicial Power and Canadian Democracy*, (Montreal: McGill-Queen's University Press, 2001).

25. See Carolyn M. Johns, "Federalism and Intergovernmental Relations," in Joan Grace and Byron Sheldrick, eds. *Canadian Politics: Democracy and Dissent*, (Toronto: Pearson Prentice Hall, 2006): 85–116; and Nathalie Des Rosiers, "Federalism and Judicial Review," in Martin Westmacott and Hugh Mellon, *Challenges to Canadian Federalism*, (Scarborough: Prentice Hall, 1998): 66.

26. Macdonald's view of Confederation is discussed in J.R. Mallory, *The Structure of Canadian Government*, (Toronto: Gage, 1971): 331–34. See also P.B. Waite, ed. *The Confederation Debates in the Province of Canada*, 1865, (Toronto: McClelland and Stewart, 1963).

27. See John Ibbitson, *Loyal No More: Ontario's Struggle for a Separate Destiny*, (Toronto: HarperCollins, 2001); and Donald Swainson, ed. *Oliver Mowat's Ontario*, (Toronto: Macmillan, 1972).

28. Keith Banting, *The Welfare State and Canadian Federalism, Second Edition*, (Kingston: McGill-Queen's University Press, 1987): 52.

29. See, for instance, David Kwavnick, *The Tremblay Report*, (Toronto: McClelland and Stewart, 1973).

30. See Gregory J. Inwood, "Federalism, Globalization and the (Anti-)Social Union," in Mike Burke, Colin Mooers and John Shields, eds. *Restructuring and Resistance: Canadian Public Policy in an Age of Global Capitalism*, (Halifax: Fernwood Press, 2000); Kathy O'Hara and Sarah Cox, *Securing the Social Union*, (Ottawa: Canadian Policy Research Networks, 1998); and Alain-G. Gagnon and Hugh Segal, eds. *The Canadian Social Union Without Quebec: Eight Critical Analyses*, (Montreal: Institute for Research on Public Policy, 2000).

31. For the provincial view, see The Council of the Federation, Advisory Panel on Fiscal Imbalance. Reconciling the Irreconcilable: Addressing Canada's Fiscal Imbalance, (Ottawa: Council of the Federation, March 2006). **www.councilofthefederation.ca/pdfs/Report_Fiscalim_Mar3106. pdf.** For the federal view, see The Expert Panel on Equalization and Territorial Formula Financing, Achieving a National Purpose: Putting Equalization Back on Track, (Ottawa: Department of Finance, May 2006). **www.eqtff-pfft.ca/english/index.asp.**

32. See Peter H. Russell, *Leading Constitutional Decisions, Fourth Edition*, (Ottawa: Carleton University Press, 1987): 54–63.

33. Russell, *Leading Constitutional Decisions*, (1987): 69–75.

34. Russell, *Leading Constitutional Decisions*, (1987): 77–81.

35. Russell, *Leading Constitutional Decisions*, (1987): 113–30.

36. See Peter H. Russell, "The Anti-Inflation Case: The Anatomy of a Constitutional Decision," *Canadian Public Administration*, 10, 4 (Winter, 1977): 632–65.

37. Russell, *Leading Constitutional Decisions*, (1987): 33–40.

38. See Brooks, *Canadian Democracy*, (2004): 194.

39. See Brooks, *Canadian Democracy*, (2004): 195.

40. Canada, Supreme Court of Canada, "Reference Re Secession of Quebec," **www.scc-csg.gc/ reference/hn.htm** Accessed August 20, 1998.

41. On intergovernmental bargaining and negotiation concerning health care, for instance, see Patricia L. O'Reilly, "The Federal/Provincial/Territorial Health Conference System," in Duane Adams, ed. *Federalism, Democracy and Canadian Health Policy*, (Montreal: McGill-Queen's University Press, 2001): 107–30.

42. See Stevenson, *Unfulfilled Union*, (2004): chapter 9.

43. See Alan Cairns, "The Past and Future of the Canadian Administrative State," in Douglas E. Williams, ed. *Reconfigurations: Canadian Citizenship and Constitutional Change*, (Toronto: McClelland and Stewart, 1995): 62–96.

44. See Carolyn M. Johns, Patricia L. O'Reilly and Gregory J. Inwood, "Intergovernmental Innovation and the Administrative State in Canada," *Governance*, 19, 4 (October 2006): 627–49; and Carolyn M. Johns, Patricia L. O'Reilly and Gregory J. Inwood, "Formal and Informal Dimensions of Intergovernmental Administrative Relations in Canada," *Canadian Public Administration*, 50, 1 (Spring, 2007): 21–41.

45. The classic analysis of this phenomenon remains Richard Simeon, *Federal-Provincial Diplomacy: The Making of Recent Policy in Canada. With a New Preface and Postscript*, (Toronto: University of Toronto Press, 2006). See also J. Peter Meekison, Hamish Telford and Harvey Lazar, eds. *Canada: The State of the Federation 2002. Reconsidering the Institutions of Canadian Federalism*, (Montreal: McGill-Queen's University Press, 2004).

46. See O'Reilly, "The Federal/Provincial/Territorial Health Conference System," (2001). On the roles and responsibilities of intergovernmental officials, see Gregory J. Inwood, Carolyn M. Johns and Patricia L. O'Reilly, "Intergovernmental Officials in Canada," in J. Peter Meekison, Hamish Telford and Harvey Lazar, eds. *Canada: The State of the Federation 2002. Reconsidering the Institutions of Canadian Federalism*, (Montreal: McGill-Queen's University Press, 2004): 249–84.

47. On executive federalism, see J. Stefan Dupre, "Reflections on the Workability of Executive Federalism," in Richard Simeon, ed. *Intergovernmental Relations*, (Toronto: University of Toronto Press, 1985): 1–32; Donald V. Smiley, "An Outsider's Observations of Federal-Provincial Relations Among Consenting Adults," in R.D. Olling and M.W. Westmacott, eds. *Perspectives on Canadian Federalism*, (Scarborough: Prentice-Hall, 1988): 279–84; and Albert Breton, "Competition and Cooperation in the Canadian Federal System," in Report of the Royal Commission on the Economic Union and Development Prospects for Canada, Volume III, (Ottawa: Minister of Supply and Services, 1985): 486–526.

48. See Jennifer Smith, *Federalism*, (Vancouver: UBC Press, 2004).

49. See Inwood, "Federalism, Globalization and the (Anti-) Social Union," (2000).

50. See Alan Leadbeater, *Council on Administration: Administrative Law Series Prepared for the Law Reform Commission of Canada*, (Ottawa: Minister of Supply and Services, 1980): 3.

51. Leadbeater, *Council on Administration*, (1980): 1.

52. Sara Blake, "An Introduction to Administrative Law in Canada," in Christopher Dunn, ed. *The Handbook of Canadian Public Administration*, (Toronto: Oxford University Press, 2002): 466.

53. See René Dussault and Louis Borgeat, *Administrative Law: A Treatise, Second Edition*, Volume 1, (Toronto: Carswell, 1985): 4.

54. David P. Jones and Anne S. de Villars, *Principles of Administrative Law, Fourth Edition*, (Toronto: Carswell, 2004): 3–4. The following discussion of administrative law is derived from their overview.

55. George E. Eaton, "Understanding Canadian Parliamentary Government," in Randy Hoffman et al. *Public Administration: Canadian Materials, Third Edition*, (North York: Captus Press, 1988): 63.

56. Dussault and Borgeat, *Administrative Law*, (1985): 13. See also Margot Priest, "Structure and Accountability of Administrative Agencies," in *Administrative Law: Principles, Practice and Pluralism: Special Lectures of the Law Society of Upper Canada*, (Toronto: Carswell, 1992): 63–78.

57. Donald J. Bourgeois, *Public Law in Canada*, (Scarborough: Nelson, 1990): 195.

58. See Des Rosiers, "Federalism and Judicial Review," (1998): 63–75.

59. Victor S. MacKinnon, "Introduction to the Legal Environment: Theories and Principles," in Randy Hoffman, et al. *Public Administration: Canadian Materials, Third Edition*, (North York: Captus Press, 1998): 199–200.

60. Paul Atkinson, *The Canadian Justice System: An Overview*, (Markham, Ontario: Butterworths, 2005): 93.

61. A.V. Dicey, *Introduction to the Study of the Law of the Constitution*, (London: Macmillan, 1920): 40.

62. See Hogg, *Constitutional Law of Canada*, (2002): 668–69.

63. Jones and de Villars, *Principles of Administrative Law*, (2004): 9.

64. Atkinson, *The Canadian Justice System*, (2005): 91.

65. See Lorne Sossin, "The Uneasy Relationship between Independence and Appointments in Canadian Administrative Law," in Grant Huscroft and Michael Taggart, eds. *Inside and Outside Canadian Administrative Law: Essays in Honour of David Mullan*, (Toronto: University of Toronto Press, 2006): 50–80.

66. See Kenneth F. Warren, *Administrative Law in the Political System, Abridged Third Edition*, (Upper Saddle River, New Jersey: Prentice Hall, 1997): 23.

Chapter 7

Public Administration *and* Public Policy

WHAT YOU WILL LEARN

The formulation, implementation, and evaluation of **public policy** are vitally important aspects of public administration. By the end of this chapter, you will be able to answer the following questions:

- What does public policy involve?
- What major theories of public policy decision making explain the way public officials make decisions on behalf of citizens?
- What is the policy cycle of formulation, implementation, and evaluation?

This chapter is divided into four sections highlighting these central issues:

1. Defining Public Policy

This brief introductory section will ask you to consider what public policy is. You will discover that a number of definitions exist.

2. Formulating Public Policy

There are several different theoretical explanations that seek to illuminate the question of how and why policy is made. This section asks the following: What goes on in the formulation of public policy? Who is involved? How do we use theoretical models to explain *how* policy is made as well as *why* policy is made (or not made)?

3. Implementing Public Policy

The issue of how policy is acted upon once it is identified is the main concern of this section. It asks, What policy instruments are available for governments to use in realizing their goals? How do they choose among these instruments?

4. — *Evaluating Public Policy*

A relatively new concern of governments has been how to test whether their policy actions have been effective. While this issue is dealt with in detail in chapter 8, we introduce it here as part of the policy framework. How do public officials and others assess the quality, utility, and success of public policies?

Defining Public Policy

Public policies in general cover a wide range of fields, and you can tell something about the interests of particular governments by the policies they emphasize.[1] One government may stress economic policy; another, social policy. Yet another might see foreign and defence policy as important, while others do not. Justice policy, language policy, multicultural policy, education policy, and environment policy are just some of the countless areas that public administration deals with. A particular prime minister may have a strong personal interest in an issue, as did former prime minister Pierre Trudeau on constitutional and national unity policy. Or interest groups may be particularly effective in persuading the government to focus its energies on one area, as did the big business lobbies with the free trade issue. In other cases, public opinion may dictate that a government proceed with a certain policy only at its peril. Sometimes a crisis, such as September 11, 2001, mad cow disease, or SARS (severe acute respiratory syndrome), will catapult an issue to the forefront. The mix of factors that determine which issues will be addressed as public policy is complex and changes over time. But whatever the public policy, it is the job of public administration to formulate, implement, and evaluate it.

There is a large, well-developed and growing literature in Canada on public policy.[2] Public policy has been defined as "a set of interrelated decisions taken by a political actor or group of actors concerning the selection of goals and the means of achieving them."[3] American political scientist Thomas Dye said public policy is "whatever governments choose to do or not to do,"[4] pointing out that "policy" can be a case of either action or inaction. Thus, passing a law is an obvious, deliberate, and conscious policy act on the part of a government. But *not* passing a law may be a conscious decision as well.

Consider, for instance, a law that the courts find violates the Constitution. Such a law is, therefore, of no force or effect. The government is then faced with a number of options. First, it can decide to redraft the law to bring it into conformity with the Constitution. It can over-ride the court's decision by employing the Charter of Rights and Freedoms (in certain select areas). Or it can do nothing. All these responses are "public policy." A case in point occurred in January 1988, when the Supreme Court of Canada struck down the government's abortion law on the basis that it violated certain sections of the Constitution. The government of the day took stock of the judgment and decided to do nothing. That is, it declined to either over-rule the court or redraft and reintroduce the law. Thus, there is currently no abortion law in Canada. Why did the government take this "inaction"? It simply weighed the political costs of taking sides in the controversial abortion debate in Canada and decided that *inaction* was, in fact, the most prudent action.

In many ways, public policy involves conscious choices by governments that lead to action or inaction. These take many forms, such as passing a law or regulation, creating a Crown corporation, spending or raising money (i.e., taxing), holding a royal commission or inquiry, and so on. But there are other less obvious examples of public policy, too. Suppose the Minister of Education came to your campus to speak on the future of post-secondary education. This may be considered part of the ongoing process of public policy making, in that the minister may use the speech to signal a new direction in government thinking, test the reaction of educators and students to existing government policy, defend the status quo, or float trial balloons. All of this activity is public policy.

A useful way to think about public policy is in terms of scope, means, and resources.[5] Simply put, this means considering how much government involvement in our lives is appropriate (scope), what form that involvement ought to take (means), and how it is to be provided (resources).

Scope

Canadian governments do more now than they have ever done. They pass more laws, create more regulations, spend and raise more money, employ more people, etc. As the scope of government activity has increased, the machinery of government and the decision making process have become more complex. This is sometimes explained with reference to the *overload thesis,* which is expressed in two ways.[6] First, it is argued that the state has taken on more functions than it can perform or afford. Second, the policy making process has become too cumbersome and complicated. The overall result is that citizens have lost faith in the capacity of their governments to deliver on promises. And there has been a backlash against "big government"—a backlash felt strongly in the realm of public policy.

The question "How much government is too much?" is central to the issue of public policy making. Once we figure out the proper scope of government, then we can know what areas government ought to be acting in. But how do we answer that question? Fundamentally, we must make value judgments to determine what areas of life government should be involved in. These value judgments are shaped and constrained by our socialization, which includes our family life, education, workplace experience, exposure to popular culture, and so on. Once we identify our core values as a society, we construct constitutional rules that influence the actions of government, and then the laws, regulations, Crown corporations, and so on, through which public policy is realized.

An alternative perspective on the question of the scope of government asks whether government can be made more democratic, regardless of its size. This view argues that the debate over the scope of the state is misplaced, that no matter what government does, empowering citizens and popular movements should be the real focus, along with training public administrators to increase citizens' democratic capacity.[7]

Thus, much of public policy making comes down to value judgments about how to achieve societal and private goals within the confines of a broad set of "rules of the game." For example, as a society we may generally agree that the education of children is a predominant value. We long ago agreed as a society to permit the state to take on the major responsibility for this function. Put another way, we determined that the "private" issue of education, once achieved in the home, should completely become a "public" issue of state concern.

Means

Once we sort out the thorny problem of whether the government *ought* to be involved in a particular issue, we must also ask what *form* that involvement should take. We need to consider how the government can achieve its goals, once they are articulated. Governments have a variety of tools at their disposal, and we refer to the selection of these tools as the "choice of **governing instruments**."

Unfortunately, the process of selecting appropriate instruments is rarely straightforward. It can be influenced by any of a number of factors, such as by the way things have been done in the past, by dominant ideas and ideologies, by the personal preferences of particular politicians or public servants, by the availability of resources, by the relative strengths of interest groups trying to influence the government, by the media, by public opinion, etc. For example, taxation on personal and corporate income has become one of the chief policy instruments of modern governments. Yet now, most governments feel severely constrained since more personal taxation may invoke a taxpayers' revolt, while more corporate taxation might provoke a "capital strike" by business.

But even knowing which policy instrument is needed leaves unanswered the question of whether the government has the *policy capacity* to achieve its goals. Since the 1990s there has been a growing literature on policy capacity,[8] defined as "the institutional ability to conduct policy analysis and implement its results effectively and efficiently."[9] In general, governments have recently experienced a reduced capacity to develop policy, which may be attributed to factors such as cutbacks and restructuring exercises, in which policy analysts and policy shops in government were the first things reduced or eliminated. At the same time, there has been increased focus on management as opposed to policy. However, as political scientist Leslie Pal reports, "policy is popular again."[10] Governments are realizing that to achieve their objectives, they must place a greater emphasis on developing strong policy capacity.

Part of the issue of determining the means by which policy is to be achieved is tied up with the notion of what goal is to be served. Justice? Efficiency? Equality? Security? What do we do when these goals clash? What standard do we use to measure the success or failure of a particular policy?[11] These are difficult questions. Consider, for instance, the great free trade debate of the late 1980s. As the Canadian government sought an economic policy to ensure growth and prosperity, it was confronted by two value-based arguments. The pro-free-traders argued that the economic gains from free trade were unassailable and that the goal of economic efficiency should guide which policy instrument (free trade) ought to be adopted. The anti-free-traders, on the other hand, argued that intangible values, such as national identity and culture, would be threatened by free trade, and, therefore, they preferred the policy option of diversified trade and limited tariffs.[12]

Related to these value problems are those associated with cost. Policies, more often than not, have some kind of price tag attached. It is up to government to determine whether a particular price—financial and/or political—is worth paying for a given policy. First of all, there is the "dollars and cents" aspect to policy: the fiscal means must be present in order to embark on policy. But there is also the political question of whether a particular action (or inaction) will cost votes. The policy of regional economic development grants, for instance, may be popular in depressed regions of the country that require economic assistance to spur employment and growth. But that policy may be unpopular in the regions that have to help pay for them via transfer payments from the rich provinces to the poorer ones. All these issues influence the question of the "means" of public policy.

Resources

Politics is said to be about who gets what, when, and how. The making of public policy partly answers that question. But when you get something in the form of policy by the government, someone else may be deprived of something since there are finite resources to spread around. For instance, you may desire a policy that calls for lower personal taxes. This may mean, however, that the quality of health care must diminish because there is now less money to spend on it or that tuition must go up since governments have less tax revenue to put into the post-secondary education system. Thus, the issue of who benefits and who pays is central to policy decisions. Given that resources are scarce and there is not enough of everything to go around for everyone at all times, governments must make difficult decisions about how to apportion the resources of society through the policies they enact.

How governments deal with this through public policy is related again to values. In Canada, one dominant value is that those least able to help themselves should be assisted by those who can. But this has led to controversy over the role of government in redistributing wealth through taxation policy, social programs, regional economic development programs, etc. Major government expenditures to the less well-off regions of Canada through policy tools—such as equalization programs, income transfers to individuals (Employment Insurance, etc.), and industrial assistance programs that subsidize businesses—are controversial, even if most Canadians subscribe to the principle that the better-off should help the less well-off. Thus, governments are constantly trying to strike a balance in devising policy that will help redistribute wealth but not infringe too much on the right to private property or on the workings of the free market.

One answer to the question of how resources are spent or apportioned by government comes from the observation that policy choices reflect the **mobilization of bias**. This means that any individual or group with a particular interest or concern (a "bias") can organize and mobilize itself to influence government to act in its favour. At first blush, this argument would tend to support the view that Canadian society is democratic, in that anyone can mobilize herself and influence government. But closer inspection reveals that, naturally, those with the fiscal and organizational means will tend to be more successful at getting the attention of government and are more likely to have their interests served by public policy than are the unorganized, the marginalized, and the less well-off. Thus, it is best to remember that the decision making process, where public policy is concerned, is weighted in favour of certain actors in Canadian society, and that the question of how the scarce resources of society are divided up is never the result of an equal competition.

Finally, besides the material or financial costs of resources, we must also consider symbolic resources that governments spend and save. Perception is vitally important in politics and public administration—and perception is often shaped by symbols. The flag is a symbol of national unity that costs relatively little to disseminate but that can reap large rewards or cause deep division. Remember that the Sponsorship Program had, at its base, the simple initiative of "showing the flag" more in Quebec to enhance the federal government's profile in *la belle province*. But careless use of resources entirely displaced the intended symbolic message and replaced it with another, involving corruption, cronyism, and misappropriation of public funds by the Liberal Party. The ensuing scandal even partly caused the defeat of a government![13] The Charter of Rights and Freedoms, language laws, multiculturalism, etc., are all powerful symbols as well, which can be invoked virtually without having to spend a cent. Thus, it is wise not to overlook the importance of symbols in calculating the resources available to governments in the making of public policy.

The concepts of scope, means, and resources, then, help us to organize our thinking about the policy making aspect of public administration. We can also think about policy making as a cyclical exercise involving three distinct but related steps. These steps are formulation, implementation, and evaluation. Figure 7.1 depicts the relationship of the three parts of the **policy cycle**. We can conceptualize each of the three as distinct stages in an ongoing process of policy making. In addition, each stage of the process is the responsibility of certain individuals and institutions. For instance, the **formulation** stage is mainly the responsibility of the Cabinet. The

FIGURE 7.1   The Policy Cycle

Legislature has a limited role here, and public servants play an advisory role at this point. **Implementation** is the responsibility primarily of the public service: the Cabinet and Legislature oversee this stage to ensure that their orders are being followed faithfully. Finally, the **evaluation** stage is the responsibility of the public service, the judiciary, and citizens. Public servants are constantly engaged in checking their own work, while citizens (often acting as interest groups or through the media) keep an eye on the government and its officials to ensure that their tax dollars are being spent wisely. In addition, the courts are ever-present to evaluate the constitutionality and legality of public policy.

But in reality, the policy making cycle is less clear-cut than Figure 7.1 depicts. In fact, the boundaries among the three stages are rather indistinct, as are the roles assigned to key actors and institutions. The process, rather than unfolding sequentially, may occur simultaneously or in some other order. In any event, the three steps constantly influence one another. Figure 7.2 depicts more realistically the overlapping nature of the three parts of the policy making process. The next three sections of this chapter deal with the formulation, implementation, and evaluation of policy.

Formulating Public Policy

The key decision-makers, where public policy is concerned, are the politicians and the public servants. More specifically, the prime minister and Cabinet enjoy the ultimate decision making authority. They are assisted by senior public servants but retain the final "yes" or "no" in determining the government's policy. Parliament plays the role of scrutinizing government and passing legislation, and the courts play the role of judging whether policy is "legal" or not. This oversimplifies the complex functions and activities of the executive, legislative, and judicial branches of government but, nonetheless, summarizes the main policy roles of each.

But let us consider the question of how public policy is made by placing it in theoretical perspective. Several models of decision making have been developed to explain how we move from the mobilization of bias to actual public policy.

FIGURE 7.2   The Policy Cycle Revisited

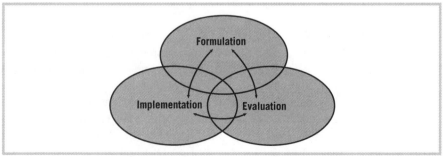

Imagine yourself, for example, as a key decision-maker in the government. How exactly do you arrive at decisions about which policies government ought to pursue? Do you try to anticipate the demands of the society you serve and initiate action accordingly? Or do you wait until various societal interests and actors have demanded action? Once you acknowledge that there are demands for government to respond to an issue, how do you then determine what the best response is: Inaction? A new law? A regulation? An inquiry? A treaty with a foreign country? Education? The huge array of policy choices demands some sort of decision making process. This is where *models* can help us. Models sketch out the parameters of the decision making process and explain why certain policy choices are made under certain circumstances.

The most basic model says that public policy making is a democratic process in which the will of the people is translated into policy through the work of competitive political parties and elected representatives, who play the crucial role in determining which issues will advance. But however appealing it is to think that public policy is a reflection of the "will of the people," this view is simplistic, for it ignores a number of realities. For one, there is no unified, single "will" out there; rather, there is a multiplicity of voices all clamouring for attention. Moreover, this view ignores the fact that sometimes governments act in the absence of public demand. The decision-makers are not simply passive receptors of instructions from the people. They are active players themselves in the development of policy initiatives. Thus, we need a more sophisticated theory than traditional democratic theory to explain public policy.

First, though, let us consider the broad framework that policy making takes place in. Political scientist Richard Simeon has suggested that there are five key variables that help us understand why we get the policies that we do. Simeon begins with the assumption that

the political machinery and the policy-makers at any point in time work within a framework which greatly restricts the alternatives they consider and the range of innovations they make. This framework, or set of constraints and opportunities, defines a set of problems considered to be important, a set of acceptable solutions or policy responses, [and] a set of procedures and rules by which they will be considered.[14]

We can approach public policy by first examining these five complementary characteristics of a society: environmental factors; the distribution of power; social attitudes and ideas; institutional structures; and procedural factors.

Environmental Factors

At the root of all policy are certain basic socio-economic realities. For instance, the geography, demography, level of industrialization, rate of urbanization, relative affluence, level of education, and similar features of a society shape government policy. One of the first concerns of the new Dominion of Canada in the late nineteenth century was to facilitate communications and transportation links across great stretches of territory. Hence, many public-policy initiatives focused on construction of a transcontinental railway and on immigration to settle the vast expanses of the Prairies. In addition, proximity to the United States means that the environment of our public policy is inevitably shaped by *continentalism*. Hence, tariff policy and free trade, as well as cultural protection and nationalism, have loomed large. Thus, these basic *environmental factors* play a significant part in shaping public policy.

Distribution of Power

This is a more nebulous concept. While we can agree that public policy reflects the exercise of power and influence, it is difficult to measure and quantify the concept of power itself, as we noted in chapter 2. What is it? Who has it? How is it measured? Some suggest that power is widely diffused in a democratic society such as Canada and that a plurality of interests have a more or less equal chance of influencing policy-makers to create policy. This is the **pluralist theory**, which argues that there is a healthy competition among groups that expresses itself through the competitive political party system. **Elite theory**, by contrast, argues that power is tightly held and concentrated in few hands, and that there is a network of corporate, political, and bureaucratic elite, which, for the most part, dominate the development of public policy in their own interests. Various interpretations of these views are elaborated next.

Social Attitudes and Ideas

Within any given society there is a set of broadly held attitudes, values, and beliefs that shape public policy by helping to determine which ideas are and are not acceptable. There are two sets of social attitudes and ideas that are especially relevant to public policy making. The first is the set of *procedural* attitudes that a society holds. These are the accepted rules of the game. For instance, nearly everyone agrees in Canada that the political system ought to be democratic and that the process of making public policy should adhere to certain procedures, such as free, fair, and open elections; free speech; parliamentary procedures; and so on. The second set of social attitudes and ideas relevant to public policy making are *substantive* values, which reflect beliefs about the scope and purpose of government. For example, historically, Canadians have been more willing than have Americans to use the state in the pursuit of societal goals, with the result that public policy in the two countries is qualitatively different in a number of ways. Overall, social attitudes and beliefs are broad and general in nature but help to define the problems and the range of policy alternatives open to government. Indeed, the great British economist John Maynard Keynes attributed a great deal of importance to the role of ideas. He wrote,

The ideas of economists and political philosophers, both when they are right and when they are wrong, are more powerful than is commonly understood. Indeed the world is ruled by little else. Practical men, who believe themselves to be exempt from any intellectual influences, are usually the slaves of some defunct economist. Madmen in authority, who hear voices in the air, are distilling their frenzy from some academic scribbler of a few years back.[15]

Keynes, of course, provided the intellectual underpinnings for the modern welfare state with his own theoretical writings, and so could speak with some authority on the influence of ideas.

Institutional Structures

The nuts and bolts of government help determine the types of public policy. The way power and authority are distributed across the structures of government has an important impact on translating will into action. As we noted in chapter 5, institutions, such as federalism and cabinet-parliamentary government, central agencies, line departments, regulatory bodies and Crown corporations, as well as the Constitution and other institutional features, all influence the exercise of power and the type of public policy produced.

Procedural Factors

This concept is closely related to the foregoing one. It refers to the way that those closest to the development of public policy (primarily politicians, public servants, and interest groups) interact in developing policy. They follow rules and processes based on certain norms, with the result that policy is formulated, implemented, and later evaluated in a certain manner. There is considerable dispute, though, over exactly how the process unfolds, which we will explore in more detail next.

Frameworks, Models, and Theories[16]

Lists of factors can go only so far in furthering our understanding of public policy. Social life is lived out in complex organizations and systems, so to understand it we must put these factors into context. For this, policy analysts, like all social scientists, use *frameworks* (which identify key elements or approaches), *models* (which set out limited hypotheses), and *theories* (which develop laws of predictable actions) in policy analysis.[17] Here, we enter a minefield of complexity because, of course, human action is complex. Some policy analysts look more to simplistic or parsimonious models of policy making, while others readily accept and even embrace the idea that policy making is complex and cannot be made to fit into simplistic models. Some focus on the role of individual decision-makers, others on more collective or societal forces affecting decision making. Furthermore, more simplistic models or theories tend to assume that both policy actors and policy analysts are capable of a high degree of rationality, which allows them to understand causal effects, such as "Gun registration will lower gun violence in the streets." The more complex models or policy stories, however, assume that neither policy actors nor policy analysts are capable of much rationality, especially with regard to causation, leading to a long history of poor policy choices.

We will look briefly at some of the most influential frameworks, models, and theories, approaching them from three interrelated perspectives, which lie (loosely) along a continuum from the individual to the collective, the simple to the complex, and the rational to the non-rational. First, we look at the micro, individual level and some of the theories and frameworks that guide this level.

Second, we will look at the models, theories, and frameworks at the more macro, collective, or social level.

The Level of the Individual At the more micro, individual level, we will look at the rational-comprehensive theory, public choice theory, incremental model, mixed-scanning model, garbage can model, and interpretive framework. Imagine the following scenario. You are a key decision-maker in the government, charged with the development of a policy on some important matter. You take as a given the following influences on your decision making: the environment that constrains you (i.e., the demographic, geographic, urban-industrial, bilingual, multicultural, and other characteristics of Canada); the current distribution of power (both within the country as a whole and within the government); the predominant ideas and attitudes that Canadians hold; the institutional constraints; and the procedural rules of the game you are required to follow. Beyond these factors, though, how do you actually make a policy decision? Consider the following options.

The Rational-Comprehensive Theory   You wake up in the morning confident that for every policy problem confronting Canadians, there is a rational solution. You arrive at work and are met by a problem. You carefully draw up a list of goals, values, or objectives related to the problem and rank them according to their importance. You next carefully consider various alternatives for dealing with the problem, and examine them thoroughly. In so doing, you weigh the consequences of each alternative by considering the costs and benefits of each, and the advantages and disadvantages of each. Next you compare the alternatives to one another. Finally, you choose the alternative that will allow you to attain your goals, values, and objectives. Voila! You have created public policy through a rational decision making process. At the end of the day you head home, confident that your rational application of problem-solving skills has saved the day for Canada!

This, in a nutshell, is the **rational-comprehensive model**.[18] This is a widely accepted approach rooted in a Weberian perspective that suggests policy making is a rational, logical process of making decisions, which involves a number of discrete steps or stages. All the decision-maker has to do is follow the steps, and the result will be effective public policy. For every policy problem a set of alternative solutions exist. One need only identify these, weigh the costs and benefits of each, and then choose the preferred course of action. This approach has a good deal of appeal, but it is not without significant criticisms.

First, problems confronting decision-makers are not always well defined. For instance, when car drivers in major urban centres begin to complain about "squeegee kids," what exactly is the problem? Is it a traffic safety problem, or is it an issue of poverty and a lack of meaningful employment opportunities? Should we treat the symptom (squeegee kids), or the cause (youth alienation)? A second criticism focuses on the unrealistic scenario of unlimited time and resources. There is the assumption that the decision-maker can collect, relatively easily, whatever data is needed to make an informed decision and take the time to reflect on it carefully and thoughtfully. This is clearly not possible in the pressure cooker of the real world. Moreover, many of the "alternatives" proposed will be derived from value judgments on the part of those affected by the issue, and on the part of the decision-makers themselves. In other words, personal biases and interests impinge on the cold, rational calculations that the model calls for. And those interests can become particularly entrenched if past policy decisions have tended to favour them. For instance, there may be broad agreement in society that health-care costs are escalating too rapidly. But health-care professions may be reluctant to accept any fiscal solution to the problem that erodes their privileged financial solution, such as reducing doctors' pay or deinstitutionalizing health care. In addition, the rational model has been criticized for excluding different modes of rationality, based as it is on a narrow Western tradition rooted in ancient Greek and European civilizations. Non-Western cultures, e.g., Aboriginal cultures, may use decision making processes that rely less on rationalistic traditions of the Western world but that are, nonetheless, every bit as valid.[19] An example is the way Aboriginal people are often portrayed by non-Aboriginal policy-makers. As one Aboriginal leader put it, "the most we can hope for is that we are paraphrased correctly."[20]

Notwithstanding criticisms of the rational-comprehensive model, it nonetheless has a good deal of appeal. In a perfect world, it would indeed be useful to follow the steps it outlines. In an imperfect world, though, perhaps the best we can hope for is to adhere to the main precepts of the model, while recognizing its shortcomings.

The Public Choice (or Rational Choice) Theory   Another variant of the individual rational model that has gained considerable prominence, particularly in the United States, is that of **rational choice**, or as it is more commonly called in Canada, **public choice**. This theory is heavily influenced by classical liberal economic theory and derived from the view that individuals are rational, self-interested, utility-maximizing creatures. It argues that our pursuit of individual fulfillment is constrained only by a world in which scarcity is the prevailing condition. As noted earlier, there is not enough of everything for everybody at all times. Therefore, we make rational calculations based on self-interest as to how to get the things we want, need, and desire. But we are in a constant competition with other individuals engaged in the same basic process of fulfilling their desires.

Decision making about how to fulfill those desires in the political realm is no different from the process in the economic marketplace, according to this theory. Thus, you make decisions in the economic marketplace on the basis of a rational calculation of your self-interest (e.g., I am hungry; how much money do I have in my pocket? How much is that pizza compared to that submarine sandwich?). So, too, will you support political parties that promote policies most likely to maximize your individual well-being. Here, as policy-maker, you would wake up in the morning confident that every policy problem has a rational solution, but, rather than draw up a list of goals, values, or objectives related to a problem and rank them according to their importance, you would rank them according to your self-interest and choose the alternative that maximizes the attainment of your own goals, values, and objectives. This might mean enacting policies that will bring you the greatest chances for re-election if you are a politician, or that will expand your bureaucratic empire or secure your own position and promotion if you are a public servant. From this perspective, it is folly to talk about some vague "public interest" or "will of the people," since all are engaged in a competition to see their own particular and narrow self-interest prevail. (There are also some important collective elements to public choice theory, to which we will return below.)

The problems with the public choice approach are several-fold. First, the theory assumes a view of human nature that is by no means universally accepted. It assumes that people are always inward-looking and self-interested competitors, while making no allowance for other values, such as altruism and co-operation. Second, even if policy-makers *do* often act in self-interest, it is unlikely that anyone could be *this* rational, for the same reasons discussed earlier in the rational-comprehensive model. Finally, this speaks to the criticism of lack of context of the public choice theory. Its proponents are often accused of leaving out important elements, such as preference formation (i.e., how do their preferences develop, and how do they choose between attractive options?) and the influences and barriers created by institutions, culture, and ideas. Public choice proponents are also criticized for being unable to deal with change—even of individuals' interests and preferences. While the simplicity of both the rational-comprehensive and the public choice theory is attractive, it is also argued to be misleading. What both gain in simplicity, they lose in truth.

The Incremental Model   Some theorists have turned to an analysis of decision making that is less dependent on full rationality. Returning to your role as decision-maker, suppose you recognize that, realistically, you can only work within a more constrained set of circumstances, considering only some of the policy alternatives and guessing at a limited number of potential consequences. You do not cast your net broadly in the search for solutions; instead, you begin by looking for solutions that require only minimal change from the status quo. In other words, you look for *incremental* change, rather than wholesale change. You engage in a process of give-and-take and mutual consent among interested parties to the issue. This approach allows you to avoid proposing radical change that might involve an all-or-nothing policy solution. Instead, you can offer pragmatic, moderate change to the status quo that does not upset entrenched interests (see Box 7.1).

Overall, the **incremental model** for understanding policy making has had many proponents. It is an approach with strong explanatory value, particularly as to why government appears to be such a lumbering beast. But the model, too, has been criticized. It has been suggested that incrementalism is really just a conservative approach to policy development, which, by its nature, favours the status quo and entrenched interests. Moreover, in crisis situations, incrementalism may actually be detrimental to finding solutions. Other critics argue that incrementalism's combination of both rationality and pragmatism (or what its leading proponent, the economist Charles Lindblom, termed "the science of

BOX 7.1　The Incremental Model

This approach avoids many of the problems associated with the rational-comprehensive approach, and may describe the actual decision making process of policy-makers more accurately.

1. The selection of goals or objectives and the empirical analysis of the action needed to attain them are closely intertwined with, rather than distinct from, one another.

2. The decision-maker considers only some of the alternatives for dealing with a problem, and these will differ only incrementally (i.e., marginally) from existing policies.

3. For each alternative, only a limited number of "important" consequences are evaluated.

4. The problem confronting the decision-maker is continuously redefined. Incrementalism allows for countless ends/means and means/ends adjustments that have the effect of making the problem more manageable.

5. There is no single decision or "right" solution for a problem. The test of a good decision is that various analysts find themselves directly agreeing on it, without necessarily agreeing that the decision is the most appropriate means to an agreed objective.

6. Incremental decision making is essentially remedial and is geared more to the amelioration of current, concrete social imperfections than to the promotion of future social goals.

Source: Charles E. Lindblom, "The Science of 'Muddling Through,'" *Public Administration Review,* 19, 2 (Spring, 1959): 79–88.

muddling through")[21] is still assuming too much rationality or science. Critics emphasize the "muddling through" part of it and de-emphasize the "science" part. Some policy analysts argue there is likely a balance between rationality and incrementalism, sometimes called mixed scanning.

The Mixed-Scanning Model　**Mixed scanning** is a model developed by sociologist Amitai Etzioni, who tried to synthesize the most useful aspects of the rational-comprehensive model with those of the incremental model.[22] In this way, the difficulty of attending to every detail inherent in the rational-comprehensive model is overcome, and more profound change is possible than the incremental model allows. In mixed scanning, you explore the main alternatives to the existing policy (rather than all possible alternatives), and thereby avoid paralyzing details and minutiae. An overview of possible change is developed that avoids the conservatism of incrementalism and the unrealistic characteristics of rational-comprehensive approaches. Some applications of the mixed scanning model suggest that the type of decision making process you employ may depend on your position within the organization's hierarchy. It may be that the lower-level functionaries will lean toward incremental means of decision making, lacking the authority and information for large-scale alterations to policy. The higher officials probably engage in a more comprehensive scanning of the alternatives, given that they have the "big picture" before them.

The Garbage Can Model   Stronger critics argue that both incrementalism and mixed scanning models assume too much human capacity for rationality. The **garbage can model** of policy making is probably the most famous of the rebuttals to these rationality-based models. Some theorists have argued that the policy process functions more like a garbage can, in which sits a mix of policy problems and potential solutions.[23] However, this is no ordinary garbage can. Even for its proponents, to have left the garbage can contents in their naturally disordered state would have set the policy analysts on the uncomfortable path to (postmodern) anarchy; so, in their quest for order and causation, they have sought process within the garbage can. There they saw "streams," "channels," "communities," and "windows" through which policies flow, with some policies percolating to the top of the policy agenda and others not. Individuals enter and exit the decision arenas/"garbage cans" such that the policy outcomes are the result of decision making within the garbage can. Because of this, policy "outcomes cannot ordinarily be predicted by rational analysis . . . (so) official presentations of orderly policy with respect to a problem generally represent post hoc rationalizatons of what has been decided largely on a non-rational basis."[24] That is, the policy-makers make policy as best they can and *then* justify it.

The garbage can model, as you could probably guess by now, is criticized for being both too complex and irrational by the analysts we have already discussed, and too simple and rational by others, particularly those adhering to an interpretive approach.

The Interpretive Framework   Critical thinkers employing an **interpretive framework** (and post-modern thinkers, following) argue that no decision-maker can ever be rational and comprehensive because organized life is socially constructed, and in social settings we can never know causation. We do not live in a laboratory, where variables can be controlled in order to understand their interactions. We cannot remove everything but mercury and fish from a lake to see if the fish die. We cannot know for sure that alternative A or B will cause X. To pretend that we can will lead us to poor policies. You, as the policy-maker, would be better off spending your work hours "de-constructing" the "story" behind each policy issue and learning to interpret the meaning behind the actions and intentions of the members of the policy community—including yours and your government's. This, it would be argued, would help avoid the lack of understanding that led, for example, to the serious problems of the gun registry in Canada or to the "short" wars in foreign territories that continue for years. Some analysts argue that politics is all one big fight over preferred interpretations.[25] Is the war in Iraq a war against terror and for democracy or against difference and for oil? Was the policy decision to support the war based on fact or interpretation?

While many analysts would accept the argument that meanings are socially constructed, particularly in the macro approaches that follow, and that how we think about the world affects the world, the problem is that the interpretive approach is atheoretical. That is, it does not postulate hypotheses and laws (which is why we are not calling it a model or theory), while much of political *science* has—in fancying itself a science—engaged in the pursuit of such hypotheses and laws. For example, if a policy-maker wants to eliminate Aboriginal child poverty, he or she would like to know what causes this poverty and might hypothesize that redistributing public funds to the "head of the Aboriginal household" would result in healthy, happy children who would grow up to be productive citizens. Unfortunately, many of these hypotheses may later prove to be most-unscientifically wrong. Many of the more science-oriented analysts (the deductive types) do not seem to worry much about this problem of erroneous hypotheses; they simply continue to use them until bad policy decisions usually lead to the demise of the hypotheses. Others (inductive, empirical "behaviouralists") go back to the drawing board when the policy fails and try to measure the causes behind the real outcome (failure to eliminate Aboriginal child poverty),[26] leading to an adjustment to their original hypotheses. Interpretive analysts would say they would both be better off just dropping the hypotheses altogether and going into the Aboriginal community to ask its members what the most effective course of action might be. Some very famous American policy failures, such as the Vietnam war and the "war on poverty," were designed by white men in suits who had never lived in, and in most cases never even visited, Vietnam or American inner city ghettos, so it is little wonder their hypotheses about jungle warfare and inner-city poverty were off the mark.[27]

Another primary objection to interpretive theory is that it does not lend itself well to comparative analysis. It goes in and teases out the meanings that shape politics, but it does so under specific conditions: for example, those of a group of Aboriginal children it studied in a particular location at a particular time. It tells "their story," not anyone else's. So, good policy analysis, although more accurate, would take a very long time and cost a great deal of money. You as a policy-maker in the public service do not have enough resources for this, and your political boss wants a new policy for the next election. So you turn to hypotheses that, although relatively uninvestigated, at least sound right—such as "more money leads to more happiness."

The Level of the Collective Moving along our continuum from the more micro, or individually oriented, to the more macro, or collective oriented, policy analyses, the latter also sit on a continuum from assumed rationality to non-rationality, and range from the more simplistic to the more complex. We will take an even quicker look (since you are getting the picture here) at the pluralist model; structural analysis (i.e., Marxist, feminist, and **cultural theories**); neo-institutional and **ideational frameworks**; and **post-positivist frameworks**. These approaches all share a concern for the broader forces that shape decision making. Many of them are also referred to as "determinists," "structuralists," or "constructionists" because they see politics and policy as socially constructed.

Pluralism The **pluralist model** of policy analysis asserts that individuals in society join together to pursue common goals and form groups or organizations to influence policy-makers. These groups are many in number, and, indeed, you probably belong to several at one time. For instance, as a student, you belong to organized interests—such as your student council, or the Canadian Federation of Students—which attempt to influence government. But at the same time, you may also be working full- or part-time, in which case you may belong to a union that puts its views regarding policy to decision-makers. Your employer may belong to a business association as well. There are countless groups and associations which, when they turn their attention toward influencing government, are generally referred to as *interest groups, pressure groups,* or *advocacy coalitions.*[28]

Pluralism suggests that there is an ongoing competition among shifting groups in society, who all attempt to influence you, the policy-maker, to create public policy that favours their interests.[29] Individuals may band together with others on the basis of common religion, ethnicity, language, class, gender, region, ideology, or other factors. Sometimes alliances between groups with common interests will be constructed, occasionally under the banner of a political party. In this view, government is seen as a neutral arbiter or referee for groups with equal opportunity to influence it toward appropriately democratic public policy.

An essential component of this theory is that power is widely diffused in society. A concentration of power is avoided, and no one individual or group can monopolize public policy. As long as groups play by the rules of the game—that is, the broadly accepted societal political values and procedures—they all have a potentially equal influence on public policy making.

More sophisticated versions of the theory point out that the main competition between groups tends to occur at the elite level. The leadership of each interest or coalition of interests engages in bargaining and negotiation with the government. The reward for the interest group elite is policies that promote their interests, and the interests of their supporters. For the political elite, the competition is for votes—and the reward is re-election.[30]

As a description of politics, pluralism provides a powerful explanation for how state policy is made. But the early proponents of this view ignored the fact that, while people do band together into groups around common interests, these groups are patently unequal in resources. Some are wealthy, sophisticated, and powerful. Others are lacking fiscal and other resources, knowledge of the political system, and influence. It is obviously easier, for instance, for the big banks to organize and mobilize their resources to influence government decision-makers than it is for the poor to do so. In a famous formulation of this critique of pluralism, political theorist E.E. Schattschneider wrote, "[T]he flaw in the pluralist heaven is that the heavenly chorus sings with a strong upper-class accent."[31] Moreover, it is argued that some issues that might otherwise be placed on the public policy agenda are actually "organized out" of politics. You will recall that our definition of public policy indicated that it is both *decisions* and *non-decisions* by governments. Thus, powerful groups influence government not only *to do* things on their behalf but also *not to do* things, effectively preventing some issues from ever seeing the light of day.

Interestingly, this theory is not far removed from public choice theory, where individuals rather than groups seek to further their interests. However, public choice departs from the pluralist view that the state is somehow a neutral arbiter among the competing interests in society; instead, public servants and politicians engage in a complex process of negotiating and bargaining to maximize their own individual self-interests. Public choice theorists, unlike pluralists, admit that this can lead to poor policy. Or as Hay puts it, "Individual rationality translates into collective irrationality."[32] This is the case in the classic example of the "tragedy of the commons," where individual people, corporations, and states each choose quite rationally to pollute the environment—an irrational action for the collective.[33]

Like all of our approaches, pluralism has metamorphosed after years of critique. In its more sophisticated contemporary form, using the language of pressure groups, political/policy communities, and networks, it now recognizes the *power* of entrenched interests and institutions—including those of (you) the policy-maker. This has led to a greater emphasis in public policy on "who and what gets left out"—for example, in the non-decisions we saw earlier in our definition of public policy. Why are street people virtually ignored in politics, until the Olympics come to town? This leads us to our next macro approach to policy analysis.

Structural Analysis   The **structural** or deterministic group of analyses argue that power relations are already structured into our system in class, gender, race, culture, ethnicity, sexuality, disability, and any category that denotes social, political, and economic exclusion. These Marxists, feminists, and cultural analysts argue that policy analysis must start by recognizing this reality, which largely determines any policy outcome. Except for Marxism, which tends to be more the product of intellectuals than of the subjects of its concern—that is, the working class—much of this is often now called "identity politics" because these groups identify with their place in the political relations of power of their society. And those who do not are often seen to be operating under a constructed false consciousness—that is, they do not know or are not conscious of their own best interests. In order to make a good policy, you the policy-maker would need to both cope with the complaints of the consciously excluded and see through the false consciousness of the unconsciously excluded—that is, you would have to believe that one group knows its own best interests and listen to that group, but not believe another group and instead decide for yourself what its best interests are on its behalf.

Critics, of course, say that the idea that someone else can decide your self-interest is false, unnecessarily patronizing, and endlessly open to abuse; plus, they criticize the "theories," especially Marxism, that treat this determinism as law. (Capitalism will *necessarily* exploit the working class, and so on.) The rebuttal to this rebuttal is that the new global world is looking more and more as Marx predicted—a world where the rich get richer and the working class get poorer, even if many of the losers in the system are accepting of their fate.

Other structural (now more often called constructivist) analysts who focus on the structured or socially constructed realities of specific groups, such as women, people of colour, Aboriginals, gays and lesbians, the disabled, etc., are critiqued for their narrow focus. The world, it is argued, is not constructed solely around these groups, as it would seem when one reads these analyses. A broader analysis would take into account their conditions of oppression as well as other factors affecting public policy—that is, their concerns are legitimate and important, but they do not the entire analysis of public policy make.

The Neo-Institutional Framework   Another of the structurally oriented analyses, **institutionalism**, is now, like pluralism, in its "neo" or new stage—which really just means some of the key elements of the old framework have been kept, but the framework has been rather seriously revamped by its critics. Given that political analysis began as institutionalist analysis, focusing on bodies like Parliament, Cabinet, the Supreme Court, the bureaucracy, and so on, institutionalism has clearly had considerable influence on the "discipline" of political science.[34] Like other structuralist or determinist theories, it has had to back off its bolder claim that institutions determine outcomes, because other analysts came in and provided evidence that *their* favoured analytical categories (for example, ideas and interest groups) had had just as much or more influence on outcome. For example, the Parliament of Canada did not decide as a singular rational institution to legalize gay marriage. The story behind this *institutional* decision is one where *interests* in a policy community of pressure groups, the media, judicial and government actors, electoral groups, and perhaps even a friend of the prime minister came together under an *ideational* climate of equality and rights discourse and succeeded in pressing the governing institutions into a policy outcome. The new or "neo" institutionalism incorporates these forces—the role of other policy community actors and the role of ideas, especially—into its analysis.

Variants of the new institutionalism either lean toward greater simplicity, where the world is more rational (historical institutionalism/path dependency, where history has determined a path toward policy outcomes) or toward greater complexity, where the world is less rational (a more interpretive institutionalism, where the analyst has to look at each case to determine the mix of institutions, ideas, and interests that have helped construct particular policy outcomes). Outright critics, of course, reject **neo-institutionalism** and utilize either the previously discussed micro or macro approaches, or they move toward the truly anarchic analysis of postmodernism.

The Postmodern Approach   As we saw earlier, the **postmodern** approach (this approach does not believe in theories, so we cannot refer to it as postmodern theory—although many textbooks do) rejects simplicity and rationalism. In the study of politics and public policy, this approach has been mostly shunned, but its influence is being felt in subtle ways. At a minimum the postmodern approach provides a check on rationalism, recognizing the randomness of life events and the importance of change as a variable in policy studies. At a maximum, however, there can only be discrete context-ridden studies, speaking only to their specific time and place. Pushed to the limit, a postmodern analysis is the "garbage can" without the processes (streams, windows, etc.). It is just a random set of events and actors. Therefore, there is no policy *theory* that will give us laws of human action in policy making. We need, this approach argues, to accept this and do the best we can in a world of imperfect knowledge. But this makes a lot of people nervous and insecure. Its vehement critics sit on both ends of the political spectrum: on the right, where conservatives crave more law and order; and on the left, where radicals see the postmodern approach as politically disempowering. Increasingly, however, more moderate critical analysts are seeing this approach as an important check on human arrogance in a field such as policy studies, which has long failed to live up to the grand promises of its early days.[35]

While we have tried to present this scattered and various literature in simplified form, generally from the individual to the collective, from the simple to the complex, and from the rational to the non-rational, this is necessarily an oversimplification. Many of these frameworks, models, and theories overlap and steal ideas and techniques from each other: for example, there is now a "rational choice institutionalism" and a "rational choice behaviouralism" (not to mention a "neo-neo-synthesis," which we have spared you). What you might take from all of this is that policy-makers exist in a complex, changing world, which they are asked to hold steady and simplify in order to make policy decisions. This is no easy job.

Implementing Public Policy: How Does Anything Get Done?

What exactly happens once a policy decision has been taken? Two things. First, the decision must be implemented. It is of little use for the government to decide on a course of action if there is no effective way of carrying out its intentions. Following this, the policy must be evaluated to see that it is successfully attaining the objectives that the government has set out.

In theory, the implementation stage of the policy process is dominated by public servants, who are mainly responsible for carrying out the will of the elected representatives who made the key decision to proceed with a particular policy. In an ideal policy making world, the politicians impart directions to the public servants, who then faithfully carry them out. The Cabinet and Legislature retain a role in this stage of the policy cycle by overseeing the actions of the public servants. Part of the implementation process involves deciding exactly which policy instrument will be used to realize the government's goals. A variety of options is available, and we will discuss the choice of governing instrument. First, though, we look at some problems associated with implementation.

When scholars initially turned their attention to the implementation process, they noticed that there was often a disturbing gap between the expectations of political actors who formulated policy, and the actions of bureaucratic actors who implemented it. For instance, if legislators passed a law to eliminate child poverty, why has poverty among children actually been increasing? If tough new environmental standards have been passed, why has pollution been getting worse? In these and countless other examples, there seems to be a disconnect between intention and action, leading to the conclusion that implementation of policy making deserves more thorough attention.[36]

In fact, the implementation of public policy is complicated by numerous factors.[37] To begin with, governments must often draft legislation in broad and general terms. Indeed, the objectives of policy are often unclear and may be expressed in fuzzy, multiple, or contradictory terms. It is then left up to the public servants to interpret the meaning of those terms and, ultimately, to provide the actual content of the policy in day-to-day implementation. What this implies is that public servants enjoy a generous amount of *discretion* in translating into action the legislative expectations of their political masters. In turn, narrow bureaucratic goals may displace those of the legislators. For instance, if legislation calls for reforming the delivery of certain social services, and if this threatens the positions of public servants in the department responsible, those reforms may be sabotaged in the implementation stage. Or conversely, the reforms may be exaggerated if their impact is to expand a bureaucratic empire. But this may then lead to conflict with other administrative agencies over the appropriate areas of involvement of the first agency, with the result that implementation is thwarted by bureaucratic in-fighting. A further layer of interference may occur when the central agencies (i.e., Finance Department, Treasury Board, the Privy Council Office, or the Prime Minister's Office) stick their noses into the process. Thus, in the implementation stage, the content of policy can be modified, elaborated, or even reversed.

Within the bureaucracy itself, then, there may be resistance to implementing policy. Old habits, ideas, and programs die hard. As a result, when a department is given instructions to draft the regulatory framework for enacting a new law, it may draft those regulations so as to minimize change to customary procedures. Or there may be costs associated with change that are difficult to overcome. Or prevailing values may be challenged, which is often compounded by the differing perspectives of the implementers relative to those of the formulators. The individuals enacting a program may decide, for whatever reason, that they will focus on the one or two objectives with which they are most comfortable—leaving the other objectives to fall by the wayside. The question of political feasibility also often gets in the way of implementation: whatever the merits of a policy, if it is too politically costly, politicians may resist implementing it.

Another actor is the front-line worker, who actually meets with the public and is responsible for delivering a policy, program, or service. These could include the people who issue your driver's licence, give you a parking ticket, pick up your garbage, collect your bus fare, etc. Consider your teachers as front-line workers, for instance. Each is instructed to follow policy that is sent down from "on high" from the Ministry of Education. But, despite the best intentions of legislators and public servants who dictate through policy that children are entitled to a "good education," they are not the ones responsible for delivering that policy to its ultimate users: children in the schools. It is the teacher—the front-line worker—who holds that responsibility. Thus, the front-line worker has a great deal of influence over the quality of the delivery of services and often has a direct influence on a given policy's success or failure.

Since Canada is a federal state, initiatives at one level of government can be affected by the other level. For instance, the federal government and the provinces are engaged in numerous shared-cost and joint federal-provincial programs. But disputes constantly arise as to how to implement these programs. For instance, under the Canada Health

Act, the federal government articulated a set of five principles that guide the delivery of health services by the provinces. Health care is a provincial responsibility, but since the federal government kicks in the lion's share of funding, it feels entitled to set some of the rules regarding implementation. This has caused a series of disputes between the two levels of government.[38]

In addition, forces outside government influence the implementation stage. Policy decisions are often the result of compromise and negotiation between interests with conflicting views. A decision will spawn both proponents and opponents, winners and losers. In many cases, the losers will not simply give up and go away once a policy is announced. Rather, they will move from trying to influence the formulation stage to influencing the implementation stage. They may, for instance, carefully monitor implementation to ensure that whatever regulations and guidelines have been enacted adhere to the letter of the law. Or they may even take the extreme step of trying to impede the policy's implementation. Lobbying, protests, strikes, and court challenges are among the range of responses available to opponents of a policy.

Ever since the enactment of the Charter of Rights and Freedoms, implementing public policy has been subjected to heightened scrutiny. The courts have always been an avenue to check the constitutional legality of legislation but primarily with regard to whether a law was within the jurisdiction of the level of government that passed it. With the advent of the Charter, however, the constitutional validity of laws can be challenged on the basis of whether they violate human rights. The range of policies subjected to Charter challenges has been incredibly broad, including abortion, fetal rights, mandatory retirement, strikes and secondary picketing, Sunday shopping, children's advertising, minority language education rights, French-only signs, official bilingualism, extradition, drunk driving, cruise missile testing,

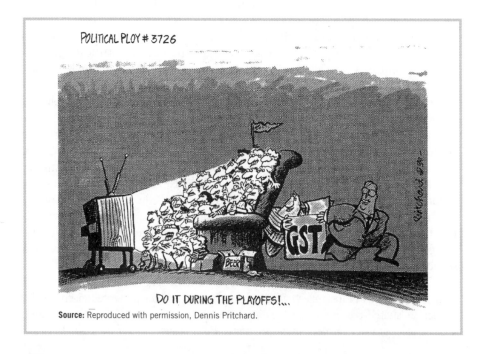

POLITICAL PLOY # 3726

DO IT DURING THE PLAYOFFS!...

Source: Reproduced with permission, Dennis Pritchard.

narcotics, Breathalyzer testing, refugees, assisted suicide, pornography, hate literature, political rights of public servants, constituency boundaries, dangerous offenders, sexual assault, battered women, prisoners' rights, prostitution, and other issues. Analysis of Charter cases in the first 10 years of the Charter's life reveals that legal rights, mainly dealing with the enforcement of criminal law, were the most common basis of Charter cases. The result, according to some analysts, is that the Charter has effectively created a "new constitutional code of conduct for Canadian police officers in dealing with suspects and accused persons, and in the process has pushed the Canadian criminal process away from the 'crime control' side of the ledger toward the 'due process' side of the ledger."[39] In other words, the legality of the implementation of policies has served as the most common form of Charter violation complaint.

As you can see, there are many interests and actors in the policy process. Analysts of public policy sometimes try to capture the full constellation of interests and actors—both governmental and non-governmental—that might have a stake in an issue and therefore seek to influence public policy. As such, they talk about a **policy community** as constituting all the actors in the policy making process that have an interest in a particular policy field. These actors can be either primary—that is, they are lead actors—or secondary—that is, actors with a tertiary interest, as with the "attentive public." A policy community can be distinguished from a **policy network**, which includes only those like-minded actors that might collaborate with other like-minded groups to advance an issue, as well as referring to the patterns of relations among members of a policy community.[40] Figure 7.3 depicts the array of interests and actors that together make up a policy community.

It may appear from this brief survey of some of the factors affecting implementation that policy as articulated by formulators does not stand a chance of being enacted as planned. Yet a tremendous amount of progress is made, year after year, by governments in enacting a panoply of policy. We now turn to the issue of the choice of governing instrument.

Choice of Governing Instrument

One of the key steps in implementing any policy involves deciding on the means by which the policy will be enacted. And one way of exploring this question is to look at governing instruments, defined as "the major ways in which governments seek to ensure compliance, support and implementation of public policy."[41] In other words, is it better to use the carrot, the stick, or the sermon?[42] Most studies of instrument choice trace their intellectual origins to the work of Theodore Lowi, who was among the first to categorize the types of instruments available to governments, as well as to differentiate them according to how coercive they were.[43] As well, a classic study of instrument choice was produced by the Economic Council of Canada over 25 years ago.[44] Recently, Canadian governments have shown an increased interest in issues of instrument choice and implementation.[45] We will look at various governing instruments in terms of their level of intrusiveness in the economy and in the lives of citizens. This expands upon the issues raised earlier regarding the scope of government, while also bringing to mind the related issues of means and resources.

Fundamentally, when government creates public policy, it is trying to get us to adjust our behaviour in some way. When it passes a law calling, for example,

FIGURE 7.3   **The Policy Community**

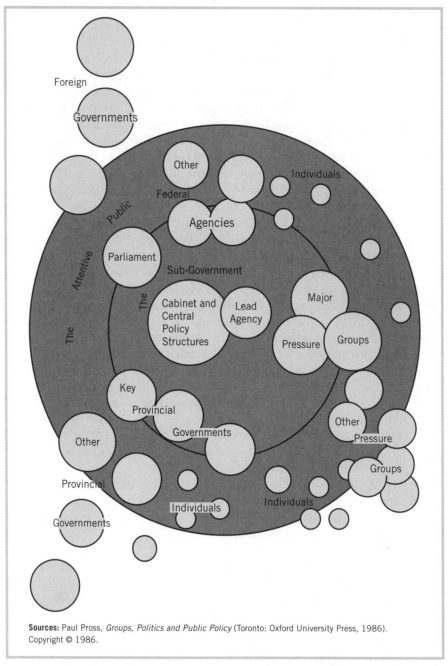

Foreign

Governments

Other

Individuals

Federal

Public

Agencies

Attentive

Parliament

Sub-Government

The

The

Cabinet and
Central
Policy
Structures

Lead
Agency

Major

Pressure

Groups

Key

Provincial

Other

Governments

Pressure

Other

Groups

Provincial

Individuals

Individuals

Governments

Sources: Paul Pross, *Groups, Politics and Public Policy* (Toronto: Oxford University Press, 1986). Copyright © 1986.

for a stop sign at the corner of Maple and Elm streets, this requires us to adjust our driving habits. When it provides tax breaks for purchasing Registered Retirement Savings Plans (RRSPs), this encourages us to adjust our savings and investment habits. And when we fail to comply with the state in these matters, various penalties can be applied. Failure to stop at a stop sign might result in a ticket. Failure to purchase RRSPs might mean higher real tax rates and a diminished quality of life when we retire. In short, the state has at its disposal a range of policy instruments to influence our behaviour, backed up by a range of sanctions and coercive measures to ensure our compliance.

But what motivates policy-makers to select certain policy instruments and not others? For one answer, consider the role of the state in terms of the level of intrusiveness of policy instruments, an approach outlined by political scientist Nicolas Baxter-Moore. *Intrusiveness* means "the extent to which various instruments as means of government intervention intrude directly and publicly on private decision making."[46] Baxter-Moore developed a scale of government intrusiveness, in which he categorized the various instruments available for government use (see Figure 7.4). The scale has the advantage of accounting for both *decisions* and *non-decisions* of government and thus accords with our definition of public policy. It ranges from minimum to maximum degrees of intrusiveness.

The scale is divided first into non-decisions and decisions. Each of these categories is then subdivided into degrees of state intrusiveness, ranging from minimum to maximum. At the minimum end of the scale is the idea that conflict between citizens is privatized. Indeed, government may concretely signal that it refuses to get involved, as in instances where certain professions are given the power to regulate themselves rather than have the government regulate them. Medicine and law, for instance, are self-governing professions. There is no government public policy at this point, but moving across the scale we encounter our first example of government intrusiveness. This takes the form of a *symbolic gesture or response,* wherein, for instance, the prime minister makes a speech or establishes a royal commission or task force to inquire into an issue without actually committing the government to take a course of action. It also includes conferences, information, studies and research, the reorganization of government departments, and other similar devices.

Privatization of conflict and symbolic responses both fall under the heading of non-decisions. Other policy instruments fall under the heading of decisions, which in turn is subdivided into incentives and directives. Incentives begin with exhortation, which means political and bureaucratic leaders attempt to secure the compliance of citizens without threats or inducements. Examples include the government's using persuasion to get us to buy into what it is trying to accomplish. Moving along the scale of intrusiveness, we next find tax expenditures, which permit individuals and corporations to retain money that would otherwise normally go to taxes. This policy instrument essentially entails the failure to do something (e.g., collect taxes) that might otherwise have been done.

Public spending is the next most intrusive category of public policy. It includes items such as subsidies, grants, and transfer payments, loans and loan guarantees, and some cases of joint public-private ownership where the government is a minority shareholder. Exhortation, tax expenditures, and public spending are examples of

FIGURE 7.4   A Reconstruction of the Policy Instruments Continuum

Non-Decisions		Decisions					
		Incentives (Indirect Public Intervention)			Directives (Direct Public Intervention)		
Privatization of Conflict	Symbolic Responses	Exhortation	Tax Expenditures	Public Spending	Regulation	Taxation	Public Ownership	State of Emergency
Minimum ----------- Degree of State Intrusiveness ----------- Maximum

Source: Nicolas Baxter-Moore, "Policy Implementation and the Role of the State: A Revised Approach to the Study of Policy Instruments," in Robert J. Jackson et al., *Contemporary Canadian Politics*, (Scarborough: Prentice-Hall, 1987).

incentives involving indirect public intervention. Directives are the final category, within which the government takes an increasingly intrusive role. Regulation is the first example of a directive but is somewhat less intrusive than taxation. Public ownership is more intrusive than either regulation or taxation. The most intrusive government public policy, however, is to declare a state of emergency. In this case, all normal civil liberties and government institutions are suspended, control is exercised autocratically, and state security forces (the army and police) are used to support the government's directives, using force if necessary.

Given this scale of intrusiveness and the range of policy choices available, how do decision-makers decide which policy to employ? The answer to this question takes us back to the issues of scope, means, and resources. Policy-makers are constrained in their choice of governing instruments by societal views regarding what the appropriate level of state involvement should be in the society. They are constrained by the appropriateness of various means at their disposal. (It would make little sense, for instance, to try to secure the compliance of citizens to obey traffic laws by imposing a state of emergency.) And finally, the resources need to be available to ensure that a policy goal is realistically achievable. The creation of a national, universally accessible federally funded day-care system seemed improbable in an age of spiralling debt and deficits. But when we entered the post-deficit era, and resources became available, we saw this issue resurface on the public policy agenda.

Recent Developments in Policy Implementation

Implementation of policy has recently undergone some important changes. As with other aspects of public administration, the trend toward transferring responsibilities to the private sector means that in some instances policy implementation is being taken over by nongovernmental actors. As we noted in chapter 4, the thinking among New Public Management (NPM) advocates is that government should "steer" rather than "row."[47] A major premise of this approach is that government should arrange for the provision of services, but not deliver (or implement) those services itself.

To put it another way, many policy decisions fall on the least intrusive end of the scale discussed above: namely, *privatization of conflict,* reflecting NPM approaches. Implementation has been affected by the recent increases in demands for greater privatization and deregulation, coupled with citizen participation and control, democracy, and responsiveness of government institutions.[48] The impact of NPM on policy implementation is summarized in Box 7.2.

Yet the outcomes of NPM policy innovations are sometimes not clear (as with other systems of management). For instance, massive restructuring of the health-care sector brought new efficiencies and cost savings in Ontario. But it also unexpectedly brought a 4000 percent increase in the incidence of certain bacterial infections in hospitals. This was because fewer staff, dealing with greater caseloads, had less time to wash their hands between treating patients, with the result being that bacterial infections soared. Unforeseen consequences frequently seem to bedevil implementation, whatever form it takes.

All in all, the concept of implementation is a difficult one to analyze, much less execute. It involves so many factors and actors: Cabinet and Legislature, courts, public servants, interest groups, citizens, etc. And it involves an evolving process of

BOX 7.2 | The Impact of the NPM on Policy Implementation

1. NPM assumes traditional government structures are rule-bound, inflexible, and incapable of adapting quickly.

2. NPM questions government involvement in a variety of traditional policy fields.

3. Policy-makers increasingly look to nongovernmental actors to deliver policies (private sector corporations, community groups, nonprofit organizations, citizens, the family, etc.).

4. There is a new emphasis on outcomes of policy in terms of quality of service.

5. NPM looks to hybrid forms of policy delivery that have greater flexibility than traditional governmental forms, including contracting out, partnerships, and other forms of nongovernmental implementation of policy.

Source: Leslie A. Pal, *Beyond Policy Analysis: Public Issue Management in Turbulent Times, Third Edition*, (Toronto: Thomson Nelson, 2006): 203.

bargaining, negotiation, incentives, decisions, log-rolling, discretion, and so on. It is also hard to say with authority where the formulation process ends and implementation begins, since the two are continuous and interrelated. Still, it is crucial to understanding the public policy aspects of public administration. In any event, once formulated and implemented, some mechanism must exist to ensure that the policy has achieved its objectives. The evaluation of policy is the third step in the policy cycle, and, although discussed in detail in chapter 8, is introduced next.

Evaluating Public Policy

Evaluation is one area that distinguishes the public sector from the private sector. It is relatively straightforward to determine whether a widget company is making a profit. On the basis of this "bottom-line" standard, an evaluation can be made. But in the public sector, as we noted in chapter 1, this clear-cut bottom-line standard does not exist. Thus, evaluation can be more of a challenge in the public sector than in the private sector. We will explore the conundrums of evaluation in some detail in chapter 8. But for now, we will simply make a few general observations about how evaluation fits in with the other two aspects of the policy cycle: formulation and implementation.

As noted above, evaluation is that part of the policy cycle that is mainly conducted by the public service and the attentive public. It is an ongoing process that can be conducted either formally and systematically, or informally and haphazardly. The former case might involve, for instance, a team of forensic accountants being contracted by a municipal government to determine if county finances are in order. The latter case might involve the casual observation by a citizen that a parking meter is not functioning properly. In both cases, some form of evaluative exercise is going on that forces government officials to account for their action (or inaction). In short, public policy is being scrutinized and assessed.

It might seem surprising that the systematic evaluation of public policy is a young art. It is only in the past 20 or 30 years that theorists of public administration acknowledged how little was being done academically in this area. Furthermore, while we could argue that practitioners of public administration had always carried on some form of evaluation of public policy—however informal it might have been—the Canadian federal government only initiated ongoing, professional, and rigorous self-evaluation in the past few decades. According to political scientist Ray Rist,

Policy evaluation began and rapidly expanded at a time in many western democratic societies when there were strong pressures to address the social problems of these same societies. The 20 years from 1960–1980 witnessed a dramatic increase in the use of the public sector to address social issues as far-ranging as drug abuse, education of poor children, crime, availability of affordable housing, environmental pollution and health care for the elderly, to name but a few. . . .

But while large sums of funds were to be spent, there was also the need to ensure that the funds were spent effectively. Stated differently, there was a need to ensure that the policies and programs delivered on what they had promised. Assessing the impacts and performances of the new initiatives fell to the emergent field of policy and program evaluation.[49]

Initial attempts to make use of the burgeoning field of evaluation theory, though, faltered on the faulty premise of rationalism. Theorists and practitioners alike assumed it was possible to make a factual, objective assessment of a policy based largely on quantitative methods derived from scientific inquiry. But, as Rist suggests, over time they realized that there was no simple linear relationship between evaluation and its use by policy-makers to produce sound policy.

As with formulation and implementation, it is possible to identify the key actors who should be involved in evaluation. These are the public servants and the public. But the boundaries are blurred between the three stages and between who performs on each stage. Thus, the Legislature has an important evaluative role through the mechanisms of the opposition parties, legislative committees, and question period in the House of Commons. As well, the courts are frequently asked to judge whether public officials are implementing what the formulators have asked, in accordance with the Constitution and the rules and regulations set out in legislation.

But once evaluation has taken place, then what? Usually, evaluation will reveal one of three things. First, the policy is working just fine, and so needs no further refinement or change. Second, the policy is deficient in certain regards but on the whole is redeemable. Perhaps it only requires some tinkering. Third, the policy is an abject failure and should be entirely scrapped, and a new approach developed. Notice that in all three cases, information is being fed back into the policy cycle that will affect the future formulation and implementation of policy. If the first scenario prevails and the policy does not need any change, then formulators can go on to another issue, and implementers can continue to do their job, secure in the knowledge that they are doing the right thing. But if either scenario two or scenario three prevails, then both formulators and implementors are confronted with a new set of challenges. Thus the process cranks (or creaks) back into gear, with either minor reform or wholesale change by the formulators and implementors. Such is the never-ending, dynamic, and evolving world of the policy cycle.

WHAT YOU HAVE LEARNED

Public policy is an important aspect of public administration, albeit difficult to define. We may think of the public policy process as a cycle, involving the continuous interplay of formulation, implementation, and evaluation of various public policies. While the three steps of the process can be conceptualized as discrete, in fact in the real world there is considerable overlap between them; each influences the other. You should now be able to answer the following questions: What is public policy? What theories of public policy decision making explain the way that public officials (both bureaucratic and political) make decisions on behalf of citizens?

Key Words and Concepts

public policy (205)
governing instruments (208)
mobilization of bias (209)
policy cycle (210)
formulation (210
implementation (211)
evaluation (211)
pluralist theory (213)
elite theory (213)
rational-comprehensive model (215)
public choice or rational
  choice theory (216)
incremental model (217)

mixed scanning (218)
garbage can model (219)
interpretive framework (219)
cultural theories (220)
ideational framework (220)
post-positivist framework (220)
pluralist model (220)
structural analysis (222)
institutionalism (223)
neo-institutionalism (223)
postmodernism (223)
policy community (227)
political network (227)

Review Questions

This chapter was divided into four main sections, each dealing with the issue of policy making in public administration. These central issues were highlighted:

1. Defining Public Policy
This brief introductory section considered what "public policy" is and explained that, while a number of definitions exist, in this text we focus on the idea that public policy is "a set of interrelated decisions taken by a political actor or group of actors concerning the selection of goals and the means of achieving them." More simply, we quoted Thomas Dye's maxim that public policy is "whatever governments choose to do or not to do." Ask yourself, Which definition best explains what public policy is?

2. Formulating Public Policy

Governments do an awful lot of things—but ask yourself after reading this section, How do governments do what they do? What theoretical explanations illuminate the question of how policy is made (or not made)?

3. Implementing Public Policy

This section dealt with the tools and means by which will is translated into action. It showed that policy is not self-executing but must be enacted to be effective. Ask yourself, How are decisions about the level of intrusiveness of government made? What are among the choices that policy-makers must consider when deciding on a policy? What policy instruments are available for policy-makers, and in what circumstances are they likely to be employed? What factors influence the choice of policy instruments? In the contemporary era, what is the capacity of the state to manage policy making? How much is being left of the private sector and the voluntary sector? What is the impact of the NPM on public policy?

4. Evaluating Public Policy

This brief section introduced the relatively new issue of testing the utility and success of various public policies, an issue we return to in detail in chapter 8. It asked, What is evaluation? Who are the key actors involved in the evaluation process? Finally, you need to ask yourself the following: What is the relationship between formulation, implementation, and evaluation? Who is responsible for each? Do these three terms adequately sum up the policy process? Or is there more to it than this apparently simple illustration would imply?

 ## Weblinks

Canadian Parliamentary Channel (CPAC)
www.cpac.ca

Institute for Policy Analysis
www.chass.utoronto.ca/ipa

Association for Public Policy Analysis and Management (APPAM)
www.appam.org

Canadian Centre for Policy Alternatives
www.policyalternatives.ca

Government of Canada Policy Research Initiative
www.policyresearch.gc.ca

Further Reading

1. Defining Public Policy

Anderson, James E. *Public Policy Making. Third Edition.* New York: Holt, Rinehart & Winston, 1984.

Brooks, Stephen. "Policy Analysis in Canada," in Christopher Dunn, ed. *The Handbook of Canadian Public Administration.* Toronto: Oxford University Press, 2002: 192–203.

Dobuzinskis, Laurent, Michael Howlett and David Laycock, eds. *Policy Analysis in Canada: The State of the Art*. Toronto: University of Toronto Press, 2007.

Howlett, Michael and M. Ramesh. *Studying Public Policy: Policy Cycles and Policy Subsystems. Second Edition*. Toronto: Oxford University Press, 2003.

Pal, Leslie A. *Beyond Policy Analysis: Public Issue Management in Turbulent Times. Third Edition*. Toronto: Thomson Nelson, 2006.

Shafritz, Jay M., Karen S. Layne and Christopher P. Borick, eds. *Classics of Public Policy*. New York: Pearson Longman, 2005.

2. Formulating Public Policy

Burke, Mike, Colin Mooers and John Shields, eds. *Restructuring and Resistance: Canadian Public Policy in an Age of Global Capitalism*. Halifax: Fernwood Press, 2000.

Simeon, Richard. "Studying Public Policy," *Canadian Journal of Political Science*, 9, 4 (December 1976): 548–80.

3. Implementing Public Policy

Eliadis, Pearl, Margaret M. Hill and Michael Howlett, eds. *Designing Government: From Instruments to Governance*. Montreal: McGill-Queen's University Press, 2005.

Prince, Michael. "The Return of Directed Incrementalism: Innovating Social Policy the Canadian Way," in G. Bruce Doern, ed. *How Ottawa Spends 2002–2003: The Security Aftermath and National Priorities*. Toronto: Oxford University Press, 2002: 176–95.

Woodside, Kenneth. "The Political Economy of Policy Instruments: Tax Expenditures and Subsidies in Canada," Barbara Wake Carroll, David Siegel and Mark Sproule-Jones, eds. *Classic Readings in Canadian Public Administration*. Toronto: Oxford University Press, 2005: 496–516.

4. Evaluating Public Policy

Posavac, Emil J. and Raymond G. Carey. *Program Evaluation: Methods and Case Studies. Seventh Edition*. Upper Saddle River, New Jersey: Prentice Hall, 2007.

Endnotes

1. See Stephen Brooks and Lydia Miljan, *Public Policy in Canada: An Introduction, Third Edition*, (Toronto: Oxford, 2003): chapters 1–2.

2. See, for example, Laurent Dobuzinskis, Michael Howlett and David Laycock, eds. *Policy Analysis in Canada: The State of the Art*, (Toronto: University of Toronto Press, 2007); Michael Orsini and Miriam Smith, eds. *Critical Policy Studies*, (Vancouver: UBC Press, 2007); André Lecours, ed. *New Institutionalism: Theory and Analysis*, (Toronto: University of Toronto Press, 2005); Leslie A. Pal, *Beyond Policy Analysis: Public Issue Management in Turbulent Times, Third Edition*, (Toronto: Thomson Nelson, 2006); Robert M. Campbell, Leslie A. Pal and Michael Howlett, *The Real Worlds of Canadian Politics: Cases in Process and Policy. Fourth Edition*, (Peterborough: Broadview Press, 2004); Michael Howlett and M. Ramesh, *Studying Public Policy: Policy Cycles and Policy Subsystems. Second Edition*, (Toronto: Oxford University Press, 2003); Brooks and Miljan, *Public Policy in Canada*, (2003); and Andrew F. Johnson and Andrew Stritch, eds. *Canadian Public Policy: Globalization and Political Parties*, (Toronto: Copp Clark, 1997).

3. W.I. Jenkins, *Policy Analysis*, (London: Martin Robertson, 1978): 15. Cited in G. Bruce Doern and Richard W. Phidd, *Canadian Public Policy: Ideas, Structure, Process*, (Toronto: Methuen, 1983): 33–34.

4. Thomas R. Dye, *Understanding Public Policy, Fifth Edition*, (Englewood Cliffs, New Jersey: Prentice-Hall, 1992): 1.

5. See Richard Simeon, "Studying Public Policy," *Canadian Journal of Political Science*, 9, 4 (December, 1976): 559–62. Brooks and Miljan refer to "scope," "choice of policy instrument," and "who benefits and who pays?" See Brooks and Miljan, *Public Policy in Canada*, (2003): 11–17.

6. Robert J. Jackson and Doreen Jackson, *Politics in Canada: Culture, Institutions, Behaviour and Public Policy, Sixth Edition*, (Toronto: Pearson Prentice Hall, 2006): 22.

7. Gregory Albo, David Langille and Leo Panitch, eds. *A Different Kind of State? Popular Power and Democratic Administration*, (Toronto: Oxford University Press, 1993): 5. See also Wendy McKeen and Ann Porter, "Politics and Transformation: Welfare State Restructuring in Canada," in Wallace Clement and Leah F. Vosko, eds. *Changing Canada: Political Economy as Transformation*, (Montreal: McGill-Queen's University Press, 2003): 109–34.

8. Canada. Strengthening Our Policy Capacity, Report of the Task Force on Strengthening the Policy Capacity of the Federal Government, (Ottawa: Canadian Centre for Management Development, April, 1995); B. Guy Peters, *The Policy Capacity of Government*, (Ottawa: Canadian Centre for Management Development, 1996); George Anderson, "The New Focus on Policy Capacity in the Federal Government," *Canadian Public Administration, 39, 4, (1996): 470–71; Canada. Policy Research Secretariat, Policy Research in Canada: A Capacity for the Future: A Discussion Document, (March, 1999); Herman Bakvis, "Rebuilding Policy Capacity in the Era of the Fiscal Dividend: A Report from Canada," *Governance, 13, 1, (2000): 71–103.

9. Pal, *Beyond Policy Analysis*, (2006): 35.

10. Pal, *Beyond Policy Analysis*, (2006): 24.

11. Brooks and Miljan, *Public Policy in Canada*, (2003): 14.

12. For an analysis of the struggle over these values related to the free trade issue see Gregory J. Inwood, *Continentalizing Canada: The Politics and Legacy of the Macdonald Royal Commission*, (Toronto: University of Toronto Press, 2005).

13. See Canada. Commission of Inquiry into the Sponsorship Program and Advertising Activities, Who is Responsible? Fact Finding Report, (Ottawa: Public Works and Government Services, 2005).

14. See Richard Simeon, "Studying Public Policy," *Canadian Journal of Political Science, 9, 4* (December, 1976): 548–80. Simeon's views, in turn, were influenced by the work of Anthony King. See "Ideas, Institutions and the Policies of Governments: A Comparative Analysis," Parts I–III, *British Journal of Political Science, 2* (July and October, 1973): 291–313 and 409–23.

15. John Maynard Keynes, *The General Theory of Employment, Interest and Money*, (London: Macmillan, 1936): 383.

16. I am indebted to my colleague Patricia O'Reilly for her lucid and comprehensive review of the current policy literature in a draft of her work on frameworks, models, and theories of public policy.

17. See Elinor Ostrom, "Institutional Rational Choice: An Assessment of the Institutional Analysis and Development Framework," in Paul A. Sabatier, ed. *Theories of the Policy Process, Second Edition*, (Cambridge, Massachusetts: Westview Press, 2002): 25.

18. Jackson and Jackson, *Politics in Canada,* (2006): 504 ff. See also James E. Anderson, *Public Policy Making, Third Edition*, (New York: Holt, Rinehart and Winston, 1984): 8–10.

19. Pal, *Beyond Policy Analysis*, (2006): 18–19.

20. Ute Lischke and David T. McNab, eds. *Walking a Tightrope: Aboriginal People and their Representations*, (Waterloo: Wilfrid Laurier Press, 2005): 1. See also Frances Abele, "Between Respect and Control: Traditional Indigenous Knowledge in Canadian Public Policy," in Michael Orsini and Miriam Smith, eds. *Critical Policy Studies*, (Vancouver: UBC Press, 2007): 233–56.

21. Charles E. Lindblom, "The Science of 'Muddling Through,'" *Public Administration Review, 19, 2* (Spring, 1959): 79–88.

22. See Amitai Etzioni, "Mixed Scanning: A 'Third' Approach to Decision Making," *Public Administration Review, 27, 5* (December, 1967); and *Modern Organizations*, (Englewood Cliffs, New Jersey: Prentice-Hall, 1964).

23. See Michael D. Cohen, James G. March, and Johan P. Olsen, "A Garbage Can Model of Organizational Choice," *Administrative Science Quarterly, 17*, (1972): 1–25; and John W. Kingdon, *Agendas, Alternatives and Public Policies, Second Edition*, (New York: Harper Collins, 1995).

24. See G. David Garson, "Garbage Can Models: Multiple Stream Theory," (2006). **www2.chass.ncsu.edu/garson/pa765/garbagecan.htm** Accessed August 14, 2007.

25. See Deborah Stone, "Policy Paradox: The Art of Political Decision Making," in Jay M. Shafritz, Karen S. Layne and Christopher P. Borick, eds. *Classics of Public Policy*, (New York: Pearson Longman, 2005): 62–71.

26. For further reading on these terms, see Colin Hay, *Political Analysis: A Critical Introduction*, (Houndmills, England: Palgrave, 2002); Paul A. Sabatier, *Theories of the Policy Process, Second Edition*, (Cambridge, Massachusetts: Westview Press, 2007); and David Marsh and Gerry Stoker, eds. *Theory and Methods in Political Science, Second Edition* (Houndmills, England: Palgrave, 2002).

27. See Peter deLeon, *Advice and Consent: The Development of the Policy Sciences*, (New York: Russell Sage Foundation, 1988).

28. See Miriam Smith, *A Civil Society? Collective Actors in Canadian Political Life*, (Peterborough: Broadview Press, 2005); Lisa Young and Joanna Everitt, *Advocacy Groups*, (Vancouver: UBC Press, 2004); Hugh G. Thorburn, "Interest Groups in the Canadian Federal System," in R.S. Blair and J.T. McLeod, eds. *The Canadian Political Tradition, Second Edition*, (Scarborough: Nelson, 1993): 316–29; and Paul Pross, *Group Politics and Public Policy*, (Toronto: Oxford University Press, 1986).

29. The classic statement of pluralist theory is Robert A. Dahl, *Who Governs?* (New Haven: Yale University Press, 1961).

30. See Joseph Schumpeter, *Capitalism, Socialism, and Democracy*, (New York: Harper, 1943).

31. E.E. Schattschneider, *The Semisovereign People: A Realist's View of Democracy in America*, (Hinsdale: Dryden Press, 1975): 34.

32. Hay, *Political Analysis*, (2002):10.

33. See Garrett Hardin, "The Tragedy of the Commons," in Morton E. Winston and Ralph D. Edelbach, eds. *Society, Ethics and Technology, Third Edition*, (Toronto: Thomson Nelson, 2006).

34. See, for example, R. MacGregor Dawson, *The Government of Canada*, (Toronto: University of Toronto Press, 1970).

35. See Hay, *Political Analysis*, (2002): chapter 7.

36. Among the important first studies of implementation as a distinct part of the policy cycle is a study by public management theorists. See Jeffrey L. Pressman and Aaron Wildavsky, *Implementation, Second Edition*, (Berkeley: University of California Press, 1979).

37. See Jeffrey D. Straussman, *Public Administration, Second Edition*, (New York: Longman, 1990): 244–45.

38. See Duane Adams, ed. *Federalism, Democracy and Health Policy in Canada,* (Montreal: McGill-Queen's University Press, 2001); and Carolyn Tuohy, *Policy and Politics in Canada: Institutionalized Ambivalence,* (Philadelphia: Temple University Press, 1992): chapter 3.

39. F.L. Morton, Peter H. Russell and Troy Riddell, "The Supreme Court's First Decade of Charter Decisions: Judging the Judges, 1982–1992," in Paul Fox and Graham White, eds. *Politics: Canada, Eighth Edition*, (Toronto: McGraw-Hill, 1995): 80.

40. On policy communities and networks see William D. Coleman and Grace Skogstad, "Policy Communities and Policy Networks," in William D. Coleman and Grace Skogstad, eds. *Organized Interests and Public Policies*, (Toronto: Copp-Clark, 1990): 14–33; Michael M. Atkinson and William D. Coleman, *The State, Business and Industrial Change in Canada*, (Toronto: University of Toronto Press, 1989); and Evert A. Lindquist, "New Agendas for Research on Policy Communities: Policy Analysis, Administration and Governance," in Laurent Dobuzinskis, Michael Howlett and David Laycock, eds. *Policy Studies in Canada: The State of the Art*, (Toronto: University of Toronto Press, 1996): 219–41.

41. G. Bruce Doern and Richard W. Phidd, *Canadian Public Policy: Ideas, Structure, Process*, (Toronto: Methuen, 1983): 110.

42. See Marie-Louise Bemelmans-Videc, Ray C. Rist and Evert Vedung, *Carrots, Sticks and Sermons: Policy Instruments and Their Evaluation*, (New Brunswick, New Jersey: Transaction Publishers, 1998).

43. Theodore Lowi, "Distribution, Regulation, Redistribution: The Functions of Government," in R.B. Ripley, ed. *Public Policies and Their Politics: Techniques of Government Control*, (New York: W.W. Norton, 1966): 27–40.

44. See Michael J. Trebilcock et al., *The Choice of Governing Instrument*, (Ottawa: Economic Council of Canada, 1982). See also Michael J. Trebilcock, "The Choice of Governing Instrument: A Retrospective," in Pearl Eliadis, Margaret M. Hill, and Michael Howlett, eds. *Designing Government: From Instruments to Governance*, eds., (Montreal: McGill-Queen's University Press, 2005): 51–73.

45. Michael Howlett, "Policy Instruments and Implementation Styles: The Evolution of Instrument Choice in Canadian Environmental Policy," in Debora L. VanNijnatten and Robert Boardman, eds. *Canadian Environmental Policy: Context and Cases*, (Toronto: Oxford University Press, 2002): 25–45. See also Susan Delacourt and Donald G. Lenihan, eds. *Collaborative Government: Is There a Canadian Way?* (Toronto: Institute of Public Administration of Canada, 2000).

46. See Nicolas Baxter-Moore, "Policy Implementation and the Role of the State: A Revised Approach to the Study of Policy Instruments," in Robert J. Jackson et al. *Contemporary Canadian Politics: Reading and Notes*, (Scarborough: Prentice Hall, 1987): 336–55. See also Rand Dyck, *Canadian Politics: Critical Approaches, Fifth Edition*, (Toronto: Thomson Nelson, 2008): 514–17; and Geoffrey Hale, *Uneasy Partnership: The Politics of Business and Government in Canada*, (Peterborough: Broadview Press, 2006).

47. David Osborne and Ted Gaebler, *Reinventing Government*, (Reading, Massachusetts: Addison-Wesley, 1992): chapter 1.

48. See Pal, *Beyond Policy Analysis*, (2006): 202 ff.

49. Ray C. Rist, "Introduction," in Ray C. Rist, ed. *Policy Evaluation: Linking Theory to Practice*, (Aldershot, England: Edward Elgar Publishing: 1995): xv.

Public Administration *and* Evaluation

WHAT YOU WILL LEARN

Canadians need to know whether or not the policies and programs instituted by government are working properly. But how is this to be determined since the public sector does not have the standard of a "bottom line" against which to measure success? The evaluation of the decision making and actions of government must be accomplished with efficiency and economy. You will consider these issues in this chapter:

■ Where and how did the field of evaluation arise in the Canadian public sector?

■ What particular difficulties are associated with evaluating government policies and programs?

■ How does government evaluate whether each department has done its job well, let alone whether the government as a whole has met citizens' expectations?

Chapter 8 examines the difficulties around effective evaluation in the public service in Canada, noting that evaluation is the third component of the policy cycle (along with formulation and implementation) introduced in chapter 7. This chapter is divided into the following sections:

1. *The Development of Evaluation*

This section provides a brief overview of the development of evaluation. It asks, What is evaluation? How is it conducted, both formally and informally? What early developments contributed to the emerging role of evaluation in the policy cycle?

2. ⌐ *Problems of Evaluation*

The exercise of evaluation studies is fraught with difficulty. This section asks, What are the major impediments to effective evaluation? How can they be overcome?

3. ⌐ *Evaluation in Action*

This section considers the actual practice of evaluation. It explores, Who is primarily responsible for evaluation? How is it undertaken? What factors contribute to successful evaluation?

4. ⌐ *Contemporary Evaluation Practices*

This section asks, How has the New Public Management had an impact on evaluation? What explains the current emphasis on results-based management and value-for-money evaluation practices?

The Development of Evaluation

Policy evaluation both *is* and *is not* a complicated affair. To begin with, we constantly evaluate even the simplest of activities we are engaged in. For instance, "cooks taste their gravy and sauce, cabinetmakers run their hands over the wood to decide when a piece is smooth enough, and basketball players watch to see whether their shots go in. Indeed, it would be most unwise after turning on the hot water to neglect to check the water temperature before stepping into the shower."[1] However, it becomes much more complicated when the object of evaluation is a large, multifunctional, complex public organization. This is partly due to the shared nature of the responsibility for policy—cabinet, public servants, Parliament, and so on. But while responsibility for evaluating our cooking rests with the individual cook, responsibility for evaluating a policy is often spread out among many disparate actors. In addition, the object of policy, usually citizens, is heterogeneous by definition, with a huge array of needs and demands. There is often a time lag between implementing a policy and the point at which we can determine whether it is working as intended or not. But even determining the criteria by which we decide it is working can be daunting, as we will see following. But most significant is the political context, which is perhaps the greatest differentiation between evaluation by individuals and evaluation in public organizations.

There is no consensus in the literature as to what, exactly, **evaluation** should entail. It is a multidisciplinary creature, drawing on political science, accounting, economics, education, industrial engineering, management sciences, medicine, psychology, sociology, statistics, mathematics, urban studies, and other areas. Evaluation should not be confused with policy analysis, which is embarked on before a policy is implemented. Rather, program evaluation is a retrospective consideration of how a policy has worked.

There are a number of problems associated with evaluation, which we review below. For now, though, think about your own experience as a student.

First, it is natural that people are reluctant to have their work assessed, for fear of being criticized. So we approach evaluation with some reluctance. Still, you hand in your first-rate essay and patiently wait for that *A+* you are sure it deserves. But your paper is now in the hands of someone who had no part in its creation, has a different perspective on what an essay ought to look like, and has extremely high expectations about its content. After receiving your *C*, you wonder what planet your professor is from. In particular, you wonder what standards of evaluation were applied to your work. If you pursue the question, you will probably find that a set of "objective" criteria exists against which every essay was graded, including proper spelling, punctuation, and grammar; a coherent thesis and argument; a clear structure and organization; and evidence of research and familiarity with the literature in your field of study. But how objective are these criteria, in reality? Your professor invariably has a strong background in certain areas but is not an expert in everything. And what if she was not feeling well when she graded your paper, or was distracted by other work or family responsibilities? How do you know that she does not hold the opposite ideological position from your essay, and disagreed with your stance, no matter how eloquently put?

All these issues colour the evaluation of your work. Similarly, a host of problems interfere with the easy and objective evaluation of the work of the public service. The purpose of program evaluation is, in part, to ensure that government can be held accountable. In addition, it is expected to assist managers in making informed decisions about how to resource programs, determine a program's worth, and provide useful advice to Cabinet. Moreover, evaluation permits the government to anticipate future problems and plan ahead to avoid them. It also sometimes promotes experimentation and innovation. Finally, evaluation helps to legitimize government programs, since evidence is presented to citizens of their effectiveness and efficiency. Still, notwithstanding all these laudable goals and effects of evaluation, the practice is often regarded with suspicion and disdain by those being evaluated.

Evaluation can be usefully categorized into three types: administrative; judicial; and political evaluation.[2] **Administrative evaluation** generally involves examining the efficient delivery of government services, and determining whether the best value for money is being realized within the framework of democracy and justice. **Audits** of budgetary systems, personnel reviews, managerial performance reviews, and the like are typical of this type of evaluation, which is usually conducted within government by specialized agencies. Methodologically, administrative evaluation tends to be technical in nature, and involves compiling and analyzing data on program costs and benefits.

Judicial evaluation is related to the practice of judicial review (see chapter 6). It is concerned with the legal issues arising out of administrative actions when government programs are implemented. Judicial evaluation is a facet of constitutional and administrative law, where the judges and the courts pass judgment on the behaviour and practices of the public service, either on their own or at the behest of a government, corporation, or citizen filing a case against a government agency.

Political evaluation is a vaguer concept, since it is an ongoing process that can occur formally or informally and lacks technical and methodological sophistication. This type of evaluation is less interested in objectively establishing the utility and value of a particular policy, and more interested in subjectively establishing a case for its demise and replacing it with a policy more favourable to the evaluator's interests. Perhaps the most visible manifestation of this type of evaluation occurs at election time when citizens are asked, in a sense, to evaluate their government's overall performance. This is evaluation as it is most broadly understood. Political evaluation also occurs, though, in royal commissions and task forces, parliamentary committees, central agencies, line departments, Cabinet, through the actions of interest groups, via protests, lobbying, the media, and so on. When you write a letter to the editor of your local newspaper or to a Member of Parliament to protest against some government program, you are engaging in an informal and uncoordinated form of government policy evaluation. In short, evaluation occurs anywhere that "politics" takes place. We will be concerned in this chapter with *administrative evaluation*.

The 1960 Royal Commission on Government Organization (the Glassco Commission) is the starting point for the evolution of evaluation from a focus on the *amounts* of government expenditures to the *results* of government expenditures. Prior to the Glassco Commission, evaluation relied mainly on the **Auditor General's** annual post-audit of government department activity and spending and pre-audits conducted by the comptroller of the Treasury Board. Each audit ensured that due process was followed and that the honesty and integrity of the expenditure process was upheld. In other words, these audits looked at the *inputs* into programs—the finances.

But despite money being raised and spent while rigorously following every rule in the book, the results expected of programs and policies were not always obtained. So eventually it was determined that not just the inputs but also the results of programs ought to be evaluated alongside their probity. The outcome of the Glassco recommendations was a more decentralized management and financial system, and more modern management techniques that broadened the traditional function of financial audits and that created a concern for evaluating programs in terms of their legislated intent and outcomes. By the 1960s, program evaluation had developed into a more sophisticated art, drawing on the new tools of social science emerging in this period.

There are three basic questions evaluation is intended to answer: Is a policy relevant? Is it successful? Is it cost effective? To answer these questions, various attempts were made from the 1960s onward to reorganize the roles of departmental managers by allowing them to assume more responsibility for managing their affairs. For instance, a new financial management approach was introduced in 1968 called the **Planning, Programming, Budgeting System (PPBS)**, designed to define program objectives and show the full cost of each government program (as opposed to simply showing the cost of departments, each of which housed many discrete programs). Moreover, PPBS was intended to produce multi-year plans so there would be some predictability in financial management. The Trudeau government briefly embraced this system, consistent as it was with the prime minister's own stated preference to bring rationality and reason to politics, as did several provincial governments. (Ironically, the U.S. government abandoned this system as unworkable just as Canadian governments were embracing it.) The Treasury Board oversaw the introduction of PPBS, encouraging all departments to state their goals and objectives, list specific costs associated with each program designed to meet those goals, and detail the resources required for each program.[3] Once these steps had been initiated, it was thought, comparisons between departments and programs for evaluation purposes could be made relatively easily. The rationalism underlying the approach made it attractive to the technocrats who dominated the senior reaches of the public service.

But "the articulation of rational budgeting philosophies is not to be equated with their actual practice. Practice could not help but part company with theory to some significant extent, since politics (viewed as both power and ideas) imposes a rationality of its own."[4] In other words, PPBS failed to live up to its advance billing, since its underlying rationalism ignored that it was being grafted onto a political rationality quite different from the one called for in PPBS. As a result, the system never quite fulfilled its promise.[5]

It did contribute to the new emphasis on approaching evaluation in a results-oriented manner, however, and influenced a trend toward more systematic and professional evaluation. An increase in computer modelling and highly sophisticated, quantitative research assisted the evolution of evaluation into more of a science and less of an art, as did the growing business of evaluation consultants and the formation of professional standards for evaluators. In 1981, the Canadian Evaluation Society was formed as a non-profit organization dedicated to the advancement of evaluation theory and practice, and the *Canadian Journal of Program Evaluation* was launched in 1986.

In 1977, formal, systematic evaluations of programs were initiated by the Treasury Board; henceforth, departments and agencies were expected to periodically review their programs to evaluate their effectiveness in meeting objectives and to evaluate their administrative efficiency. But as political scientist Sharon Sutherland reported, there were important differences between the original PPBS initiative and subsequent Treasury Board guidelines that followed in 1977 and 1981. To begin with, the PPBS framework implicitly called for automatic evaluations of programs. Moreover, they would consist primarily of cost-benefit analyses, and generate comparisons across government departments. But the updated policy was looser than this in its expectations. It left in the hands of administrators much of the decision making about when and what kinds of evaluations to undertake—and left out any serious requirements for comparisons.[6] Political scientist Leslie Pal concluded that "with a kind of logic that would delight Lewis Carroll, program evaluation became both universally mandated for all federal government programs over time, and yet was left up to the discretion of departmental managers as to targets and techniques of evaluation."[7] As a result, evaluation as a tool of accountability declined.

Other developments, though, breathed new life into the moribund practices of evaluation. In the mid-1970s, a professional accountant named J.J. Macdonnell was appointed Auditor General. He wanted the federal government to adopt private sector accounting practices, and pushed for the creation of an **Office of the Comptroller General** to oversee the government's evaluation systems. The government was galvanized into action when Macdonnell imperiously announced in his 1976 annual report to Parliament, "I am deeply concerned that Parliament—and indeed the Government—has lost, or is close to losing, effective control of the public purse."[8] The ensuing storm resulted in a royal commission on financial management and accountability and, ultimately, establishment of the Office of the Comptroller General (OCG). Although part of the motivation was to head off political criticism, the OCG nonetheless played an important role in the design, development, implementation, and monitoring of evaluation systems. As a result, according to Savoie, "[P]rogram evaluation did indeed develop into a growth industry, and it grew around the Office of the Comptroller General."[9] The OCG was created in 1978 and was headed by a deputy minister reporting directly to the president of the Treasury Board, and was given broad authority and responsibility for administrative practices and controls in financial management and procedures for program evaluation, and for ensuring that departments and agencies established program evaluation processes consistent with policy as articulated by the Treasury Board.[10]

The Treasury Board evaluation guidelines of 1981 were updated in 1991 in response to the growing influence of New Public Management (NPM) and to **PS2000**, which called for a new emphasis on "quality of service" to the public. PS2000 was a major review of the public service arising from a period of low morale and an apparent gap in understanding between the higher and lower echelons of the public service (see chapter 9). The OCG published "Into the '90s: Government Program Evaluation Perspectives," a document that laid out the relationship of PS2000 to evaluation.[11] A link was drawn between successful and careful evaluations and better quality service to the public. The document also emphasized broadening the evaluative process beyond simply consulting with direct stakeholders about how a program affects them, to a more participatory model of assessing the quality of service to the public as part of a broader change-based environment.

But by the early 1990s, the original zeal for evaluation diminished. The Auditor General was critical of a trend that saw a quantitative and qualitative decline in evaluations. This is not to suggest that evaluation was inconsequential. Indeed, in this period many useful reforms arose as a result of a variety of evaluation studies. But as Savoie pointed out in 1990, the question of "who was evaluating the evaluators" was left unanswered. The OCG and program evaluation "seem to be concerned only with methodologies and how many programs have been evaluated," according to Savoie. "Put more bluntly, evaluators seem to be kept busy turning cranks not connected to anything. The result is that one would be hard-pressed to point to even a handful of programs that have been reduced or eliminated as a result of an evaluation study."[12] Given the problems that plagued its existence, the OCG was closed in 1993, with its evaluation functions integrated into TBS.

Then, in 1994, the Treasury Board issued an updated framework for evaluation that, in concert with **Program Review**, superseded PS2000. Program Review was a wide-ranging initiative introduced by the Chrétien government in 1994 to review all government programs in order to identify cost savings that would help reduce the deficit. This marks a distinction that developed between the evaluation concerns of traditional management practices in the public service and those arising in the early 1990s as a result of NPM. The traditional approach focused on effectiveness, efficiency, and economy, and on government processes rather than outcomes. It placed much less emphasis on issues such as customer satisfaction, public participation, and procedural due process, all of which came to the forefront in reconfiguring evaluation. Most important, a clear link was established between the purposes of evaluation and deficit control. The Treasury Board argued that "the fiscal burden carried by Canadian taxpayers, pressures to control and reduce the cost of government programs and operations, and management reform within the Public Service are all factors that make it essential to have information on results."[13]

We see this again in the Annual Report to Parliament in 1996 by the president of the Treasury Board, which said, "[W]e must equip ourselves with better systems for evaluating the actions of government so that we can genuinely answer for our actions, first and foremost to our fellow citizens who are both clients and taxpayers. This is the only way our government can evaluate and debate the merits of the decisions we make every day on the public's behalf."[14] Government performance, then, was to be measured not only in terms of the benefits citizens derive from programs, but also on its success in reducing total government expenditures and in establishing a more results-oriented management culture in the public service. Program Review was perhaps the largest macro exercise ever undertaken in evaluation of government programs. Program Review sought to provide the rationale and means by which government could be "shrunk" to a more manageable size, which involved evaluating existing practices and programs. The results included ending inappropriate programs, changing the way some programs were delivered, and improving the efficiency of ongoing initiatives. But, most significantly, it is estimated that Program Review effected savings of some $11 billion in direct program spending over the period 1994–1995 to 1998–1999.

With the advent of the NPM, evaluation exercises increasingly concluded that many services traditionally provided by government could be provided by others outside government. Part of restructuring, then, meant undertaking new arrangements, such as devolving authority to provincial or municipal governments, creating alternative service delivery vehicles, and developing new mechanisms and partnerships. While these initiatives may indeed increase the flexibility of program delivery, they raised important questions about evaluation and accountability. As a result, actors outside government became more engaged in evaluation. As the government relied increasingly on third parties, and empowered employees to achieve public purposes, new methods were developed to evaluate the effectiveness of policy. For instance, where the government contracted out a service, it usually required specific observable and measurable performance requirements that could be assessed. Scheduled and surprise inspections by government personnel, client surveys, "hot lines," and other strategies were built into evaluation processes. Clearly, though, these new activities raised serious questions about accountability. This point is explored more thoroughly in chapter 12.

Related to these developments is the introduction of the **business planning** process, first initiated by the government of Alberta (see chapter 10). This is a means by which departmental planning is put on a more businesslike footing, involving the identification of core results and programs as well as statements of performance expectations and reviews. Performance is measured in terms of what is being delivered by a given department (for instance, new policies, or improvements in existing ones), or the impact of programs (for instance, new job creation or economic growth). Evaluation results are fed back into the system to determine the future course of action, and decisions are made about how to better manage programs and make continuous improvements in providing services. Business plans and reports to Parliament incorporate the evaluation information as feedback in their development. And citizens (now referred to as "clients" in the business plans) are sounded out for further feedback and results monitoring.

This was the main outline of the evolution of evaluation to the end of the 1990s. You can clearly see the influence of NPM in these developments. Before picking up the story in the twenty-first century, a slight digression is in order to report on the difficulties in the evolving emphasis on evaluation. We will return to more recent developments following. But first we provide an overview of the many problems associated with operationalizing evaluation in the public service.

Problems of Evaluation

Program evaluation is fraught with difficulties. Program objectives are not always straightforward or clearly defined. Politicians and public servants are often reluctant to expressly state the goals of a particular program, lest it offend those not served by it. In addition, they may want to avoid blame, should something go wrong, so legislation objectives are sometimes vaguely worded. Politicians often derive their support from broad coalitions of interests in society; they frame legislation in terms that appeal to disparate groups so that each can interpret the intent of the legislation as serving their own goals.[15]

The root of the problem is that program objectives are not always easily measurable. If the government increases funding for scholarships for post-secondary students, and there is a decrease in student indebtedness, did the one cause the other? Perhaps more students found summer or part-time work; perhaps more well-off students entered the system; perhaps Kraft Dinner was on sale more often in the year under review! Or consider the program objectives of the Department of External Affairs. How does one determine whether improved relations with foreign countries has been attained? Or that trade has been increased due to the efforts of our ambassadors, schmoozing with foreign dignitaries?

Where goals are measurable, things that are easily measured will attract the eye of those conducting evaluations. This contorts the rationale of evaluation and may result in influencing the program to conform with that which is measurable (see Box 8.1). Political scientist Alan Maslove states,

Indicators may emerge from the political-bureaucratic process which minimize problems or make them more amenable to solutions and which suit the emotional commitments and interests of the decision-makers and those who influence them. Indicators may be selected to promote the adoption of desired policies, to make these policies appear as successful as possible, and to direct public discussion in the desired directions.[16]

BOX 8.1 | **How Bureaucrats Explain Negative Findings**

According to political scientist Thomas Dye:

Government administrators and program supporters are ingenious in devising reasons why negative findings about policy impacts should be rejected. Even in the face of clear evidence that their favourite programs are useless or even counterproductive, they will argue that:

1. *The effects of the program are long range and cannot be measured at the present time.*

2. *The effects of the program are diffuse and general in nature, no single criterion or index adequately measures what is being accomplished.*

3. *The effects of the program are subtle and cannot be identified by crude measures or statistics.*

4. *Experimental research cannot be carried out effectively because to withhold services from some persons to observe the impact of such withholding would be unfair to them.*

5. *The fact that no difference was found between persons receiving the services and those not receiving them means that the program is not sufficiently intensive and indicates the need to spend more resources on the program.*

6. *The failure to identify any positive effects of a program is attributable to inadequacy or bias in the research itself, not in the program.*

Source: Thomas R. Dye, *Understanding Public Policy. Ninth Edition,* (Upper Saddle River, New Jersey, 1998): 349.

Furthermore, establishing control groups to test whether a policy applied to one group but not to another is effective is next to impossible. Even establishing causality—that is, showing that program X caused a certain result—can be challenging because of the difficulty of isolating the impact of a particular program. Outside factors may intrude on the success or failure of a program. For instance, is a decline in drunk driving the result of increased educational campaigns, increased police spot checks, or an aging population less inclined to consume alcohol? Another problem is that some programs themselves comprise several subprograms. Does the measurement of the success of the subprograms add up to the measurement of the success of the overall program? Or consider that the world of public policy is constantly changing. Programs may have a short shelf life, and there may simply not be enough data about a program to make a reasonable assessment of its utility.

In some cases goals—for example, those regarding national security or sensitive financial information—cannot be stated publicly or explicitly. In other cases, new and innovative programs may defy easy assessment simply because they are in uncharted waters. Programs devised to promote racial tolerance or gender equality may fall into this category. More specifically, objectives for these types of programs may be deliberately left vague to permit flexibility in their implementation. And then, there are some things governments do not want to know. For instance, if a government is committed ideologically or politically to a course of action, it may not want to know that it will not work. The opponents of the Free Trade Agreement (FTA) and the North American Free Trade Agreement (NAFTA), for example, argued that trade deals were to blame when tens of thousands of workers were thrown out of work in the early 1990s. But the government insisted that it had conducted no evaluations of the impact of free trade, so it could not confirm that free trade was responsible for the recession that gripped the country.

Evaluation proposals must first scale the wall of skepticism that surrounds policy-makers, convincing them to commit sufficient resources to projects that might in the end criticize their work. They must then traverse the minefield of policy reversals, changes in funding and personnel, and changing priorities in public policy. In addition, mustering capable troops to conduct evaluations has been a problem given the lack of expertise in this relatively new field. Given the wide range of disciplines that evaluation draws on, findings may be contested by "experts" from disparate fields. In addition, the assumption that only the "experts" know best sometimes flies in the face of the real, lived experiences of people affected by government programs. For instance, scientists working for the Ministry of Fisheries may scientifically assess a fishery and determine that it should be closed to preserve the dwindling stock of fish. But for the fishers who make their livelihood there, that recommendation is disastrous. Moreover, the fishers' evaluation of previous attempts by scientists to monitor the stock may have pointed out gross errors in their calculations. But because the fishers are not "experts," their concerns may be ignored.[17]

In addition, some programs serve several masters, and public service managers are accountable to more than one agency. This may result in the manager being pulled in several different directions at once, which may in turn detract from the overall quality of the program. Public servants are often reluctant to subject their work to critical examination. It is often said in this context that a dog will not fetch the stick with which it will be beaten. Public servants also resist evaluation because it is costly. In 2005, total expenditure by the federal government for evaluations was $54.8 million. However, this figure should be placed in perspective: it represents only 0.16 percent of departmental expenditures, and only 11 of 47 small agencies had evaluation budgets totalling $1 million—and 60 percent of that related to just two small agencies.[18] They also perceive evalution as time-consuming (see Figure 8.1). Political scientist Timothy Plumptre rather pithily summarized the problems with evaluation when he compared it to chastity. "People support it in principle," he suggests, "but in practice they prefer if it is mandatory for others and optional for them. . . ."[19]

FIGURE 8.1   **Number of Months Evaluation Takes 2004–2005***

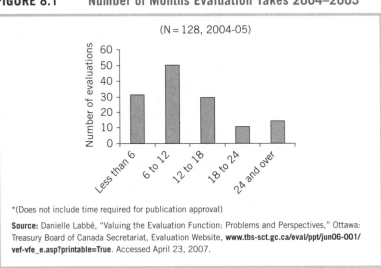

(N = 128, 2004-05)

*(Does not include time required for publication approval)

Source: Danielle Labbé, "Valuing the Evaluation Function: Problems and Perspectives," Ottawa: Treasury Board of Canada Secretariat, Evaluation Website, **www.tbs-sct.gc.ca/eval/ppt/jun06-001/ vef-vfe_e.asp?printable=True**. Accessed April 23, 2007.

Evaluation in Action

Notwithstanding these difficulties, a culture of evaluation has gradually infused the public service, and evaluation is seen as an important aspect of accountability— almost all evaluations conducted by the public service are available for public scrutiny. The government uses a range of types of evaluations; methods as complex as econometric modelling and computer simulations exist alongside traditional interviewing of program beneficiaries and experts in a field. Great care must be taken in determining what type of evaluation is suitable for a particular program. Indeed, many exercises have floundered on the rocks of inadequate consideration for "appropriate" evaluation. Hence, evaluation assessment studies are a part of the evaluation landscape.

An appropriate evaluation study of a program requires consideration of six factors.[20] First, the nature of the program to be evaluated must be considered. This includes a definition or description of what is to be evaluated; the length of time that a program has been running, since a program should be "field-tested" before attempts are made to evaluate; and the type of state intervention used in the program, whether it involves regulation, expenditure, taxation, or other policy instruments.

Second, the questions to be addressed by the evaluation must be carefully thought through. Evaluators need to consider whether their evaluation is dealing with the rationale of the program, its impacts and effects, its objective achievements, or alternatives to the program. Each of these will prompt a different set of questions.

Third, the client of the evaluation study must be clearly identified. Potential clients include Cabinet, the media, Parliament, program planners and managers, the public, researchers, and senior public servants. Consider again a program designed to ease student debt load. Cabinet might ask if the program is having a demonstrable effect on fiscal resources dedicated to student loans, and the political impact of garnering the electoral support of students. The students themselves might ask whether enough is being done to ease their debt load, and why the government is not doing more. The program manager might ask whether the program is being delivered effectively and efficiently, or whether a new computer system or other technology or redeployment of staff would help in the program's delivery.

The fourth component of an evaluation study relates to the actual technique used to conduct the evaluation. A range of methodologies is available to program evaluators, and great care must be taken to ensure the right type of evaluation is conducted. Decisions must be made about whether to employ quantitative or qualitative methods, analysis, description, surveys, polling, interviews, focus groups, etc. Questions must be asked about how rigorous and systematic the evaluation needs to be, or how casual and informal, and so on.

Fifth, every program evaluation study must carefully consider the resources and time available. Almost invariably, trade-offs must be made that may sometimes compromise the process. The short-term perspective of the governmental budget cycle means that long, languorous, time-consuming studies are a luxury. Moreover, clients often want results "yesterday." Evaluations that report to Parliament must subscribe to the parliamentary cycle and timelines. The costs involved must be justified. This in itself can entail considerable effort that detracts from the actual evaluation.

Sixth, evaluation studies must be credible and have legitimacy—in the eyes of clients as well as other observers. Credibility can be enhanced if the evaluator has an arm's-length relationship from the subject being evaluated, as well as from the client being served. This is where institutions such as the OCG, the Office of the Auditor General, and the Treasury Board are useful. They establish criteria and guidelines for evaluation that help ensure the evaluation is objective. Ultimately, though, the test of credibility is in the hands of the public. If a program is perceived by citizens to be a boondoggle, all the evaluation studies in the world are unlikely to change their minds. In this regard, recent Access to Information legislation has given citizens (as well as public servants) improved tools with which to conduct their own evaluations of government programs.

Contemporary Evaluation Practices

You will recall that earlier in this chapter we traced the evolution of evaluation up to the end of the 1990s. We pick up the story here by noting that the advent of contemporary management practices, including those inspired by the NPM, reinvigorated the practice of evaluation even as it changed its character to more overtly focus on results.[21] It has been pointed out that "many governments are now engaged in what is commonly described as results-based management, involving the development of performance indicators and measures related to an organization's business objectives, measuring the outputs and outcomes of programs and services, and using these data to evaluate the performance of the organization and its employees."[22] Indeed, internationally there was an explosion of interest in new program evaluation techniques and development in the 1990s and early 2000s. The European Evaluation Society was formed in 1994, as was the United Kingdom Evaluation Society. As well, evaluation societies appeared in Australia in 1991, France in 1996, Germany, Italy, and Switzerland in 1997, Malaysia in 1999, and more recently in Russia, Belgium, Ethiopia, Finland, Ghana, Israel, and Kenya.[23] The Canadian government created the Centre for Excellence in Evaluation in 2001 as part of a capacity-building exercise to enable it to conduct better evaluations. However, overall "the extent that the Canadian federal government has influenced the development of the field of program evaluation and evaluation capacity in Canada is less clear and direct than in the United States and United Kingdom."[24]

In 2001, the Treasury Board updated its policy on evaluation, re-emphasizing the importance with which evaluation should be regarded by public service managers and focusing sharply on the practice of "managing for results." The policy was based on three fundamental principles:

- first, that achieving and accurately reporting on results is a primary responsibility of public service managers;

- second, that rigorous and objective evaluation is an important tool in helping managers to manage for results; and

- third, that departments, with the support of the Treasury Board Secretariat, are responsible to ensure that the rigour and discipline of evaluation are sufficiently deployed within their jurisdictions.[25]

Managing for results has become the mantra for public service managers, who are now expected, as a matter of routine, to define the anticipated results of their work, continuously focus attention on results achievements, and measure performance regularly, all with an eye on improving efficiency and effectiveness. In addition, as a contemporary management tool, evaluation increasingly is entangled with new forms of service delivery, such as partnerships within government bodies, across departments, and with outside actors.

According to the Treasury Board Secretariat, managers are expected to "embed the discipline of evaluation into the lifecycle management of policies, programs and initiatives."[26] Furthermore, it argues the following:

The success of evaluation depends on a number of important factors. It requires clarity of roles, application of sound standards, ongoing support for rigorous, professional practice, and developing a conducive environment where managers embed the discipline of evaluation into their work. The organizational positioning of evaluation should reflect the unique needs of the department. Evaluation discipline should be used in synergy with other management tools to improve decision making. Heads of evaluation should work to ensure that evaluation in their organization is healthy in respect of all these factors. The Treasury Board Secretariat, in its role as the government's management board, should support the practice of evaluation in departments by providing advice on best practices, setting standards, monitoring the evaluation capacity in departments and using the products of evaluation to inform decision making at the centre.[27]

By the start of the twenty-first century, the federal government had developed a sophisticated, though not problem-free, infrastructure for evaluating policy. All of the main departments and agencies had internal audit and evaluation sections, and they regularly published their findings of their audits and evaluations. The Centre of Excellence for Evaluation served as a focal point for leadership of the evaluation function in the federal Public Service, to launch new initiatives, and to support capacity building and strengthening of the evaluation community. And the Office of the Auditor General conducted performance audits of departments and agencies.[28]

In addition, the Office of the Comptroller General was resurrected in 2003 by the Paul Martin government and charged with enhancing and strengthening comptrollership in all government departments. The government published two documents entitled *Responsible and Prudent Financial Management* and *Strengthening Public Sector Management,* which outlined a new expenditure management system and the place of evaluation therein.[29] But again, politics seemed to be a prime motivation as the government was feeling the pressure of the Sponsorship Program scandal (see chapter 12) and wanted to be seen enhancing accountability. The current mandate and priorities of the Office of the Comptroller General are shown in Box 8.2.

In 2006, with the arrival of a new government came a new approach to evaluation tied to a new emphasis on accountability in government, of which the Federal Accountability Act was the centrepiece. The government's budget speech of that year said,

. . . our government's approach to spending control is based on the following three principles: government programs should focus on results and value-for-money; government programs must be consistent with federal responsibilities; and programs that no longer serve the purpose for which they were created should be eliminated.

With those principles in mind, the Government is launching a review of its expenditure management system.[30]

BOX 8.2 | **The Mandate and Ongoing Priorities of the Office of the Comptroller General**

The Comptroller General is responsible for providing government-wide functional direction and assurance for financial management and internal audit. Through the Office of the Comptroller General (OCG) and its operating sectors/directorates, which have policy centre mandates, ongoing activities are conducted in the following priority areas:

- *Promoting stronger financial and audit controls that are essential to ensuring rigorous stewardship of public funds and value for money;*

- *Setting and reviewing financial, accounting, and auditing standards and policies for the Government of Canada and providing leadership to ensure and enforce* appropriate financial controls and cultivate sound resource stewardship at all levels across the federal public service;

■ Nurturing and managing the professional development of the financial and internal audit communities;

■ Leading the introduction of modern, timely, "enterprise-wide" financial information systems to track all spending and provide appropriate tools for effective scrutiny and decision making;

■ Overseeing government spending, including review and sign-off on new spending initiatives, and monitoring and reporting on how well financial management and internal audit are being managed in departments and agencies;

■ Providing guidance for the preparation of departmental financial statements and the Public Accounts of Canada; and

■ Providing ongoing financial management and internal audit, advice, and support to the President, the Secretary, TBS Branches and Sectors, Deputy Ministers, other central agencies & functional specialists.

Source: Canada. Treasury Board Secretariat. *TBS Organization—Office of the Comptroller General.* Ottawa: Treasury Board Secretariat **www.tbs-sct.gc.ca/organisation/ocg-bcg-PR_e.asp?printable=True**. Accessed April 20, 2007.

In addition, the budget speech required that every department undertake a review of all federal grants and contributions at least once every five years.

But evaluation issues consider to bedevil the government, particularly those problems associated with the concept of "measurement." Although the idiom "what gets measured gets managed" emerged to encapsulate the advantages of performance measurement, at least three main problems persisted:

■ Conceptual problems (how far are the measures meaningful and understandable to the various social, political, and public service groups which are affected by them?)

■ Motivational problems (mainly—though not entirely—small "p" problems of bureaucratic politics: who measures who, for what purposes and with what safeguards against distortion and misuse?)

■ Technical problems (can everything important be measured, and measured reliably, at reasonable cost and without too much delay?)[31]

One recent report on the views of deputy ministers toward evaluation identified a number of ongoing problems. For instance, there is a lack of resources and competent evaluators, and weak linkages with policy and the expenditure management system. In addition, for heads of evaluation, access to competent evaluators is a major problem. Despite the Treasury Board Secretariat's call for more evaluations on the effectiveness of horizontal initiatives and programs, lack of capacity and coordination of horizontal evaluations is a major obstacle.[32] Moreover, evaluation has not been well-integrated with senior management decision making, there is a lack of feedback between evaluation findings and policy development, and the cutbacks of the 1990s continue to adversely affect the government's ability to conduct evaluation to the extent that many evaluation studies are still contracted out, limiting the development of in-house government experts.[33]

One recent approach to wrestle with these broad problems and further refine the system of evaluation has been to adopt value-for-money auditing, framed by two key questions:

1. *Relevance—Are we doing the right thing?*
   - *Program addresses a demonstrable need, is appropriate to the federal government, and is responsive to Canadians.*

2. *Performance—Are we achieving value?*
   - *Economy: Are tax-payer resources well utilized?*
   - *Efficiency: Are program outputs (services and products) achieved in an affordable manner?*
   - *Effectiveness: Extent to which program objectives have been achieved? That is, what results were produced? Are the costs of achieving program outcomes minimized?*[34]

The new approach to evaluation is summarized in Table 8.1.

As we can see, the contemporary face of evaluation is evolving, and there are continuous calls for a change of focus. But, according to one public servant, the real focus must always ultimately be on the public good:

Part of the problem, in my view, is that evaluations have focused on the program manager as the primary client. Program managers are largely concerned with questions of efficiency and effectiveness that guide service delivery and program improvements. While critical to the conduct of an evaluation, focusing evaluation solely on the needs of this group reduces its utility to decision makers such as deputies, central agencies, Ministers, Parliament, and ultimately Canadians. The information demands of these stakeholders requires a focus on larger issues centred on the public good as opposed to program operations.[35]

A similar concern was raised by Christopher Pollitt, who invoked Oscar Wilde's quip about "a man who knows the price of everything and the value of nothing" in warning about the real importance of evaluation. Pollitt wrote that "governments may end up knowing how much everything costs, how long everything takes, what percentage of errors are committed in processing various kinds of claims, how many output targets have been met and many other things, yet will remain ignorant of the values which different groups of citizens place upon different public services, and of the reasons why those values are held."[36]

This overview of recent developments in the world of the evaluation of public policy shows that interest in the process has waxed and waned over time. After an initial outburst of interest in the 1960s and 1970s, the place of evaluation in the realm of government activities declined in stature and status. Many of the difficulties associated with the practice asserted themselves, and no sustained effort was made to ensure that evaluation became a regular feature of government accountability. A renewed interest in evaluation arose in the 1990s and early 2000s, with the advent of new management philosophies and techniques. Evaluation is now linked to the overarching goals of

TABLE 8.1 New Approaches to Evaluation Through Value-For-Money

- The value-for-money (VFM) tool focuses on two areas of inquiry:

Program Relevance	Program Performance
• Need	• Economy of inputs
• Appropriateness	• Efficiency of outputs
• Consistency with government objectives	• Cost-Effectiveness of direct, immediate outcomes

The VFM Tool assesses a program's relevance by rating the following criteria as low, medium, or high

1. Source of program authority
2. Continuing need for program
3. Consistency with current government priorities
4. Appropriateness to government

The VFM Tool then assesses a program's performance by rating the following criteria as low, medium, or high

Economy:

- Assessment of input costs (e.g., trends and understanding of cost drivers)
- Management practices that promote economy (e.g., asset management, HR mix, understanding and application of best practices)

Efficiency:

- Assessment of output costs (e.g., targets or benchmarking)
- Management practices (e.g., service standards)

Cost-Effectiveness:

- Assessment of outcome costs (e.g., targets or benchmarking)
- Management practices (e.g., client satisfaction)

The quality and availability of information to assess these criteria is also rated as low, medium, or high.

Source: Canada. Treasury Board of Canada Secretariat. *Modernizing Evaluation Tools: Value-For-Money Profile.* Ottawa: Treasury Board of Canada, Evaluation Website, November 2006. **www.tbs-sct.gc.ca/eval/ppt/dec06-001/vfmp-por_e. asp?printable=True**. Accessed April 23, 2006.

fiscal prudence, quality of service, program review, management for results, performance measurement, and other related issues that have arisen in contemporary governance. Peter Aucoin summarizes the importance of this evolutionary process:

The advent of Program Evaluation as a component of decision making in the Canadian government in the 1970s constituted a significant innovation that was internationally recognized. Although a great deal has changed over the past three decades, the current emphasis on Result-Based Management as well as Results-Based Reporting indicates the extent to which the pursuit of continuous improvement through the evaluation of performance continues to be front and centre on the governance and public management reform agenda.[37]

So, the next time you feel aggrieved by a government action (or inaction), rest assured that it has probably undergone a process of evaluation that has concluded that—like cod liver oil—it is good for you.

WHAT YOU HAVE LEARNED

Evaluation, as the third element in the policy cycle, can be an elusive concept. Ironically, nearly everyone recognizes, at least intuitively, that some measure of the worth of public policies needs to be taken. Citizens want to know, and have a right to know, whether they are getting value for their tax dollars. They also need to know and have a right to know that the rules of the game are being followed—that fairness, objectivity, and honesty are applied to all cases. Evaluation should go some way toward telling citizens whether this is the case. But because of the difficulties associated with evaluation, it is not always clear-cut. The recent emphasis on evaluation is motivated less by traditional concerns of probity and honesty than by the values of the three *Es*. This generalization does not apply in all cases, of course, but sufficiently illustrates the differing emphases of the art and science of evaluation, past and present.

Key Words and Concepts

evaluation (241)
administrative evaluation (242)
audits (242)
judicial evaluation (242)
political evaluation (243)
Auditor General (243)
Planning, Programming,
  Budgeting System (243)

Office of the Comptroller
  General (245)
PS2000 (245)
Program Review (245)
business planning (247)

Review Questions

This chapter reviewed the important role of policy evaluation as a key part of the policy cycle. It was divided into four sections:

1. *The Development of Evaluation*
In considering the development of evaluation, ask yourself, What is evaluation, and how different is the model of evaluation that was predominant at the time of the Glassco Commission from that of NPM?

2. Problems of Evaluation

The difficulties of conducting evaluation in the public service are legion. Ask yourself, What methodological and other problems confront evaluators? Can evaluation practices be made effective enough to assure the public that it is getting the most bang for its buck?

3. Evaluation in Action

Notwithstanding the difficulties of evaluation, it is an important tool. This section asks you, Who are the primary actors and institutions involved in evaluation? What are the conditions under which evaluation is likely to be successful?

4. Contemporary Evaluation Practices

In looking at recent developments, ask yourself, What influence has New Public Management had on evaluation? What changes in perspective have been brought to the process of evaluation by the new emphasis on running government like a business? What results have been produced in the area of evaluation by various reforms over the years?

Weblinks

Treasury Board of Canada Secretariat
www.tbs-sct.gc.ca

Expenditure Management System
www.tbs-sct.gc.ca/Pubs_pol/opepubs/TB_H/EXMA_e.asp

Treasury Board of Canada Secretariat: Evaluation Web Site
www.tbs-sct.gc.ca/eval/eval_e.asp

Canadian Evaluation Society
www.evaluationcanada.ca

Canadian Journal of Program Evaluation
www.evaluationcanada.ca/site.cgi?s=4&ss=2&_lang=en

Further Reading

1. The Development of Evaluation

Braybrooke, David and Charles E. Lindblom. *A Strategy of Decision*. New York: Free Press of Glencoe, 1963.

Muller-Clemm, W.J. and Maria Paulette Barnes. "A Historical Perspective on Federal Program Evaluation in Canada," *Canadian Journal of Program Evaluation*, 12, 1, (Summer, 1997): 47–70.

Rist, Ray C., ed. *Policy Evaluation: Linking Theory to Practice*. Aldershot, England: Edward Elgar Publishing Limited, 1995.

Weiss, Carol H. *Evaluation. Second Edition*. Upper Saddle River, New Jersey: Prentice Hall, 1998.

2. Problems of Evaluation

Pal, Leslie A. *Beyond Policy Analysis: Public Issue Management in Turbulent Times. Third Edition*. Toronto: Thomson Nelson, 2006: chapter 7.

Seidle, F. Leslie. *Rethinking the Delivery of Public Services to Citizens*. Montreal: Institute for Research on Public Policy, 1995.

3. Evaluation in Action

Dobell, Rodney and David Zussman. "An Evaluation System for Government: If Politics Is Theatre, Then Evaluation Is (Mostly) Art," in Barbara Wake Carroll, David Siegel and Mark Sproule Jones, eds. *Classic Readings in Canadian Public Administration*. Toronto: Oxford University Press, 2005: 353–74.

Doern, G. Bruce. *Progress and Constraints in Five Canadian Federal Agencies: The Road to Better Public Services*. Montreal: Institute for Research on Public Policy, 1994.

Howlett, Michael and M. Ramesh, *Studying Public Policy: Policy Cycles and Policy Subsystems, Second Edition*. Toronto: Oxford University Press, 2003: chapter 9.

Wholey, Joseph S., Harry P. Hatry and Kathryn E. Newcomer, eds. *Handbook of Practical Program Evaluation*. San Francisco: Jossey-Bass Publishers, 1994.

4. Contemporary Evaluation Practices

Carroll, Barbara Wake and David I. Dewar. "Performance Management: Panacea or Fools' Gold?" in Christopher Dunn, ed. *The Handbook of Canadian Public Administration*. Toronto: Oxford University Press, 2002: 413–29.

Leclerc, G. "Institutionalizing Evaluation in Canada," in J. Mayne, J. Hudson, M.L. Bemelmans-Videc and R. Conner, eds. *Advancing Public Policy Evaluation: Learning From International Experiences*. Amsterdam: North Holland, 1992: 49–58.

Endnotes

1. Emil J. Posavac and Raymond G. Carey, *Program Evaluation: Methods and Case Studies. Seventh Edition*, (Upper Saddle River, New Jersey: Pearson Prentice Hall, 2007): 1–2.

2. See Michael Howlett and M. Ramesh, *Studying Public Policy: Policy Cycles and Policy Subsystems, Second Edition*, (Toronto: Oxford University Press, 2003): 210–16.

3. See Government of Canada, *Planning, Programming and Budgeting Guide*, (Ottawa: Information Canada, 1969).

4. Allan M. Maslove, Richard Schultz and G. Bruce Doern, *Federal and Provincial Budgeting*, (Toronto: University of Toronto Press, 1985): 18. See also Donald J. Savoie, *The Politics of Public Spending in Canada*, (Toronto: University of Toronto Press, 1990).

5. See Sharon L. Sutherland, "The Evolution of Program Budget Ideas in Canada: Does Parliament Benefit From Estimates Reform?" *Canadian Public Administration*, 33 (Summer, 1990): 133–64. See also Evert Lindquist, "Getting Results Right: Reforming Ottawa's Estimates," in Leslie A. Pal, ed. *How Ottawa Spends 1998–1999: Balancing Act: The Post-Deficit Mandate*, (Toronto: Oxford University Press, 1998): 153–90.

6. Sutherland, "The Evolution of Program Budget Ideas in Canada," (1990): 144–45.

7. Leslie A. Pal, *Beyond Policy Analysis: Public Issue Management in Turbulent Times, Third Edition*, (Toronto: Thomson Nelson, 2006): 311.

8. Canada, Auditor General of Canada, *Annual Report 1976*, (Ottawa: Information Canada, 1976): 9.

9. Savoie, *The Politics of Public Spending in Canada*, (1990): 114.

10. See Donald J. Savoie, *Governing From the Centre: The Concentration of Power in Canadian Politics*, (Toronto: University of Toronto Press, 1999): 205.

11. See Canada, Treasury Board of Canada Secretariat, *Into the 90s: Government Program Evaluation Perspectives*, (Ottawa: Office of the Comptroller General, 1991).

12. Savoie, *The Politics of Public Spending in Canada*, (1990): 115.

13. See Canada, Treasury Board of Canada Secretariat, Treasury Board Manual—Review, Internal Audit and Evaluation, Amendment RIE/94-1, (Ottawa: Treasury Board of Canada, July 1994): 2.

14. Canada, Treasury Board of Canada Secretariat, "Getting Government Right: Improving Results Measurement and Accountability," (Ottawa: Minister of Public Works and Government Services Canada, 1996): preface. Online: **www.tbs-sct.gc/rma/communic/prr96/PRR96.e.htm**.

15. See, for example, James E. Anderson, *Public Policy Making,* (New York: Holt, Rinehart and Winston, 1984): 139–43.

16. Alan M. Maslove, "Indicators and Policy Formation," *Canadian Public Administration,* 18, 3 (Fall, 1975): 483.

17. See Susan McCorquodale, "Federal Spending on the Atlantic Fisheries," in Susan Phillips, ed. *How Ottawa Spends 1995–1996: Mid-Life Crisis,* (Ottawa: Carleton University Press, 1995): 364.

18. T.K. Gussman Associates, "Improving the Profession of Evaluation," (Ottawa: Treasury Board of Canada Secretariat, Evaluation Web Site, May 31, 2005). **www.tbs-sct.gc.ca/eval/dev/Professionalism/profession_e.asp.** Accessed April 23, 2007.

19. Timothy Plumptre, *Beyond the Bottom Line: Management in Government,* (Halifax: The Institute for Research on Public Policy, 1988): 267.

20. See Canada, Treasury Board of Canada, "Guide for the Development of Results-Based Management and Accountability Frameworks," (August 2000) **www.tbs-sct.gc.ca/eval/pubs/rmafcgrr-PR_e.asp**

21. See Christopher Pollitt, "Management Techniques for the Public Sector: Pulpit and Practice," in B. Guy Peters and Donald J. Savoie, eds. *Governance in a Changing Environment,* (Kingston: McGill–Queen's University Press, 1995): 226–31.

22. Ken Kernaghan, Brian Marson and Sandford Borins, *The New Public Organization*, (Toronto: Institute of Public Administration of Canada, 2000): 273.

23. See Ian Greene, "Lessons Learned from Two Decades of Program Evaluation in Canada," (August 2, 2005).**www.yorku.ca/igreene/progeval.html.** Accessed April 23, 2007. See also Christopher Pollitt, "How Do We Know How Good Public Services Are?" in B. Guy Peters and Donald J. Savoie, eds. *Governance in the Twenty-First Century: Revitalizing the Public Service,* (Montreal: McGill-Queen's University Press, 2000): 119–52.

24. J. Bradley Cousins and Tim Aubry, Roles for Government in Evaluation Quality Assurance: Discussion Paper, (Ottawa: Treasury Board of Canada, Evaluation Website, April 2006).**www.tbs-sct.gc.ca/eval/tools_outils/qae-aqe/rgeqa_e.asp?printable=True.** Accessed April 23, 2007.

25. Canada, Treasury Board of Canada Secretariat, *Evaluation Policy*, (April 1, 2001): 1.

26. Canada, Treasury Board of Canada Secretariat, *Evaluation Policy*, (April 1, 2001): 2.

27. Canada, Treasury Board of Canada Secretariat, *Evaluation Policy*, (April 1, 2001): 2.

28. Danielle Labbé, "Valuing the Evaluation Function: Problems and Perspectives," (Ottawa: Treasury Board of Canada Secretariat, Evaluation Website, June 1, 2006).**www.tbs-sct.gc.ca/eval/ppt/jun06-001/vef-vfe_e.asp?printable=True.** Accessed April 23, 2007.

29. See Evert Lindquist, Ian Clark and James Mitchell, "Reshaping Ottawa's Centre of Government: Martin's Reforms in Historical Perspective," in G. Bruce Doern, ed. *How Ottawa Spends 2004–2005: Mandate Change in the Paul Martin Era,* (Montreal: McGill-Queen's University Press, 2004): 337.

30. Canada. Department of Finance, *The Budget Speech,* (Ottawa: Department of Finance, 2006): 18.

31. Pollitt, "How Do We Know How Good Public Services Are?" (2000): 122. See also Barbara Wake Carroll and David I. Dewar, "Performance Management: Panacea or Fools' Gold?" in Christopher Dunn, ed. *The Handbook of Canadian Public Administration,* (Toronto: Oxford University Press, 2002): 413–29.

32. Cousins and Aubry, "Roles for Government in Evaluation Quality Assurance," (2006). **www.tbs-sct.gc.ca/eval/tools_outils/qae-aqe/rgeqa_e.asp?printable=True.** Accessed April 23, 2007.

33. Labbé, "Valuing the Evaluation Function," (2006). **www.tbs-sct.gc.ca/eval/ppt/jun06-001/vef-vfe_e.asp?printable=True.** Accessed April 23, 2007.

34. Canada. Treasury Board of Canada Secretariat. *Modernizing Evaluation Tools: Value-For-Money Profile,* (Ottawa: Treasury Board of Canada Secretariat, Evaluation Website, 2006). **www.tbs-sct.gc.ca/eval/ppt/dec06-001/vfmp-por_e.asp?printable=True.** Accessed April 23, 2007.

35. Terry Hunt, "The Role of Culture and the Future of the Evaluation Function: Considerations and Key Functions," *Canadian Journal of Program Evaluation,* 21, 3 (2006): 125.

36. Pollitt, "How Do We Know How Good Public Services Are?" (2000): 122.

37. Peter Aucoin, "Decision Making in Government: The Role of Program Evaluation," (Ottawa: Treasury Board of Canada Secretariat, Evaluation Website: March 29, 2005). **www.tbs-sct.gc.ca/eval/tools_outils/Aucoin/Aucoin_e.asp.** Accessed April 23, 2007.

Chapter 9

Public Administration *and the* Management *of* Human Resources

WHAT YOU WILL LEARN

In chapter 1, we identified personnel as a key issue in the study and practice of public administration. Under the guidance of their political masters, public servants—the people who work in the central agencies, departments, regulatory bodies, Crown corporations, and other government institutions—are responsible for formulating, implementing, and evaluating public policies. To coordinate and manage the vast range of services government offers, a large, sophisticated merit-based public service has emerged, made up of professionals from many occupations, who offer an astonishing array of skills.[1]

The federal government is the largest enterprise in the country. It is more than four times larger than the next largest employer, with seven times more revenue than the next largest organization, with more than 1600 programs and 2000 points of service in Canada and overseas.[2] Because it is a *public* sector organization rather than a private sector one, the issues relating to the organization and structure of the federal workforce are of particular importance, including the following:

- What and who constitutes the public service?
- What has been the historical development of the public service?
- What are the main organizational features of the public service?
- What contemporary issues concern human resource management in the public sector?

We consider these issues in the following sections:

1. — A Brief History of the Public Service: Who Works There, Anyway?

This section provides a brief history of the public sector and introduces some of the basic issues therein. It asks, What issues have animated the evolution of the public service over the past 140 years? How is the public service workforce organized, and who works there? Merit and patronage have been raised as important issues several times already in this book, but we take another look at them here. This section also asks, What steps have been taken to find a balance between patronage and merit?

2. — The Public Service Today: An Overview

In many respects, the public sector has pioneered progressive change in the workplace but not without a struggle. This section asks, What factors affect its current composition? Why are region, language, equity, and unionization important? Which have the most important equity issues? How has the public service changed to reflect the face of Canada? What is the importance of representativeness? How was the right to collective bargaining achieved in the public service? What political rights do public servants enjoy? What is the doctrine of political neutrality? What trends currently dominate in the relationship between public servants and the political system?

3. — Human Resources Management

The issue of how the tens of thousands of public servants in the federal government are organized and managed requires consideration. To this end, this section asks, How are systems of accountability established and maintained in the public service? What opportunities and constraints do managers have in the hiring and firing of personnel, and in setting pay levels and conditions of employment? How do merit and representativeness mesh or conflict with one another? Recent demographic shifts have left the public service in a precarious position. So this section also asks: What is being done around issues of recruitment, retention, and succession planning?

A Brief History of the Public Service: Who Works There, Anyway?

A famous National Film Board documentary by the late, great Canadian filmmaker Donald Brittain captured the disparaging attitude many people have toward the bureaucrat, whom Brittain characterized in this way:

He is that most despised of human creatures. His activities have brought down upon his shoulders the scorn and outrage of history's multitude. He is homo bureaucratus; the bureaucrat. He is the paper-pusher of the world. . . . He has been compared to the cockroach. Like the cockroach, he appears to have no useful function. Like the cockroach, he has many enemies. Like the cockroach, he has survived all attempts at extinction.[3]

This tongue-in-cheek characterization reflects a popularly held attitude. Compared to private sector organizations, the public service has made a very poor impression in the minds of many Canadians. Yet part of this perception depends on what citizens understand by *public service*. As Table 9.1 reveals, when asked which professions Canadians trust most, six of the top eight are actually public servants (firefighters, nurses, teachers, doctors, police officers, and judges). Senior public servants do not fare so well, it is true, coming in at 15th out of 23; and politicians rate ahead only of used car salespeople. But government, and indeed society, could scarcely function without the legions of public servants who every day protect us from danger, process our forms, regulate our behaviour, and punish our crimes and misdemeanours. Despite this, negative—if facile—attitudes about public servants persist.

TABLE 9.1   Professions Barometer
(percentage of Canadians who trust)

	Difference 2006–07	2007	2006	2005	2004	2003	2002
Firefighters	+1	97%	96%	97%	97%	96%	98%
Nurses	−1	94%	95%	94%	95%	94%	96%
Farmers	—	92%	92%	91%	91%	91%	93%
Teachers	+1	89%	88%	88%	88%	88%	—
Doctors	−2	87%	89%	89%	89%	89%	92%
Police officers	+3	84%	81%	83%	79%	80%	88%
Engineers	−5	83%	88%	—	—	—	—
Judges	−4	74%	78%	72%	75%	73%	80%
Notaries	−2	73%	75%	71%	72%	71%	82%
Bankers	−4	68%	72%	65%	67%	70%	72%
Church representatives	−3	61%	64%	65%	65%	65%	73%
Pollsters	−4	59%	63%	65%	63%	62%	70%
Economists	−5	57%	62%	—	—	—	—
Lawyers	+4	52%	48%	45%	44%	48%	54%
Senior public servants	—	50%	50%	45%	49%	50%	56%
Insurance brokers	+4	50%	46%	44%	41%	46%	51%
Journalists	−1	48%	49%	49%	46%	46%	53%
Real estate agents	+4	46%	42%	40%	39%	40%	44%
Unionists	+3	41%	38%	38%	36%	39%	41%
New car salespeople	NA	35%	—	—	—	—	—
Publicists	−9	31%	40%	37%	35%	38%	47%
Politicians	+1	15%	14%	16%	14%	14%	18%
Used car salespeople	NA	12%	—	—	—	—	—

Source: Leger Marketing Profession Barometer 2007. **www.legermarketing.com/eng/** Accessed June 10, 2007.

Love it or hate it, the public service in Canada is always striving to improve itself. Indeed, reform of the public service reaches back to the earliest days of Confederation. Mind you, Canada is not alone in this regard. The United States, Britain, Finland, New Zealand, Australia, Sweden, Singapore, Malaysia, and countless other jurisdictions are responding to globalization, fiscal issues, and citizens' growing disillusionment with government by changing the way their public services do their jobs. But the history of public service reform in Canada includes a series of pitfalls whenever *reform* has been understood to mean "reduce." When Pierre Trudeau became prime minister in 1968, he promised to reduce the number of government employees by 25 000. Ten years later, their numbers had grown by 40 000. Brian Mulroney assumed office in 1984 with the promise that he would issue "pink slips and running shoes" to the public service. By the time he left in 1993, the public service had increased by over 13 000. The Chrétien government reversed this between 1993 and 1999, when there was a 23 percent reduction in the federal public service. By the end of 1999, public service employment had reached a historic low of 186 314.[4] But these reductions created serious workload issues, as we will see following. In 1999 the first employment increase in seven years took place, and the public service grew by 2.6 percent or 3800 employees.

To place this in some context, let us consider the history of the public service through the lens of patronage and merit. The origins of patronage in the Canadian public service reach back to the colonies of New France and British North America. The political culture of both was shaped by the fact that they were primarily military colonies: that is, hierarchically organized societies in which personal ambition was rewarded through service to the King, who held centralized political control, and whose functionaries doled out patronage positions. Thus, the patterns of public service human resources management were established in colonial times when public servants received their posts for life. This generated stability for the governance of the colony, and laid the basis for a "professional" career-based civil service, despite the presence of patronage politics. For instance,

[I]mmediately prior to Confederation, out of nine deputy departmental heads in the Province of Canada, six had risen through the ranks by promotion, four had over twenty years' experience, and the most senior among them, the clerk of the Executive Council, could claim well over forty years' public service employment! The pattern was continued after 1867. At the time of the First World War, for example, the two dozen deputies at the federal level had an average of twenty years' experience.[5]

So, while we generally assume that the major "human resources policy" of the early days of this country was essentially the widespread use of patronage to reward friends of the government, in fact, a "meritocracy" of sorts was evident quite early on at the upper reaches of the civil service. But by the mid-1800s, the importance of patronage had changed, as the following quote indicates:

[P]atronage played an important role in nineteenth-century Canadian political culture because of its role as a vehicle for social promotion for the professional middle classes. In

a largely pre-industrial economy, the many employment possibilities offered by an expanding state—from customs inspectors and postal clerks to appointments to the judicial bench—were irresistibly attractive to the middle classes in search of security and prestige. The pursuit of such social rewards provided the foundation for political life in nineteenth-century Canada and gave rise to an intensely partisan political culture. . . . [Sir] John A. Macdonald used the patronage potential of an expanding state with mastery to build up his federal Conservative Party across the new federation and to dissolve, as far as possible, the forces of regionalism which threatened the stability of the new federal state. However, his success and example stimulated emulation and competition at the level of provincial governments, especially in Ontario, where long-serving Liberal Premier Oliver Mowat built up a smoothly functioning patronage machine based on an expanding and centralizing provincial state that eclipsed even Macdonald's federal Conservative machine for impartial and impersonal efficiency.[6]

However, citizen outrage over the pettiness of patronage lower down in the public service, coupled with the example of merit systems introduced in Great Britain and the United States, prompted reforms. Indeed, between 1867 and 1918, five federal royal commissions devoted at least part of their investigations to the evils of patronage.

Political scientist Laurent Dobuzinskis suggests that the move toward a meritocratic system of administration along Weberian lines began in Western Europe but had spread to North America by the 1880s.[7] By then, the need for professional administrators in both government and industry had become increasingly obvious; the drive for a merit-based professional civil service mixed with the scientific management approaches wafting up from the United States. The result was a sort of hybrid of British and American traditions.[8] The **Civil Service Acts of 1908 and 1918**, the creation of the **Civil Service Commission** in 1908, and the extension of its authority in the 1918 reforms marked the drive toward professionalization of the Canadian public service. Moreover, it reinforced the independence of the public service from political interference—a factor that remains a cornerstone of the modern **Public Service Commission** today.

The reforms of 1918 were directly predicated, strangely enough, on a U.S. model not particularly suited to Canadian conditions. Political pressures surrounding the government of Sir Robert Borden during the First World War forced the prime minister to reform the civil service to end the squabbling between Conservatives and Liberals over patronage appointments. As a result, a U.S. consulting firm was called in to make recommendations for reform. The firm devised a blueprint for a complex, inflexible, and highly centralized human resources system designed for the conditions of corrupt machine politics in U.S. cities. This was Taylor's scientific management with a vengeance. According to one observer, the 1918 reforms contained the following:

. . . a mechanistic view of the world of work, of clear-cut and precise specialization of labour, one that assumed considerable organizational stability—so much stability that each step in the process of classifying and filling jobs should be done thoroughly

even if it took many months, because each appointment was expected to last for years and years. This resulted in heavy, time-consuming processes and not a great deal of concern for human resource management. Employees were, in essence, seen as cogs in a large machine.[9]

Nonetheless, a generation of public service managers took the reforms of 1918 to heart. They desired a professional, technically skilled, and competent career public service, and actually constructed one. But it was one firmly dominated by the Tayloristic model. Thus, the pattern of human resource management was set and reinforced by these developments.

While Woodrow Wilson's distinction between politics and administration stood as the standard against which the quality of administration was measured for many decades, by the middle of the twentieth century, public servants were, in fact, playing an active role in policy formulation. The emergence of the welfare state was indeed partly attributable to the increasingly activist role of public servants. They provided the technical, managerial, and professional capability to mobilize the resources of the Canadian government toward a massive shift in the traditional relationship between the state and society. These senior civil servants played a vital role in shaping the managerial class and human resources policy and outlook of the Canadian public service. A new intellectual community, rooted mainly in the universities (especially the University of Toronto and Queen's University in Kingston), began to emerge, turning its attention to how the state could better manage the new issues of rapid industrialization and urbanization that were becoming prominent government concerns. Specifically, a cadre of individuals trained in the social sciences developed the conceit that they could play a role in making Canada a better country through improved human resource management and, ultimately—with a professional, skilled public service in place—in public policy making.[10] Individuals such as O.D. Skelton and Clifford Clark left Queen's University in the 1920s and 1930s to become deputy ministers (of External Affairs and Finance, respectively), attracting a new generation of like-minded university graduates, many of them economists, to form what historian J.L. Granatstein termed a new "mandarin" class of influential senior public managers.[11] Through the 1940s and 1950s, this small group played an influential role in professionalizing the public service. Recruitment to the ranks of the upper reaches of the public service is noteworthy because of the way it reinforced the mandarins' position and power. For instance, over the past 50 years, nearly 95 percent of the deputy ministers (DMs) have come up from the ranks of assistant or associate deputy ministers. And even though the authority to appoint DMs is widely regarded as one of the more potent aspects of prime ministerial power, DMs are rarely, in fact, recruited directly by the prime minister. Instead, most are recommended and approved on the advice of the secretary to the Cabinet (who, you will recall, is the senior-most civil servant). This has led two observers to conclude that "the senior public service in Canada, then, has developed a pattern of internal recruitment, professionalism and political neutrality, although some deputy ministers in later life have become Cabinet ministers or senators."[12] But in the past it also meant that the senior levels of the public service were remarkably homogeneous, a fact remarked upon in a groundbreaking study by sociologist John Porter. He noted in his 1965 book *The Vertical Mosaic* that the senior public servants were part of an interconnected political, economic, social, and intellectual elite that shared certain characteristics: they tended to be white, Anglo-Saxon, Christian males who were well educated, moved in the same social circles, and acted as "gatekeepers" to keep out others who were not like themselves.[13] But perhaps more to the point, this group of managers seemed to regard human resources management as almost incidental to their work. They were greatly concerned with the broad picture of policy making, and with macro-economic management of the country and related issues. But they paid little concrete attention to the day-to-day issues of employee satisfaction, morale, working conditions, or even the performance and competence of their underlings. Indeed, it is not an exaggeration to suggest that despite its huge significance, human resources management has been a central concern of government for only the past 30 years.

However, the rapid changes brought about by immigration, as well as the changing role of women in Canadian society, made anachronistic this "clubby" public service elite. Gradually, new attitudes crept into the thinking of public service managers, not the least of which was the notion that the entire public service, and most particularly its senior levels, should bear some resemblance to the society it serves. Hence, the more recent era of wholesale reform of human resource policies, such as affirmative action, employment equity, pay equity, and so on. Ironically, attention was finally paid to this area during an era of financial constraint—such that the much-needed reforms were severely impeded by fiscal realities.

By the 1950s and 1960s, the state was assuming an ever-larger role in the management of the economy and the day-to-day lives of Canadians. The earlier metaphors derived from Weber's and Taylor's views of a mechanistic, rule-bound hierarchical organization were reinforced by increasingly rigid structures and processes and, simultaneously, challenged by new thinking about the roles of public servants. Two post-war developments, in particular, changed the nature and role of the public service in profound ways. The first was a rudimentary affirmative action plan to provide employment for Canadian soldiers returning from the Second World War (a similar, more modest effort had been initiated after the First World War, as well). Over about 12 years from 1940, the public service tripled in size, absorbing surplus labour and helping to prevent a return to the conditions of the Great Depression of the 1930s. However, this development, while impressive quantitatively, had relatively little qualitative effect. As Nicole Morgan, an authority on public service management, put it,

[T]he first period of growth was unparalleled but had no effect on the traditional structure of the public service. In this instance, growth was carefully managed; it was concentrated in a few departments, distributed fairly evenly across the country, and made up of older men whose outlook had been shaped by the Hungry Thirties and the war. In a period of intensive growth, the civil service, as it was then called, was modeled on our military.[14]

The post-war years saw a massive expansion of government at all levels in response to the growth of society and technological change but a lag in renewing human resources policy. Departmental expansion meant that more employees were brought into the public service, but, more important, qualitative changes to human resources policy were needed. Moreover, a variety of new professional, technical, and managerial careers were needed in the public service. For example, the widespread introduction of computerized systems meant that positions for technically skilled computer technicians had to be created and categorized, and their pay levels and job descriptions had to be formalized. Given the rigid and bureaucratic nature of human resources management in this era, this was no easy task. It also had to be done for the countless other new positions created to keep pace with the broader changes in Canadian society. The depths of the difficulties in this era of rapid expansion were encapsulated in the Glassco Commission of 1961, and were expressed in the need to make the management of human resources (and indeed of government generally) more efficient, economical, and effective.[15]

Moreover, as the 1960s and 1970s unfolded, the issues of language training and bilingualism, unionization, affirmative action, and departmental reorganization converged. By this time, the literature of business management was replete with theories derived from the human relations school of organizational theory (see chapters 3 and 4). New management techniques were washing over the public service, and a new public service ethos was emerging that saw the public servant as an agent of change in the community, and not just a passive servant of the people, awaiting policy directives and instructions from Parliament. Participatory democracy became the watchword (although in practice it meant "you participate, we'll decide"), and the rapidly changing public sector scrambled to keep up.

Renewal of the public service became a pressing concern, and the strong expectation developed that new recruits to the upper levels would produce a more representative public service. Today, contemporary demographic patterns, and the reality that so many senior managers have left the public service in recent years (as noted following), means that recruitment from outside the ranks of the public service is now becoming more commonplace.[16] And since the broader society from which those recruits are coming has changed, it is axiomatic that the public service will continue to evolve into an institution far removed from the days of the old boys' network. Another striking development occurred when the first cohort of baby boomers began to graduate from the expanded university system in the 1960s and 1970s. From 1965 to 1975, the public service doubled in size. Many of these new, young employees began to see themselves not just as loyal servants but as agents of change. Morgan suggests that "although the second period of growth was less important in terms of numbers, it revolutionized both the structure and role of the public service."[17] These highly skilled and well-trained graduates, mainly from business schools, the social sciences, and economics, increasingly challenged civil servants' traditional views, pursuing organizational objectives and career goals that greatly transformed the public service. A new climate developed that encouraged policy experimentation and initiative. The technocratic expert who could provide sophisticated work based on the new sciences of cybernetics, computer modelling, systems theory, and other innovations came to be valued. The number of government departments, regulatory bodies, and Crown corporations mushroomed. New planning techniques were introduced, including financial management systems, such as Planning, Programming, Budgeting Systems (PPBS) (discussed in chapter 8) and its successors. But this explosion of new systems left a troubling legacy. As Dobuzinskis reports,

[T]raditional administrative tasks (e.g. personnel management) received relatively less attention; thus a gap was created between the macro-policy concerns of the upper echelons of the public service and the more strictly managerial concerns of middle-ranking officials. This gap was to become more and more pronounced, until it was finally acknowledged in the late 1980s. The same preoccupation with policy issues, as distinguished from the study of public administration, also gripped the academic community in the same period. (For instance, most graduate programs offering a Master's degree in public administration placed a greater emphasis on policy analysis than on organizational and managerial problems).[18]

Moreover, even the merit system began to reveal itself as a barrier to sound management practices. By the 1980s, it was apparent that the rules governing recruitment and promotion had set up systemic barriers to certain socio-economic groups and that, consequently, the public service was disproportionately staffed by white Anglophone males, especially at the upper levels. This failure of public service to be representative of society developed into a contentious issue.

Organizationally, the public service experienced growing pains in the post-war years, and a new legislative framework was put in place. For instance, the *Civil Service Act of 1961* was passed after it became apparent that the Civil Service Commission and the Treasury Board were stepping on each other's toes in terms of authority over government personnel. The Act gave the Treasury Board sole responsibility for determining pay levels and administrative organization. That was when the Public Service Employment Act (PSEA) established the Public Service Commission (PSC) and gave it responsibility for appointments to the public service, and oversight regarding the political activities of public servants. In addition, the Public Service Staff Relations Act (PSSRA) established the Public Service Staff Relations Board, which was given the responsibility to administer the Act and which confirmed the role of the Treasury Board (TB) as the "employer" in collective bargaining and negotiating with public service employees. In addition, the Financial Administration Act (FAA) also gave the Treasury Board certain human resources management authority for the public service. The independence of the Public Service Commission from interference by government was maintained by having it report to Parliament rather than to Cabinet, although the three commissioners who head the Public Service Commission are appointed by the Cabinet for a set term of 10 years. A number of other Acts also came into force and gave more definition to the overall human resources framework. These included the Official Languages Act, the Employment Equity Act, the Canadian Charter of Rights and Freedoms, the Canadian Human Rights Act, the Privacy Act, and Part II of the Canada Labour Code.

As well, a variety of societal changes affected the public service in the post-war years. First, this was, in part, a response to the necessity of keeping up with the rapid technological changes of the twentieth century.[19] Second, the public service had to respond to the rise of new social movements in areas such as women's rights and gender equality, environmentalism, gay and lesbian rights, animal rights, seniors' rights, and the rising militancy of youth, "engaged in the politics of identity and . . . interested in the democratization of both everyday life and governance."[20] Finally, a fiscal crisis gripped the state from the 1970s, reshaping thinking about what the public service should be doing and what it should look like. Public sector managers, as a result, were forced to shift their attention from designing grand systems for policy to the more prosaic details of managerial and administrative concerns. By the 1980s and 1990s, these factors seemed to overwhelm the public service, and a malaise settled over it. When this was coupled with the cutbacks and layoffs of the period, it became apparent that renewal of the public service was an emerging issue.

Yet another factor profoundly affecting the public service was ideological in nature. The rise of neoconservatism, first in Great Britain under Margaret Thatcher, then in the United States under Ronald Reagan, and finally in Canada under Brian Mulroney, Jean Chrétien, Paul Martin, and Stephen Harper, brought increased disparagement of the public service. A concerted attack was launched by those who believed the state had become too large, complex, and unwieldy and a primary instrument of obstruction to the free operation of markets. Globalization reinforced these perspectives by raising the idea that states (that is, the public sector) interfere with the flow of goods and services in the global marketplace. The growing chorus of demands to reduce the size of government and to put the art of governing on a more businesslike footing based on the theories of New Public Management (NPM) profoundly affected the public service's identity, role, composition, and morale.

Neoconservative arguments were challenged, however, by those who saw a legitimate role for government intervention in the economy. Jocelyne Bourgon, then clerk of the Privy Council and Secretary to the Cabinet (the top civil servant in the public service) reminded Canadians that those reinventing government, while perhaps doing the inevitable, must not make government more businesslike, since the public and private sectors are inherently different. She also argued that the challenges of reinventing government were tremendously more complex than in the private sector. "The management of change in the private sector may be a question of financial survival," she argued, "but for those of us in the public sector, it is about the future of the country, the national interest and the public good. We must guard against the simplistic notion that the public sector should be run like a private enterprise."[21] But these arguments largely succumbed to the powerful juggernaut of the professional economists, business lobbies, and think tanks propounding the neoconservative doctrine.

As a result of the spread of neoconservative and NPM, the public service has undergone a major self-examination over the past 25 years. In her *Report to the Prime Minister on the Public Service of Canada,* Jocelyne Bourgon described a "quiet crisis" in the Canadian public service. The years of downsizing and pay freezes, criticism, and insufficient recruitment efforts made it difficult to retain, motivate, and attract people to the public service. This is related to another factor affecting the public service: demographic changes. The departure of experienced public servants who took early retirement buyouts or simply left in frustration, coupled with insufficient hiring of new young blood, means that the public service is bulging with middle-aged managers and workers. The historical memory, institutional experience, and knowledge of the "old-timers" were drained away. As well, there was an absence of the invigorating new ideas and perspectives that new recruits would normally bring to an organization. It was as if someone had cut off the head and feet of the organization and left the bloated body (see Figure 9.1).

Thus, reform exercises such as PS2000, La Relève, and the Public Service Modernization Act were launched (discussed in greater detail following), resulting in some changes to the public service. For instance, in 1992, as a result of PS2000, the Public Service Reform Act was passed, which helped lessen the bureaucratic red tape around hiring and firing. Perhaps more significantly, it also mandated employment equity programs. These reforms did, however, lead to some contention over the extent to which the merit principle was compromised for the goal of increased efficiency.[22]

Moreover, a general rethinking of the place of the public service ensued. The key issues included merit, the ability to perform duties without political interference, **representativeness**, and access by all Canadians to employment opportunities within the public service.[23] Some important institutional changes were also

FIGURE 9.1   **Age Distribution of Public Service Management vs. Canadian Labour Force Senior Management (1996 Census)**

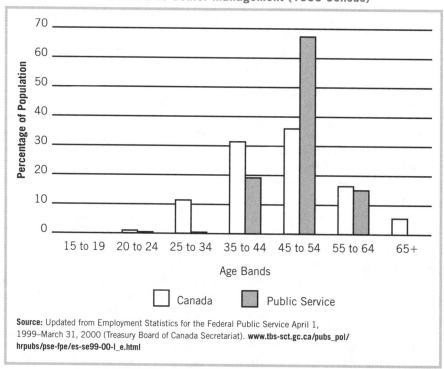

Source: Updated from Employment Statistics for the Federal Public Service April 1, 1999–March 31, 2000 (Treasury Board of Canada Secretariat). **www.tbs-sct.gc.ca/pubs_pol/ hrpubs/pse-fpe/es-se99-00-l_e.html**

made. For instance, in 1999–2000, two new federal agencies were created that significantly reduced the number of employees traditionally under the purview of the Treasury Board. First, Parks Canada was created in April 1999, resulting in the transfer of 3900 employees from the Ministry of Canadian Heritage. In November 1999, Revenue Canada became a separate agency known as the Canada Customs and Revenue Agency (now the Canada Revenue Agency), resulting in the transfer of about 40 000 employees. These innovations represented new ways to contain the growth of the public service and to reconfigure the universe of government human resources management since they fall outside the Public Service Staff Relations Act (the legislation that gives the Treasury Board the authority to act as the manager and employer of the federal public service).

Still, severe stresses and strains were produced by these various issues intersecting with one another. As a result, re-evaluation of human resources management has been a constant feature of the public service. Organizational confusion as to who should be doing what continuously challenges the regime of accountability. As well, in the 1990s, the PSEA and the PSSRA were reformed to better facilitate changing staffing and people management. Investment in leadership and management training was invigorated through the creation of an institution "to inculcate corporate values and prepare senior managers to work in rapidly changing internal and external environments. The idea of a 'university' for senior managers had been in circulation for over 20 years and, in 1988, the Canadian Centre for Management Development (CCMD) was established . . . its mandate included commissioning research from public servants and from academics on public management issues, and providing a forum for the exchange of ideas."[24] In 2003, its mandate was altered to provide training for public servants at all levels, and its name was changed to the Canada School of Public Service (CSPS). As well, as mentioned earlier, an initiative called "La Relève" (discussed in chapter 10) introduced new succession planning and corporate development programs.

Given the organization and structure of management where human resources is concerned, it is no wonder that specialized training, such as that being developed by the CSPS, is needed. Consider, for instance, the complexity of the organizational duties and roles of the main bodies responsible for human resources management. Figure 9.2 depicts the responsibilities of the four main actors in contemporary human resource management, and Box 9.1 provides a summary of some of the main reforms to human resource management of the past 50 years.

Clearly, many changes have occurred in the public service in Canada since 1867. Originally a relatively small, patronage-based haven for friends of the governing party, it has evolved into a huge, complex, merit-based professional institution composed of legions of highly skilled and technically gifted people. It has changed in other important ways, too. For instance, it has become more representative in nature. Once the preserve of white, Anglophone middle- and upper-class males, the public service has recently taken proactive and progressive steps to become a more inclusive equal opportunity employer. To ensure that the public service reflects the regional, multicultural, linguistic, and gender makeup

FIGURE 9.2   Responsibilities in Human Resources Management in the Federal Public Service

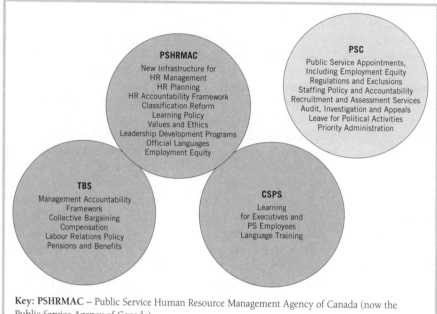

PSHRMAC
New Infrastructure for
HR Management
HR Planning
HR Accountability Framework
Classification Reform
Learning Policy
Values and Ethics
Leadership Development Programs
Official Languages
Employment Equity

PSC
Public Service Appointments,
Including Employment Equity
Regulations and Exclusions
Staffing Policy and Accountability
Recruitment and Assessment Services
Audit, Investigation and Appeals
Leave for Political Activities
Priority Administration

TBS
Management Accountability
Framework
Collective Bargaining
Compensation
Labour Relations Policy
Pensions and Benefits

CSPS
Learning
for Executives and
PS Employees
Language Training

Key: PSHRMAC – Public Service Human Resource Management Agency of Canada (now the Public Service Agency of Canada)

PSC – Public Service Commission

TBS – Treasury Board Secretariat

CSPS – Canada School of Public Service

Sources: Canada. Public Service Human Resources Management Agency of Canada. Roles and Responsibilities. www.psagency-agencefp.gc.ca/common/fs-fi/bubblediagram_e.asp Accessed June 10, 2007.

BOX 9.1 | Human Resources Reports and Studies

A large number of investigations into human resources management have taken place in the federal government over the years. Following is a brief synopsis of some of the most important.

Past Studies and Reports

- The Royal Commission on Government Organization ("*Glassco Report*"—1962) *proposed that "departments and agencies be given the necessary authority and be held responsible for the management of money and staff—with greater powers . . . especially to select, classify, train, promote and discipline their personnel." It also proposed that the Civil Service Commission (the PSC's predecessor) continue to carry out functions requiring independence from executive authority (such as certifying initial public service appointments, and acting as the final point of appeal for grievances).*

- The Royal Commission on Financial Management and Accountability ("*Lambert Report*"—1979) *recommended that the authority of the PSC over staffing be transferred to a Board of Management (the Treasury Board) with delegation to Deputy Heads. It was proposed that the PSC be reconstituted as a Parliamentary agency to ensure that appointments in the public service are made on the basis of merit.*

■ The report of the Special Committee on the Review of Personnel Management and the Merit Principle *("D'Avignon Report"—1979) proposed that human resources management be consolidated under the responsibility of a Management Board, including operational responsibilities under the PSEA. It recommended that the PSC continue to act on behalf of Parliament to uphold the merit principle, as well as audit departmental human resources management in a broad sense (including conducting investigations and staffing appeals, for example).*

■ In 1990, the Public Service 2000 *White Paper recommended that clearer accountability for HR management be given to Deputy Heads and managers, arguing that the current system " . . . favours the exercise of external control rather than the exercise of individual responsibility . . . favours error prevention rather than accountability, [and] . . . relies on rules rather than judgement." The report advocated holding public service managers and employees to account for their actions and for achieving results, rather than relying on onerous central control by prescribing detailed processes and procedures.*

Recent Studies and Reports

■ *The final report of the tripartite labour-management-academic Advisory Committee on Labour-Management Relations in the Federal Public Service ("Fryer Report"—June 2001) recommended major changes in the legislation governing labour-management relations. In particular, it underscored the need for a co-operative approach and partnership between employers and bargaining agents in addressing workplace issues. The Fryer Report also recommended an integrated approach to recourse that responds to the needs of both employees and managers, including the use of mediation and alternative forms of dispute resolution as appropriate. Most employees will continue to be represented by bargaining agents in collective bargaining (more than 85 percent of employees are now).*

■ The Report of the Auditor General (2000) *found ". . . a clear lack of co-ordination in dealing with the Government's recruitment priority partly because of unclear roles and responsibilities." In 2001, the Auditor General further recommended that both legislative and non-legislative changes be made to clarify the roles of the key players, improve HR planning, and provide for a more strategic approach to human resources management. That included a call for an overhaul of ". . . a complex rules-driven staffing system that has been an obstacle to recruiting qualified applicants in the public service for 40 years . . . to secure the long-term effectiveness of the public service."*

■ In December 2001, the House of Commons Standing Committee on Public Accounts, *reflecting on the reports of the Auditor General and other information provided to it, noted its "high level of concern" about how well the Government manages its human resources and concluded that the federal government's human resources needs must be better addressed.*

> ■ *The PSC, in its annual report to Parliament in October 2002, recognized the many challenges facing the public service in the areas of recruitment and staffing. It noted that the current system has continued to provide a competent, non-partisan work force serving Canadians. It has also noted the desirability of increased flexibility as part of the modernization of human resources management, with a simplified system and greater authority and accountability for managers, and with continuing independent oversight to ensure that recruitment into and promotion within the public service are based on merit.*
>
> **Source:** Canada. Treasury Board Secretariat. *Public Service Modernization Act: Backgrounder.* **www.tbs-sct.gc.ca/media/nr-cp/2003/0206_e.asp** Accessed December 18, 2006.

of Canada, procedures such as affirmative action, employment equity, and pay equity programs have been introduced to encourage and promote the employment of women, visible minorities, the disabled, and Aboriginals. Moreover, since the Second World War, the public sector has been the fastest-unionizing sector of the Canadian economy. This development—the culmination of a long struggle—has given workers in the public service collective agreements and expanded their political rights, which were once severely circumscribed.

Each of these developments has contributed significantly to Canadians' enjoying a very high standard of living in a country with a well-developed and sophisticated provision of public services. Indeed, Canada has always ranked extremely high in the United Nations Human Development Index, a scale devised to measure purchasing power, life expectancy, literacy, and educational attainment: from first (in 1996) to sixth (in 2006).[25] But at the same time, each of the developments cited above has also been marked by controversy, reflecting disputes over what the public service (that is, the state) should or should not do.

The Public Service Today: An Overview

Attitudes about the public service in Canada are currently changing. Recognizing some of the damage that has been done to a once-great institution, efforts are being made to restore a sense of pride and worth to a public service career. In his Annual Report to the Prime Minister, the clerk of the Privy Council, Kevin Lynch, said that "many would say that the Public Service seems to have been renewing itself for much of the past 20 years. Is this process never going to end? Why is it necessary to put people and institutions through still more change and, some would say, upheaval, when there are so many other things to be done by government in the service of Canadians?" In answering his own question, the clerk went on to suggest,

The answer, to put it simply, is: if the Public Service as a core national institution, does not renew itself for future as well as for current service to the government and people of Canada, it risks becoming less relevant, less useful and less respected as the years go by. If we do not

commit ourselves to a continuing process of renewal, the Public Service will not remain a creative national institution, central to the governance and development of our country.[26]

Even if you have never worked in the public sector, chances are that you know someone who has or does. Indeed, when you account for federal, provincial, and local governments, the public sector in Canada employs about one in four Canadians. By comparison, prior to Confederation, the public service employed about 2700 people, and by 1896 it had grown to about 10 000.[27] In 1993, 196 674 people were employed under the authority of the federal Public Service Commission alone. By 1999, however, this number had been reduced to 142 906.[28] But if the transitions involving Parks Canada and the Canada Customs and Revenue Agency are taken out of the equation, the public service actually began to grow again in 2000. The rest of the federal workforce is under the jurisdiction of the Armed Forces, RCMP, Crown corporations, agencies, and other bodies that together make up the broader public service. Indeed, when you take into consideration employment at the federal, provincial, territorial, and local government levels, the pattern is one of bottoming out in the late 1990s followed by considerable rebuilding (see Figure 9.3).

According to the 2006 Census, federal, provincial and territorial, and local governments as well as government business enterprise employment reached an annual average of 3.1 million employees, with about 2.9 million of these employees working in the federal, provincial and territorial, and local governments (see Table 9.2). This contrasts with the figure for 1999, when government employment hit a low of just over 2.5 million. The breakdown of employment by level of government shows that in 2006, the provinces and territories accounted for 51.0 percent of total government employment, or nearly 1.5 million. The federal government accounted for 13.6 percent, or 393 000 employees, and local governments accounted for 35.4 percent, or slightly over 1 million employees. The

FIGURE 9.3 **Number of Employees, Government Sector, Canada 1991–2005**

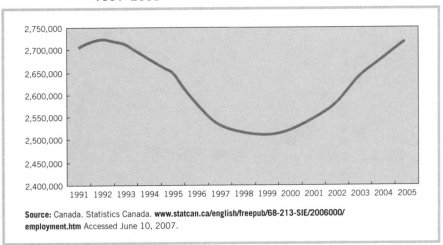

Source: Canada. Statistics Canada. **www.statcan.ca/english/freepub/68-213-SIE/2006000/ employment.htm** Accessed June 10, 2007.

TABLE 9.2   Public Sector Employment in Canada

Year	Federal Government	Provincial and Territorial Government	Local Government	Total Government	Government Business Enterprises	Total Public Sector
			Thousands			
1991	415	1,402	889	2,706	351	3,057
1992	411	1,409	904	2,725	338	3,063
1993	405	1,397	910	2,712	326	3,037
1994	394	1,376	909	2,679	324	3,003
1995	371	1,370	907	2,649	309	2,958
1996	356	1,315	907	2,579	273	2,851
1997	338	1,302	891	2,531	258	2,789
1998	331	1,300	888	2,518	261	2,779
1999	328	1,295	885	2,508	262	2,770
2000	335	1,304	882	2,521	266	2,787
2001	351	1,336	943	2,630	266	2,897
2002	359	1,367	963	2,689	264	2,953
2003	366	1,419	972	2,757	267	3,024
2004	367	1,427	980	2,774	265	3,039
2005	376	1,449	999	2,825	263	3,088
2006	393	1,471	1,021	2,886	263	3,149

Note: Numbers may not add up due to rounding.

Source: Canada. Statistics Canada. "Public Sector Employment," *The Daily Mirror.* May 30, 2007. **www.statcan.ca/Daily/English/070530/d070530c.htm** Accessed June 12, 2007.

relative sizes of the three levels of government in terms of numbers of employees have remained relatively stable over the years. But, overall, government employment has risen moderately. For instance, between 2003 and 2006, federal government employment rose 7.4 percent (just under 2.5 percent per year), or 27 000. Provincial and territorial government employment advanced 3.7 percent (just over 1.2 percent per year), or 52 000. Local governments saw an increase of 5.0 percent (nearly 1.7 percent per year), or 49 000. About half of employees at the provincial and territorial level of government worked in the health and social service sector; about one-quarter worked in ministries, departments, agencies, and similar institutions; and the rest worked in colleges and universities.[29]

The question of how to organize all those people is vital to the smooth functioning of government. Until recently, the federal public service was divided into six occupational categories: executive group, consisting of about 4322 employees; scientific and professional, with 23 920 employees; administrative and foreign service, with 69 868 employees; technical, with 17 567 employees; administrative support, with 31 736 employees; and operational, with 18 563 employees.[30] In 2005, a new classification standard was applied to the Foreign Service group, and a new Border Services classification group was created. These categories are used to help determine pay levels and occupations. According to the Treasury Board's guidelines, the policy objective of the classification system is "to ensure that the relative value of all jobs in the Public Service is established in an equitable, consistent and effective manner and provides a basis for the compensation of public servants."[31] Within these six categories, virtually every profession and trade known to modern society is found, organized in a uniform manner that permits rational staffing and appointments consistent with the merit principle. No matter which department an employee works in, he receives the same remuneration as any other employee in that level and category. The categorization of jobs in this manner reflects a clear chain of command and responsibility, and within each department a descending order of command is organized, such that each employee is responsible to a superior.

Currently, job categorization is undergoing major reform. The Classification Modernization Program was launched in 2003 in concert with key management modernization priorities of the federal government, including the Public Service Modernization Act (PSMA). It was also aligned with the 2006 Federal Accountability Act and the clerk of the Privy Council's public service renewal initiatives, relating to recruitment, knowledge transfer, succession planning, learning and training, talent management, and retention.[32]

Even earlier, in 2001, the government initiated a new approach to modernizing human resources management. The prime minister announced the formation of the Task Force on Modernizing Human Resources Management in the Public Service to recommend a modern institutional framework for managing human resources. The Task Force was guided by three principles: protecting the merit principle, delegating human resource management matters to the lowest possible managerial level, and ensuring that managers were accountable for results. The work of the Task Force resulted in the 2003 Public Service Modernization Act.[33]

The purposes of the Act included the following:

- *increased flexibility in staffing and managing people with reinforced safeguards to sustain a merit-based, non-partisan public service;*

- *more constructive, co-operative labour-management relations to support a healthy, productive workplace;*

- *more coherent training and learning to help employees pursue professional development and meet the corporate needs of the public service;*

- *and clarified roles and strengthened accountability for the institutions and individuals responsible for managing the public service.[34]*

Following this, also in 2003, the government created the Public Service Human Resources Management Agency of Canada, reporting to the president of the Treasury Board. This Agency changed its name to the more succinct Canada Public Service Agency in 2007. There are now four agencies with some responsibility for human resources management in the federal government: the Treasury Board Secretariat, the Public Service Commission, the Canada Public Service Agency, and the Canada School of Public Service.[35]

Also in 2003, the Treasury Board introduced the Management Accountability Framework (MAF), partly in response to the various accountability scandals that were rocking government at the time. The MAF set out the Treasury Board's expectations of senior public service managers for good management. Consisting of 10 key elements, the MAF is depicted and explained in Figure 9.4.

Currently, the major issues confronting human resource managers in the public service are focused on the ongoing implementation of the Public Service Modernization Act, a major aspect of which is to shift "responsibility for HR management away from central agencies into the hands of deputy heads and from HR professionals to line managers, thereby giving managers more authority and flexibility—but also more responsibility and accountability—to manage their people."[36] Other issues include capacity building in human resources planning and accountability; embedding public service values and ethics at all levels of the public service, including the implementation of legislation regarding the disclosure of wrongdoing; the modernization of the classification system; the re-engineering of corporate human resources processes and information systems; achieving targets and required cultural changes in the areas of official languages and employment equity; creating a more inclusive, representative, and accessible public service; the management and development of leadership; and implementing a new learning policy for employees.[37]

In 2006, the prime minister created yet another task force to investigate the state of human resources management. The Prime Minister's Advisory Committee on the Public Service issued its first report on March 30, 2007. In it, the Task Force articulated concerns about recruitment and retention; policy and legislative barriers; development programs; human resources management policies and practices; and branding the public service.[38]

As you can see, the agenda of major issues confronting human resource managers in the public service is large and daunting. Consider demographic trends, for example. One of the most significant factors is a growing concentration of the 45–54 age group, which now constitutes over 50 percent of all federal employees.

FIGURE 9.4　　The Management Accountability Framework

Public Service Values
Through their actions, departmental leaders continually reinforce the importance of all public service values and ethics in the delivery of results to Canadians (e.g., democratic, professional, ethical and people values)

Governance and Strategic Directions
The essential conditions—internal conference, corporate discipline and alignment to customers—are in place for providing effective strategic directions, support to the minister and parliament and the delivery of results.

Policy and Programs
Departmental research and analytic capacity is developed and sustained to assume high quality policy options, program design and advice to ministers

People
The department has the peoples work environment and focus on building capacity and leadership to assume its success and a confident future for the Public Service of Canada

Citizen-focussed Service
Services are citizen-centred, polices and programs are developed from the "outside in" and partnerships are encouraged and effectively managed.

Risk Management
The executive team clearly defines the corporate context and practice for managing risk proactively

Stewardship
The departmental control regime (assets, money, people, service, etc) is integrated and effective, and its underlying principles are clear to all staff.

Accountability
Accountabilities for results are clearly assigned and consistent with resources, and delegations are appropriate to capabilities.

Results and Performance
Relevent information on results internal, service and program is gathered and used to make departmental decisions, and public reporting is balanced transparent, and easy to understand.

Learning, Innovation and Change Management
The departmental manager through continuous innovation and transformation promotes organizational learning, values corporate knowledge, and learns from its performance

The Management Accountability Framework (MAF) is:

- **A vision for good management**
  - It defines the conditions that need to be in place to ensure government is well-managed and to promote management excellence.
- **A process**
  - This process includes annual MAF assessments of most departments and agencies, engagement between deputy heads and TBS/PSHRMAC where warranted, joint agreement on specific management improvement action plans and ultimately public reporting on the state of management.
- **An analytical tool**
  - The government uses MAF assessment to identify management strengths and weaknesses in individual departments and agencies and ultimately on a government wide basis.

Note: TBS—Treasury Board Secretariat; PSHRMAC—Public Service Human Resources Agency of Canada

Source: Canada. Treasury Board Secretariat. **www.tbs-sct.gc.ca/maf-crg/index_e.asp** Accessed June 10, 2007.

Furthermore, the number of employees aged 55 or over is expected to almost double over the next 10 years, imposing a greater strain on the public service in terms of sick leave and higher health-care costs. The rate at which employees leave the public service is also expected to dramatically increase, especially at the senior levels of the public service. In fact, the age profile of the federal public service is reversed from that of 15 years ago, when employees aged 24–44 comprised 60 percent of the workforce, and fewer than 30 percent were over 45. Today more than 50 percent of all public servants are over 45. Currently, about 10 percent of public servants have 30-plus years of pensionable service, and about 8 percent are eligible to retire. One in five employees is forecast to leave by 2009–2010.

The numbers are particularly acute in the executive category of the federal public service. For example, of the 4639 executives (March 1, 2006), 75 percent are between the ages of 45 and 59, with an average age over 50, and about 18 percent of those 4639 are currently eligible to retire. Since 2000, the number of executives under the age of 45 has increased about 48 percent, from 618 to 917. Clearly, demographic trends pose a serious challenge here.

The good news is that governments at all levels are thinking seriously about recruitment. So, suppose you decide on a career in the federal public service—how do you get in? First, the Public Service Commission sponsors various recruitment programs for students and others. The Post-Secondary Recruitment Program (PSR) seeks post-secondary graduates who have the qualifications needed to fill entry-level positions. Jobs are advertised by means of recruitment campaigns, which generally begin in the fall and winter. In addition, there is a general inventory open year-round to university students of all fields of study. There are also targeted recruitment campaigns aimed at attracting the "best and the brightest" among university graduates to the public service. Typically, you will have to write an entrance exam to determine whether you are a qualified candidate. Once you secure a position, there are competitions for promotions, as well as an appeal process to ensure that every employee has a fair chance to advance. In some cases, new job openings will be deemed "open," meaning that individuals from outside the public service can apply. In other circumstances, the candidate search will be "closed," meaning that it is limited to those who already work within the public service.[39]

The merit of your application to the public service is a key factor in whether you are hired, of course. But the government is also committed to employment equity (discussed following). As a result,

The Government of Canada is committed to a public service that reflects the rich diversity of the Canadian society it serves. Canada is becoming more diverse and the fabric of Canadian society is changing. This is creating a need for policies, programs, and services that address these changes. As our labour market evolves, the talents required for a dynamic and innovative public service will be increasingly found by attracting the best talent from employment equity groups.[40]

Therefore, analyzing employment in the public service is not simply a matter of "How many?" Looking at a variety of factors will give us a more nuanced picture. We will consider the following issues: region, language, equity, and unionization. But first we will consider the extent to which the public service is, or ought to be, representative of the society it serves.

The Theory of Representativeness

The Public Service Employment Act, as amended in 1992, forbids discrimination in hiring or promotion on the basis of race, national or ethnic origin, colour, religion, age, sex, marital status, disability, or conviction for an offence for which a pardon has been granted. Since the 1992 reforms, the Public Service Commission's staffing decisions are still guided by the merit principle, but it has also initiated employment equity plans for historically under-represented groups: women, Aboriginal peoples, persons with disabilities, and visible minorities. The broad goal has been to make the public service more representative of the society it serves. Social changes have seen more women enter the paid workforce, and immigration has brought about demographic change. The difficult question is how to adapt the public service to these changes so that it reflects the broader Canadian society.[41]

Essentially, the theory behind representativeness is that if the public service reflects the population, it will make decisions in the best interests of those it serves and ensure that the values of both are commensurate. Of course, there is no guarantee that the values of an individual public servant will be the same as those of the group she comes from, since socialization is a complex thing. Thus, critics of the theory of representativeness suggest that you cannot guarantee a responsive public service simply by creating one composed of individuals whose numbers are in proportion to the size of their group in society. In any event, the public service has its own institutional values and interests that often supersede those of individuals, no matter how those individuals were previously socialized. The other side of this coin, though, is that there is no guarantee that a responsive public service need be representative. There are countless examples in Canadian history of the elite, exclusive upper echelons of the public service enacting policy that benefits groups different from those who hold offices of power.

In any event, the theoretical arguments about representativeness seem moot in light of real-life experience. A regime of representativeness is under construction in Canada, and has been for more than 40 years. Proactive steps have been taken in a number of areas to promote regional and linguistic representativeness. Moreover, various equity initiatives concerning women, visible minorities, Aboriginals, and the disabled have been enacted (see Table 9.3). We will now consider each in turn, bearing in mind that despite these recent efforts, the Canadian public service is still not a "microcosm" of the society it serves, and that the further up the hierarchy you go, the truer this is.

Region

It may not seem obvious at first, but where public servants work is an important consideration. The assumption that the "government" is in Ottawa is a mistaken one. Consider the following:

- *In 2006, 42 percent of federal public servants worked in the National Capital Region (Ottawa-Gatineau).*

- *About 13 percent work in Ontario; 12 percent in Quebec outside the National Capital Region (roughly equal to their proportion of the overall population when you factor in employees in the National Capital Region).*

- *About 11 percent work in the Atlantic provinces (slightly more than their proportion of the overall population).*

- *About 12 percent work in the prairies; 10 percent in British Columbia or the Territories (slightly less than their proportion of the overall population).*

- *About 1 percent work outside Canada in our embassies and trade missions.[42]*

The proportion of public servants found in each region of the country has both symbolic and pragmatic importance. First, there has been a deliberate effort to decentralize the functions of government away from Ottawa to help combat

TABLE 9.3 **Representation of Federal Public Service Employees by Designated Group and Occupational Category as of March 31, 2004**

Occupation Category	All Employees		Women		Aboriginal Peoples		Persons with Disabilities		Members of Visible Minorities	
	#	%	#	%	#	%	#	%	#	%
Executive	4,322	100.0	1,510	34.9	124	2.9	213	4.9	208	4.8
Scientific & Professional	23,920	100.0	9,912	41.4	585	2.4	894	3.7	2,846	11.9
Administration & Foreign Service	69,868	100.0	41,697	59.7	2,857	4.1	4,171	6.0	5,386	7.7
Technical	17,567	100.0	5,521	31.4	521	3.0	780	4.4	915	5.2
Administrative Support	31,736	100.0	26,260	82.7	1,654	5.2	2,525	8.0	2,942	9.3
Operational	18,563	100.0	3,275	17.6	982	5.3	869	4.7	704	3.8
Total	**165,976**	**100.0**	**88,175**	**53.1**	**6,723**	**4.1**	**9,452**	**5.7**	**13,001**	**7.8**

Source: Canada. Human Resources and Development Canada. *Public Service Employment Equity Annual Report 2005–2006*. www.hrsdc.gc.ca/cgi-bin/hrsdc-rhdsc/print/print.asp?Page_Url=/en/lp/lo/lswe/we/ee_tools/reports/annual/2005/appendix-c-table4.shtml alienation from the nation's capital, by putting the face of the government in the very communities that it affects. In other words, establishing field offices across the country lets Canadians see their tax dollars at work, and in a sense personalizes the distant and aloof structures of power found in Ottawa. Second, and more pragmatically, locating government offices outside Ottawa creates jobs in regions that might lack other employment opportunities. Nothing puts a smile on the face of a Cabinet minister like the prospect of opening a federal facility in his or her riding!

Language

Linguistic considerations have always played a prominent role in the development of the public service. In the era of patronage, French Canadians could always count on receiving appointments from the handful of French-Canadian Cabinet ministers. But when patronage was eliminated as the basis of hiring, there was no mechanism put in place to ensure that the proportion of French-speaking civil servants matched the proportion of the French-speaking population in Canada. As a result, the use and importance of French within the halls of power diminished over time. Political scientist J.E. Hodgetts reported that between 1918 and 1945, for instance, the number of French-speaking civil servants dropped by more than 10 percent.[43] At the senior levels of the public service, the numbers were particularly dismal. Former prime minister Pierre Trudeau recalled arriving in Ottawa in the late 1950s to work as a public servant in the Privy Council Office, and being astonished to discover that if he wanted to write a memo to another French-Canadian civil servant, he had to do so in English!

Political scientists Robert and Doreen Jackson explain the under-representation of French-Canadians in the civil service this way:

Many factors combined during these years to reduce levels of francophone recruitment in the federal bureaucracy. The public service became less attractive for French-Canadians because no provisions were made to ensure service to French-Canadians. Nor were francophones' bilingual skills included in an assessment of their qualifications. Francophones were also hindered by the merit system's examinations and interviews, which reflected the patterns of thought and cultural styles of English-speaking Canada. The competitions also emphasized the technical and commercial skills taught in the English educational system, placing French-Canadians, with their classical education, at a disadvantage.[44]

Incidents like the one experienced by Trudeau in an ostensibly bilingual country and federal public service prompted him to pass the Official Languages Act in 1969 to rectify this type of discrimination. Trudeau embarked upon an ambitious exercise to make "French power" a reality in Ottawa, and to make the federal government truly bilingual.

Much of the groundwork for this process was laid by the Royal Commission on Bilingualism and Biculturalism, which reported between 1967 and 1970.[45] The Royal Commission handed the Public Service Commission the responsibility for language training, instructing it to walk a tightrope between, on the one hand, promoting the use of French in the federal public service and recruiting more bilingual workers, and, on the other hand, ensuring that the merit principle was respected. Progress has been slow, especially at the upper reaches, but today the numbers of French Canadians in each of the occupational categories of the public service match or exceed the percentage of French Canadians overall (which is about 24 percent). The Office of the Commissioner of Official Languages is the body responsible for monitoring and reporting on the implementation of the Official Languages Act, and does so annually with its Report to Parliament.[46]

Equity

Employment equity—a term coined by Judge Rosalie Abella in her groundbreaking Royal Commission Report on Equality in Employment—came into widespread use in the 1980s and is similar in meaning to **affirmative action**.[47] The Public Service Commission defines *employment equity* as "employment practices designed to ensure that the regular staffing process is free of attitudinal and systemic barriers in order that the Public Service reflects all groups present in the Canadian labour force, and designed to ensure that corrective measures are applied to erase any historical disadvantage experienced by certain designated groups."[48] Judge Abella intended it to help eliminate discrimination in the workplace, which, she noted, had affected various groups in Canadian society. "One hundred years ago, the role for women was almost exclusively domestic," she wrote. "Fifty years ago some visible minorities were disenfranchised; 25 years ago, native people lacked a policy voice; and 10 years ago, disabled persons were routinely kept dependent. Today, none of these exclusionary assumptions is acceptable."[49]

Let's consider the position of women first. In 1967, women made up only 27 percent of the employees in the public service, compared to 53 percent today. However, women have historically been heavily "ghettoized" in "pink-collar" occupations. For instance, 83 percent worked in "office and administrative support" positions in 1967, compared to about 30 percent today. Whereas only 12 percent of those working in program administration 30 years ago were women, today 47 percent are women. Figure 9.5 shows the upward trend in women's participation in the federal public service between 1988 and 2005. These gains are impressive, but there are several occupational groups where women have made virtually no progress. Consider, for instance, that women constitute only about 9 percent of engineers and land surveyors, 3 percent of electronics experts, 2 percent of firefighters, and 3 percent of general labour and trades, and it is evident that progress is uneven across the public service.

At the executive level of the public service, for example, fewer than 1 percent of senior officers were women in 1967, whereas today 37 percent are women, revealing progress but continued under-representation overall. The first woman to be appointed to the position of the top public servant—the clerk of the Privy Council—was Jocelyne Bourgon, who served in that role from 1994 to 1999, and in 2007, eight of 25 Deputy Ministers were women. Overall, the percentage of female public servants who work in the executive, scientific and professional, or administrative and foreign service categories has been rising since the 1980s, while women hold a proportionately smaller number of administrative support

FIGURE 9.5   Representation of Women in the Federal Public Service 1988–2005

Representation of women, 1988 to 2005 (%)

Workforce Availablity: 52.2

53.5

Source: Canada. Treasury Board Secretariat of Canada. Employment Equity in the Public Service 2004–05 Annual Report to Parliament. **www.psagency-agencefp.gc.ca/reports-rapports/ee-0501_e.asp#_Toc143307355** Accessed June 20, 2007.

jobs than in the past. Moreover, women constitute the greatest numbers of all persons hired into the scientific and professional category (54.8 percent). And women are being promoted at a greater rate than men, with women receiving approximately 6 out of 10 promotions. Interestingly, though, 4 in 10 women continue to enter the public service through the administrative support category (see Figures 9.5 and 9.6).

However, a more focused assessment reveals some lingering problems.[50] For instance, there is a significant difference between the genders in the percentages of employees in term and casual positions, with female employees constituting 60 percent of hiring in this category. While the overall number of women in the

FIGURE 9.6   Distribution of Women by Occupational Category

3.345 — 1.601
10.313
25.327
42.511
5.605

☐ Executive (1.8%)

☐ Scientific and professional (11.5%)

☐ Administrative and foreign service (47.9%)

☐ Technical (6.3%)

☐ Administrative support (28.6%)

☐ Operational (3.2%)

Source: Canada. Treasury Board Secretariat of Canada. Employment Equity in the Public Service 2004–05 Annual Report to Parliament. **www.psagency-agencefp.gc.ca/reports-rapports/ee-0501_e.asp#_Toc143307355** Accessed June 20, 2007.

executive category has increased, most are concentrated in the lower reaches of that group. However, a spate of retirements means that up to 70 percent of the executive category could leave in the next few years, although political scientist Jonathan Malloy argues that we are witnessing "evolutionary" rather than "revolutionary" demographic shifts in the public service—that is, the spate of sudden retirements is not happening all at once.[51] But since most potential retirees are men, and more men than women overall are leaving the public service, this could open the doors for women in senior management positions. However, under conditions of downsizing and budget cutbacks, most federal departments reduced external recruitment and demand for management trainees. Moreover, downsizing means more work for fewer people. Since women are disproportionately responsible for "home work" and child rearing, they are at a distinct disadvantage in a work climate where expectations are that ever more time will be spent at the office.

In any event, attitudes toward women working in the public service have been slow to change. Hiring, promotion, sick leave, and handling of absenteeism have all been implemented differently for women than for men. Consider that until 1955, there was a prohibition against married women even being employed in the public service! This reflected the view that men were the natural breadwinners and that women belonged in the home. Prior to 1969, it was permissible for hiring requests going to the Public Service Commission to specify either male or female, and, even more recently, it was considered normal to ask female employees about their plans to marry and have children, as part of any assessment of their qualifications! Camilla Stivers, a professor of public administration, argues that both the study and the practice of public administration are structurally male. She claims that the "images of expertise, leadership, and virtue that mark defences of administrative power contain dilemmas of gender. They not only have masculine features, but help to keep in place or bestow political and economic privilege on the bearers of culturally masculine qualities at the expense of those who display culturally feminine ones."[52]

But it is further argued that differences between the way men and women relate to their work environment mean that traditional "male" approaches are still overused in the public service. In particular, fostering a "competitive" management style reflects a male way of thinking. As Martha Hynna, a management consultant and former senior public service mandarin, explains, "[T]he contrasting 'integrative' style of management, which values team-building, participation, responsiveness, and the ability to integrate various points of view, more closely reflects the way in which many women have been socialized and behave in a work environment . . . ." She further suggests that "there are important differences in the way men and women communicate. These differences can lead to misinterpretation and misunderstanding, and, in a culture where 'toughness' is valued, this can sometimes result in men underestimating the competence and effectiveness of women."[53] But while the Public Service Commission lauds the goal of developing a truly representative workforce, it admits the results are mixed in relation not only to women but also to Aboriginals, persons with disabilities, and members of visible

FIGURE 9.7 **Representation of Aboriginal Peoples 1988 to 2005 (%)**

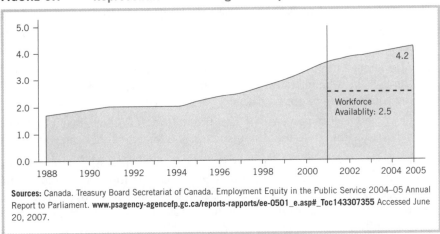

Sources: Canada. Treasury Board Secretariat of Canada. Employment Equity in the Public Service 2004–05 Annual Report to Parliament. **www.psagency-agencefp.gc.ca/reports-rapports/ee-0501_e.asp#_Toc143307355** Accessed June 20, 2007.

minorities. According to the Treasury Board, more than 4 percent of public service employees are Aboriginal, higher than their workforce availability of 2.5 percent. Aboriginal peoples make up 3 percent of all public service executives—double the proportion of five years ago[54] (see Figures 9.7 and 9.8). Other important facts include the following:

■ Just under 2 percent of Aboriginal employees are in the executive category, compared to 2.5 percent of all employees. Aboriginal employees make up 3.0 percent of the executive category.

■ The highest proportions of Aboriginal employees are in the administrative and foreign service category (43.4 percent) and administrative support (23.4 percent).

FIGURE 9.8 **Distribution of Aboriginal Peoples by Occupational Categories**

Source: Canada. Treasury Board Secretariat of Canada. Employment Equity in the Public Service 2004–05 Annual Report to Parliament. **www.psagency-agencefp.gc.ca/reports-rapports/ee-0501_e.asp#_Toc143307355** Accessed June 20, 2007.

■ Over 40 percent of Aboriginal employees work west of Ontario, while 42 percent of all employees work in the National Capital Region (NCR).

■ Aboriginal peoples represented 4.3 percent of all new hires into the public service, with almost one quarter being hired in the NCR.

■ Aboriginal employees continued to enter the public service primarily through the administrative and foreign service category (33.7 percent) and the administrative support category (27.6 percent).

■ Over half (54.6 percent) of the promotions of Aboriginal employees occurred within or to the administration and foreign service category.

In general, however, Aboriginals (including status and non-status Indians, Metis, and Inuit) face an appalling number of barriers to representation in the public service. Isolated culturally, they lack role models in the upper reaches of the public service. As well, poor educational opportunities make entry to and advancement in the public service prohibitively difficult. Moreover, the traditional emphasis in the public service on formal educational qualifications over life experience has discriminated against Aboriginals. Some Aboriginals do not recognize Ottawa as their legitimate government, which dissuades them from entering the federal public service. To overcome these barriers, the federal government has instituted programs and strategies (used earlier in its history to promote French Canadians and women), including aggressive recruitment campaigns and training assistance.

Some progress has been made in the area of persons with disabilities (see Figures 9.9 and 9.10). Nearly 6 percent of federal public service employees are persons with disabilities, which is still below their level of availability in the

FIGURE 9.9   Representation of Persons with Disabilities 1988 to 2005 (%)

Source: Canada. Treasury Board Secretariat of Canada. Employment Equity in the Public Service 2004–05 Annual Report to Parliament. **www.psagency-agencefp.gc.ca/reports-rapports/ee-0501_e.asp#_Toc143307355** Accessed June 20, 2007.

FIGURE 9.10   **Distribution of Persons with Disabilities by Occupational Category**

Executive (2.5%)

Scientific and professional (9.8%)

Administrative and foreign service (44.7%)

Technical (8.2%)

Administrative support (25.8%)

Operational (9.0%)

Source: Canada. Treasury Board Secretariat of Canada. Employment Equity in the Public Service 2004–05 Annual Report to Parliament. **www.psagency-agencefp.gc.ca/reports-rapports/ee-0501_e.asp#_Toc143307355** Accessed June 20, 2007.

Canadian workforce (about 10 percent). About 5.5 percent of executives in the public service are persons with disabilities. The administrative and foreign service category (44.7 percent) and the administrative support category (25.8 percent) continue to be the main points of entry for persons with disabilities. The demographic profile of persons with disabilities shows that just over two-thirds (68.0 percent) are 45 years of age or older, and persons with disabilities comprise 3.1 percent of all new hires. Of the large departments, Human Resources and Skills Development Canada (8.8 percent), Social Development Canada (7.8 percent), and Veterans Affairs Canada (7.5 percent) continue to employ the highest proportions of individuals with disabilities. Among small and mid-sized departments and agencies, with 100 employees or more, the Canadian Human Rights Commission continues to have the highest proportion of employees with disabilities, at 11.9 percent, followed by the Office of the Chief Electoral Officer, at 10.0 percent.

According to the Treasury Board, 8 percent of public service employees are members of a visible minority, more than 2 percentage points below their workforce availability of 10.4 percent (see Figures 9.11 and 9.12). Just over 5 percent of all executives, moreover, are members of visible minority groups, more than twice the proportion in 2000. Following are some additional numbers:

■ For the past few years, the highest proportion of persons in a visible minority group has been in the administrative and foreign service category (41.7 percent).

■ Of all new hires, 9.5 percent were members of visible minorities.

■ Visible minority employees entered the public service primarily through the administrative support (32.7 percent), and administrative and foreign service categories (27.8 percent). Over 20 percent entered via the scientific and professional category, higher than for any other designated group.

FIGURE 9.11 Representation of Persons in a Visible Minority Group 1988 to 2005 (%)

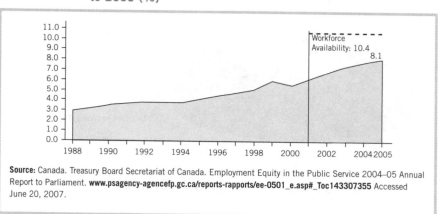

Source: Canada. Treasury Board Secretariat of Canada. Employment Equity in the Public Service 2004–05 Annual Report to Parliament. **www.psagency-agencefp.gc.ca/reports-rapports/ee-0501_e.asp#_Toc143307355** Accessed June 20, 2007.

- Among large departments and agencies, Citizenship and Immigration Canada (14.8 percent) and Health Canada (13.3 percent) continue to employ the highest proportions of persons in a visible minority group.

- The Immigration and Refugee Board had the highest percentage, 21.8 percent, among small departments (those with 100 employees or more).

The initiation of the 1995 Employment Equity Act and other progressive changes to the public service have brought a variety of challenges, including that of "managing diversity."[55] For example, there is the difficulty of promoting changes in organizational values and ensuring that managers are sensitive to cultural and other differences. In addition, there is the view that many equity

FIGURE 9.12 Distribution of Persons in a Visible Minority Group by Occupational Category

Source: Canada. Treasury Board Secretariat of Canada. Employment Equity in the Public Service 2004–05 Annual Report to Parliament. **www.psagency-agencefp.gc.ca/reports-rapports/ee-0501_e.asp#_Toc143307355** Accessed June 20, 2007.

initiatives constitute reverse discrimination. Moreover, in times of fiscal conservatism, the view is put forward that equity is not "affordable," as the opponents of **pay equity** argued, which involves determining equal pay for work of equal value.

Constitutional and administrative law heavily influence the equity regime in Canada. For instance, the provinces and federal government have enacted human rights codes, the first of which was created by the CCF government of Saskatchewan more than 40 years ago. These codes generally prohibit discrimination in employment against women, visible minorities, and other designated groups. Moreover, section 15 of the 1982 Charter of Rights and Freedoms guarantees "equal protection and equal benefit of the law without discrimination," but importantly, it goes on to suggest that this guarantee "does not preclude any law, program or activity that has as its object the amelioration of conditions of disadvantaged individuals or groups, including those that are disadvantaged because of race, national or ethnic origin, colour, religion, sex, age or mental or physical disability." In addition, the Canadian Human Rights Act, passed in 1977, established the Canadian Human Rights Commission to investigate complaints about discrimination by federal departments, Crown corporations, and business under federal jurisdiction. A variety of other federal and provincial legislation reinforces the equity regime.

Women, Aboriginals, visible minorities, and persons with disabilities all face a variety of barriers, both inside the public service and in the broader society, which make the achievement of representativeness an ongoing challenge. Overall, despite some progress in this area, as the title of a recent report by the Standing Senate Committee on Human Rights suggested, the federal public service is "not there yet" where employment equity is concerned.[56]

Unionization of the Public Service

The struggle by Canadian public servants to unionize was a long and arduous one. Prior to 1872, trade unions were illegal in Canada. After that, public service unionization was put off by the convenient fiction that the rights of government workers could be restricted because of the principle of the supremacy of Parliament. Even when federal civil servants finally won the right to **collective bargaining** in 1967, the government imposed restrictions on their rights well beyond those imposed on private sector workers. "Vital issues, including pensions, job classifications, technological change, staffing, and use of part-time or casual labour, were wholly or partly excluded from the scope of bargaining," according to political economists Leo Panitch and Donald Swartz. "Serious consideration was given to denying federal workers the right to strike as well, but in the end, the right to strike was granted, largely because the postal employees, particularly in British Columbia and Quebec, waged a number of what, in effect, were recognition strikes in the mid-1960s."[57] Public sector employees make up slightly more than half of all union members; in fact, the three largest unions in Canada are public sector unions. The unique nature of public sector bargaining gives rise to a number of issues absent in the private sector. As one observer states, in the public service, *collective bargaining, which is generally an exercise in economic power, becomes an exercise in political power. Public opinion and the prospects of re-election substitute for profit maximization in the employer's calculus. A related issue is whether government policy should be decided at the bargaining table, instead of the appropriate legislature.*[58]

Prior to the era of collective bargaining, the federal government established a National Joint Council of the Public Service, made up of representatives of staff associations and managers representing the government.[59] This was intended as a mechanism through which employees could be consulted regarding matters such as conditions of employment. It proved unsatisfactory, however, and by the late 1950s and 1960s, public servants were increasingly agitating for full unionization. In 1961, a new Civil Service Act gave employees the right to be consulted on pay determination, a major point of contention that was not covered under the National Joint Council. But even this advance proved difficult to realize, due to the complex way in which consultations were structured. Still, the 1961 reforms meant that, henceforth, public servants would be paid as a matter of right rather than as a matter of privilege of the Crown, as was previously the case.

The three main political parties campaigned in the 1963 election with a promise, if elected, to introduce collective bargaining in the public service. Legislation followed in 1967, when the Public Service Staff Relations Act was passed, giving employee organizations the right to negotiate directly with the government as trade unions, with the right to compulsory arbitration conciliation, and the right to strike. The Act is administered by the Public Service Staff Relations Board.

In fact, the legal framework for unionization of the public service is found in three statutes. First, the **Financial Administration Act** was amended to make the Treasury Board the "employer" for purposes of collective bargaining. As well, it assumed responsibilities for staff requirements, pay, job classification, and training policy from the Civil Service Commission. Second, the **Public Service Employment Act** was passed, replacing the Civil Service Commission with the Public Service Commission. It became the central staffing agency of the government. Finally, the **Public Service Staff Relations Act** was passed to provide the "machinery" of collective bargaining. For example, the authority to certify bargaining units and administer dispute resolution was handed to the Public Service Staff Relations Board. In 2003, a new Public Service Employment Act and Public Service Labour Relations Act were passed to improve collective bargaining, offer greater opportunities for mediation, and resolve conflict in a more flexible manner.

Despite these advances for public sector workers, certain public servants are denied the right to strike, since they are considered to provide "essential services" for public safety or security. Moreover, there are restrictions on what the government deems "negotiable." Job security, classification, and other issues have been excluded in the past from the set of issues that public servants can bargain over with their employer. As well, several classes of employees are specifically excluded from the legislation governing collective bargaining. Still, the introduction of collective bargaining in the federal public service in 1967 significantly altered relations between the government, as employer, and its employees.[60]

Public Servants and Politics

The political rights of public servants are also protected by the Public Service Commission, as is the responsibility to see to it that public servants can speak the truth to those in power without fear of reprisal. The fact that Cabinet ministers cannot recruit, assign, transfer, promote, or make any other decision regarding the career of a public servant serves to maintain the integrity and nonpartisanship of the public service and keep it free from undue political interference.

Ultimately, politicians must be able to trust that their public servants will not engage in partisan politics, but will serve them loyally:

[T]here is nothing more important to the effectiveness of the Public Service than that Ministers of successive Governments have confidence in the loyalty of Public Servants. Those who advise them . . . must be without partisan associations. . . . These conditions form the basis of careers in the Public Service, enabling Public Servants to carry out their essential duty of serving successive Governments of different political parties without any legitimate questioning of their loyalty and commitment.[61]

Indeed, when reforms to the Civil Service were enacted in 1918, serious penalties were imposed on any public servant engaging in political activities. The zeal with which reformers sought to eradicate patronage meant that, though they could still vote, public servants suffered the curtailment of virtually all other political rights that we, as citizens, take for granted.

This continued until 1967, when the Public Service Employment Act loosened the constraints on the political rights of public servants. It allowed public servants below the rank of deputy minister to run for election under certain circumstances, and to attend political meetings and donate funds to candidates or parties. They still could not work for or against a candidate or political party, however. In 1991, the Supreme Court struck down the sections of the Public Service Employment Act containing these remaining prohibitions, on the grounds that they violated public servants' political rights. As lawyer Michael Mandel reports, "[T]he Supreme Court held that the limits on federal civil servants' partisan political activity were too broad in that they included every employee without any distinctions for type of job and type of political activity."[62] As a result, today's federal public servants, with the exception of deputy ministers, are free to participate fully in the political system. Current Public Service Employment Act regulations state that public servants who seek to be nominated as candidates and to stand for election in the House of Commons, or any other legislature in Canada, must apply to the Commission for a leave of absence without pay.

There are some particular principles that set the parameters of the relationship between the public service and the political system.[63] Prominent among them is the doctrine of **political neutrality**.[64] In short, this convention states that public servants must consistently act in ways that assure their political impartiality. They are not members of the governing party, nor are they party activists who happen to be working within the government. Instead, they occupy a special position of trust through which they are expected to serve the government of the day faithfully, no matter which party is in power.

The doctrine of political neutrality is made up of several elements. First is the politics-administration dichotomy, which, you will recall, states that policy and administration are separate activities. Politicians make policy; public servants administer it. Second is the merit principle, which, in this setting, implies that positions are awarded not on the basis of political affiliation but on the person's skills and qualifications. Third, and related, is the notion that public servants do not engage in partisan political activities. To do so would compromise their positions as neutral advisors to the government. Fourth, although public servants have their own personal views of the quality of the government's policy and administration, it is not their place to express those views publicly. Fifth, in return for honest and straightforward advice to their political masters, public servants' anonymity is guaranteed. Thus, politicians accept public responsibility for the government's action or inaction; they take the blame when things go wrong and the praise when things go right. The public servant, on the other hand, toils anonymously in the background. Finally, public servants enjoy tenure in their positions as long as they perform their jobs satisfactorily. In return, they are expected to offer loyal service and to execute the government's decisions, irrespective of their personal opinions.

Overall, striking a balance between the need for political neutrality and the political rights of public servants is a challenging task. But recent developments, both federally and provincially, suggest a trend toward broadening public servants' political rights. The extent to which this trend may compromise the quality of advice and service provided to politicians is yet to be seen. But indications are that erring on the side of democratic freedom has not diminished the public service's professionalism or effectiveness.

Human Resources Management

At this point, it may be worth reflecting on the administrative complexity of the picture so far. Consider all the bodies to which you are accountable if you are a senior administrator in a department about to make a hiring decision. You must ensure that you comply with the regulations of the main bodies responsible for human resources management. You must also act in accordance with the directives of your own superiors within the department, and with whatever rules they impose on the selection of the person for the job. You must be versed in the merit principle but also be sensitive to the value of representativeness, and be aware of the latest government policies with regard to employment equity. But the list of bureaucratic and administrative responsibilities does not end here, since several other government sectors have a stake in your hiring decision. These include the Human Rights Commission, whose provisions you must not violate, and the Privy Council Office, especially if the hiring is for a senior position. And even this is not a comprehensive list of the government bodies that could potentially be involved, at some level, in your decision. Moreover, you must determine what job classification to use, how your hire fits into your department's broad human resource planning goals, what your staffing needs will be for the new position, whether the candidates have all had an equal chance to meet the selection criteria for the job (including language requirements), and so on. To say that the process is complex is an understatement.

Now imagine that you must make a firing decision. There is a widespread assumption that once a person has been hired in the public service, he or she is essentially "set" for life. This is inaccurate, as recent mass layoffs and firings at all levels of government amply demonstrate. Nonetheless, there is a complex procedure that must be followed before any public servant can be let go. Every employee is subject to a rigorous performance assessment on an annual basis that has an important bearing on pay, opportunities for training and upgrading, and promotion. A government-wide system of staff assessment is administered by management. The Performance Review and Appraisal Report, developed by the Treasury Board and the Public Service Commission, is used to rank an employee's performance on a five-point scale, from Outstanding to Unsatisfactory. It also assesses an employee's abilities, also on a five-point scale, for purposes of determining promotion, probation, transfer, and other actions. As political scientist James Simeon reports, this process "provides a structured method for assessing their employees and assisting them in realizing their full potential. In fact, managers are assessed on how well they do staff performance reviews and appraisals."[65]

Simeon goes on to point out that disciplinary measures are another important aspect of human resources management. There are five measures used in the federal public service in relation to discipline. In ascending order of severity, these are as follows: oral reprimand, written reprimand, suspension, financial penalty, and discharge. Immediate supervisors may dispense the first two, but a senior manager must deal with more serious offences and penalties. The deputy minister ultimately has the discretion to determine which penalty should be applied for various sorts of misconduct. These penalties are partly determined, though, by guidelines set through established precedents within the public service. In setting penalties, managers must not violate collective agreements. And employees have the right to appeal disciplinary measures and be represented in a hearing by legal counsel (see chapter 6 on administrative law). Furthermore, there are prescribed steps that must be followed prior to taking disciplinary action, including giving the employee an opportunity to explain the circumstances surrounding her actions. "Determining an appropriate penalty for misconduct always requires good judgement," according to Simeon. "With respect to the federal government, its explicit policy is that the primary object of discipline is not punishment but to rehabilitate the employee, to make them a better and more productive worker. This is referred to as 'corrective discipline.'"[66] At the very least, all of this suggests that where human resources is concerned, management is far more difficult in the public sector than in the private.

Finally, managers in today's public service are increasingly consumed with the issues of retention and recruitment as part of a broader process of human resources modernization.[67] Recruitment is a concern due to the steady erosion in the public's faith in the public service, coupled with the denigration of public service careers from within. The institutions of government have been suffering for a long time now from a serious image problem in the public mind, and have been overseen by political masters whose own view is that the public service is an inefficient, slow, ponderous, expensive, and ineffective machine. As a result, the idea of the "career public servant" has eroded. Where once it was commonplace to work toward a lifetime of service to the public, today there is a much higher rate of outward migration to the private sector, the not-for-profit sector, the voluntary sector, and so on.

As a result, public sector managers are faced with the task of reinvigorating the public service and making it into an "employer of choice" for prospective job-seekers. The challenge, according to professor of public administration Evert Lindquist, is to offer opportunities for a career that is challenging; allows for knowledge-building; provides opportunities to work with people from diverse backgrounds; allows for learning from experienced staff; enables people to move from position to position to work in a variety of areas; permits creativity; makes a difference and has an impact on the community and public policy; compensates well in a manner which is competitive with other sectors; and provides people with recognition for a job well done.[68]

The recruitment challenge is partly derived from the demographic reality noted above—namely, that the public service is aging and is not being renewed. Public service employers now face a "seller's market" when looking to hire and must aggressively compete with other employers for a limited pool of talent. Hence, the clerk of the Privy Council said in 2007 that "success in recruitment requires effective 'branding'—that is, identifying the Public Service as a career of choice in the minds young Canadians."[69] Many of those who would traditionally seek a career in the public service—such as new graduates in public administration, political science, and other disciplines—are choosing other career paths. Some of the new strategies used by public service recruiters to win these people back have included aggressive on-campus recruiting at universities and colleges; emphasizing public sector strengths and learning opportunities to prospective employees; expanding beyond their usual recruitment sources (to, for example, electronic recruitment strategies); and developing selling points to make the idea of a career in the public service more appealing.[70]

Of course, once recruitment efforts are successful, retention becomes an issue. So, too, are succession planning and employee development. Skilled employees will continue to be in demand, there will be a high level of job mobility, and competitors (in both public and private sectors) will be recruiting aggressively. Knowledge workers are especially valued, as governments embrace technological innovations in the delivery of programs and services. Thus, governments will have to continue to innovate and flexibly respond to changing labour market conditions in order to fulfill the ongoing demand for the provision of public goods and services.

WHAT YOU HAVE LEARNED

Can the public service move forward in the area of human resources management under the current stresses and strains that it faces? Issues such as patronage versus merit, the growth of government, the return of war veterans and arrival of new university graduates, and bilingualism challenged the public service in the early years. Later, issues such as shrinking government, affirmative action, employment equity and pay equity, as well as the need to do more with less in an era hostile to the very institution of the public service lowered morale and brought other new problems. Currently, retention, recruitment, and succession planning are among the most significant challenges. In sum, the public service has had to change constantly. What, then, are the expectations that Canadians currently hold of their public service? According to the Public Service Commission,

Canadians want some things to change, but they wish that basic Public Service values be protected. The Public Service Commission plays a key role in addressing this requirement. Its role is to meet the dual challenge of preserving the values of merit-based, non-partisan and representative staffing that are the cornerstone of our staffing process, while helping create for managers and public servants the conditions for creativity and innovation that will need to be the hallmarks of the Public Service of the future.[71]

The extent to which the challenges of the current era have been met is a matter of some dispute. Certainly the Auditor General has been critical of the human resources reforms of the 1990s, calling human resource management "a major weakness" of government.[72] The jury is still out on the reforms of the early twenty-first century, though. The next chapter focuses on the management of the public service, including fiscal management, to place the issues raised in chapter 9 in a broader context.

Key Words and Concepts

Civil Service Act, 1908 (266)	pay equity (293)
Civil Service Act, 1918 (266)	collective bargaining (293)
Civil Service Commission (266)	Financial Administration Act (294)
Public Service Commission (266)	Public Service Employment Act (294)
representative (272)	Public Service Staff Relations Act (294)
employment equity (286)	political neutrality (295)
affirmative action (286)	

Review Questions

1. A Brief History of the Public Service: Who Works There, Anyway?
This section provided an overview of the composition of the public sector workforce and introduced some of the basic issues that have confronted the public service over time. It focused on merit and patronage and the tension between these. Ask yourself, What is the public service? What historical developments shaped the public service? What issues have recently emerged, and how are they being addressed? How can the merit principle be reconciled with new developments?

2. The Public Service Today: An Overview

The public sector's response to the questions raised in the first section is evident in the many progressive changes it has pioneered in the workplace. This section addressed some of those changes, as well as those produced by attaining collective bargaining rights by public servants. Can you answer these questions: How large is the public service? How have equity issues come to the forefront within the public service? How has the public service changed recently? What is the significance of representativeness? How has unionization of the public service affected the union movement in Canada, the political rights of workers in the public service, and their relationship to the government?

Public servants clearly have a special relationship to the political system. Historically, their political rights were severely circumscribed. More recently, there has been a trend toward loosening the strictures against political activity. But the notion that public servants' political rights are different from those of ordinary citizens has been difficult to overcome, running headlong, as it does, into principles such as the doctrine of political neutrality. As a result, ask yourself, What grounds existed to limit the political rights of public servants, and how has this changed? What is the doctrine of political neutrality? How has it affected the work that public servants do? What is the relationship between public servants and the political system?

3. Human Resources Management

The issue of how the tens of thousands of public servants in the federal government are organized and managed was assessed from the perspective of managers' responsibilities. Ask yourself, How do you as a manager hire and fire personnel, set pay levels, and determine conditions of employment? How do you reconcile merit and representativeness? What is the contemporary importance of recruitment, retention, and succession planning in the public service?

Weblinks

Public Service Commission of Canada—Career Recruitment
www.jobs.gc.ca

Canadian Union of Public Employees
www.cupe.ca

Public Service Alliance of Canada
www.psac.com

Canada Public Service Agency (formerly Public Service Agency of Canada)
www.psagency-agencefp.gc.ca

Canada Public Service Agency Responsibilities
www.psagency-agencefp.gc.ca/common/resp_e.asp

Human Resources Management Modernization
www.psagency-agencefp.gc.ca/hrmm-mgrh/index_e.asp

Classification Modernization
www.psagency-agencefp.gc.ca/classification/index_e.asp

Leadership Network
www.psagency-agencefp.gc.ca/leadership/ld_e.asp

Employment Equity
www.psagency-agencefp.gc.ca/ee/index_e.asp

Official Languages Act
http://laws.justice.gc.ca/en/O-3.01/index.html

Public Service Modernization Act
http://laws.justice.gc.ca/en/p-33.4/

Employment Equity Act
http://laws.justice.gc.ca/en/E-5.401/index.html

Results for Canadians: A Management Framework for the Government of Canada
www.tbs-sct.gc.ca/report/res_can/siglist_e.asp

Canada School of Public Service
www.myschool-monecole.gc.ca

Treasury Board of Canada Secretariat
www.tbs-sct.gc.ca

Further Reading

1. A Brief History of the Public Service: Who Works There, Anyway?

Dwivedi, O.P., ed. *The Administrative State in Canada: Essays in Honour of J.E. Hodgetts*. Toronto: University of Toronto Press, 1981.

Johnson, A.W. *Dream No Little Dreams: A Biography of the Douglas Government of Saskatchewan 1944–1961*. Toronto: University of Toronto Press, 2004.

Lindquist, Evert. *A Critical Moment: Capturing and Conveying the Evolution of the Canadian Public Service*. Ottawa: Canada School of Public Service, 2006.

2. The Public Service Today: An Overview

Canada. Public Service Commission of Canada. Representativeness: An Integral Part of Merit. Ottawa: Public Service Commission of Canada, February, 2002. **www.psc-cfp.gc.ca/cgi-bin/clf-upe/prn-impr.pl**

Dwivedi O.P. and John Halligan, "The Canadian Public Service: Balancing Values and Management," in John Halligan, ed. *Civil Service Systems in Anglo-American Countries*. Cheltenham, UK: Edward Elgar, 2003: 148–73.

Malloy, Jonathan. "The Next Generation? Recruitment and Renewal in the Federal Public Service," in G. Bruce Doern, ed. *How Ottawa Spends 2004–2005: Mandate Change in the Paul Martin Era*. Montreal: McGill-Queen's University Press, 2004: 277–95.

Ruemper, Fred. "Beyond Merit: The Representative Principle," in Randy Hoffman, et al., *Public Administration: Canadian Materials. Third Edition*. Toronto: Captus Press, 1998: 252–71.

Wernick, Michael. *French to Follow? Revitalizing the Official Languages in the Workplace*. Ottawa: Canadian Centre for Management Development, 2003.

3. Human Resources Management

Agocs, Carol and Jack Roberts. "Is Employment Equity Fair and Necessary?" in Paul Barker and Mark Charlton, eds. *Crosscurrents: Contemporary Political Issues*. Scarborough: Nelson, 1991: 392–418.

Canada. Public Service Commission of Canada. *The Road Ahead: Recruitment and Retention Challenges for the Public Service*. Ottawa: Public Service Commission of Canada, February, 2002.

Endnotes

1. See Reginald Whitaker, "Politics Versus Administration: Politicians and Bureaucrats," in Michael Whittington and Glenn Williams, eds. *Canadian Politics in the 21st Century, Sixth Edition,* (Toronto: Thomson Nelson, 2004): chapter 3.

2. Canada. Treasury Board Secretariat. *Strengthening Public Sector Management: An Overview of the Government Action Plan and Key Initiatives,* (Ottawa: President of the Treasury Board, 2004): 2.

3. Donald Brittain, *Paperland: The Bureaucrat Observed,* (Ottawa: National Film Board of Canada, 1979).

4. This number refers to all federal public service employees working in departments and agencies listed under Schedule 1, Part 1 of the Public Service Staff Relations Act. See Canada. Treasury Board of Canada Secretariat. *Employment Statistics for the Federal Public Service April 1, 1999–March 31, 2000.* Ottawa: Treasury Board Secretariat, 2000:2. **www.tbs-sct.gc.ca/ pubs_pol/hrpubs/pse-fpe/ es-se99-00-1_e.html**

5. Ralph Heintzman, "Introduction: Canada and Public Administration," in Jacques Bourgault, Maurice Demers and Cynthia Williams, eds. *Public Administration and Public Management: Experiences in Canada,* (Sainte-Foy, Quebec: Les Publications du Quebec, 1997): 5.

6. Heintzman, "Introduction," (1997). On the role of patronage in pre-Confederation Ontario, see S.J.R. Noel, *Patrons, Clients, Brokers: Ontario Society and Politics 1791–1896,* (Toronto: University of Toronto Press, 1990).

7. Laurent Dobuzinskis, "Public Administration," in Michael Howlett and David Laycock, eds. *Puzzles of Power: An Introduction to Political Science, Second Edition,* (Toronto: Oxford University Press, 1998): 156. The following paragraphs are derived from Dobuzinskis's overview of the development of the public service.

8. See O.P. Dwivedi and John Halligan, "The Canadian Public Service: Balancing Values and Management," in John Halligan, ed. *Civil Service Systems in Anglo-American Countries,* (Cheltenham, UK: Edward Elgar, 2003): 148–73.

9. Cited in Alasdair Roberts, *So-Called Experts: How American Consultants Remade the Canadian Civil Service, 1918–21,* (Toronto: Institute of Public Administration of Canada, 1996): 3–4.

10. See Doug Owram, *The Government Generation: Canadian Intellectuals and the State 1900–1945,* (Toronto: University of Toronto Press, 1986).

11. See J.L. Granatstein, *The Ottawa Men: The Civil Service Mandarins, 1835–1957. With a New Introduction,* (Toronto: University of Toronto Press, 1998).

12. Jacques Bourgault and Barbara Wake Carroll, "The Canadian Senior Public Service: The Last Vestigaes of the Whitehall Model?" in Jacques Bourgault, Maurice Demers and Cynthia Williams, eds. *Public Administration and Public Management: Experiences in Canada,* (Sainte-Foy, Quebec: Les Publications du Quebec, 1997): 98.

13. See John Porter, *The Vertical Mosaic: An Analysis of Social Class and Power in Canada,* (Toronto: University of Toronto Press, 1965).

14. See Nicole Morgan, *Implosion: An Analysis of the Growth of the Federal Public Service in Canada 1945–1985,* (Montreal: Institute for Research on Public Policy, 1986): xvi–xvii.

15. See Canada, Royal Commission on Government Organization, *Report,* Five Volumes, (Ottawa: Queen's Printer, 1962–1963).

16. See Arthur Kroeger and Jeff Heynen, *Making Transitions Work: Integrating External Executives into the Federal Public Service,* (Ottawa: Canadian Centre for Management Development, 2003).

17. Morgan, *Implosion,* (1986): xvii.

18. Dobuzinskis, "Public Administration," (1998): 157.

19. See Gary Teeple, *Globalization and the Decline of Social Reform: Into the Twenty-First Century,* (Toronto: Garamond Press, 2000).

20. See Susan D. Phillips, "A More Democratic Canada . . . ?" in Susan D. Phillips, ed. *How Canada Spends: A More Democratic Canada? 1993–1994,* (Ottawa: Carleton University Press, 1993): 6–7.

21. Canada, Public Service Commission, "Change and Management in the Public Service. Talking Points for Mme. Jocelyne Bourgon, Clerk of the Privy Council and Secretary to the Cabinet to the Association of Professional Executives of the Public Service of Canada," (Ottawa: Public Service Commission of Canada, May 11, 1994): 3. Online **www.pco-bcp.gc.ca/ClerkSP/ Manageme.htm** See also Isabella Bakker, "The Politics of Scarcity: Deficits and the Debt" in Michael S. Whittington and Glen Williams, eds. *Canadian Politics in the 1990s, Fourth Edition,* (Scarborough: Nelson, 1995): 55–79.

22. See Trevor Bhupsingh and Peter Edwards. *Tracking the Role of the PSC in the Government System of the Federal Public Service.* (Ottawa: Public Service Commission of Canada, April, 1997). **www.psc-cfp.gc.ca**

23. Canada, *The Public Service Commission,* (Ottawa, The Public Service Commission, 1998). Online **www.psc-cfp.gc.ca/mission/pscrre2.htm**

24. Ian D. Clark, "Restraint, Renewal, and the Treasury Board Secretariat," *Canadian Public Administration,* 37, 2 (Summer, 1994): 216.

25. United Nations, *Human Development Report 2006,* **http://hdr.undp.org/hdr2006/statistics/** Accessed June 12, 2007.

26. Canada. Privy Council Office, *Fourteenth Annual Report to the Prime Minister on the Public Service of Canada,* (Ottawa: Privy Council Office, 2007): 2. See also Evert Lindquist, *A Critical Moment: Capturing and Conveying the Evolution of the Canadian Public Service,* (Ottawa: Canada School of Public Service, 2006). **www.sft-ddt.gc.ca/sftddt_e.htm**

27. Heintzman, "Introduction," (1997): 5.

28. Canada. Treasury Board of Canada Secretariat. *Employment Statistics for the Federal Public Service April 1, 1999–March 31, 2000.* Ottawa: Treasury Board Secretariat, 2000: 2. **www.tbs-sct.gc.ca/ pubs_pol/hrpubs/pse-fpe/es-se99-00-1_e.html** Canada. Treasury Board Secretariat. *Classification System.***www.tbs-sct.gc.ca/Pubs_pol/hrpubs/TBM_111/CHAPT1_e.html**

29. Canada. Statistics Canada. "Public Sector Employment," *The Daily Mirror.* May 30, 2007. **www.statcan.ca/Daily/English/070530/d070530c.htm** Accessed June 12, 2007. According to Statistics Canada, for the purposes of the Census, "the public sector includes all economic entities controlled by government. It is comprised of four major components: federal government (ministries, departments, agencies and non-autonomous funds, and autonomous funds and organizations); provincial and territorial government (ministries, departments, agencies and non-autonomous funds, autonomous funds and organizations, universities and colleges, and health and social service institutions); local government (municipalities and non-autonomous funds, autonomous funds and organizations, and school boards); and government business enterprises (at the federal, provincial/territorial and local levels)."

30. Canada. Human Resources and Social Development Canada. *2005 Employment Equity Report.* Ottawa: Human Resources and Social Development Canada. **www.hrsdc.gc.ca/en/lp/lo/lswe/ we/ee_tools/reports/annual/2005/index-we.shtml** Accessed June 14, 2007.

31. Canada. Treasury Board of Canada Secretariat. *Employment Statistics for the Federal Public Service April 1, 1999–March 31, 2000.* Ottawa: Treasury Board Secretariat, 2000: 1. **www.tbs-sct.gc.ca/ pubs_pol/hrpubs/pse-fpe/es-se99-00-1_e.html**

32. See Canada. Public Service Agency. *Modernizing the Classification System—Annual Report 2005–06,* (Ottawa: Public Service Agency); and Canada. Public Service Human Resources Management Agency. *2006–2007 Estimates: Report on Progress,* (Ottawa: Public Service Human Resources Management Agency, 2007).

33. Canada. Treasury Board Secretariat. *Public Service Modernization Act: Backgrounder.* **www.tbs-sct.gc. ca/media/nr-cp/2003/0206_e.asp** Accessed December 18, 2006.

34. Canada. Treasury Board Secretariat. *Public Service Modernization Act: Backgrounder.* **www.tbs-sct. gc.ca/media/nr-cp/2003/0206_e.asp** Accessed December 18, 2006.

35. Canada. Treasury Board Secretariat. *Public Service Modernization Act: Backgrounder.* **www.tbs-sct.gc.ca/ media/nr-cp/2003/0206_e.asp** Accessed December 18, 2006.

36. Canada. Public Service Human Resources Management Agency. 2006–2007 Estimates: *Report on Progress,* (Ottawa: Public Service Human Resources Management Agency, 2007): 8.

37. Canada. Treasury Board Secretariat. Public Service Human Resources Management Agency of Canada 2006–07 Estimates: Report on Plans and Priorities. **www.tbs-sct.gc.ca/rpp/0607/ pshrmac-agrhfpc/pshrmac-agrhfpc_e.pdf** Accessed June 19, 2007.

38. Canada. Privy Council Office. *Fourteenth Annual Report to the Prime Minister on the Public Service of Canada: Annex 3. The First Report by the Prime Minister's Advisory Committee on the Public Service,* (Ottawa: Privy Council Office, 2007).

39. For a current listing of career opportunities in the public service go to **jobs.gc.ca**

40. Canada. Public Service Agency. *Employment Equity in the Federal Public Service 2004–05. Annual Report to Parliament.* **www.psagency-agencefp.gc.ca/reports-rapports/ee-05-PR_e.asp? printable=True** Accessed June 21, 2007.

41. For an early consideration of these issues, see V. Seymour Wilson and Willard A. Mullins, "Representative Bureaucracy: Linguistic/Ethnic Aspects in Canadian Public Policy," *Canadian Public Administration,* 21 (Winter, 1978): 513–38.

42. Canada. Privy Council Office. *Fourteenth Annual Report to the Prime Minister on the Public Service of Canada.* (Ottawa: Privy Council Office, 2007): 38.

43. J.E. Hodgetts, et al. *The Biography of an Institution: The Civil Service Commission of Canada 1908–1967,* (Montreal: McGill–Queen's University Press, 1972): 473.

44. Robert J. Jackson and Doreen Jackson, *Politics in Canada: Culture, Institutions, Behaviour and Public Policy, Sixth Edition,* (Toronto: Pearson Prentice Hall, 2006): 358.

45. Canada, Royal Commission on Bilingualism and Biculturalism, Report, Five Volumes, (Ottawa: Queen's Printer, 1967–1970).

46. See, for example, Canada. Office of the Commissioner of Official Languages. *Annual Report 2006–2007,* (Ottawa: Public Works and Services Canada, 2007).

47. See Judge Rosalie Silberman Abella, *Equality in Employment: A Royal Commission Report,* (Ottawa: Supply and Services Canada, 1984): 7.

48. Canada, Public Service Commission, *Annual Report 1992,* (Ottawa: Supply and Services, 1993): 46.

49. Abella, *Equality in Employment,* (1984): 1.

50. See Susan D. Phillips, Brian R. Little and Laura A. Goodine, "Reconsidering Gender and Public Administration: Five Steps Beyond Conventional Research," *Canadian Public Administration,* 40, 4 (Winter, 1994): 576. See also Sandra Burt and Sonya Lynn Hardman, "The Case of the Disappearing Targets: The Liberals and Gender Equality," in Leslie A. Pal, ed. *How Ottawa Spends 2001–2002: Power in Transition,* (Toronto: Oxford University Press, 2001): 201–22.

51. Jonathan Malloy, "The Next Generation? Recruitment and Renewal in the Federal Public Service," in G. Bruce Doern, ed. *How Ottawa Spends 2004–2005: Mandate Change in the Paul Martin Era,* (Montreal: McGill-Queen's University Press, 2004): 283.

52. Camilla Stivers, *Gender Images in Public Administration,* (Newbury Park, California: Sage, 1993): 4.

53. Martha Hynna, "Women in the Public Service—A Thirty-Year Perspective," *Canadian Public Administration,* 40, 4 (Winter, 1997):

54. The following data concerning women, Aboriginals, persons with disabilities, and visible minorities are derived from Canada. Treasury Board Secretariat of Canada. *Employment Equity in the Public Service 2004–05 Annual Report to Parliament.* **www.psagency-agencefp.gc.ca/ reports-rapports/ee-0501_e.asp#_Toc143307355** Accessed June 20, 2007.

55. See Kenneth Kernaghan and Mohamed Charih, "The Challenge of Change: Emerging Issues in Contemporary Public Administration," *Canadian Public Administration,* 40, 2 (Summer, 1997): 227–28.

56. Canada. The Senate of Canada. *Employement Equity in the Federal Public Service—Not There Yet: Preliminary Findings of the Senate Standing Committee on Human Rights.* (Ottawa: Senate Standing Committee on Human Rights, February, 2007).

57. Leo Panitch and Donald Swartz, *From Consent to Coercion: The Assault on Trade Union Freedoms. Third Edition,* (Aurora: Garamond Press, 2003): 18–19.

58. Gene Swimmer, "Critical Issues in Public Sector Industrial Relations," in Amarjit S. Sethi, ed. *Collective Bargaining in Canada,* (Scarborough: Nelson, 1989): 401.

59. The following discussion is derived from P.K. Kuruvilla, "Collective Bargaining in the Canadian Public Service," in Kenneth Kernaghan, ed. *Public Administration in Canada: Selected Readings, Fifth Edition,* (Toronto: Methuen, 1985): 224–35.

60. See Audrey D. Doer, *The Machinery of Government in Canada,* (Toronto: Methuen, 1981): 63.

61. Canada, *Public Service 2000: The Renewal of the Public Service of Canada,* (Ottawa: Supply and Services, 1990): 63, 64.

62. Michael Mandel, *The Charter of Rights and the Legalization of Politics in Canada,* (Toronto: Thomson Educational Publishing, 1994): 294.

63. See Michael Cassidy, ed. *Democratic Rights and Electoral Reform in Canada,* (Toronto: Dundurn Press, for the Royal Commission on Electoral Reform and Party Financing, 1991).

64. For an early statement of this doctrine, see Kenneth Kernaghan, "Politics, Policy and Public Servants: Political Neutrality Revised," *Canadian Public Administration,* 21 (Fall, 1976) 432–56.

65. James C. Simeon, "Canadian Public Administration and Government," in Randy Hoffman et al. *Public Administration: Canadian Materials, Third Edition,* (North York: Captus Press, 1998): 34.

66. Simeon, "Canadian Public Administration and Government," (1998): 35.

67. See Canada, Public Service Commission of Canada, *The Road Ahead: Recruitment and Retention Challenges for the Public Service*, (Ottawa: Public Service Commission of Canada, February, 2002).

68. Evert Lindquist, "Are Public Service Careers Changing? Images, Challenges, Strategies," Presentation to the *New Professionals Driving a New Public Service Conference*, (Toronto: October 22, 2001). **www.newpublicservice.ca/en_indexframes.asp**

69. Canada. Privy Council Office. *Fourteenth Annual Report,* (2007): 21.

70. Canada, Public Service Commission of Canada, *The Road Ahead,* (2002): 26.

71. Canada, Public Service Commission of Canada, *The Road Ahead* (2002): 26.

72. Canada, Office of the Auditor-General of Canada, *Public Service Management Reform: Progress, Setbacks and Challenges*, (Ottawa: Minister of Public Works and Services, February, 2001).

Chapter 10

Public Administration, Management Reform, *and* Financial Management

WHAT YOU WILL LEARN

Two central elements of public administration permit governments to do what they need to do. These are *money* and *personnel*. This chapter looks at the following:

- What are the pre-eminent issues in management reform in the public service?
- How does the management of financial resources involve making decisions about how to divide the government "pie"?
- How do governments try to answer the question of "who gets what, when, and how?"
- How have complex and elaborate systems of budget making and financial management evolved, and how are they subject to ongoing review and reform, audit, and evaluation?

Chapter 9 showed that the management of human resources in the public sector is a complex affair. In this chapter, we examine some of the major reforms in the management of human resources affecting what the managers of the public service do and how they do it. We also note that even in times when government coffers are full, financial management is complicated, but in an era of diminishing revenues, it is hotly disputed. To resolve disputes over how financial resources are raised and spent, someone has to ensure that financial resources are being used wisely, and that every dollar of taxpayers' money can be accounted for. This results in some of the most contentious political debate within government and society. In their attempts to create a transparent and fair system of budgeting, Canadian governments have experimented with a variety of models, but, so far, no one system or model has been able to address all the issues surrounding the administration and management of government finances.

This chapter examines issues related both to management reform and to financial management. In reality, the two are often linked. The chapter is divided into the following sections:

1. — Restructuring the Public Service: The Management View

Recent changes have altered the composition of the public service. Downsizing, re-engineering, pay freezes, cutbacks, layoffs, and firings were endemic throughout the 1990s. This section asks the following: What are the most important recent reforms to the management of the public service? How has restructuring affected the public service? What has it done to the morale of those remaining in the public service? How has it affected the delivery of services to the public? What are the implications of privatizing and contracting out? What does the future hold for those seeking a career in the Canadian public service?

2. — Financial Management

The issues of power and politics raised in chapter 2 revolved around this question: Who gets what, when, and how? We return to this by examining that most fundamental of issues related to government—money. Some observers of public administration have indeed concluded that to get anything done, governments need three things: money, money, and money.[1] Canadian governments manage billions of dollars of taxpayers' money (that is, *your* money) every year. How is that money managed? What budgeting systems have been established to ensure that probity, honesty, economy, efficiency, and accountability are maintained? Who is ultimately responsible for the management of funds? What kinds of competition do departments engage in to ensure that they get their share of the loot? What is the budgetary cycle?

Restructuring the Public Service: The Management View

The last decade of the twentieth century was a difficult one for the public service in Canada. Recognizing the debilitating trends of low morale, cutbacks, wage freezes, and the general disparagement aimed at public servants, managers have recently turned their attention to the vexing issue of how to rebuild a once-proud institution. Since 1999, public service renewal has again moved to the forefront of the agenda of many Canadian governments. At the federal level, many new initiatives have been launched, including adoption of performance management measures; an increased focus on human resources planning, with emphasis on identifying and addressing retention and recruitment problems; exploration of other forms of partnerships, such as employee takeovers; and development of a new employment classification structure.[2] Before we explore the specifics of these issues, we need to review the depth and breadth of change in the public service over the years.

Imagine that it is 1970 and that you're fresh out of university. You are attracted to the prospect of a career in the public service because you have always understood that serving your country in this way is a lofty and honourable ambition. Your instructors in public administration courses have regaled you with tales of the proud and powerful mandarinate that dominated the halls of bureaucratic power in the post-war years, reconstructing the country after the war, building the great edifice known as the "social welfare state," and contributing in no small way to the greatest era of sustained prosperity in the country's history. You are versed in the literature of Keynesian macro-economic management, as well as the latest systems approaches and modern social science management techniques. The world is your oyster, and you confidently accept your responsibility as a management trainee in an important federal department, content in the knowledge that your long and satisfying career will lead you, in no time, right to the deputy minister's office.

Now flash ahead to 2007. You have somehow survived the various purges that decimated the ranks of your colleagues in the 1980s and 1990s. You are a few short years from retirement and are being pressured to leave early, even though it will adversely affect your pension and post-work lifestyle. The much-vaunted Keynesian management systems that you were taught have long been discredited by newfangled approaches known as monetarism and neoconservatism, the underlying premises of which are that you are a useless parasite sucking the lifeblood out of the nation. Successive prime ministers, from Trudeau to Harper, have denigrated your work. The negative impression of the public service has been adopted by the public and the media, who regularly vilify you and your colleagues. You are held responsible for everything from the national debt to the lack of competitiveness of Canadian industry to the sorry state of the health care system to the rise in crime to the decline in morality, and on and on! And somewhere along the way, you found your march up the career ladder blocked by a huge cohort of your fellow public servants, all around your age and with the same ambitions. At some point, you realized that you had been "shelved."

What on earth happened in the intervening years?

Managing the public service has always been a challenging task. Notwithstanding the nostalgic recollections of the "glory years" after the Second World War, there have always been stresses and strains, conflicts and challenges for public service managers. But from the 1970s onward, the nature and set of issues and challenges seem to have both altered and intensified, and the management of the public service ran into serious—and heretofore largely unknown—difficulties. A variety of internal problems coincided with a change in societal views about the role and place of the public service. Just as the transition between the minimalist state and the Keynesian welfare state was difficult (the Great Depression of the 1930s), so, too, was the transformation from the Keynesian welfare state to the neoconservative state. (These terms, you will recall, were used in chapter 1.)

Government surpluses, deficits and debt, technological change, globalization, and the rise of new social movements and interest groups, coupled with a more assertive and skeptical citizenry, have created new problems for public service managers. These have been exacerbated by two issues. First, managers' ability to respond to the forces of change has been hampered by inadequate internal systems and processes for managing their departments. Second, widespread external criticism has emerged that the public service has grown out of control and is incapable of doing its job.

Moreover, the Auditor General's infamous statement in 1976 that "Parliament—and indeed the government—had lost or was close to losing effective control of the public purse" shocked Canadians and galvanized the public sector.[3] In 1978, the Auditor General reported that public servants had developed the attitude that the government was a bottomless pit of money, were engaged in empire-building, and had little regard for efficiency and economy, or the interests of the taxpayer.[4] Subsequent reports, while couched in more moderate language, frequently reinforced these negative impressions of government management.

Have these concerns been adequately addressed? In 2001, the Auditor General identified four key areas where the management of the federal public service remains especially problematic:

The erosion of parliamentary control over how the government raises money and spends it. Canadians have the right to control how public funds are collected and used, and ultimately it is the members of Parliament we elect who carry out this control on our behalf. That is why I am concerned about recent examples of the erosion of parliamentary control, involving billions of dollars of revenue and expenditure. Strengthening fiscal and financial management. Over the last five years there has been a significant change in the federal government's fiscal position. The transparency and discipline that have yielded impressive results so far are critical to continued success. Steps have also been taken to improve financial management in departments and agencies. Money must be managed prudently in the interest of the public. The undermanagement of grant and contribution programs. The recent attention paid to grants and contributions has not yet translated into an overall improvement in the way they are managed across government. Government-wide problems require government-wide solutions. The internal health of the federal public service. The government has established an ambitious schedule for modernizing human resource management. Good government depends on the performance of the public service. I will be watching these modernization efforts closely.[5]

Similarly, in 2003 the Auditor General authored a scathing report after investigating the Sponsorship Program (see Box 10.1). It would seem that many of the same themes that animated the consternation of the Auditors General 20 and 30 years ago persist.

The second set of challenges, derived from the widespread external criticism that the public service had grown out of control, has had a profound effect on the notion of the public service as a lofty and honourable calling, and has contributed to the strikingly low levels of morale in the public service. This impression was confirmed forcefully by the clerk of the Privy Council's warnings of a "quiet crisis" in the public service (discussed in chapter 9). The overall result was confusion, insecurity, hopelessness, anger, and frustration among many

BOX 10.1　The Sponsorship Program

After nearly losing the 1995 Quebec referendum, the federal government launched the Sponsorship Program. Its intent was simple—to raise the profile of the federal government in Quebec and promote Canadian federalism there. Prime Minister Chrétien thought spending federal money to promote cultural programs, the arts, and sporting events would help endear Quebecers to Canada. Between 1996 and 2003, some $250 million was spent in this way. However, it gradually emerged that at least some of the money was being misappropriated and that criminal fraud and corruption was at play.

Auditor General Sheila Fraser recommended that the RCMP investigate. She used a rather colourful turn of phrase in suggesting that federal public servants "broke every rule in the book" in their relationships with certain Quebec advertising firms with ties to the Liberal Party of Canada by funnelling contracts and money to them. In turn, some of these agencies funnelled the money both into their own pockets without delivering any substantial product, or into the coffers of the Liberal Party. In her 2004 Annual Report, the Auditor General announced that up to $100 million had been misspent in this way, and that the senior officials running the Sponsorship Program had essentially disregarded every rule for proper financial management of the funds.

As a result of the Auditor General's investigations, and the subsequent pressure from the opposition parties and media, Prime Minister Martin called a public inquiry into the matter in February 2004. Justice John Gomery was directed to head it up. The televised proceedings of the inquiry and the almost daily barrage of front-page headlines about the scandal caught the attention of the public, who witnessed, among other things, the unprecedented live testimony of a former and current prime minister as part of the inquiry. The Gomery Commission issued a two-volume report, a set of recommendations for future reform, and a three-volume set of research studies. But its legacy also includes contributing to the defeat of the Martin government and its replacement by the Harper Conservatives, although with only a minority government, in January 2006. In addition, several of the key actors in the scandal were tried and convicted in criminal court.

public servants. It has also meant that the management of the public sector has been undergoing a virtually continuous process of reform, at least since former prime minister John Diefenbaker unleashed the Glassco Commission on the world of Canadian public administration in 1960, with its admonition to "let the managers manage." Al Johnson served in the government of Saskatchewan and federally at the senior-most level, and by his reckoning there have been reforms concerning the effective and efficient management of the public service about every two to five years since the Glassco Commission.[6] This is in itself a factor contributing to the ennui felt in this once-respected institution.

Reform is not a factor exclusive to the Canadian public sector, of course. Much has been written and noted about similar trends in countries such as New Zealand, Great Britain, and Australia.[7] Contemporary reforms include borrowing "best practices" from the private sector; focusing on "clients" (instead of serving "citizens"); forming strategic alliances with the private sector and other levels of government; relying increasingly on volunteer and nonprofit organizations for the delivery and development of services; using new technologies to improve service delivery and communication with Canadians.

In Canada, the preoccupation with renewal has brought continual attitudinal, institutional, and structural changes throughout the 1980s and 1990s. But it was renewal within a new paradigm—one in which government was made to run more like business, and in which public servants were therefore expected to become more and more entrepreneurial in their work. And this renewal took place within a public service where managers were suffering "death by a thousand cuts." These "cuts" included a lack of vision and leadership among senior managers and political executives; a lack of autonomy among front-line managers; a rapid turnover of senior managers (for example, deputy ministers rotate their positions on average every 22 months); a "vertical solitude" between senior and middle managers in which trust and respect is lacking; a stale organizational culture; severe financial cutbacks; and other related problems.[8] As well as PS2000 and La Relève, several other initiatives were launched with varying degrees of success, to address these serious problems.[9] We cannot review them all here, but will consider some of the more important ones over the past 20 years. The point here is to give you a picture of the ongoing upheaval that has beset the public service, and that has in some ways only sustained the problems reforms were meant to address. In several cases you will note that it appears "the patient died, but the operation was a success."

PS2000

The current era of reform arguably has its roots as far back as the early 1960s with the Glassco Commission. It was also given impetus in the 1970s and 1980s with exercises like the **Productivity Improvement Program** started by the Trudeau government, and the **Ministerial Task Force on Program Review** and the **Increased Ministerial Authority and Accountability** exercise in the Mulroney years. **PS2000** followed on the heels of these initiatives. Surveys of public sector managers in 1986 and 1988 by two Ottawa University professors revealed striking differences from the attitudes of private sector managers.[10] Low morale was endemic, and the further down the hierarchy, the lower it was. Thus, there was a disjunction between the attitudes of senior managers and their subordinates. Moreover, the scores obtained from rating various attitudes tended to be lower in the public service than in the private sector. The results of the surveys provided the impetus for PS2000, announced by the prime minister in December 1989. It was led by the clerk of the Privy Council, Paul Tellier, with the intent that the public service would engage in a thorough self-examination, and "heal itself."

Ten task forces were set up under the leadership of deputy ministers, who were charged with finding ways to simplify personnel policies, to loosen central agency controls and increase the managerial freedom of department managers, and to increase efficiency and program delivery.[11] Thousands of public servants and others outside government were consulted, and a White Paper was issued, summarizing the findings of the exercise:

The white paper highlighted several challenges, including fast-paced economic and social changes, the growing complexity of policy issues, the need for a simpler and more transparent political process, the multiplication of controls, too many procedures hindering change, low morale among public servants, low public administration productivity, growing financial constraints, and the citizens' lack of confidence in the public service. These challenges begged for a more open relationship between Canadians and the public service, as well as for greater flexibility in government procedures. A change in bureaucratic culture was called for to pave the way to a culture based on consultation and service to the citizens.[12]

PS2000 suggested that each department should produce that 1990s business-school contrivance, the *mission statement*. Managers would delineate specific service-oriented goals, and embrace notions of participatory management. PS2000 called for department managers to consult broadly, not only with their own employees but also with citizens, to establish service standards and a more service-oriented culture. And organizational reform was achieved by flattening structures such that no more than three executive levels existed under each deputy minister. (Recall our discussion of span of control in chapter 3.) The goal here was to improve communication and to empower managers. Furthermore, it was suggested that the number of categories and levels within groups be reduced to simplify both personnel matters and decision making procedures. Finally, the government decided to reinforce the importance of new organizational models of service delivery, called Special Operating Agencies (SOA), which had been introduced earlier by the Treasury Board.

Ian Clark called the budget reforms resulting from PS2000, which allowed managers more control over their funds, its most important recommendation.[13] But as one observer of this process concluded, "[E]mpowerment of public servants was the cornerstone of Public Service 2000."[14] Whether it worked or not is the subject of some dispute. The Auditor General concluded in his 1993 report that while some progress had been made, there was still a feeling of skepticism among public service managers.[15] Political scientist Peter Aucoin echoed this sentiment in his assessment of PS2000.[16] But even the head of the public service at the time, Paul Tellier, whose job it was to develop and implement PS2000, described it as a failure. He claimed his plan was defeated by the "culture of caution" that permeates the public service, especially among managers.[17] In any event, many middle-level managers regarded it as fiat passed down from above: an executive-level exercise removed from the real day-to-day concerns of the middle-level manager. To them, it lacked legitimacy. By the end of 1993, PS2000 had faded from view as a reform program, supplanted by other, newer reform attempts and unable to recover.

Program Review

When the Liberals came to power on the heels of the demise of PS2000, a major restructuring of government had already begun. Chrétien's predecessor, Conservative Kim Campbell, had reduced the number of government ministries from 32 to 23. This necessitated building new management structures and consolidating the activities and operations of the old departments into the fewer new ones. Chrétien opted for a similar streamlined government, and created 24 ministries. He also dedicated his government to three main tasks: renewing federalism, reviewing all government programs, and reforming the public service. Significantly, he designated one of his Cabinet members as Minister for Public Sector Renewal. Marcel Massé was given this job, and proceeded to implement the new goals of public service management.[18] Of these three goals, the one that most interests us here is the **Program Review** (raised in earlier chapters).[19] The driving force behind this round of reforms was deficit reduction. During the 1993 election campaign, the Liberals had promised to reduce the deficit to 3 percent of GDP by 1997–1998. Beyond this, according to two observers of the public administration process, Program Review involved

clarifying the core responsibilities of the federal government and rebalancing the division of labour among the different levels of government and the private and not-for-profit sectors in the Canadian governance system, and equipping the federal public service with the tools necessary to improve the efficiency of public sector management.[20]

In spring 1994, all government departments and government agencies were given expenditure targets, and were expected to reform their programs to fit these targets. Six "tests" of Program Review were instituted, which all programs were to be measured against. These tests asked the following questions: Was there a public interest at stake? Was there a legitimate role for government in the issue? Was the federal government the right level of government jurisdictionally? Could the activities of the program be transferred to the private or voluntary sector? How could efficiency be improved? And was the program in question affordable?[21] In his February 1995 budget, then Finance Minister Paul Martin called for reductions in program spending of $29 billion over a three-year period, as well as the elimination of 45 000 civil servant jobs (14 percent of the entire public service). Transfer payments to the provinces for health, welfare, and post-secondary education were unilaterally reduced by $4.5 billion, although the provinces were given greater flexibility in how they were to spend whatever sums they did receive. Expenditure reductions varied across departments and agencies, with some having to cut as little as 5 percent from their budgets, and others having to cut as much as 60 percent. Only the Department of Indian Affairs and Northern Development was spared. The most deeply affected departments were Transport, Industry, and Natural Resources.[22] A Program Review Secretariat was created within the Privy Council Office to oversee these developments.

According to two analysts of Program Review, the exercise did not meet its expectations. "Our general diagnosis is that it has not been as effective as it might have been," they suggest. "It has undoubtedly triggered some expenditure reductions, and these are likely to continue." However, it did not fundamentally reform the governance of the system, which was a basic goal of Program Review.[23] Part of the problem lay in the fact that, as with PS2000, the Program Review was conducted largely by "insiders." And it was also a top-down process, for the most part. It should be obvious why it was difficult to get middle-level public servants to embrace reform that was not based on consultation, especially when it might have adversely affected the very programs that they administered. Moreover, those people outside government who would be most affected by the program cutbacks resulting from expenditure cutbacks were not consulted either. In the end, the results of Program Review were assessed by a senior public servant as falling far short of its ambitious goals:

From my perspective, the Federal Program Review, while producing dramatic results in terms of dollars or job cuts, was primarily a scramble for cash, and did not represent a "re-design" or "re-invention" of government as had been claimed by some. Federal Departments cut what could be cut, and little real attention was paid to the six starting criteria. There was little or no attempt made to examine the structure and process of government on a horizontal basis, to lessen the pressures which require departments to incur such enormous overhead costs (e.g., the massive impact of bloated Central Agencies and their multiple controls and demands on departments, the costs of the unwieldy, obsolete and ineffective personnel system—which every critic since Glassco has vainly tried to reform— and the unwieldy centralized and control-oriented financial and administrative systems).[24]

Yet another round of reforms ultimately failed to achieve the fundamental reorientation of the public service called for by the various crises confronting it. These reforms may even have worsened the situation, as morale among public servants plummeted and the malaise noted earlier deepened with each brilliant new scheme launched.

La Relève and the Leadership Network

The battering of public service morale led to the declaration of a "quiet crisis" by the clerk of the Privy Council, who launched **La Relève** as a means of plumbing the depths of public servant dissatisfaction and of finding solutions to renew the institution. The "quiet crisis" resulted from a number of factors: "the loss of talent through many years of downsizing; a demographic skew after years of limited recruitment; constant criticism of the public sector which seriously affected morale; many years of pay freezes; and increasing interest by the private sector in acquiring the skills possessed by public servants."[25] The term *La Relève* itself is an acronym for Leadership, Action, Renewal, Energy, Learning, Expertise, Values, and Excellence. Beginning in January 1997, more than 15 000 public servants from all departments and regions were consulted about their perceptions of working in the public service. Conferences were staged across the country, and parliamentarians were briefed on the La Relève Task Force findings, as were interested academics, professional associations, the provincial governments, foreign countries, and the media. The

La Relève Task Force identified the key challenges confronting the modern public service as globalization, new information technologies, and changing attitudes toward traditional hierarchical institutions. It urged a more responsible and participatory role for managers at all levels, and a "democratization" of the decision making process, which emphasized leadership across the public service.

One result of La Relève was the targeting of demographics, representativeness, and recruitment as three important contemporary challenges to the public service. Student work programs and co-operative education programs were instituted to address the demographic reality of a civil service in need of new blood. Departments and agencies made a concerted effort to renew the public service workforce through recruitment, training, and development initiatives. As well, the high level of departures by senior managers inspired an effort to renew the leadership cadre of the civil service. As we noted in chapter 9, campaigns to recruit university graduates and professionals with specialized skills were developed, along with ones to better train public servants and increase their mobility within the organization. This approach involved investing in experienced public servants and recruiting new ones. Career management planning, advisory services, and support for continuous learning were implemented across the public service. Then, in 1998, La Relève evolved into the Leadership Network, which was established as an agency reporting to the Cabinet Secretary and focusing on effective management training and education for assistant deputy ministers. The Leadership Network was eventually placed under the umbrella of the Canada Public Service Human Resources Management Agency (now Canada Public Service Agency) in 2003. While there is still a long way to go, Box 10.2 reveals that some career public servants do retain a latent and powerful sense of pride.

BOX 10.2 | **At Your Service with Pride**

The following article was written by a career public servant, Bob Chartier of Saskatoon, who works in the Department of Indian and Northern Affairs.

I am a public servant. In the 30 years of my career, there have been more times than I would care to admit when I was not very comfortable saying that out loud, much less in print. However, like everyone lately, my world has been rocked. The embassy bombings, the bombing of the federal building in Oklahoma City and the Sept. 11 images of public servants—police officers and firefighters—running towards the horror instead of away from it will stay with us forever. I have had to recognize that many terrorists target governments and, as we know, public servants are the front line of governance.

For years, public servants struggled with a "poor cousin" image in the workplace. It was insinuated that the brightest and the best would always go into the private sector. The rest of us, for many different reasons, made the decision to spend our lives teaching your kids, hooking up your intravenous, protecting your border, checking the maintenance record on the aircraft taking you to Cancun and responding to 911 calls.

Oh, we heard your snickers over the years.

We have heard your comments about road crews leaning on their shovels, striking nurses, mindless clerks processing paper, lazy teachers and cops in doughnut shops. And this was the tame stuff. I believe it's time to rethink our views on public service. First of all, understand that we do the things that no one else really wants to do and that there is no real money in it. Try to buy police services from a street vendor. What price would the market pay to find an illegal immigrant? Ask a major private-sector company to write a new fair-trade policy. Try to shop around for a good deal on a passport.

The private-enterprise capitalist system is fine by me. It is adept at doing those things it is supposed to do, but it can't do it all. When it comes to writing good policy on parole violations, we don't freelance the contract; we ask a public servant with a weighty academic background, a wealth of experience and an ear to the street to compose it. When we need protection, high standards in our goods, food and water, we again look to the public servant. Whoa, let's stop right there. On that water thing. You're right. We have Walkerton and North Battleford to consider. I grew up in North Battleford and, as a working government guy, I was appalled that, for decades, city workers there drew drinking water a kilometre downstream from the spot they dumped the sewage. Let's be honest. Public servants make mistakes. Big ones, little ones and some really stupid ones. But so does the private sector. Our trouble, as public servants, is that our mistakes can cause a lot more grief.

It is true, we are notorious for our red tape, our obsession with paper and our slowness. But we are working really hard. We can and will be just as fast, as effective and as quality-minded as the private sector, even more. We have many masters, however, and sometimes when we try to cut the red tape we get beat up for what is then called a lack of accountability. It's always hard for us to know whom we really serve—politicians or citizens. But I believe we can serve both and do it with accountability and effectiveness.

So what have we got here? Well, we have jobs that have no market value. We are under constant public scrutiny. We get paid what citizens, not the market, think we are worth and we provide always essential but often hidden services. And most of us really like our work. We love your kids, we fell for you in the intensive-care unit, we want to find the bad guys and we are driven to develop policy that reflects Canadian values.

Public servants may now feel even more like a target for evil, but they will go to work every day. They will be here for us, the first to run into the trouble and to lead in the rebuilding. The war on terrorism will not be fought in the market, it will be defended at the border, in policy making decisions on privacy and in the day by day readiness of emergency workers. And that is why I serve the public, with pride.

Source: *Maclean's*, 115, 2 (January 14, 2002): 9.

The Policy Research Initiative (PRI)

One of government's major deficiencies, it became evident, was in its capacity to formulate and implement policy. The cutbacks of the 1990s had gutted many policy shops and cost many policy analysts their jobs. Two Deputy Ministers Task Forces were constituted to investigate and report on the government's policy capacity.[26] Therefore, in 1996 the government launched the Policy Review Committee, which morphed into the Policy Research Initiative (PRI), whose mandate was to strengthen the government's policy research capacity. According to its mandate,

The federal government requires a strong knowledge base and policy capacity to meet the increasingly complex challenges facing Canada. To respond to this need, the Policy Research Initiative conducts research in support of the Government of Canada's medium term agenda. Its core mandate is to advance research on emerging horizontal issues, and to ensure the effective transfer of acquired knowledge to policy-makers.[27]

Currently, the PRI conducts independent policy research projects, is attached to Human Resources and Social Development Canada (HRSDC), and receives guidance from a Deputy Minister Steering Committee.

The Public Service Modernization Act

As we noted in chapter 9, in 2001 the government promised in its Speech from the Throne yet another set of reforms. It created a Task Force on Modernizing Human Resources Management, which recommended a modern framework for human resources management. The task force assessed reforms in other countries, such as Australia, the U.K., and New Zealand. Legislation to modernize the public service was subsequently introduced in 2003. The Public Service Modernization Act (PMSA) (also discussed in chapter 9) created a new Public Service Employment Act and a new Public Service Labour Relations Act, as well as amending other pieces of legislation. According to two theorists of public administration, the PSMA aims to provide:

(a) increased flexibility in staffing and managing people with safeguards to continue a merit-oriented, and politically neutral public service; (b) cooperative labour-management relations; (c) a coherent training and learning programme to meet the professional development and corporate needs of the government; and (d) a clear role and strengthened accountability for the government institutions and individuals responsible for managing the public service.[28]

In addition, a number of other reports and initiatives came together in the early twenty-first century to continue with the reform agenda in public administration. The Auditor General's report of 2000 found a lack of coordination in government appointment practices. The Auditor General's report of 2003 exposed the issues that ultimately led to the sponsorship and advertising contracts inquiry known as the Gomery Commission. The House of Commons Standing Committee on Public Accounts report in December, 2001, expressed concern about the management of human resources in the public service. And the annual reports of the Public Service Commission as well as the clerk of the Privy Council repeatedly spoke to the need for increased flexibility in managing human resources as well as simplifying processes therein. But few of these had the dramatic impact of the Commission of Inquiry into the Sponsorship Program and Advertising Activities, also known as the Gomery Commission.

The Gomery Commission

While in itself the Gomery Commission was not a reform per se, it nonetheless had considerable influence on the Harper government's decision to make reform of the accountability regime a centrepiece of its agenda. We examine Harper's Federal Accountability Act in more depth in chapter 12. Here we will simply highlight the major areas that the Gomery Commission suggested needed attention by the government and that contributed to the climate of reform by shifting more attention to the issue of accountability.

On February 19, 2004, an Order in Council was issued defining the terms of reference for the Commission of Inquiry into the Sponsorship Program and Advertising Activities. Mr. Justice John H. Gomery was named Commissioner. According to the terms of reference, the Commission was given a double mandate. The first required the Commission to investigate and report on questions raised, directly or indirectly, by chapters 3 and 4 of the 2003 Report of the Auditor General of Canada. The second mandate called for recommendations to the Government of Canada, based upon the Commission's factual findings, to prevent mismanagement of sponsorship programs and advertising activities in the future.

Justice Gomery released two reports on the Sponsorship Program, on November 1, 2005, and February 6, 2006.[29] The Commission identified the need to rebalance power in Parliament by limiting the power of the prime minister and Cabinet while enhancing the power of ordinary MPs and parliamentary committees. If this could be achieved, the report argued, the elected legislature could better hold the government to account, consonant with the principle of responsible government. Among the 19 recommendations were the following:

- increased funding for parliamentary committees;
- a public service charter entrenched in law;
- substantially increased funding for the Public Accounts Committee for more research personnel, legal and administrative staff, and experts as needed;
- a clear and unequivocal statement delineating the responsibilities and accountabilities of ministers and public servants;
- an open and competitive process for the selection of deputy ministers, with appointments to terms of at least three years, with the expectation that the posting would normally last at least five years.[30]

While the Gomery Commission has been influential in some ways, it is the broader package and general climate of reform that will likely have more lasting significance. The early results of these various initiatives suggest that a corner may have been turned, and that the public service is emerging from its darkest days. What is less clear is whether this corner has been turned as a result of reforms associated with the NPM generally, or because of the new fiscal realities of balanced budgets and reduced government debt, or because of reduced public tolerance for mismanagement, or for some combination of these and other reasons. For now it may be worth noting that in the absence of financial resources, public sector renewal appears to be a self-defeating exercise, since it mainly requires self-inflicted denigration of the institution in the face of hostile external attacks. However, if the rationale for public sector reform is fiscal constraint, and that rationale is removed, we can conclude that the future of the public service looks brighter now than it has for a long time. We turn now to a consideration of financial management.

Financial Management

Financial management of an enterprise that generates and spends billions of dollars of taxpayers' money is no small task. The complexities of budgeting have spawned an extensive literature dedicated to developing the best possible system for the management of the public's fiscal resources. We will consider these developments briefly in historical perspective before turning to the nuts and bolts of public sector financial management, as it is currently practised. Keep in mind, though, that financial management is mainly about "who gets what" from government and society.

The State and Economy

The rise of a new class of "mandarins" in the post-war years (as noted in chapter 9) coincided with and made possible a huge expansion of the role of the state in Canada. While the state in Canada has always had some role in the economic life of the nation (see chapter 1), in the 1930s and 1940s the federal government shifted its attention from such things as tariffs and transportation—the pillars of Canada's "national policy" of the late-nineteenth century—to new responsibilities. Monetary policy and the construction of a new welfare state on the basis of Keynesian theory emerged as what some observers called a "new national policy." The federal government consequently expanded its role into areas where it had previously feared to tread. The crises of the Great Depression in the 1930s and the Second World War in the 1940s accelerated this process, with profound consequences for the management of the federal public service:

As a result, by 1945 the federal civil service had swollen to 115 000 employees, compared to the 10 000 estimated in 1896. The wages alone for these government employees represented a sum five times larger than the total government budget 50 years earlier. The total 1945 budget was $5.25 billion, compared to $36 million in 1896. The range of federal government activities had expanded to include such responsibilities as old-age pensions, unemployment insurance, family allowances, subsidized housing and other social policies, as well as a new conception of the federal government's role in economic management.[31]

The implications for the financial management of the government's business were huge. The result has been a dramatic growth in government spending until recently. Donald Savoie sums up the trend in the following way:[32] he points out that the total federal government budgetary spending in 1920–1921 was $476 million. This figure actually dropped in 1923–1924 to $352 million. But from then on it gradually climbed higher. In 1939, total expenditures were $533 million. By 1950–1951, they had risen to $2.4 billion; in 1960–1961, they reached $6.7 billion; in 1970–1971, they were $15.3 billion; in 1980–1981, $62 billion; in 1983–1984, $96.6 billion; and in 1987–1988, total government expenditures reached $122.5 billion. Strikingly, after more than a decade of restructuring, total expenditures climbed to $175.2 billion by 2000–2001, and in 2006–2007, they sat at $205 billion.

These numbers are difficult to contemplate; they are abstractions that are hard to conceptualize. So look at them this way: the total value of the goods and services produced by a country is referred to as its Gross Domestic Product (GDP). If we look at the percentage of GDP accounted for by government, we get another perspective on the growth of the state. In 1930–1931, federal government expenditures represented 6.8 percent of GDP. They represented 16 percent of GDP by 1940–1941, levelled off to 12.8 percent in 1950–1951, reached 17.6 percent in 1960–1961, 21 percent in 1976–1977, 23.6 percent in 1982–1983, and 23 percent in 1986–1987. In the 1990s and early 2000s expenditures hovered around 12–13 percent, which suggests that the federal government has always been and still is a key player in the economy (see Figures 10.1 and 10.2).

FIGURE 10.1   Government Expenditures as a Percentage of GDP

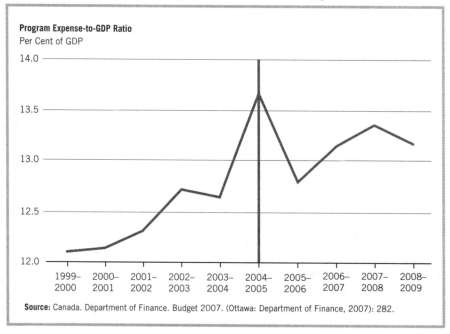

Source: Canada. Department of Finance. Budget 2007. (Ottawa: Department of Finance, 2007): 282.

FIGURE 10.2   Government Revenues as a Percentage of GDP

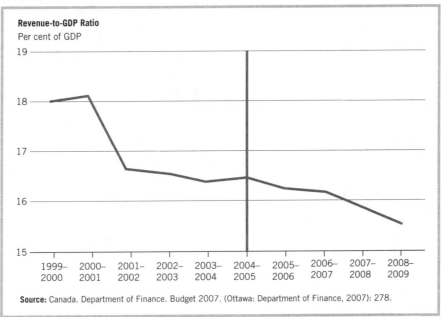

Source: Canada. Department of Finance. Budget 2007. (Ottawa: Department of Finance, 2007): 278.

The issue of raising and spending money can usefully be conceptualized by thinking about some government departments as "savers" and others as "spenders." The key "savers" are the Department of Finance and the Treasury Board, and the Privy Council Office also plays an important part. The spenders are virtually all the other departments. The two types are engaged in a constant struggle. Each has its own set of clients, both within government and out in the broader society, pressuring the government to take action—or not to take action; each has its champions and villains within Cabinet, Parliament, interest groups, the media, and the public. For example, the Ministry of Agriculture, a "spender" department, wants government to dedicate sufficient resources to agricultural interests in Canada in order to guarantee the ongoing viability and vitality of this sector of the economy. The ministry is pressured by the farming community, manufacturers of farm equipment, chemical, pesticide, and herbicide makers, rural Canadians, and others to make sure that agricultural ways of life are protected and promoted. The Finance Department, on the other hand, is chief among the "saver" departments. It has ultimate responsibility for the government's overall fiscal health, and keeps a firm hand on the purse strings. It is constantly pressured by "spender" departments, such as Agriculture, to reapportion the government pie. But it is simultaneously pressured by other actors, as well: the big business community might be asking for tax breaks; organized interests and think tanks might be producing studies showing the importance of reducing the debt; the Auditor General may be demanding an end to the government's profligate ways. The Finance Department bears the brunt of all these and countless other pressures in managing the government's financial resources. Overall, for many years it seemed as though the "spenders" were winning the battle, if not the war. But through the 1980s and 1990s, the "savers" launched a forceful counteroffensive, resulting in significant downsizing and a deliberate and concerted effort to wrestle the deficit and debt to the ground. Moreover, there was an increased emphasis on improving the various financial controls and reporting mechanisms used to oversee the entire government budgetary process. Now, however, the spenders have re-emerged in this era of surpluses.[33] The key question remains, though, of how best to design and implement controls and mechanisms for financial management. As two observers put it, "[I]ndeed, the authorities granted to governments by legislatures to collect and expend public funds, and the obligations to report on the use of these funds, are at the heart of parliamentary governance and democracy."[34]

Budgeting involves many actors and institutions, making it a highly complex exercise. Parliament, Cabinet, departments, central agencies, and the Auditor General are key players within government. The media and interest groups have historically been keen observers of the process, often acting as watchdogs to uncover government malfeasance, while ordinary citizens are increasingly being consulted on the budget-making exercise that dominates the life of governments—an exercise that was once closed, secretive, and exclusive to a handful of mandarins and the finance minister. Nonetheless, there are elements of the contemporary budgetary process that political scientist Geoffrey Hale calls "managed fiscal illusion," originating in the Chrétien years. He states:

Having inherited a fiscal regime in which Finance officials always under-estimated deficits and Finance ministers usually over-promised results, the Martin-era Finance Department always kept a surplus of fiscal cushions in stock. Growth rates were estimated conservatively. Spending projections—particularly for Employment Insurance—were often padded. Estimates of interest rates were usually pessimistic. And if all else failed, Martin maintained a $3 billion Contingency Reserve against unanticipated economic shocks.[35]

The most recent important reforms to the budgeting process can be summed up in three initiatives: the Expenditure Management System (EMS); departmental business plans; and improved reporting to Parliament. At the root of the system we are about to explore is one fundamental principle, which we briefly looked at in earlier chapters: responsible government. At the end of the day, the government is held responsible by Parliament for its actions to the citizens of the country. In particular, the government is held responsible for its handling of the taxpayers' money, and it can only hold power as long as it demonstrates that it has acted reasonably and responsibly in managing those monies.

Consider the organizational features of government financial management that underpin this theory. At Confederation in 1867, the statutory basis of financial management was established in the BNA Act, section 102, which gives Parliament the right to control public money, and which also calls for the creation of a single consolidated revenue fund to receive all money belonging to Canada. As well, authority to pay money out of the consolidated revenue fund is given to Parliament in section 106. Thus, it is Parliament that formally and constitutionally is responsible for approving the raising and spending of public money. Donald Savoie explains the importance of this point:

Several principles underpin Parliament's role in the budget process. The first is that the government—or the executive—can have no revenue which is not sanctioned by Parliament, and the second is that the government can make no expenditures except those approved by Parliament. In addition, Parliament does not grant a permanent right to spend, so that the government must submit a new budget every year. Thus funds allocated by Parliament but not spent must lapse. Detailed spending plans are submitted annually in the form of spending "estimates." The government must also account to Parliament for its management of public moneys, both revenues and expenditures.[36]

Once again, though, we should note that there is a disjuncture between theory and practice. In the real world of Canadian politics, control over the public purse is in the hands of the executive (that is, the Cabinet). Because of the practice of party discipline, the executive receives support for its budgetary plans virtually automatically. So, in reality, the role played by Parliament is more one of "watchdog," "legitimating" the government's financial plans, rather than setting them. In times of minority government, Parliament's role may be enhanced since the executive often must bargain with one or more of the opposition parties to support the budget. In return, those parties may be able to negotiate out of the budget those items they find most objectionable, or have included items close to their own hearts, as did the NDP under Jack Layton in the 2005 Liberal budget.

Canadians are apprised of the state of their finances through four major reports that are made annually to Parliament. The most visible and politically significant of these is the budget by the minister of finance, "which includes a comprehensive financial statement, including a forecast of financial requirements for government operations for the forthcoming year, and the ways and means proposed by the government to achieve its multiple objectives."[37] The budget speech delivered by the minister of finance each year has been described as "the focal point of the federal government's efforts to define and mobilize public support for its fiscal and economic agenda. As such, it is an opportunity for the federal government to define its priorities, exercise leadership, and obtain legal and political support for its policies, through both the formal processes of Parliament and direct appeals for public support."[38] Second, the government annually provides estimates to inform Parliament of its spending plans for the coming year. The estimates provide the basis for the legislation that Parliament passes to authorize government spending. Third, every month in the *Canada Gazette*, a Statement of Financial Operations is published. This provides detailed information on financial transactions for the previous month, as well as a running total for the year. Finally, the government's annual audited financial statements are found in the Public Accounts of Canada, presented to Parliament by the president of the Treasury Board on behalf of the government, although they are prepared under the direction of the Treasury Board president and the minister of finance by the Receiver General of Canada. The reports are also presented to the Auditor General, who reviews them and presents to Parliament his or her independent assessment of the management of Canada's finances. In turn, the Auditor General's Report becomes part of the Public Accounts of Canada. These are reviewed by a parliamentary committee called the Standing Committee on Public Accounts, which also reports to Parliament.

This brief sketch only scratches the surface of the process, which, as you can see, is complex and involves many important actors. Before taking a more in-depth look at the process in the context of the annual budgetary timetable, it will be useful to review the major trends in reporting and control of the public purse. We briefly introduced the **Planning, Programming, Budgeting System (PPBS)** in chapter 8. Here we expand on it and other subsequent budgeting systems that have come and gone over the years in Ottawa.

Managing Government Fiscal Resources

As with many recent reform developments, our discussion of financial control systems begins with the Glassco Commission, which set the stage for reform of financial management systems and improved reporting to Parliament; it continues to influence developments in this area to this day. Prior to Glassco, there was an emphasis on accountability in terms of ensuring accuracy and probity in raising and spending money. And this is still true. But less attention used to be paid to the budget as a tool of effective management, planning, and evaluation. And the budget was not considered a tool of macro-economic management of the Canadian economy until after the rise of Keynesianism. Typically, control of the budget was in the hands of the Department of Finance. Other departments would negotiate with Finance over the increased dollars they would receive to run their programs after accounting for inflation or the establishment of new programs. The process was incremental, with a little bit added each year, and with little attention paid to the cumulative impact of the many decisions that went into the annual budget.

The key problem that Glassco identified in financial management was the practice of setting departmental (and hence governmental) budgets by approving transactions before they occurred. This meant that individual managers would offer their best "guesstimate" of how much money they would need to offer services and run programs for the upcoming fiscal year. This technique, besides not being particularly systematic, had the effect of putting upward pressure on the government's overall expenditures. Few managers would admit to needing fewer resources than in previous years, since this might imply that their program or service was of diminishing importance, and therefore disposable. Moreover, this system monopolized power over the government's overall financial resources, and managers had little opportunity to see the "big picture" of governmental budgeting.

So, in this context, Glassco's rallying cry of "let the managers manage" meant increasing managers' authority as well as their responsibility and accountability. The Glassco Commission suggested introducing methods by which the value and efficiency of expenditures could be measured (see chapter 8), and introducing a five-year budgetary planning cycle. Shortly thereafter, in 1966, the Treasury

Board was separated from the Department of Finance. It was given its own minister and department, and took over control of budget, personnel, and administrative policy.

By the 1970s, after 30 years, economic growth had slowed. The new challenge was to figure out how to do more with less: that is, how to provide the same or even higher levels of service with less and less funding. Flattened tax revenues, a decline in business confidence and investment, new overseas competition in sectors of the economy that Canada had traditionally been strong in—all combined to exert pressure on the state's ability to carry on "business as usual." As well, the tax burden had gradually shifted, so that corporations were now paying a smaller proportion of the overall burden while individuals were paying a greater one. The government's extensive use of tax breaks and tax expenditures began to catch up with it. The positivist, activist vision of the Canadian state eroded as taxpayers increasingly came to see many government programs as wasteful, although this did not necessarily stop them from demanding that services still be provided.

As a result, and following from Glassco, a veritable alphabet soup of decision-making systems was introduced into financial management. The thrust of these systems was to introduce rationality, planning, and advanced management techniques into the process. The first step along this path was to change the nature of expenditure requests by managers. In the past, such requests had been based on a rudimentary **line-item method of budgeting**, which simply involves listing the main objects of expenditure (e.g., How many paper clips does the department need? How much will be paid out in salaries? How much does it cost to rent office space?). Little or no attempt was made to evaluate the effectiveness of these expenditures. But henceforth, a manager would be expected to produce formal statements outlining his department's objectives, and how he planned to systematically evaluate the effectiveness of the programs the department administered. The Planning, Programming, Budgeting System (PPBS) was the first attempt to reorganize financial management in this way.

PPBS was based on the budgeting techniques in vogue in the United States, and was adopted by the Treasury Board in 1969. It sought to provide a framework for budgeting that went beyond line-item budgeting to analyze new initiatives and develop longer-range plans to meet departmental and governmental objectives. This became known as **program budgeting**. There were also to be ongoing assessments of the impact of programs, and of whether they met the government's stated goals and objectives in the most efficient way. Also, "an important objective was to improve policy analysis, program evaluation, and performance measurement throughout the public service in order to better hold department managers to account and to better inform decision making and resource allocation."[39] PPBS introduced the idea of the "A" budget, the "B" budget, and the "X" budget into each department. Managers would design the "A" budget to cover the costs of ongoing programs. The "B" budget was intended for new or expanded programs. And the "X" budget was meant to cover low-priority items that might be reduced or eliminated.

But while the beauty of PPBS was its rational basis, its fatal flaw was the added bureaucracy required to administer it. Copious amounts of paperwork and reporting were necessary to keep it afloat, and gradually the Cabinet decision making process it was supposed to support was swamped. Moreover, the introduction of PPBS coincided with a serious downturn in the Canadian economy, and the resulting mishmash of financial management resulted in the commissioning of yet another inquiry to sort out the mess. The Lambert Commission (the Royal Commission on Financial Management and Accountability) was struck in 1976 to investigate standards for financial management and accountability. Even before the commission reported, however, the government created the position of Comptroller General to do just that. While most of the Lambert Commission's recommendations were initially ignored by the government, it did contribute to the general climate that suggested a need for improved financial management.

In fact, the next set of reforms actually resembled several of the suggestions put forth by Lambert. In 1979, the Conservative government of Joe Clark introduced a new system called the **Policy and Expenditure Management System (PEMS)**.[40] While Clark's government lasted only nine months in office, his innovations were adopted by the successive Trudeau administration. The goal of PEMS was similar to those of many earlier reforms: it improved ministerial control over financial management in the area of priority setting and allowed ministers to more easily appraise both the medium- and long-term picture of policy development and financial management. Moreover, PEMS was meant to promote a more collegial decision making process in Cabinet with respect to allocating fiscal resources across the government. An "envelope" system was introduced regarding expenditures, in which ministers were figuratively handed an envelope with a set amount of cash in it, and expected to make their department's spending fit the amount; cabinet committees determined how much went into each departmental envelope.[41] To assist them in this work, departments were required to submit Strategic Overviews of their activities, as well as Multi-Year Operational Plans.

Through the 1980s, piecemeal changes were made to PEMS, including a shift away from the envelope system in favour of *reference levels* for departments, a more flexible way of apportioning resources. In addition, the delivery of the minister of finance's annual budget was brought in line with the annual expenditure cycle (usually in February). And consultations with groups outside government became a regular feature of the budgetary process, in contrast to the highly secretive methods of the past. Once again, however, the excessive bureaucratic and administrative work required to keep PEMS alive proved daunting. Gradually, it too fell into disrepute, particularly as the problems of growing deficits and debt continued to bedevil the government, notwithstanding the introduction of these rational planning and financial management techniques.[42] As a result, PEMS gave way to **EMS**—the **Expenditure Management System**—in January 1995.

Under EMS, there was a heavy emphasis on "getting government right," which had become the buzz-phrase of the day. Where budgeting was concerned, this meant focusing on efficiency, and EMS introduced the practice of having departments produce annual **business plans**. These were documents based on a private sector model of reporting that would replace the Multi-Year Operational Plans introduced under PEMS. Business plans, delivered to the Treasury Board by each department in the fall of each year, were meant to show how departments planned to improve or restructure programs—increasingly referred to now as *lines of service*—over a three-year period. The business plans were also intended to signal ways in which departments could adjust their activities to promote efficiencies and improvements in services to clients, as well as measure performance.[43] The business planning process was introduced by the Treasury Board Secretariat as part of an initiative called "Managing for Results."

An increased emphasis was also placed on "results-based" reporting and evaluation. To place these developments in the context of the overall budget system, it is necessary to go back to the observation above, that Parliament alone can authorize the spending and raising of money, which it does in the Estimates. The Estimates are the means by which the government seeks Parliament's permission to access the Consolidated Revenue Fund. The Estimates comprise three parts: Part I summarizes the government's expenditure plans for the year, while Part II shows the amounts that the government requires for specific votes (that is, for each department or agency). But it was Part III of the Estimates that contained the most detailed information regarding each department's expenditure requirements. Part III was added to the Estimates in 1981, as a result of the reforms made during the PEMS era, and was influenced in its design and presentation by the Office of the Comptroller General. Unfortunately, the Estimates were often so convoluted and difficult to read that they were of little use as accountability mechanisms for Parliament. Thus, they have been simplified through the Business Plan format to make it easier for Parliament to hold the government accountable. Since 2005, the Estimates have also set out results as well as simply reporting spending by departments. Concerted efforts have also been made to improve the reporting functions of departments, and to improve performance measurement and evaluation, through EMS. Figure 10.3 shows the objectives, inputs, and players in the EMS.

In her 2006 Annual Report, the Auditor General underscored the importance of EMS by saying,

The EMS is at the heart of the operation of government. It touches everything the government does, since all government activities involve spending. A system that works well promotes efficient, responsive, and accountable government. Without a good system, nothing departments and agencies do individually will result in sound overall management of government spending. An effective EMS is essential to getting the results the government wants and to being accountable to Canadians for what is done on their behalf.[44]

Alas, as with all previous financial management systems, EMS, too, has spawned its own sets of problems. These were recognized when, in 2006, the government announced it was reviewing the EMS. The government is wrestling with the linkage (or lack thereof) between the stated goals of budgeting and of service to citizens through improved management of their resources, as allocated through the bud-

FIGURE 10.3   The Main Objectives, Inputs, and Players of the Expenditure
Management System

Basic Objectives	Main Inputs	Key Players
Overall fiscal control	• Fiscal strategy • Spending and revenue forecasts • Budget preparation	• The Cabinet • The Department of Finance
Efficient allocation of resources	• Priority setting • Policy development • New spending approvals • Production of Estimates	• The Cabinet • The Privy Council Office • The Department of Finance • The Treasury Board and its Secretariat • The departments
Operational efficiency	• Operational planning • Financial management and controls • Performance monitoring and measurement	• The Treasury Board and its Secretariat • The departments
Parliamentary control	• Examination and approval of the Estimates • Review of Public Accounts and program performance	• The House of Commons • Parliamentary committees • The Auditor General

Source: Canada. Auditor General of Canada. Report of the Auditor General of Canada to the House of Commons: An Overview of the Federal Government's Expenditure Management System. **www.oag-bvg.gc.ca/domino/reports.nsf/html/ 20061100xe01.html** Accessed June 24, 2007.

getary process. In part this concern is connected to the ongoing problem of declining citizen trust in government (as with the sponsorship and other scandals) as much as to the need to improve on-the-ground service provision. Therefore, government is reviewing roles and responsibilities of key actors, including the central agencies as well as the managers of service delivery, in an attempt to close the gap between expectations and deliverables. So, for instance, the Treasury Board initiated a review of EMS, focusing on accountability and on its role as an oversight body aimed at cultivating management excellence. To this end, performance measurement is receiving intensified attention, including an annual assessment of the role of deputy ministers in the financial management pantheon. The Expenditure Management Information System (EMIS) project is a key part of this ongoing process.

In its 2006 budget, the government announced it would seek to strengthen the EMS, reallocate resources to new priorities, implement cyclical departmental and horizontal program reviews, and link planning and results management. According to the Treasury Board, "as of March 2004, EMIS' objectives included providing the Government's Budget Office and Management Board with the information and analytical tools needed to deliver on its stewardship functions. The overall objective is to create an environment that supports the integration of analysis of information for effective expenditure management decisions."[45]

When EMS was instituted, the government was fixated on eliminating the deficit, which led to another set of concerns. In the words of the Auditor General,

The current Expenditure Management System was designed in the mid-1990s when, facing budget deficits, the government was trying to reduce its spending. Departments and agencies had to operate in a fiscal environment that restricted new funding as much as possible. However, a system suited to times of fiscal restraint is not necessarily the best one for periods of fiscal abundance—for example, a budget surplus. Changes in the scale and nature of government spending will call for corresponding changes in how spending is managed.[46]

In other words, questions about value-for-money had been put on the back burner while questions about expenditure reduction held everyone's attention. But while officials busily examined their A-base budgets each year, looking for waste and duplication to eliminate, they neglected the quality of the implementation of programs and services. Cabinet committee activity reflected this as well. Ministers were so preoccupied with deficits that they paid little attention to results. Subsequently, when surpluses emerged, cabinet was quite conditioned to simply seek to add new spending without really looking at existing programs in terms of value-for-money or results.

In short, the service delivery oversight role had been neglected. As this reality dawned, a new effort developed to improve oversight of service delivery. Service improvement initiatives were launched, and emphasis was placed on looking more critically at the so-called "back-office" functions of units within departments: that is, on budgets and personnel practices. In addition, attention began to be given over to examining the complex administrative systems that had been allowed to develop while everyone was fixated on deficits. For example, it was found that there were over 100 separate finance and human resources systems, which could be reduced to just 7 finance and 4 HR systems. Despite these advances, however, the systems, though fewer in number, could not easily talk to one another. For instance, pay offices in different departments were, in some instances, using different software systems, so managers could not easily share data.

In addition, when EMS was examined closely, it became apparent that there needed to be an improved balance between following the rules and exercising discretion, and between oversight and flexibility. The federal government decided that the litmus test would be **risk management**. Senior public servants noticed that as a consequence of the various scandals rocking government citizens had become quite risk-averse. So, too, had public servants. But heeding the growing number of rules designed to prevent abuse meant slowdowns and reductions in efficiency as well as muddled, overly bureaucratized accountability systems. Therefore, there had been a gradual loss of innovation, creativity, and imaginative initiatives on the part of the public service. So the government sought to overcome these problems by encouraging a more risk-taking culture that empowered managers within a framework of careful articulated values.[47] The Management Accountability Framework (discussed in chapter 9) was a part of this process. The "web of rules" that existed was reduced, and a rationale was constructed against which rules could be measured. For example, rules had to meet the following objectives: match the values of the public service, allow managers to manage risk to the operations of their departments, and promote consistent management across the whole of government. To accomplish these objectives, the oversight role had to be taken away from central agencies and returned to departments. For instance, the Treasury Board reduced its number of auditors from 900 to 400, as audit functions were decentralized and oversight of fiscal matters was allowed to take place within departments themselves. Meanwhile, the Treasury Board undertook to systematically review the over 180 sets of rules regarding oversight and accountability in an effort to reduce them to under 45. Deputy ministers were given more tools to manage oversight within their own departments, rather than having central agencies looking over their shoulders.

The grants and contributions program is a case in point. The rules regarding applications and reporting for federal grants had become so cumbersome that many small agencies and individuals simply could not cope with them administratively. It made little sense to offer funding for a social program if the agencies that could deliver the program were too intimidated by the mountain of forms and mid-term and annual reporting requirements of the application process. And those that could, often found their organizations bogged down in "administrivia" rather than program and service provision. As a consequence of this problem, the government set up a Blue Ribbon Panel, which reported on ways to streamline and improve the grants and contributions program.

Government also tackled the risk management issue by devising a grid of low, medium, and high-risk activities to help determine those situations where central agency intervention was desirable. As a result, the "bottom line" has become the process of linking existing spending to new spending with an eye on outcomes and results in a culture of risk management and service to citizens.

Finally, the Auditor General identified one other growing concern with EMS. While the Main Estimates support the government's annual request to Parliament for authorization to spend money, there are also what are called Supplementary Estimates, which are usually presented in the fall and again toward the end of the fiscal year. The issue is that since the late 1990s, the proportion of spending proposals made through these Supplementary Estimates, rather than through the Main Estimates, has increased significantly. Supplementary Estimates are necessary in certain circumstances, since the government cannot always forecast when it might need additional funds for some discrete, unforeseen circumstance. But the Auditor General noted with concern "their routine use for spending that could be proposed in the Main Estimates. What is troubling about the increased reliance on Supplementary Estimates is that it limits parliamentarians' opportunity to examine the full range of proposed government spending." In addition, she said, "I am also concerned about the approval of Supplementary Estimates late in the fiscal year. Departments start to spend on programs and initiatives and charge the expenditures against the existing appropriations by 'cash managing' until the Supplementary Estimates are approved. This puts program spending at risk, because Parliament could reduce or reject the Supplementary Estimates. It also undermines parliamentary control of government spending because the money is spent before Parliament has examined and approved the spending proposal."[48] In other words, the very principle of responsible government was subtly being undermined by the increased resorting to Supplementary Estimates.

Clearly, EMS—and the budgetary process in general—is a complex system that is a challenge to understand. Perhaps a look at the day-to-day process of budget making and the various roles by the key actors in that process will help clarify this most important aspect of public administration. To this end, we now turn to an examination of the budgetary cycle as it unfolds within the EMS framework.

The Budgetary Cycle

The budget has been described as "a financial expression of the government's priorities, policies and plans."[49] Historically, the budget was released after the presentation of the Main Estimates, which were the documents that announced the government's detailed spending plans. The budget, therefore, focused on the measures needed to fund the government's plans, or the "ways and means," like taxes and other measures. But more recently the budget has evolved into the central tool for announcing new spending measures as well as tax measures. The budget itself has no legal authority. Although measures announced in the budget may come into effect immediately, formally speaking they must be presented to Parliament as legislative proposals before they can become law.

It may appear that the central focus of the budget process is on the minister of finance when he or she delivers the budget speech to the House of Commons. And this is undoubtedly a key moment in the life of the government. But it is important to understand that the budget, and financial management in general, go on throughout the year, as Figure 10.4 reveals. We outline the cycle and the key actors within EMS following.[50]

In the spring, from March to June, the Cabinet conducts strategy sessions that examine the results of the last budget, determining priorities largely on the basis of advice received from the Cabinet policy committees. Then, in the summer, Cabinet uses this information to guide the process of determining and defining reallocation and policy options for the consultation process that will take place in the fall. The Cabinet policy committees oversee the design and implementation of new initiatives announced in the previous budget, and decide on new policy proposals in response to the strategic directions laid out by Cabinet. Meanwhile, departments and agencies prepare their multi-year business plans based on resources allocated in the previous budget. Their goal is to figure out how to match up their business plans and programs within available

FIGURE 10.4   The Expenditure Management System

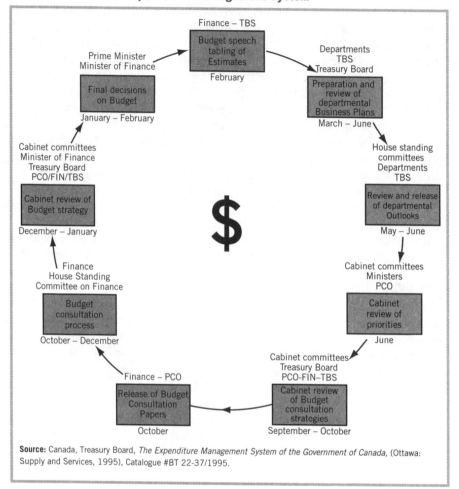

Source: Canada, Treasury Board, *The Expenditure Management System of the Government of Canada,* (Ottawa: Supply and Services, 1995), Catalogue #BT 22-37/1995.

resources. At this time, departments also release documents called Outlooks on Program Priorities and Expenditures for review by the standing committees.

The Treasury Board reviews departmental business plans to ensure that departments are sticking to budget targets, and to assess the implications of these plans on the government overall. It also identifies areas where it feels intervention or support might be needed to ensure that departments adhere to their strategies and targets. The Treasury Board will also identify new reallocation options, while flagging areas that need more performance information.

Parliamentary committees use the departmental outlooks as the starting point for their reviews of the process. They look at expenditure trends, priorities, and performance, and report their conclusions to Parliament before the end of June.

During the summer, from June to September, while most of us are relaxing, various central agencies play an important part in the unfolding drama. In particular, the Privy Council Office, the Department of Finance, and the Treasury Board work with departments to integrate the advice from Cabinet policy committees, the Treasury Board, and the parliamentary committees. They then present strategies and options to the minister of finance for his consideration during the budgetary consultation stage. Meanwhile, the Department of Finance also prepares an update on the general fiscal and economic outlook.

In the fall, from September to December, Cabinet as a whole considers and approves the budget consultation strategies devised by the minister of finance. The Department of Finance, assisted by other central agencies and departments, prepares Budget Consultation Papers as the basis of discussions with Canadians about what ought to go into the upcoming budget. These Consultation Papers cover the economic and fiscal outlook, and prospective fiscal and expenditure targets. The minister of finance releases these papers and then begins consultation with the Standing Committee on Finance, provincial finance ministers, interest groups, and the public. Meanwhile, work is going on in the central agencies, departments, and Cabinet policy committees to refine their contributions to the budgetary process in light of evolving circumstances. The Standing Committee on Finance submits its report at this time as well, commenting on the fiscal strategy being drafted for the upcoming budget. Meanwhile, the minister of finance busily tries to incorporate all these inputs into the development of the budget.

In the winter, Cabinet reviews the budget strategy by considering the government's fiscal targets, any new spending initiatives and reallocations, and any proposed reductions in spending. The Department of Finance puts the finishing touches on the budget, while the Treasury Board finalizes the Estimates. Finally, as the country breathlessly awaits, the minister of finance stands up in the House of Commons, sometime around the end of February, and delivers the budget, while the president of the Treasury Board tables the Estimates.

While this may appear to be the end of the story, it is in fact only the beginning... of the next round of budget preparation. For, upon delivery of the budget by the minister of finance, the departments go back to the task of preparing their business plans all over again. And the cycle continues. Box 10.3 shows the reporting cycle attached to the EMS.

BOX 10.3 | **The Reporting Cycle**

The Treasury Board summarizes the reporting cycle involved in the EMS in the following way:

The Reporting Cycle illustrates the timing, events, and reports related to the provision of financial and non-financial planning and performance information to parliament. The documents within the cycle support both the Government's efforts to effectively plan and evaluate its performance, and Parliament's budgetary, appropriation and accountability functions.

The Budget, *which is typically tabled six weeks prior to the beginning of the fiscal year (April 1), identifies the broad spending priorities of the Government, and details how the Government plans to collect and invest taxpayers' money. The spending plans of the Government are outlined in greater detail within Parts I and II of the Estimates, which delineate the total voted and statutory expenditures of the Government and individual departments and agencies. Parliamentarians consider the information included in the* Main Estimates *when voting on the Budget and appropriations bills in Parliament. Parts I and II are supported by Part III of the* Estimates, *which is composed of two parts:* Departmental Reports on Plans and Priorities (RPPs), *and* Departmental Performance Reports (DPRs). Canada's Performance *report is tabled by the President of the Treasury Board, and is a chapeau piece to the DPRs that outlines how the Government of Canada contributes to Canada's performance as a nation. The* Public Accounts of Canada *is the annual report summarizing the financial transactions made by the Government of Canada during a given fiscal year ending at Mach 31. The Pre-budget consultation process begins in the fall with the tabling of the* Economic and Fiscal Update, *which provides an annual update on the national economic and federal fiscal situation leading to the budget-planning process. The fiscal projections in it form the basis for pre-budget policy discussions. The President of the Treasury Board tables* Supplementary Estimates *to obtain authority of Parliament to adjust the Government's expenditure plan, as reflected in the Estimates for that fiscal year.*

Fall (Sept/Oct/Nov)

- Pre-budget consultation begins
- Economic and Fiscal Update
- First Regular Supplementary Estimates
- Fully Supply for First Regular Supplementary Estimates
- Fully Performance Package
  - Canada's Performance Reports
  - Departmental Performance Reports
  - Public Accounts
  - Annual Financial Report for the Government of Canada

SUMMER (Jun/Jun/Aug)

- Full Supply for Main Estimates (part II)

WINTER (Dec/Jan/Feb)

- Budget
- The Government Expense Plan (Estimates - Parts I)
- Main Estimates (Estimates - Parts II)
- Final Supplementary Estimates

SPRING (Mar/Apr/May)

- Final Supply for Final Supplementary Estimates
- Interim Supply for Main Estimates (Part II)
- Departmental Reports on Plans and Priorities (Estimates - Part III)
- Committees
  - Report on Estimates
  - Make recommendations on supply

Source: Canada. Treasury Board Secretariat of Canada. *The Reporting Cycle.* www.tbs-sct.gc.ca/audience/pp-PR_e.asp?printable=True Accessed May 5, 2007.

FIGURE 10.5   Roles in the Expenditure Management System

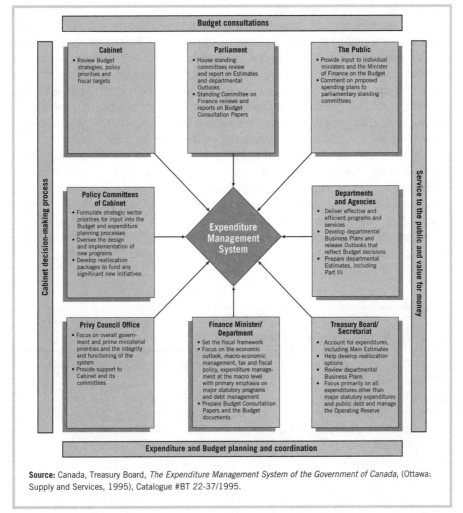

Source: Canada, Treasury Board, *The Expenditure Management System of the Government of Canada,* (Ottawa: Supply and Services, 1995), Catalogue #BT 22-37/1995.

As should be obvious, EMS involves a veritable army of actors playing a variety of important roles (see Figure 10.5). It is a complex process whose importance cannot be underestimated, since, once again, it is in the budget that the age-old political question of "Who gets what, when, and how?" is answered.

WHAT YOU HAVE LEARNED

When public sector managers use new human resource or financial management systems, they must ensure that the cure is not worse than the disease. Clearly, there has been a lot of experimentation in public sector management. The quantity and, more important, the quality of public services that Canadians have come to expect hang in the balance.[51] In this chapter, we addressed the complexity of managing the public service, and we considered what the managers of the public service do and how they do it, in the context of ongoing reform and in relation to money.

The management of financial resources involves elaborate decision making systems dedicated to dividing the "pie" of government and answering the fundamental question, "Who gets what, when, and how?" We noted the impact of both deficits and surpluses, and other contemporary stresses and strains confronted by managers in the public service. And we noted the increased emphasis on auditing and evaluation (as suggested in chapter 8), as well as performance assessment, efficiency, and the importation of private sector business techniques to accompany the traditional concerns of probity and honesty.

In their attempt to resolve disputes and create a transparent and fair system of budgeting, successive Canadian governments have experimented with a variety of budgeting models. But so far, no one system or model has been able to address all the hotly contested issues around the administration and management of government finances. This chapter examined issues related to financial management by tracing the development of budgetary reform inspired by the Glassco Commission and actualized by PPBS, PEMS, and EMS.

Key Words and Concepts

Productivity Improvement Program (311)	La Relève (314)
	PPBS (324)
Ministerial Task Force on Program Review (311)	line-item budgeting (325)
	program budgeting (325)
Increased Ministerial Authority and Accountability (311)	PEMS (326)
	EMS (326)
PS2000 (311)	business plans (326)
Program Review (313)	risk management (329)

Review Questions

1. Restructuring the Public Service: The Management View
The composition of the public service has undergone significant changes over time, as have approaches to managing, from an era in which downsizing, re-engineering, pay freezes, cutbacks, layoffs, and firings were endemic to the current era of reinvestment and growth. After reviewing the most recent trends in human resources management, ask yourself, Why has wholesale and ongoing reform of the public sector management been necessary? Has the public sector really turned the corner and overcome its past liabilities, or is it still mired in the same old problems? What are your future prospects should you decide on a career in the Canadian public service?

2. Financial Management

The fundamental questions of power politics raised in chapter 2 revolved around the question of "Who gets what, when, and how?" We returned here to this question by examining that most fundamental of issues related to government: money. Ask yourself, Does the complexity of managing the public's money pose special problems compared to managing money in the private sector? What is the "public interest" in relation to the management of money in the public sector? How do we know if the public's money is being well managed? Do the systems of budgetary management control and oversight give citizens the requisite "bang for the buck" they deserve?

Weblinks

Department of Finance
www.fin.gc.ca

Canada School of Public Service
www.myschool-monecole.gc.ca

Public Service Commission of Canada
www.psc-cfp.gc.ca

Treasury Board Secretariat of Canada
www.tbs-sct.gc.ca

Canada Public Service Agency
www.psagency-agencefp.gc.ca

Office of the Auditor General
www.oag-bvg.gc.ca/domino/oag-bvg.nsf/html/menue.html

Further Reading

1. Restructuring the Public Service: The Management View

Albo, Gregory. "Democratic Citizenship and the Future of Public Management." In G. Albo, D. Langille and L. Panitch, eds. *A Different Kind of State? Popular Power and Democratic Administration*. Toronto: Oxford University Press, 1993.

Campbell, Colin and George Szablowski. *The Superbureaucrats: Structure and Behaviour in Central Agencies*. Toronto: Macmillan, 1979.

Canada. Public Service Commission of Canada. *A Timeline of the Public Service Commission of Canada*. Ottawa: Public Service Commission of Canada, 1998: 7–10. **www.psc-cfp.gc.ca/research/ timeline/psc_timeline_e.htm**

Good, David. *The Politics of Public Management: The HRDC Audit of Grants and Contributions*. Toronto: University of Toronto Press, 2003.

Hodgetts, J.E., William McCloskey, Reginald Whitaker and V. Seymour Wilson. *The Biography of an Institution: The Civil Service of Canada, 1908–1967*. Montreal: McGill-Queen's University Press, 1972.

Shields, John and B. Mitchell Evans. *Shrinking the State: Globalization and Public Administration "Reform."* Halifax: Fernwood Press, 1998.

2. Financial Management

Hale, Geoffrey. *The Politics of Taxation in Canada*. Peterborough: Broadview Press, 2002.

Lewis, Timothy. *In the Long Run We're All Dead: The Canadian Turn to Fiscal Restraint*. Vancouver: UBC Press, 2003.

Lindquist, Evert. "How Ottawa Reviews Spending: Moving Beyond Adhocracy?" in G. Bruce Doern, ed. *How Ottawa Spends 2006–2007: In From the Cold: The Tory Rise and the Liberal Demise*. Montreal: McGill-Queen's University Press, 2006: 185–207.

Strick, John C. *The Public Sector in Canada: Programs, Finance and Policy*. Toronto: Thompson Educational Publishing, 1999.

Endnotes

1. Robert F. Adie and Paul G. Thomas, *Canadian Public Administration: Problematical Perspectives, Second Edition*, (Scarborough: Prentice Hall, 1987): 252.

2. Canada. Treasury Board of Canada Secretariat. *Employment Statistics for the Federal Public Service April 1, 1999–March 31, 2000*. Ottawa: Treasury Board Secretariat, 2000: 1. **www.tbs-sct.gc.ca/ pubs_pol/hrpubs/pse-fpe/es-se99-00-1_e.html**

3. Canada, Auditor General, *Annual Report 1976*, (Ottawa: Supply and Services, 1976): 10.

4. Canada, Auditor General, *Annual Report 1978*, (Ottawa: Supply and Services, 1979).

5. Canada, Office of the Auditor General, *Report of the Auditor General of Canada—2001*, (Ottawa: Office of the Auditor General, 2001). **www.oag-bvg.gc.ca/domino/reports.nsf/ html/01sice.html**

6. See A.W. Johnson, *Reflections on Administrative Reform in the Government of Canada 1962–1991*, (Ottawa: Office of the Auditor General of Canada, 1992).

7. See John Halligan, ed. *Civil Service Systems in Anglo-American Countries*, (Cheltenham, UK: Edward Elgar, 2003); and Peter Aucoin, *The New Public Management: Canada in Comparative Perspective*, (Montreal: Institute for Research on Public Policy, 1995).

8. Gilles Paquet and Robert Shepherd, "The Program Review Process: A Deconstruction," in Gene Swimmer, ed. *How Ottawa Spends 1996–1997: Life Under the Knife*, (Ottawa: Carleton University Press, 1996): 42. The phrase "vertical solitude" is from D. Zussman and J. Jabes, *The Vertical Solitude: Managing in the Public Sector*, (Halifax: Institute for Research on Public Policy, 1989).

9. For an overview, see Michel Paquin, "Administrative Modernization within the Canadian Government," in Jacques Bourgault, Maurice Demers and Cynthia Williams, eds. *Public Administration and Public Management: Experiences in Canada*, (Sainte-Foy, Quebec: Les Publications du Quebec, 1997): 144–54.

10. See Zussman and Jabes, *The Vertical Solitude*, (1989).

11. On the mandate of PS2000, see Government of Canada, *Public Service 2000: The Renewal of the Public Service of Canada*, (Ottawa: Supply and Services Canada, 1990): 3–4; and P.M. Tellier, "Public Service 2000: The Renewal of the Public Service," *Canadian Public Administration*, 33, 2 (Summer, 1990): 123–32.

12. Paquin, "Administrative Modernization within the Canadian Government," (1997): 147.

13. Ian D. Clark, "Restraint, Renewal, and the Treasury Board Secretariat," *Canadian Public Administration*, 37, 2 (Summer 1994): 290–340.

14. Paquin, "Administrative Modernization within the Canadian Government," (1997): 148.

15. Canada, Auditor General of Canada, *Auditor General's Report to the House of Commons*, (Ottawa: Ministry of Supply and Services, 1993).

16. Aucoin, *The New Public Management* (1995).

17. Sandro Contenta, "A New Attack on Red Tape," *Toronto Star*, (Saturday, March 12, 1994): B4.

18. See Marcel Massé, "Getting Government 'Right': The Challenges of Governing Canada," in James John Guy, ed. *Expanding Our Political Horizons: Readings in Canadian Politics and Government*, (Toronto: Harcourt, Brace, 1997): 8–14.

19. See Paquin, "Administrative Modernization within the Canadian Government," (1994): 152–53.

20. Gilles Paquet and Robert Shepherd, "The Program Review Process: A Deconstruction," in Gene Swimmer, ed. *How Ottawa Spends 1996–1997: Life Under the Knife,* (1996): 39–40.

21. See Canada, Privy Council Office, *Getting Government Right: A Progress Report,* (Ottawa: Minister of Supply and Services, 1996).

22. See Susan D. Phillips, "The Liberals' Mid-Life Crises: Aspirations versus Achievements," in Susan D. Phillips, ed. *How Ottawa Spends 1995–1996: Mid-Life Crisis,* (Ottawa: Carleton University Press, 1995): 15.

23. Paquet and Shepherd, "The Program Review Process," (1996): 40.

24. Cited in Paquet and Shepherd, "The Program Review Process," (1996): 51–52.

25. Canada, *First Progress Report on La Relève: A Commitment to Action,* (Ottawa: La Relève Task Force, 1998): 2.

26. Canada. Canadian Centre for Management Development. *Deputy Minister's Task Force on the Management of Horizontal Issues,* (Ottawa: Canadian Centre for Management Development, 1996); and Canada. Canadian Centre for Management Development. *Strengthening Our Policy Capacity: Report of the Task Force on Strengthening the Policy Capacity of the Federal Government,* (Ottawa: Canadian Centre for Management Development, 1995).

27. Canada. Policy Research Initiative *About the PRI*, **www.policyresearch.gc.ca/page.asp?pagenm=pri_index** Accessed July 24, 2007.

28. O.P. Dwivedi and John Halligan, "The Canadian Public Service: Balancing Values and Management," in John Halligan, ed. *Civil Service Systems in Anglo-American Countries*, (Cheltenham, UK: Edward Elgar, 2003): 168. See also Evert Lindquist, Ian Clark, and James Mitchell, "Reshaping Ottawa's Centre of Government: Martin's Reforms in Historical Perspective," in G. Bruce Doern, ed. *How Ottawa Spends 2004–2005: Mandate Change in the Paul Martin Era,* (Montreal: McGill-Queen's University Press, 2004): 317–47.

29. For a chronology of the Sponsorship scandal, see Canada. Public Works and Government Services Canada. *Chronology of the Sponsorship Activities.* **www.pwgsc.gc.ca/sponsorship/text/sponsorship-timeline-e.html#top** Accessed June 27, 2007.

30. Canada. Commission of Inquiry into the Sponsorship Program and Advertising Activities. *Restoring Accountability: Recommendations*, (Ottawa: Public Works and Government Services Canada, 2006): 197–204.

31. Ralph Heintzman, "Introduction: Canada and Public Administration," in Jacques Bourgault, Maurice Demers, and Cynthia Williams, eds. *Public Administration and Public Management: Experiences in Canada,* (Sainte-Foy, Quebec: Les Publications du Quebec, 1997): 8.

32. Donald J. Savoie, *The Politics of Public Spending in Canada,* (Toronto: University of Toronto Press, 1990): 4.

33. See Michael J. Prince, "Budgetary Trilogies: The Phases of Budget Reform in Canada," in Christopher Dunn, ed. *The Handbook of Canadian Public Administration*, (Toronto: Oxford Press, 2002).

34. Pater Harder and Evert Lindquist, "Expenditure Management and Reporting in the Government of Canada: Recent Developments and Backgrounds," in Jacques Bourgault, Maurice Demers and Cynthia Williams, eds. *Public Administration and Public Management: Experiences in Canada,* (Sainte-Foy, Quebec: Les Public Actions du Quebec, 1997): 72. The following discussion is partly derived from this source.

35. Geoffrey E. Hale, "Trading Up or Treading Water? Federal Fiscal and Budgetary Policies in Search of a New Mandate," in G. Bruce Doern, ed. *How Ottawa Spends 2006–2007: In From the Cold: The Tory Rise and the Liberal Demise*, (Montreal: McGill-Queen's University Press, 2006): 32.

36. Savoie, *The Politics of Public Spending in Canada,* (1990): 26.

37. Harder and Lindquist, "Expenditure Management and Reporting in the Government of Canada," (1997): 73.

38. Geoffrey Hale, *The Politics of Taxation in Canada*, (Peterborough: Broadview Press, 2002): 120.

39. Harder and Lindquist, "Expenditure Management and Reporting in the Government of Canada," (1997): 76. See also O.P. Dwivedi and John Halligan, "The Canadian Public Service: Balancing Values and Management," in John Halligan, ed. *Civil Service Systems in Anglo-American Countries,* (Cheltenham, UK: Edward Elgar, 2003): 148–73.

40. See Richard Van Loon, "The Policy and Expenditure Management System in the Federal Government: The First Three Years," *Canadian Public Administration,* 26 (Summer, 1983): 255–85.

41. See Ian D. Clark, "Recent Changes in the Cabinet Decision Making System in Ottawa," *Canadian Public Administration,* 28, 2 (Summer, 1985): 185–201.

42. See Peter Aucoin, "Organizational Change in the Machinery of Canadian Government: From Rational Management to Brokerage Politics," *Canadian Journal of Political Science,* 19, 1 (March, 1986): 3–27.

43. See Evert A. Lindquist, "On the Cutting Edge: Program Review, Government Restructuring and the Treasury Board of Canada," in Gene Swimmer, ed. *How Ottawa Spends 1996–1997: Life Under the Knife,* (Ottawa: Carleton University Press, 1996): 205–52; Evert A. Lindquist, "Business Planning Comes to Ottawa: Critical Issues and Future Directions," in Peter Aucoin and Donald J. Savoie, eds. *Managing Strategic Change: Learning From Program Review,* (Ottawa: Canadian Centre for Management Development, 1998); and Harder and Lindquist, "Expenditure Management and Reporting in the Government of Canada," (1997): 85–86.

44. Canada. Auditor General of Canada. *Auditor General Report 2006*, **www.oag-bvg.gc.ca/domino/ reports.nsf/html/200611sice.html#hd4a** Accessed June 14, 2007.

45. Canada. Treasury Board Secretariat of Canada. *Audit of the Development of the Expenditure Management Information System (EMIS)—Final Report—Management Response—November 25, 2005.* **www.tbs-sct.gc.ca/report/orp/2005/ia-vi/emis-sigd01-PR_e.asp?printable=True** Accessed June 26, 2007.

46. Canada. Auditor General of Canada. *Auditor General Report 2006,* **www.oag-bvg.gc.ca/domino/ reports.nsf/html/200611sice.html#hd4a** Accessed June 14, 2007.

47. On risk management as applied in the British experience, see Bridget Hutter, "Risk Management and Governance," in Pearl Eliadis, Margaret M. Hill and Michael Howlett, eds. *Designing Government: From Instruments to Governance,* (Montreal: McGill-Queen's University Press, 2005): 303–21.

48. Canada. Auditor General of Canada. *Auditor General Report 2006,* **www.oag-bvg.gc.ca/domino/ reports.nsf/html/200611sice.html#hd4a** Accessed June 14, 2007.

49. Canada. Auditor General of Canada. *Auditor General Report 2006,* **www.oag-bvg.gc.ca/domino/ reports.nsf/html/200611sice.html#hd4a** Accessed June 14, 2007.

50. This description is derived from Canada, Treasury Board, *The Expenditure Management System of Canada,* (Ottawa: Minister of Supply and Services Canada, 1995).

51. See Peter Aucoin, "The Politics and Management of Restraint Budgeting," in André Blais and Stèphane Dion, eds. *The Budget-Maximizing Bureaucrat: Appraisals and Evidence,* (Pittsburgh: University of Pittsburgh Press, 1991): 119–41.

Chapter (11)

Public Administration *and* Ethics

WHAT YOU WILL LEARN

One of the distinguishing features of public administration is that in the interests of accountability, public servants are subject to ethical guidelines that are often absent in the private sector. This chapter asks:

- How do we ensure the honesty and integrity of those dedicated to serving the public interest?
- What if the guidelines promoting ethical behaviour impede efficiency in providing services—which values should prevail?
- How is the behaviour of public servants shaped and constrained in the context of ethical dilemmas?
- What measures have been taken to ensure the highest standards of conduct by public servants?

This chapter is divided into the following sections:

1. Ethical Dilemmas in the Public Service

This section sketches out some of the broad controversies surrounding the ethical standards of behaviour in the public sector. It asks these questions: What behaviours are acceptable within the public sector, and what are not? Are standards of behaviour in the public sector significantly different from those in the private sector? What is the "public interest"? What is the importance of discretion, partisanship, public comment, conflict of interest, lying to the public, and public versus private-sector ethics?

2. — *Codes of Conduct*

Powerful arguments have been put forth to suggest that ethical behaviour can only be maintained if public sector employees are subject to written codes of conduct that spell out both acceptable activities and penalties for failure to comply. Others have suggested that written codes are unsuitable and that education and role models are preferable means for ensuring ethical behaviour. This section addresses this debate and asks the following: What are ethical codes of conduct? How do they work, and are they effective? Why is it felt that codes of conduct are required? What other mechanisms can be used to ensure that the highest ethical standards are upheld? What alternative means exist to ensure public servants' integrity?

Ethical Dilemmas in the Public Service

The question of the ethical behaviour of public office holders is an ancient one. Consider that in fifth-century Greece, at the age of 17, Athenians took the following pledge:

We will never bring disgrace on this our city by an act of dishonesty or cowardice. We will fight for the ideals and sacred things of the city both alone and with others.

We will revere and obey the city's laws, and will do our best to incite a like reverence and respect in those above us who are prone to annul them or set them at naught.

We will strive increasingly to quicken the public's sense of civic duty.

Thus, in all those ways we will transmit this city, not only, not less, but greater and more beautiful than it was transmitted to us.[1]

Ethical conduct among public servants and their political masters is important. It has long been established that public officials must not use their offices for private gain. Nor may they disclose confidential information or place themselves in positions of conflict of interest. As a result of these and other considerations (discussed following), the strictures on the behaviour of public servants are considerable, as are the opportunities and temptations that present themselves. They are also unique, compared to the private sector. Public servants may find themselves in untenable situations as a result of their overriding need to behave in an ethical manner. To behave ethically requires a sense of personal integrity shaped in part by the standards of the profession, but also by personal socialization outside the workplace. Reconciling these two sources of ethical and moral principle can be tremendously difficult.

The issue of **ethics** in the public service is relatively new as a subject of study in Canadian public administration. It has also recently spawned new practices, institutions, and behaviours. But questionable ethical behaviour has been a feature of Canadian political life since before Confederation. As two observers put it,

Scandals and rumours of scandals have been an ever-present curse within the Canadian political system from well before Confederation. Canadian history is replete with "horror stories" involving the Château Clique and the Family Compact, the Grand Trunk and the

CPR, the Ross rifle and liquor licensing. Of more recent vintage, allegations and verified incidents of unethical political party financing arrangements, as well as conflicts of interest involving government contracting, influence-peddling, favouritism and nepotism have attracted attention on the federal and provincial stages.[2]

Moreover, the Civil Service reforms of 1918, while ushering in a meritocracy, said little or nothing about ethical behaviour. More recently, as noted elsewhere in this book, a spate of scandals in the 1990s and early 2000s have reminded us of the ongoing need to ensure the highest ethical conduct of officials is upheld.

One of the reasons ethics has garnered more attention of late is the changing nature of public administration, much of which we documented in earlier chapters. In the days when government was small, a coterie of mandarins controlled the public service and infused it with a set of shared values, attitudes, and beliefs. Ethical norms and standards were derived largely from these role models at the apex of the bureaucracy. But as government grew and became more complex and unwieldy, and as scores of new recruits brought their own ethical "baggage" with them, the shared values of an earlier era gave way to new ones. Control, in the form of inculcating public servants with the same values as the mandarins, eroded. As the public service grew, the chains of command lengthened; and as they lengthened, they loosened, making room for new interpretations of what constituted ethical behaviour.

Related to these developments was an increase in opportunities for bureaucratic **discretion**, as well as a change in attitude about the appropriate role of public servants. More and more, public servants were seen as agents of change, rather than simply as passive servants of the public will, and the old distinctions between politics and administration were increasingly challenged. Moreover, as morale in the public sector plunged, the notion of a "career" public servant underwent a metamorphosis, so the core values that used to characterize the career also have undergone change. In addition, the new climate of evaluation emerging in Canadian public administration meant taking a closer look, not just at management, but at the ethical and moral behaviour of public servants, and ways to evaluate it. Freedom of information and privacy acts and commissioners proliferated, as did ombuds offices. The practices of Auditors General and comptrollers provided the templates for considering ways in which the ethical behaviour of public servants could be measured, and calls for establishing **ethics commissioners** emerged, and have been heeded in many jurisdictions.[3]

In 1996, a groundbreaking report entitled *A Strong Foundation* was published, which provided in-depth discussion of values and ethics in the federal public service.[4] Also known as the Tait Report, after its author John Tait, it called for government bodies to identify core corporate values and standards of ethical conduct. The Tait Report looked at core values in the public service, such as democratic values (respect for elected officials, accountability, nonpartisanship); professional values (innovation, resourcefulness); ethical values (probity, public interests); and people values (openness, fairness, courage). Following the Tait Report, in 1999 the clerk of the Privy Council named two senior public servants as "co-champions" of a government-wide dialogue on ethics in the public service. They worked to impress upon the broader public service the centrality of values and ethics in the work of public servants, and contributed to the development of a comprehensive framework for values and ethics in the public service. Also in 1999, the Office of Values and Ethics was created to undertake public service–wide initiatives to promote values and ethics (see Box 11.1). The office

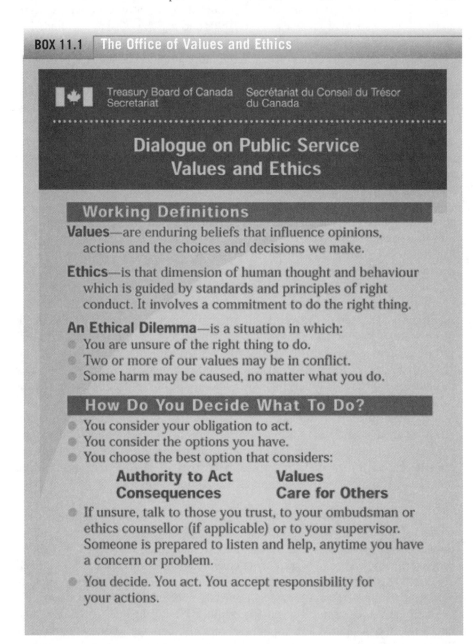

BOX 11.1 | **The Office of Values and Ethics**

Treasury Board of Canada Secretariat — Secrétariat du Conseil du Trésor du Canada

Dialogue on Public Service Values and Ethics

Working Definitions

Values—are enduring beliefs that influence opinions, actions and the choices and decisions we make.

Ethics—is that dimension of human thought and behaviour which is guided by standards and principles of right conduct. It involves a commitment to do the right thing.

An Ethical Dilemma—is a situation in which:
- You are unsure of the right thing to do.
- Two or more of our values may be in conflict.
- Some harm may be caused, no matter what you do.

How Do You Decide What To Do?

- You consider your obligation to act.
- You consider the options you have.
- You choose the best option that considers:

| Authority to Act | Values |
| Consequences | Care for Others |

- If unsure, talk to those you trust, to your ombudsman or ethics counsellor (if applicable) or to your supervisor. Someone is prepared to listen and help, anytime you have a concern or problem.

- You decide. You act. You accept responsibility for your actions.

www.tbs-sct.gc.ca/veo-bve

Office of Values and Ethics
(613) 957-2458

Public Service Values and Ethics
Extract from *A Summary* of the Tait Report (Feb 97)

The four families of core values:

The Democratic Values of:

Responsible government ● Rule of law ● Support for democracy ● Loyalty ● Respect for authority of elected office holders ●Neutrality/non-partisanship ● Accountability ● Due process ● Public interest/public good

The "Traditional" Professional Values of:

Neutrality ● Merit ● Excellence ● Effectiveness ● Economy ● Frankness ● Objectivity and impartiality in advice ● Speaking truth to power ● Balancing complexity ● Fidelity to the public trust

The "New" Professional Values of:

Quality ● Innovation ● Initiative ● Creativity ● Resourcefulness ● Service to clients/citizens ● Horizontality (collaboration) ● Teamwork

The Ethical Values of:

Integrity ● Honesty ● Probity ● Prudence ● Impartiality ● Equity ● Selflessness ● Discretion ● Public trust

The People Values of:

Respect ● Concern/caring ● Civility/courtesy ● Tolerance ● Openness ● Collegiality/participation ● Fairness ● Moderation ● Decency ● Reasonableness ● Humanity ● Courage

Canadä

was also made responsible for the conflict of interest code for public servants and for developing an internal disclosure policy.[5] Recent changes rooted in neoconservative approaches and the New Public Management (NPM) have created a new orientation toward ethics. For instance, the trends toward "partnering" and contracting out and toward merging public and private sector practices have meant that the value systems of the two are increasingly bumping up against one another, posing new challenges.

Ethical behaviour in the public service is particularly important because it contributes to the public's perception of our political institutions: it promotes trust and efficacy. Since public servants and politicians are the guardians of the public's interests, there should be a special bond between the state and its citizens, expressed through the latter's belief that public officials can be depended upon to act in their best interests. Lately, though, public confidence in government has diminished. Canadians are reported to be more cynical and disrespectful of public institutions. Not all of this can be blamed on the unethical behaviour of public officials, but a considerable amount of the public's perceptions are shaped by this factor. For example, the resignation of a half-dozen Cabinet ministers from the Mulroney government for a variety of offences, both real and perceived, and an unsavoury series of scandals in the Chrétien and Martin governments contributed heavily to the growing public disgust with politicians. Changing attitudes toward authority seem to be a part of the contemporary political culture, and they influence the public's attitude regarding the ethical standards that should be applied to public servants and their political masters. According to political scientist Neil Nevitte, there has recently been a marked decline in the public confidence in government institutions. For example, in 1981, about 36.9 percent surveyed claimed to have "high" confidence in government institutions in Canada. By 1990, this number had dropped to 29.4 percent.[6] More recent polling data shows that since the 1990s, the percentage of Canadians who have trust in the government has remained at about 30 percent.[7]

In 2004, the government began to construct a broader and deeper ethics regime, focusing on Parliament but with effects on the public service, too. A process for creating a code of conduct for Members of Parliament and a tougher code for Cabinet ministers was introduced. As well, an independent Ethics Commissioner for the House of Commons, Cabinet, and order-in-council appointees was established. An independent ethics officer for the Senate was created, as was a process for the Senate to create its own code of conduct. These steps followed similar ethics regimes created at the provincial level as early as 1988 (see Table 11.1).

The concept of the **public interest** underscores the expectation of ethical behaviour in the public service. One of the early considerations of this issue was undertaken by E. Pendleton Herring in his 1936 book, *Public Administration and the Public Interest*.[8] Herring was concerned with the tremendous growth in the scope of government activity and, in particular, with the growing bureaucratic discretion in decision making. He noted that laws and regulations were often vague in their wording, and that, as such, public servants were left to interpret what the politicians meant before actually implementing their instructions. This called into question who was really in charge, as we noted in chapter 1—the

TABLE 11.1   Dates of Establishment of Offices of Independent Ethics Commissioners in Canada

• Ontario	1988
• British Columbia	1990
• Nova Scotia	1991
• Alberta	1992
• Newfoundland and Labrador	1993
• Saskatchewan	1994
• Northwest Territories	1998
• Prince Edward Island	1999
• New Brunswick	2000
• Nunavut	2000
• Manitoba	2002
• Yukon	2002
• Quebec	2002
• Ottawa—House of Commons	2004
• Ottawa—Senate	2005

Sources: Ian Greene, "The Harper Impact on the Federal Ethics Regime," paper presented to the Annual Meeting of the Canadian Political Science Association, Saskatoon, June 1, 2007. **www.cpsa-acsp.ca/papers-2007/Greene.pdf** Accessed July 24, 2007.

public servants or the politicians? More to the point, the public servant may be required to make determinations about what constitutes the public interest. According to Herring, the most effective way this can be accomplished, while still remaining true to the spirit and intent of the legislation at hand, is for the public servant to establish a sound working relationship with the societal interest most affected by the legislation, and "broker" differences between competing groups. An added concern, Herring points out, is that between the time a law is passed and the time an administrative agency is responsible for its implementation, societal conditions that inspired the law may well have changed. Thus, to implement the law as originally intended may actually run counter to the public interest as newly expressed.

Unfortunately, Herring also argues, the concept of the public interest that ought to guide public servants in these circumstances is an ambiguous one. It is defined in part by the subjective perceptions of the public servant involved. Thus, the ethical standards of these individuals must be beyond reproach. But in any event, we rely tremendously on their discretion in the administrative process. We elaborate on the issue of discretion following.

The notion of the public interest is perhaps the single most important concept guiding the ethical dimension of administrative behaviour.[9] John Tait wrote,

The ideal of service is one of the deepest sources of public service motivation. In the heart of most public servants lies the conviction that service to the public, to the public good, or to the public interest is what makes their profession like no other. It is why they chose it, for the most part; and why they keep at it, with enthusiasm and conviction, despite difficulties and frustrations along the way. Service to the public and to the public interest is the vision of the public service, and it is a creative, essential and compelling vision.[10]

But developing a set of guidelines so that every decision can objectively be said to serve the public interest is impossible. There are too many variables involved. And the concept itself is too ambiguous. It changes over time and under different circumstances. And it often differs according to whether one is politician, public servant or citizen. This does not mean, though, that we should throw our hands up in despair and declare that there is no ethical standard that can be used to determine the public interest.

How, then, is a standard arrived at? One answer is for various groups in society to mobilize themselves to influence government. Government, in turn, acts as a neutral referee between these groups, determining whose interests are met and whose are declined. In this scenario, the objective application of a set of guidelines is all that government requires in order to determine as fairly and honestly as possible who the winners and losers are. However, what this ignores is that not all the groups involved in this struggle have equal resources. Some are well-financed, sophisticated organizations with access to the halls of power. Others are relatively penniless, with little knowledge of how government works, and are shut out of the network. Under these circumstances, can we still say that the public interest is being served if some are able to get their views across to government and others aren't?

This raises ethical issues, because the objects of attention of these groups are politicians and public servants. The question that arises is this: Can we be sure that ethical values of fairness and honesty are being followed in circumstances in which some citizens seem able to achieve privileged access to decision-makers and others do not? Indeed, what happens when decision-makers succumb to the blandishments of the well organized? Do they override the broader public interest? More directly, what if some material reward is offered by those interests—the promise of a job after leaving office, for instance, or cash or services? Or, to consider the issue from a slightly different perspective, is the public servant who responds only to the voices he or she can hear doing a proper job? Or is the public servant who actively seeks out the marginalized, the dispossessed, and the unorganized—that is, all interests related to a particular issue—doing the ethical thing? Is it the job of the public servant to solicit the views of societal interests, or merely to respond to them? To simply respond is to leave some citizens out. But if the public servant solicits views, he or she must invariably do so on the basis of his or her own personal value judgments about what groups should be heard. In other words, the public servant is injecting his or her own ethical and moral value system into the process of public administration. Is it ethical to sit back and accept that the public interest is defined somewhere else, knowing that some societal interest will not get a fair hearing? Is it ethical to step forward and try to shape the "public interest" by injecting your own views into the struggle, even though this would seem to run counter to the job of public servant? The resolution of these conflicts is rooted in the debate over how to ensure ethical standards of behaviour among public servants. There are no easy answers to these questions.

"Administrative ethics," according to one observer, "involves the application of moral principles to the conduct of officials in organizations."[11] As you will recall from our discussion of organizational theory in chapters 3 and 4, understanding the behaviour of individuals in organizations is a challenging and complex undertaking. Even assuming you can understand their motives, it is still not certain that all the members of an organization subscribe to the same general moral code. In other words, it is not always clear what rights and duties individuals respect when they engage in activity that affects the public interest. At the root of the problem is the fact that moral behaviour in organizations requires individuals to assume an objective and disengaged perspective. It requires them, in other words, to separate their own self-interest from the interest of those they are serving, and to be as unbiased in the application of rules and procedures as is humanly possible. However, the complicating factor is that we are all humans, and we all carry biases with us. Moreover, finding common moral ground with others in the organization is a challenge for two reasons. First, questions need to be answered about who *may judge*; second, questions need to be answered about who *is to be judged*. The former raises the notion that public servants are supposed to be neutral in fulfilling their duties: that is, they should not be guided by their own personal morality or principles but by those of the organization. The latter suggests that responsibility for the organization's decisions should rest not with the individuals, but with the organization itself (through its senior officers).

In an ideal organizational world, public servants carry out their superiors' orders and implement the government's policies. In this scenario, they are ethically neutral vessels or instruments. They need not exercise independent moral judgment, and are not expected to act on moral principles that they may themselves hold. Instead, they simply act on the principles contained in the orders they are given and the policies they are to implement. Simply put, "They serve the organization so that the organization may serve society."[12]

This is not to deny that individual public servants have moral and ethical belief systems of their own. Clearly, they do. But the theory described above suggests that, in effect, they park those belief systems at the door when they arrive at work. Their goal is to understand what policy their political masters intend, and to faithfully enact it. If there is a conflict, they do not fall back on their own personal moral code but, rather, look to whatever legal or constitutional guidelines exist that might apply in the given case. This view sees administrators as instruments serving the organization's goals. If they find themselves in a position of unbearable moral or ethical conflict, they have the option to resign. Thus, it is argued, the organization is made capable of serving any social end, regardless of the personal views of those who hold office.

Is this a realistic view of the roles of individuals within organizations where ethical issues are concerned? It may seem as though it requires humans to become automatons—robotic in their behaviour. This criticism is not far off the mark. Requiring people to suspend their own morality to serve the organization's greater ends seems like a hyper-Weberian recipe—geared solely toward efficiency at the expense of other, more human values. And yet, consider an organization at the other end of the spectrum. Think of one in which all decisions and actions are subject to the moral and ethical belief systems of each and every individual concerned. Would anything get done? *Could* anything get done? Surely, paralysis of the organization would result. Ideally, then, a smoothly functioning and responsible organization must somehow strike a balance between the strictures of pure neutrality described above, and the chaos of moral relativism that would result if each individual in the organization was left to inject her own personal morality into every decision and action.

The dilemmas posed by trying to strike that balance are many and varied. To illustrate, we will now turn to some particular examples, including the following issues: discretion, partisanship, public comment, conflict of interest, lying to the public, and the ethics of the public versus private sector.[13] In each of the following scenarios, imagine that you are a public servant confronted with the ethical dilemma. How would you respond?

Discretion

The first issue concerns discretion, which means simply the power of free decision of choice within certain legal bounds. It reflects our abilities to exercise judgment and discriminate between courses of action. Public servants exercise a certain amount of power. As a result, they are frequently placed in situations where their own personal judgment of the integrity of their actions comes into play. So, public servants enjoy a high level of discretion in their conduct.

For example, a directive may come down the chain of command from the minister, through the deputy minister, to the assistant deputy minister, and so on, down to you, working in the front lines of a government service-providing agency. But by the time the directive gets to you, its instructions, while well intentioned, bear little relation to the issues you face on a day-to-day basis. And they may even run counter in some ways to citizens' expectations about the type of service you provide. For example, suppose you issue support payments to social assistance recipients. The rules from on high dictate that recipients must produce proof of residence before you can give them a cheque. Now suppose a regular client comes in and tells you that he has been kicked out of his apartment but has a new place lined up for next week. Technically, without proof of residence, you cannot issue the cheque. But you have come to know this individual and some of the problems he is experiencing in trying to get his life in order. What do you do?

Your own personal sense of integrity and compassion suggest that issuing a cheque just this once will not hurt anyone, and will certainly benefit this individual, who faces the prospect of a few nights in a shelter. But your institutional training warns you that issuing the cheque is a breach of rules. Clearly, your own discretion comes into play in these circumstances.

Discretion in small cases may be acceptable, providing the law is not transgressed and no one is denied what they are entitled to from the government. But we enter a hazy area when discretion is applied too liberally or too frequently, so that the rules are made a mockery of, the law is broken, or citizens are denied their entitlements. When discretion is abused, we enter the realm of unethical conduct. Public servants enjoy a certain amount of discretion in fulfilling their duties, which means there is scope for misconduct—for instance, in handling confidential information. As with many of our examples, the issue often comes down to a question of whether the means justify the end. In other words, do public servants' discretionary acts justify the outcome?

Partisanship

Partisanship is another pitfall that public servants must be aware of. This refers to the notion that public servants should remain loyal to the government in the execution of their duties, and not to the political party that happens to hold power. In other words, they are to be politically neutral in discharging their duties. The Statement of Principles of the Institute of Public Administration of Canada puts it this way:

Public employees should be sensitive to the political process and knowledgable about the laws and traditions regarding political neutrality that are applicable to their spheres of employment.

It is the responsibility of public employees to provide forthright and objective advice to, and carry out the directions of, their political superiors.

Public employees have a duty to carry out government decisions loyally, irrespective of the party or persons in power and irrespective of their personal opinions.[14]

But consider this example: What if you, as a public servant, are ordered to conceal information that might affect the outcome of an election? In this instance, you are pulled in two directions at once. On the one hand, you have a duty to follow the orders of your superiors; on the other hand, you have a responsibility to serve the public interest. You are trained to be nonpartisan, yet by taking no action, you are perhaps tilting the balance of an election toward one party over another.

This dilemma is related to several features of public administration discussed earlier in this book. For instance, it reflects the associated problems of the politics-administration dichotomy: that is, politicians make the rules and public servants implement them. It raises again the question of merit and patronage. Presumably, in an era of widespread patronage appointments, nonpartisanship was largely irrelevant—indeed, even antithetical—to the workings of government. But in a merit-based era, the opposite is true. And finally, it raises the issue of loyalty. Public servants are required to loyally serve the government, irrespective of their personal feelings about that government's policies. The reward for loyalty is tenure; public servants cannot be arbitrarily dismissed as long as they perform their jobs satisfactorily. But clearly, these principles are severely tested by the type of ethical issue alluded to above.

Public Comment

The notion of **public comment** reflects the idea that public servants should remain anonymous and stay out of the public limelight. But the temptation to go public with information may be hard to resist, if not doing so conflicts with an individual's personal integrity. Consider this example: You receive confidential ministry documents that suggest a possible coverup of government neglect regarding the discharge of toxic chemicals into the environment. Coincidentally, an old friend who works as a journalist calls you up and invites you for lunch. Do you reveal the information to her?

Or consider this example: You are a senior public servant in possession of facts that reveal that the government's policy in a certain area is marginally damaging to some Canadians, although overall the policy benefits those it was intended to help. You are required to appear before a parliamentary committee to testify about certain aspects of the legislation; however, you are not questioned directly on the material in your possession. Do you nonetheless explicitly criticize your minister and department by revealing the information publicly? It is worth noting that a recent trend in Canadian public administration has seen senior public servants being called into the public limelight more and more often to explain their departments' actions. This would seem to undermine the principle of refraining from commenting publicly. We explore this development in more detail in chapter 12, when we consider the changing nature of accountability.

Conflict of Interest

Conflicts of interest can bedevil public servants in large and small ways. For instance, is it a conflict of interest to accept a modest gift or a dinner from a corporation seeking a government contract? And should there be a "cooling-off period" after you, as a former high-level public servant, leave a post to work in the private sector, before you can turn around and begin to lobby your former department? Or what if you are pressured from on high to award a contract to a particular firm, even though you know that firm did not present the best bid? What if you possess financial information concerning an upcoming budget and could profit from that information by playing the stock market? Should you tell your family or friends? Is it a conflict to "moonlight"—that is, to accept employment outside your regular public sector job?[15]

Conflict of interest is a common ethical dilemma in the public service. It arises when there is a possibility that public servants will materially benefit from activities related to their employment, or in situations where the objective performance of their job is interfered with. The Institute of Public Administration of Canada's Statement of Principles cites the following prohibitions concerning conflicts of interest:

Public employees should not engage in any business or transaction or have any financial or other personal interest that is, or may appear to be, incompatible with the performance of their official duties.

Public employees should not, in the performance of their official duties, seek personal or private gain by granting preferential treatment to any persons.

Public employees should not solicit nor, unless duly authorized, accept transfers of economic value from persons with whom they have contact in their official capacity.

Public employees should not use, or permit the use of, government property of any kind for activities not associated with the performance of their official duties, unless they are authorized to do so.

Public employees should not seek or obtain personal or private gain from the use of information acquired during the course of their official duties which is not generally available to the public.[16]

These are guidelines only, of course. But they indicate the scope of potential conflicts that the public servant is confronted with and that he must avoid. A complicating factor is that there are differences between real, apparent, and potential conflicts of interest. In other words, appearances can be as important as reality. So conflict of interest is a slippery concept, but a significant one in the realm of public servants' ethical conduct.

Lying for the Public Good

Other sorts of ethical dilemmas confront public servants. Are there ever circumstances in which public servants ought to lie to the public? The issue of **lying for the public good** has been considered since the earliest of times. For instance, "Plato, in *The Republic*, used the expression the 'noble lie' in presenting a fanciful story to persuade people to accept class distinctions and thereby safeguard social harmony; and Machiavelli's prince was most certainly encouraged to engage in deceit, if it was in his interest to do so."[17]

Imagine a case involving scientists in the Ministry of Agriculture allegedly being required to suppress information concerning the harmful effects on humans of drinking milk from cattle treated with a particular growth hormone. Allegations are made that senior public servants ordered a coverup, and may have shredded sensitive documents that could have substantiated the claims of the scientists counselling caution. Millions of dollars in the Canadian agri-business sector are at stake, as was the livelihood of countless dairy farmers and their families. Is it possible that senior public servants, and perhaps even their political masters, are "captured" by the interests promoting the use of the hormone, prompting a web of deceit to descend over the issue? To put it more directly, if you were a public official in this case, would you withhold the entire truth about the harmful effects of the hormone if you knew so much was at stake? If there was 100 percent scientifically validated evidence that the hormone was harmful, probably not. But what if there was only a 50 percent chance? Or a 10 percent chance? Or a 1 percent chance?

It is conceivable that there are circumstances under which lying actually promotes the public good, and this fact complicates the search for ethical guidelines all the more. Consider the following three examples, for instance.[18] First, imagine that you are confronted with an overwhelming national crisis wherein harm can only be averted by deceit. Second, consider the opposite case, where the effect of the lie is so harmless that it hardly seems to matter. Third, consider a situation in which the release of vital information invades the privacy of individuals whom you are sworn to protect. Is lying justifiable in any of these cases?

It is probably safe to say that most people abide by a personal moral code that tells them that lying is wrong. Yet in the public service, are there situations in which lies are justifiable? Is it ethically and morally wrong, for instance, to withhold the truth about national security issues? Is it wrong to withhold potentially damaging information about a government policy? Should public servants be guided by the admonition, "Don't do or say anything you don't want to read about in the papers"? Again, there are no easy answers to these questions; they indicate the depth of the ethical dilemma confronting public servants.

Public Sector versus Private Sector Ethics

Should you implement policies with which you disagree, or from which you can visualize damage resulting? In other words, do public servants owe their primary allegiance to the public, to their political masters, or to their own personal moral code and conscience? Can the rules be bent for particular cases, or must they be rigidly adhered to in all cases? Is the measure of acceptable behaviour the consequences of actions taken, or is there some other higher moral standard? These are questions that are wrestled with daily in the public service.

If we search for answers to them by comparing practices in the public sector to those in the private sector, we may be frustrated by what we find. Some argue that, in their obligations to the public, public servants have an additional, more rigorous set of standards and constraints than those found in the private sector. The former

Sources: Theo Moudakis, *Toronto Star*, Monday, June 17, 2002: A20.

chairman and chief executive officer of Imperial Oil argued that "there is an added ethical dimension expected of those in the public service" due to the fact that they must uphold the public trust.[19] Many acceptable practices in the private sector are either forbidden or frowned on in the public sector. These include the following: accepting certain kinds of gifts; discussing certain kinds of appointments; promising or threatening government action under certain circumstances; receiving or holding large amounts of cash; withholding information contrary to the public's need to know; leaking information that should be kept private. These activities underline the differences between the private and public sector, where ethical behaviour is concerned—differences further illustrated by the following:

A democratic government is not a family business, dominated by its patriarch; nor is it a military battalion, or a political campaign headquarters. It is a producing organization which belongs to its members, and it is the only such organization whose members include all the citizens within its jurisdiction. Those who work for and are paid by the government are ultimately servants of the whole country, which owns and supports the government.[20]

Moreover, there is a regime of constitutional and administrative law that informs the actions of public servants and that applies to their work in a more direct manner than in the private sector. As a result, it is generally recognized that citizens expect higher standards of ethical conduct from public servants than they do from business persons. In addition, when government functions are moved outside the traditional bureaucracy, concerns arise over

the extent to which it is possible to infuse program delivery agencies (e.g., service agencies in Canada) with core public service values, especially if the organizations are headed by persons brought in from the private sector to manage them on a more "businesslike" basis. The creation of agencies at arm's-length from ministerial control raises concern as to ministers' responsibility for the agencies' decisions. Moreover, the appointment of business people to head public agencies and the increased mobility of employees between the public and private sectors threaten political neutrality by increasing the likelihood of partisanship and patronage.[21]

Finally, the two have different motivations. As we noted in chapter 1, private sector activity is motivated by the bottom line, whereas the public sector has no such motivation. These qualitative differences should not be overlooked.

Now, however, we have entered an era in which governments are supposed to be run in a more businesslike fashion. Does this mean importing the private sector's ethics along with its management practices? Moreover, the trend now is for governments to increasingly share responsibility with stakeholders, creating a new balance between the private and public worlds. As one observer puts it, "We are witnessing a shift from emphasis on the government as regulator to the government as co-regulator. Interdependency is what creates the new balance— and this has definite moral implications."[22] No longer will the government be the sole or most important watchdog of the public good under these conditions. But are private sector actors willing and able to assume this part of government's traditional role, along with the benefits accruing from these new partnerships? From an ethical point of view, is it appropriate to expect commercial associations, whose goal is profit maximization, to develop and implement policy, and to self-regulate? These questions have not yet been satisfactorily answered.

This is not a comprehensive list of all possible ethical dilemmas public servants face. But it should give you some sense of the complexity of the issues. There is, unfortunately, not always a straightforward "correct" answer to many of the situations cited above, which has led to the call for some sort of institutionalization of ethical conduct. It is argued that only by putting rules, regulations, and guidelines on paper for all to see and read can the proper ethical standards needed in the public sector be understood and upheld. As a result, arguments for standardized "codes of ethics" have become increasingly common. But as we will see, this solution is not without its detractors.

Codes of Conduct

According to two professors of public administration, there are seven "commandments" to which the responsible public servant is expected to adhere. They are as follows:

[A]ct in the public interest; be politically neutral; do not disclose confidential information; protect the privacy of citizens and employees; provide efficient, effective and fair service to the public; avoid conflicts of interest; and be accountable.[23]

To ensure that the public retains confidence in the administrative machinery of the government, these issues must be managed sensitively. This explains the codes of conduct, regulations, guidelines, and laws that have evolved over the past few decades. Today, a whole "ethics bureaucracy" has emerged. Interestingly, in an era of reform marked by, among other things, a trend toward deregulation, some literature points to ethics regulations within government as a key area of growth. "Beginning with Prime Minister Pearson, successive political leaders have developed rules to guide the conduct of, at first, ministers, then bureaucrats, and now members of Parliament."[24] Indeed it is highly ironic—and a topic worthy of further research—that as the era of managerialism proceeded with deregulation as one of its hallmarks, regulatory efforts and initiatives in the area of ethics, values, and accountability have mushroomed. Langford and Tupper go so far as to say,

Ottawa's many ethics initiatives now constitute an "ethics program" or "business line"— a collection of interrelated activities directed toward a common goal. . . . The federal ethics program is a sprawling collection of laws, general statements of government intent, administrative regulations and processes. It engages numerous government agencies, tens of thousands of appointed and elected officials, lobbyists, political parties and, by implication, considerable time, effort and public expenditure.[25]

The connection between years of downsizing and deregulation and the apparent rise in unethical behaviour has not been established empirically. But it is a noteworthy phenomenon that hyper-regulatory efforts in ethics, values, and accountability are occurring in step with the new managerialism's efforts to *reduce* government.

But clearly, some of the issues raised above defy easy resort to written or codified rules of conduct. Thus, the issue of codifying the ethical behaviour of public servants is contentious. So, some believe that other means are needed to achieve the objectives intended by a code of conduct approach. This section will consider the pros and cons of codes of ethics, as well as two other techniques for reinforcing ethical behaviour: training and education, and role models.[26]

Do Codes of Conduct Work?

According to one view, responsible behaviour by public servants should be measured against the expectation that ethical behaviour in government should reinforce the democratic process. It should be ensured that officials respect the rights of citizens and uphold values seen by the broader society as essential to democracy. But it is not always easy to ensure that officials in public service are sensitive to these values. Nor is it obvious that they are sufficiently self-questioning about the bigger ethical concerns in their daily decision making or execution of policies.[27]

Consequently, the drive toward codifying ethical behaviour has gained momentum. In the 1970s and 1980s, governments began to trip over themselves in issuing "codes of conduct" and "ethical guidelines to behaviour" and "conflict of interest regulations." A veritable explosion of interest developed in the issue of ethics. This was partly in response to major scandals such as Watergate in the United States during the 1970s, when U.S. president Richard Nixon was forced to resign after having been charged with unethical and illegal behaviour. It was also a response to the increasing role of the media in uncovering government malfeasance.[28] While many of these codes of conduct related primarily to political actors, concern spread to the actions of public servants, too. The Canadian government jumped on the bandwagon and introduced a Conflict of Interest Code in 1985, after having staged a Task Force on Conflict of Interest the year before.[29]

In 1995, the clerk of the Privy Council formed a Task Force on Public Service Values and Ethics, composed of deputy ministers, to investigate contemporary issues and developments in this area.[30] And, as noted above, an Office of Values and Ethics was created in 1999. In 2003, the Office of Values and Ethics released a Code of Conduct for Public Servants, which set out the expectations, rules, and behaviours expected of public officials (see Box 11.2).

The media has played a prominent role in placing these issues of ethical dilemmas before the public. It was a story in the *Globe and Mail*, for instance, that aroused suspicions about the federal Sponsorship Program. The media plays two roles simultaneously: as investigator, it uncovers malfeasance and brings it to light for the public; and as watchdog, it acts as a deterrent to public servants and politicians fearful of having their names splashed across the front pages of the newspaper. But as one award-winning analysis showed, the media can sometimes contribute to gross distortions of the level and amount of "corruption" perceived to exist.[31]

BOX 11.2 Statement of Public Service Values and Ethics

The following is excerpted from a longer Statement of Public Service Values and Ethics developed by the Office of Values and Ethics of the Treasury Board Secretariat of Canada:

Public Servants

This Code forms part of the conditions of employment in the Public Service of Canada. At the time of signing their letter of offer, public servants acknowledge that the Values and Ethics Code for the Public Service is a condition of employment. All public servants are responsible for ensuring that they comply with this Code and that they exemplify, in all their actions and behaviours, the values of public service. In particular, they have the following obligations:

a. Public servants must report, within 60 days of their first appointment or any subsequent appointment, transfer or deployment, all outside activities, assets, and direct and contingent liabilities that might give rise to a conflict of interest with respect to their official duties. To this end, a Confidential Report must be filed with their Deputy Head.

b. Every time a major change occurs in the personal affairs or official duties of public servants, they must review their obligations under this Code. If a real, apparent or potential conflict of interest exists, they must file a new Confidential Report with their Deputy Head.

c. When negotiating financial arrangements with outside parties, public servants must assure compliance with the Conflict of Interest and Post-Employment Measures in accordance with directives on this matter issued by Treasury Board. When in doubt, public servants must immediately report the situation to their supervisors in order to seek advice or direction on how to proceed.

When faced with an ethical dilemma, public servants are encouraged to use the opportunities and mechanisms established by their Deputy Head to raise, discuss and resolve issues of concern related to this Code.

Source: Canada. Treasury Board of Canada Secretariat. *Values and Ethics Code for the Public Service.* www.tbs-sct.gc.ca/pubs_pol/hrpubs/TB_851/vec-cve1_e.asp#_Toc46202800 Accessed July 24, 2007.

Ultimately, it would seem that the effectiveness of codes of conduct depends on ongoing scrutiny of public officials' activities by their colleagues within the organization, by other organizations, by the media, and by an attentive public. This, of course, depends on openness and accountability. But there is no sure-fire way of ensuring ethical behaviour that is consonant with the public interest. It ultimately depends on the individuals who aspire to public office, and on the system of values that they have been socialized into. This, of course, creates a contemporary dilemma for governance, since public institutions are held in less regard than they once were. Thus, a vicious cycle has been set up in which the low quality of public servants attracts the scorn of the public, which feeds the perception that the public service is no longer a higher calling, which means "quality" people avoid making their careers there, which means that the scorn of the public is reinforced, and so on. Recent attempts by schools of public administration and by the public sector itself have sought to break the cycle by placing more emphasis on public service ethics.

Written codes of ethics are one way of achieving this. Another is better training, and yet another is providing role models in the upper ranks of the public service who subscribe to and demonstrate the highest standards of ethical conduct (discussed following). According to one observer, interrelated objectives in seeking improved ethical standards in the public service include the following:

(1) to promote public trust and confidence in the ethical performance of public servants; (2) to decrease and, if possible, to eliminate, unethical practices by discouraging and punishing them; (3) to legitimate the imposition of sanctions for unethical behaviour; (4) to sensitize both current and aspiring public servants to the ethical and value dimensions of bureaucratic decisions; (5) to reduce uncertainty as to what constitutes ethical and unethical behaviour; (6) to develop skills in the analysis of ethical and value issues; (7) to assist public servants to resolve ethical and value dilemmas; and (8) to promote moral development.[32]

But are written codes of conduct the best way to ensure ethical behaviour in the public sector? Critics suggest that for a number of reasons, codes may not be as useful in promoting ethical behaviour as they seem.[33] First, the guidelines set out in codes are often difficult to apply in real-life situations. As the examples of ethical dilemmas above suggest, it would be impossible to develop a single code to comprehensively account for every situation that might arise in the course of a public servant's job. As well, codes of ethics are often difficult to enforce—indeed, many codes contain no reference to how their provisions should be enforced. Third, given modern governments' complexity, is it reasonable to assume that a generalized code of ethics can be drafted that applies to all government departments, regulatory bodies, and agencies? Surely, the differences in organization and structure, policy focus, and activities mitigate against a sort of one-size-fits-all approach to codifying ethical behaviour. Fourth, codes of behaviour sometimes cast their nets so wide that innocents are caught up in them, as when public servants are required to disclose not only their own personal financial interests, but those of immediate family members. Fifth, managing some ethical issues by referring to a code of ethics is inappropriate. For instance, no code can set out what level of risk to the public is acceptable in a given policy decision. The specificity of some ethical decisions belies the generality of codes of ethics. Finally, where widespread or systematic corruption commonly informs the actions and decisions of public servants, these will override the most elegantly and articulately formulated code.

Still, these criticisms assume, perhaps, that codes of ethics can do more than, in reality, they are intended to. It may well be the case that the existence of a code of ethics raises expectations about the standards of behaviour in the public service beyond that which can be reasonably expected. Thus, rather than throw the baby out with the bathwater by accepting all these criticisms as an indictment of codes of ethics, it is more advisable to acknowledge that no single code is going to "solve" all ethical dilemmas. What a code might do is contribute to an environment in which the highest standards of behaviour are aspired to by the organization and the individuals working therein.

Two other effective means of compelling public servants to act ethically include training and education, and role models.

Training and Education

Arguments have been made that improved training is the key to improved ethics in the public service. By focusing on developing the ability to identify ethical issues in day-to-day work scenarios, public servants can be stimulated to recognize ethical dilemmas and, perhaps, solve them. This allows for a deepening comprehension of ethical issues, and provides them with some tools with which to engage in ethical analysis. By drawing attention to exemplary ethical behaviour, the hope is that public servants can be socialized into the profession's highest ethical norms.[34]

The importance of training and education does not lie in the expectation that a previously amoral or unethical individual will, somehow, suddenly "find" morality or ethics. It is not argued that these things can be "taught" to an individual whose lifelong socialization has shaped him in ways that no course in ethical behaviour is going to undo. Instead, the expectation is that this kind of training will simply promote an awareness of ethical dilemmas confronted by public servants. The point is to sensitize public servants to the issues and assist them in developing the analytical skills and the practical means of dealing with the issues. It is further argued that this approach is most effective for those at the early stages of their public service career.[35]

But the role of training and education needs more explicit attention. As law professor Lorne Sossin notes, "training and education are the cornerstones to the building of a new and vigorous administrative culture for the public service in which political/public service boundaries and the commitment of the public service to uphold the rule of law figure prominently."[36] But after interviewing public servants with respect to how newly hired public servants learned the boundaries between public service and political staff and ministers, Sossin reports "most of the answers indicate that this is left to 'osmosis' and 'mentorship' and 'learning by example,' but virtually no formal instruction for training of any kind specifically addressed these issues." He concludes that "this situation must change."[37]

However, the spurt of interest in ethics education in public administration schools that occurred in the 1980s may have tapered off. A recent survey comparing Canadian master's programs in public administration, public management, and public policy noted that only one full-time MPA has a dedicated ethics course. Several schools claim that ethical concerns permeate all of their offerings, but most schools appear to simply educate students about the institutional features and mechanisms of public administration.[38] Students are well versed in the skeletal features—executive, legislative, judicial, and bureaucratic branches and the accountability relationships between them. What seems to be lacking, however, is a systematic examination of the "guts" of those relationships—that is, the values and ethics that animate public service behaviour.[39]

Finally, part of the training of new employees in the federal public service at the level of supervisor includes a program called "Orientation to the Public Service" offered by the Canada School for Public Service (CSPS). The description of this program states,

If you are an employee newly appointed to the public service, you will receive basic orientation training in the nation's capital. You will spend two days in Ottawa participating in a program designed to introduce you to the function, culture, values and ethics of the Public Service of Canada. . . . As a supervisor, you are an important catalyst in ensuring that all public servants understand the unique values and culture of the public service. To this end, the Orientation program is a great way of welcoming your new employees into the public service and to help them gain a common understanding of their role. Employees must register within two months of appointment. . . . The Orientation to the Public Service is designed to welcome new employees into the public service and to help them gain a common understanding of their role as public servants. It is an excellent learning experience, committed to: instilling a sense of pride in the opportunity to serve Canadians; and equipping new recruits with the foundational understanding of government and the values, ethics and accountability that they will draw upon throughout their careers in the Public Service.[40]

Role Models

Finally, it is also argued that inculcating ethical standards of behaviour depends on the presence of ethical leadership at the top of the organization. It is often suggested, for instance, that codes of conduct fail to provide the "living, breathing" consequences of ethical behaviour. Senior public servants can create a climate and set examples to be emulated by their junior colleagues, who, studies show, are significantly influenced by the tone set by their superiors.

However, the examples that exist of senior public servants effectively socializing their charges into a regime of ethical behaviour and standards tend to have happened in the past, when government was smaller and relations between public servants were more intimate. Today, government departments are so large that personal contact with the most senior administrators is rare for most public servants. As a result, it is more difficult for their influence to reach down through the organization, the way it did in the past. Thus, "it is unrealistic to argue that the role model provided by bureaucratic leaders can serve as the sole means of promoting ethical behaviour in the public service. Like a code of ethics, ethical leadership is necessary but insufficient."[41]

In any event, contemporary demographic realities within the public service create new challenges. As the Director of the Office of Values and Ethics reported,

We are about to witness a massive change in the demographics of the federal public service. The expected turnover in the next ten years, with 60–70% of employees eligible

to retire, has two major implications for government. As many have said already, we will need to attract a huge influx of new recruits—our share of the best and brightest—who will need to acquire quickly a sense of "self" as a public servant. Less often noted is the need to capture and transfer the legacy of the public service that exists now—not only the "corporate memory" but the culture, the traditions and the values that will be the solid foundation for these young people as they grapple with their own new challenges.[42]

Moreover, the role and place of the public servant is constantly changing. It has been argued that governments are moving away from strict hierarchical accountability, which means that public servants continue to obey orders, of course, but that they do not *merely* obey orders. "Instead they take responsibility for the work they do. The stereotype of the timid, reactive and rule-bound official has become passé."[43] This point, again, raises the importance of discretion, which we discussed earlier.

Ultimately, it would seem that some combination of a code of ethics, training and education, and role models is required to ensure that a standard of ethical behaviour prevails in the public service (see Box 11.3). However, there is one other factor that is required: an attentive public.

BOX 11.3 | An Ethics Regime for Government

Professor of public administration Kenneth Kernaghan suggests the following items ought to be included as part of government's ethics regime:

1. The evaluation of ethical performance as a basis for appointing and promoting all members of the public service, but especially its leadership.

2. A statement of values, including ethical values, either as part of a strategic plan or as a separate document.

3. A code of ethics (or conduct), linked to a value statement (if one exists) that sets out general principles or ethical conduct.

4. Elaboration on the code, usually as commentary under each principle, which explains more fully the meaning of the principle and/or provides illustrations of violations of the principle.

5. Reference to the existence of ethics rules (statutes, regulations, etc.) related to the problem areas covered in the code and/or to problem areas covered elsewhere.

6. Elaboration on the code, either following each principle or in a separate part, which adapts the code's principles to the particular needs of individual organizations.

7. Provisions for administering the code, including publicity, penalties for violations and provisions for grievance.

8. An ethics counsellor to perform advisory and administrative functions for senior public servants across the government.

9. An ethics counsellor, ombudsman or committee to provide advice on ethics rules and ethics issues within a single department or agency.

10. Ethics education and training for public servants, beginning with the senior echelons and new employees.

Additional, less common, measures that may be adapted are these:

11. An ethics audit to evaluate the organization's policies and procedures for preserving and nurturing ethical behaviour.

12. The raising of ethical considerations in a deliberate and regular way at meetings and through other means of communication, such as newsletters.

13. The provision of a confidential hotline that public servants can use to discuss concerns about their personal ethical behaviour or that of others.

14. The inclusion of exit interviews (i.e., interviews with employees leaving the organization) to ask questions about the employee's view of the ethical culture of the organization.

Source: Kenneth Kernaghan, "Values, Ethics and Public Service," in Jacques Bourgault, Maurice Demers and Cynthia Williams, eds. *Public Administration and Public Management: Experiences in Canada.* Sainte-Foy, Quebec: Les Publications du Quebec, 1997: 110–111.

An Attentive Public

It is only by being vigilant that citizens can realistically expect to receive public administration of the highest ethical calibre.

At the end of the day, ethics in public service is an issue of crucial importance. In the modern world much of life, both qualitatively and quantitatively, depends on government. Because government is now so big and deals with more than basic needs and elements of protection, the professionalism of public servants is even more important than in the past.

Consequently the qualities of individual public servants are also important. Public servants must be trusted to exercise judgements wisely, and they must be carefully selected for that trust. It is in their crucial work involving discretion and advice, as well as policy making, that the ethical standards of public service are evident. Nevertheless, it remains the ultimate responsibility of citizens, through their governments, to ensure that all the structures and procedures of government are best suited to their purposes, in good working order, continuously reviewed, and positively supportive to public servants when they carry out their satisfying and demanding, but also very responsible work.[44]

Clearly, a variety of influences affect the ethical dimensions of behaviour. Research on environmental influences on ethical behaviour shows "generally, there is support that ethical decision making is affected by the behaviour of peers and associates, by the actions of supervisors and top management, by the existence of policies and codes of conduct, by the rewards and punishments, and by the general atmosphere or climate of the organization."[45]

WHAT YOU HAVE LEARNED

A distinguishing feature of public administration—a rigorous regime of ethical standards to which public servants are subject—makes already complicated work even more so. But at some level, the public interest must be served, and it cannot be served by nefarious, corrupt, self-serving scoundrels abusing the public's trust (or their hard-earned dollars). This means that guidelines that are often absent in the private sector play a key role in shaping our expectations about public servants' behaviour. It is of the utmost importance to ensure the honesty and integrity of those dedicated to serving the public interest. And while there are many ways to do this (e.g., codes of conduct, ethics commissioners, education and training, role models), it is ultimately up to the public to keep a watchful eye. In turn, this implies that accountability of public officials is also a significant factor in public administration. It is to an examination of the issue of accountability that we next turn in chapter 12.

Key Words and Concepts

ethics (342)	partisanship (351)
discretion (343)	public comment (352)
ethics commissioners (343)	conflict of interest (352)
public interest (346)	lying for the public good (353)

Review Questions

1. Ethical Dilemmas in the Public Service
Some of the broad controversies surrounding the ethical standards of behaviour in the public sector were introduced in this section. Ask yourself, What does the public expect of public servants' behaviour? What dilemmas are posed for public servants in the course of their work? What is the "public interest," and how is it served? What potential ethical dilemmas can you think of that might emerge in the setting of the public sector?

2. Codes of Conduct
This section addressed the debate over whether written codes of conduct are useful tools in securing the highest ethical behaviour among public officials. It also suggested other ways that this might be achieved. Ask yourself, What are ethical codes of conduct, and how effective are they? What alternative measures can be taken to ensure the ethical conduct of public servants? In what way can training and education, and role models, supplement and complement codes of conduct? What role do you as a member of the "attentive public" have to play?

Weblinks

The Institute for Global Ethics
www.globalethics.org

The Office of Public Service Values and Ethics
www.psagency-agencefp.gc.ca/veo-bve/index_e.asp

Further Reading

1. Ethical Dilemmas in the Public Service

Atkinson, Michael M. and Gerald Bierling, "Politicians, the Public and Political Ethics: Worlds Apart," *Canadian Journal of Political Science,* 38, 4 (December 2005): 1003–28.

Greene, Ian and David P. Shugarman. "Commission of Inquiry into the Sponsorship Program and Advertising Activities, Phase I Report and Phase II Report," *Canadian Public Administration,* 49, 2 (2006): 220–32.

Greene, Ian and David P. Shugarman. *Honest Politics: Seeking Integrity in Canadian Public Life.* Toronto: James Lorimer, 1997.

Walzer, Michael and David P. Shugarman, "Are 'Dirty Hands' Necessary in Politics?" in Mark Charlton and Paul Barker, eds. *Crosscurrents: Contemporary Political Issues.* Toronto: Thomson Nelson, 2006: 323–43.

2. Codes of Conduct

Canada, Report of the Auditor General. *Values and Ethics in the Federal Public Service.* Ottawa: Supply and Services, 2000.

Canada, Task Force on Conflict of Interest. *Ethical Conduct in the Public Sector.* Ottawa: Supply and Services Canada, 1984.

Greene, Ian. "Conflicts of Interest and the Canadian Constitution: An Analysis of Conflict of Interest Rules for Canadian Cabinet Ministers." *Canadian Journal of Political Science,* 23, 2 (June, 1990): 233–56.

Endnotes

1. Cited in Thomas S. Axworthy, "The Responsibility Crisis in Canada," *Canadian Parliamentary Review,* 28, 2 (Summer, 2005): 12.

2. Warren R. Bailie and David Johnson, "Government Ethics and Ethics Agencies," *Canadian Public Administration,* 34, 1 (Spring, 1991): 158. See also Desmond Morton, "Reflecting on Gomery: Political Scandals and the Canadian Memory," *Policy Options,* 26, 5, (June, 2005): 14–21.

3. See Ian Greene, "Government Ethics Commissioners: The Way of the Future?" *Canadian Public Administration,* 34, 1 (Spring, 1991): 165–70. See also Luc Juillet "The Office of Ethics Commissioner, Accountability and Public Trust," in G. Bruce Doern, ed. *How Ottawa Spends 2004–2005: Mandate Change in the Paul Martin Era,* (Montreal: McGill-Queen's University Press, 2004): 296–316; and Denis Saint-Martin, "Should the Federal Ethics Counsellor Become an Independent Officer of Parliament?" *Canadian Public Policy,* 29, (2003): 197–212.

4. See John Tait, "A Strong Foundation: The Report of the Task Force on Public Service Values and Ethics (the summary)," *Canadian Public Administration,* 40, 1 (Spring, 1997). See also Canada, Treasury Board of Canada Secretariat, *Building on a Strong Foundation—The Dialogue Continues Volume II: Further Case Studies on Values and Ethics in the Public Service,* (Ottawa: Canadian Centre for Management Development, 2001).

5. The recent history of the issue of values and ethics in the public service is outlined in: Canada, Treasury Board of Canada Secretariat, "Creating a Value Based Public Service: Remarks by

Catherine MacQuarrie, Director, Office of Values and Ethics, Treasury Board Secretariat," (Ottawa: Treasury Board of Canada Secretariat, July 11, 2001).

6. Neil Nevitte, *The Decline of Deference: Canadian Value Change in Cross-National Perspective,* (Peterborough: Broadview Press, 1996): 56.

7. See Ekos Research Associates, "Rethinking Government: Exploring Changing Relationships Among Individuals, Governments and Business," (2001): 10. **www.http://ekos.ca/studies/default.asp**

8. E. Pendleton Herring, *Public Administration and the Public Interest,* (New York: McGraw-Hill, 1936).

9. See W.T. Stanbury, "Definitions of the Public Interest," in Douglas G. Hartle, *Public Policy Decision Making and Regulation,* (Montreal: Institute for Research on Public Policy, 1979): 213–18.

10. Tait, "A Strong Foundation," (1996): 32.

11. Dennis F. Thompson, "The Possibility of Administrative Ethics," in Jay M. Shafritz and Albert C. Hyde, eds. *Classics of Public Administration, Third Edition,* (Pacific Cove, California: Brooks/Cole Publishing, 1992): 523.

12. Thompson, "The Possibility of Administrative Ethics," (1992): 524.

13. The Canadian Centre for Management Development (now the Canada School of Public Service) and the Treasury Board Secretariat sponsored an ongoing series of discussions and case studies of ethics in the public service. See Canada, Treasury Board of Canada Secretariat, *Building on a Strong Foundation—The Dialogue Continues Volume II: Further Case Studies on Values and Ethics in the Public Service,* (Ottawa: Canadian Centre for Management Development, 2001). See also Kenneth Kernaghan, *Professional Ethics and Standards for the Evaluation Community in the Government of Canada,* (Ottawa: Treasury Board Secreatariat of Canada, 2006).

14. Institute of Public Administration of Canada, Statement of Principles Regarding the Conduct of Public Employees, **www.ipac.ca/ethics/revisit_principles.html** Accessed July 24, 2007. This Statement, produced in 1987, was updated in 2005. See Institute of Public Administration of Canada, A Public Servant's Commitments, **www.ipac.ca/ethics/a_public_servants_commitments/index.html** Accessed July 24, 2007. See also Kenneth Kernaghan and John W. Langford, *The Responsible Public Servant,* (Halifax: The Institute for Research on Public Policy, 1990): 205.

15. See John W. Langford, "Moonlighting and Mobility," *Canadian Public Administration,* 34, 1 (Spring, 1991): 62–72.

16. Institute of Public Administration of Canada, Statement of Principles Regarding the Conduct of Public Employees, **www.ipac.ca/ethics/revisit_principles.html** Accessed July 24, 2007.

17. Richard A. Chapman, "Ethics in Public Service," in Richard A. Chapman, ed. *Ethics in Public Service,* (Ottawa: Carleton University Press, 1993): 158–59.

18. See Sissela Bok, *Lying: Moral Choice in Public and Private Life,* (New York: Pantheon, 1978).

19. Arden R. Haynes, "The Ethical Dimension in Business and Government," *Canadian Public Administration,* 34, 1 (Spring, 1991): 18.

20. Frederick C. Mosher et al. *Watergate: Implications for Responsible Government,* (Washington, D.C.: National Academy of Public Administration, 1974). Cited in Jay M. Shafritz and Albert C. Hyde, eds. *Classics of Public Administration, Third Edition,* (1992): 416–17.

21. Kenneth Kernaghan, "East Block and Westminster: Conventions, Values and Public Service," in Christopher Dunn, ed., *Handbook of Canadian Public Administration,* (Toronto: Oxford University Press, 2002): 113.

22. Elaine Todres, "The Ethical Dimension in Public Service," *Canadian Public Administration,* 34, 1 (Spring, 1991): 12.

23. Kenneth Kernaghan and John Langford, *The Responsible Public Servant,* (Halifax: Institute for Research on Public Policy, 1990): 2.

24. Michael M. Atkinson and Gerald Bierling, "Politicians, the Public and Political Ethics: Worlds Apart," *Canadian Journal of Political Science,* 38, 4 (December 2005): 1004.

25. John Langford and Allan Tupper, "How Ottawa Does Business: Ethics as a Government Program," in G. Bruce Doern, ed. *How Ottawa Spends 2006–2007: In From the Cold: The Tory Rise and the Liberal Fall*, (Montreal: McGill-Queen's University Press, 2006): 116–17.

26. See George Thomson, "Personal Morality in a Professional Context," *Canadian Public Administration,* 34, 1 (Spring, 1991).

27. Richard A. Chapman, "Introduction," in Richard A. Chapman, ed. *Ethics in Public Service,* (Ottawa: Carleton University Press, 1993): 2.

28. See Bailie and Johnson, "Governmental Ethics and Ethics Agencies," (1991): 159.

29. See Canada, Treasury Board, *Conflict of Interest and Post-Employment Code for the Public Service,* (Ottawa: Supply and Services, 1985).

30. Tait, "A Strong Foundation," (1997): 1–22. See also Peter Aucoin, "A Profession of Public Administration?: A Commentary on 'A Strong Foundation,'" *Canadian Public Administration,* 40, 1 (Spring, 1997): 23–39.

31. See David Good, *The Politics of Public Management: The HRDC Audit of Grants and Contributions*, (Toronto: University of Toronto Press, 2003).

32. Kenneth Kernaghan, "Promoting Public Service Ethics: The Codification Option," in Richard W. Chapman, ed. *Ethics in Public Service,* (Ottawa: Carleton University Press, 1993): 18.

33. The following reasons are derived from Kernaghan, "Promoting Public Service Ethics," (1993): 19.

34. See M.W. Jackson, "How Can Ethics be Taught?" in Richard A. Chapman, ed. *Ethics in Public Service,* (Ottawa: Carleton University Press, 1993): 31–42.

35. Kernaghan, "Promoting Public Service Ethics," (1993): 25–26.

36. Lorne Sossin, "Defining Boundaries: The Constitutional Argument for Bureaucratic Independence and its Implications for the Accountability of the Public Service," in Donald Savoie, ed. *Restoring Accountability: Research Studies Volume 2. The Public Service and Transparency. Commission of Inquiry into the Sponsorship Program and Advertising Activities.* (Ottawa: Minister of Public Works and Government Services, 2006): 64.

37. Sossin, "Defining Boundaries," (2006): 64.

38. James Iain Gow and Sharon L. Sutherland, "Comparison of Canadian Master's Programs in Public Administration, Public Management and Public Policy," *Canadian Public Administration,* 47, 3, (Fall, 2004): 401.

39. See Gregory J. Inwood, "Teaching Accountability to Public Servants," paper presented to the 2006 Law and Parliament Conference, Ottawa, November 3, 2006.

40. Canada. Canada School of Public Service, "Orientation to the Public Service," **www.myschool-monecole.gc.ca/ops-ofp/index_e.asp?lang=e&loid=507** Accessed November 5, 2006.

41. Kernaghan, "Promoting Public Service Ethics," (1993): 25.

42. Canada, "Creating a Value Based Public Service" (2001): 3.

43. Todres, "The Ethical Dimension in Public Service," (1991): 15.

44. Chapman, "Ethics in Public Service," (1993): 170.

45. Dennis P. Wittmer, "Developing a Behavioral Model for Ethical Decision Making in Organizations: Conceptual and Empirical Research," in H. George Frederickson and Richard K. Ghere, eds. *Ethics in Public Management*, (Armonk, New York: M.E. Sharpe, 2005): 63–64.

Chapter 12

Public Administration *and* Accountability

WHAT YOU WILL LEARN

Many references have been made throughout this book to the important concept of *accountability*, which simply means being required to explain one's actions by answering to someone else. It is a central feature of public administration, which raises several interrelated issues:

■ What is accountability, and how is it related to the principle of responsible government?

■ How does the concept of accountability inform the public service decision making process?

■ Who is accountable to whom, for what, and under what circumstances?

This chapter is divided into the following sections:

1. Accountability and Democracy

This section reviews the central principle of responsible government, first raised in chapter 2. It then establishes the link between accountability and democracy by asking, What is the significance of the principle of responsible government? How does it work in theory and in practice in the Canadian setting in relation specifically to accountability?

2. Ministerial Responsibility

Responsible government depends in part on the doctrine of ministerial responsibility. This doctrine sets the parameters of ministerial action, and the guidelines that establish how government can be held to account. This section explains the pure theory of ministerial responsibility, and reveals how it has been altered by contemporary developments, by asking, What is the theory of ministerial responsibility? What is individual ministerial responsibility? What is collective ministerial responsibility? What is the doctrine of answerability? How has the traditional expectation about how responsibility is realized in the political system changed over time? What does the doctrine look like now?

3. ― *Accountability and Public Servants*

The traditional doctrine of ministerial authority combines with the politics-administration dichotomy to set the expectations of public servant account-ability. But recent changes to the concept of accountability have left public servants on unfamiliar ground. This section addresses both the traditional and newly evolving role of public servants, and asks, How have public servants been held accountable for their actions? How has the concept of ministerial responsibility and the politics-administration dichotomy influenced the way public servants do their jobs? How have changes to these doctrines altered the role of public servants in terms of accountability?

4. ― *Accountability in Action: The Role of the Office of the Auditor General*

There are many links in the chain of accountability. One of the most significant is the Office of the Auditor General. Here, we review briefly the role of this important actor in terms of its contribution to the accountability process by asking, How does the government get objective, unbiased assessment of its policies? What role does the Office of the Auditor General play in this process? If the auditor general watches over government, who, in turn, watches over the auditor general?

5. ― *Contemporary Issues of Accountability and Control*

Recent developments have seen some of the traditional precepts of accountability change. The traditional notions of ministerial responsibility and the role of public servants have altered as new organizational norms and systems, such as the New Public Management, come into play. This section asks, What impact has reform of public administration had on traditional notions of accountability? How has the New Public Management altered the usual relationships within government where responsibility is concerned?

Accountability and Democracy

Central to any democracy is the ability of the people to hold their elected officials **accountable** for their actions. This point has been made several times in this book. The most general sense in which this is exercised is through the ballot box. If you do not believe your representatives have been doing a good job, or if you believe they have failed to account properly for their actions, you can "throw the rascals out." It is, after all, *power* that the citizens are vesting in their elected officials. If that power is abused or poorly exercised, the people have the right to take it back and give it to someone else. Therefore, the government ought to act in a responsible manner and be accountable to the people, or it may lose the reins of power.

While this generally describes conditions in democratic societies, it was not always thus. Imagine a time before the rise of democracy. As Weber tells us, the basis of the right to rule was often either divine intervention or the charisma of individual leaders. But what this meant in terms of accountability was that the masses dared not question their leaders, for to do so would anger the gods and invite divine retribution and whatever punishment this might bring in the afterlife (that is, to question the king was to question the deity that anointed the king). To question the charismatic leader was to invite scorn, ostracism, and perhaps imprisonment or death. When societies began to move toward systems of government in which the people could choose their leaders and remove them at will, the modern notion of accountability came into play. As one observer reports, "It took several centuries in the tortuous evolution of the modern nation state to develop a coherent, binding, respected ideology of public accountability, together with efficient means of enforcement that would permit the peaceful transfer of power and the voluntary ceding of public office."[1] It was only when the absolute rule of a single leader was replaced by the rule of representative legislative assemblies overseen by an appointed executive—which could be held collectively and individually responsible for running the affairs of the state—that accountability emerged in its modern guise.

This is the basis of the principle of **responsible government** (see Box 12.1), which was achieved in Canada in the 1840s.[2] It was first adopted by Nova Scotia and the Province of Canada (now Quebec and Ontario) in 1848, Prince Edward Island in 1851, New Brunswick in 1854, and Newfoundland in 1855. Its origins can be found in the earlier development of responsible government in the British political system, the model from which the Canadian system is largely derived.[3] The British Crown had been bound by the principle of seeking the consent of the Lords before it could tax them, a principle that was incorporated in the *Magna Carta* in the twelfth century. But it was not until the seventeenth century that the king's obligation to consult the elected representatives of the people (which eventually meant the House of Commons) was established. At the time, however, the king's ministers were *not* also members of the House of Commons. But with the growing importance of the House, it gradually dawned on people that ministers ought to be Members of Parliament, and, in that way, their responsibility and accountability as representatives of the people would be more direct and could be better managed. The next step in this evolutionary process saw the rise of organized political parties in the eighteenth century, and it was largely this model that emerged in Canada.

You might ask yourself why the achievement of responsible government was a significant development in the evolution of the Canadian political system, and what bearing it has on public administration today. Consider the motivations behind vesting power in the hands of the people's representative and making the government (that is, the Cabinet) responsible to them. You might come up with two strikingly different perspectives: one arguing that responsible government is a bulwark of democracy; the other suggesting that it

BOX 12.1 | Definitions of Responsible Government

In order to govern . . . the Prime Minister and the Cabinet require the confidence of the elected House of Commons. This constitutional principle is called responsible government. If a government loses the confidence of the House—this would be either through a defeat on an important piece of legislation (i.e., the annual budget or legislation related to government spending) or on a motion of no confidence proposed by an opposition party—it loses the right to govern.[a]

***

The term responsible government defines the relationship of Cabinet ministers to the House, the Crown, and to each other. Collectively, the Cabinet is responsible to the House of Commons in that the government must maintain the support of a majority of MPs if it is to continue in office. If Cabinet loses the "confidence" of the House through a specific "want of confidence" or non-confidence vote, or through the defeat of a major government bill, unwritten constitutional convention calls for the government to tender its resignation. In practice, the prime minister would usually ask the Governor General for the "dissolution" of Parliament, and would go to the people in a general election.[b]

***

Responsible government means that the political executive is not able to act without the support of a majority in the legislature (the chamber of representatives).[c]

***

The democratic principle is that all public officials are accountable to the people and can rule only by their consent.[d]

Sources: *a.* Stephen Brooks, *Canadian Democracy: An Introduction, Fourth Edition,* (Toronto: Oxford University Press, 2004): 132. *b.* Roger Gibbins, *Conflict and Unity: An Introduction to Canadian Political Life, Second Edition,* (Scarborough: Nelson, 1990): 30. *c.* Larry Johnston, *Politics: An Introduction to the Modern Democratic State. Third Edition,* (Peterborough: Broadview Press, 2007): 138–39. *d.* Leonard T. Hobhouse, *Liberalism,* (New York: Oxford University Press, 1911). Cited in James John Guy, *People, Politics and Government: A Canadian Perspective, Sixth Edition,* (Toronto: Pearson Prentice Hall, 2006): 76.

is an elaborate system to actually check the power of the people, and protect the privileged position of the elite.

The first argument—that responsibility is meant to democratize government by giving more power to the people (or, in the context of the 1800s, less power to the Crown)—was supported by those who saw in responsible government the opportunity to transfer power from an unaccountable sovereign (as represented by the Governor General and the Governor General's appointees in Cabinet) to the people through their representatives in Parliament. We will call the people who supported these view *democrats*. The underlying assumption of the democrats was that power rightly belongs to the people and that, short of involving every citizen in the direct governance of the country (recall our discussion of direct democracy in chapter 2), it is sufficient to maximize ordinary citizens' power by giving their representatives real power.

Ironically, the opposite viewpoint also supported the concept of responsible government, but for a different set of reasons. Assuming that society was naturally divided into the *ruled* and the *rulers,* this group of people—which we will call the *conservatives*—saw in responsible government an opportunity to shelter the exercise of power from the direct interference of the "great unwashed"—that is, the people. The conservatives were inherently suspicious of democracy as we understand it today, because they saw rule by the people as destabilizing and dangerous. The mass of the citizenry was seen as too uneducated, too prone to fall under the sway of demagogues, and too likely to ignore the rights of minorities to be trusted with power.[4] But by establishing institutions such as responsible government, power would be transferred not to the people but to their representatives, who tended always to come from the class of society deserving to rule. In any event, if certain undesirable democrats managed to get themselves elected, they could always be checked in their unsavory ambitions to further democratize government by the countervailing weight of the executive branch of government (that is, the Cabinet) and the Upper House in Parliament (the Senate), whose members are appointed by the Crown. Thus, the drive to responsible government was supported by these two groups, but for quite different reasons.[5]

Whichever perspective you find most compelling, the conventional notion has developed that accountability is enforced primarily through the ballot box. Of course, responsible government is made up of several other components, too, through which this underlying principle is reinforced. For instance, the institutions of parliamentary government have a number of mechanisms through which the government is held to account, such as the daily question period in the House of Commons, Parliamentary committees, and opposition parties. Outside Parliament, the media and interest groups also play an important part in holding the government to account. The judiciary, of course, also forces the government to be accountable, as when a citizen, interest group, corporation, or other government challenges a government's actions in a court of law. It is noteworthy that the emergence of modern democratic government was accompanied by the proscription that no one—not even the leaders of the government—was beyond the law. As a result, accountability is reinforced by the judicial system through constitutional and administrative law as well. Thus, "The law would further reduce official discretion by prescribing the precise arrangements whereby public business was to be conducted, arrangements that included the structure of the machinery of government, the number and tenure of public officials, the handling of public property and monies, the code of conduct governing official behaviour, and methods for handling citizens and aliens."[6] All of these institutions are meant to support democratic governance. But it is ultimately elections that allow the people to pass judgment on a government.

For public administration, this means that, at some level, everything public officials do should in some way relate to the *will of the people* as expressed through their selection of representatives in Parliament. As a result, the focus of policy formulation, implementation, and evaluation is Parliament: it receives advice from public servants, it instructs them, and it evaluates their work, all in the name of the people. In other words, Parliament is the sun around which the planets and stars in the constellation of public administration revolve. In turn, this also contributes to the uniqueness of the public service compared to the private sector:

Public service exists to satisfy certain needs of the community. Its existence depends upon the trust, confidence and support (both financial, through taxation, and legal, through obedience to laws and regulations enforced by public servants) it derives from the public through their representatives. Unlike the private sector, it cannot (as expected) become too self-seeking and obscure. Its every action and inaction is subject to thorough scrutiny. The community expects public servants to be fair, ethical and dedicated in administering public policies and programs. And public trust and confidence is assured when public servants are found managing public programs soundly, and are found to be held accountable for their actions.[7]

But note also that the concept of *accountability* is an empty shell unless it is connected to a system of rewards and punishments. If there is no tangible benefit from acting in an accountable manner, can people be counted on to act responsibly? Not always. Similarly, if there are no punishments or sanctions for failing to act responsibly, can people be relied upon to do so? Again, not always. As a result, a complex system of rewards and punishments has evolved to ensure compliance with measures designed to promote accountability and responsibility. At the most general level, failure of the government overall to act responsibly will result in its losing power at the next election. Moving to a more specific level, failure of a Cabinet minister or Member of Parliament to act responsibly could result in a range of sanctions—from a reprimand from the prime minister, to dismissal from Cabinet, to being passed over for plum positions, to being kicked out of the political party. For public servants, the motivation to act responsibly is tied to the system of job-related rewards (raises, promotions, status, etc.) and punishments (reprimand, suspension, dismissal, etc.). At a more extreme level, legal sanctions can be invoked against either politicians or public servants in the event of criminal abuses of power. Together, this package of rewards and punishments serves to reinforce and remind public officials that their primary duty is not to themselves, but to the public interest. Compliance with the rules and regulations meant to support accountability will bring rewards, but any breach of trust or failure to act responsibly will be dealt with in a serious manner.

Society cannot allow public servants to simply act on their own whims and fancies; public servants must be answerable to someone. We can think of the institutions that enforce answerability as the political, legal, and administrative arrangements that seek to ensure that the power of the rulers is controlled ultimately by the ruled. The trick is to balance the requirement for some constraints with the need to be able to act. As one observer put it, "Too much independence and too few constraints have allowed too much wrongdoing. Too many controls and too little trust have stultified government and prevented rapid, flexible action."[8]

Further complicating our understanding of accountability and democracy is the idea that we can subdivide accountability by looking at both administrative responsibility and political responsibility. This will remind us of the admonition from the politics-administration dichotomy that politicians lead and public servants follow. Thus, it is conceptually useful to try to distinguish when and where purely political actions and decisions can be separated from purely administrative ones. For example, the decision to build a bridge in one riding and not another is a political decision. The decision to locate that bridge at what engineers say is the safest and most accessible point on the river, where it will serve the greatest amount of traffic in the most efficient manner possible, is an administrative decision. If the public is outraged because the bridge is built in a particular riding solely to create jobs so that the local Member of Parliament might more easily get re-elected, there may be a political price to pay. But if the bridge falls down because of poor construction or technical miscalculations about the strength of the riverbank to support the pylons, there are administrative and legal sanctions. Of course, in the real world, the neat division over responsibilities is less clear-cut. For instance, the decision to award a particular firm the contract to construct the pylons may have been influenced by that firm's financial support of the party in power, in which case the political and administrative boundaries over responsibility are blurred. It is exactly this type of scenario that makes it challenging to analyze and apply doctrines of accountability in a precise manner. (See Box 12.2.)

According to political scientist Paul Thomas, accountability consists of "an obligation to explain and justify how one discharges responsibilities, the origins of which may be political, constitutional, statutory, hierarchical, or contractual. Different origins give rise to several variants of accountability, which in turn differ in the degree of direct control and public disclosure involved."[9] He suggests there are five components in any accountability relationship. First is the assignment of responsibilities related to agreed-upon goals. Second is the provision of authority, resources, and a supportive environment. Third is the obligation to answer for the fulfilling of those responsibilities, while the fourth is the evaluation of performance to make sure that instructions have been complied with. And fifth is sanctions or penalties for nonperformance, as well as rewards for good performance.[10] Together, assignment, support, obligation, evaluation, and sanctions and rewards constitute a framework within which we can assess any accountability regime.

To further refine our thinking about these complex matters, we can look at accountability in another way. It is useful to think of the issues we have been exploring so far in terms of three interrelated key elements: responsibility, accountability, and liability.

BOX 12.2 How Specs Live Forever

It is sometimes difficult to figure out the origins of a particular policy and, thus, who should be accountable for it. Consider the following example that has been making the rounds in various incarnations on the internet and via email.

Can a horse's back-end be responsible for modern-day U.S. railroad specifications? Yes—sort of. The U.S. Standard railroad gauge—the distance between the rails—is four feet, eight-and-a-half inches. Many early U.S. railway lines were designed to accommodate British-built standard-gauge locomotives. These locomotives were, in turn, based on northern English tramway lines used for transporting coal. These tramways used a four-foot-eight-inch gauge.

The four-foot-eight-inch gauge was derived from wagon-wheel ruts, which were most commonly spaced at five feet. Why five feet? Five feet allowed for the wagons to comfortably fit behind a team of two draft animals. Adjusting for two, two-inch-wide rails (with a half-inch leeway) resulted in a four-foot-eight-inch gauge. Therefore, twenty-first-century engineers designing high-speed locomotives are still bound by specifications that began on mud-covered paths a thousand years ago.

Source: Cecil Adams, "Was Standard Railroad Gauge (4'8") Determined by Roman Chariot Ruts?" **www.straightdope.com/columns/000218.html** Accessed July 25, 2007.

To be responsible is to have the authority to act, power to control, freedom to decide, the ability to distinguish (as between right and wrong) and to behave rationally and reliably and with consistency and trustworthiness in exercising internal judgement. To be accountable is to answer for one's responsibilities, to report, to explain, to give reasons, to respond, to assume obligations, to render a reckoning and to submit to an outside or external judgement. To be liable is to assume the duty of making good, to restore, to compensate, to recompense for wrongdoing or poor judgement.[11]

The mechanisms for ensuring realization of these three interrelated goals have been surveyed in earlier chapters. We now return to some of the features of public administration outlined earlier, to assess their usefulness in meeting these goals.

Ministerial Responsibility

One problematic aspect of accountability is the question of who is directly and personally responsible when the government screws something up. As you now know, the theory of **ministerial responsibility** tells us that individual Cabinet ministers are ultimately responsible for all the actions of their departments, and must answer for them when they make a mistake. If the mistake is significant enough and the mistake is the result of actions that can be attributed personally and directly to the minister involved, the minister may have to resign his or her position as a sign that the minister has taken responsibility. No minister in Canada has ever resigned because of a mistake made directly by a subordinate in his or her ministry, unless the minister has been seen to be personally responsible. "If one of the minister's officials makes a mistake, the requirements of ministerial responsibility are satisfied when the minister answers to the House for the mistake and implements the necessary remedial action."[12] This is sometimes referred to as the **doctrine of answerability**, and is regarded as a somewhat watered-down version of the doctrine of individual ministerial responsibility.[13] Aucoin and Jarvis suggest there are three interrelated dimensions to ministerial responsibility:

First, the minister is the chief executive of a department, the person in charge of the officials, the one with the statutory authority to take action so that the purposes of the law are realized. Second, the minister has been assigned the duties or obligations that are also set forth in statutes. And, third, the minister must provide an account and may be held to account for his or her actions, or the actions of officials, whether or not the minister had knowledge of these actions. In short, the term responsible encompasses three dimensions of ministerial responsibility: authority, responsibility and accountability.[14]

Another aspect of ministerial responsibility is that the Cabinet acts collectively in every government decision, and therefore must accept **collective ministerial responsibility** for any errors. This convention of government is tested when votes are held in the House of Commons. When a majority supports the government by voting in favour of its policies, it is signalling confidence in the government's ability to carry on. But if a majority votes against the government, it must resign, signalling that it collectively takes responsibility for its actions. In this way accountability is realized.

The doctrine of collective ministerial responsibility is also important in terms of maintaining government stability and confidentiality.[15] It requires ministers to support Cabinet decisions publicly, the main advantage of which is to promote consensus and, as a result, political stability. This is closely linked to the notion of Cabinet confidentiality; even when individual ministers disagree with decisions taken at the Cabinet table, they keep their disagreements to themselves. Confidentiality of discussions within Cabinet promotes consensus, as it encourages open debate and a frank assessment of all alternatives in the privacy of the Cabinet, and leaves ministers secure in the knowledge that divisions within government will not be publicly aired.

One Privy Council Office official sums up the doctrines of both individual and collective ministerial responsibility this way:

As a general rule, ministerial responsibility, both collective and individual, is a "guarantee" that the political executive's decision making power will be exercised responsibly, that is, in accordance with the will of the people. Collective responsibility enables the House of Commons, and therefore the people of Canada, to hold the Cabinet accountable for its collective decisions. As for individual responsibility, it enables the House of Commons to exercise control over the public service through the responsible ministers.[16]

What exactly are ministers responsible for in the real world of government?[17] There are currently more than 135 organizations that, through ministers, are accountable to Parliament, including departments, Crown corporations, tribunals and quasi-judicial bodies, and service organizations of various kinds. As an illustration of the extent of ministerial involvement, one study indicated that in one year the Ministry of Industry, Trade, and Commerce took about 4700 decisions. And while only 190 of these were kept under the minister's direct control, they accounted for well over half of the department's expenditures.[18] Ministers are responsible for each of these types of organizations, although the exact number and type varies by ministry. There are diminishing levels of direct ministerial oversight as you move from departments to service agencies to Crown corporations to tribunals and quasi-judicial bodies. For example, departments are under direct ministerial control, and ministers can and do intervene on any departmental matters, as they wish. Service agencies, which are established by law to deliver services within an established policy and legal framework, are also closely controlled by the minister responsible. Crown corporations are less directly in the minister's purview. Generally, the minister responsible simply approves the corporation's business plans and the presentation of annual reports to Parliament. Finally, administrative tribunals and quasi-judicial bodies are subject to the least direct ministerial control. They generally require an arm's-length relationship with the minister responsible for them, to be able to do their work without fear of political interference or reprisal. Still, the minister has responsibility for them, and plays an important role in allocating their financial resources. Still other organizations, such as the Office of the Auditor General, report directly to Parliament, and effectively bypass direct ministerial control. In short, the levels of ministerial responsibility are many and complex, and indicate different degrees of responsibility. The ability to successfully juggle these different degrees of responsibility is a feat in itself, but must be managed if the underlying principles of responsible government are to be upheld.

Another aspect of accountability has to do with the way in which ministers delegate authority to their officials. In this case, authority to act is essentially transferred from the minister to officials who are expected to act on behalf of the minister. In general, "the minister is not involved personally and does not know precisely what actions are being taken. A minister is expected to give general direction, receive reports, ask questions, and respond to matters that require his or her personal involvement, including things that have gone wrong and require corrective action."[19] The important point to keep in mind is that the doctrine of ministerial responsibility allows ministers to delegate authority but not accountability.

Recently, there has been a trend toward a form of accountability that undermines the theory of ministerial responsibility. Public servants traditionally toil anonymously behind the scenes, allowing the elected representatives (their bosses) to take both the credit and blame for government actions. But there is now a strong movement toward holding public servants publicly accountable for the results achieved by their departments. This reflects the fact that Cabinet ministers cannot realistically be expected to be on top of every single development within their ministries, which may employ thousands of people and run hundreds of distinct programs. A case in point is the so-called Al-Mashat affair, in which Iraq's former ambassador to the United States entered Canada as a landed immigrant only a month after applying to get in to Canada. He and his family thereby jumped the immigration queue and bypassed the usual long, drawn-out process that most immigrants must go through. The Mulroney government pinned the blame for this mistake directly on the senior public servants involved, rather than having the minister accept responsibility.[20] However, the government has moved to clarify the distinction between ministers' accountability to Parliament for the use of powers vested in them by statute, as opposed to arm's-length bodies for which their responsibility is more indirect. Ministers remain accountable for the former but are answerable for the latter.[21] In addition, the government has supplemented the doctrine of answerability by amending the Financial Administration Act in 2007 to designate deputy ministers as **accounting officers** for their organizations. This means they now have a legal obligation to appear before Parliamentary committees and answer questions on their management responsibilities within the framework of ministerial responsibility and account-ability. As the Privy Council Office explains this new development, "although the accounting officer is legally obliged to appear, he or she appears in support of the minister's accountability."[22]

Another difficulty with ministerial accountability relates to the politics-administration dichotomy. As we have seen in earlier chapters, at the top of the public service sits a cadre of senior managers, who generally are career public servants specially trained in the art of public sector administration. They are extremely powerful because of their knowledge of the workings of government. Some people regard this as problematic, in that these individuals may be able to challenge their political masters (Cabinet ministers) in setting public policy by virtue of their greater knowledge of government administration. In theory, at least, the elected representatives are supposed to direct government, while the appointed officials simply assist. But if the senior managers have knowledge, expertise, and experience, and the elected politicians lack these traits, it is possi-ble that the traditional relationship between politicians and public servants is turned on its head. Moreover, Cabinet ministers are not only responsible for running their ministries; they also perform a variety of other roles that take them away from their departments. For instance, they must attend question period in the House of Commons and perform other legislative duties; they must respond to the demands of the constituents in their ridings; they are party members with responsibilities to their political party and caucus; and so on.

But most important, most Cabinet ministers are not "experts" in the field over which they are given responsibility. As a result, long-serving senior public servants, such as deputy ministers, assistant deputy ministers, heads of regulatory bodies and Crown corporations, and senior managerial staff can all become major actors in the formulation, implementation, and evaluation of policy because they are the ones with greater expertise. This problem reflects a weakness in the politics-administration dichotomy, which says that ministers should be "on top," while public servants should be "on tap."[23] But ministers who must rely extensively on the expertise of their appointed aides may be at a disadvantage and become overly dependent. This implies that there is a grey area where accountability is concerned.

This reality is widely recognized within public administration, and various reforms have been implemented over the years to try to ensure that the proper relationship between politicians and senior public servants is maintained. The aforementioned central agencies (Finance Department, Privy Council Office, Prime Minister's Office, and Treasury Board Secretariat) were developed in part to give the ministers sources of information and guidance apart from their own departmental officials. Attempts to limit public servants' influence and power can also be seen in the complex Cabinet committee systems that have been developed to allow ministers in related policy fields to come together on a formal basis to exchange information and advice regarding policy. Whether these innovations have actually promoted democratic government is a matter of some contention. Some people argue that while these reforms do provide ministers with countervailing sources of information and advice, they also immensely increase the bureaucratization of decision making and that, in any case, ministers are simply substituting one set of bureaucratic advisors for another.[24]

A relatively new twist to the accountability issue is the recent trend toward restructuring of the public service. Ministers are increasingly seeking advice from outside consultants, given the cutbacks in their own ministries, with the result that the chain of accountability is broken, since outsiders have no relationship to the traditional structures of decision making in government. And just as problematic is the trend toward calling public servants onto the carpet for the mistakes of these outside consultants, as was the case with the spate of advertising contract scandals that beleaguered the Chrétien and Martin governments in the early 2000s.[25] We explore these issues in more detail following.

While accountability comprises a number of aspects, it ultimately comes down to the notion that in a democratic society, elected officials must accept responsibility for the actions of their public servants and the government on behalf of the people. One former Cabinet minister in British Columbia, who had previously been a poultry farmer, put it this way:

Eggs have to be candled to check the interior quality as well as examining the exterior. I did not lay the eggs, but if a customer complained to me about the quality of one of those eggs that I was selling him, there was no point in me blaming the chicken, finding out which hen laid it and saying that she was to blame. I was responsible. I was the proprietor and it was my responsibility.[26]

Where wrongdoing has occurred, the doctrine of ministerial responsibility suggests that the minister ought to resign if the offence is a serious enough one. Of course, the definition of "serious" here is open to considerable debate, and largely depends on whether you happen to sit on the government side of the House of Commons, or on the opposition benches. But most would agree that no one individual minister can possibly be held personally liable for all the actions of his department. Thus, one of the ongoing struggles of governing involves trying to determine where the line can be drawn between minor breaches of responsibility and more serious ones requiring the resignation of a minister. Box 12.3 summarizes the key principles of the doctrine of ministerial responsibility. This issue,

BOX 12.3 | Accountable Government: a Guide for Ministers and Secretaries of State, 2007

In 2007, Prime Minister Harper outlined his expectations for ministers and secretaries of state (junior ministers) with regard to responsibility and accountability. He wrote the following:

■ *Ministers and Secretaries of State must act with integrity. To ensure public trust and confidence, not only in our Government but in government generally, Ministers and Secretaries of State must uphold the highest standards of honesty and impartiality. Both the performance of your official duties and the arrangement of your private affairs should bear the closest public scrutiny.*

■ *Ministers are responsible for ensuring that their departments are managed soundly and with complete integrity. They must discharge their portfolio responsibilities with careful regard to the particular powers, duties and functions assigned to them by statute and convention.*

■ *Ministers are accountable to Parliament for the use of all powers vested in them. This demands constant attention to their parliamentary duties, including being present in Parliament to answer honestly and accurately about their areas of responsibility, and taking corrective action, as appropriate and within their authority, to address any problems that may arise within their portfolios. Should Ministers make any inadvertent error in answering to Parliament, they must take steps to correct it at the earliest opportunity.*

■ *Ministers and Secretaries of State are bound by their oath as Privy Councillors. This oath reflects parliamentary government's core convention of Cabinet solidarity, by which Ministers share collective responsibility for the actions of government and speak to Parliament and Canadians with a single voice. This requires frank discussion in Cabinet and confidentiality in Cabinet decision making. Although they are not members of the Cabinet, Secretaries of State are part of the Ministry and will attend the meetings of the Cabinet committee relevant to their area of assigned responsibility. They must uphold the confidentiality of any Cabinet information to which they have access.*

■ *Ministers and Secretaries of State must respect the non-partisanship of the public service of Canada and not seek to engage public servants in work that is outside their appropriate role. In this way, successive governments can have confidence that the public service will provide the support they need to fulfil their ministerial functions and mandate without regard to political partisanship.*

Source: Canada. Privy Council Office. *Accountable Government: A Guide for Ministers and Secretaries of State—2007*. Ottawa: Privy Council Office, 2007: 4.

already complex in itself, has become even more so with the latest developments in public administration associated with the New Public Management (NPM). We will turn our attention later to the set of issues this has raised. But for now, we will explain more fully what the concept of *accountability* means to public servants.

Accountability and Public Servants

There are five overlapping contexts within which accountability is applied to public servants:

- accountability to a superior
- accountability to elected officials
- accountability under the law
- accountability to professional norms and institutions
- accountability to the public[27]

The first context in which accountability is applied is derived from the Weberian notion of bureaucracies as hierarchical organizations defined by a chain of command. Each employee is responsible to a superior, and each office in the hierarchy is sanctioned by and established through administrative procedures and law. The organization charts of government departments in chapter 5 reflect these points. Rewards and penalties are prescribed for both observing accountability and transgressing it. In some parts of the organization, accountability crosses from administrative lines (say, from a manager to a director) to political lines (from a deputy minister to his or her minister). In this way, the entire organization is held accountable to elected officials.

In addition, the strictures of accountability are derived from the public servant's responsibility to uphold the law in the course of administering programs and policies. Thus, the various acts and regulations passed by government are (hopefully) dutifully observed and upheld by responsible, conscientious public servants. This extends throughout the entire organization, from the most senior officers to the lowest clerk. But it is the senior-most officer—the deputy minister—who, under the Financial Administration Act, is given particular financial responsibilities for the department, and for personnel responsibilities under delegated authority from the Treasury Board and Public Service Commission.

In addition, though, there is another context of accountability that may be less obvious than those we have identified so far. This relates to the fact that since government is such a large and complex system, it requires the services of a variety of skilled and specially trained individuals to deliver services to the public. For instance, legions of scientists, engineers, doctors, nurses, lawyers, accountants, teachers and professors, surveyors, geologists, architects, real estate agents, urban planners, and countless other professionals work either directly or indirectly for the government. In many cases, these individuals have a responsibility not just to the government, but also to the norms and standards of their profession as well. Various professions have their own codes of conduct, professional criteria, standards of behaviour, conflict of interest regulations, and so on, to which their members must be responsible. Even the right to practise in a given field may be determined by the professional body that oversees the field. Public servants who work in careers that have professional organizations overseeing them are, in effect, doubly accountable: once to the government, and once to their professional organization.

Finally, of course, there is accountability to the public, a point we have emphasized elsewhere. Suffice it to say that accountability to the public is something of a professional ethos for public servants. While there is no firm basis in law or administration for this context of accountability, there is, nonetheless, a powerful convention derived from the subjective responsibility that public servants feel toward the public. This is reinforced by the public's expectation that public servants will behave in a responsible manner toward them.

These contexts can be expressed in a slightly different way.[28] We can think about *administrative accountability* in terms of superior–subordinate relationships; *legal accountability* in terms of the mandates of departments, reporting requirements for public servants, and contractual requirements; *constitutional accountability,* including ministerial responsibility, in terms of the approval of taxing and spending by Parliament; *professional accountability,* which refers to the need to adhere to professional standards and norms; and *political accountability,* which refers to competitive elections, and the relationship between representatives and their constituents and other societal interests. These categories roughly coincide with the five contexts above, but provide a slightly different perspective on accountability.

These five contexts and categories for accountability are not unconnected. Indeed, there is a considerable amount of overlap among them, conceptually and in practice, prompting one public administration practitioner to comment that "public servants sometimes feel like flies trapped in a spider's web of accountabilities."[29] In some cases, the duty to one form of accountability comes into conflict with another. For instance, a doctor's professional duty to observe the Hippocratic Oath may conflict with instructions from the minister to fudge scientific evidence regarding a particular health risk.

Perhaps even more interesting is the apparent division within the public service itself over the relative importance of the various contexts of accountability. The higher the public servant is on the hierarchy ladder, the more inclined she is to feel responsible primarily to the minister and the government of the day. The lower down on the hierarchy, the more inclined public servants are to feel responsible to the public, and especially to the clients they serve directly.[30] This creates tensions within the public service, some of which manifested themselves when exercises such as PS2000 and La Relève (discussed in chapters 9 and 10) provoked complaints that senior public servants were out of touch with their subordinates' concerns.

Finally, the recent erosion of the pure doctrine of ministerial responsibility and the emergence of the doctrine of answerability have created a new conundrum for public servants: increasingly, as part of this process, public servants are being called on the carpet to answer for their actions. But this betrays the traditional precepts of anonymity, neutrality, and tenure of service that should characterize the public service. You will recall that public servants "are appointed on the basis of merit, they provide frank and objective advice to ministers in private, they do not express their personal views in public or engage in partisan activities, they execute policies faithfully and to the best of their abilities, and in return for their support and loyalty they are protected from being personally named for mistakes and enjoy reactive job security based upon satisfactory performance."[31]

A couple of noteworthy developments are altering the traditional concept of ministerial responsibility where public servants are concerned. For instance, public servants are, more and more, being required to appear before parliamentary committees. These are very public forums, and this development means that the anonymity of public servants is being eroded. As Paul Thomas reports, public servants theoretically appear before these committees simply to provide background information to Members of Parliament. However, "the rules to govern the interactions between public servants and politicians in what are essentially partisan areas are unwritten or vague at best. This new procedure means that public servants must be cautious and agile in order to avoid being drawn into partisan controversies."[32] An episode of the British sitcom *Yes, Prime Minister* depicts the Cabinet secretary being called before a parliamentary committee, which questions him on certain improprieties committed by the government. "That is a political matter, and therefore only the prime minister can answer your questions," he sniffs. In the next scene, the prime minister is before the committee, to which he suggests that the matters under consideration "really are administrative matters" and therefore should be answered by his Cabinet secretary. Moreover, the increased emphasis on public–private partnerships and consultations with interest groups also exposes public servants to the light of day in forums that are very public in nature, which undermines the tradition of confidentiality between ministers and their public servants since more information is being shared in ever-wider circles.

The evolving role of the media has also had an impact on public servants' traditional accountability. Increased coverage of government activities, as well as a more investigative and adversarial media (perhaps copying their U.S. cousins), has also shifted the spotlight such that it focuses more on public servants. The media has also become very savvy at using access-to-information legislation to see documents that previously might have stayed under lock and key. "These trends have not brought us to the point where public servants are recognizable household names," according to Thomas, "but they are better known in the sense that parliamentarians, pressure group representatives, and interested members of the public are better able today to identify the occupants of important positions within the bureaucracy, and may even feel confident in attributing certain policy perspectives to such individuals."[33]

The recent alterations to the doctrine of ministerial responsibility raise an important concern about this traditional view of the role of public servants. If ministers do not take responsibility and public servants are not *supposed to* or are not *expected to* take responsibility, then who will? The public has both the right and the need to know who is responsible for government action (or inaction). So who will now step forward and claim responsibility? The answer seems to be that, increasingly, public servants are being exposed as the culprits when things go awry in government even though, traditionally, they were not to be held responsible. But surely if this trend is allowed to persist, it will adversely affect the work that public servants do. They may react by being overly cautious in their recommendations to their political masters. Or they may slow down the process for fear of supplying advice that could later be used against them if a policy mistake emerges. This was the result, for instance, after the Human Resources and Development Canada (HRDC) scandal that broke in 1999.[34] In this case, media and opposition party allegations suggested the department had let $1 billion in contracts without properly accounting for the money or following proper procedures in awarding the contracts. But in fact, after audits were done, it was concluded that only $85 000 was unaccounted for. Subsequently, though, HRDC staff adopted a "do-it-by-the-book" mentality, involving scrupulous attention to paperwork and risk avoidance. The result was delays of several weeks in the processing of services, as public servants sought to ensure that a complete and thorough paper trail accompanied every action.[35]

It is one of the great ironies of public administration that this new emphasis on accountability can actually promote dysfunction in government. Accountability is seen largely as being about assigning blame when things go wrong. But no one likes to accept blame, especially if it might curtail his or her career ambitions. As a result, some have observed that one of the impediments to accountability is that the emphasis on blame may lead to more "buckpassing and scapegoating by both politicians and appointed officials. In other words, because of its potential negative consequences, accountability may become something to be avoided at all costs."[36] Overall, the jury is still out on the erosion of the doctrine of ministerial responsibility and the emergence of the doctrine of answerability. But so far, it is hard to see much benefit.

Accountability in Action: The Role of the Office of the Auditor General

Much of the discussion about accountability thus far may seem abstract and disconnected from the real world. It might be useful, therefore, to briefly examine at least one mechanism through which accountability is realized. There are many links in the chain of accountability, including—besides Parliament and Cabinet—several specialized agencies and offices, such as the Information and Privacy Commission, the Commissioner of Official Languages, and the Human Rights Commission. Rather than survey all these bodies, we will now turn our attention to the Office of the Auditor General (OAG), which stands out for both its unique status (as an independent, arm's-length body) and its reporting function (it reports directly to Parliament, not to a minister). This body is one of the most significant institutions directly engaged in holding the government to account.[37] Indeed, the profile of the Office is perhaps at an all-time high, with the release of its annual report anticipated almost as much as the seventh game of the Stanley Cup final in some quarters. (Well, maybe not quite that much.) But there is no doubt that the Auditor General has become a key institution in the efforts to promote accountability in government.

As we pointed out earlier in this chapter, the public wants and needs to know that government is managing public monies effectively and efficiently, and that this management is based on the public trust. Confidence in democracy and government are reinforced when public funds are raised carefully and spent wisely; in short, when there is *value for money* spent. Parliament is the institution that has primary responsibility for this important task and that acts on behalf of the people. The government cannot raise or spend a single penny without Parliament's authorization and must explain to Parliament both the reasons for expending public money and the results of the expenditures. To maintain accountability in this process, the government must report on its performance by submitting spending plans (estimates) for each department, as well as reports of the previous year's activities. In addition, it must produce annual financial statements showing all spending, borrowing, and taxing, which are known as the Public Accounts of Canada. The result is that Parliament is inundated with information with which to hold the government to account. But also needed is independent assessment of all that information so that members of Parliament can effectively assess the government's performance while feeling comfortable that the information that they are basing their assessment on is unbiased and objective. This is where the Auditor General comes into play. In her 2007 Report, Auditor General Sheila Fraser explained the following:

In the reports we present to Parliament, we provide answers to some important questions about the management of government programs and services. Are they managed with due regard to economy, efficiency, and their impact on the environment? And does the government have measures in place to determine if programs and services are effective in achieving the objectives set for them?

Our audit mandate covers the full range of activities of the federal government. Given the size of government and the scope of its activities, deciding what to audit is a challenging exercise. We may decide to audit an activity carried out in a single department or in several; we may select an issue that affects many departments. Choosing audit subjects well is essential to producing reports that are useful to Parliament.

We select areas for audit based partly on the risks they may involve. Examples of high-risk areas include those that cost taxpayers significant amounts of money or that involve public safety or national security. We may decide to audit an area that offers potential for improving government results or is of great interest to Parliament and the Canadian public. We pay particular attention to requests by parliamentary committees for audits of specific areas of concern to them, and we try to incorporate such requests into our audit planning where our resources and mandate permit.[38]

The position and office of an independent Auditor General was established in 1878. Early reports to Parliament listed every single transaction government undertook and reported on whether public money had been spent by government in the way Parliament intended. The contemporary OAG began to take shape in the 1950s but ran into some controversy when it began to overstep the bounds of its mandate by pronouncing on the *quality* of the government's policy choices.

Later, the 1977 Auditor General Act gave the OAG a broader mandate and clarified that the office does not comment on policy choices by the government (that is, it does not pronounce this policy "bad," and that policy "good") but, rather, focuses on how those policies were implemented. More recently, in 1995, amendments to the Act established the position of Commissioner of the Environment and Sustainable Development within the OAG, reflecting contemporary concerns with these issues and the role of government therein. The vision and mission of the OAG is provided in Box 12.4.

The Auditor General is independent of the government of the day, and is appointed for a 10-year term to help reinforce the objectivity needed to support that independence. The Auditor General Act provided three questions to which the Auditor General must address himself or herself. These are as follows:

- Is the government keeping proper accounts and records and presenting its financial information accurately?

- Did the government collect or spend the authorized amount of money, and for the purposes intended by Parliament?

- Were programs run economically and efficiently? And does the government have the means to measure their effectiveness?

BOX 12.4 Vision and Mission of the Office of the Auditor General of Canada

Vision: We are committed to making a difference for the Canadian people by promoting, in all our work for Parliament, answerable, honest and productive government.

Mission: The Office of the Auditor General of Canada conducts independent audits and examinations that provide objective information, advice and assurance to Parliament. We promote accountability and best practices in government operations.

Elaboration of Mission: In achieving our mission, we want to make a difference by promoting

- *a fair and frank accounting of government's stewardship of financial and other resources*
- *efficiency and productivity in the public service*
- *cost effectiveness of government activities*
- *collection of revenues owed to the Crown.*

  Other effects we want to produce through our work are

- *objective assurance on matters found to be satisfactory and unsatisfactory*
- *compliance with authority*
- *deterrence of fraud and dishonesty.*

Source: Canada, Office of the Auditor General, *Auditing for Parliament*, (Ottawa: Minister of Public Works and Government Services Canada, 1997).

Each question corresponds to a particular type of audit that must be carried out by the Auditor General. The first question calls for *attest* auditing, which simply means that the auditor attests to or verifies the accuracy of financial statements. The second question calls for *compliance* auditing, in which the Auditor General reveals whether the government has complied with Parliament's wishes. The third question calls for *value-for-money* auditing, sometimes called *performance* auditing, in which the Auditor General investigates whether or not taxpayers got value for their tax dollars. In short, the accountability function of the Auditor General is a thorough one, contained in a broad framework intended to allow for a penetrating examination of the government's activities.

Beyond the audit functions, the Auditor General has added a number of other activities, including reviewing the sustainable development strategies of departments, special examinations of Crown corporations, and progress reports on various initiatives to reform the public service. Since 1995, the Commissioner of the Environment and Sustainable Development (CESD) has reported to the House on the environment and sustainable development, departmental strategies and action plans in this realm, and petitions from Canadians relating to the environment and sustainable development.

Public awareness about the activities of government is a key aspect of the Auditor General's work. To publicize what government has and has not done, the Auditor General issues an annual report to the House of Commons. As of 1994, with amendment of the Auditor General Act, as many as three reports are now produced each year. These reports contain the results of comprehensive audits of federal departments and agencies, government-wide audits, follow-up reports concerning previous audits, and audit observations, which are important matters not covered in any of the other reports. Other forms of reporting take place in regard to Crown corporations through the minister responsible or, in some cases, directly to the boards of directors; through the Public Accounts every autumn; and through special audits ordered by Cabinet and not included in the regular reporting process. In addition, audits of the governments of the Yukon, Nunavut, and the Northwest Territories are reported annually to their legislative assemblies.

The 2002 and 2004 OAG reports stand out in recent history as examples of the influence of the Auditor General. You will recall that in the 2002 report, the Auditor General raised the alarm that federal public servants broke "just about every rule in the book" in dealing with certain Quebec advertising agencies, and she followed that up in 2004 with a serious indictment of rampant financial abuses in the Sponsorship Program. These were the reports that led indirectly to the Gomery Commission of Inquiry and the downfall of the Martin Liberal government. But as Thomas suggests, the OAG must walk a fine line between attracting attention to its reports and wading into controversial partisan areas:

To ensure parliamentary, media, and public attention for its findings, it must present reports that are controversial enough to be noticed. At the same time it must avoid drifting into policy controversies and focusing only on negative developments because such approaches will produce a backlash and lack of co-operation from ministers and departments. There is also a balance to be maintained between identifying waste and error and emphasizing constructive criticism and organizational learning.[39]

Finally, with all this reporting going on, it is reasonable to wonder who reports on the OAG. What mechanisms exist to ensure that the government "watcher" is adequately "watched"? This is accomplished by an external auditor annually appointed by the Treasury Board. This report is presented to the Treasury Board and tabled in the House of Commons. As well, the Auditor General's work is the focus of 15 different parliamentary committees, and its own spending is subject to review and inspection by the Public Accounts Committee of Parliament and to the scrutiny of the Official Languages Commissioner on language issues, the Public Service Commission on staffing and classification practices, and the Privacy Commissioner through the Privacy Act.

In short, as this brief overview reveals, multiple and reinforcing sources of accountability ripple throughout the organization of government. The process is complex and convoluted, and in part explains why government business sometimes takes so long to be completed. The multiple checks within the system may seem overly bureaucratic, time-consuming, and inefficient. But the alternative may be even less palatable to citizens, who have every right to expect their tax dollars to be used wisely. Recent developments have introduced new issues and problems where accountability is concerned, resulting in the need for ongoing review of the functions and roles of bodies such as the Auditor General and, indeed, more broadly of government itself. We now turn our attention to some of these developments.

Contemporary Issues of Accountability and Control

The advent of the **New Public Management (NPM)** and the general trend toward making government more businesslike has had important implications for accountability. As we've pointed out, the concept and practice of accountability are different in the private sector than in the public sector. So what happens when you begin to import the practices of the former into the latter? This final section addresses this issue, bearing as it does directly on the future of public administration in Canada.

One observer suggests that the accountability regime under which public servants served in the past has changed:

Management principles like decentralization, achieving measurable results, and empowerment (key features of "managerialism") imply that public-sector managers are to be held accountable for performance results rather than for adhering to due process and to the equitable treatment of individuals. In addition, if the federal experience is any guide, individual public servants may now be held directly accountable for their own actions or those of their subordinates by parliamentary committees or their surrogates in provincial legislatures or on municipal councils (as the Al-Mashat Affair demonstrated), to say nothing of the potential for damages resulting from the increasing tendency for the public to file civil suits against particular public servants.[40]

And as we noted earlier, there is a trend toward reducing public servants' traditional anonymity. This, too, has intensified due to NPM. As professor of public administration Donald Savoie reports, this has been occurring not just at the senior-most levels of the public service, "but even career officials down the line have become active participants in the elaborate public consultative process and thereby abandoned their anonymity."[41] These developments imply that our traditional understanding of who should be held to account for government action or inaction needs to be rethought. Other factors related to NPM, such as downsizing and privatization, have had significant impacts on accountability, as has an increasing tendency to resort to private sector management techniques focusing on improved efficiency and client service. For example, when a government downloads to the private sector its responsibility to provide a particular service or, indeed, privatizes that service, who is accountable when things go awry? The answer to this question is not as clear-cut as you might assume.

Take the issue of responsibility for roads, for instance. Increasingly, governments in Canada are "selling" highways to private sector corporations, who would assume responsibility for their upkeep and maintenance by collecting tolls. But what if the roads fall into disrepair, and the corporations find it less and less profitable to maintain them? They could raise the tolls, but they would risk losing customers, which would translate into a loss of revenue for road repair. In the worst-case scenario, suppose a company abrogates its responsibilities altogether, perhaps by claiming that revenues cannot keep up with expenses, and that the company has no choice but to declare bankruptcy. The state is left to assume responsibility, using taxpayers' dollars, for the lack of accountability inherent in the original arrangement.

Yet another consequence of NPM is the emergence and development of the so-called hidden or shadow bureaucracy.[42] Relatively little is known about the hidden bureaucracy since no agency or organization is charged with keeping track of it. It is composed of the thousands of former government public servants who were terminated and/or seconded to or contracted out to the private sector and voluntary or not-for-profit sectors. Reasonable suspicions exist about the absence of a clear accountability framework or regime governing the relationship of this growing sector to the traditional government public service. Speaking of the American experience, Frederickson notes that "the hidden bureaucracy is exquisitely fragmented into dozens of agencies and thousands of contracts. . . . [and] is so complex and so far back in the shadows that it is unreasonable to expect the media to make it transparent."[43] Frederickson also notes the following:

For the new public service the central question is one of values. It is clear that the government employees are to pursue the public interest, as they see it. . . . The value question is how to achieve the public interest when power is shared with organizations that have other interests and values. . . . The pursuit of public policy usually means making difficult tradeoffs between competing values such as equality and efficiency. When such policy choices are even partially delegated to or controlled by the hidden bureaucracy, we are face to face with the issue of accountability.[44]

Or consider another emerging trend. Introducing private sector management techniques into the public service often involves "letting the managers manage"—that is, decentralizing control over the actions of subordinates, giving them more flexibility in their roles, and permitting them to make more decisions regarding the provision of services to clients (i.e., citizens). These attempts to empower public servants and make them more responsive to Canadians may seem laudable. But surely at some level they conflict with certain traditional values of accountability. Emphasizing efficiency and responsiveness substitutes the private sector's value system for the public sector's. This may mean that, in the pursuit of efficiency, due process will have to be sacrificed. As Savoie suggests, incorporating private-sector management practices into the public sector "means rejecting traditional public-administration concerns with accountability and control, and giving way to the business-management emphasis on productivity, performance, and service to clients."[45] The overriding concern is that public servants operate in a political environment involving the public trust, whereas business operates in a different environment altogether. As Savoie also says, "In business it does not much matter if you get it wrong 10 percent of the time as long as you turn a profit at the end of the year. In government, it does not much matter if you get it right 90 percent of the time because the focus will be on the 10 percent of the time you got it wrong."[46] Another view, however, is that if "managerialism enables objectives to be expressed more clearly and encourages better measurement of results, it can actually make control more meaningful and provide better information to ministers, thereby enhancing, not diminishing, their ability to account for the use they make of public funds."[47]

A variety of organizational models have been introduced into public administration recently that test the traditional doctrine of ministerial responsibility and the concept of accountability in general. Greater decentralization and more autonomy for public servants seem to be recurring themes in these models, and practices in other countries have been noted by the Canadian government. In Great Britain, for instance, the concept of *executive agencies* has been introduced. These are bodies that are delegated a certain amount of responsibility by the minister concerned. The chief executives of these agencies are accountable to the minister through certain performance contracts rather than through traditional hierarchical channels. This model leaves responsibility for overall policy making in the hands of the minister, but it transfers responsibility for operations to the chief executives. New Zealand has introduced something called the *state-owned enterprise,* in which a higher level of independence is granted to these enterprises than is traditionally the case with the older Crown corporation model. In Canada, a number of similar initiatives are underway. For instance, as a result of Program Review, the air navigation system under the auspices of Transport Canada now operates on a commercial basis. The Translation Bureau in the Department of Public Works and Government

Services became a Special Operating Agency (SOA), a body that provides some operational autonomy from its department, although not as much as a Crown corporation enjoys. New agencies were developed in areas such as parks management, food inspection, revenue, and securities, some of which add another layer of complication to the responsibility issue, since they cross over from federal into provincial jurisdiction. These examples and others implicitly strain the conventional understanding of accountability, leaving some observers to conclude that "the question of ministerial responsibility and the structures within which the new service delivery agencies are to be held accountable to Parliament must be seriously examined." Moreover, "to fail to do so would jeopardize the doctrine of ministerial responsibility, which could in turn undermine an important part of the Canadian democratic system."[48] As an example of the changing nature of accountability brought on by NPM, consider the idea of empowerment of public servants through more decentralized decision making and the encouragement of risk taking.[49] These developments potentially conflict with traditional notions of accountability. In the first place, existing structures and institutions (like central agencies) tend to constrain empowerment and risk taking, and so new structures and approaches need to be developed. In the second place, public-sector managers, unlike their private-sector counterparts, are typically risk-averse, fearing that mistakes will attract the attention of the media, interest groups, and opposition parties, thus curtailing their career potential. Third, and related, notions of neutrality and anonymity are compromised, as public servants using their increased decision making powers come to be more and more identified with government initiatives.

Still, governments are increasingly redefining accountability, through the lens of empowerment and other precepts of the NPM, to place greater emphasis on *results* rather than *process*. As some observers suggest, "governments are more aware that holding public servants accountable through a variety of formal controls is a necessary but insufficient means of ensuring responsible administrative conduct." Further, "empowerment envisages increased emphasis on psychological or personal responsibility, in the sense of loyalty to, or identification with, organizational and program goals."[50] But, again, we bump up against a potential conflict between a sense of personal responsibility on the part of individual public servants, and the larger framework of ministerial responsibility. Unless ministers are willing to broaden their conception of ministerial responsibility to include a defence of risk taking by public servants and of the mistakes that inevitably will be made, there seems little chance that the tensions between old and new forms of accountability will dissipate.

Political scientist Paul Thomas identifies a clear trend in relation to the erosion of the tradition of the anonymous career public servant. He suggests that "under the sway of NPM ideas there is a growing insistence that public servants be personally accountable for results through, for example, the development and publication of performance indicators."[51] As political scientist J.E. Hodgetts foresaw in the early 1990s,

if the inevitable drift of public management into the political realm of governance itself . . . is to be the path of the future, then we must be prepared to see senior managers assume the role of scapegoats for the failures of others who, in our system of responsible cabinet government, have hitherto been elected to bear that direct responsibility.[52]

Flushing public servants out from the shadows where they traditionally reside is problematic, if for no other reason than that there is no one else, other than their own superiors within the hierarchical chain of command, to whom they are required to answer directly. The recent use of parliamentary committees (as in the Al-Mashat affair) to roast public servants on the open fires of Parliament is inappropriate, since the committees were intended as accountability mechanisms that ministers—not their public servants—answer to. In any event, only ministers can impose penalties or sanctions for errors committed by public servants; parliamentary committees do not possess that right. But, at the same time, public servants' reputations and careers can be severely damaged in the partisan arena of Parliament, leading Thomas to conclude that "placing public servants before parliamentary committees creates risks in terms of inappropriate and unfair questions by politicians, and not just from those on the opposition benches."[53]

Thomas cites some other concerns with these developments. He suggests, "The NPM literature tends to denigrate existing approaches to accountability as mistaking adherence to procedures for the achievement of results, stifling creativity and initiative and adding to the costs of running government. Control is seen only in negative terms of adding to red tape."[54] Yet control through accountability measures may actually improve efficiency and effectiveness by preventing abuses that lead to waste. Thus, while the NPM is dismissive of traditional mechanisms and systems of accountability it tends to ignore the fact that the bureaucracy of accountability actually fosters the values NPM supports.

The implications of many of the contemporary developments related to accountability can be traced right back to our discussion of constitutional and administrative law in chapter 6. The Constitution, you will recall, sets out the relationship between individuals and the state, and among the different institutions of government. It does this in order to promote the rule of law, the premise of which is that no one in society—not even the most politically, economically, or socially powerful—is above the law. This includes, of course, the government itself and those who work in it. In this sense, the courts have played a prominent role in accountability, being a primary mechanism by which penalties are imposed for transgressions. The courts uphold the rule of law, and hence the Constitution, in ensuring that politicians and public servants do not overstep the bounds of accountability imposed upon them by the myriad rules and institutions we have surveyed previously. However, the NPM may be changing the role and impact of the rule of law, as well as the courts, in maintaining accountability. The NPM draws for its inspiration on the literature and language of private management. Traditional public administration, in contrast, draws on the literature and language of law and political science. Clearly, the latter is more directly concerned with issues of justice and legality, the Constitution, the rule of law, and related matters. The former is more concerned with management techniques that promote efficiency, effectiveness, and economy. Yet again, we see another manifestation of the conflicting-values problem in public administration, this time related to the issue of accountability.

A large problem in accountability lies, ironically, in the premises of various recent reforms of the public service, many of which were aimed at improving accountability. First, cutting red tape and budget restrictions often focused on reducing capacity in the areas of monitoring and auditing, thereby compromising accountability.[55] Second, the new paradigm of public management disparaged traditional public service values and ethics and the mechanisms designed to promote control and compliance. Third, the increasing tendency to politicize the public service has undermined its nonpartisan character.[56] As Aucoin and Jarvis suggest,

In each of these three respects, the public service was confronted with major challenges that it sought to address. At the time of Program Review in the early to mid-1990s, the attitude in many quarters was that the monitoring, auditing and challenge functions were essentially "bureaucratic overhead." Scaling back on the administrative resources to carry out these functions was seen by many as a good thing to do. Second the initial attack on traditional public administration as rule-bound bureaucracy emanated from the private sector. However, the importance of public service values and ethics has recently resurfaced as a result of several wrongdoings, in Canada and elsewhere, and then perhaps only because similar ethical lapses began to occur in the private sector. And finally, the past two decades have witnessed an increasing number of political staff who have insisted on involving themselves in public administration, and an increasing number of ministers who wish their public servants to be responsive in promoting the implementation of their agenda.[57]

Nonetheless, these developments reinforced concerns that institutions and standards in the federal government were defective. Prime Ministers Chrétien and Martin consequently put forward an agenda of reform meant to strengthen integrity and transparency of government.[58] Prime Minister Harper then followed the trail that had been blazed ahead of his ascension to office and introduced the Federal Accountability Act (FAA) in 2006 to reinforce compliance and enforcement of rules, enhance independent oversight and review, increase transparency and disclosure, and streamline current rules to increase efficiency.[59]

The FAA represented attempts by government to move from a "culture of entitlement" to a "culture of accountability." This legislation, emerging directly in the wake of the Sponsorship scandal, sought to strengthen institutional arrangements in oversight bodies like the OAG and Ethics Commissioner as well as to make government overall more accountable. The Act was a long and complex document that amended several existing acts as well as introducing new ones and was accompanied by a Federal Accountability Action Plan to aid in the process of implementation. Among the goals of the FAA were the following:

- reforming the financing of political parties
- banning secret donations to political candidates
- strengthening the role of the Ethics Commissioner
- toughening the Lobbyists Registration Act

- ensuring truth in budgeting with a Parliamentary Budget Authority
- making qualified government appointments
- cleaning up the procurement of government contracts
- cleaning up government polling and advertising
- providing real protection for whistleblowers
- strengthening access to information legislation
- strengthening the power of the Auditor General
- strengthening auditing and accountability within departments
- creating a Director of Public Prosecutions[60]

The various controversies currently swirling around the issue of accountability are unlikely to be resolved any time soon. It is not as though there is a single easy answer. Instead, gradual change is called for, vis-à-vis reforms and experimentation, new initiatives, and careful consideration and analysis of existing systems of accountability. But remember that accountability is based on the underlying principle of responsible government. This fundamental democratic premise of the Canadian system of government should drive all attempts at coordinating the actors, institutions, ideas, and formal and informal systems and processes that animate the regime of accountability. Failure to focus on this basic point means that citizens will be ill-served, since both politicians and public servants may be less inclined to "pay attention to their respective assigned and accepted responsibilities [and] to understand that it does matter."[61]

WHAT YOU HAVE LEARNED

The concept of *accountability* embraces several different aspects of public administration; it is vital to democratic government, yet it is not always clearly understood. When modern society created democratic systems of government, the convention developed that public office was a matter of public trust, that the powers associated with public office should be used for the betterment of society (and not just the office-holder's personal gain), and that in pursuing this goal, office-holders were expected to act with integrity, honesty, and responsibility. Moreover, they were to constantly account for their actions and for the exercise of power entrusted to them. This meant that they would have to report regularly on their activities in a public and visible way; that they would make themselves available to public scrutiny and be able to justify all their actions and decisions; that they would follow constitutional and administrative law in so doing; and that they would ultimately work toward improved provision of public services. Moreover, they would assume liability if they misused office. It is often suggested that public administration, in this conception, was not the administration *of* the public, but administration *for* the public. In short, notwithstanding the new trends in Canadian public administration, the responsibilities of the public servant were unlike those of an individual in private business, wherein the regime of accountability is less comprehensive, more limited, and different in orientation.

Key Words and Concepts

accountable (369)

responsible government (370)

ministerial responsibility (375)

doctrine of answerability (376)

collective ministerial responsibility (376)

accounting officer (378)

New Public Management (NPM) (388)

Review Questions

1. Accountability and Democracy

The central principle of responsible government, which lies at the root of the accountability issue and was first raised in chapter 2, was the focus of discussion here. This principle lies, in fact, at the root of the accountability issue. This section explained the link between accountability and democracy. Ask yourself, How is the principle of responsible government significant where accountability is concerned? How does the principle work in theory and in practice in the context of Canadian public administration?

2. Ministerial Responsibility

Responsible government, we determined, depends in part on the doctrine of ministerial responsibility, which sets the boundaries of ministerial action. It also establishes the guidelines that state how government can be held to account. This section explained the pure theory of ministerial responsibility, and showed how contemporary trends and developments have affected the original theory. Ask yourself, Do I understand the theory of ministerial responsibility, including both individual and collective ministerial responsibility? How has the doctrine of answerability modified the accountability of ministers? How has the traditional approach to ministerial responsibility in the political system changed over time? What does this mean for the concept of accountability now?

3. Accountability and Public Servants

Where the traditional doctrine of ministerial authority meets the politics-administration dichotomy, certain expectations about the role and behaviour of public servants emerge. But recent changes to the concept of accountability have altered the conventional set of expectations, leaving public servants on unfamiliar ground. This section addressed both the traditional role of public servants and the newly emerging one. Ask yourself, In what ways have public servants traditionally been held accountable for their actions? How have the concepts of ministerial responsibility, the doctrine of answerability, and the politics-administration dichotomy affected the position and work of public servants in terms of accountability? What problems do public servants face in trying to live up to the accountability regime? How do public servants respond to the multiple demands of executives, legislatures, judiciary, interest groups, professional associations, regulatory boards, the media, clients, and citizens when responsibility demands conflict? Which take precedence?

4. *Accountability in Action: The Role of the Office of the Auditor General*

The Office of the Auditor General is one of the most important links in the chain of accountability. We briefly reviewed the role of this important actor in terms of how it contributes to accountability. Ask yourself, What role does the Office of the Auditor General play in the process promoting accountability by providing the government with objective, unbiased assessments of its work?

5. *Contemporary Issues of Accountability and Control*

This section revealed that the accountability regime is in flux. Recent developments have altered the traditional understanding of who is responsible to whom for what. Traditional notions of ministerial responsibility and the role of public servants have altered due to the emergence of new organizational norms, and systems such as the New Public Management. The drive to put government on a more businesslike footing is behind a large number of these changes. Ask yourself, How have traditional notions of accountability been altered under the influence of new developments in Canadian public administration? What impact has the New Public Management had on the usual relationships within government, and between government and citizens? Are these developments helpful or hurtful to the accountability regime?

Weblinks

Auditor General of Canada
www.oag-bvg.gc.ca

Commissioner of the Environment and Sustainable Development
www.oag-bvg.gc.ca/domino/cesd_cedd.nsf/html/cesd_index_e.html

Privy Council Office
www.pco-bcp.gc.ca

Federal Accountability Act
www.faa-lfi.gc.ca

Democracy Watch
www.dwatch.ca

Privacy Commissioner of Canada
www.privcom.gc.ca

Further Reading

1. *Accountability and Democracy*

Johnson, David. *Thinking Government: Public Sector Management in Canada. Second Edition.* Peterborough: Broadview Press, 2006.

Mosher, Frederick C. *Democracy and the Public Service.* New York: Oxford University Press, 1968.

2. *Ministerial Responsibility*

d'Ombrain, Nicholas. "Ministerial Responsibility and the Machinery of Government," *Canadian Public Administration,* 50, 2 (Summer, 2007): 195–217.

Savoie, Donald, ed. *Restoring Accountability: Research Studies Volumes 1, 2 and 3. Commission of Inquiry into the Sponsorship Program and Advertising Activities.* Ottawa: Public Works and Government Services, 2006.

Sutherland, S.L. "Responsible Government and Ministerial Responsibility," *Canadian Journal of Political Science,* 24, 1 (March, 1991): 91–120.

3. Accountability and Public Servants

Finer, Herman. "Administrative Responsibility in Democratic Government," *Public Administration Review,* 1, 4 (1941): 335–50.

Friedrich, Carl J. "Public Policy and the Nature of Administrative Responsibility," in Carl J. Friedrich and Edward S. Mason, eds. *Public Policy.* Cambridge: Harvard University Press, 1940: 3–24.

Kernaghan, Kenneth and John Langford. *The Responsible Public Servant.* Halifax: Institute for Research on Public Policy, 1990.

Osbaldeston, Gordon. *Keeping Deputy Ministers Accountable.* Toronto: McGraw-Hill Ryerson, 1989.

Savoie, Donald J. *Breaking the Bargain: Public Servants, Ministers and Parliament.* Toronto: University of Toronto Press, 2003.

Segal, Hugh. "The Accountability of Public Servants: Our Government Would be Better if Senior Mandarins Were Less Secure," in Barbara Wake Carroll, David Seigel and Mark Sproule-Jones, eds. *Classic Readings in Canadian Public Administration.* Toronto: Oxford University Press, 2005: 84–86.

Thomas, Paul C. "Parliament and the Public Service," in Christopher Dunn, ed. *The Handbook of Canadian Public Administration.* Toronto: Oxford University Press, 2002: 341–68.

4. Accountability in Action: The Role of the Office of the Auditor General

Saint-Martin, Denis. "Managerialist Advocate or 'Control Freak'? The Janus-Faced Office of the Auditor General," *Canadian Public Administration,* 47, 2 (Summer 2004): 121–40.

Sutherland, Sharon L. "The Office of the Auditor General: Government in Exile?" Kingston: Queen's University School of Policy Studies, 2002.

5. Contemporary Issues of Accountability and Control

Aucoin, Peter. "The Design of Public Organizations for the 21st Century: Why Bureaucracy Will Survive in Public Management," *Canadian Public Administration,* 40, 2 (Summer, 1997): 290–306.

Aucoin, Peter. *The New Public Management: Canada in Comparative Perspective.* Montreal: Institute for Research on Public Policy, 1995.

Aucoin, Peter and Mark D. Jarvis, *Modernizing Government Accountability: A Framework for Reform.* Ottawa: Canada School of Public Service, 2005.

Carroll, Barbara Wake and David I. Dewar. "Performance Management: Panacea or Fools' Gold?" in Christopher Dunn, ed. *The Handbook of Canadian Public Administration.* Toronto: Oxford University Press, 2002: 413–29.

Thomas, Paul G. "The Swirling Meanings and Practices of Accountability in Canadian Government," in Ken Rasmussen and David Siegel, eds. *Professionalism and Public Service: Essays in Honour of Kenneth Kernaghan.* Toronto: University of Toronto Press, 2007.

Endnotes

1. Gerald E. Caiden, "The Problem of Ensuring the Public Accountability of Public Officials," in Joseph G. Jabbra and O.P. Dwivedi, eds. *Public Service Accountability,* (West Hartford, Connecticut: Kumarian Press, 1988): 19.

2. See J.R. Mallory, *The Structure of Canadian Government,* (Toronto: Gage, 1971).

3. See Canada, Privy Council Office, *Responsibility in the Constitution,* (Ottawa: Minister of Supply and Services, 1993): 11–27.

4. James John Guy, *How We Are Governed: The Basics of Canadian Politics and Government,* (Toronto: Harcourt Brace and Company, 1995): 35.

5. See Keith Archer et al., *Parameters of Power: Canada's Political Institutions,* (Scarborough: Nelson, 1995): 72.

6. Caiden, "The Problem of Ensuring the Public Accountability of Public Officials," (1988): 20.

7. O.P. Dwivedi, "The Issue of Accountability in the Public Service of Canada," in Joseph G. Jabbra and O.P. Dwivedi, eds. *Public Service Accountability: A Comparative Perspective,* (West Hartford, Connecticut: Kumarian Press, 1988): 86.

8. Caiden, "The Problem of Ensuring the Public Accountability of Public Officials," (1988): 17.

9. Paul G. Thomas, "The Changing Nature of Accountability," in B. Guy Peters and Donald J. Savoie, eds. *Taking Stock: Assessing Public Sector Reforms,* (Montreal: McGill–Queen's University Press, 1998): 352.

10. Paul G. Thomas, "The Crisis of Trust in Government: Rhetoric or Reality?" Public Policy Forum (March 29, 2007). **www.ppforum.ca/common/assets/summaries/en/paul_thomas_march29_presentation.pdf** Accessed July 25, 2007.

11. Caiden, "The Problem of Ensuring the Public Accountability of Public Officials," (1988): 25.

12. Nicole Jauvin, "Government, Ministers, Macro-Organization Chart and Networks," in Jacques Bourgault, Maurice Demers and Cynthia Williams, eds. *Public Administration and Public Management: Experiences in Canada,* (St. Foy, Quebec: Les Publications du Quebec, 1997): 49. See also David E. Smith, "Clarifying the Doctrine of Ministerial Responsibility as it Applies to the Government and Parliament of Canada," in Donald Savoie, ed. *Restoring Accountability: Research Studies Volumes 1. Commission of Inquiry into the Sponsorship Program and Advertising Activities,* (Ottawa: Public Works and Government Services, 2006): 106–07.

13. Thomas, "The Changing Nature of Accountability," (1998): 359. See also Peter Aucoin and Mark D. Jarvis, *Modernizing Government Accountability: A Framework for Reform,* (Ottawa: Canada School of Public Service, 2005).

14. Aucoin and Jarvis, *Modernizing Government Accountability,* (2005): 14.

15. See Jauvin, "Government, Ministers, Macro-Organization Chart and Networks," (1997): 48.

16. Jauvin, "Government, Ministers, Macro-Organization Chart and Networks," (1997): 49.

17. The following section is derived largely from Jauvin, "Government, Ministers, Macro-Organization Chart and Networks," (1997): 55–56.

18. Ian Clark, "A 'Back to Basics' Look at the Government Decision Making Process," unpublished paper, (November 4, 1983): 13. Cited in Robert J. Jackson and Doreen Jackson, *Politics in Canada: Culture, Institutions, Behaviour and Public Policy, Sixth Edition,* (Toronto: Pearson Prentice Hall, 2006): 279.

19. Aucoin and Jarvis, *Modernizing Government Accountability,* (2005): 15.

20. See S.L. Sutherland, "The Al-Mashat Affair: Administrative Accountability in Parliamentary Institutions," *Canadian Public Administration,* 34, 4 (Winter, 1991): 573–603.

21. Canada. Privy Council Office. *Accountable Government: A Guide for Ministers and Secretaries of State—2007,* (Ottawa: Privy Council Office, 2007): 6.

22. Canada. Privy Council Office. *Accounting Officers: Guidelines on Roles, Responsibilities and Appearances Before Parliamentary Committees,* (Ottawa: Privy Council Office, 2007): 1. See also C.E.S. (Ned) Franks, "The Respective Responsibilities and Accountabilities of Ministers and Public Servants: A Study of the British Accounting Officer System and Its Relevance for Canada," in Donald Savoie, ed. *Restoring Accountability: Research Studies Volume 3. Commission of Inquiry into the Sponsorship Program and Advertising Activities,* (Ottawa: Public Works and Government Services, 2006): 157–230.

23. See Flora MacDonald, "Who Is on Top? The Minister or the Mandarins?" and Mitchell Sharp, "A Reply From a Former Minister and Mandarin," in Paul W. Fox and Graham White, eds. *Politics Canada, Eighth Edition,* (Toronto: McGraw-Hill, 1995): 448–56.

24. See Richard J. Van Loon and Michael S. Whittington, *The Canadian Political System, Fourth Edition,* (Toronto: McGraw-Hill Ryerson, 1987): chapters 15 and 17; and Evert

A. Lindquist, "Has Federal Cabinet Decision Making Come Full Circle?" in Paul W. Fox and Graham White, eds. *Politics Canada, Eighth Edition,* (Toronto: McGraw-Hill, 1995): 544–52.

25. See Graham Fraser, "Civil Service a Victim in Sponsorship Scandals," *Toronto Star* (June 16, 2002).

26. Cited in Sutherland, "The Al-Mashat Affair," (1991): 582.

27. See R.L. Gagne, "Accountability and Public Administration," *Canadian Public Administration,* 39, 2 (Summer, 1996): 214.

28. See Thomas, "The Changing Nature of Accountability," (1998): 356.

29. J. David Wright, "Exposing the Chameleon: Response to 'Accountability and Public Administration,'" *Canadian Public Administration,* 39, 2 (Summer, 1996): 229.

30. Donald J. Savoie, *Thatcher, Reagan, Mulroney: In Search of a New Bureaucracy,* (Pittsburgh: University of Pittsburgh Press, 1994): 216–17.

31. Thomas, "The Changing Nature of Accountability," (1998): 360.

32. Thomas, "The Changing Nature of Accountability," (1998): 360–61. See also Paul C. Thomas, "Parliament and the Public Service," in Christopher Dunn, ed. *The Handbook of Canadian Public Administration,* (Toronto: Oxford University Press, 2002): 341–68.

33. Thomas, "The Changing Nature of Accountability," (1998): 361.

34. The definitive account of the HRDC affair is David Good, *The Politics of Public Management: The HRDC Audit of Government Grants and Contributions,* (Toronto: University of Toronto Press, 2003).

35. See Good, *The Politics of Public Management,* (2003); and Graham Fraser, "Scandal Leaves Ottawa Swamped in Paperwork," *Toronto Star,* (December 13, 2000): A23. The HRDC scandal is reviewed in Canada, Treasury Board of Canada Secretariat, *Building on a Strong Foundation—The Dialogue Continues Volume II: Further Case Studies on Values and Ethics in the Public Service,* (Ottawa: Canadian Centre for Management Development, 2001): 41–48. See also Sharon L. Sutherland, "'Biggest Scandal in Canadian History': HRDC Audit Starts Probity War," (Kingston: Queen's University Working Paper 23, August, 2001).

36. Thomas, "The Changing Nature of Accountability," (1998): 353.

37. The following description of the Auditor General's role is derived from Canada, Office of the Auditor General, *Auditing for Parliament,* (Ottawa: Minister of Public Works and Government Services Canada, 1997). For a critical review of the work of the Auditor General during the HRDC scandal, see Sutherland, "Biggest Scandal in Canadian History" (2001).

38. Canada. Office of the Auditor General of Canada, "A Message from the Auditor General—May 2007," Report of the Auditor General of Canada 2007, (Ottawa: Office of the Auditor General, 2007). **www.oag-bvg.gc.ca/domino/reports.nsf/html/20070500ce.html** Accessed July 26, 2007.

39. Thomas, "Parliament and the Public Service," (2002): 354.

40. Gagne, "Accountability and Public Administration," (1996): 220.

41. Donald J. Savoie, *Breaking the Bargain: Public Servants, Ministers and Parliament*, (Toronto: University of Toronto Press, 2003): 247.

42. See H. George Frederickson, "Public Ethics and the New Managerialism," in H. George Frederickson and Richard K. Ghere, eds. *Ethics in Public Management,* (Armonk, New York: M.E. Sharpe, 2005): 174.

43. Frederickson, "Public Ethics and the New Managerialism," (2005): 175.

44. Frederickson, "Public Ethics and the New Managerialism," (2005): 175.

45. Savoie, *Thatcher, Reagan, Mulroney,* (1994): 283.

46. Donald J. Savoie, "What Is Wrong With the New Public Management?" *Canadian Public Administration,* 38, 1 (Spring, 1995): 115.

47. Wright, "Exposing the Chameleon," (1996): 232.

48. Jauvin, "Government, Ministers, Macro-Organization Chart and Networks," (1997): 58.

49. See Kenneth Kernaghan, Brian Marson and Sandford Borins, *The New Public Organization,* (Toronto: Institute of Public Administration of Canada, 2000): 175–77.

50. Kernaghan, Marson and Borins, *The New Public Organization*, (2000): 176.

51. Thomas, "The Changing Nature of Accountability," (1998): 382.

52. J.E. Hodgetts, *Public Management: Emblem of Reform for the Canadian Public Service*, (Ottawa: Canadian Centre for Management Development, 1991): 13. Cited in O.P. Dwivedi and James Iain Gow, *From Bureaucracy to Public Management: The Administrative Culture of the Government of Canada*, (Peterborough: Broadview Press, 1999): 176.

53. Thomas, "The Changing Nature of Accountability," (1998): 382.

54. Thomas, "The Changing Nature of Accountability," (1998): 383.

55. See Good, *The Politics of Public Management*, (2003).

56. These points are made by Aucoin and Jarvis, *Modernizing Government Accountability*, (2005): 61.

57. Aucoin and Jarvis, *Modernizing Government Accountability* (2005): 62.

58. See Luc Juillet, "The Office of Ethics Commissioner, Accountability and Public Trust," in G. Bruce Doern, ed. *How Ottawa Spends 2004–2005: Mandate Change in the Paul Martin Era*, (Montreal: McGill-Queen's University Press, 2004): 296–316.

59. Canada, Treasury Board Secretariat of Canada, "Canada's New Government: Federal Accountability Action Plan: Turning a New Leaf," (Ottawa: Treasury Board Secretariat of Canada, 2006): 1–2.

60. Canada. The Federal Accountability Act, **www.faa-lfi.gc.ca/fs-fi/fs-fi_e.asp** Accessed July 27, 2007.

61. Canada, Royal Commission on Financial Management and Accountability, *Final Report*, (Ottawa: Supply and Services, 1979): 9.

Chapter (13)

A Canadian Public Administration

WHAT YOU WILL LEARN

You have worked through this book and become engaged in the study of public administration, and are now among a select few with a deeper and more comprehensive understanding and appreciation of this complex field. You now know that it is both an area of study derived from several academic disciplines as well as a practice rooted in the activities and structures of the state. In addition, you now have gleaned an appreciation of the many issues animating public administration, including the following:

- the importance of democracy, power, and influence, authority, legitimacy, and related concepts;
- the tensions between democracy and efficiency;
- the relative weight of public versus private sector values;
- the theoretical basis of the field;
- the politics-administration dichotomy;
- the various organizational institutions of government;
- the relationship between public administration and law;
- public policy formulation, implementation, and evaluation;
- the challenges of human and financial resource management;
- the evolution of ethical regimes in the public service;
- the significance of accountability of public officials.

You should now be able to dazzle your family and friends with your deep, intimate knowledge. But there is one more question you might consider, one that is the concern of this final chapter: to what extent can we speak of a distinctly *Canadian* public administration?

To pursue this intriguing issue, the chapter is divided into two sections.

1. *Models of Canadian Public Administration*

In this section we review the core features of Canadian public administration. We ask, what are those core features? How have they evolved over time? How do they compare to the classical Weberian model of bureaucracy?

2. *A Canadian Public Administration?*

In this section we consider the case made by a former clerk of the Privy Council that there is, indeed, a unique Canadian public administration, and we review some of the literature that addresses this question. We ask, How does contemporary Canadian public administration reflect that of other countries? How does it differ? Where does Canada stand in comparison to other countries seeking to reform their public sectors?

Models of Canadian Public Administration

As you have learned in your studies, the Canadian public service has a long and notable history (see Box 13.1). It has helped propel Canada to the forefront of nations as an eminently liveable and civilized country. Yet, in true Canadian style, we are continually critical of the institutions that seek to serve our needs. But in fact, in recent years the Canadian public service has done an enviable job by world standards:

Yet, after more than a decade of grappling with many governance challenges, some unique to Canada and most encountered by all OECD governments, and as well as a series of reform initiatives by governments and public service leaders, there are decidedly mixed reviews about what has been accomplished and the state of the public service. On the one hand, there has been considerable restructuring and innovation to

---

BOX 13.1 | **Sir John A. Macdonald on the Canadian Public Service**

". . . the civil service of Canada would compare favourably with that of any country in the world; here there are poets, men of science and men of literary tastes and habits, some of whom had even European fame, and if they had not more public acknowledgement, it was rather because of a limited sphere of action than of capacity."

—Sir John A. Macdonald, quoted in the *Ottawa Times*, March 2, 1872.

Source: Cited in Paul G. Thomas, "The Crisis of Trust in Government: Rhetoric or Reality?" Public Policy Forum (March 29, 2007). **www.ppforum.ca/common/assets/summaries/en/paul_thomas_march29_presentation.pdf** Accessed July 25, 2007.

address significant challenges, resulting in deserved pride about accomplishments. On the other, there is appreciation that the Canadian government has been less bold and coherent in its approach to public sector reform. More recently, several breaches of the public trust fuelled concerns about the quality of the Canadian public service, despite its considerable strengths, and stimulated interest in rebuilding confidence in the eyes of key stakeholders. For these reasons, leaders and academic observers have become interested in defining the contemporary Canadian model of public service.[1]

According to a Commonwealth Secretariat study of Canadian public sector management, after many years of continuous reform, "Canada continues to be seen as a leading example of excellence in public administration and a distinctive Canadian approach has begun to emerge."[2] This same study describes the factors that contributed to the reform agenda, both in Canada and elsewhere, including, most importantly, the financial crisis of the 1980s and 1990s, which posed a potential threat to Canada's status as a developed country; globalization; the rapid development of information technologies; and the growing expectations of well-informed citizens.[3] The study goes on to suggest that a set of key challenges emerged, including "the need to change the role of government and get government right; the need to overhaul service delivery; how to engage citizens in the development of policies, programmes and services; the need to reduce and restructure the public service workforce and make effective use of information technology."[4] As discussed earlier in this book, Canadian governments initiated several attempts to address these issues, including Program Review, La Relève, Citizens First, Government-On-Line, Modern Comptrollership, Human Resource Modernization, the Public Service Modernization Act, and the Federal Accountability Act. Alongside these steps, action was taken in the areas of values and ethics, official languages, diversity, and the growth of a learning organization and culture in the public sector.

We might suggest three relatively distinct eras that have characterized Canadian public administration since the country's inception, plus the current "hybrid," which features characteristics of all three articulated through the new managerialism. Ian Gow, professor emeritus of public administration, briefly sums up our administrative history by suggesting the following:

Previously, we have had colonial administration, partisan administration that came with the granting of responsible government, bureaucratic administration for good for the 50 years after 1918, and then a growing hybrid in which public servants were supposed to reconcile the bureaucratic virtues of impartiality, probity and legality with the managerial values of efficiency, effectiveness, flexibility and innovation.[5]

One means of discerning whether a distinctly Canadian model exists is by examining the Canadian experience through the lens of the classical Weberian model, as Gow has done. If you recall from chapter 3, Weber identified certain key characteristics of bureaucracies, including **permanence, hierarchy, impersonality and universality,** and **rationality**. The first era of traditional Canadian public administration was based on and drew its primary values and institutions from the Westminster system of parliamentary government. It was one suited to the needs of a small, post-colonial society in which the responsibilities of governments were relatively few compared to today and in which public servants and politicians were faced with managing a much less complicated set of institutions in a more personalized setting. It was also an era in which permanence was compromised by patronage, albeit in a rules-based hierarchical structure partly derived from the militaristic practices of colonial rule. Impersonality and universality were not highly regarded values. Instead, a system of spoils prevailed in which connections and ties to the ruling elite could be the harbinger of success in attaining land, status, appointments, or privilege.[6] Some aspects of rationality, however, were present—for instance, in the functional distribution of activities across government departments (agricultural affairs became the concern of the Department of Agriculture, etc.).

A second era in Canadian public administration evolved after the 1918 reforms of the public service with the embrace of a system of merit-based appointments. Then, a non-partisan professional public service emerged, heavily influenced by Weberian and Taylorist approaches.[7] A cadre of senior public servants dominated the government and set the tone for the culture and practices of the public service.[8] The infusion of a large number of veterans after the First and Second World Wars reinforced the authoritarian, highly regimented nature of government as a profession, but this was challenged as the baby boomers swamped the public service from the 1960s onward.[9] In this third era, an ethos of activism emerged, as did approaches more consistent with the human relations school of thought, though Weberian features were still prominent. Permanence became a cornerstone of this era, with an increasing emphasis on the idea of public service as a professional career with continuity and tenure. Hierarchy prevailed and was seen as the key organizing principle of governmental organizations. The values of impersonality and universality were enshrined in numerous initiatives, from informal cultural practices and emerging traditions to the legal-rational basis of the public service as found in a growing body of legislation, central agency controls, rules, and regulations. The politics-administration dichotomy came to be seen as a core part of the "bargain" between public servants and politicians.[10] As a result of the rapid and far-reaching changes in both the state and society, "insofar as the Westminster system approximated the Weberian model of bureaucracy, the challenges presented by the rise of the administrative state was that of accommodating political arrangements worked out for the most part in the 19th century within this new, complex and technically sophisticated administration."[11] We look at the new managerial hybrid following.

Lindquist suggests that since the 1960s, new expectations emerged concerning public administration in Canada that brought changes to the traditional model. These included the following:

■ *Representation. Bilingualism and later minority-group representation became important new ideas in the public service. They reflected the new desire to make the public service reflect the diversity of the citizens and to give all Canadians equal access to public service employment. Moreover, with such diversity, the public service could also provide better advice to ministers and better service to citizens.*

■ **Employee protection.** *The Public Service Employment Act and the Public Service Staff Relations Act adopted in the late 1960s formally recognized bargaining agents for different groups of public servants and introduced collective bargaining. This led to more job protection for public servants, regularized procedures for hiring, promoting and disciplining staff, and created opportunities to challenge the decisions of managers and their departments.*

■ **Planning and coordination.** *Since the 1960s, the number of government programs grew dramatically, as did the number of employees, departments and agencies. Beginning with the Pearson government, Prime Ministers instituted more complex cabinet and decision making systems. Along with new statutory obligations, this increased the number and scope of central agencies.*

■ **Control and accountability.** *The rapid increase in the scope and size of government activities lead to new approaches to budgeting, such as the Program, Planning and Budgeting System (PPBS). Worry about the government's ability to monitor and control financial affairs led to the appointment of the Glassco Commission on Government Organization in 1960 and the Lambert Commission on Financial Management and Accountability in 1976. The Auditor General's role expanded, and the Office of the Comptroller General was created to improve the government's financial management capabilities. The government also reformed the Estimates and introduced the Policy and Expenditure Management System in the late 1970s.*[12]

These developments helped pave the way for the contemporary hybrid of Canadian public administration. In the past 30 or 40 years, received nostrums of public administration have been severely tested, leading several other countries to move to new models to meet the challenges of contemporary life. In Canada, the public service went through a period of rapid and intense experimentation with innovation, as the notion of permanence in the public service was challenged by contracting out, flexible partnerships, alternative service delivery models, career fluidity, cutbacks, and downsizing. While hierarchy persisted, attempts were made to flatten it and create more horizontal relationships. Hierarchy was also compromised by an increasing resort to public–private partnerships in which lines of command and control were less obvious, as were lines of accountability. Impersonality and universality was severely eroded as the move toward a "blame and shame" culture exposed public servants to the glare of the public spotlight in unprecedented ways. As well, rationality was strongly emphasized through the construction of an elaborate "web of rules," which, ironically, created the conditions for retrenchment toward decentralization and "letting the managers manage." An imperfect marriage resulted, in which moves toward greater flexibility were countered by moves toward increasing rules (often in the wake of public scandals). Attempts were made to further entrench rationality by infusing a results-based orientation into the public service, changing the focus to managing outcomes, though with dubious results overall.

As we noted elsewhere in this book, by the 1980s a new manner of thinking about the role of government had emerged. Loosely agglomerated around a core set of ideas and principles, the ideologically driven **New Public Management (NPM)** posed serious challenges to the practice and theory of public administration in Canada and abroad. Based largely on private sector values, NPM proved a useful paradigm in an era in which deficit reduction and the concomitant shrinking of the state were prioritized. The mixed message of improving public services while reducing the public service was a key element of NPM. Interestingly, much of the discourse of NPM echoes the language of earlier reform efforts, including the Glassco Commission, the Lambert Commission, PS2000, and others.[13]

But the Canadian variant of NPM did not fundamentally re-orient public administration. Instead, public sector reform was driven by deficit reduction and cost saving, rather than by some broader philosophical, overarching set of principles and goals. According to management professor Sanford Borins, even when Canadian governments invoked NPM they embraced ideas for public sector change that were more like those in vogue in the United States than the "hard-edged public choice and agency theories that motivated reform in the U.K. and New Zealand [which] were not often heard in Canada."[14] Borins concludes that "if we were to liken the new public administration paradigm to a buffet, we would conclude that the Canadian government has sampled everything but not made a full meal of any dish."[15] Lindquist suggests that in Canada NPM did "not require wholesale restructuring of government machinery,"[16] although this does not imply its impact was unimportant in select areas. Dwivedi and Halligan concluded that "Canada has followed its own pathway in reshaping the public service that has sought to avoid the more extreme positions that entailed less government as an end itself, reliance on competition and private sector models, and a heavy emphasis on individualisation, contractualisation and perfor-mance management. These elements exist but not as overriding approaches."[17] Exceptions to these observations were the provincial governments of Alberta under Ralph Klein, British Columbia under Gordon Campbell, and Ontario under Mike Harris, all of whom more fully and aggressively embraced NPM rostrums and practices. But their actions were quite out of step with the federal and most other provincial and territorial governments.

Thus, we can identify the broad parameters of these eras of public administration in Canada and can see the foreign influences alongside the domestic developments unique to the Canadian experience. Our next concern is mainly with the contemporary era, and the extent to which we can now say we have a predominantly "made-in-Canada" model of public administration.

While it has been remarked that politicians are rarely interested in the nuts-and-bolts of administering government, given Canada's executive-dominated system of government it is not surprising that many administrative reforms are, nonetheless, associated with particular prime ministers. Table 13.1 shows the major developments in public administration under several Canadian prime ministers.

TABLE 13.1 Canadian Prime Ministers and Their Influence on Public Service Reforms

Period	Prime Minister	Challenges	Reforms
1867–1873	Sir John A. Macdonald	Nation-building and transition from colonial government to Dominion	BNA Act and established first administration of the new Dominion
1911–1920	Sir Robert Borden	Politically neutral civil service, patronage appointments, and independent Civil Service Commission	Civil Service Acts of 1917 and 1918, and introduced the merit system in the civil service
1921–1930 and 1935–1948	William Lyon Mackenzie King	Professionalism and position-classification in the civil service, management of the budget, need for the welfare state	Introduced Keynesian budgeting, increased the hiring of intellectuals in the public service; established the Royal Commission on Classification Administrative (Gordon Commission)
1930–1935	R.B. Bennett	Impact of the Great Depression, fiscal accountability	Fiscal conservative stringent controls, consolidated Revenue and Audit Act, balanced budget
1948–1957	Louis St. Laurent	Demand for governmental intervention in the economy and society	Gordon Commission on Canada's Long-Term Economic Prospects
1957–1963	John G. Diefenbaker	Demand for social expansion, managing the administrative state	Critical of the public service, established Royal Commission on Government Organization (Glassco Commission), which emphasized management within government
1963–1968	Lester B. Pearson	Demand for trade union rights in the civil service,	Introduced collective bargaining legislation for public servants.

(Continued)

TABLE 13.1   Continued

Period	Prime Minister	Challenges	Reforms
1968–1979 and 1980–1984	Pierre Elliott Trudeau	equal status for French language, rights of women Francophone representation in the public service, government by management, gender issues, privatization	Royal Commission on Bilingualism and Biculturalism, and Status of Women Political management, improved the Cabinet Committee system, passed Official Languages Act, Charter of Rights and Freedoms
1979	Joe Clark	Desire to restrain growth of state	Policy Expenditure Management System (PEMS)
1984–1993	Brian Mulroney	Neoconservatism, restraining government spending, rising national debt	Nielson Task Force, downsizing, deregulation, privatization, PS2000 Task Force
1993	Kim Campbell	Downsizing of government operations	Initiative in downsizing and restructuring of government to eight broad functional areas
1993–2004	Jean Chrétien	Restructuring, doing more with fewer human and financial resources, privatization	Expenditure Management System replaced PEMS, fiscally driven downsizing of government, Program Review, and deficit management
2004–2006	Paul Martin	Sponsorship scandal, accountability, ethics, public service modernization, minority government	Commission of Inquiry into the Sponsorship Scandal (Gomery Commission), Public Service Modernization Act, Public Service Employment Act
2006–2007	Stephen Harper	Accountability, ethics, minority government	Federal Accountability Act

Source: Adapted from O.P. Dwivedi and R.W. Phidd, "Public Service Reform in Canada," in John Halligan, ed. *Public Service Reform*, (Canberra: Centre for Research in Public Sector Management and International Association of Schools and Institutes of Administration, 1999): 50–51.

A *Canadian* Public Administration?

The search for the distinctively Canadian features of public administration in the contemporary era can probably be traced to assertions made in 1998 by a former clerk of the Privy Council, Jocelyne Bourgon, that such a model existed. She suggested that reforms in a variety of countries around service delivery, citizen-centred initiatives, results-based management, best practices borrowed from the private sector, and so on, had produced "models" associated with those countries. Thus, there was a "New Zealand" model, an "Australian model," and a "U.K. model." But was there a "Canadian model" with a catalogue of reforms and approaches unique to this country? Yes, according to Bourgon (see Box 13.2). She argued that,

---

BOX 13.2 | **A Canadian Model of Public Service Reform**

Compared to other countries, "the 'Canadian model' is less well known," according to the clerk of the Privy Council. But "while none of its elements are uniquely Canadian, taken together they amount to an approach that is sufficiently different from all the others to warrant attention." She describes the key attributes of the Canadian model in the following way:

The Canadian model is based on the belief that government and government institutions are essential to a well-performing society. While it rejects the philosophy that less government is synonymous with better government, the Canadian model recognizes the importance of affordable government. It endorses the idea that democracy working side by side with a market economy is the key to national prosperity and the well-being of citizens.

The Canadian model asserts that public sector reform must start by examining the role that government is expected to play in the future. It recognizes that public sector reform must be anchored in a reasonable understanding of the strategic contribution that government is expected to make to the prosperity of Canada and to the well-being of its citizens. It recognizes that government cannot act alone. It acknowledges that the role of government can vary depending on the circumstances: it must be able to lead, to play the role of catalyst, to build partnerships, to create strategic alliances, and to rely on the commitment of all those who are willing and able to contribute to the collective good.

The Canadian model affirms that a well-performing public sector requires both a strong policy capacity and a modern service delivery function. Over the past few years, the public service has sought to strengthen its capacity for policy research, analysis and development and, at the same time, to modernize its approach to service delivery. Along the way it discovered that both functions were facing very similar challenges.

In service delivery, it means integrating services among departments and among governments, building partnerships and strategic alliances and exploiting the potential of information technology to better meet the needs of citizens. In policy, it means taking a broader, more comprehensive approach to the public interest, ahead of the departmental interest; working co-operatively to develop more integrated policy responses; and cultivating more open, participatory and transparent policy development processes.

The Canadian model rejects the notion that "one size fits all." It encourages experimentation and the emergence of a diversity of institutional models to put before decision makers. Portfolio management is a recent Canadian innovation. It recognizes that a minister is responsible to Parliament for a family of organizations, and it encourages greater flexibility within each organization and greater cohesion among the organizations reporting to a single minister.

The Canadian model does not accept that the policy and service delivery functions should be separated as a universal principle. Instead, it follows a more pragmatic route in which separating the policy and service delivery functions is contemplated whenever it can be demonstrated that it will bring about substantive gains in the quality of service to citizens.

The Canadian model recognizes the importance of a well-performing, professional, non-partisan public service. *It recognizes that public servants have a key role to play in shaping policies and delivering services. The Canadian model recognizes that to build a modern and vibrant professional, non-partisan public service, it is necessary to commit as much time and energy to human resources management as to policy development or service delivery. It recognizes that to retain, motivate and attract a corps of talented and dedicated public servants requires profound change. The public service must be able to provide its people with the breadth of knowledge and experience necessary to advise and serve in a modern and global environment.*

The Canadian model requires leadership from both elected and appointed officials. *Political leadership has been essential to realign the role of government, to ensure balance and fairness and to stay the course over a number of years. Public service leadership has been relied upon to put bold and creative ideas before ministers, to marshal support for change and to ensure smooth implementation. Each group has played its role well and all have reason to be proud of the results they have accomplished together.*

Source: Canada. Privy Council Office. *Fifth Annual Report to the Prime Minister on the Public Service of Canada.* Ottawa: Privy Council Office, 1998.

"I decided the world wasn't ready for the wheel, so I invented the desk."

Source: www.cartoonstock.com

after a decade or more of disruption in the Canadian public service and in other countries, the Canadian model represented a more temperate voice among the more dramatic initiatives in places like New Zealand and the U.K. She also warned against the easy assumption that government could—or should—be run like a business, acknowledging the important differences in values, objectives, cultures, and purposes between the public and private sectors. Bourgon further suggested that, in looking to future reforms, it was possible to discern the outlines or an approach that was Canadian first by virtue of this country's continued assumption that government institutions were essential to a healthy, well-performing society. Second, she argued that reforms must be cognizant of the strategic place government plays in fostering prosperity and citizen well-being. Third, a well-performing public sector required a strong policy capacity and modern service-delivery capabilities. Fourth, she acknowledged the need for a well-performing, professional, non-partisan public service. And, finally, Bourgon said the Canadian model required leadership from both elected and appointed officials.[18] However, Bourgon's model was not very thoroughly articulated; it was a skeleton, really. But it provided some food for thought that was taken up by others.

Peter Aucoin, professor of public administration, suggests that political leadership in Canada at the federal level has been reluctant to adopt the neoconservative ideological underpinnings of NPM with nearly as much zeal as leaders have in other countries, and in this regard the Canadian approach has been distinctive.[19] Gow underscores this point by also suggesting that Canadian public servants have not been as ideological as their counterparts in other places. "We in Canada have not had doctrinaire senior bureaucrats who, as in the case of New Zealand, persuaded ministers that reform was necessary."[20] Second, Aucoin argues that the NPM approach toward strategic partnerships and alliances with non-governmental groups has been embraced to a degree but that the Canadian state has retained the idea of collective public action to pursue public purposes. He suggests that, again unlike in other countries, there is a rejection here of the idea that government has no role to play. A third feature of the Canadian model, according to Aucoin, is pragmatism. He argues that Canadian governments have demonstrated for the most part a willingness to put aside ideology or "conviction politics" in favour of instrumental pragmatism. Fourth, unlike Thatcher in the U.K., Reagan in the U.S., or others, Canadian leaders have not seen the public service as an impediment to the pursuit of their agendas. This flows partly from the tradition of a strong bureaucratic centre located in the central agencies, whose role importantly includes assisting ministers to rein in the more free-spending and independent impulses of line departments. Moreover, it also reflects the observation that Canadian politicians have generally been more willing to trust their public servants to implement their agenda, lacking the "pathological suspicion of public servants that was seen in Britain, the United States and New Zealand. In other words, like their senior advisors, they [politicians] have been moderates, not conviction-driven ideologues."[21]

Another related set of observations about the Canadian model is provided by David Good, a professor of public administration and former senior public servant. Good notes that NPM has not been seen by Canadian practitioners as a single unified theoretical approach. Quoting two students of public administration, Good says, "whether there is in fact a single 'new public management' or whether NPM is better seen as something like a flu virus, continuously mutating and having several different strains at once, is debatable."[22] Good, commenting on Bourgon's model, describes that Canadian model:

Its distinguishing features were pragmatic and non-ideological. Its approach was practical and not doctrinaire, reflecting the evolutionary history in the practice of public administration within a Westminster system of cabinet government in a decentralized federation. It also reflected a broadly shared set of values about the role of government in a country of large geography, close proximity to the United States, and a society with diverse ethnic origins and different regional experiences.[23]

For Good, the Canadian model has its roots in the concept of a professional public service, even as it adapts to some elements of NPM. Hence, issues like privatization, politicization of the public service, and performance measurement are moderated and conditioned by the Canadian perspective. The importance of a professional public service should not be underestimated in discerning the distinctiveness of the Canadian approach, and is partly attributable to the point raised by Aucoin that Canadian governments have not generally seen the public service as an obstacle to its policy and political objectives. Hence, the focus of ministers has been more on how to use the public service to achieve goals, rather than how to reform the public service to get it out of the way of its goals.

Good also suggests that the Canadian model incorporates a professional public service that is politically sensitive at all levels. He argues that, as such, public servants are able to deal with conflicting values. Indeed, the recent explosion of interest in values and ethics, which we discussed in chapter 11, may be reflective of this characteristic of the Canadian public service. Professionalism, thus, is reinforced in that every time the government changes its political stripes, it needs to be reassured that the public service will be sensitive to its new priorities and approaches. At the same time, a professional public service with political sensitivity must be able to "speak truth to power." In this sense, the Canadian public service fosters learning and the cultivation of "knowledge workers" who can propose innovations and find solutions to complex issues without fear of political reprisal. Finally, the Canadian model, in comparative perspective, has been far less attuned to monitoring results and measuring performance than the models of other countries.

Iain Gow has suggested that there are five main features of the Canadian model, which have developed since World War II: 1) strong political control, restrained by the federal system, the Charter of Rights and Freedoms, autonomous parliamentary agents, and public opinion; 2) a strong legal framework, backed up by the Charter and the courts; 3) an autonomous nonpartisan, professional public service; 4) a tradition of moderation and pragmatism with both political and public service leaders; 5) fairly strong tolerance for ambiguity, as present in federal–provincial relations, equal opportunity for minorities and new forms of government for the northern territories and self-governing Native communities.[24] Moderation in all things seems to be the Canadian mantra. Gow suggests that in the area of administrative reforms in the 1980s, for instance, Canadian initiatives were not just moderate, they were even timid. He goes on to suggest the following:

Even the policy initiatives to downsize the state were moderate. Nothing much came of the [1984] Nielsen Review, which might have led to a rigorous and selective downsizing. A serious attempt was made to get program spending under control, but its progress was swept away by the uncontrollable surge of spending caused by the recession of the early 1990s. In comparative context, Canadian privatizations and deregulation were moderate. There was increased recourse to contracting out, but few cases of exaggerated or wholesale abandonment of functions. At the same time, the Mulroney government adopted important access-to-equality legislation in 1985, strengthened the Official Languages Act in 1988, and reformed the Public Service Employment Act in 1992 in the wake of the Public Service 2000 exercise. These were all the work of reform, not the dismantlement of the state.

In the1990s, more hardy innovations occurred, in the Program Review, alternative service delivery (ASD), and information technologies (IT). As in the U.S., campaigns and competitions were introduced to encourage individual and organizational innovation. Still, the Canadian experience puts us in the middle of OECD countries for the number and extent of reforms introduced.[25]

Paul Thomas, professor of public administration, has asked why Canadian public service reforms generally have been less noticed and celebrated on the international scene, and suggests two possible answers. First, he argues,

the scope, depth and pace of public service reform in any country reflects a range of factors: the political culture of the country, the constitutional and legal structure of the political system, the scope of the public sector, the history and traditions of the public service, the ideas and leadership skills of the political and administrative elites, the changing economic and social circumstances and even serendipity![26]

In Canada these factors have combined to produce a pragmatic, cautious, trial-and-error approach, reflecting the fact that the public service is not an island unto itself. Thomas suggests "Canada's national government had less public sector to reform than countries like the United Kingdom and New Zealand which are usually mentioned as leaders of the NPM parade. Unlike those countries, Canada lacked political leaders with strong convictions about the importance of transforming the role of government."[27] Consequently, public service reform has largely been left to the public servants themselves and has lacked political champions. So we ended up in a situation where "insisting upon 'error free government,' ministers (and the central agencies which serve them) adopted the rhetoric of public service reform, but refused to act fully on the slogan of empowering public managers and others to act in the public interest."[28]

Returning to our comparison between the Canadian model and the classical Weberian model of permanence, hierarchy, impersonality and universality, and rationality, Gow assesses the current Canadian experience and reaches the following conclusions:

At the level of permanence, we still have a career service and indeed are trying to improve it to ensure its ability to produce new generations of quality leaders. Conflict-of-interest provisions still separate the public function from private life, but partnerships blur the line between them. Concern seems greater for creativity and innovation than for continuity, but the overall stress on moderate reforms means that continuity is preferred to revolutionary change and there is recognition of the need to preserve institutional memory.

Hierarchy is still respected in the system, political direction is assured, and any devolutions of power are supposed to be accompanied by corresponding requirements to report on results achieved. Access to information has reduced the level of secrecy, but it is a continuing battle and in no way authorizes public servants to disclose information on their own. There seems to be moderate satisfaction with the workings of internal accountability, that various recent crises have shown us that external accountability (i.e., to Parliament) still works mainly by crisis.

Impersonality and universality, in the forms of objectivity and impartiality, are still qualities required of the professional public service. However, partnerships introduce something less than universality, as the partner has a privileged position with the administration. Devolution also means that a greater variety of norms and standards is being applied. Finally, and most important, the recognition of collective rights under the Charter, access to equality, language legislation and native self government have seriously undermined the universal state (if it ever existed).

Rationality is still very much with us, represented today above all by results-based management. Citizen-centered management has led to the promotion of horizontal management, which counteracts the divisive effects of the division of labour. The specialty that Weber was thinking of, law, was given a big boost by the adoption of the Charter Of Rights And Freedoms, but it is undermined by partnerships, which are more pragmatic in nature. The attempt to measure and increase client or citizen satisfaction is also diluting the weight of law in our administrations.[29]

The comparative dimension has been alluded to in several places in this chapter. Several studies have been undertaken over the past few years to discern where Canada sits in the pantheon of countries that have embraced administrative reform. Generally, there seems to be a rough consensus that Canada is neither the most- nor the least-active country. Instead, in typical Canadian fashion, perhaps, we have exercised moderations and constraint, flirting with elements of some reforms here and there as it suited our purposes, but, with few exceptions, avoiding a headlong rush into a full-blown embrace. For example, John Halligan studied five Anglo-American countries (Canada, the U.S., the U.K., New Zealand, and Australia) and found that in the fundamental features of their public service systems, there were differences in terms of presidential (the U.S.) versus parliamentarian systems, open and closed models of recruitment, size of the public sectors relative to GDP (with the U.S. and Australia being relatively small and the rest falling in the middle range of OECD countries), the role of the career public service, and modes of accountability. He observes that in terms of differences, "the breadth of the spectrum is most obvious in political-bureaucratic relations; the U.K. lies at one end, with a mix of political and professional appointments. The United States remains unique in some respects, and neighbouring Canada occupies something of an intermediate position between its North American neighbour and the others."[30] This middle position need not surprise us since, as you will recall, "the public service system reflects both the Westminster tradition and the influence of the neighbouring United States," according to Dwivedi and Halligan, who go on to suggest "yet the country's administrative tradition and its public service remain distinctively Canada."[31] This distinctiveness is characterized by an apparent willingness to appropriate and experiment with reforms but a hesitation to fully implement those same reforms. This has resulted in a paradoxically Canadian stance:

Canada was the first to explore management reform but was slow to incorporate and institutionalize it, and in some respects the public service remained undermanagerialised; second, despite having never fully embraced managerialism, the Canadian public service exhibits many standard management features and has experienced the tensions and conflicts produced by attempts to change the administrative culture.[32]

More broadly, Lindquist summarizes several studies comparing Canada to other OECD countries.[33] In one analysis of public sector reform, Australia, New Zealand, and the U.K. were held to be at one extreme as "comprehensive" reformers, while Germany, Switzerland, Japan, and Norway underwent comparatively little reform. Canada and the U.S. stand somewhere between these points on the spectrum along with Finland, Denmark, Sweden, and the Netherlands as more active reformers. In another analysis, Canada was characterized as a "modernizer" along with Finland, France, the Netherlands, and Sweden. Germany and the European Commission were characterized as "maintainers," while Australia, New Zealand, and the U.K. were termed "marketizers." Finally, Lindquist notes a 2003 World Bank study that characterized Canada as sitting somewhere in the middle of countries that had undergone extensive versus selective reforms.

Assuming we have identified a Canadian public administration, it would be a mistake to suggest that today's paradigms of public administration will provide us with all of tomorrow's answers. All the various reforms of recent times—privatization, contracting out, empowerment, deregulation, new operating agencies, downsizing, de-layering of management levels, a focus on clients rather than citizens—aimed at modernizing government by making it more businesslike have influenced the institutions of government. But current fashions in public administration come and go in response to broader socio-economic and political forces in society. The current mania for businesslike solutions may turn out to be a passing fancy. Now that conditions are changing again, new schools of thought will invariably arise as to how to practise public administration. And it is this constant dynamism and change that makes the study of public administration so engaging.

WHAT YOU HAVE LEARNED

It is important to note that certain traditional and long-standing concerns of public administration, which were highlighted throughout this book, remain prominent among the concerns of both practitioners and academics. Thus, the lens through which the issues are viewed may be fogged-over from time to time. But the core concerns persist. For the foreseeable future, underlying developments in public administration will include the following: the nature of state–market relations; the tensions between democracy and efficiency; the relative weight of public versus private sector values; the politics-administration dichotomy; the proper organizational form for government; the relationship between public administration and law; the enhancement of public policy formulation, implementation, and evaluation; the challenges of human and financial resource management; the evolution of the ethical regime in the public service; the ongoing struggle around the accountability of public officials; and other related matters. As students of public administration, we all can look forward to the myriad challenges and opportunities inherent in this most vital and fascinating of human endeavours.

Key Words and Concepts

permanence (403)

hierarchy (403)

impersonality and universality (403)

rationality (403)

New Public Management (NPM) (406)

Review Questions

1. Models of Canadian Public Administration

In this section we reviewed the core features of Canadian public administration. Ask yourself, Can I identify the eras of Canadian public administration as it has evolved over time? Do I know what its core features are? Can I effectively compare it to the classical Weberian model of bureaucracy?

2. A Canadian *Public Administration?*

While there is a growing body of literature that posits a Canadian public administration, ask yourself, Do I agree that the characteristics cited in the literature add up to something distinctly Canadian? Can I say how contemporary Canadian public administration reflects as well as stands apart from that of other countries? Is a path to the future of Canadian public administration discernable from the ongoing reforms of today?

Weblinks

Commonwealth Secretariat
www.thecommonwealth.org

Canadian Association of Programs in Public Administration
www.cappa.ca

Institute of Public Administration of Canada
www.ipac.ca

Canada School of Public Service
www.csps-efpc.gc.ca

Networked Government
www.networkedgovernment.ca

International Association of Schools and Institutes of Administration
www.iiasiisa.be/schools/aeacc.htm

United Nations Public Administration Network
www.unpan.org/discover.asp

Further Reading

1. Models of Canadian Public Administration

Halligan, John. "Comparing Public Sector Reform in the OECD," in Brendan C. Nolan, ed. *Public Sector Reform: An International Perspective*. Basingstoke, U.K.: Macmillan, 2001.

Peters, B. Guy and Donald J. Savoie, eds. *Governance in a Changing Environment*. Montreal: McGill–Queen's University Press, 1995.

Peters, B. Guy and Donald J. Savoie, eds. *Governance in the Twenty-First Century*. Montreal: McGill–Queen's University Press, 2000.

Peters, B. Guy and Donald J. Savoie, eds. *Taking Stock: Assessing Public Sector Reforms*. Montreal: McGill–Queen's University Press, 1998.

Public Policy Forum. *Canada's Public Service in the 21st Century: Discussion Paper*. Ottawa: Public Policy Forum, April 2007.

2. A Canadian *Public Administration?*

Aucoin, Peter. *The New Public Management: Canada in Comparative Perspective*. Montreal: Institute for Research on Public Policy, 1995.

Candler, Gaylord George. "The Comparative Evolution of Public Administration in Australia, Brazil and Canada," *Canadian Public Administration*, 49, 3 (Fall, 2006): 334–49.

McQuaig, Linda. *Shooting the Hippo: Death by Deficit and Other Canadian Myths*. Toronto: Penguin Books, 1995.

Saint-Martin, Denis. *Building the New Managerialist State: Consultants and the Politics of Public Sector Reform in Comparative Perspective*. Toronto: Oxford University Press, 2000.

Savoie, Donald. *Reagan, Thatcher and Mulroney: In Search of a New Bureaucracy*. Toronto: University of Toronto Press, 1994.

Endnotes

1. Evert Lindquist, *A Critical Moment: Capturing and Conveying the Evolution of the Canadian Public Service*, (Ottawa: Canada School of Public Service, 2006): 1.

2. Commonwealth Secretariat, "The Canadian Experience of Public Sector Management Reform 1995–2002," *A Profile of the Public Service of Canada: Current Good Practices and New Developments in Public Sector Service Management*, (London: Commonwealth Secretariat, 2003): vii.

3. Commonwealth Secretariat, "The Canadian Experience," (2003): vii.

4. Commonwealth Secretariat, "The Canadian Experience," (2003): vii.

5. Iain Gow, *A Canadian Model of Public Administration?* (Ottawa: Canada School of Public Service, 2004): 22.

6. See S.J.R. Noel Patrons, *Clients, Brokers: Ontario Society and Politics, 1791–1896*, (Toronto: University of Toronto Press, 1990).

7. See Alisdair Roberts, "A Fragile State: Federal Public Administration in the Twentieth Century," in Christopher Dunn, ed. *The Handbook of Canadian Public Administration*, (Toronto: Oxford University Press, 2002): 18–36.

8. See J. L. Granatstein, *The Ottawa Men: The Civil Service Mandarins, 1935–1957. With a New Introduction*, (Toronto: University of Toronto Press, 1998).

9. Nicole Morgan, *Implosion: An Analysis of the Growth of the Federal Public Service in Canada 1945–1985*, (Montreal: Institute for Research on Public Policy, 1986).

10. See Donald J. Savoie, *Breaking the Bargain: Public Servants, Ministers, and Parliament*, (Toronto: University of Toronto Press, 2003).

11. O.P. Dwivedi and John Halligan, "The Canadian Public Service: Balancing Values and Management," in John Halligan, ed. *Civil Service Systems in Anglo-American Countries*, (Cheltenham, U.K.: Edward Elgar, 2003): 150.

12. Lindquist, *A Critical Moment* (2006): 6–7.

13. Dwivedi and Halligan, "The Canadian Public Service," (2003); See also O.P. Dwivedi, and Iain Gow, "The New Public Management Comes to Canada," in O.P. Dwivedi and Iain Gow, eds. *From Bureaucracy to Public Management: The Administrative Culture of the Government of Canada*, (Toronto: Institute of Public Administration of Canada, 1999).

14. Sandford Borins, "Transformation of the Public Sector: Canada in Comparative Perspective," in Christopher Dunn, ed. *The Handbook of Canadian Public Administration*, (Toronto: Oxford University Press, 2002): 7.

15. Borins, "Transformation of the Public Sector," (2002):12.

16. Lindquist, *A Critical Moment* (2006): 8.

17. Dwivedi and Halligan, "The Canadian Public Service," (2003): 170.

18. Canada. Privy Council Office. Fifth Annual Report to the Prime Minister on the Public Service of Canada, (Ottawa: Privy Council Office, 1998).

19. See Peter Aucoin, "Beyond the 'New' in Public Management Reform in Canada: Catching the Next Wave?" in Christopher Dunn, ed. *The Handbook of Canadian Public Administration*, (Toronto: Oxford University Press, 2002): 37–52.

20. Gow, *A Canadian Model of Public Administration?* (2004): 10.

21. Gow, *A Canadian Model of Public Administration?* (2004): 11.

22. David Good, *The Politics of Public Management: The HRDC Audit of Grants and Contributions*, (Toronto: University of Toronto Press, 2003): 154.

23. Good, *The Politics of Public Management*, (2003): 154–55.

24. Gow, *A Canadian Model of Public Administration?* (2004): 21.

25. Gow, *A Canadian Model of Public Administration?* (2004): 11.

26. Paul G. Thomas, "The Crisis of Trust in Government: Rhetoric or Reality?" Public Policy Forum (March 29, 2007): 1. **www.ppforum.ca/common/assets/summaries/en/paul_thomas_ march29_ presentation.pdf** Accessed July 25, 2007.

27. Paul G. Thomas, "A Canadian Perspective on the 'New Public Service,'" Commentary by Paul G. Thomas on the presentation by Robert Denhardt to the Annual Conference of the Institute of Public Administration of Canada, (Toronto, August 25, 2003): 1.

28. Thomas, "A Canadian Perspective," (2003): 1.

29. Gow, *A Canadian Model of Public Administration?* (2006): 19–21.

30. John Halligan, "Anglo-American Civil Service Systems: An Overview," in John Halligan, ed. *Civil Service Systems in Anglo-American Countries*, (Cheltenham, U.K.: Edward Elgar, 2003): 3. See also Lindquist, *A Critical Moment,* (2006): 12–13.

31. Dwivedi and Halligan, "The Canadian Public Service," (2003): 148.

32. Dwivedi and Halligan, "The Canadian Public Service," (2003): 148.

33. See Lindquist, *A Critical Moment* (2006): 13. Lindquist usefully critiques the methodological and analytical limitations in comparing these various studies, since most start with different orientations.

Glossary

accountability—a fundamental principle of democratic government that states that those who hold governmental power must be answerable and responsive to the people for the way in which that power is exercised. *See also* administrative responsibility.

accountable— *see* accountability.

accounting officer—designation assigned to deputy ministers, giving them the legal obligation to appear before parliamentary committees to answer questions on their management responsibilities within the framework of ministerial responsibility and accountability.

accumulation—a concept used in neo-Marxist theory referring to the need for capital to generate (accumulate) profits and for government to formulate policies that foster the conditions to make profitability possible.

administrative evaluation— the examination of the efficiency of delivery of government services. This evaluation is performed in order to determine if the best value for money is being realized within the framework of democracy and justice, using technical methodologies involving the compilation and analysis of data on program costs and benefits. *See also* policy evaluation.

administrative law—that part of the law that is concerned with the legal limitations on the actions of government officials and the remedies available to anyone affected by a transgression of these limits.

administrative responsibility— the requirement that public servants be answerable and accountable in fulfilling their duties as authorized by a superior.

advisory board— an organization composed of citizens and created by the government, but outside of the normal bureaucracy, to provide independent advice to a minister.

affirmative action— *see* employment equity.

alienation— a concept used in Marxist analysis to describe the condition in which citizens see the bureaucracy and/or state as a distant, impersonal, and oppressive force.

alternative service delivery (ASD)— organizational bodies developed to deliver government services more efficiently and innovatively than traditional departments and agencies.

amending formula—a procedure introduced in the Constitution Act, 1982, to formally change the Constitution. Generally, the amending formula requires the agreement of Ottawa and seven out of ten provinces, representing at least 50 percent of the population. Some constitutional amendments, however, require the unanimous agreement of all 11 governments.

audit— a process of examining government accounts to see that they are correct. *See also* comprehensive audit.

Auditor General— responsible directly to Parliament, the Auditor General is the financial "watchdog" who performs an audit each year of the Public Accounts and prepares an annual report on the financial management of the government. The results of these audits are released to the public.

authority—the basis of state rule, in which the right to rule others and to legitimately compel obedience in the behaviour of citizens is held by state officials.

autonomy—freedom of action. This term is used by Marxists in connection with the freedom of state officials to formulate policies independently of the control or influence of capital.

budget—an annual statement of the government's revenues and expenditures.

bureaucracy—a form of organization characterized by hierarchy, a division of labour, a system of hiring and promotion based on merit, and management by detailed but impersonal rules.

bureaucratic discretion—the degree of freedom of judgment and action that bureaucrats have in implementing public policies.

bureaucratic pathology—a phenomenon in which the strict adherence to rigid rules and regulations supplants the real goals of a bureaucratic organization.

bureaucratization—the organization of human behaviour into formal organizations and structures for the purposes of efficiency and control.

business planning—*see* business plans.

business plans—a private sector managerial technique increasingly adopted by the public sector as part of the New Public Management movement. These are detailed plans of the multi-year objectives of line departments and their strategies for achieving the best possible service delivery at the least possible cost.

Cabinet—the political executive, which formulates government policies and is responsible for initiating most government legislation, the priorities of government, and the administration of policies. Cabinet generally consists of 20 to 40 Members of Parliament chosen by the prime minister to head government ministries.

central agency—a coordinating agency of government with the authority to intervene and direct the affairs of other government departments. Currently, there are four central agencies in the federal government: the Prime Minister's Office; the Privy Council Office; the Department of Finance; and the Treasury Board.

charismatic legitimacy—a form of legitimacy outlined by Max Weber in which citizens accept that an individual has the right to rule over them by virtue of his or her personal characteristics and strength of personality. *See also* legal-rational legitimacy and traditional legitimacy.

Charter of Rights and Freedoms—added to the Canadian Constitution in 1982, the Charter protects Canadians' fundamental freedoms, democratic rights, mobility rights, legal rights, equality rights, language rights, and Aboriginal rights.

civil law—law based on the French Napoleonic Code and Roman Law, in which the law is codified, unlike English-based common law. Civil law is the basis of the legal system in Quebec.

Civil Service Acts, 1908 and 1918—reforms to the federal civil service that eliminated patronage as the basis of hiring in the public service and set in motion the movement toward a merit-based, professional public service.

Civil Service Commission—*see* Public Service Commission.

class conflict—a central premise of Marxist theory, which argues that capitalist societies are divided into mutually antagonistic classes whose fundamental interests are ultimately irreconcilable.

code of ethics—a written set of regulations setting out the boundaries of acceptable and unacceptable behaviour for public servants and promoting the highest ethical conduct and standards required of public servants. Codes of ethics generally govern such matters as conflicts of interest, moonlighting, nonpartisanship, confidentiality, lying to the public, and similar issues.

collective bargaining—a means of determining wages, hours, and working conditions through negotiation between an employer and a union.

collective ministerial responsibility—the principle that members of the Cabinet (the executive branch of government) are collectively responsible for the policies and management of the government as a whole. *See also* individual ministerial responsibility.

common law—the rules developed by the courts and based on the principle of *stare decisis* (that is, established legal precedents guide current judgments).

comprehensive audit—an audit of a program focusing on its economy, efficiency, and effectiveness.

conflict of interest—a circumstance in which a politician or public servant has a personal interest in a policy or program such that his or her professional position and role is compromised.

conservatism—in Canada, traditionally an ideology that values hierarchy, order, and security above individual freedom and advocates a certain level of state intervention to restrain personal freedom for the greater good of the community.

conservative—*see* conservatism.

constitution—the supreme law of the land. Constitutions delineate the relationship between the state and citizens, between the parts of the state (executive, legislative, and judicial) and, in a federal system, between levels of government (national and provincial).

constitutional convention—the unwritten part of the constitution which is derived from habit, tradition, and past practices. Although not legally enforceable, constitutional conventions carry important political weight.

constitutional law—that part of the constitution composed of written documents and the common law, which is enforceable through the courts.

contracting out—the practice by government of employing the private sector to deliver services in order to save money.

Crown corporation—a corporation that the state owns wholly or in part in order to promote the national interest but that operates at arm's length from direct government control. Crown corporations are part of the arsenal of governing instruments available to the state.

cultural analysis—a type of policy analysis that focuses on the role culture plays in policy making. It tends to be structuralist and/or interpretive in approach. *See also* structural analysis and interpretive framework.

debt—the accumulation of deficits over the years.

deficit—the amount by which government expenditures exceed revenues during a specified period of time (usually one year).

democratic society—*see* direct democracy and representative democracy.

department—an organizational unit of government headed by a minister.

deputy minister—the administrative head of a government department appointed by the prime minister.

deregulation—the process of removing government regulations over an industry or sector of the economy, so that it may operate according to the dictates of the free market.

direct democracy—a form of government by the people in which citizens make all important community decisions as a whole, usually in some form of public assembly. This stands in contrast to a system of representative democracy, in which citizens choose representatives to make decisions on their behalf.

disallowance—section 56 of the Constitution Act, 1867 (formerly the British North America Act, 1867), which permits the federal government to disallow provincial legislation.

discretion—*see* bureaucratic discretion.

division of labour—a principle of organization in which specialization in the organization of work is imposed in order to narrow the range of tasks each person is responsible for. The goal is to improve the overall efficiency of the organization and thus boost productivity.

division of powers—those sections of the constitution that set out the jurisdictional responsibilities of each level of government. In general, federal powers are spelled out in section 91 and provincial powers in section 92 of the Canadian Constitution.

doctrine of answerability—a watered-down version of the principle of ministerial responsibility in which the minister of a department is required simply to explain the errors of her subordinates, but not actually resign as a result of those actions.

elite—a small group of people who exercise considerable power in society—politically, economically, socially, and/or bureaucratically.

employment equity—a set of programs and policies aimed at removing systemic barriers to employment and promotion among groups historically under-represented in the public service. *See also* representativeness.

estimates—the government's annual request to Parliament for an appropriation of funds to support its programs.

ethics—rules and codes of morality guiding human behaviour.

ethics commissioners—officials appointed by government to oversee ethical rules and codes governing the behaviour of public servants.

evaluation—*see* policy evaluation.

executive branch of government—composed of the monarch and Governor General at the formal (or symbolic) level, and the prime minister, Cabinet, and bureaucracy at the political level, the executive is the organizational centre of power in the political system.

Expenditure Management System (EMS)—the system of budgeting introduced by the Chrétien government to promote greater control over government expenditures.

federalism—a system of governing in which the activities of government are divided in a written constitution between a national government and regional governments, each of which is coordinate with but independent of the other in its own jurisdictional areas.

Financial Administration Act—the statute that governs financial accountability for federal departments, agencies, and Crown corporations, and that defines the responsibilities of the Treasury Board and the Department of Finance in the area of financial management.

formulation—part of the policy cycle involving the development of public policy. *See also* public policy and policy cycle.

Free Trade Agreement (FTA)—the Free Trade Agreement between Canada and the United States was passed by the Conservative government of Brian Mulroney in 1988 and took effect in 1989. It created a tariff-free border while institutionalizing the Canada–U.S. relationship to an unprecedented degree. *See also* North American Free Trade Agreement.

garbage can model—a theory of public policy formulation for analyzing decision making in situations of "organized anarchy," where goals are ambiguous and methods uncertain.

governing instruments—the array of tools available to government to realize its policy goals, ranging from the privatization of conflict to direct government intervention.

Governor General—the representative of the monarch in Canada, appointed by the monarch on the recommendation of the prime minister. The legal and constitutional powers of the Governor General are impressive on paper but are almost entirely symbolic in practice.

Hawthorne experiments—experiments conducted by industrial psychologists at the Hawthorne Works plant of Western Electric (near Chicago), beginning in 1924, to determine how physical conditions of work could be adjusted to improve productivity. The experiments are generally regarded as the origin of the human relations school of organizational theory. *See also* humanist theories.

hierarchy—the ordering of individuals or groups within an organization and their relationships of power and control.

hierarchy of human needs—a theory developed by Abraham Maslow that argues that humans are motivated by the satisfaction of a variety of needs, ranging from basic physical requirements (food, shelter, clothing) to self-actualization. As lower level needs are realized, people move on to fulfill higher level ones.

homogeneity—the principle that asserts that similar activities ought to be grouped together in the same unit under a single supervisor and a single plan. Thus, in public administration, things related to health care ought to be grouped in one department, those related to education in another, and so on. Moreover, within departments, there is a further division of labour, with scientists grouped in one unit, policy analysts in another, clerical staff in another, and so on, for the purposes of job function, promotion, and wages. Also referred to as *unity of direction*.

humanist theories—a school of thought about organizing and managing workplaces, which focuses on the inherent worth of individual workers and their needs. It originated with the Hawthorne studies on workplace organization in the 1920s and 1930s.

ideational framework—a type of framework for policy analysis that focuses on the role of ideas in policy making, including how they shape the inclusion and exclusion of policy agendas, strategies, and actors. *See also* neo-institutionalism.

implementation—the part of the policy cycle involving the realization of public policy. *See also* public policy and policy cycle.

Increased Ministerial Authority and Accountability—the 1986 reform by the Mulroney government intended to allow for more flexibility in the roles and functions of ministers and their departments relative to their control by central agencies.

incremental model—an approach to policy making in which small, incremental changes are made to the status quo.

individual ministerial responsibility—the principle that states that individual ministers are responsible for the actions of their departments and accountable for their departments to Parliament and the Canadian people. *See also* collective ministerial responsibility.

informal group—term used to describe the phenomenon discovered by the Hawthorne experiment researchers that the dominant factor in employee productivity was workers' membership in casual associations of fellow employees, who together motivated each other to perform at certain levels by influencing values and attitudes and establishing social norms of behaviour in the workplace. *See also* Hawthorne experiments.

institutionalism—a framework for policy analysis that focuses on the institutions of policy making and how they shape policy debates and outcomes. *See also* neo-institutionalism and structuralism.

interest group—an organized association that attempts to influence the government to pursue policies favourable to its own interests.

interpretive framework—a type of framework for policy analysis that attempts to understand people's meanings and inter-pretations of reality and the contests between these interpretations as they are played out in policy making. *See also* post-positivism.

intra vires—a legal phrase that describes a federal or provincial statute as being within the constitutional jurisdiction of that level of government, as determined through judicial review of the Constitution Act.

judicial branch of government—the Supreme Court and justices and all the other courts and justices below it. The judi-ciary in Canada is appointed rather than elected, and is separate from and indepen-dent of the other two branches of govern-ment (the executive and legislative branches).

judicial committee of the Privy Council—the British law Lords who acted as the court of final appeal for Canadians until 1949, when the Supreme Court of Canada was made the final arbiter of Canadian legal cases.

judicial evaluation—concerned with the legal issues arising out of administrative actions, judicial evaluation is a facet of administrative and constitutional law that involves the judges and the courts passing judgment on the behaviour and practices of the public service. *See also* judicial review.

judicial review—the power of the court to determine if the actions of other branches of the government are constitutional or not.

Keynesian welfare state—a broad term used to encompass the social welfare state constructed in the post–Second World War years on the basis of a theoretical model developed by British economist John Meynard Keynes, which promoted an activist role for government in the macroeconomic management of the economy.

La Relève—the internal review of the public service launched by the clerk of the Privy Council in 1996 to deal with the "quiet crisis" within the federal bureaucracy. The term is an acronym for Leadership, Action, Renewal, Energy, Learning, Expertise, Values, and Excellence.

legal-rational legitimacy—a form of legitimacy outlined by Max Weber, in which citizens accept that an individual has the right to rule over them by virtue of the law. *See also* charismatic legitimacy and traditional legitimacy.

legislative branch of government—that branch of government charged with passing and amending laws. In Canada it is composed of the Parliament, which is made up of the elected House of Commons and the appointed Senate.

legitimation—a concept employed in neo-Marxist theory, referring to the need for the state to pass policies that legitimate capitalism in the eyes of those oppressed by it. Thus, social policies such as welfare and unemployment insurance are seen as policies that legitimate the system for the working class, so that they do not rise up and overthrow it.

line-item budgeting—a rudimentary system of budgeting, emphasizing the objects of expenditures (e.g., how many paper clips are needed, how much office space must be rented, etc.) rather than the purpose of expenditures.

Management by Objectives (MBO)—a management system associated with the work of Peter Drucker and others that focuses on co-operation between managers and workers in the establishment of broad-based annual goals and objectives for the organization.

market—an arena in which the organization of the economy and society for the production and distribution of goods and services takes place through the mechanism of exchange predicated on the voluntary actions of individuals. The human and social costs of relying on self-regulating markets have been so great that governments have been forced over time to step in and limit or regulate certain market excesses.

Marx, Karl—influential German philosopher (1818–1883) and founder of the political philosophy of Communism. *See also* Marxist analysis and neo-Marxist theory.

Marxist analysis—a broad school of thought premised on the idea that modern capitalist societies are based on class conflict, and positing that the role of the state is to promote policies of accumulation for the capitalist class and policies of legitimation for the working class. *See also* neo-Marxist theory.

merit principle—the principle that all citizens should have an equal opportunity to be considered for employment in the public service based on their qualifications and skills, and should be promoted on the basis of their abilities and talents.

minimalist state—term used to describe the relatively minor role played by the Canadian state in the social and economic affairs of Canadians from the Confederation period to the 1930s.

minister—the political head of a department of government, appointed by the prime minister.

ministerial responsibility—*see* collective ministerial responsibility and individual ministerial responsibility.

Ministerial Task Force on Program Review—task force set up in 1984 by the Mulroney government under the leadership of Deputy Prime Minister Eric Nielsen to conduct a government-wide review of programs, with the goal of cutting waste and inefficiencies.

ministry—*see* department.

mixed-scanning—a theoretical approach to explaining policy making, which suggests that policy-makers combine rationality and incrementalism in the process of determining what action (or inaction) to take. *See also* incremental model and rational-comprehensive theory.

mobilization of bias—term derived from pluralist theory to describe policy

formulation as the result of a process of interest groups acting to influence government decision-makers.

neoconservative state—term used to describe contemporary governments that focus on reducing the size and intrusiveness of government through policies of deregulation, privatization, reducing taxes, reducing public services and reducing spending. It is premised on an ideological world-view which favours the free market over the state.

neo-institutionalism—a framework for policy analysis that maintains the institutionalist analysis's focus on institutions in policy making but also looks to the role of ideas and interest groups or policy networks in policy making. *See also* institutionalism.

neo-Marxist theory—a broad school of thought that reconceptualizes the original theories about the capitalist state put forward by Karl Marx. *See also* Marxist analysis.

New Public Management (NPM)—a school of thought originating in Margaret Thatcher's Britain, advocating changes to organizational design and managerial practices consistent with neoconservative ideas. It is broadly aimed at making the state more responsive to political direction and to citizens, and at introducing more private sector practices into the public sector.

North American Free Trade Agreement (NAFTA)—the extension in 1994 of the Free Trade Agreement between Canada and the U.S. to include Mexico.

Office of the Comptroller General—created in 1978, this body has authority over administrative practices and controls in the areas of financial management and procedures for program evaluation.

Organization Development (OD)—a team-based approach to management decision making and problem solving.

participatory management—a management style that incorporates the views of workers in the decision making process.

partisanship—the degree of loyalty members of a political party feel toward one another.

party discipline—a key pillar of responsible government, party discipline means that party members support their leaders and act in unison in the legislature.

It is supported by a system of rewards and punishments.

patronage—the awarding of contracts and the appointment of individuals to government positions on the basis of partisan support for, or contributions to, the governing party, rather than of merit.

pay equity—a shorthand term for equal pay for work of equal value, in which comparisons are made between different jobs for the same employer.

performance budgeting—a system of budgeting in which expenditures are related to specific activities to determine the costs of providing services.

Planning, Programming, Budgeting System (PPBS)—a broad-based budgeting system introduced in Canada in the 1960s and 1970s in an effort to impose greater rationality over the budget process. It was premised on the view that expenditure requests should be presented in terms of the objective of spending rather than in terms of input costs and particular functions, but ultimately fell out of favour due to the layers of complexity it added to the process.

pluralist theory—the view that power in society is widely dispersed between diverse groups that vie to influence government to produce policies favourable to their own interests.

Policy and Expenditure Management System (PEMS)—a system involving the use of Cabinet committees to coordinate, plan, and integrate government budgeting and policy making. It was introduced in 1979 by the Joe Clark government to improve ministerial control over financial management in the areas of priority setting and to allow ministers to see the longer-range view of government policy development and financial activities.

policy community—comprised of actors in the policy making process with an interest in a particular policy field. These actors can be in the public sector (for example a ministry) and/or the private sector (for example a business association) and/or the "attentive public."

policy cycle—the theoretical construction that suggests that public policy can best be understood as a process of formulation, implementation, and evaluation. *See also* public policy; policy formulation; policy implementation; and policy evaluation.

policy evaluation—the part of the policy cycle involving the determination of needed policy or administrative changes through a process of in-depth analysis of institutions, programs, and policies. *See also* public policy and policy cycle.

policy formulation—the part of the policy cycle involving the development of public policy. *See also* public policy and policy cycle.

policy implementation—the part of the policy cycle involving the realization of public policy. *See also* public policy and policy cycle.

policy network—the interactions among members in a policy community.

political culture—the broad pattern of beliefs, values, and attitudes citizens hold toward politics and the political system.

political evaluation—the ongoing process by which the electorate determines the worth of government policy by supporting or opposing the governing party in elections or through the expression of views in royal commissions, task forces, parliamentary committees, or to Cabinet, central agencies, or line departments through the actions of citizens, interest groups, the media, and so on. *See also* policy evaluation.

political neutrality—the principle that public servants must not engage in partisan politics but should, rather, remain politically impartial and neutral, serving the government of the day, *not* the political party that happens to hold power.

political parties—organizations designed to secure the power of the state for their leaders.

politics-administration dichotomy—the notion that there is a distinction between the duties and responsibilities of politicians who make public policy, and their public servants, who faithfully execute it.

POSDCORB—an acronym defining the administrative process by classifying the functions of top executives in an organization as planning, organizing, staffing, directing, coordinating, reporting, and budgeting. It was devised by Luther Gulick.

post-modern analysis—a type of policy analysis that rejects the simplistic, rationality-based frameworks, models, and theories. It argues that society is too complex to be understood as a science. It can only be studied on a case-by-case basis, and there are no predictable laws of political action. *See also* post-positivism.

post-positivism—an approach to knowledge that denies our ability to know causation or laws of social or political action. It argues we can never really know our reality, only interpret it through our own biases and tell stories or narratives about it. *See also* interpretive ramework and post-modern analysis.

power—the ability to influence or coerce others to conform to one's own goals and values.

pressure group—*see* interest group.

Prime Minister's Office—a central agency of government staffed by appointees of the prime minister to provide partisan advice and monitor political developments for the prime minister.

private sector—that part of the economy not under government control.

privatization—the act of selling or turning over Crown corporations to the private sector.

Privy Council—a largely ceremonial body composed of current and former ministers of the Crown and other individuals recommended by the prime minister and appointed for life by the Governor General.

Privy Council Office—a central agency that provides policy advice and administrative support to the Cabinet and its committees. It is the main organization responsible for developing and coordinating government policy.

Productivity Improvement Program—a set of reforms introduced in the dying days of the last Trudeau government to cut red tape and procedures hampering the efficient provision of government services through initiatives undertaken by the Treasury Board.

program budgeting—a system of budgeting that seeks to measure the impact of expenditures on the goals of the organization.

Program Review—a wide-reaching initiative introduced by the Chrétien government in 1994 to review all government programs, with the goal of identifying potential cost savings.

The Review was driven by the government's desire to eliminate the deficit.

province building—the process of aggressive and assertive provincial premiers and governments seeking enhanced powers and responsibilities, while also seeking to diminish the role of the federal government.

PS2000—a review of the public service meant to address the low morale and disjunction between the senior and lower levels of public servants. Launched in late 1989, it was organized around 10 task forces headed by deputy ministers charged with finding ways to simplify personnel policies, loosen central agency controls, increase the managerial freedom of department managers, and increase program efficiency.

public administration—the ways in which governments conduct themselves through bureaucratic processes. This includes the norms and values of government officials, the organization of the bureaucracy, the accountability of public servants, the relationship between politicians and bureaucrats, and the decision making systems used to formulate, implement, and evaluate public policy.

public choice theory—a theoretical approach derived from classical economics, which is premised on the notion that individuals act on the basis of a rational calculation of self-interest. Also referred to as rational choice theory.

public comment—an aspect of the doctrine of political neutrality, through which public servants are expected not to express publicly their personal views on government policy or administration. *See also* political neutrality.

public policy—what governments choose to do or not to do.

public sector—the collective term used to describe the institutions and personnel of the state.

Public Service Commission—called the Civil Service Commission until 1967, this independent agency is responsible for recruiting employees through competitive examinations and interviews, and for staffing and promotion using the merit principle.

Public Service Employment Act—passed in 1967, this Act granted the Public Service Commission the exclusive authority to appoint persons to and within the public service according to the merit principle, and to administer appeals, layoffs, and dismissals. As well, it liberalized the restrictions on political activities by public servants.

Public Service Staff Relations Act—passed in 1967, this Act sets out the responsibilities of the quasi-judicial Public Service Staff Relations Board and provides for the structure and operation of the collective bargaining process in the public service. It also oversees the resolution of disputes and grievances, and conducts research on matters relevant to contract negotiations, such as rates of pay, benefits, and working conditions.

rational choice theory—*see* public choice theory.

rational-comprehensive theory—a theoretical model that seeks to explain public policy decision making as the product of a reasoned and thorough consideration of all the available options and their consequences.

recall—the procedure by which an elected official is removed from office by a vote of the electorate.

referendum—a means by which a particular question is put directly to the total electorate rather than to the elected representatives of the people.

regulatory agency—a government body that administers economic, environmental, social, or other activities in the public interest according to guidelines and regulations established by government.

representative democracy—*see* representative government.

representative government—a political system with an elected legislature.

representativeness—the notion that the public service should reflect the social composition of the population it serves.

reservation—section 57 of the Constitution Act, 1867 (formerly the British North America Act, 1867), which permits the Lieutenant-Governor of a province to withhold assent to a piece of provincial legislation pending review by the federal Cabinet.

responsible government—a system of government in which the executive branch of government requires the support and

confidence of the legislative branch (and through it, the people) in order to govern.

risk management—the process of measuring or assessing risk and then developing strategies to manage the risk. A systematic approach to setting the best course of action under uncertainty by identifying, assessing, understanding, acting on, and communicating risk issues.

rule of law—the principle that both the ruled and the rulers are answerable to the law.

scientific management—generally associated with the work of Frederick Winslow Taylor, scientific management is a management style that emphasized finding the "one best way" of accomplishing a task. It introduced the use of time and motion studies into the workplace with the goal of improving productivity by increasing efficiency.

social movements—informal networks of groups of citizens with shared values and identities oriented toward influencing the government on various social policies and issues through social and/or political struggle. *See also* interest group.

social welfare state—the term used to describe the interventionist state in postwar Western, industrialized countries, wherein governments took on an ever-expanding set of responsibilities in the areas of social welfare policy, health care, education, housing, pensions, unemployment insurance, etc.

span of control—an organizational mechanism indicating the number of subordinates reporting to a particular supervisor.

spending power—the power of the federal government to spend money on programs even if the programs are within provincial jurisdiction. This power is nowhere written in the Constitution but is nonetheless a powerful federal tool in intergovernmental relations.

state—a form of political organization encompassing governmental institutions and personnel that are capable of maintaining order and implementing rules and laws over a given population within a given territory.

structural analysis—a type of policy analysis that focuses on how the structured elements of social organization (such as class, race, and gender) predetermine policy outcomes, predominantly through the power relations they entail.

structuralist theory—the school of organization theory that is premised on a view of workers as little more than interchangeable parts in a machine. The goal of structuralist organization theory is to devise structures within which the work of individuals could be maximized through rigid rules and regulations so as to increase the organization's efficiency. Little regard is paid to the needs or views of individual workers.

Supreme Court of Canada—composed of nine justices appointed by the prime minister, the Supreme Court is Canada's highest court for civil, criminal, and constitutional cases.

three Es—the three *Es* are efficiency, effectiveness, and economy. They represent a particular set of values underlying reforms to improve the functioning of organizations within the private sector, but they have increasingly been adopted in the public sector as well, where they compete with other values such as democracy, justice, and accountability.

time and motion studies—an innovation introduced by Frederick Winslow Taylor, father of scientific management, in his effort to discover the "one best way" of routinizing workplace functions. Taylor used a stop-watch to record the time it took to complete every motion in a particular piece of work, allegedly to improve efficiency by eliminating unnecessary motions.

Total Quality Management (TQM)—a participatory management approach that developed in the 1980s and early 1990s, advocating changing an organization's culture to focus on high standards of quality throughout the organization. The guiding principle of TQM is "get it right the first time," and it was famously embraced first by Japanese car makers.

traditional legitimacy—a form of legitimacy outlined by Max Weber, in which citizens accept that an individual has the right to rule over them by virtue of divine right— that is, that the gods anointed an individual as leader. *See also* charismatic legitimacy and legal-rational legitimacy.

Treasury Board—a Cabinet committee composed of six Cabinet ministers (including the president of the Treasury Board and the Minister of Finance), responsible for the preparation of the expenditure budget and for administrative management of government departments.

Treasury Board Secretariat—a central agency that supports the Treasury Board.

ultra vires—a legal phrase that describes a federal or provincial statute as beyond the constitutional jurisdiction of that level of government, as determined through judicial review of the Constitution Act.

unity of direction—*see* homogeneity.

user fees—the practice by governments of charging fees to citizens for services previously provided free or for a nominal charge, to cover the cost of providing the service as a strategy for fighting deficits. User fees are a regressive form of taxation.

Weber, Max—German sociologist (1864–1920) generally regarded as the most influential writer on the subject of bureaucracy.

Index

1984 (Orwell), 83

A

Aboriginal Canadians
  contribution to legal system, 170
  as founding culture, 42
  public service employees, 289–290
abortion debate, 206–207
accountability, 145, 369–395
  see also Gomery Commission
  contemporary issues of, 388–394
  and democracy, 369–375
  ministerial responsibility, 375–380
  and the Office of the Auditor General, 384–388
  in public bureaucracies, 8, 9, 13
  and public servants, 381–384
  in responsible government, 51–52
accounting officers, 378
accumulation (capital), 67
administrative evaluation, 242
administrative law, 189–197
  administration of power, 197
  appointments of, 196–197
  judicial branch and, 128–129
  judicial review, 194–196
  overview of, 189–194
affirmative action, 286
Agrarian Socialism (Lipset), 72
Agri-Food, 138
Air Canada, 36, 152, 158, 159
air navigation system, 390
Al-Mashat affair, 377–378, 389, 392
alienation, 64
Almond, Gabriel, 34, 39
alternative service delivery (ASD), 143–144
amending formula, 179
American National Academy of Sciences, 84
American Revolution, 43
anomie, 87, 92
Anti-Inflation Act (1975), 186
Appeals Division, 172
assistant deputy ministers (ADMs), 138
Atomic Energy Control Board, 150
Attorney General, 172–173
audi alteram partem, 193
Auditor General. *See* Office of the
  Auditor General
Auditor General Act (1977), 386–387

audits, 242, 387
Australia, 415, 416
authority, 28
autonomy (of bureaucracy), 65

B

Balzac, Honoré de, 7
Barnard, Chester, 86–87
Bennett, Bill, 18
Bennett, R.B., 185–186, 407
bilingualism, 285–286, 404
Bill of Rights, 179
Bismarck, Otto von, 31
Bloc Québecois, 45, 54
Blue Ribbon Panel, 330
Board of Commerce Act (1919), 185
Borden, Sir Robert, 15, 266, 407
Bourgon, Jocelyn, 271, 286, 409–411
Brandeis, Louis D., 78
Bre-X, 13
British Columbia treaty process, 170
British Judicial Committee of the Privy
  Council (JCPC), 184–186, 187
British North America Act (1867)
  division of powers, 48, 178, 182–183
  financial management, 322
  overview of, 48, 178–179, 181, 182–183
  proposed amendments, 187
  taxation, 182
Brittain, Donald, 263
budgetary cycle, 331–335
budgetary process, 324–331
bureaucracy
  see also organizational theory
  described, 7–9, 39
  emergence of, 3
  features of traditional, 109
  impersonal nature of, 73–75
"Bureaucratic Structure and Personality"
  (Merton), 73–74
business plans, 247, 326–327

C

Cabinet, 125
  budgetary cycle, 331–333
  central agencies and, 138
  collective ministerial responsibility, 376

composition of, 132–133
elite background of ministers, 102
and ministerial responsibility, 144–145
political rights of public servants, 295
and public policy, 210, 211, 224
role and duties of, 51, 127–128, 378
Cabinet Directive on Streamlining Regulation, 154
cabinet-parliamentary structure, 125–130
Campbell, Gordon, 19, 406
Campbell, Kim, 133, 313, 408
Canada Act (1982), 180
Canada and its Provinces, 4
Canada Gazette, 323
Canada Health Act, 124–125
Canada Public Service Agency, 139, 315
Canada Public Service Human Resources Management Agency, 315
Canada Revenue Agency, 103, 273
Canada School for Public Service (CSPS), 273, 274, 361
Canada-United States relations
American investment in Canada, 46–47
continentalism and, 42–43
influence of US on public administration, 4
Canadian Alliance, 54
Canadian Association of Programs in Public Administration (CAPPA), 5
Canadian Centre for Management Development (CCMD), 273
Canadian Constitution. *See* Constitution
Canadian court system, 171–174, 175
Canadian Evaluation Society, 244
Canadian government
see also Canadian political culture; Canadian public administration; organizational structure of government
democracy, 33–36
depiction of systems theory, 94, 95
revenue and expenditure (1950, 2001), 19
Canadian Human Rights Act (1977), 293
Canadian Human Rights Commission, 13, 14, 291, 293
Canadian Journal of Program Evaluation, 244
Canadian judicial system, 169–174
see also administrative law; constitutional law
common and civil law, 170
court system, 171–174
judicial review, 194–196
rule of law, 169–170
Canadian Labour Relations Board, 150
Canadian National Railway, 156

Canadian Pension Commission, 150
Canadian political culture, 39–50
see also parliamentary extra-parliamentary actors
versus American, 157, 158
Canadian Constitution, 48–49
continentalism, 42–43
demography, 42
federalism, 50
geography, 41–42
interpretations of, 43–48
North American Free Trade Agreement (NAFTA), 49–50
overview of, 39–41
three founding cultures, 42
Canadian Public Administration, 5
Canadian public administration, 48–56
see also organizational structure of government; politics-administration dichotomy
American influence on, 4
Constitution, 48–49
distinctiveness of Canadian model, 409–416
extra-parliamentary actors, 54–56
federalism, 50
free trade agreements, 49–50
history of, 4–5
international comparisons, 415–416
models of, 402–408
parliamentary actors, 51–54
professionalism and ethics, 15–17, 413
restructuring of, 17–20
size of, 130
Canadian Radio-television and Telecommunications Commission (CRTC), 56, 150, 152
Canadian Wheat Board, 157
Cape Breton Development Corporation, 156
capitalism
and democracy, 122–123
Marxist view of, 66, 222
neo-Marxist view of, 67–68
Carleton College, 5
Carleton University, 5
CBC, 36, 56, 156, 158
CCF (Co-operative Commonwealth Federation), 54, 72, 293
central agencies, 138–142
budgetary cycle, 332–333
Department of Finance, 138–139
overview of, 138, 379
Prime Minister's Office (PMO), 141–143
Privy Council Office (PCO), 139–141
public policy implementation, 225
Treasury Board Secretariat, 139

Centre for Excellence in Evaluation (2001), 252
Chaplin, Charlie, 82, 83
charismatic legitimacy, 28–30
Charlottetown Accord, 180
Charter of Rights and Freedoms
  Aboriginal rights, 170
  administrative law, 193
  creation of, 49, 179
  discrimination, 293
  importance of, 49, 128, 181, 206
  Justice Department and, 173
  public policy implementation, 226–227
China, ancient, 3
Chrétien, Jean, 19, 131, 133, 152, 265, 271
  Clarity Bill and Quebec independence, 180
  fiscal legacy, 322
  influence on public service, 408
  policy evaluation, 245–246
  Sponsorship Program, 310
Churchill, Winston, 7,161
CIGOL v. Government of Saskatchewan (1978), 187
Citizenship and Immigration Canada, 292
Civic Culture (Almond and Verba), 34
Civil Code, 170
civil law, 170
Civil Service Act (1908), 266
Civil Service Act (1918), 16, 103, 266
Civil Service Act (1961), 270, 294
Civil Service Commission, 16, 103, 266, 270, 294
Civil Service of Canada (Dawson), 5
Civil Service Reform Act (1918), 103
Clarity Act, 180, 187
Clark, Joe, 133, 145, 326, 408
class conflict, 64
Classification Modernization Program, 279
clients, needs of, 74
co-operation, 30
Co-operative Commonwealth Federation (CCF), 54, 72, 293
Code of Babylonia, 169
Code of Conduct for Public Servants, 357, 358
Code of Hammurabi, 169
codes of conduct, 356–364
  an attentive public, 363–364
  role models, 361–363
  training and education, 360–361
  usefulness of, 357–360

collective bargaining, 92, 293–294, 404
collective ministerial responsibility, 144, 376
Combines and Fair Prices Act (1919), 185
Commissioner of Official Languages, 160
Commissioner of the Environment and Sustainable Development, 386, 387
common law, 170
communism, 67
Communist Manifesto (Marx), 37
"Comparative Political Systems" (Almond), 39–40
Confederation, 15, 17, 322
conflict
  in industry, 91
  in politics, 30
Conflict of Interest Code (1985), 357
conflicts of interest, 352–353
consent (of the governed), 38–39
conservatism, 158
Conservative Party, 15–16, 18, 19, 54, 131
  see also Harper, Stephen; Mulroney, Brian
Constitution, 48–49, 174–184
  see also Charter of Rights and Freedoms; constitutional law; division of powers
  federalism and, 181–184
  history of, 177–181
  powers conferred by, 126–127
  purpose of, 174–177
  rights and freedoms, 34
  rule of law, 174, 392
Constitution Act (1867), 50
Constitution Act (1982), 128, 179, 180
constitutional convention, 127
constitutional law, 177, 184–189
  federal-provincial bargaining, 186–189
  overview of, 184–186
consultants, 379
Continental Divide (Lipset), 43
continentalism, 42–43
contingency theory, 94
contracting out, 113, 115, 116, 246
conventions of behaviour, 8–9
Court Challenges Program of Canada, 181
court system, 171–174, 175, 392
criminal law, 178
Crown corporations, 154–160, 387
CRTC (Canadian Radio-television and Telecommunications Commission), 56, 150, 152
cultural theories, 220
cybernetics, 94, 96

D

Dalhousie University, 5
Dark Ages, 3
Darwinism, 95
Dawson, R. MacGregor, 4–5
Death of a Salesman (Miller), 83
decentralization, 104
deficits, 18
Deming, W. Edwards, 107
democracy, 32–36
 accountability and, 369–375
 bureaucracy and, 71
 capitalist, 122–123
 defined, 32
 direct, 32–33
 economic, 35–36
 versus efficiency, 9
 political, 33–35
 public administration and, 6–7
 representative, 33
democratic administration, 88
democratic society, 6
demography (of Canada), 42
Department of Agriculture, 138
Department of Energy, Mines and
  Resources, 107
Department of Finance, 138–139,
  321, 333
Department of Foreign Affairs and
  International Trade, 137–138
Department of Industry, Science and
  Technology, 107
Department of Justice, 172–174
Department of Public Works and
  Government Services, 390–391
departmental organizations (of government),
  132–149
 alternative service delivery, 143–144
 central agencies, 138–142
 deputy minister, 145–149
 described, 132–138
 ministerial responsibility, 144–145
 summary of, 134, 136
 typical structure of, 137–138
departments, 132
deputy minister, 145–149
 accountability, 378
 appointment of, 146, 267
 and minister of justice, 173
 role and duties of, 146–149, 381
Deputy Minister of Justice, 173
deregulation, 19, 113, 116, 152–153
Dickson, William, 87

Diefenbaker, John, 179, 310, 407
direct democracy, 32–33
disabled persons, in public service,
  290–291
disallowance, 182–183
disciplinary measures, 297
discretion, 193, 350–351
discrimination
 under Charter, 293
 in public administration, 110–112, 113
 theory of representativeness, 282–285
dismissal, 297
division of labour, 82, 103
division of powers, 182–186
 conflict surrounding, 50, 184–186
 history of, 48, 178, 182–183
 spending power and, 124–125
doctrine of answerability, 376
Donne, John, 92
downsizing, 389
Drucker, Peter, 105
Duplessis, Maurice, 195
Durham, Lord, 42
Durkheim, Emile, 87

E

Easton, David, 30–31
École Nationale D'Administration
  Publique, 5
Economic Council of Canada, 150, 227
economic democracy, 35–36
education
 ethics courses, 360–361
 public administration programs, 5
efficiency
 in Crown corporations, 158
 lack of, in government, 9
 of public versus private sectors, 12, 14–15
Egypt, ancient, 3, 75–76, 169
elite, 102
elite theory, 213
Employment and Social Service Act Reference
  (1937), 186
employment equity, 286–293
Employment Equity Act (1995), 292
Enlightenment, 3
Enron, 13
environmental factors (and public policy),
  212–213
equality (in democracy), 34, 35–36
equity, 12, 286–293
Estimates, 327, 330–335, 405

ethics, 342–356
  see also codes of conduct
  conflicts of interest, 352–353
  discretion, 350–351
  lying for the public good, 353–354
  overview of, 342–350
  partisanship, 351
  public comment, 352
  public relations reforms, 343–347
  of public versus private sector, 16–17, 354–356
Ethics Commissioner, 343, 346, 347, 393
ethics courses, 360–361
European Evaluation Society, 252
evaluation, 232–234, 241–257
  in action, 250–251
  business planning, 246
  contemporary practices, 251–257
  development of, 241–247
  Planning, Programming, Budgeting System, 243–244
  problems of, 247–250
  Program Review, 245–246
  PS2000, 245
  value-for-money (VFM) tool, 256
evaluation stage of policy, 211
Exchequer Court, 172
executive agencies, 390
executive branch of government, 51–52, 125–128
executive federalism, 50
Expenditure Management System (EMS), 322–323, 326–331
  budgetary cycle, 331–335
  problems with, 327–331
  purpose of, 326–327

F

Fascism, 82
Fayol, Henri, 80
Federal Accountability Act (2006), 145, 253, 279, 393–394
Federal Court of Canada, 172
federalism, 50, 123–125
feminist theory, 110–112
Financial Administration Act, 133, 149, 378, 381
financial management, 319–335, 405
  budgetary cycle, 331–335
  managing fiscal resources, 324–331
  state and economy, 319–324
First Ministers' Conference, 45
"fiscal imbalance", 125, 182, 183–184

Follett, Mary Parker, 84, 110, 111
Ford, Henry, 82
foreign investment regulation, 47
Foreign Investment Review Agency, 47
formal rules (of bureaucracies), 8
formulation stage of policy cycle, 210
  see also policy formulation
Fort Frances Pulp and Power Company v. the Manitoba Free Press (1923), 185
Fortier, Michael, 133
Founding of New Societies (Hartz), 43
Fraser, Sheila, 310, 385
free trade
  debates on, 208–209, 249
  North American Free Trade Agreement (NAFTA), 47, 49–50, 131, 153, 249
Free Trade Agreement (FTA), 47, 49, 249
French-Canadians
  see also Quebec
  in public sector, 285–286
French-English relationship, 42, 44–45
FTA (Free Trade Agreement), 47, 49
Fulton-Favreau formula (1964), 180
Function of the Executive (Barnard), 86–87

G

Gaebler, Ted, 114
garbage can model, 219
GDP (gross domestic product), 19, 320
gender bias, in public administration, 110–112, 113
geography (of Canada), 41–42
"Giving of Orders" (Follett), 84
Glassco Commission, 104, 243, 274, 310–311, 324–325
global corporations, 153
global trade, 153
globalization, 18
Globe and Mail, 10–11, 357
goals, of public versus private sectors, 12–14
Gomery Commission, 310, 317–318, 318–319, 387
Goodnow, Frank J., 75
Goods and Services Tax (GST), 38, 131
Gouldner, Alvin, 74–75
government. *See* Canadian government; state
government business enterprises (GBEs). *See* Crown Corporations
government intrusiveness, 229–231

Government of Canada, (Dawson), 5
government organizational structure. *See*
    organizational structure of government
Governor General, 51, 125, 127, 179
Great Depression, 18, 86, 185–186, 268,
    308, 319
Great Shelf Principle, 75
Gross Domestic Product (GDP), 19, 320
group values, influence of, 86, 88
GST (Goods and Services Tax), 38, 131
Gulick, Luther, 80–81, 136–137

H

Harper, Stephen, 19, 133, 152, 271
    accountability, 145, 318, 393
    accounting officer provisions, 149
    defeat of Liberal Party, 310
    dismantling of Court Challenges
        Program, 181
    influence on public service, 408
    judicial appointments, 49
    privy council office structure, 140
    senate selection controversy, 133
Harris, Mike, 19, 406
Hartz, Louis, 43
Harvard Business School, 86
Harvard University, 79
Hawthorne experiments, 84–86, 90, 105
Health Canada, 292
Hegel, G.W.F., 65, 66
Herring, E. Pendleton, 346
hidden bureaucracy, 389–390
hierarchy
    adverse effects of, 65, 70
    of departmental organizations, 137–138
    division of labour, 82
    of government structure, 65, 68, 381, 414
    span of control, 75–76
hierarchy of human needs, 89
Hobbes, Thomas, 157
Hollinger, 13
homogeneity, 103
House of Commons, 45, 54, 125, 127
    accountability to, 149
    collective ministerial responsibility, 376
    members of, 132–133
    reports of regulatory bodies, 150
    role of, 52–53, 128
human relations approach, 83–92
    basic principles of, 88
    criticisms of, 90–92
    Hawthorne experiments, 84–86
    Maslow's hierarchy of human needs, 89

Mayo's observations, 86, 87–88
    participatory management, 84
Human Resources and Development
    Canada (HRDC) scandal, 384
Human Resources and Skills Development
    Canada, 291
human resources legislation, 270
    see also Charter of Rights and Freedoms
human resources management, 296–298
    public service bodies responsible for, 274
    public versus private sectors, 12
    reform of, 279–282
    reports and studies, 274–276
human rights, 34, 35–36, 293
Human Rights Commission, 296
human rights legislation, 293
    see also Charter of Rights and Freedoms
humanist theories, 83
    see also human relations approach

I

ideational frameworks, 220
Immigration and Refugee Board, 292
implementation of policy. *See* public policy
    implementation
Increased Ministerial Authority and
    Accountability, 311
incremental model, 217–218
industrial psychology, 83–86
industrialization, 81, 87
inequality, in public administration, 110–112
informal group, 86
Innis, Harold Adams, 44, 45
Institute of Public Administration of Canada
    (IPAC), 5
institutionalism, 223
institutions (of bureaucracies), 9
interest groups, 54–55
interpretive framework, 219–220
Interstate Commerce Commission, 78
Investment Canada, 47
"iron law of oligarchy", 91
Italian Fascists, 82

J

Japanese management techniques, 107
Jehovah Witnesses, arrest of, 195
job structure, and human relations, 91
judicial branch of government. *See* judiciary
judicial committee of the Privy Council, 53
judicial evaluation, 242

judicial review, 194–196
judicial system, 169–174, 372
judiciary
    appointments of, 49
    composition of, 125
    function of, 53–54, 128–129
    role in federalism, 50

K

Katz, Daniel, 92
Kerr, Clark, 91
Kesey, Ken, 73
Keynes, John Maynard, 18, 213–214
Keynesian welfare state, 18, 267, 308, 319
Khan, Robert, 92
King, William Lyon Mackenzie, 186, 407
Klein, Ralph, 19, 406

L

La Relève, 272, 273, 314–316, 382
Labour Code, 158
labour movements, 31, 82, 84
Lambert Commission, 274, 326, 405
Lang, Fritz, 82
language legislation, 285–286
Leadership Network, 314–316
legal-rational legitimacy, 28–30
legislation
    see also administrative law; constitutional law
    accountability, 145, 253, 279, 393
    employee protection, 404
    foreign competition, 17–18
    human resource management, 317
    human rights, 292–293
    language, 285–286
    Office of the Auditor General, 386–387
    for public service organizations, 16, 272,
        279, 295
legislative branch of government.
        See Legislature
Legislature, 52–53, 125, 128, 224, 233
legitimation, 67
Lenin, Vladimir, 31, 82
Lévesque, René, 180
Lewin, Kurt, 105–106
Liberal Party, 19, 54, 187–188
    see also Chrétien, Jean; Martin, Paul;
        Trudeau, Pierre Eliot
liberalism, 157–158
Lieutenant-Governor, 127, 182–183
line-item method of budgeting, 325
Lipset, Seymour Martin, 43, 72

literature on public administration, 5–6
Local Prohibition, 184–185
Locke, John, 157
Loyalists, 43
lying for the public good, 353–354
Lynch, Kevin, 276
Lyon, Sterling, 18

M

MacDonald, Flora, 145–146
MacDonald, Sir John A., 15, 188
    on Canadian Public Service, 402
    federalism, 181–182
    government involvement in economy, 156
    justice administration, 172
    influence on public service, 407
    National Policy, 17
    on Senate, 52
Macdonnell, J.J., 244–245
Machiavelli, 353
Magna Carta, 370
Main Estimates, 330–331, 334
majority rule, 34
Management Accountability Framework
        (MAF), 280, 281, 330
Management and the Worker (Roethlisberger
        and Dickson), 87
Management by Objectives, 105
Martin, Paul, 19, 133, 152, 253, 271
    influence on public service, 408
    policy evaluation, 253
    Program Review, 313
    Sponsorship Program, 310, 387
Marx, Karl, 31, 37
    see also Marxist theory of bureaucracy
Marxist theory of bureaucracy, 64–68, 96,
        132, 222
    and Canadian public administration, 102
    criticism of, 68
    described, 64–67
    neo-Marxists, 67–68
    view of the State, 37
Maslow, Abraham, 88–89
Massé, Marcel, 313
Mayo, Elton, 86, 87–88, 92
McGregor, Douglas, 92, 93
media, influence on public administration,
        55–56, 357–360, 383
Meech Lake Accord, 180
Members of Parliament, 52–53
Mercier, Honoré, 188
merit principle, 6, 296

merit system, 266, 270, 404
Merton, Robert, 73–74
Metropolis, 82
Mexico, trade with. *See* North American
    Free Trade Agreement (NAFTA)
Michels, Robert, 91
Midvale Steel Company, 91
Miller, Arthur, 83
minimalist state, 17–18
minister, 132
    see also Cabinet
Minister for Public Service Renewal, 313
Minister of Public Safety, 173
ministerial responsibility, 144–146,
    375–380, 382
Ministerial Task Force on Program
    Review, 311
ministries, 132
    see also departmental organizations
        (of government)
Ministry of Canadian Heritage, 273
minority rights, 34
mixed-scanning model, 218–219
mobilization of bias, 209–211
Modern Organizations (Thompson), 74–75
Modern Times, 82, 83
monarch, powers of, 127
Montcalm, Marquis de, 44
motivation
    hierarchy of human needs, 89
    human relation influences on, 86, 88–90
    under scientific management, 81
Mowat, Oliver, 182, 188
Mulroney, Brian, 19, 112, 133, 152, 265,
    271, 311
    Al-Mashat affair, 377–378
    the Constitution and Quebec, 180
    de-indexing of old age pensions, 41
    influence on public service, 408, 413
    Multi-Year Operational Plan, 326

N
NAFTA (North American Free Trade
    Agreement), 47, 49–50, 131, 153, 249
Napoleon, 74
National Film Board, 263
National Joint Council of the
    Public Service, 294
National Policy (1878)
neo-institutionalism, 223
neo-Marxists, 67–68
neoconservatism, 18–20, 271–272

neoconservative state, 18–20
New Democratic Party (NDP), 54, 72
New Jersey Telephone Company, 86
New Public Management (NPM), 105, 110
    112–117, 271, 406
    accountability and control, 388–392
    Canadian approach to, 115–116, 412–413
    criticisms of, 115–117, 391–392
    philosophy of, 112–115
    public policy implementation, 231–232
New Zealand, 115, 390, 414, 416
Nicholas I, Czar, 7
Nicholson, Jack, 73
Nielson Review (1984), 413
Nixon, Richard, 357
Nobel Prize, 75
North American Free Trade Agreement
    (NAFTA), 47, 49–50, 131, 153, 249
NPM. *See* New Public Management (NPM)

O
OCG (Office of the Comptroller General),
    14, 245, 251, 253, 326, 327, 405
Office of the Auditor General, 107, 160
    duties and role of, 13, 14, 251
    financial management, 324, 330–331,
        384–388
    Gomery Commission, 309, 310, 317
    on government management, 309
    human resource management, 275
    ministerial responsibility, 377
    political evaluation, 243, 245, 251
Office of the Chief Electoral Officer, 291
Office of the Commissioner of Official
    Languages, 286
Office of the Comptroller General, 14, 245,
    251, 253, 326, 327, 405
Office of the Governor General, 51, 125,
    127, 179
Office of Values and Ethics, 344–346,
    357, 358
Official Languages Act (1969), 285, 286
Official Languages Commissioner, 387
old-age pensions, de-indexing, 43
On the Art of Cutting Metal (Taylor), 79
One Flew Over the Cuckoo's Nest (Kesey),
    73, 74
Ontario Hydro, 156, 158
Organisation for Economic Co-operation
    and Development (OECD), 153
Organization Development (OD),
    105–107, 108

organization theory, 92–96
  see also humanist theory; Marxist theory of
    bureaucracy; stucturalist theory; Weber's
    model of bureaucracy
  bureaucratic organization perspectives, 63–65
  and co-operation, 30
  cybernetics, 94
  discrimination in, 110–112, 113
  feminist theory, 110–112
  impact of, 102–103
  population ecology theory, 94–95
  systems theory, 92–94
  Theory X/Theory Y, 92, 93
organization theory and Canadian public
    administration, 102–104
  see also New Public Management (NPM);
    participatory management
  contemporary developments, 102–104
  impact of, 102–103
organizational structure of government,
    51–53, 122–132, 214
  see also departmental organizations (of gov-
    ernment)
  advantages and disadvantages of, 160–161
  cabinet-parliamentary structure, 125–130
  capitalist democracy, 122–123
  crown corporations, 154–160
  departmental structure, 137–138
  executive, 51–52
  federalism, 123–125
  judiciary, 53-54
  legislature, 52–53
  political-administrative relationships,
    131–132
  regulatory agencies, 150–154
Organizations in Action (Thompson), 92
Orwell, George, 83
Osborne, David, 114
Ottawa University, 311
Outlooks on Program Priorities and
    Expenditures, 332

P
"Papers on the Science of Administration"
    (Gulick and Urwick), 80
Parliament, 52–53, 125
  see also parliamentary/extra-parliamentary
    actors
  accountability of government, 149, 385, 387
  budgetary cycle, 332
  financial management, 322–323
Parliament Hill, 41
parliamentary/extra-parliamentary
    actors, 51–56

  executive, 51–52
  interest groups, 54–55
  judiciary, 53–54
  legislature, 52–53
  media, 55–56
  political parties, 54
Parsons case, 186
Parti Québecois, 188
participatory management, 84, 105–112
  challenges of implementing, 107–112
  defined, 104–105
  Management by Objectives, 105
  Organization Development (OD), 105–107
  Total Quality Management (TQM), 107
partisanship, 351
party discipline, 46
Patriation Reference (1981), 187
patronage, 15–16, 265–266
Patterns of Industrial Behaviour
    (Gouldner), 74–75
pay equity, 293
"Peace, Order and Good Government"
    (P.O.G.G.), 184–186
Pearson, Lester B., 133, 356, 404, 407
pensions, de-indexing of old-age, 43
Performance Review and Appraisal Board, 297
personnel of bureaucracies, 8
PESA (Public Service Employment Act),
    133, 270, 282, 294, 295, 405
Peter Principle, 75
Peters, Thomas, 114
Petro-Canada, 156, 159
Philosophy of Right (Hegel), 66
Plains of Abraham, 44
Planning, Programming, Budgeting System
    (PPBS), 243–244, 270, 325–326
Plato, 353
plebiscite, 33
pluralist model, 220–222
pluralist theory, 213
PODSCROB, 81
Policy and Expenditure Management
    System (PEMS), 326
policy community, 227
policy cycle, 210, 211–212
policy instruments, 8
policy network, 227
Policy Research Initiative (PRI), 317
political culture. *See* Canadian political
    culture
political democracy, 33–35, 35–36
political evaluation, 243

political neutrality, 295–296
political parties, 54
political rights of public servants, 295–296
political systems (under systems theory), 94, 95
politics, and public administration, 28–32
politics-administration dichotomy, 6–7, 75, 131–132
  deputy minister and, 148
  emergence of, 404
  and ministerial responsibility, 378
  and political neutrality, 296
Politics and Administration (Goodnow), 75
population ecology theory, 94–95
Porter, John, 43, 268
post-positivist frameworks, 220
Post-Secondary Recruitment Program (PSR), 282
postmodern approach, 223–224
power
  within cabinet-parliamentary structure, 126–127
  distribution of, 213
  of Lieutenant Governors, 182–183
  in public administration and politics, 28–32, 176
Prime Minister's Advisory Committee on the Public Service, 280
Prime Minister(s) of Canada
  role of, 51
  summary of achievements, 407–408
Prime Minister's Office (PMO), 141–143
Principle of Official Independence, The (Dawson), 5
Principles of Scientific Management (Taylor), 78, 80
Privacy Act, 387
Privacy Commissioner, 387
private sector. *See* public sector versus private sector
private sector malfeasance, 13
privitization, 19, 113, 115
  and accountability, 389
  of Crown corporations, 159–160
Privy Council, 127
  see also Cabinet
Privy Council Office (PCO), 139–141, 296
  budgetary responsibility, 333
  human resources management, 296
  fiscal responsibility, 321
  public service reform, 312, 313, 314
  Secretariat, 142
  value and ethics, 357
Privy Council Office (PCO) Secretariat, 142

Productivity Improvement Program, 311
professionalism, 15–17
profitability, 14
program budgeting, 325
Program Review, 115, 245–246, 313, 390–391, 393
Progressive Conservative Party. *See* Conservative Party
province building, 188
provincial jurisdiction, 20
PS2000 (Public Service 2000), 108, 115, 245, 272, 311–313, 382
PSSRA (Public Service Staff Relations Act), 270, 273, 294
public, accountability to, 381–382
Public Accounts Committee of Parliament, 387
Public Accounts of Canada, 323–324, 334, 385
public administration, 2–9
  see also Canadian public administration; public sector versus private sector
  bureaucracy, 7–9
  definition and background of, 2–6
  and democratic government, 6–7
  power, politics and, 28–32
  top ten concerns of, 20–21
Public Administration and the Public Interest (Pendleton), 346–347
public administration texts, 5
public choice, 216–217
public comment, 352
public goods, 13
public ownership, 158
public policy, 206–211
  see also evaluation; public policy formulation; public policy implementation
  defining, 206
  means of, 208–209
  resources, 209–211
  scope of, 207–208
public policy formulation, 210–214
  see also public policy models and theories
  distribution of power, 213
  environmental factors, 212–213
  institutional structure, 214
  overview of, 211–212
  procedural factors, 214
  social attitudes and ideas, 213–214
public policy implementation, 211, 224–232
  governing instruments, 227–231
  overview of, 224–227
  recent developments, 231–232

public policy models and theories, 214–224
  garbage can model, 219
  incremental model, 217–218
  interpretive framework, 219–220
  mixed-scanning model, 218–219
  neo-institutional framework, 223
  overview of, 214–215
  pluralism, 220–222
  postmodern approach, 223–224
  public choice (rational choice) theory, 216–217
  rational-comprehensive model, 215–216
  structural analysis, 222–223
public sector versus private sector, 9–17
  accountability issues, 389–390
  efficiency and service, 14–15
  ethics, 354–356
  mandate and goals, 12–14
  professionalism and ethics, 15–17
public servants
  accountability, 381–384
  and administrative law, 191
  and bureaucracy, 8
  political influence of, 72
  roles and actions of, 6–7, 131
public service, 276–294
  see also public servants; public service history;
      public service reform
  equity, 286–293
  human resource management, 296–298
  language, 285–286
  overview of, 276–282
  and politics, 295–296
  purpose of, 125
  recruitment, 282–283, 297–298
  regional aspects, 283–285
  size of, 277–279
  staff demographic trends, 281–282
  theory of representativeness, 282–283, 284
  unionization, 293–295
Public Service 2000 (PS2000), 108, 115,
    245, 272, 311–313, 382
Public Service Agency of Canada, 274,
    280, 314
Public Service Board v. Dionne (1978), 187
Public Service Commission, 16
  employment equity, 286, 288
  establishment of, 294
  financial management, 381
  human resource management, 135, 276
  independence of, 266, 270
  language training, 285
  public service values, 299
  recruitment, 145, 282–283
  staffing assessment, 297
Public Service Employment Act (PSEA) 133,
    270, 282, 294, 295, 405

public service history, 263–276
  elitism of, 267–268
  employee numbers, 265
  modernization of, 269–270
  negative view of, 263–264
  neoconservatism and NPM, 271–273
  patronage, 265–266
  post-war developments, 268–269, 270,
      319–320
  reforms of 1918, 266–267
Public Service Human Resources
    Management Agency of Canada,
    274, 280
Public Service Labour Relations Act, 317
Public Service Modernization Act (PSMA)
    (2003), 16, 272, 279, 280, 317–318
Public Service Rearrangement and Transfer
    Duties Act, 133
public service reform, 16, 279–280,
    307–319, 402–416
  see also New Public Management (NPM)
  background of need for, 307–311
  Canadian model for, 402–416
  Canadian Prime Ministers and, 407–408
  Gomery Commission, 318–319
  international comparisons, 409–416
  La Relève and Leadership Network,
      314–316
  Lambert Commission, 274, 326, 405
  Policy Research Initiative, 317
  Program Review, 313
  PS2000, 311–313
  Public Service Modernization Act, 317–318
Public Service Reform Act, 272
Public Service Staff Relations Act (PSSRA)
    (1967), 270, 273, 294, 404
Public Services Employment Act (1967), 16
public spending, 229

Q
Quality Service Initiative (1995), 115
Quebec
  civil code, 170
  opposition to constitutional
      amendments, 180
  referendums, 33, 180
  secessionist movement, 187–188
  self-definition and self-determination of, 44
  Sponsorship Program scandal, 210, 310, 387
  voting power of, 34
Quebec Act (1774), 44, 170
Quebec referendums, 33, 180
Queen Elizabeth, 180
Queen's University, 267

R

rational choice, 216–217
rational-comprehensive model, 215–216
Reagan, Ronald, 112, 271, 412
rebellions of 1837/1838, 43
Receiver General of Canada, 323
recruitment, 282–283, 297–298
"red tape", 8, 9
referenda, 33, 180
Reform Party, 54
regional economic development, 157
regionalism, 45–46
Registered Retirement Savings Plans
    (RRSPs), 227–228
regulatory agencies, 150–154
regulatory reform, 153–154
Reinventing Government (Osborne and
    Gaebler), 114
religion, 29
representation. *See* representativeness
representative democracy, 33
representativeness, 272, 282–283, 284,
    404–405
reservation, 182–183
resource industries, 91
resource scarcity, 30
resources, distribution of, 209
responsible government, 46
    BNA Act and, 179
    executive branch and, 127
    legislative branch and, 128
    origins of, 370–372
Revenue Canada, 273
Riel rebellions, 43
risk management, 329
Roethlisberger, F.J., 87
Roman Catholic Church, 3
Roman Empire, 3
Roncarelli v. Duplessis, 195
Royal Canadian Mounted Police (RCMP), 173
Royal Commission on Aboriginal Peoples
    (RCAP), 170
Royal Commission on Bilingualism
    and Biculturalism, 285
Royal Commission on Financial
    Management and Accountability,
    274, 326, 405
Royal Commission on Government
    Organization (1965). *See* Glassco
    Commission
Royal Commission Report on Equality in
    Employment, 286

rule of law, 30, 195, 392
Russell v. The Queen (1982), 184
Ryerson University, 5

S

scandals
    see also Sponsorship Program
    Human Resources and Development Canada
        (HRDC), 384
scarcity, 30
scientific management, 77–83, 86, 96
    and Canadian public administration, 103
    criticisms of, 82–83
    described, 77–82
    gender bias, 110
Search of Excellence (Peters and
    Waterman), 114
Second World War, 319
Senate, 125, 149
    ineffectiveness of purpose, 46, 52, 132–133
    elite background of, 102
senators. *See* Senate
September 11, 2001, 46, 206
shadow bureaucracy. *See* hidden
    bureaucracy
Siegel, Abraham, 91
Simon, Herbert, 75–76
Skelton, O.D., 267
Smart Regulation, 153–154
Social Credit Party, 18, 54
Social Development Canada, 291
social inequality, in political democracy,
    35–36
Social Psychology of Organizations (Katz
    and Kahn), 92
social rewards, 88
Social Union Framework Agreement
    (SUFA), 183
social values (and public policy), 213–214
socialism, 157
Solicitor General, 173
span of control, 75–76
Special Operating Agencies (SOAs), 144,
    312, 391
spending power, 124, 183
Sponsorship Program
    Auditor General and, 310, 387
    impact of, 210, 310
    media and, 357
    recommendations of Gomery Commission,
        318–319
St. Laurant, Louis, 407
Standing Committee on Finance, 333

Standing Committee on Public Accounts, 317–318
staples approach, 44
state, 17–20, 36–39
    government intrusiveness, 229–231
    and government relationships, 38–39
    Keynesian welfare state, 18, 267, 308, 319
    minimalist state, 17–18
    neoconservative state, 18–20
    views of, 36–39
state of emergency, 231
state-owned enterprise, 390
Strategic Overviews, 326
Strong Foundation (Tait), 343
structural analysis, 222–223
structuralist theory, 77
    see also scientific management
supervision, 88
Supplementary Estimates, 330–331
Supreme Court of Canada, 53, 125
    abortion law, 206–207
    composition of, 172
    constitutional reform, 180
    establishment of, 172, 179
    federal-provincial bargaining, **187**
    political rights of public servants, 295
    on provincial secession, 180, 187
    role of, 171
symbolism (of flag), 210
"systems" approach to the study of politics, 30–31
systems theory, 92–94

T

Tait Report, 343, 347–348
tariffs, 17–18
Task Force on Modernizing Human Resources Management, 317
taxation, 36, 182
Taylor, Frederick Winslow, 78–82, 86, 96, 103
Taylorism. *See* scientific management
technological growth, and regulation, 152
television broadcasting jurisdiction, 187
Tellier, Paul, 312
textile industry, 91
Thatcher, Margaret, 112, 271, 412
Theory X and Theory Y, 92, 93
Thompson, James D., 92
Thompson, Victor, 74–75
time and motion studies, 79–80
Toronto Electric Commissioners v. Snider (1925), 185

Total Quality Management (TQM), 107
trade. *See* free trade
traditional legitimacy, 28–30
Translation Bureau, 390
Transport Canada, 390
Treasury Board, 14, 312
    and Auditor General, 387
    budgetary cycle, 332–333, 334
    budgets of regulatory bodies, 150
    collective bargaining, 294
    financial management, 321, 324, 325, 328, 330
    policy evaluation, 244–246, 251, 252
    public service administration, 270, 280
    regulatory reform, 153–154
    staff assessment, 297
Treasury Board Secretariat, 139, 252, 254, 274, 358
Trial Division, 172
Trotsky, Leon, 37
Trudeau, Pierre Eliot, 133, 142, 206, 265, 311
    bilingualism, 285
    constitutional change, 180
    deregulation, 152
    financial management reform, 326
    influence on public service, 408
    political evaluation, 243–244
    systems theory, 94
Turner, John, 133

U

ultra vires, 187, 194
unemployed, and bureaucracy, 74
unionization of public service, 293–295
unions, human relations view on, 92
United Empire Loyalists, 43
United Kingdom
    executive agencies, 390
    influence on Canadian constitutional system, 178
    influence on Canadian public administration, 266, 403–404
    public service reform, 112, 115, 266, 414, 415, 416
    and responsible government, 370
    as a social model, 158
United Kingdom Evaluation Society, 252
United Nations Human Development Index, 276
United States, 216
    see also Canada-United States relations
    gender in public administration studies, 111
    political culture, 157, 158
    public service reform, 75, 266, 415, 416

unity of direction, 103
University of Ottawa, 5
University of Toronto, 5, 267
Upper and Lower Canada rebellions, 43
Urwick, Lyndall, 80
U.S. Congress, 80
user fees, 113

V

value-for-money (VFM) tool, 256
Vander Zalm, Bill, 18
Verba, Sidney, 34
Vertical Mosaic (Porter), 43, 268
Veterans Affairs Canada, 291
Victoria Charter (1971), 180
Virginia Tech's Center for Public
    Administration and Policy, 111
visible minorities, in public service,
    291–292

W

watchdog agencies, 13
Watergate, 357
Waterman, Robert, 114
Weber, Max
    see also Weber's model of bureaucracy
    right to rule, 370
    view of the State, 37

Weber's model of bureaucracy, 28, 68–77,
    96, 160–161
    and Canadian public administration,
        102–103, 403–404, 414–415
    criticisms of, 70–77
    described, 68–70
    gender bias, 110
welfare state, 18, 267, 308, 319
Western Canada, 39, 52
Western Electric Company's Hawthorne
    Works, 84–86
Westminster political system, 147
Whitehall model, 147
Wilde, Oscar, 255
Wilson, Woodrow, 4, 10, 75, 267
Wolfe, James, 44
women, in public service, 286–288
women's movement, 31
World War II, 46
WorldCom, 13

Y

Yes, Prime Minister, 145, 383
York University, 5

Z

Zedong, Mao, 31